REGNUM STUDIES IN MISSION

Mission to the World

Communicating the Gospel in the 21st Century

Essays in Honour of Knud Jørgensen

Series Preface

Regnum Studies in Mission are born from the lived experience of Christians and Christian communities in mission, especially but not solely in the fast growing churches among the poor of the world. These churches have more to tell than stories of growth. They are making significant impacts on their cultures in the cause of Christ. They are producing 'cultural products' which express the reality of Christian faith, hope and love in their societies.

Regnum Studies in Mission are the fruit often of rigorous research to the highest international standards and always of authentic Christian engagement in the transformation of people and societies. And these are for the world. The formation of Christian theology, missiology and practice in the twenty-first century will depend to a great extent on the active participation of growing churches contributing biblical and culturally appropriate expressions of Christian practice to inform World Christianity.

Series Editors

REGNUM STUDIES IN MISSION

Mission to the World

Communicating the Gospel in the 21st Century
Essays in Honour of Knud Jørgensen

Edited by
Tormod Engelsviken,
Ernst Harbakk,
Rolv Olsen and
Thor Strandenæs

regnum

areopagos

First published 2008 by Regnum in cooperation with
Egede Instituttet and Areopagos

Regnum is an Imprint of The Oxford Centre for Mission Studies,
P.O. Box 70, Oxford, OX2 6HB
www.ocms.ac.uk/regnum
and Paternoster Press
P.O. Box 300, Carlisle, Cumbria, CA3 0QS, UK
and
P.O. Box 1047, Waynesboro, GA 30830–2047, USA

09 08 07 06 05 04 03 8 7 6 5 4 3 2 1

British Library Cataloguing in Publication Data
A catalogue record for this book is available from the British Library

ISBN 978-1-506477-68-8

Typeset by BB Ltd

Distributed by 1517 Media in the US and Canada

Contents

PREFACE

Director of Areopagos, Dr. Knud Jørgensen, is 65 years on September 29, 2007. On this occasion an editorial committee, under the sponsorship of Areopagos and Egede Instituttet in Oslo, has taken the initiative to publish a festschrift in his honour.

Knud Jørgensen is a Dane who for most of his life has lived in Norway. He is now directing an organization with home base both in Denmark and Norway. His life has been one of a series of various ministries in Denmark, Norway, Ethiopia, Switzerland, USA and China, to mention the most important countries. But he is an international church and mission leader with connections and contacts in most parts of the global church.

In planning the festschrift we have taken, as points of departure, the countries in which Jørgensen has ministered, as well as the major themes in his ministry and writings.

The title of the festschrift, *Mission to the World. Communicating the Gospel in the 21st Century. Essays in Honour of Knud Jørgensen*, indicates a program: It reflects the various main areas of Knud Jørgensen's commitment to mission. At the same time it focuses on the main frontier of mission, the *world*, the content of mission, the *Gospel*, the fact that the Gospel has to be *communicated*, and the *context* of contemporary mission: the *21st century*.

On this background the festschrift is divided into three main parts, which again are divided into two subsections each.

The first part, *Mission to the World –In Word and Deed*, deals in the first subsection with important aspects of the history and contemporary situation of the church in mission, including international diaconia, and in the second subsection with missional and contextual spirituality.

The second part, *Communicating the Gospel in the 21st Century*, deals in the first subsection with some central features of the church's task to communicate and contextualize the Gospel in various circumstances, and in the second subsection with encounters and dialogue with other religions in today's pluralistic and conflict-filled world.

The third part, *Leadership and Training in Mission*, deals in the first subsection with some historical and theological perspectives on how leadership in church and mission has been practiced and understood, as well as outlining some challenges for contemporary and future leadership preparation and development. The second subsection focuses on the calling of missionaries, and on the role of mission and missiology in theological education.

The whole festschrift is framed by a first chapter presenting the life and writings of Knud Jørgensen and a last chapter presenting his bibliography.

The editorial committee has met with an overwhelming interest for the festschrift, a fact that is documented both by the long *Tabula Gratulatoria* which probably could have been much longer if more information about the festschrift had been published, and by the willingness of almost everybody to contribute. The contributors represent different countries, such as Denmark, Norway, China/Hong Kong, USA and Great Britain, various organisations, universities and churches, as well as various theological and ecclesiastical positions. The committee regrets that it did not succeed in finding an African contributor, but would like to refer to the several chapters that have clear African perspectives.

The editorial committee would like to thank Regnum Books for its willingness to publish the festschrift in its Mission Studies series, Egede Instituttet for its support in the preparation and production of the manuscript, and Areopagos that (without Knud Jørgensen's knowledge!) has subsidized the festschrift.

With this the festschrift is presented for study and reflection.

Oslo, July 2, 2007
Tormod Engelsviken, Ernst Harbakk, Rolv Olsen, Thor Strandenæs
Editorial Committee

KNUD JØRGENSEN: MISSIONART STATESMAN
A BIOGRAPHICAL AND BIBLIOGRAPHICAL SKETCH

Tormod Engelsviken

Prof Dr Tormod Engelsviken, MF Norwegian School of Theology, Oslo, Norway

Introduction

Who is this man who is 65 years in September 2007, and whom we want to honour with this festschrift? He is both a missionary thinker and doer, and extremely good at both. But he is first and foremost a human being and a Christian. In this essay I would like to draw a picture of Knud Jørgensen as I see him as a long-time friend and co-worker. It will obviously not be a complete picture; Jørgensen's person and life are too varied and rich for that. It will be a personal picture drawn from my own experience, from reading of his writings, and from information that he himself graciously has provided concerning his own life and the influences that have contributed to make him into the missionary statesman that he in my opinion has been and is today.[1]

It is one of the main characteristics of Jørgensen that he combines in an almost unique way the ability to think and write as a scholar while at the same time being intensely involved in strategic planning and action on the practical level. He has not in any major way been employed in formal academic work, although he has significant teaching experience in several academic institutions. Most of his teaching and writing have been done while he has held

---

[1] This is not the place and I am not the person for a thorough and critical analysis and evaluation of Knud Jørgensen's writings. I have received information from him in writing and in oral conversation. I have used this in this essay together with other information that I have. Although some of the material may reflect Jørgensen's own perspectives, I am fully responsible for the views expressed and for possible mistakes.

important administrative positions as consultant, director, principal, etc. in seminaries, schools, institutes, and organizations.

This combination of theoretical reflection and practical engagement have given Jørgensen a unique perspective that in my opinion is one of the most characteristic and valuable features in his work: He is a missiological scholar who is not engaged in scholarship for scholarship's own sake, but for the importance and significance it may have for the church in mission. All his theological and missiological efforts are geared towards one major goal: the extension of the kingdom of God to all people. He is an example of a theologian where theory and praxis go hand in hand, and where theory serves the praxis of mission both in a critical and constructive way. Although he is not a card carrying liberation theologian, his understanding of theology is very similar to the definition "theology is critical reflection on praxis in light of the Word".[2] Jørgensen's work on missiology is, however, not primarily occupied with the past, but with the future. He is deeply concerned with the future of the Christian church. This comes to expression through his orientation towards strategic thinking and planning. It is the relevance and fruitfulness of missiological reflection and missionary work that are most important. This does not mean that historical questions and the truth and value questions are not important, but they will always be seen in light of their relevance for the future of the church and in the light of the normative Biblical revelation.

With these introductory words we have established a perspective on the person and work of Knud Jørgensen, a perspective that will, I hope, be expanded and confirmed through a more detailed account of his life and accomplishments. I will follow a chronological framework and attempt to mark certain periods in Jørgensen's life depending upon his major areas of work and corresponding main interests. There will also be a special emphasis on some of his most important writings in those periods.

Period one: Childhood and Youth 1942-1961

Jørgensen was born in the small town of Slagelse in Denmark on September 29, 1942. His home was a Christian home with strong values for personal and social life. Strongest among these values were integrity and responsibility. At the same time his Christian surroundings were focused on the need for appropriating faith in a personal way through conversion, and living out that faith in church and society. Both inner and foreign mission figured strongly in his parents' lives and examples. The possibility of serving God fulltime was a real option from his early youth.

While Jørgensen was a high school student his family had a close relation to

[2] For theology as reflection on practice in light of the Word, see e.g. Samuel Escobar, *Changing Tides. Latin Ámerica and World Mission Today* (Maryknoll, N.Y.: Orbis, 2002), pp. 12-13

the local Lutheran pastor Boyen Rasmussen, whom the young student often criticized for the lack of youth work in the congregation. One day the pastor turned to him and said: "I am tired of your criticism. Why don't *you* take the initiative to start youth work?" The challenge hit him and a few months later he got started on what for almost a decade became his primary Christian service: Building up *Emdrup Kristelige Ungdomsforening* in Copenhagen. This youth work attracted for several years up to 200 youngsters, many of whom were converted through Bible study groups, preaching and other forms of evangelism. Several of them occupy leading positions in the Church of Denmark today. It became a model of youth work for Copenhagen – with drama, magazine, theatre, selling Christmas trees, arranging summer meetings and summer camps, etc. Close links were also established with similar work in Norway, especially with *Nordberg Kristelige Ungdomsforening* in Oslo. There Jørgensen also became close friends with leaders such Pedro Lund, Finn Bjørndal, Finn Wagle (presently bishop in Nidaros diocese, Trondheim, Norway) and many others, and received significant influences from them. The common aim in Copenhagen and Oslo was to create a room, a space, where youngsters were welcomed, challenged, used and called to a living faith in a living Lord. It was this involvement in youth work that formed his life and faith during his young years. It was a Christian work that challenged the whole person to commitment and to experience the joy of living with Jesus.

Already at this early stage at least two of Knud Jørgensen's most important characteristics became visible: his leadership ability and his ability to create and maintain friendships in a large network. We will come back to him as a leader and to his reflections on leadership as they are expressed in some of his writings. As for friends, few have the same ability to establish personal close friendships and to maintain them faithfully over many years as Knud Jørgensen. The enormous response to the invitation to sign the *Tabula Gratulatoria* of this festschrift, and the willingness of so many to contribute to it, is but one sign of this. Jørgensen has a very large number of personal, close friends with whom he is in frequent contact. He (and his wife Eva) follow them up in times of need and exercise a human and spiritual mentorship that has meant a lot for many.

The challenge that the young student gave to the pastor is also characteristic of Jørgensen's direct, sometimes rather blunt, way of approaching people. He does not shrink from criticism and personal challenge when it seems justified. Some have initially reacted negatively to this, but have soon found out that his concern is based on care and love for persons and their total situation. Often the encounters have led to new and deeper self insight and to transformed and improved relations.

Period two: Studies and Radio Work in Denmark 1962-1970

Soon Knud Jørgensen moved from local Christian youth work in Copenhagen to work with a larger audience. An interest for media that has followed him throughout his life was awakened by a summer job in the Danish newspaper Politiken. The step from the newspaper to Radio Denmark was short. However, between these two jobs an important intermezzo took place. Ironically, it happened almost by mistake. A friend of his had enrolled in Fiellhaug Bible School in Oslo in order to be away from her fiancée as he finished his studies. Since Knud did not know exactly what to do after having graduated from high school in 1961, his friend suggested that he come along to Oslo. Knud saw this as a good opportunity to be close to his friends in Nordberg, not knowing that he would end up in a setting influenced by the conservative, pietistic Norwegian Lutheran Mission (*Norsk Luthersk Misjonssamband*) that owned and ran the school. Knud Jørgensen attended a three months Bible school, and he tells that these months profoundly changed his life.

The change was due to two major factors. Firstly, Jørgensen was exposed to the teaching of the Norwegian theologian and preacher Øivind Andersen and to the writings and influence of the 19th century famous Swedish Lutheran pastor, preacher and writer Carl Olof Rosenius. Andersen's lectures on Romans with a strong focus on justification by faith alone[3] and the heritage from Rosenius[4] became in many ways his own heritage. It was a strong focus on being "in Christ", similar to what he later in his theological studies met in Dietrich Bonhoeffer's thinking: What happened to Christ, happened to me. When he was crucified, I was crucified, and when he rose, I rose (1 Cor. 5:17, Rom. 6).

---

3 Øyvind Andersen was for many years the main teacher of dogmatics at Fjellhaug Mission Seminary. He exercised a strong influence as teacher and preacher in evangelical, low-church, revivalist circles of the Church of Norway, and particularly in the Norwegian Lutheran Mission, which is the largest mission society in Northern Europe. He emphasized especially justification by faith based on Christ's substitutionary death as an expression of God's free grace. He was instrumental through his ministry to bring people into a strong and lasting experience of evangelical freedom from a conscience burdened by guilt and the judgment of God. His most famous book is his commentary on Romans, see Øyvind Andersen, *Grunnsannheter til frelse*: *Romerbrevet 1-8* (Oslo: Gry, 1958)

4 Carl Olof Rosenius was a Swedish theologian, preacher and author who through his ministry had a widespread influence on revivalist circles in Scandinavia in the late 19th and early 20th centuries. He edited the magazine *Pietisten* and wrote several books. His articles and books were read with great interest in Norway. He inspired many pastors and lay preachers in Norway and his liberating message of grace and justification by faith was seen by many as a welcome correction to the more legalistic Lutheran revival tradition going back to the Norwegian lay preacher Hans Nielsen Hauge. See also the chapter by Vidar L. Haanes in this festschrift.

Secondly, it so happened that Knud's future wife, Eva Berger, also attended the school during the same months. Eva's Christian background was the Norwegian evangelical, low-church and strongly mission minded "bedehus" (prayer house) tradition. She had grown up in Fredrikstad in South-East Norway, and had already as a young woman developed a ministry as youth leader and lay preacher.[5] Since their wedding in August 1965 she has accompanied Knud to his various places of ministry while at the same time having a significant ministry of her own. In addition to her preaching ministry she has in recent years concentrated more on pastoral counselling. Together, Knud and Eva, have had an open home for guests through their long marriage, and it is impossible to envisage Knud's far-flung ministry without Eva at his side. Together they have two sons and one daughter.

When Jørgensen returned from Oslo to Copenhagen, he began his theological studies in 1962 at the theological faculty at the University of Copenhagen almost at the same time as he started working in Radio Denmark, first as a speaker in the music radio and later also involved in producing both radio and TV programmes. His life, as he remembers it, was filled with heavy theology in one hand and the Beatles in the other. And much of what happened in his thoughts was aimed at trying to build a bridge between the two. He also had to relate theology to the workplace as his radio colleagues constantly challenged him to give an account for the hope that was in him. In a way he became their "little radio pastor". During this time Jørgensen's learned the difficult task of moving between the secular world and the Christian, and to communicate his Christian convictions in everyday life and to audiences outside the church. His sermons and articles from this time bear ample evidence of this.

The strongest theological influence on the young student came from Professor Kristian Skydsgård, one of the top Protestant scholars on Roman Catholic theology who among other things was a Lutheran observer during Vatican II. It was Skydsgård who taught him always to be ready to rethink or think again and never be finished. Like Pope John XXIII he talked about 'aggiornamento'. And it was him who led Jørgensen to Bonhoeffer, first his *Sanctorum Communio*,[6] then his *Ethik*,[7] and later his book on *Nachfolge*.[8] The latter book, *Nachfolge*, made a profound impact on Jørgensen and has followed

[5] Eva Berger's ministry was also within the Norwegian Lutheran Mission and the Rosenius tradition.

[6] Dietrich Bonhoeffer, *Sanctorum Communio. Eine dogmatische Untersuchung zur Soziologie der Kirche,* herausggegeben von Joachim von Soosten (Munich: Chr. Kaiser Verlag, 1986)

[7] Dietrich Bonhoeffer, *Ethik,* herausgegeben von Ilse Tödt *et al.* (Munich: Chr. Kaiser Verlag, 1992)

[8] Dietrich Bonhoeffer, *Nachfolge,* herausgegeben von Martin Kuske und Ilse Tödt (Munich: Chr. Kaiser Verlag, 1989)

him since. He still is inspired by it and uses it extensively in sermon preparation. What struck him most were the radical call to follow Jesus and the close connection between faith and obedience: Only the obedient is able to believe, and only the believer is able to follow. This leads to 'costly grace', costly because it has cost God his only Son. This is a strong feature in Jørgensen's theology. The emphasis on free grace in the Rosenius tradition has not led to what is called "cheap grace" when one seeks comfort in God's grace while continuing to live in sin. Jørgensen has reacted strongly against many types of "cheap grace" that he has often sensed in the Western version of faith, a "grace" that leads many astray because it allows people to remain in their sins rather than calling them out of a sinful situation. This perspective was also later strengthened by Jørgensen's encounter with the East African Revival movement and the Charismatic movement.[9]

The study that led up to "teologisk embedseksamen" (state examination or cand. theol.) in Denmark and Norway was a thorough study of Latin, Biblical languages, and all the major disiplines of theology. It lasted normally from 6 to 7 years. Jørgensen graduated in 1970 with excellent grades. He was ready to embark on his fulltime Christian ministry.

Period three: Mission and Media Ministry in Africa 1970-1977

The 1960s were in many ways a time of spiritual formation and preparation through studies and work for his later ministry. When the 1970s arrived Jørgensen was ready for even greater challenges.

It was a Norwegian, Dr. Sigurd Aske,[10] who became instrumental in bringing Knud and Eva Jørgensen to Ethiopia – as it was him who later brought them to Geneva and to Norway. From 1970 and until his death in 1990 Aske exercised a very strong influence on the geography of Jørgensen's life and on his understanding of mission and the world. He became a friend and a mentor, and shared willingly with his younger colleague his enormous network of contacts and friends in Africa, China, and Scandinavia. He opened up Jørgensen's vision and gave him "eyes and glasses" to see God's mission in a global and local perspective. In remembering Aske, Jørgensen says, "he gave me advice, input, critique and functioned in many ways as a second father to me." The influence of Aske may go even deeper than Jørgensen realizes. Jørgensen who has been a mentor for many received himself mentorship

---

[9] See below

[10] Sigurd Aske belonged to the Evangelical Lutheran Free Church of Norway. He was strongly involved in media ministry on national and international levels. Aske is seen as the founder of Radio Voice of the Gospel in Ethiopia and worked for many years as director of communication in the Lutheran World Federation in Geneva. He was an inspiring leader and for some time chair of the Norwegian Lausanne Committee.

through several years from Aske. Not only Aske's views but also his personality, spirituality and form of ministry may have influenced him. It is possible to see many of the same traits in Jørgensen as in Aske: the global mission vision, the emphasis on personal relations, the effective use of media to communicate the gospel, the enormous international network, and the extraordinary leadership skills. Whether these similarities were due to their own personalities and gifts or influences from one on the other, is hard to say. Probably it is a combination of both as well as other factors. Yet, Jørgensen was not an uncritical follower or copy of Aske, but developed a ministry that also in many ways was different from Aske's. While Aske first and foremost was a practitioner and Christian entrepreneur, is Jørgensen more of a pastor, theological thinker and writer.

Radio Voice of the Gospel (RVOG) was a radio station built and run by the Lutheran World Federation in Addis Ababa, Ethiopia, with an aim to reach Africa with the gospel message but also with useful programmes of various kinds under a holistic vision of people. The years at RVOG were, according to Jørgensen, among the most happy and satisfying years in his life, with plenty of challenges and plenty of work. The work at the radio station created a platform where media, communication and mission were intertwined as they continued to be in his life ever since.

At this point I wish to insert a personal note. It was in 1971 I got to know Knud Jørgensen in a personal way, as we both worked as missionaries in Addis Ababa. I had the privilege to participate in some of the radio programs, and I particularly remember two incidents. One may illustrate Jørgensen's ability to connect the Christian message to popular culture as he used the popular song, "What the world needs now, is love, sweet love" to introduce the Christian message of God's abounding love for humankind. The other may illustrate the need to show wisdom, sensitivity and creativity in communicating Christian values in a country where freedom of speech was not much in evidence. In 1972 Pentecostals belonging to the Mulu Wongel church were persecuted and imprisoned by the Ethiopian police with support from the leadership of the Ethiopian Orthodox Church. The atrocities could not be openly criticized. Instead Jørgensen made a program where he invited me and others to discuss the persecution and incarceration of Jehovah's Witnesses in Malawi at the same time. In this way we could condemn religious persecution and express our support for human rights and particularly for freedom of religion. I do believe that many of the more informed listeners knew what we were really talking about!

My personal friendship with Knud, which also has been an opportunity for close cooperation leading to many common projects,[11] has lasted for more than

---

[11] E.g. the missiology textbook, Berentsen, Jan-Martin, Tormod Engelsviken & Knud Jørgensen (eds.), *Missiologi i dag*, (Oslo: Universitetsforlaget, 2nd ed., 2004) and the work in the Lausanne Theology Working Group. We have also

35 years and been one of the most rewarding friendships – and may I say – mentorships I have had in my life.

It is almost impossible to work in Africa without getting fascinated by African culture and Christianity. Jørgensen became part and parcel of the Ethiopian Evangelical Church Mekane Yesus (EECMY) that was growing, from 157.000 in December 1970 when he landed in Addis Ababa to almost five million believers today! As Jørgensen sees it, it is a miracle of receptivity and of the Spirit. Obviously social and political factors played a strong role, especially from the beginning of the revolution in 1974. But there were other factors: The focus on prayer, proclamation that brought together both reconciliation and the victory of Christ, openness (eventually) for the work of the Holy Spirit, and spontaneous evangelism, especially among the students and the youth, that was partly ignited by the charismatic renewal among the students in the late 1960s and the 1970s.

In the midst of the rather dramatic developments in the Ethiopian church and in Ethiopian politics, there were two pillars that touched and formed Jørgensen's life in a decisive manner: One was Dr. Emmanuel Gebre Selassie, former church president, friend of the emperor, advisor at RVOG – a man who after 1974 lost his power and should have been broken, but instead remained standing, reminding everybody that "the Lord is still on the throne". Even after the Communist revolution of 1974 had mocked him, he stuck to his faithfulness to Christ.

The other was Rev. Gudina Tumsa,[12] the EECMY general secretary, who taught and demonstrated the close connection between the Gospel and social responsibility. It was Gudina who led the church and the missionaries into a reflective criticism of the emperor's regime and who guided the church under the new regime, the *Dergue*, until he disappeared. Some of the EECMY leaders accused Jørgensen of having leaked information from Gudina to the Orthodox leaders and in that way been instrumental in his imprisonment. Fortunately Gudina was released again and could verify that it was not because of Jørgensen that he had been imprisoned. A few weeks later he disappeared again for good. He was later killed by the Communist regime, and became a martyr

---

arranged conferences and taught several missiological courses together at MF Norwegian School of Theology and other places.

[12] Gudina Tumsa was perhaps the most outstanding and visionary of the church leaders in Ethiopia, and his memory has been kept by the Gudina Tumsa Foundation which has arranged several seminars and published books on his legacy, see *The Life and Ministry of Rev. Gudina Tumsa, General Secretary of the Ethiopian Evangelical Church Mekane Yesus* (Addis Ababa: The Gudina Tumsa Foundation, 2003); *Witness and Discipleship. Leadership of the Church in Multi-Ethnic Ethiopia in a Time of Revolution. The Essential Writings of Gudina Tumsa, General Secretary of the Ethiopian Evangelical Church Mekane Yesus (1929-1979)* (Addis Ababa: Gudina Tumsa Foundation, 2003).

for the church. It took, however, many years for Jørgensen to recover from this accusation, and it was not until 1994 that he could sit down with the person who had made the accusation, talk it through, and be reconciled.

Jørgensen worked at the RVOG from 1970 to 1977, and his life and work became increasingly international, especially after he became program director in 1975. He had to visit studios in India, the Middle East, and all parts of Africa. In that way he came to know the world, a world that he saw was filled both with monsters and with God's angels. He came to believe literally in the spirit world and the activity of the devil, simply because he saw the results. This conviction, and the theological reflection that went along with it, have followed Jørgensen over the years and have come to expression in several lectures and articles. He was chair of the Lausanne consultation "Deliver Us From Evil" in Nairobi in 2000, and contributed significantly to it.[13] In this respect as in others he has been open to listen to and learn from Christians in the Global South.

As Jørgensen became acquainted with God's people everywhere, he also got involved in the East African revival through a friendship with John Wilson, Festo Kivengere and Michael Cassidy. He tells how they shared with him that faith meant "to walk in the light – and if you are not in the light, then you need to sit down and confess your sins to the brothers so that the blood may cleanse you, and the devil may not catch you in the dark." The blood of Christ became like a gateway into fellowship with the Lord. This is still very much part of Jørgensen's daily way of being a Christian, and one hears him often quote the warning about walking in the dark.

Through the African Evangelistic Enterprise that grew out of the East African revival he also became part of a brotherhood for strategic evangelism in the cities of Africa. He was elected member of its International Partnership Board, a position he has retained ever since.

It was in Africa, through the Mekane Yesus Church and the African Evangelistic Enterprise, that Jørgensen came to appreciate another central feature of mission theology, what has later, with the words of Paul Hiebert, been called "the flaw of the excluded middle".[14] He came to the realization that what we sing about in Luther's famous hymn "A mighty fortress is our God" is actually true, that mission is to go out and regain the territory that the devil has occupied. This spiritual battle requires spiritual gifts; it cannot be won through

---

[13] Knud Jørgensen, "Spiritual conflict in socio-cultural context", in: A. Scott Moreau *et al.* (eds.), *Deliver Us From Evil. An Uneasy Frontier in Christian Mission* (Monrovia, Ca.: MARC, 2002), pp. 213-230. See also Knud Jørgensen, "Åndskamp – mer enn slagord", in: *Impulser til kristenliv i Norge i nitti-årene* (Oslo: Luther og Credo, 1991) and Knud Jørgensen, "Spiritualitet og åndskamp", *Ung Teologi,* Vol. 36 (2003), No. 2, pp. 57-65

[14] Paul G. Hiebert, "The Flaw of the Excluded Middle", *Missiology: An International Review,* No. 10, 1982, pp. 35-47

our own efforts. "We must pray down over one another the blessings, baptism and gifts of the Spirit. Call it a charismatic renewal, yes, it probably was – and it has followed me since: the focus on spiritual gifts, the need always to listen to the still voice of the Spirit, the belief that He is a go-between God who opens our eyes so that we may see what Christ has done for us on the cross."

This emphasis on spiritual conflict, charismatic renewal and ministry in the Spirit may seem somewhat surprising taking into account the scepticism and resistance that the most conservative Lutheranism, and especially parts of the Pietistic revival movements have had towards the Pentecostal and charismatic movements. It shows, however, the deep influence the encounter with African Christianity had on Jørgensen. Revival movements in Africa will almost inevitably take on a Pentecostal or charismatic character, not primarily as a result of influence from similar movements in the West, but first and foremost as a result of the African worldview and spiritual experience encountering the stories and teaching of the Bible. Africans recognize experiences of the spirits and of the Holy Spirit as they read the Scriptures and apply it to their own spiritual context. Then their own experiences are similar to those in the Bible, including healing, exorcism, prophecy, dreams, visions etc.[15]. The Malaysian missiologist Hwa Yung has emphasized especially the need to take Asian cultures and worldviews seriously in order to contextualize the Christian message in the area of evangelism and pastoral ministry. This will necessarily involve "the practice of "power encounter" in the healing and exorcism ministries".[16] A similar approach should be taken *mutatis mutandis* with regard to Africa.

This approach also corresponds with a more comprehensive and holistic emphasis, where not only the relation between right theory and practice, expressed as orthodoxy and orthopraxy, but also a right commitment and allegiance, including feelings and sentiments, called orthopathy is emphasized as part of Christian spirituality.[17] Jørgensen has been able to integrate this dimension of spirituality, especially as a fruit of his interaction with African church leaders, which makes him in some ways exceptional, especially as far as Western church leaders are concerned.

Knud Jørgensen's continuous emphasis on prayer, and especially

---

[15] See e.g. Tormod Engelsviken, *Besettelse og åndsutdrivelse i Bibelen, historien og vår egen tid* (Oslo: Lunde, 1978); and "Exorcism and Healing in the Evangelical churches in Ethiopia", *Journal of Mission Theology,* Vol.1, Fasc. 1 (1991), pp.41-48.

[16] Hwa Yung, *Mangoes or Bananas. The Quest for an Authentic Asian Christian Theology* (Oxford: Regnum, 1997), pp. 71-76.

[17] Cf. the terminology introduced by the Pentecostal scholar Steven J. Land to analyze the spirituality of Pentecostalism in Stephen J. Land, *Pentecostal Spirituality: a Passion for the Kingdom* (Sheffield: Sheffield Academic Press, 1993).

intercessory prayer, can be seen in light of this holistic spirituality. He says that since his time in Africa one important focus is to ensure that he has had faithful intercessors. This focus was later strongly reinforced by Peter Wagner at Fuller Theological Seminary when he challenged him and the other teachers at the time to have someone who would lift the hands like Moses, while others, like Joshua, were involved in the battle. Jørgensen says that in his life it resulted in having four intercessors who for many years followed him closely and lifted him up to the Lord. "Without them I do not know where I would have been."

Period four: Media and Communication Ministry in Europe 1978-1988

In 1977 Knud Jørgensen returned back from Africa to Europe. His international ministry continued, however, but now with a basis in Geneva, as Executive Secretary for Consultative Services in the Department of Communication within the Lutheran World Federation (LWF). A person with Jørgensen's leadership capabilities almost inevitably would be thrown into management positions. It happened towards the end of his ministry in Ethiopia and later in Europe.

Jørgensen's ministry in the Ecumenical Center in Geneva where also the World Council of Churches (WCC) and other ecumenical bodies were located, raises the question of Jørgensen's ecumenical stance. He says himself that he in many ways is an "an ecumenical evangelical." This was in large measure a result of his years in Geneva where he was in charge of media and communication projects in all the corners of the world. His evangelical theology was challenged in the Ecumenical Centre, by LWF and WCC colleagues.

In 1974 he had as a young radio reporter been attending the Lasusanne Congress on World Evangelization. The entire congress had deeply influenced him, especially people like John Stott, Rene Padilla, Samuel Escobar, and Ralph Winter. He signed the Lausanne Covenant there and then and he says that he has never "regretted or gone back on (his) basic adherence to that covenant." It was with that baggage he arrived in Geneva. That was not easy. He often clashed or reacted, but slowly learned to listen and to see that there were actually committed people within the WCC. He even discovered new aspects of the gospel that he had not seen before: the social, political dimensions. His picture of the WCC had largely been determined by the Uppsala Assembly in 1968 and the conference of the WCC Commission on World Mission and Evangelism (CWME) with the theme "Salvation Today" in Bangkok 1972/73. The WCC in 1978-81 was very different, however, from Uppsala and Bangkok, and much more coloured by the Assembly in Nairobi in 1975 and later by the CWME conference in Melbourne with its focus on the poor.[18] Jørgensen reacted against the reading of the materially poor into all the Biblical texts, especially in light of the massive New Testament study by prof. Hans Kvalbein on "Jesus and the Poor" which he had read at this time.[19] His time in Ethiopia had at the same time left strong dents on an evangelical thinking that did not take the situation of the poor seriously enough. Out of this grew a new understanding of "prophetic diaconia", of combining the individual with the social dimensions of diaconia. The Geneva experience also opened his eyes to the role of dialogue as a way of living and a way of communicating. Both these perspectives should later be especially important as he worked for Norwegian Church Aid, a Christian relief and development organization, and for Areopagos that especially emphasizes dialogue.[20] He continued to be part of the Lausanne network and shared its fundamental convictions and values, and yet he was also very much part of the ecumenical scene. He has seen it as his duty to build bridges between the two whenever possible. With a certain pride Jørgensen relates that in February 2007 he took the chairman of the Lausanne Committee for World Evangelization (LCWE), Doug Birdsall on a guided tour of Geneva and the Ecumenical Center and made him sit down with the ecumenical leaders in LWF and WCC to find out that they can after all talk together.[21]

---

[18] To the development of mission theology within the ecumenical and evangelical movements in the 1960s and 70s, see James A. Scherer, *Gospel, Church & Kingdom. Comparative Studies in World Mission Theology* (Minneapolis, Minn.: Augsburg Publishing House, 1987), and Tormod Engelsviken, "Misjonstenkningen fra 1900 til vår tid", in: Jan-Martin Berentsen, Tormod Engelsviken and Knud Jørgensen (eds.), *Missiologi i dag*, 2nd ed. (Oslo: Universitetsforlaget, 2004), pp. 140-158

[19] Hans Kvalbein, *Jesus og de fattige og hans bruk av ord for "fattig"* (Oslo: Luther, 1981)

[20] See below

[21] This openness towards the ecumenical movement does not sit well with many representatives of the Norwegian mission movements. The Norwegian Missionary Council was the only one in the world that withdrew from the International Missionary Council when it was merged with the CWME in New Delhi in 1961. The ecumenical climate in Norway has, however, changed in recent years, as has the climate towards the Evangelicals in the WCC. Today the constituency of the CWME is wider than that of the WCC, including as full members representatives from the Roman Catholic Church, the Evangelical movement and the Pentecostal movement. The ecumenical statements on mission of the period 1980-2005 are also much more open to evangelical viewpoints than the earlier documents, cf. *"You are the light of the world". Statements on Mission by the World Council of Churches 1980-2005* (Geneva: WCC Publications, 2005) and Tormod Engelsviken, "Divergene or Convergence? The Relationship between Recent Ecumenical and Evangelical

In spite of his openness to the Ecumenical Movement Jørgensen sees the Lausanne fellowship as his theological "home base". Here he finds hearts that vibrate for communicating the Gospel to others and for the costly discipleship of Bonhoeffer. He has served in the Communication Working Group, the Administrative Committee, and until today in the Theology Working Group. He has personal connections with Lausanne leaders such as John Stott, Leighton Ford, Paul Cedar, Tom Houston, Gottfried Osei-Mensah, Robin Claydon, Hwa Yung and many others.

In 1981 Knud Jørgensen moved to Norway to take up a new position as Director of Planning at the International Mass Media Institute (IMMI) in Kristiansand. In 1982 he took over as Director, a position he held until 1988. When he arrived in Norway it was on the threshold of a new media situation. The monopoly of the state-owned Norwegian Broadcasting Corporation (NRK) was broken by the new conservative government. As a result, everybody, including mission organisations and congregations, threw themselves on the new bandwagon: Local or community radio was almost overnight seen as a God-given medium for evangelism. Jørgensen had been recruited by Sigurd Aske and another Norwegian lay leader, Leif Haanes, to take over from Aske as director of IMMI, that at the time was a rather small operation with a couple of people employed and with almost no funds. Seven years later, in 1988, it had become a major consultative agency for Christian communication in Norway and abroad with about 12 employees, with a TV/video company, with courses and seminars in Norway and abroad. It was seven busy years of riding the waves of the liberalisation of the media situation in Scandinavia, even taking over the production of the daily devotions from NRK. The optimism was great, and during this period Jørgensen taught and wrote extensively about media, communication, journalism, communication strategy, information society, satellites, etc.

A look at Jørgensen's bibliography will show how productive he and his fellow workers were during this time of media euphoria. He and his co-workers wrote and edited books and articles, like *New and Old Media in Norway* (1983),[22] *Misjon og kommunikasjon* (Mission and Communication, 1983), *Nærradio, nærmiljø og lokalmenighet: Veiledningshefte for menigheter og organisasjoner* (Local radio, local environment and local church: A Guide for congregations and organizations, 1984), *Radioarbeid: programproduksjon og radiojournalistikk* (Radio Work: Program production and Radio Journalism, 1984), *Proclaiming Christ to His World* (1984), *Medie- og kommunikasjonsstrategi* (A Strategy for Media and Communication, 1985), *Åpen kanal: misjon og medier* (Open channel: Mission and Media, 1987), *Det*

Mission Documents", *Swedish Missiological Themes*, No. 2 (2001), pp. 197-220

[22] For the bibliographical data of these titles, see Knud Jørgensen's bibliography.

trykte ord (The Printed Word, 1987), and many others.

The expressed aim of this intense activity was to call the church, the organisations within the churches, and the many eager amateurs to order: Involvement in media demands professionalism and knowledge of both media and communication. One cannot just open a local radio and then believe that this will result in a stream of new converts. "In the media you can only advertise what is already available inside the shop", as Jørgensen phrases it.

This statement could also be seen as a program for his major achievement during this period: his doctoral dissertation in missiology at Fuller Theological Seminary in Pasadena, California, *The Role and Function of the Media in the Mission of the Church.*[23] The title contains a program: The role of the media is to support and not replace. They should support the living witness and diaconia of the church. Jørgensen in his dissertation links the use of the media very closely to local evangelism and follow-up of a 'mediatized' laity on the ground. He sees Christian communication as incarnational, based on 1 John 1: "What we have seen and heard and touched with our own hands, that is what we pass on." Therefore it is crucial that the communicators themselves receive the message. "Communication does not start with getting the message across, but with getting the message". Also in the doctoral dissertation we see the influence of Jørgensen's African experience and the fruits of his ministry in RVOG, especially in two interesting case studies. A study of the Fulani people illustrates how one can win a hearing "through media communication to the extent that the media have participated significantly in preparing a people movement", while another case study of the EECMY in Ethiopia shows a situation and a church where the media have served as an adjunct or complement to other already ongoing processes in culture, society and Church".[24]

Even though IMMI primarily served a limited audience in Norway, Jørgensen's international focus remained. Together with Aske and others he concentrated his interest on broadcasting to China. This was controversial since the Chinese Bishop Ting was critical and tried his best to stop their dreams. Yet they went ahead and established an agency called *Kairos Communication Service* in Los Angeles, producing and broadcasting daily programs to China. It was often an uphill battle, but they persevered and Jørgensen's friend David Chao from Hong Kong became the pioneer who made it happen. The program is still very much alive. It was probably there that Jørgensen's love and concern for China began in earnest.

---

[23] Knud Jørgensen, *The Role and Function of the Media in the Mission of the Church (with Particular Reference to Africa),* (Unpublished doctoral dissertation, Pasadena, Ca.: Fuller Theological Seminary, School of World Mission, 1986)

[24] Jørgensen, *The Role and Function*, pp.344-411

Period five: Studies in America, 1988-89

Knud Jørgensen has studied altogether three years in America at Fuller Theological Seminary in Pasadena. California. The studies are interspersed over a period of time, namely 1974-75, 1977-78 and 1988-89. We regard it here as one of the separate important periods in his life since the last year followed after the period of ministry in IMMI, Norway. It is not accidental that Fuller became Jørgensen's *Alma Mater* in America. At Fuller he could develop his visions and ideas in an environment that emphasized mission, church growth, communication and leadership, all based in an evangelical theology. Although the term "church growth" today is somewhat out of fashion, Jørgensen for many years was keenly interested in it. Actually the two first works in his bibliography deal with church growth, *Evangelisation og kirkevækst* (Evangelization and Church Growth, 1976), and *Kirkevækst: et forsøg på en indføring* (Church Growth: an Attempt at an Introduction, 1976). The theme has followed him up through the years,[25] and has led to an intensive occupation with the relationship between church and mission.[26]

During the two first periods at Fuller Jørgensen focused primarily on his doctorate and church growth. He studied church growth with such men as Donald McGavran, Peter Wagner and Eddie Gibbs. He says that a lot of the church growth thinking became second nature to him, such as receptivity, homogeneous units, and contextualisation. But he did not accept everything he was taught. He was also often critical: Does not this become too American, too preoccupied with methods? Is there not too little theological reflection? He went to people like Arthur Glasser and Charles Kraft with his sometimes angry reactions to what he felt was superficial thinking, and experienced that they listened to him, and even encouraged him. Some of this is reflected in his dissertation, especially in the chapters on communication and on biblical models.[27]

Jørgensen did, however, not concentrate solely on church growth and communication. He relates how he studied anthropology and sociology with Paul Hiebert, Allan Tippett, and Charles Kraft, and read and read until he was hospitalised with a severe attack of muscle cramps in back and legs. During this time especially Charles Kraft became his mentor and close friend. Jørgensen

---

[25] "Kirkevækst og missionsforskning" (Church Growth and Missionary Research), in: *Mission*, Vol. 93, No. 4, 1982, pp. 155-159. His doctoral dissertation has also as an overarching perspective how media can contribute to church growth, "Recognizing the relation between communication and incorporation, and the complexity of church growth, media communication may contribute towards the receptivity to the Christian message, thus functioning as *preparatio evangelica* within an overall network of Christian communication", Abstract, in Jørgensen, *The Role and Function*, p. ii.

[26] See below

[27] Jørgensen, *The Role and Function*, pp. 118-224

regards Fuller Theological Seminary in many ways as his "missiological home".

His last period at Fuller in 1988-89 was an expression of a new direction of his interest. During his work at IMMI he had received an increasing number of demands for developing strategies for organisations and churches. And again and again he found that the problem was not strategy or the lack of it, but leadership. This led him back to Fuller and to studies on leadership in society and in church. In a way it was experienced as studying the same scenario as before but from a different and more focused perspective. In these studies he also had the advantage of reflecting on his own leadership through the years – and actually reflecting on his entire life and its various influences since the pastor of his youth had challenged him. This study opened up new vistas and avenues, both in his own life and in the life of the church. He was able to reflect on his own experiences in the areas such as spirituality, spiritual gifts and the understanding of education and formation. The studies also led him to become more and more critical of what he calls "the Rambo-style leadership" of the church, with the focus on the priest and pastor. He came to see this as part of the Constantinian imprisonment of the church where the civil religion of Constantine's empire invaded the concepts and structures of the church and resulted in a number of reductions of the Gospel. He remembers his surprise when he realised that a word for laity is not found in Scripture – and that it actually is a translation of the Latin *idiotes.* He saw a need for a new reformation to realise the priesthood of all believers and at the same time regain the biblical, broader perspective on leadership.

The leadership studies also convinced him of the crucial importance of leadership in missiological terms. Too many of the problems in mission are due to poor or irrelevant leadership – imitation leaders who may look like well dressed Westerners in black suits, but whose leadership does not grow out of the local patterns for leadership. Also mission societies should therefore give priority to all forms of leadership formation.

Jørgensen leadership studies gave birth to the second large book in his theological production, *Visjon og hverdag: lederskap i misjon og menighet* (Vision and everyday: leadership in mission and congregation, 1991).[28] After having discussed a number of leadership models and issues analytically and critically he concludes in a final chapter, Challenges for Leadership, where he writes (my translation), "It (leadership) is less about prestige than about being a servant first. It is less about being held in high esteem by others than about suffering as a good soldier for Christ. It is less about a dynamic personality than

[28] Knud Jørgensen, *Visjon og hverdag: lederskap i misjon og menighet* (Oslo: Verbum ,1991). During these years he also wrote several articles on leadership, e.g. "Lederskap på tvers av grenser" (Crosscultural leadership), *Santalen*, Vol. 107, No. 24, 1989, pp. 18-19

about spiritual authority."[29] In the final challenge he writes that the basic Biblical model of leadership is servant leadership in clear contrast to the ideal of "the strong leader".[30] However, at this point one may see an almost paradoxical situation: While Jørgensen strongly (*sic*!) espouses servant leadership, he represents himself in many ways both the strong leader, sometimes even dominating, as well as the humble, vulnerable leader who is in need of correction and intercession. He does not fit with his own negative description of the "strong leader" (*Führer*), and yet he is a strong leader, both in terms of his personality as well as his spiritual authority. This may be an indication that leadership theory not always squares with human experience, and that Christian leadership is a very complex reality.

Period six: Missionary Education in Norway, 1989-1992

In 1989, after his studies at Fuller, Jørgensen seemed to move into a completely new area of work: teaching and preaching as principal of *Gå Ut Senteret* (GUS, Go Out Centre) in Hurdal, north of Oslo. This was a small school primarily aimed at the training of missionaries for the Norwegian Santal Mission.[31] However, there was a significant continuity. Jørgensen had always enjoyed teaching, and in this school he plunged into teaching all sorts of subjects from his newly gained perspective of leadership formation. The focus on missionary training forced him to broaden his reading in missiology. This resulted in a comprehensive textbook *Missiologi i dag* (Missiology Today) which was published in 1994. [32] It was a team work where Jørgensen worked together with Jan-Martin Berentsen at the School for Mission and Theology in Stavanger and Tormod Engelsviken at the MF Norwegian School of Theology in Oslo. The book was an almost 500p textbook on missiology dealing with mission in the Bible, mission history, mission theology and mission strategy. It had contributions from all the Scandinavian countries and has been the major

---

[29] Jørgensen, *Visjon og hverdag*, p. 227

[30] Jørgensen, *Visjon og hverdag*, pp. 233-235

[31] The Santal Mission was founded by the famous Norwegian missionary, Lars Skrefsrud, who was a missionary to Santal Parganas in India. His established the Ebenezer Mission Station in 1967, and this year is seen as the founding year of the Santal Mission. The mission is one of the three large missions within the (Lutheran) Church of Norway. The others are the Norwegian Missionary Society (founded 1842) and the Norwegian Lutheran Mission (founded 1991). The Santal Mission in 2001 merged with the Inner Mission Society to form Normisjon. See the chapters by Vidar L. Haanes and Jan-Martin Berentsen in this festschrift for more details.

[32] Jan-Martin Berentsen, Tormod Engelsviken og Knud Jørgensen (red.), *Missiologi i dag* (Oslo: Universitetsforlaget, 1994). A second, revised edition was published by the same publisher in 2004.

missiological textbook in a Scandinavian language for the last decade. It has an evangelical profile inspired by the Lausanne movement. Jørgensen wrote the chapter on church and mission, a task that led him to go even deeper into the subject. The same happened within other fields such as tentmaking,[33] new forms of mission,[34] spiritual battle,[35] and the role of diaconia in mission.

The time at GUS also brought Jørgensen into close fellowhip with Gunnleik Seierstad, the general secretary of the Santal Mission. He was trained in science and was a layman, yet according to Jørgensen he was the theologically best "non-theologian" he knew. His humility, his integrity and his ability to pursue new visions impressed him, and they both shared the desire to lift up the priesthood of all believers within a pastor-dominated church.

The time at GUS gave Jørgensen an opportunity to use one of the other gifts he had. It gave him a platform to preach. The fact that he was Danish and continued to speak Danish in Norway[36] had often prevented people from asking him to preach. In the Santal Mission, however, that did not seem to be a hindrance. There is no doubt that Jørgensen has a strong gift for preaching, a gift that probably over the years has not been sufficiently appreciated in Norway. It is a preaching that combines Biblical and doctrinal content with a strong appeal for commitment. It is obvious that he enjoys the ministry of preaching as much as teaching.

This aspect of ministry also came to the fore while he was actively involved in the *Oase* (Oasis) Movement, which is the charismatic movement within the Church of Norway. Here he was part of the Leadership and a much used speaker at conferences and seminars. The inspiration from Oase, and in particular John Wimber, made him regard "power evangelism" as an essential component in the evangelism of the church.[37]

[33] Knud Jørgensen og Berit Helgøy Kloster, *Vitner i arbeid og fritid: teltmakertjenesten til jordens ender* (Witnesses during work and leisure time: tentmaker ministry to the ends of the earth) (Oslo: Credo, 1991)

[34]Knud Jørgensen, "Misjonærrollen under lupen" (The missionary role under the magnifying glass), *Santalen* Vol. 110, No. 6/7, 1992, pp. 16-19

[35] Knud Jørgensen, "Misjon er åndskamp" (Mission is spiritual battle), *Santalen*, Vol. 107, No. 12/13, p. 14; "Åndskamp – mer enn slagord" (Spiritual battle – more than slogans), in *Reis deg Guds menighet. Impulser til kristenliv i Norge i nitti-årene* (Oslo: Credo, 1991).

[36] Danish and Norwegian are very similar in writing, but quite different in pronunciation.

[37] John Wimber, *Power Evangelism. Signs and Wonders Today* (London: Hodder and Stoughton, 1985)

Period seven: Diaconia and Management in Norway and Ethiopia, 1992-1998

Jørgensen's period as principal at GUS was relatively short, three years. It may be that the size and location of the school in a certain sense limited the scope of his ministry. It is also indicative of a certain restlessness that he always has been open to new challenges. So in 1992 he once again made a major switch in his career as he responded to the challenge of joining the largest Norwegian relief and development organization, Norwegian Church Aid (NCA), as Director of Information. In some sense he was back in the business of communication and mission, this time, however, with a strong emphasis on international diaconia.

He worked with NCA both in Norway and in Ethiopia from 1992 to 1998. The years in Norway as Director of Information were very hectic, both because of the nature of the work and because it was a time of transition and leadership change. Once again he had to widen his perspective and his studies: This time he had to think through diaconia and development. Slightly differently from the emphasis of NCA, Jørgensen argues for the importance of the role of the church and the gospel in diaconia and development. He maintains that the church is called to be, to do and to speak in the world; that diaconia relates both to being and doing and should, if possible, be placed in a context where God's people give their testimony. Thus diaconia is a goal in itself and not something that is done in order to gain an opportunity to preach. "At the same time", he says, "I came to see that the key component in development assistance from a Christian perspective is the Gospel itself – because only the Gospel can set me free from my marred identity and from the web of lies surrounding my life."[38] In light of this conviction he has often been concerned when mission organisations in Norway are overly eager to separate their development activities from the Christian witness, for fear that they may lose NORAD-support[39] if the two are mixed. "If we do not place the power of the Gospel in the centre of our development efforts, what is it then that should set people free?" says Jørgensen somewhat provocatively.

---

38 This language strongly resembles the language of one of Jørgensen's friend in the Lausanne network, Bryant Myers, in his book *Walking with the Poor. Principles and Practices of Transformational Development* (Maryknoll,N.Y.: Orbis, 1999)

39 NORAD is the development agency of the Norwegian government. As part of its work it also supports the relief and development work of Norwegian Christian NGOs. It has, however, made it a condition that government funds may not be used for evangelism or church work. This may cause a problem for a more holistic understanding of mission as well as development. The relation between humanitarian aid and development on the one hand and evangelism and church work on the other has been a topic of heated public debate in Norway.

In his work in NCA he also learned to see that all diaconia has political implications, and that the church therefore should focus much more on advocacy both at home and internationally. In a relief organization like NCA he was exposed to some of the most catastrophic humanitarian disasters of our time and they made a deep impression on him, "I saw in new and terrible ways how the devil can rip life apart and destroy societies. My worst experience was the genocide in Rwanda where the devil was let loose in such a way that even Christians got involved in the bloodbath. I was shaken and terrified by what I saw. The same applied to Southern Sudan, Ethiopia-Eritrea, Guatemala."

These experiences, however, did not prevent Jørgensen from returning to his early love, Ethiopia, for a new period of service. In 1994 he went to Ethiopia, seconded by NCA to the Mẹkane Yesus Theological Seminary. The task was to develop and establish a new faculty or department on leadership, management and communication. The growing church was in sore need of leaders, a broad spectrum of leaders who could break with the traditional pattern of control from above and fear from below, i.e. the feudal pattern of leadership which had governed the Ethiopian scene since Emperor Haile Selassie.[40] These years were very happy years; both Knud and Eva Jørgensen felt that they were home again among Ethiopian friends and in the Ethiopian culture. Jørgensen succeeded in finding the funds (more than 2.5 mill USD) to rebuild and expand the seminary. Staff was recruited and students enrolled in a two years program. The establishment of the Department of Leadership, Management and Communication at the Mekane Yesus Theological Seminary was a success, largely due to Jørgensen's vision and leadership, and the students came out of their studies as changed people. It was an immense joy for Jørgensen to see that his model of leadership formation also functioned in the real world.

In the course of these years Jørgensen came to appreciate two of his expatriate colleagues, the Norwegian Johnny Bakke and the Swede Agne Nordlander. Bakke had a long and distinguished service in Etiopia as theological professor from 1969 until 2006. He was a counsellor for Jørgensen, and carried a major part of the burden with regard to the construction project. Nordlander was a brilliant evangelical theologian and an outstanding teacher and preacher who warmed the hearts of the students.[41]

Jørgensen also developed a close relationship with several of the Ethiopian

---

[40] See the chapter on leadership and the references to Ethiopian traditions in Jørn Lemvik's chapter in this festschrift.

[41] Both Johnny Bakke and Agne Nordlander have also contributed significantly to the studies of the church in Ethiopia, see e.g. Johnny Bakke, *Christian Ministry: Patterns and Functions within the Ethiopian Evangelical Church Mekane Yesus* (Oslo: Solum Farlag, 19871978) and Agne Nordlander, *Väckelse och växtvärk i Etiopien* (Revival and growth pains in Ethiopia, Stockholm: Verbum, 1996); *Med smak av nåd. Festskrift til Agne Nordlander* (Ôrebro: Libris, 2000).

church leaders. Although he was an expatriate he was taken into their confidence and exerted a considerable influence as advisor. Among these church leaders were its President Yadessa Daba, whom he admired for his willingness to admit mistakes and openly asking for forgiveness. Also the later President Iteffa Gobena, and the Associate General Secretary Abebe Yohannes forged close ties with Jørgensen and became his friends.

The good years in Ethiopia came to an abrupt end when Jørgensen in 1997 got a severe heart attack and was shipped home for a bypass operation. The recovery was slow and was marked by depression. It was an uphill battle where he was helped very much by his wife, Eva, whom he calls a "lighthouse that gives direction and new strength".

Period eight: Director of Areopagos in Norway and China, 1998-

After having recovered from the heart attack and worked one more year with NCA in Norway as Senior Advisor, he was in 1998 offered the directorship of Christian Mission to Buddhists. It was the beginning of the latest period of his life. The Christian Mission to Buddhists was one of the smallest mission organizations in Scandinavia with a rather narrow support basis and a weak economy. It had, however, a major asset in Tao Fong Shan, a mission centre on a mountain top in Hong Kong.[42] By selling off a bit of this property for an amount of almost 100 mill. USD, the organization changed from collecting money to becoming a major donor organization. It had been somewhere on the margin of Scandinavian mission and church but with its enormous free funds (at least in a Scandinavian context) and its new leader it soon became a major player at the centre of the church. Now Jørgensen had got the freedom and platform to pursue several of his visions by influencing and supporting cooperation and mission initiatives of different kinds both in the home base in Norway and Denmark, in the traditional mission areas Hong Kong and China and in the world at large. Instead of doing things alone Areopagos under Jørgensen's leadership developed into a network organisation cooperating closely with the Church of Norway and the Church of Denmark, with educational institutions, with the LWF and WCC and LCWE. In a number of major activities related to spirituality, mission and dialogue, Areopagos played a central and essential role, both because of its money, but also because it had developed the necessary expertise.

Jørgensen's longstanding interest in church and mission came to expression in a new emphasis on the missional church. It seems that Jørgensen in the encounter with the legacy of Lesslie Newbigin and the movement "the Gospel and Our Culture" in America found a new and clear focus for his ecclesiological thinking. It led to a significant contribution in a book on

---

[42] To the history of Tao Fong Shan, see the chapter by Rolv Olsen in this festschrift.

missional ecclesiology.[43] He is inspired by missiologists like Craig Van Gelder,[44] Darrell L. Guder,[45] George Hunsberger,[46] Alan Roxburgh,[47] Eddie Gibbs,[48] Wilbert R. Shenk,[49] and of course Lesslie Newbigin.[50] In his ecclesiological thinking Jørgensen is very critical of the "Constantinian identity" of the church as opposed to a "missional identity" and this involves not least a critique of the Scandinavian state church system.[51] At the same time he stresses the missional nature of the church as being sent to the world with the gospel. Missionary activities are a result of the missional nature or essence of the church.

Jørgensen did not stop at thinking, talking and writing about the missional church. In both Norway and Denmark he and his co-workers were instrumental in lifting up the concept of missional church in such a way that it resulted in two major programmatic activities *Menighet i bevegelse* (Congregation in motion) in Norway and *Kirke hos os* (Church with us) in Denmark. Jørgensen has also been strongly involved in *Samarbeidsråd for menighet og misjon* (Cooperative Council for Church and Mission) in Norway which is an instrument of cooperation between the official state church with its congregations and most of the voluntary Lutheran mission organizations within the church. This is another almost paradoxical situation: that one of the sharpest critics of the state church/mission organization system in Norway, at the same time, without hiding his views, is able to cooperate with these structures and make them cooperate with each other! All of this is carried by a missional

---

[43] Knud Jørgensen, "Trenger kirken omvendelse? På vei mot en misjonal ekklesiologi" (Does the church need conversion? On the way towards a missional ecclesiologi), in: Tormod Engelsviken og Kjell Olav Sannes (eds.): *Hva vil det si å være kirke? Kirkens vesen og oppdrag* (Trondheim: Tapir, 2004), pp. 51-68.

[44] Craig Van Gelder, *The Essence of the Church* (Grand Rapids, Mich.: Baker Books, 1998)

[45] Especially Darrell L. Guder, *The Continuing Conversion of the Church* (Grand Rapids, Mich.: Eerdmans, 1999)

[46] George Hunsberger and Craig Van Gelder, *The Church between Gospel and Culture* (Grand Rapids, Mich.: Eerdmans, 1996)

[47] Alan Roxburgh, *Constructing the Bridge: Developing Missional Ledareship* (Unpublished manuscript, 2003)

[48] Eddie Gibbs and Ian Coffey, *Church Next. Quantum Changes in Christian Ministry* (Downers Grove: InterVarsity Press, 2001)

[49] Wilbert R. Shenk, *Changing Frontiers of Mission* (Maryknoll, N.Y.: Orbis, 1999)

[50] Especially Lesslie Newbigin, *Foolishness to the Greeks. The Gospel and Western Culture* (Grand Rapids, Mich.: Eerdmans, 1986)

[51] Jørgensen, "Trenger kirken omvendelse", 2004, p.60-61. See to the Danish state church the chapter by Hans Raun Iversen in this festschrift

vision and purpose.

With its emphasis on spirituality, Areopagos has also strategically built up the focus on spirituality and pilgrimage in both countries, especially through its two mission pastors, Knut Grønvik in Norway and Ole Skjerbæk Madsen in Denmark. Skjerbæk Madsen has become a leading expert on how the church should relate in new ways to the new spirituality (New Age).

Internationally, Jørgensen and Areopagos have recently taken much financial responsibility for bringing different partners together to plan for the celebration of Edinburgh 2010. The vision is that the preparatory study process may bring together the various traditions that grew out of Edinburgh 1910, especially the conciliar and the evangelical camps. This is an attempt to build bridges and reconnect.

The third pillar in the work of Areopagos is religious dialogue. The influence of Lesslie Newbigin has not only been in the area of missional church, but in his views on theology of religion. The theology of religion has been a challenge for Jørgensen within Areopagos. It is an organisation with a great span of various views on the uniqueness of Christ. This has led him to carry out studies within this field. Newbigin often talks about *committed pluralism.* Jørgensen likes this term because, he says, "it takes seriously the multireligious context, as the same time as it says that we in the midst of the plural context are committed to give an account for our faith in Christ as the only saviour of mankind." In a recent article,[52] Jørgensen rejects the traditional threefold typology of exclusivism, inclusivism and pluralism, and seemingly opts for other categories in which he seems to support Thiessen's notion of "accessibilism".[53] His conclusion is as follows, "God does give everyone revelation that is sufficient for salvation if it is responded to properly, but that the necessary faith varies with the kind of revelation an individual receives."[54]

---

[52] Jørgensen is planning on publishing a book on this subject in the future. So far he has written a chapter in a festschrift for Notto R.Thelle: Knud Jørgensen, "Steps into a pluralist world: Commitment and Accessibilism", *Norsk tidsskrift for misjon*, Vol. 60, No. 3/4 2006, pp. 255-268.

[53] Jørgensen, Steps, 2006, pp.262; cp. Terrance L. Thiessen, *Who Can Be Saved? Reassessing Salvation in Christ and World Religions* (Downers Grove: InterVarsity Press, 2004)

[54] Jørgensen, Steps, 2006, pp.264-5. This article drew a negative response from Rolf Kjøde, the general secretary of Normisjon and a reply from Jørgensen where he insists that he still believes in the possibility of being lost, a view he also had expressed in the original article, cf. Knud Jørgensen, "Misjon og fortapelse", *Luthersk Kirketidende,* Vol. 142, No. 5, 2007, pp. 144-146, Jørgensen, Steps, 2006, p. 265: "Perdition or being lost is therefore a result of the disobedience that says no to the word of the Gospel about salvation. I dare believe that all of us in one way or another shall have an opportunity to choose between faith and unbelief."

It will be interesting to see where Jørgensen's thinking will take him in this area so crucial for an evangelical identity.

Professor Notto R. Thelle at the University of Oslo is a central figure within Areopagos. Jørgensen says that he has inspired him – and sometimes provoked him. His wisdom and intimate knowledge of Japan and Buddhism have been inspiring, but in the field of theology of religion they have disagreed, as Jørgensen also has disagreed with the Emmaus people within his own organisation. Yet, he feels that "learning to give room for and living together with other viewpoints have been exciting challenges".

Last but not least, the work as director of Areopagos has taken Jørgensen back to Hong Kong and China, to Tao Fong Shan with all its activities, to the universities in China, to diaconal projects among the poor segments in China, and to cultural projects. Particularly the encounter with the so-called cultural Christians at the many secular universities has meant a lot to him. Areopagos has been deeply involved in providing theological literature to Chinese universities, and Jørgensen has lectured repeatedly in China. In this work he has been aided by the Asia secretary of Areopagos, Ernst Harbakk, and his huge knowledge of Chinese history, culture and church life.

Jørgensen's sees how the centre of gravity for the Christian church has moved to the global South. His experiences in China and Africa and elsewhere have convinced him that the winds of Christian renewal come from the East and South, a renewal that the West sorely needs. This renewal in the West will certainly look differently than that in the South. It is Jørgensen's vision that Areopagos to a higher degree could become a bridge into Scandinavia for such a renewal.

Conclusion

We have followed Knud Jørgensen through his life until his 65th year and tried to highlight some of his characteristics and achievements. We started by calling him a "missionary statesman", and I hope that by the end of this brief essay the reader may agree. May be we could summarize in a few sentences some reasons for using such a designation:

Knud Jørgensen is firmly planted in the Christian church, with a strong Evangelical, Ecumenical, Charismatic, and Lutheran spirituality expressed in clear theological convictions. He is a man with great vision for the future of the church in mission in a global perspective, a vision which he has pursued with strength, wisdom and integrity. By using his gifts he has functioned as a theological teacher, an inspiring preacher and thoughtful advisor in many contexts and to a variety of people. His leadership qualities have brought him into leading positions in several organizations on the local, national and global level and made him able to lead others to achieve high common goals. He is a man with unusual energy and effectiveness who is able to carry through his plans and visions in practice.

After all this is said, it should nevertheless be underlined that he is first and foremost a simple, humble Christian who wants to serve the Lord, the church and his family and friends faithfully in the best possible way.

For all this and much more many of us are grateful and want to thank him and honour him at this significant point in his life.

PART ONE

MISSION TO THE WORLD IN WORD AND DEED

(1) Church, Mission And Diaconia

Background and Emergence of Norwegian Missions: Historical Sketch and Brief Outlook[1]

Jan-Martin Berentsen

Prof. Em. Dr. Jan-Martin Berentsen; School of Mission and Theology, Stavanger, Norway

Introduction

Norway has for years been widely known as a country of expansive missionary work. Compared to its small size in terms of inhabitants (4.5 million) a surprisingly high number of missionaries from various organizations and churches have been sent to different parts of the world for more than 150 years. Guests visiting Norway from different churches around the world – particularly from the South – often ask questions about this particular feature of Norwegian church life. Leaders as well as ordinary members of many churches in daily co-operation with Norwegian missions and missionaries do the same.

It would take much more than a short chapter to present the background and emergence of this broad and varied movement in a comprehensive and scholarly way. The modest purpose of this rather popular contribution is to provide the outsider with a sketch of some of the historical presuppositions and conditions from which Norwegian missions eventually sprang forth. Who knows, new outsiders may catch interest and join the movement with constructive and critical insight as our honoured co-worker Knud Jørgensen did when he immigrated from Denmark a generation ago.

I shall be selective and limit myself to a brief presentation of why and how the Norwegian missionary movement as a whole came into being in the 19th century. It is an interesting history with its peculiar Norwegian features. There are, however, strong links to theological, sociological and political developments in Europe at large. As we shall try to cover both aspects we need to be content with a few broad strokes, first to the *background* of the

---

[1] The main part of the article is published in Japanese translation in the journal *Senkyo to shingaku* of Kobe Lutheran Theological Seminary, fall 2006. See *Senkyo to shingaku* 28 (2006): 15-25.

movement, then to the *emergence* of its three largest and most influential groups. The three are – in historical order – Norwegian Missionary Society, Norwegian Mission to the Santals (today: Normisjon), and Norwegian Lutheran Mission. In summarising my presentation I shall add some personal comments in terms of an actualising outlook.

Background

European history from the time of the Reformation through the Enlightenment era until the beginning of the 19th century was a turbulent period as well as a period when decisive new ideas emerged in philosophy and theology. Of special interest to us is the shift in the understanding of the missionary mandate of the church which evolved in Protestantism through these couple of centuries.

Missiological renewal in European Protestantism

The point of departure for a proper understanding and appraisal of this shift is to keep in mind the medieval relationship between state and church in Europe. The guiding principle had for long been that a nation's king (or emperor) was the one to decide upon the faith of his people(s) – *cuius regio eius religio*. Ideas like democracy and freedom of religion were still unknown. The monarch had in his power to rule over politics and religion, state and church. After the Reformation, then, Europe was divided along geo-political lines in Catholic and Protestant countries, and the boundaries between Christian and non-Christian lands were decided according to similar principles.

This had implications for the understanding of mission in Lutheran (and Reformed) Orthodoxy in the 17th century. In the controversies with Rome on what it meant to be apostolic, Orthodoxy emphasized that the missionary mandate in Matt 28:18-20 was a personal privilege given to the first apostles, and they had already fulfilled the command by proclaiming the gospel "to every creature under heaven" (Col 1:23). Nobody, said Othodoxy, not even the Pope was to be successor of the first apostles in this respect. The missionary mandate in Matt 28 therefore was not to be taken as a mandate to the church in post-apostolic times. Moreover, the duty to further the cause of Christianity among the peoples belonged to the state, i.e. to the monarch, and to nobody else. Along these lines Lutheran Orthodoxy rejected the idea of mission among non-Christian peoples.

Lutheran Orthodoxy at this point met opposition in the church, and when the leaders of Pietism presented another way of theological reasoning, things started to change. Even though Matt 28 may be seen as a personal privilege for the first apostles, they said, and even though the apostles may have "preached everywhere" (Mk 16:20), the fact is that the light of the gospel is not shining among the non-Christian peoples any more. Therefore, God's mercy simply demands that it be lit again, a task that first of all belongs to the believing church to fulfil.

The person who more than anyone else came to implement Pietism's new understanding of the missionary mandate as an actual challenge for a Christ-believing church was Count Zinzendorf (1700-1760). Certain aspects of his theology made him quite controversial with the consequence that his missiology did not gain immediate recognition in the Lutheran churches. His followers however, the Moravians, immediately started missionary work in a number of countries and came to play a decisive role in the emergence of Norwegian missions.

Another person of interest and importance for developments in Norway is Hans Egede (1686-1758). While serving as a local pastor in the Church of Norway, he struggled with a personal missionary calling. According to the rules of the day he wrote to the king – altogether three letters – to persuade him as head of the church to release him from his parish and send him as missionary to Greenland. In his letters Egede gave theological arguments for mission as a continuous duty for the church. He did not see any other possibility for its practical implementation, however, than a sending by the king – the head of the state and the head of the church. The king was persuaded and Egede finally left for Greenland in 1721. His second, most thorough letter from 1711 has later been called "a monument in the Norwegian history of missions".

Another 100 years passed before Egede's seminal ideas really started to bear fruit in Norway, and when that eventually happened significant developments had taken place further south and west in Europe. It is a well established fact that the breakthrough of Protestant missions is related to England, not least to William Carey and his famous little book from 1792 briefly referred to as *Enquiry*. Carey's book was a last and decisive confrontation with the idea that Mt 28 is a binding mandate for the first apostles only. He gives good reasons why this view is misguided and must be discarded. The Great Commission commissions the church at all times, said Carey.

At the same time developments in Europe towards the end of the 18th century proved conducive to the idea of mission in several ways: the industrial revolution carried deep material and social needs in its wake, a spiritual revival led by John Wesley swept through England, and a growing concern over the way the country treated the people of its colonies was brewing. In the midst of all this the French Revolution in 1789 shook all Europe and created an almost apocalyptic mood in many churches. Some people saw the revolution as a precursor of Antichrist, others as a sign that the glorious Millennium was close at hand. In any case the need for the gospel presented itself as demanding. Parallel to this the Enlightenment and the industrial revolution had paved the way for voluntary initiatives and individual entrepreneurship in society. Inspired by this people joined together and formed missionary societies – first in England with William Carey's Baptist Missionary Society in 1792, London Missionary Society in 1795, and Church Missionary Society in 1799. A few years later the same happened in Germany. Thirty years into the 19th century seven missionary societies, some confessional, some inter-confessional, were born in that country. The breakthrough of Protestant missions was a fact.

Features of early 19th century Norway

The developments in England and Germany influenced Norway in many ways. Politically the year 1814 marks the start of a new era. Norway had for more than 400 years been part of the kingdom of Denmark and was eventually ruled by a system of absolute monarchy. In 1814 Norway formed its own, new constitution. Although the country for some time – as a result of the Napoleon wars – had to go into political union with Sweden, the new constitution brought democratic monarchy to life in the nation. The constitution of 1814 was deeply influenced by modern ideas from the American and French revolutions and changed Norwegian society in many ways, sociologically and religiously. It opened up for a whole new middle class to emerge and make themselves influential through commerce, shipping and industry of various kinds.

Although the idea of freedom of religion needed quite some time to be implemented, the old system's power of the king to rule over religious life was broken in many ways. This is well illustrated through the life of Hans Nielsen Hauge (1771-1824), a most remarkable person in Norwegian history. Hauge was converted as a young man and experienced a strong personal calling to follow Christ and witness to the gospel. For that purpose he started to travel the country from south to north and gathered people for religious meetings in private homes in towns and villages. He soon proved to be extremely gifted both as preacher, industrialist and entrepreneur. Religious revival together with new industry and commerce grew in his footsteps as he taught his followers to be both faithful believers and diligent citizens.

Hauge's religious activities were unlawful, however. According to a law of 1741 no religious gathering could take place except under the auspices of an ordained pastor in the Lutheran state church. Hauge – who was a lay preacher – had therefore to serve tough sentences in prison for his unlawful preaching. Nevertheless, the revival grew and the rule of 1741 was eventually repealed in 1842. The Hauge movement evolved as one of the forming factors of modern Norway both religiously, sociologically and politically. The *Haugians* – as his followers were called – became pillars in the church and, as we shall see, were among the founders of Norwegian missions.

A third factor of importance in our context must be mentioned. The Haugians was not the only lay movement at work in early 19th century Norway. Count Zinzendorf's followers, the *Moravians*, had made themselves known in the country already since the 1730s. Local groups had established themselves from Oslo along the coast to Stavanger and Trondheim. These were all mission-minded people. A few Norwegians had even served with the movement's work in Greenland. In some respects the Moravian groups differed from the Haugians. Generally they recruited their members from higher strata of the population. Both local pastors and other civil servants were among their leaders. Theologically they were strongly evangelical with a somewhat emotional emphasis in their presentation of Christ.

Together with the great political and social changes in early 19th century Norway the Haugians and the Moravians represent features of religious life of the greatest importance for the emergence of Norwegian missions.

Emergence

Various circumstances and incidents in the 1820-1830s make up the concrete point of departure for the first missionary society to be formed in Norway. They also show that close contact with Denmark and Germany/Switzerland played a crucial role. In the Moravian group in Oslo strong interest in missions developed around its leader Niels Johannes Holm. He obtained permission by the government to conduct open meetings on Sundays where he informed about – and collected money for – Moravian missionary enterprises from Denmark and Germany. In 1824 a young student from the Moravian milieu, J.W. Cappelen, travelled to Basel, Switzerland where he studied for two years at the Mission School. He was supported by Danish Missionary Society, established three years before. The plan was for Cappelen to go as a missionary to the Danish colony Guinea. Due to ill health, however, he had to return to Oslo in 1826 where he succeeded in starting a committee for the Basel Mission with support from Moravians, Haugians, and local pastors.

A second stronghold for the Moravians had emerged in the Stavanger area where similar activities for mission support took place both on Moravian and other initiatives. In December 1826 a local association for mission was formed. From the beginning it drew its members mostly from the Moravian group, but after a few years of clarification of purpose and confessional basis some of the influential Haugians involved themselves. Even here there was close contact with the drive for mission further south and west in Europe.

The committee in Oslo and the association in Stavanger are indicators of a peculiar development that proved to be of great significance in the years to come. In town after town small associations for mission were formed. Central in this development were the Moravian dyer F.T. Knudsen and his son, H.C. Knudsen, from Lista, a village on the south-west coast. From 1835 to 1839 the father arranged for his son to study with the newly established Rhenish Missionary Society's school in Barmen, Germany. The winter of 1839-1840 H.C. Knudsen was back in Norway travelling with his father along the coast with a twofold aim in mind: to form local mission associations, and to have the small, local associations form a joint missionary society. His hope was that such a society on a national level could send himself out as missionary. He approached the association in Stavanger with his plan. Time was not yet ripe for such an initiative, however. In 1841 H.C. Knudsen left Norway for South Africa, sent by the Rhenish Missionary Society.

Norwegian Missionary Society

It did not last long before H.C. Knudsen's dream came true. To see a Norwegian missionary society like the ones established further west and south in Europe was a dream shared by quite a few. Already the same year as Knudsen left for South Africa – 1841 – a prominent industrialist and Haugian leader in Stavanger, J. Hougvaldstad, went to Germany to visit the North German Missionary Society in Hamburg. Even Hougvaldstad had a double aim in mind: to see how such a society was organized, and to learn how missionaries were educated.

Hougvaldstad was convinced by what he saw in Hamburg. Well back in Stavanger plans were prepared for a national gathering of all local mission associations. In the spring of 1842 a written invitation was sent to all groups to have delegates meet in Stavanger in order to organize a Norwegian society for mission. At the same time interesting news came from the committee in Oslo where Hans Nielsen Hauge's son, Pastor Andreas Hauge, was now the leader. A young, bright graduate from the theological faculty at the University of Oslo, H.P.S. Schreuder, had made known his missionary calling and published a challenging pamphlet with the title "A word to the Church of Norway on its Christian duty with regard to care for the salvation of non-Christian brothers". There was great interest in Oslo to have this young man ordained by a bishop and sent.

On the 8th of August 1842, then, delegates – mostly lay people – from 65 local associations met in Stavanger. The *Norwegian Missionary Society* (NMS) was formed with the expressed purpose of "working for the extension of the Kingdom of God especially among the heathens through education, sending and support of missionaries". Late the following year H.P.S. Schreuder was sent to South Africa as the first NMS missionary.

Implied in the decision mentioned was the intention to establish a theological school for education of missionaries. This was implemented the following year. The Mission School in Stavanger – today: the School of Mission and Theology – accepted its first three students in 1843.

These events mark the decisive breakthrough of missions in Norway. In order to understand the further development in terms of Norwegian missions later in the 19th century a few comments need to be made.

Three main groups were behind the formation of NMS: Moravians, Haugians and some pastors in the Church of Norway. The movement had grown largely on the concern, initiative and vision of lay people, not by inspiration and official decisions promoted by the church leadership. Seen in the context of early 19th century Norway with its rigid state-church set-up it is no surprise that such a development caused tensions within the church. The lay movement (Haugians and Moravians) and the official structure of the church had still to find a *modus vivendi* in terms of constructive relationships. The tensions had somehow to be sorted out in connection with the formation of NMS. H.P.S. Schreuder had openly advocated the view that the Church of

Norway ought to be his sending agent rather than a "society" organized according to modern voluntary and democratic principles. This remained a problem in Schreuder's relationship with NMS until he finally broke with the organization in 1873.

NMS did not aim at a break with the Church of Norway, however, but rather wanted to see itself as an agent for the missionary calling of the church. This is obvious from the fact that NMS from the very beginning sought to have missionary candidates who met the qualifications ordained by the church. This was granted in 1864, a fact which shows that the church accepted and regarded NMS as its representative agent for mission.

Norwegian Mission to the Santals (today: Normisjon)

The Mission School of 1843 very soon proved to be decisive for developments far beyond the NMS, at times in unexpected ways. When the school was about to accept new students in 1862, the 22 year old L. Skrefsrud (1840-1910) from north of Oslo went all the way to Stavanger to apply for admission. The young man was special in many ways. He had already proved himself a genius in languages. The problem was that he had just been released from prison after a four year sentence for thefts and robbery! He was radically converted while in prison and experienced a strong missionary calling.

The school turned down his application. Little did NMS know that they turned down the person who was to become the most famous Norwegian missionary in the 19th century. Again we see how important the contact with Germany was in the emergence of Norwegian missions. Some Moravians in Stavanger took care of the young man, had confidence in the former convict and helped him go to Berlin to realize his call. In Berlin Skrefsrud met the Dane H.P. Børresen and wife Caroline. The three entered into a deep, friendly relationship which eventually took them through decades of common missionary service in India. Børresen introduced Skrefsrud to the thirty year old Gossner Mission. Skrefsrud got some training at their institute and was sent to India at the end of 1863 together with the Børresens.

The three's service with the Gossner Mission lasted for only a couple of years. They then went into cooperation with the Baptist Missionary Society of England, but after some time organized their own work under the name of Indian Home Mission to the Santals. This was an independent society with its own board formed and located in India. On the 26th of September 1867 the cornerstone was laid for their first mission station in Santal Parganas, a date usually regarded as the date of foundation for the Norwegian Mission to the Santals.

The work of Skrefsrud and Børresen had as yet no organizational basis in Norway. However, as Skrefsrud was an extremely able missionary both as linguist and social reformer among the Santals, he soon gained a reputation in India which eventually reached England and Scandinavia. On his few visits to Norway he inspired great crowds and impressed even some of the country's intellectual elite. Support for his work grew and after a visit by Børresen in 1876 the Central Committee for Mission among the Santals was organized in Oslo. Attempts were made by some of its leaders to have the committee integrated with the NMS, but this did not materialize. The first gathering as a nationwide organization was held in Oslo in 1908.

The further history of the Norwegian Mission to the Santals is not of interest here. Suffice it to say that in 2001 the mission merged with the Norwegian Lutheran Inner Mission and formed Normisjon.

Norwegian Lutheran Mission

With the NMS established and the formation of the Norwegian Mission to the Santals under way interest in foreign mission increased remarkably in Norway. The information from foreign countries provided by *Misjonstidende*, the journal of NMS, was rare for its day. For some time the journal had in fact higher subscription than the largest secular newspaper.

As we have seen, close contact with Germany had so far been of great importance for the emergence of Norwegian missions. From the 1870ies influence from England came to play a major role, especially after Hudson Taylor formed China Inland Mission (CIM) in 1865. Influence from England was thus coupled with increasing interest in China, and in 1884 two young Norwegian women from Kristiansand went to this new field in the service of CIM. Again the Mission School in Stavanger inadvertently came to play a role. In 1887 Ole Naestegaard presented himself for entrance exams but did not pass. He felt a strong call for China, however, and in 1888 he went there as a missionary on his own, supported by friends in Stavanger and Oslo. When Hudson Taylor himself visited Oslo in 1889 some of Naestegaard's supporters formed a committee to work in close contact with CIM.

Naestegaard was not the only one who failed admission to the Mission School in 1887, Sivert Gjerde was another. Even Gjerde found supporters in Stavanger for his call to China. During a visit by Gjerde to Bergen a group of women was moved to form an association for mission to China. Some men joined and in March 1890 a board was formed to lead "The Bergen committee for mission to China". The key person in the committee was Johannes Brandtzaeg (1861-1931).

The interest in China had resulted in supporting committees and associations in various parts of Norway, and a suggestion was made that these local groups be gathered as one organization. Others would rather like to see the concern for China integrated into NMS. The Bergen committee eventually invited to consultations on the issue in October 1890. Lars Dahle, General Secretary of NMS, made clear that it was not possible for NMS to start missions in a new field for the time being. He also voiced concern that some of the proponents of missions to China were not in agreement with the Lutheran confession. Representatives of the CIM committee in Oslo on their part made it clear that they were not ready to enter into a co-operation based on Lutheran doctrine.

The Bergen committee, however, saw such a confessional basis as necessary for their work.

The result of the consultations was clear: a new national organization for the China cause was to be established. On 18th-19th May 1891 the *Norwegian Lutheran Federation for Missions in China* (popularly called The China-federation) was constituted in Bergen. Late in September the same year its first eight missionaries left Bergen for the new field. Among the eight was also Johannes Brandtzaeg. Due to ill health, however, he had to return to Norway a year later and was entrusted with the task to lead the new organization. In 1898 Brandtzaeg started a school close to Bergen for the education of the federation's missionaries, and in 1915 he moved both the headquarters and the school to Fjellhaug, Oslo, where they are still located. The organization's work expanded rapidly both in China and Norway. When Western missionaries had to leave China towards the end of the 1940ies, The China-federation started work in other countries (as Japan and Ethiopia) and therefore changed its name to *Norwegian Lutheran Mission* (NLM).

As we have seen, concern for the Chinese people and NMS' reluctance to take up the task in 1890 may be regarded as the two immediate reasons why NLM emerged as a third Norwegian mission. One further reason needs some comments. The China-federation had emerged decisively as a lay movement. Tension between the lay movement and the Church of Norway's official structure was felt already in the formation of NMS, as we have pointed out above. When NMS decided to have its missionaries ordained in the church by a bishop and had that granted in 1864, it was not readily accepted in all quarters of the lay movement. Some opted for a more independent stand in relation to the church with its structure and clergy and favoured the formation of a new mission for such reasons.

The issue of ordination of missionaries, then, very soon became a burning issue in NLM. Different opinions were found at grass roots level as well as in the board and among the missionaries. The bishops of the Church of Norway were also not ready to grant ordination. When the board asked for Johannes Brandtzaeg – himself a theological candidate from the University of Oslo – to be ordained in 1891, the bishops turned the application down. The debate then continued in NLM through the 1890s. One party advocated that the organization should continue to seek ordination in the church for missionaries who met the qualifications. Another party argued that the organization itself should consecrate its missionaries in a special ceremony. When the General Assembly in 1899 and 1901 finally decided in favour of the latter, NLM had chosen a stand different from that of NMS in relation to the official structure of the church, a stand that has manifested itself in various ways until the present.

Summary and outlook

We have briefly surveyed an important period in Norwegian church history. Let me summarize in four points.

Firstly, the background and emergence of Norwegian missions are closely related to the history of Protestantism in Europe. The breakthrough of the modern missionary movement in England towards the end of the 18th century with subsequent developments in Germany in the beginning of the 19th influenced church life in Norway. This is seen for example in the role of the *Moravians*.

Secondly, at the same time life in general in Norway underwent great changes, illustrated by the history of Hans Nielsen Hauge. The lay movement within the Church of Norway which grew out of the *Haugean revival* became a decisive factor in the emergence of Norwegian missions.

Thirdly, the emergence of Norwegian missions is intimately linked to the life story of *particular individuals*, most often young lay people who experienced a personal call from God. This holds true for all three missions in our survey. Some of these people came to play significant roles in the life of the church both in Norway and in far-away countries.

Fourthly, the most adequate way to explain – from a Christian point of view – why and how these individuals came to be of such importance is to acknowledge that *God* was at work in and through them. The emergence of Norwegian missions in the 19th century is not a human endeavour to be applauded, but the gracious work of the Lord of the church.

The background and emergence of Norwegian missions are not simply of historical interest however. We do well to reflect upon some elements in this story with a view to the mission of the church today.

First of all we notice the consistent and faithful *orientation towards "the other"* which was exhibited in people behind the emerging missions. At a time when hardships of daily life at home were at a level that could have absorbed physical and mental strength a hundred percent, fellow humans in far-away countries and in very different circumstances caught the interest of the mission minded men and women. People in the movement demonstrated concern for humans whom they had never seen. This is all the more noteworthy as we know that the level of knowledge about Africa in the middle of the 19th century was very low; little if anything was taught in school, and daily newspapers as channels of information were not yet in circulation in any significant way. Nevertheless, from scarce information people caught fire and proved willing to invest from whatever little they had for the benefit of "the other". Most important of all was that she/he be given a fair chance to hear the gospel.

In recent years the emerging movement has certainly got its share of "pepper" because it adopted some of the negative stereotypes of the African. The criticism, valid as it at points may be, is obviously anachronistic. What else could be expected? The stereotypes were not primarily promoted by the emerging missionary movement. They were established and argued for by the learned European scholarship of the day. That some of the same resounded on grass root level cannot surprise. More surprising is the fact that NMS brought

Moses from South Africa (in the 1860s) and Rabeony from Madagascar (in the 1880s) to study theology in Stavanger at a time when it was a widely held opinion in academia that the peoples to which the two belonged were not yet capable of understanding such an "advanced" religion as Christianity. The orientation towards "the other" did not only subscribe to popular opinions, it prepared new paths towards the future.

There are lessons to be learned at this point for the church in the affluent West. Orientation towards "the other" is not the most salient feature of today's society, to say the least, neither in the church nor outside. On the one hand we have knowledge about "the other" in abundance; the flow of information about people's living conditions around the world is without limit. On the other hand we go on enjoying plenty of opportunities to live comfortably with our affluence for ourselves. The situation seems to breed narcissistic egotism and self-centredness – materially and spiritually – rather than concern for "the other". The emergence of Norwegian missions was carried forward by people who knew quite well the meaning of "godliness with contentment" (1 Tim 6:6). Have we lost the apostolic perspective of godliness and contentment to the effect that orientation towards "the other" has had to give way for preoccupation with "the self"?

Secondly we notice the role of *the young* in the breakthrough and emergence of Norwegian missions. Of course, the Haugean and Moravian groups included people of all age groups, even most vital and active seniors. A person like John Hougvaldstad, for example, was already 70 when he went to Germany to learn how to run a missionary society. This fact gives us no reason to conclude, however, that the movement was mostly the work of bearded old men. H.N. Hauge himself was only 25 when he experienced his spiritual breakthrough, and he had travelled all across Norway as a powerful preacher before turning 35. As for the formation of the organizations covered above, the role of the young is even more conspicuous. A young theological candidate just out of university – Schreuder – was of crucial importance for the formation of NMS. A young convict – Skrefsrud – eventually became the founder of the Norwegian Mission to the Santals. And neither Gjerde nor Brandtzaeg had turned 30 when they were instrumental in the formation of "The Bergen committee for mission to China" in 1890. Young people with a calling and a vision won confidence and support and became central forces in the emergence of Norwegian missions. Not only were they young, they came out of very different backgrounds and some did not immediately exhibit the kind of qualifications which would seem to guarantee success.

Even this may be a memento for us to heed. Churches and missions of our days are elaborate bureaucracies, and high academic and other qualifications are expected from the ones who want to play a role. This may well be necessary; times have changed and we have to meet the standards of our own days in church and mission. Nevertheless, is it too difficult for the young with a calling and a vision to obtain a hearing and find important roles to play in a missional church today? Is there anything in the way we move and operate in traditional missions that give the impression that mission is first of all a concern for the old? If so, we are obviously out of step with our roots.

Finally, a point closely related to what we just said; the agenda of the young forerunners in Norwegian missions was not uncontroversial. The spiritual renewal that swept through the church was met with scepticism and opposition both for theological and structural reasons. It is probably more than an interesting coincidence that the law of 1741 saying that no religious gathering could be conducted except under the auspices of an ordained pastor, was repealed in 1842 – the year NMS was formed! The Haugian renewal had proved that the gifts of the Spirit could not be contained and restrained by legal rulings. *Spiritual renewal* called for *renewed structures* in the church. When the need to share the gospel with "the heathen" eventually took root as a theological conviction, the problem was how this could materialise in practice. The structural set-up of the church was not geared to take on the theological challenge. Furthermore, how an issue like the gifts of the Spirit was to be understood in relation to emerging ideas like democracy and freedom in the church was presenting itself as an intriguing and most controversial question.

In such a context of spiritual and structural reorientation the founders of Norwegian missions struggled towards a missional renewal of their church. The outcome was missionary organisations structurally independent from the bureaucracy of the Church of Norway, but at the same time conscious of being missional agents for the church to which their people belonged. Thus a symbiosis developed which has continued – in different forms and to various degrees of tension – until the present.

The lesson for today seems obvious. Tension between freedom and structure, renewal and continuity, belongs to the church as such and has followed her all the way. All too often, however, the tension has ruined the unity and resulted in controversy and open split. There is, in other words, a constant need to work for a structural flexibility in the church that allows for spiritual renewal and updated missional approaches. Young people with a calling and a vision may still be in a unique position to lead the way just as they were at the time of the breakthrough of Norwegian missions, guiding the church towards a renewed orientation towards "the other".

How can a Folk Church be Missional Church?

Hans Raun Iversen

Associate Professor Hans Raun Iversen, Faculty of Theology, University of Copenhagen, Denmark

How can a Folk Church not be missional?

> "The Church exists by mission, just as the fire exists by burning" (Emil Brunner 1931), mission meaning: making Christ known and believed as far at this is possible for human beings. As congregations must be missional, mission must be congregational.

Lutheran definitions of Church often emphasize the functional aspect, i.e. the Church is the Church insofar as it is a community preaching the Gospel and administering the Sacraments.[1] *Karl Barth*'s contemporary in dialectic theology, *Emil Brunner*, put it bluntly when stating that "the Church exists by mission, just as the fire exists by burning".[2] The fire has various functions, heating, lightening, spoiling, consuming, cleaning and/or polluting. If the fire is not burning, however, there is no fire. The Church too has a number of functions, such as building community, celebrating, serving people in various ways etc. If the church is not making Christ known and believed as a basic dimension of whatever it is, the Church is no longer a Christian Church, belonging to Christ.

I was educated as a missiologist during the 1970s in the wave after the study program on *The Missionary Structure of the Congregation*, launched by the *World Council of Churches* after the merger between the WCC and the *International Missionary Council* in New Delhi in 1961. The relationship between Church and mission has therefore always been a key issue for me. Basically I am convinced that congregations must be missional, just as mission must be congregational. Mission and Church belong together as two interwoven dimensions of the same reality.[3] The good news is only news if it is

---

[1] *Confessio Augustana* 1530, article 7.

[2] Emil Brunner, *The Word in the World* (London: SCM Press, 1931), 11.

[3] Charles van Engen has written one of the better books on this issue in *God's Missionary People. Rethinking the Purpose of the Local Church* (Grand

communicated. There is not a message if there are no messengers. Christian faith can only stay alive in us when we practice and communicate our faith (1 Cor 9:16 and 23).

A Folk Church like any other church does have its anti-missional sides. It is, for example, very much an established, even bureaucratic, Church. The Danish Folk Church is in fact a state-governed Church – with a secular state as its legal subject at the national level. It is a church in Babylonian captivity; to a far extent run by other criteria than those of the Gospel. But the Folk Church may also have potential for mission: it has good relationships with, and easy access to, the great majority of the Danish people, most of whom are in fact members paying their Church tax. There is a fairly high degree of general confidence and trust among the various actors around the local Folk Church, and it also enjoys stable funding through the above-mentioned tax, which is collected by the state alongside the municipality and state taxes.

A Folk Church at its best is as much and often more a facilitator for various activities going on in the midst of the lives of ordinary people than an organization over and against the people. In this respect the missional potential of a Folk Church may be even better than that of other church forms. This was also the experience at the time of the revivals: any good Danish revivalist pastor 120 years ago might revive major numbers of his parishioners, whereas foreigners like *Billy Graham* and *Luis Palau* never made any significant impact during their campaigns in Denmark.[4]

On the other hand a Folk Church with a long history is often experienced as a power from above and thus as a pacifying factor in terms of religion: it demands nothing and expects very little from its members – except their Church tax! It is indeed a striking fact that the Nordic countries, which have had the longest and strongest state-governed (Lutheran) national Churches, are also generally the most secularised societies in the world, according to the conventional definition of secularization.[5]

Rapids: Baker Book House 1991). I developed my own simple thesis that "proper congregational life in the local context is proper mission and vice versa" during two years of participant observations in eight different local congregations in eight different ethnic groups in Northern Tanzania in 1977 and 1978, cf. my book *Tanzania tur/retur. Syv tekster om socialisme og missio*n (Århus: FK-Tryk, 1981). A concentrated discussion on my point of view is found in "Incarnation, Congregation and Mission", in *Identity and Conflict. Essays in Honour of Johannes Aagaard* (New Delhi, Munshiram Manoharlal Publishers Pvt. Ltd., 1998): 203-218.

[4] Cf. my evaluation in "Palau og Ansgar", *Nordisk Missionstidsskrift* 100/1 (1989): 8-12.

[5] Cf. Hans Raun Iversen, "Secular Religion and Religious Secularism", *Nordic Journal of Religion and Society*, 19/2 (2006): 75-92.

Decisive characteristics of Danish/Nordic Societies today

> Danish (Nordic) Society is tribal and almost communist in terms of economy, welfare, culture and mentality. Danes have much in common in terms of 1) primary socialization in families and child care institutions, 2) a comprehensive folk school system (*single state school*), 3) strong Public Service mass media with converging socializing entertainment, 4) a labour market with flexicurity, 5) a Protestant-inspired universal welfare system, 6) consensus seeking practices in civil society and 7) a common park of religious traditions.

In recent years we have seen a number of studies seeking to establish what the Nordic countries have in common – as a special part of Europe.[6] Major areas of history and traditions and not least the similar languages (apart from Finnish) are common to the Nordic countries. The seven above-mentioned factors are found in all the Nordic countries – in slightly different forms – and are probably even stronger as unifying factors among Nordic people. It is to be assumed that they also determine the common conditions of work for our Folk Churches.

Three teachers from three faculties at the University of Copenhagen are currently attempting to study what we initially called *The Heart-Beat in Denmark – Patterns of Mentality and its Institutional Form in a Protestant Welfare Society*. The ambition is to write a book on Denmark inspired among others by Robert Bellah's *Habits of the Heart. Individualism and Commitment in American Life* from 1985. The study is based on interviews and with no initial thesis to prove. So far the result seem to be that common institutions as the seven above mentioned go hand in hand with a common mentality, and an extremely high degree of satisfaction with life in Denmark. The Danes do not consider themselves to be the best in the world. They feel, however, that they are good at being who they are! Therefore they fit for Denmark and Denmark fits for them.

In spite of many variations in the Nordic countries, e.g. among Swedes who want to be the best and Danes who want to be the Danes[7], from an international perspective the common factors, denominators and patterns are predominant. After all, our societies are structured in similar ways. At the same time it is significant that all of our countries have Folk Churches with approx. 80 % of the people as members – in spite of many years with freedom of religion (in Denmark since 1849) and significant groups of immigrants with other religions.

A difficult topic for discussion is whether the religious traditions and their

---

[6] Cf. e.g. Øystein Sørensen and Bo Stråth (eds.), *The Cultural Construction of Norden* (Copenhagen: Scandinavian University Press, 1997), and Björn Ryman et al (eds.), *Nordic Folk Churches. A Contemporary Church History* (Grand Rapids: William B. Eerdsmans Publishing Company, 2005).

[7] Cf. Hanne Sanders, *Nyfiken på Danmark –klokare på Sverige* (Göteborg: Makadam/Center for Danmarksstudier, 2006).

subsequent secularization, into the "Parks of Religions", as I like to call it, is mainly a dependent or a determining factor in Nordic societies. It is obvious that the Folk Church is vitally dependent on the development of the other common arenas. For example in the late 1960s and early 1970s, when a large number of mothers left home to work full-time on the labour market, we saw a decrease in Church practice, and especially in infant baptism, a rite that is essential for the survival of Folk Churches.[8] In the same way the work of the Folk Churches depends on the access of the Church to cooperation with the Folk School, as the Danish comprehensive school system is called. This is entirely legal in Demark but depends on the goodwill of the teachers involved. On the other hand it is strongly argued that the fact that at the Reformation the king and thus the state expropriated not only the property and leadership but also the infrastructure and project of the church, is the major historical factor behind the development of the universalistic welfare state system in Nordic countries.[9] In many ways our societies can be understood as encompassing a sort of secularised Lutheranism.[10] In the above mentioned study in progress it appears that Danes are very much committed to work and to relations to friends and family. Thus they emphasise vocation or work and placement (*kald og stand*) above anything else, which may be interpreted as a form of secular Lutheranism.

> The comprehensive Folk School teaches its pupils that some people believe in God, and that you are also allowed to do so, with the reservation that God may not exist. The most popular forms of "Church" are TV, Cinema and Literature. Here deeply-felt ethical and existential concerns can be fleshed out in a way where no authority (*ecclesia*) tells you what to think and do. The media leave it to you to be "Christian in your own way", as Scandinavians like to put it.

A recent study of how belief in God is present in various arenas of Danish society points out that the basic form of faith in God among Danes is the one formed in the Folk School, where children in Form 3 (aged 8-9) have already learnt that there are these stories about God, but where the teachers, when asked if they are true, always answer, "I don't know, but some people believe so". With the combination of religious story-telling and scientifically-based teaching in the Folk School children and after them adults are likely to end up with a rather unarticulated, conditional and reserved faith in God. Most people

---

[8] Cf. Hans Raun Iversen: Gudstro i den danske religionspark, in Morten Thomsen Højsgaard and Hans Raun Iversen: *Gudstro i Danmark* (Copenhagen: Anis, 2005), 105.

[9] Cf. Jens Holger Schjørring and Jens Thorkild Bak (red.): *Velfærdsstat og kirke* (Copenhagen: Anis, 2005).

[10] Uffe Østergaard: *Europas ansigter. Nationale stater og politiske kulturer i en ny, gammel verden*, (Copenhagen: Rosinante, 1992), 336ff.

when urged to respond place themselves not too far from the centre of the national Park of Religion, when they say, "Yes, I believe in God, but maybe there is no God". A precise picture of the Danish state of religious affairs is given in the following brief dialogue by Woody Allen:

> A: Do you believe in God? B: I'm not sure… A: Well, Kierkegaard says that if you're not sure, then you don't! B: Okay! Then I guess I do! [11]

According to the *European Value Studies* Danes rank top of the scale in relation to social solidarity and willingness to pay high taxes to maintain their welfare state, but at the bottom when it comes to confidence in collective decisions and common authorities on ethical and existential questions. They therefore have no idea that the Church might have anything important to say when personal or political decisions are to be taken on questions such as the use of genetic embryo examinations leading to abortion. However, the Danes are much concerned about moral responsibility, such as the criteria for life and death. At present the majority of the best-attended Danish films deal with just such questions with great success. Danes who would never think of going to their Church with such questions deliberately turn to Cinema, TV, Literature, Internet etc. and sometimes to family and friends – but rarely to the Church.[12] *The Da Vinci Code* has become extremely popular and read by many more people than the Bible. In Denmark the secret to the success of Dan Brown's book is not that it brings a lot of occult stuff, but rather that it emphasises the importance of churchless Christianity, where what matters is not who you are but whom you choose to be for the time being. In that respect it is helpful that the old "Great Code"[13] (i.e. the Bible) is now being supplemented if not replaced by new "Christian" codes such as the *Da Vinci Code*.

> Danes live on the plains and among the green hills of the North, without mountains and valleys like Norway: "To researchers who are legion in the Scandinavian region, I really must make plain: A Norwegian is more Norwegian than a Dane is ever Dane" (Piet Hein). If Norwegians traditionally believe too much in too little, Danes believe too little in too much.

When it comes to ethical and existential questions, Danes are even more individualistic than Norwegians, who are used to belonging to a certain valley with a particular identity in terms of culture and religion. It is significant that approx. 10 % of the life circle rituals (*casualia*) in Norway are conducted by

---

[11] Quoted from Morten Warmind. "Ateisme i Danmark", in Højsgaard and Iversen (eds.) 2005, 290.

[12] Cf. Stig Hjarvard. "Medialisering af religiøse forestillinger", in Højsgaard and Iversen (eds.) 2005, 175ff.

[13] Cf. Jan Ulrik Dyrkøb, *Northrop Fryes litteraturteori* (København: Berlingske Forlag 1979), 61ff.

the *Human Ethical Society*, whereas there is practically no such alternative to the rituals of the Folk Church in Denmark[14]. Even though there are controversial pastors on both political wings and differing religious and political styles in various congregations, the general outlook of the Danish Folk Church is mainstream, comprehensive and uncontroversial.

A very few people who take a strong political or religious stand may leave the Folk Church because of its inability to make collective decisions on any controversy. If you only say a little and are heard by very few you will not provoke many people. If – as happened on Christmas Eve 2005 – 300 pastors collectively decide to preach against the lack of lodging for foreigners in the Danish house, you may have a little unrest but you will soon be back to business as usual – not mixing politics and Christianity, as the self-contradictory slogan goes in the politically governed Danish Folk Church. Generally speaking the Folk Church in Denmark is fairly stable in terms of membership. The general rule is that only those people who have had too few or only negative experience in their church cancel their membership, at present a few thousands a year and equivalent to the number rejoining the church. As the only Church in the Nordic countries the Folk Church in Denmark has never faced a real campaign encouraging people to leave the church. Even if atheists are mobilising today, the general feeling seem to be that campaigning against religion is being too serious about religion.

Thousands of social and political gatherings in Denmark open with one of the famous national songs, *Langt højere bjerge* (Far higher hills), which concludes as follows:

> Far more metal, so red and so white
> Others got from mountains and plunder.
> Danes, nonetheless, have daily bread,
> Even in the hut of the poor man.
> That's when in richness we have come far,
> When few have too much and fewer too little.

This song was composed by the Danish national bard and modern father of Church and nation, *N. F. S. Grundtvig* (1783-1872) on the occasion of a Danish expedition to the West Indies in 1820. The idea of a social welfare state, where each individual citizen has the right to economic help from the common basket of state and municipality, was far from his mind. Even so, as a Christian he wanted there to be food for the poor Lazarus – and he certainly wanted there to be as few poor people as possible in our small country. Presumably, Grundtvig here is drawing on the story of how God nurtured the Israelites by sending

[14] In the antireligious wave after some years with religion as the most debated issue in Denmark a majority of the city magistrate in Copenhagen in April 2007wants to open the first non-consecrated funeral place in Copenhagen.

manna to them in the desert: the people were instructed to gather as much as needed, two quarts for each member of a household, with the result that "those who gathered much did not have too much, and those who gathered less did not have too little. Each had gathered just what he needed" (Ex 26:18). It is a similar vision of the divine distribution of God's own gifts that is behind the words of Grundtvig in this famous Danish national song.

Denmark has followed a silent and almost totally peaceful way from a rural, agricultural country in the 19th century via a modern, industrialised country in the 20th century[15] to a highly competitive "flexicurity" economy in the globalisation of the 21st century. [16] Thus the Danes repeatedly are ranked as the most "happy" people in the world in international surveys. As mentioned above the Danes are very much satisfied with their own performance, institutions and mentality. Exactly this makes them turn their backs to people "who are not like us" as seen in current immigrant politics and the Muhammad Cartoon Crises 2006[17].

Denmark is one of the most egalitarian countries in the world. The 10 % richest have only 2.8 times more money available than the 10 % poorest. Having more in common and being more egalitarian we are more communist than the communists ever were. For this project the Folk Church and the Folk State are supposed to stand together, excluding those who do not belong to "we Danes". Like the Russians support the dictatorship of Putin, who is making the majority of Russians richer, the majority of the Danes, among whom 5/6 are becoming richer these years, are happy having a bourgeois government dependent on the nationalist Danish Folk Party, whose new slogan is "Strict politics with regard to foreigners and true welfare" (Stram udlændingepolitik og ægte *velfærd*).[18]

[15] Not least due to the influence of Grundtvig, cf. Stephen Boris, *The Land of the Living. The Danish Folk High Schools and Denmark's Non-violent Path to Modernization* (Nevada City: Blue Dolphin, 1991).

[16] Cf. John L. Campbell, John A Halland and Ove K. Pedersen (eds.) *National Identity and the Varieties of Capitalism* (Copenhagen: DJØF Publishing, 2006).

[17] Cf. Lisbet Christoffersen (ed.): *Gudebilleder.Ytringsfrihed og religion i en globaliseret verden* (Copenhagen: Tiderne Skifter, 2006). An English edition of this book is under preparation.

[18] It is noteworthy that the majority of pastors and probably also of church Christians are not at all in favor of present Danish politics, cf. Hans Raun Iversen, "Kan præsterne anerkende de anderledes troende og samtidig være i mission blandt dem?" in *Karma, koran, kirke – religiøs mangfoldighed som folkekirkelig udfordring* (Århus: Forlaget Univers, 2006).

Determining characteristics of Nordic/Danish Folk Churches today

A (Nordic sort of) Folk Church is what you have between the autocratic King's Church and what comes after the Folk Church (Krister Stendahl). The Danish Folk Church was created politically as a changeling (Kløvedal Reich), as the only solution politically possible when Denmark acquired its democratic constitution in 1849. Currently the Folk Church in Denmark is taken hostage in an iron triangle between state, church and native folk – leaving Muslims, for example, outside as non-recognized.

If St. Peter had asked, as the last point on the agenda at the first assembly of the apostles in Jerusalem (Acts 15), what sort of church the heathen people of the countries of Northern Europe should have, the meeting might have come up with many and various suggestions. The only one they would never have invented is the Folk Church. Only history can invent a Folk Church.

A Folk Church is what you have *after* the state church and *before* what comes after the folk church, the Swedish professor and bishop, *Krister Stendahl*, once said.[19] In the process of introducing secular democracy and freedom of religion in the 19th and 20th centuries the old Lutheran state Churches kept the great majority of the population as members and were more or less formally labelled Folk Churches, even though the state church legislation was only gradually changed to democratic church rule. The Folk Churches have contributed considerably to the cultural and political coherence of people and nations in Scandinavia. To a varying degree they also prevented strong free churches from developing, this being the case especially in Denmark. The Folk Churches of Scandinavia at one and the same time have kept the majority of the people as Church members and have served as insurance against too *much* religion, as the German political theologian Dorothee Sölle once put it.

A recent minor prophet in Denmark, *Ebbe Kløvedal Reich,* pointed out in one of his many historical surveys that the Danish Folk Church was born a weakling and a changeling that nobody really cared for.[20] Even though up to the Second World War the Social Democrats as well as Christian-inspired Conservatives in principle wanted a split between Church and state, nothing happened to this effect, as the Church "as such" never had any organisation and standpoint of its own. These days the Social Democratic opposition to the Liberal-Conservative government wants to discuss Church-state relations, but they have no voice in a situation of national "crisis" such as the one that

---

[19] Krister Stendahl, "De nordiske folkekirkers fremtid" in Kjell Ove Nilsson (ed.), *Folkekirkerne i Norden* (Uppsala: Nordiska Ekumeniska Instituttet, 1986), 143.

[20] Ebbe Kløvedal Reich, *Kun et gæstekammer. Historien om den danske folkekirkes fødse*l (Aarhus: Landsforeningen af Menighedsrådsmedlemmer, 1999), 96. See further 109.

followed the publication of the Muhammed cartoons in 2006.

Since the reformation in 1536 (bringing a civil war to its end) Denmark never had a 1) revolution, 2) civil war, 3) occupation (sic!), 4) serious cultural war, 5) revival leading to splinter churches, 6) immigration seriously challenging the hegemony of the ethnic Danish group. Thus the triangle people, state and church may still be seen as a unity.[21] Currently the Folk Church in Denmark is thus taken hostage by its own history in an iron triangle between state, church and native people – leaving e. g. Muslims outside as non-recognized.[22]

> The Danish Folk Church (the only church called Folk Church in a national constitution) is the weakest monopoly church in the world. It is what Danish people want to have instead of the "*ecclesia*" (the religious folk assembly gathered at the square), which they have no sense of. The Folk Church is respected and used by its members in the same way as public hospitals.

In the debate about "believing" or "belonging" I label the Danes as "belonging without believing" or even better "belonging without even believing in belonging".[23] Few Danes ever left the Folk Church, of which their forefathers were forced to be members in its proper state Church edition until 1849. On the other hand most of them never took a firm decision to be full and responsible members of their Church. Thus at the most 15 % of the members vote at the elections of congregational boards in the approx. 10 % of the parishes where there is more than a single list of candidates at the elections every fourth year. When we examine what they do in terms of attending Church, conforming to the faith of their Church and having positive expectations of their Church the Danes together with the Swedes are the most secular people in the world, at a maximum distance to their Church.

The Danes are extremely afraid of too much religion, especially as they perceive it among Muslims. Politicians are very successful in exploiting this fear. Paradoxically at one and the same time Danes have the feeling that religion should play a more significant role – as a stabilizing factor behind their fragile Cultural Christianity.[24] When asked what is most important about the

---

[21] Iversen 2006.

[22] In a recent study (Peter Gundelach and Ester Nørregaard Nielsen, *Etniske gruppers værdier* (Copenhagen: Ministeriet for Integration, 2007), 126 and 129) it appears that only app. 40% of ethnic Danes emphasises full political freedom for all groups and freedom to perform all sort of religious rituals. App. 85% of immigrant Danes supports these freedoms.

[23] Hans Raun Iversen, "Leaving the distant Church. The Danish Experience" in Mordecai Bar-Lev and William Shaffir (eds.), *Leaving Religion and Religious Life*, (London: Jai Press Inc.1997), 156.

[24] Christian A. Larsen, *Danskernes forhold til religionen – en afrapportering af ISSP98* (Ålborg: Aalborg Universitetscenter, 2002), 86-88.

Church, Danes point to the old buildings, the life-circle ritual and Christmas – with a very low priority to ordinary Sunday Services. When asked how the Church should prioritize its work, the result is similar with one striking exception: the Church should first of all "help elderly and sick people" and "contribute to international relief work".[25] This of course is totally unrealistic, as 99 % of social work has long ago been taken over by the state and the municipalities. It does, however, signify that the Danes want the Church to be there to do what they – on the background of their Cultural Christianity – think that all of us should do. Knowing that we do not do it, they believe that at least the Church, that taught us Cultural Christianity's law of loving one's neighbour should do so itself!

Life circle rituals, family traditions and the role of the Church as a sort of guarantor behind our Cultural Christianity make the Church almost as legitimate as the National Health Service. The Church is an institution which should be respected. On the other hand it also means that the churches are treated just like the hospitals. Danes pay the taxes necessary but rarely come to church except when badly needed, i.e. when they or their friends and relatives need to have something done.

> 83 % of the Danish population are members of the Folk Church, 75.5 % of babies are baptised at the time of name-giving, 72 % of the youth are confirmed at age 14, 43 % of all marriages are conducted in church, and 89 % of all funerals (figures from 2005/2006). App. 2% of the Danes use to attend church on a given Sunday.

As we have more elderly Church members dying than babies being baptised, membership of the Danish Folk Church is decreasing by roughly 0.5 % per annum. For the time being the most severe decrease is found in the figures for confirmation, which dropped from 77% to 72 % between 2001 and 2005. An even more drastic fall has been seen in the percentage of marriages conducted in the Church. These dropped from 74 % in 1966 to 43 % in 2001. On the other hand the figures for infant baptism and Church funerals are fairly stable.

The present cultural situation is characterised by individualism in the sense that the only choice you do not have is not to choose. It has become culturally illegitimate just to do as your family used to do. Everybody has to be the responsible editor of his or her own CV. This seems to be the explanation for the decrease in the numbers of confirmations and weddings in Church, where as an individual you do have various options. You can be married at the Town

[25] Gallup Opinion Poll April-May 1998 on "What is most important in the church". For similar findings covering all Nordic countries, see Göran Gustaffsson and Thorleif Pettersson (eds.), *Folkkyrkor och religiös pluralism – den nordiska religiösa modellen* (Borås, Verbum Förlag. 2000), 62ff. and 101ff.

Hall – and have the Church celebration for your new family at the time of the baptism of the first child. And youth may decide that they want to have a family party (and hopefully "confirmation" gifts) without attending confirmation classes and being confirmed in Church. It is no big thing for the non-confirmed young persons, nor is it for the Church. However, a decrease in contact to the Church as well as in basic knowledge of Christianity does loosen the links between the Church and its members, and may eventually lead to the members' full withdrawal from the Church. Still, infant baptisms and Church funerals are more stable, as in practice these are not left so much to the individuals to choose for themselves. Practically there are no regular alternatives to baptism and a Church funeral.

The Missional Functions of the Danish Folk Church

> The Folk Church attempts to bring up its baptised children to be Church Christians (e.g. by confirmation classes and by offering various activities to school classes, as museums do). The Folk Church thereby maintains Cultural Christianity (non-religious Christianity) as common ethical and cultural ballast in Denmark.

We do not have any membership surveys or other good indications of the outcome of the work of the Danish Folk Church. In her ethnological Ph.D. thesis 16 years ago *Inger-Marie Børgesen*, listening to the life stories of Folk Church members in different settings, found that they obviously became what they call "Christian in my own way" on the background of various experiences of encounters with the Folk Church, e.g. at life-circle rituals.[26] People do not expect much from the church. When they are given guidance and help at funerals, for example, they are thus positively surprised.[27] On a daily basis the great majority of the members of the Folk Church do not think of the Church as something to which they "belong". On the other hand to a considerable extent they become what they become due to the actual work of the Folk Church, towards which they generally have a positive attitude.

71 % of the Danes state that they are "*believing*" ("troende"), meaning people who want to live with positive and trusting attitudes to their own lives as well as to their neighbours. 69 % state that they are Christians, and 62 % that they believe in some kind of God. Only 15 % state that they are agnostics and 5 % atheists.[28] The 69 % of the Danes who label themselves Christians – and in

---

[26] Inger-Marie Børgesen, *Folk og folkekirken. Kirkens plads i menneskers hverdagsliv og tankeverden (*Copenhagen: Akademisk Forlag, 1991).

[27] Cf. Birthe Lund and Hans Raun Iversen (eds.), *Livshjælp. Undersøgelser af begravelsespraksis og begravelseskultur i Danmark* (Århus: Landsforeningen af Menighedsrådsmedlemmer, 1993).

[28] Højsgaard and Iversen (eds.) 2005: 68.

fact quite a few more – I designate "Cultural Christians".

Cultural Christianity as found in Scandinavia consists of a Christian-influenced world view, a concept of humans and some basic ethical and existential values deriving from Christianity, together with a preference for using Christian-inspired language in important situations. For Cultural Christians a major part of their culture is Christian, whereas their entire culture is most certainly not, nor are their religious beliefs if they have any.[29] Cultural Christianity does not come alive – nor is it being kept alive – by itself. It is the child of the teaching of the Folk Churches through the centuries. Cultural Christians have no ways or rituals of their own for the transmission of Cultural Christianity to their children. Cultural Christians are thus dependent on the Folk Churches, which in turn rely on the existence of Cultural Christianity.

Historically, Cultural Christianity was established as a result of compulsory confirmation classes, in Denmark from 1736. Also today confirmation classes teach young people Church Christianity with the result that they become Cultural Christians. What is heard by those attending the rituals of the Folk Churches also seems to contribute to the upholding of Cultural Christianity among Scandinavian people. This may be the major political and existential contribution of the Folk Church to the culture and identity of the Danes.

> In almost all activities of the Danish Folk Church 1) Church Christians, 3) Cultural Christians and often also 3) Charismatic Christians, meet and exchange their views of Christianity in subtle ways. The Folk Church at its best functions as a switchboard making the three forms of Christianity mutually inform, respect and inspire one another. In this way the Folk Church is broadcasting Christianity.

For more than ten years it has been my argument – partially inspired by the studies conducted by Harald Hegstad in Norway – that the mission of the Danish Folk Church is mainly found in the positive exchange which continually takes place between Church Christians, Cultural Christians and often also Charismatic Christians, i.e. people working and living enthusiastically for the purpose of Christianity.[30] I still believe this argument to be valid – and probably even more so in Denmark than in Norway – as we have fewer examples of hostile relations between revival-like core groups and more secular or liberal

---

[29] For a more detailed discussion of the concept see Hans Raun Iversen: "Folk Church as Mission to Cultural Christians", *Swedish Missiological Themes*, 85/3-4, (1997), 237-264 and "Kulturkristendom, kirkekristendom og karismatisk kristendom. Kristendomsformernes baggrund og samspil i folkekirken", in Jørn Henrik Olsen (ed.): *Kulturkristendom og kirke*. Ny Mission 1 (Copenhagen: Unitas Forlag, 1999), 6-43.

[30] Cf. Harald Hegstad, *Folkekirke og trosfellesskap. Et kirkesociologisk og ekklesiologisk grunnproblem belyst gjennon en undersøkelse av tre norske lokalmenigheter*. (Trondheim: Tapir Forlag, 1995). See also my works mentioned in footnote 4.

Folk Church members in Denmark than in Norway. Obviously only little positive can come out of this encounter and exchange (be it in the congregational boards, at life circle rituals, at Sunday services, or in children's work etc.) if there is no mutual respect and basic trust among the groups and individuals involved.

The importance of this exchange is decreasing as the old core groups of Church Christians are disappearing in the Danish Folk Church. This is mainly due to the recent development in the life-forms in Nordic societies. In the mainly agricultural-based society in the 18th century our communities were the given ones in the local parishes, even though some revivalists and a few atheists broke out from life under *the sacred canopy* as it was interpreted and administered by the parish pastor. In the mainly industrial-based society in the 19th century we learned how to choose between *various solidarities and sectors* and the Church tended to become a sector of its own remote from the busy life of industry and business. At its best the Church gathered some temporary groups who took the responsibility of being core groups. In the mainly service-based society of the 21st century, where we are at one and the same time becoming more global and more eager to live in small circles of friends, we have adopted *fluid relations* as we seek places and experiences where we can acquire strengths and orientation in our lives. [31]

> As we are moving from *given or chosen* communities via *temporary* communities to *fluid* communities the question is no longer *who* or *what* but *where* God is. As the old congregational core-group culture disappears, the Churches – as temples, not as synagogues – serve as arenas and offer relationships for the new fluid communities. Obvious examples of the growth of the fluid Church are Night-Churches, Street-Pastors, Baby-Hymns, Alfa-Courses, Bible-Marathons, Pilgrimages, Road-Churches, Cyber-Churches and from 2006 a weekly TV-Church on Danish Public Service TV.

As are your days, so shall your strength be, said our forefathers, quoting Ecclesiastes. As your events and experiences of orientation are, so your strength shall be, we seem to say today. The Folk Church in Denmark is tentatively, even hesitantly, attempting to face this new form of life by trying out new ways of work. In a series of seminars at Vartov in the autumn of 2007 new forms of congregational life are being explored under four headings: The *temporary congregations*, where people come for a special rituals or events, the

---

[31] See Figure 14.1 in Anders Bäckström, *Svenska Kyrkan som välfärdsaktör i en global kultur (* Stockholm: Verbum, 1999). Cf. further Anders Bäckström et al: *Religious Change in Northern Europe. The Case of Sweden* (Stockholm: Verbum, 2004).

singing congregations, where our Nordic record in hymn singing[32] is renewed in new forms, the *conversational congregations*, where dialogues are taking place between e.g. immigrants, social outcasts, New Age adherents and Folk Church Christians in all sort of ways and places, and the *churchless congregations*, where people, who basically want to be independent of any church, seek the churches, including Cyber-churches and the Tent Church at Roskilde Festival, as pilgrims or tourists.

More people seek the churches in Denmark today than 25 years ago. Most often they have more positive experiences by doing so today than in former times. They have, however, no intention to build stable congregations in the synagogue way as promoted by the children of the old revival movements. They look a lot more like the medieval Christians who respected and used the churches as temples whenever needed – a few times a year or at least during life time.[33]

Sometimes I think that the Danish Folk Church is beginning to look a bit like St. Francis of Assisi preaching to the birds. The Folk Church is serving people who stop by at the oddest times and places to see if there is anything for them to pick up today. In following them the Church itself may become fluid – journeying along the roads like Jesus – from *Galilee* with the heathen migrants via *Samaria* with its mixture of religions to *Judea* with the Folk Church Temple in Jerusalem. Probably almost half of the more than 2000 congregations in Denmark have today involved themselves in inter-religious work in contact with Muslims and adherents of other religions[34]. Hopefully they will learn from the experiences – moving from Galilee via Samaria to Judea and back again.

Is the Danish Folk Church a missional church?

> There is most often no clear missionary intention in the work of the Danish Folk Church. There is, however, often a missionary dimension in the same work. There is little *centripetal, community building light* in the folk church. There is, however, quite a bit of *centrifugal, formational salt* in its work (cf. Matt 5:13-16).

Even if the work of the Folk Church for *Christian information* does not result in much it does not mean that there are no results in terms of *Christian and Culture Christian formation* among church members. The church can point to

---

32 Cf. Hans Raun Iversen, "Tidevarv komma, tidevarv försvinna... Overvejelser omkring en spørgeskemaundersøgelse af salmesang i de nordiske lande" in *Hymnologiske Meddelelser* 31/1 (2992): 76-82.

33 Cf. Oskar Skarsaune, "Noe overveielser om norsk folkereligiøsitet", and "Hvor mange Typer menigheder huser folkekirken?" in *Halvårsskrift for Praktisk teologi*, 2/1993, 1/1997.

34 Cf. *Karma, Koran og Kirke. Religiøs mangfoldighed som folkekirkelig udfordring* (Aarhus: Nivers, 2007).

little results in terms of regular church attendance, conformity with the official teaching of the church and identification with church Christianity. Even so an apostolic dimension of the work of the church may be found in its widespread work for Christian formation. If it is the goal to make people believe e.g. that "All scripture is inspired by God" (2 Tim 3:16) the Danish Folk Church is not doing well. It does, however seem to be doing somewhat better, if the goal is to "equip for every good work" (2 Tim 2:17).

In his important book *The continuing Conversion of the Church* the reformed missiologist *Darrell L. Guder* tightens the concepts of church and mission up saying: "Whatever is not mission is not part of the church's vocation"[35]. In his lecture at the Mission Conference of the Danish Folk Church at Nyborg Strand June 9 2006 he elaborated his point in this way:

> A leading Mennonite missiologist in the United States has said that 'Christendom is Christianity without mission'. That is, as I have told him, a historical over-simplification. But it does describe our theological traditions accurately. We have done our theology of the church with virtually no attention to its fundamentally missional purpose and action.[36]

Historically seen this is literally true for the Danish Folk Church: It is possible to point to only a limited missional impact of the work of the church. Generally speaking it is correct to label the work of the church an attempt to maintain the status quo of a rather passive majority Church. What really matters to the folk church seems to be that people continue belonging to the Church. In the words of Guder:

> It has become possible for people to compartmentalize their religion, to unlink the message of gathered worship on Sunday from the practices and decision-making Monday through Saturday. It has become possible for missional vocation to be reduced to religious observance.[37]

At the annual meeting of the *International Research Consortium Congregational Mission and the Social Sciences* in the buildings of *Dietrich Bonhoeffer*'s first Pastoral Seminary at Zingst March 2007 a participant, black South African Church leader told the following story from one of the first occasions he was sitting one evening with a white South African Church leader. "10 years ago I did not think that I should ever sit together with a white Christian", the black Christian said. "I know, but trust me, we really tried to be serious Christians, reading a lot in the Bible", the white Church leader retorted.

---

35 Darrell L. Guder, *The continuing Conversion of the Church* (Grand Rapids, Michigan: William B. Eerdmans Publishing Company, 2000), 207.
36 Darrell L. Guder, *Mission in a Pluralist Society – Why and How?* Mission Conference of the Folk Church at Nyborg Strand June 9 2006, Presentation I, 7.
37 Guder 2006: Presentation II, 7.

"Yes, but you never read the Bible together with us" the black Church leader commented. "You are right, and that was exactly where we failed", the white Christian concluded.

The white churches in South Africa have had to learn the hard way by realizing their own wrongdoings. The Danish Folk Church never faced any hardship from which it could learn. Its leaders can still boast of their church having "the best church order in the world". The Danish Folk Church may be excused in as far as it has been taken hostage by its own history and by secular, nationalist politicians. The Folk Church looks like a church in Babylonian captivity. But it is also as a church unprepared and undecided to leave the Egyptian fleshpots of the security in the arms of the successful Danish State. The question remains when the Danish Folk Church will ever learn by sharing in the way described by Guder:

> The history of Western theology can be described as a sequence of learned attempts to explain why the Sermon on the Mount does not apply to us. When we enter discussion with our sister churches around the world and explore our shared understanding of our calling and our mission, then we can certainly share what we have learned from our long history....[38]

[38] Guder 2006, Presentation I, 13.

The Conversion of Immigrants to Christianity in a Danish Context

Mogens S. Mogensen

Dr Mogens S. Mogensen, Faculty of Theology, University of Copenhagen

Over the last 30 – 40 years Denmark has developed from a very mono-religious to a more multi-religious society. The background for this change has primarily been migration of workers and of refugees. Migrants from Africa, Asia and the Balkans with an Islamic, Hindu, Buddhist or another religious background have established new non-Christian religious communities in Denmark.

In the same period we have seen an increasing number of religious conversions. In the 1970s and 1980s the focus was on Danes converting to religions from the East and to the so-called New Age movements, and since the 1990s conversions to Islam have attracted a lot of attention. Most studies of conversion in Denmark have analysed the conversion of Danes (most often with a Christian background) to these new religions, which were brought to Denmark by immigrants. This study, however, will focus on the often overlooked phenomenon of immigrants converting from Islam and other religions to Christianity.

Migration and religious change

Often there is a connection between migration and religious change. We may distinguish between three processes of religious change that are related to the migrants' adaptation to and survival in their new host society.

(1) The migrants stick to their pre-migration religion, which, however, often undergoes changes in the new context.[1]

In a study of South Asian immigrants in the US Raymond Bradley Williams concludes that:

[1] Williams, Raymond Bradley, *Religions of Immigrants from India and Pakistan: New Threads in the American Tapestry* (Cambridge: Cambridge University Press, 1988) :11.

> Immigrants are religious – by all counts more religious than they were before they left home – because religion is one of the important identity markers that help them preserve individual self-awareness and cohesion in a group. … Apart from its spiritual dimension, religion is a major force in social participation; it develops and at the same time sacralises one's self-identity, and thus the religious bond is one of the strongest social ties.

While they continue to adhere to the religion they belonged to in their original home country, they will often – under the influence of the new context – reinterpret their religion in a way that leads to changes in religious practice, doctrines and organisation. This adherence to their original religion (and culture) has the potential both to impede and to further the integration of the immigrants. It may lead to a separation from the surrounding society and the creation of ghettos. Their adherence to their pre-migration religion, however, may also in the long run advance their integration. For immigrants, cultural and religious communities rooted in the culture and religion of their homeland may stabilise their identity in a difficult transition period and give them a sense of safety and security and thereby become for them a solid platform from which they may venture into the new host society and enter into the process of integration.[2]

(2) Migrants who stick to their pre-migration religion contribute to the spreading of their own religion to the indigenous people in their new host country.

Processes of religious change may be explained with reference to diffusion-theories. When talking about diffusion of innovations, including religious innovations, we may distinguish between "expansion diffusion", when people adopt the religious innovation through direct contact, and "relocation diffusion", when the religious innovation is brought to new places for example through migration. The most common process of diffusion, also regarding the spread of religions, however, involves a combination of the two forms of diffusion. A physical "relocation" leads a group of religious people to a new place, thereby bringing the religious innovation to this place. Then follows an "expansion diffusion", when this religious group enters into direct contact on a daily basis with the indigenous people. This type of "expansion diffusion" may be called "contagious diffusion", but might also in our context be described as

---

[2] Martin Bauman, "Religion und ihre Bedeutung für Migranten". in *Religion – Migration – Integration*, Beauftragte der Bundesregierung für Migration (red.), Flüchtlinge und Integration, 19-30. Berlin & Bonn: Beauftragte der Bundesregierung für Migration, Flüchtlinge und Integration, 2004:26pp; "Religion und ihre Bedeutung für Migranten". Antrittsvorlesung 20.06.2002 in Luzern, http://backupuni.bison-web.com/gf/3259_9399.htm 06-11-2006:7-10.

"contact conversion".[3]

(3) Migrants adapt to the new context by leaving their pre-migration religion and perhaps joining the predominant religion of the country to which they have migrated.

The desire to achieve a social integration and to gain acceptance in their new host country may lead some immigrants to choose to lay aside their cultural and religious peculiarities (de-conversion), and some may go all to way and join the religion of the majority (conversion). Based on studies in Germany Martin Baumann has observed that

> In der neuen Umwelt können die heimatlichen religiösen Bindungen und Orientierungen verloren gehen, manch einer legt sie auch bewusst ab. "Verloren gehen" bedeutet hier, dass sie die Zuwanderer nicht nur in sozialen und ökonomischen, sondern auch in kulturellen und religiösen Anschauungen weitgehend der Aufnahmegesellschaft anpassen. Eine solche Assimilation bedeutet mit Blick auf der Religion Konversion, die Aufgabe der mitgebrachten religiösen Orientierung. Der Prozess kann schon in der ersten Generation, stärker jedoch in den Folgegenerationen einsetzen.[4]

In the remaining part of this study the focus will be on the third type of processes of change where migration leads to conversion.

Integration and Conversion

Immigration may lead to different forms of incorporation into the new host society, from segregation and ghetto-life to an actual assimilation. As Alejandro Portes has shown in an American context, the process of incorporation and the result of this process will depend on a number of factors in the host society and with the immigrants: the policy of the host society towards various segments of immigrants (welcoming, indifferent or hostile), the attitudes towards the immigrants in the labour market (neutral, positive, discriminatory) and the characteristics of the communities of immigrants.[5]

When in the following I talk about integration, I follow Viggo Mortensen's definition, according to which integration is "a process which unites what was separated and thus brings about another greater entity ("sammenhæng") which

---

[3] Park, Chris C., *Sacred Worlds. An Introduction to Geography and Religion* (London & New York: Routledge, 1994): 99-100.

[4] Bauman 2002/06:6.

[5] Referred to in Heisler, Barbara Schmitter, "The Sociology of Immigration. From Assimilation to Segmented Integration, from the American Experience to the Global Arena", in *Migration Theory. Talking across Disciplines*, Caroline B. Brettell & James F. Hollifield (New York & London: Routledge, 2000): 83-84.

makes an increased understanding possible." The integration of immigrants is "thus a process which should bring the immigrant into that entity ("sammenhæng") which is called 'Denmark', whereby a common understanding and peaceful coexistence is made possible".[6] Integration is a mutual process, but here we will look at that part of the process that has to do with the role of the immigrant. Integration of immigrants involves that they become a part of the Danish society and that they become Danish.

Such integration may lead to various processes of religious change, one of which is the conversion of immigrants. I follow Lewis R. Rambo's understanding of conversion as "a process of religious change that takes place in dynamic force field of people, events, ideologies, institutions, expectations, and orientations".[7] Conversion then may be seen as the outcome of the interactions of the longings, needs and attitudes of the convert and the characteristics of the group to which he or she converts and the specific social contest in which these processes take place. Seen from another perspective we may also describe conversion as it has been done by Brad Kallenberg, as "the emergence of new mode of life occasioned by a self-involving participation in the shared life, language, and paradigm of the believing community." According to this understanding conversion involves a change in religious community, discourse and paradigm (Kallenberg 1995:385).

Empirical Study of Conversion and Baptism in Denmark

In order to remedy the apparent lack of data concerning conversion of adherents of other religions to Christianity in Denmark, I conducted in the period from September 2004 to April 2005 an empirical study of conversion of Muslims, Buddhist, Hindus etc. to Christianity.[8] The vast majority of those who were baptised were people with a migration background, either as first or second generation immigrants.

It is often very complicated to find fairly precise numbers of converts between religions, but what makes the data of converts to Christianity from other religions more readily accessible is the fact these conversions almost always take place together with baptisms, which are almost exclusively carried out by pastors, and which are registered by the churches. In a Christian understanding of conversion baptism is often seen as the decisive point in the process. At the same time membership of a church in most denominations is linked to baptism, so that baptism for converts from other religions is a

---

6 Mortensen, Viggo, *Betydningen af religion og religiøsitet for integrationsprocesserne*. Aarhus, Denmark, 2002:14. My translation.

7 Rambo, Lewis R., *Understanding Religious Conversion* (New Haven: Yale University Press, USA, 1993): 5.

8 Mogensen, Mogens S., *Dåb og religionsskifte* (Frederiksberg: Unitas, Denmark, 2005a).

condition for membership.

The study is based on a questionnaire survey, in which all 2057 pastors in The Evangelical Lutheran Church in Denmark, in the following called the Folk Church (Folkekirken), the pastors or other leaders of 328 congregations from the Roman Catholic Church, the free churches and migrant congregations[9] were contacted. Answers to the questionnaire were received from 68 % in the Folk Church and 67 % from the other churches. The pastors (or church leaders) were asked to inform how many people had converted from non-Christian religions and been baptised within the five year period from 2000 to 2004.[10] In the questionnaire the respondents were not asked to indicate the number of baptisms of children from families where one of the parents was a Christian and the other belonged to another religion, but many pastors in the Folk Church on their own initiative listed how many baptisms of children from such religiously mixed families they had conducted.

As the table shows 660 converts from other religions were baptised in this five year period. Added to these are the baptisms of 160 children, young people and adults, who grew up in religiously mixed families.

I had expected that most baptisms would have taken place in the free churches because of their mission activities and also their more free and charismatic services and their closer fellowships, which might be more attractive to non-Western immigrants. The survey, however, shows that almost half of all baptisms of converts took place in the Folk Church, and that the

---

[9] In her book *Andre stemmer. Migrantkirker i Danmark* from 2004 the leader Tværkulturelt Center (Cross Cultural Centre) in Copenhagen Birthe Munck-Fairwood in cooperation with others has mapped this group of ethnic and international congregations. A migrant congregation is here understood as "a Christian congregation of at least 10 adults who regularly conduct Sunday services or similar services in a language other than Danish led by a pastor/leader who is not born in Denmark" (174, my translation). The groups that were not contacted were smaller groups that were attached to the Folk Church, The Roman Catholic Church or other churches in such a way that the baptisms would be registered there. 45 of these migrant congregations were contacted and 31 answered the questionnaire.

[10] Those pastors and congregational leaders who did not initially respond to the questionnaire were contacted by e-mail, letter or telephone and asked to respond. Since not all pastors or leaders have been active in their congregation during all the five years of the survey, there will be baptisms that are not reflected in this survey. Some pastors and leaders may of course not have been able to remember exactly how many baptisms of people with another religious background than Christianity they had baptised, but conversations with a number of pastors during the survey indicate that these conversions and baptisms had made such an impression on them that they most often vividly remembered the situations or were able to find the records of them.

majority of the rest took place in the migrant congregations.

Baptism of people with another religious background than Christianity 2000 – 2004										
	Folk[11]	RCC	Adv	Apost	Bapt	Meth	Coven	Pent	Migr	Total
Islam	158	4	0	6	5	1	2	15	113	304
Buddhism	29	27	0	0	2	0	0	5	17	80
Hinduism	19	1	0	2	0	0	0	7	111	140
Judaism	18	0	0	0	0	0	0	0	0	18
Other religions[12]	86	0	5	1	0	0	0	8	20	118
Children of mixed marriages[13]	160									160
Total	470	32	5	9	7	1	2	33	261	820

It was also to be expected that most baptisms would have taken place in larger cities such as Copenhagen and Aarhus, because of the high number of immigrants living there. But as may be seen from the table below, those baptisms that took place in the Folk Church were relatively equally distributed among the ten dioceses, although with the highest numbers in Copenhagen and Aarhus. These baptisms are furthermore distributed among 91 of the 111 deaneries in the Folk Church, and 10 % of all pastors in this church have conducted such conversion baptisms during the five year period in question.

---

[11] The abbreviations refer to the following churches: the Folk Church, the Roman Catholic Church, the Adventist Church, the Apostolic Church, the Baptist Church, the Methodist Church, the Covenant Church (Missionsforbundet), the Pentecostal Church and migrant congregations.

[12] Other religions include adherents of Falun Gong, Confucianism, Mandean religion, Mormonism, old Nordic religion, and a number of traditional Asian and African religions and a number of New Religious Movements.

[13] When the non-Christian parent and the child are baptised at the same time, the baptism of the child is still registered in this category. A son or a daughter from such a religiously mixed family who does not convert to Christianity until he or she is an adult is also registered in this category. About a third of these children have a Muslim parent, most often a Muslim father. About a fourth have of them has a Buddhist parent, most often a Buddhist mother.

Baptism of people with another religious background than Christianity in the dioceses of the Folk Church 2000-2004											
	Kbh[14]	Hel	Ros	L-F	Fyn	Aalb	Vib	Aarh	Ribe	Had	Total
Islam	37	14	12	2	8	18	10	24	8	25	158
Buddhism	7	1	3	0	1	5	1	2	7	2	29
Hinduism	4	1	3	0	0	4	3	2	1	1	19
Judaism	7	9	0	0	0	0	0	2	0	0	18
Other religions[15]	22	4	7	18	1	5	7	9	11	5	86
Children of mixed marriages	13	16	17	3	9	19	22	33	13	15	160
Total	87	45	42	23	19	51	43	72	40	48	470

As previously mentioned the survey is based on answers from about two thirds of all the pastors (or leaders) in the Folk Church and the other churches. Most likely the answers represent more than two thirds of the baptisms conducted by the pastors contacted in this survey, since those pastors who had been involved in baptisms of converts would probably be more motivated to participate in the survey than other pastors. If the results of the survey represent 90 % of all baptisms of converts, the total number of baptisms of converts will be 735 (excluding baptisms of children from religiously mixed marriages).

The survey covers baptisms of converts that took place in the five year period from 2000 to 2004, but also before this period Muslims, Hindus and Buddhists have converted and been baptised. The question is how many people have converted and have been baptised during the 25 year period from 1980 to 2004. Earlier in this period the number of Muslims, Hindus and Buddhists in the Danish population was much smaller than in the period which was surveyed, and since also a lot of conversion research emphasise the critical importance of personal contact for conversion, it is likely that the number of conversions per year will have been significantly lower at that time. If the number of converts from these three religions to Christianity has doubled in each of the five year periods from 1980 to 2004, the total number of converts in the period 1980 – 2004 may be about 655 from a Muslim background, 302 from a Hindu background and 172 from a Buddhist background.[16]

---

[14] The abbreviations refer to the following dioceses: København (Copenhagen), Helsingør, Roskilde, Lolland-Falster, Fyn, Aalborg, Viborg, Aarhus, Ribe and Haderslev.

[15] Other religions include adherents of Falun Gong, Confucianism, Mandean religion, Mormonism, old Nordic religion, and a number of traditional Asian and African religions and a number of New Religious Movements.

[16] If the rate of increase from one five year period to the nest only had been 50 %, then the total number of converts in the period 1980 – 2004 would have

The Integration-conversion Pattern in the Folk Church

Together with the quantitative survey of baptisms of converts, another set of qualitative data was collected from the pastors in the Folk Church. The pastors who conducted the baptisms of the converts were asked the write short reports on how they perceived the circumstances around the conversions. An analysis of this data indicates that a number of dynamics are at work and that there are various patterns and processes leading to the conversion and baptism of people with another religious background than Christianity. There are Muslims, who already before they fled from Iran for various reason wanted to leave Islam in order to become Christians, but first had the opportunity to do so when they came to Denmark. Others have had specific mystical experiences. In dreams they had seen Jesus or they felt that they in a very special way have received help from Jesus in times of crisis.

Apart from these patterns, however, it is also possible to trace a pattern that links the conversion of immigrants to Christianity closely to their integration into the Danish society. It becomes apparent in the pastors' reports of baptisms of adults and even more in the case of baptisms of children. In a family where the mother was a Christian and the father a Muslim, the father decided that their two children should be baptised "since they lived in a Christian country."

The same way of reasoning can also be traced in reports about baptism of children of parents who both belonged to a non-Christian religion. A pastor reports on a Hindu-family:

> Many years ago the family fled from Sri Lanka to Denmark and has in a very fine way been integrated into the Danish society. Therefore the parents also thought that it was important for their children to learn something about the Danish culture and about Christianity. Consequently both of the children should follow the mini-confirmand education, and when the oldest child was to be confirmed, the parents in consultation with their children decided that their children, both the oldest son [who was to be confirmed] and his younger sister should be baptised.

A Muslim couple wanted "that their children should live as Christians in a Christian country", and an African couple with a traditional African religious background "wanted that their child should grow up as a 'Dane'".

This integration-conversion pattern may be traced among both young people and adults. A pastor who baptised a young boy understood that his desire to be baptised had to do with the importance he attached to being part of the group of Danish young people and not being different from them. A young Buddhist who participated in confirmation classes wanted primarily to be baptised "in order to be in a religious fellowship with his friends". A young Muslim man, who lived together with his Danish girlfriend, said that he would like to be

---

been 880 from a Muslim background, 406 from a Hindu background and 232 from a Buddhist background.

baptised in order to be a real Dane and so that he could more easily get a job. For various reasons, however, he was not baptised after all.

Many of the conversions to Christianity took place in connection with a marriage between a Christian and a person with another religious background. A Hindu women who was to be wedded to a Christian Dane wanted to be baptised together with their child because – as she explained to the pastor – "now she and her family wanted to be really Danish and therefore also Christian".[17]

There are clear indications of a special integration-conversion pattern in the current situation in Denmark. What characterises this conversion-pattern is among other things the following:

Those who covert are migrants and their children. These migrants have come to Denmark from countries with a culture very different from the one in Denmark.

Migrants and their children convert to the religion which is predominant in the culture to which they come, i.e., they convert to Christianity in the Christian dominated Danish society.

Migrants and their children convert and are baptised within the church which is the church of the vast majority and which has the status of being the official church, the Folk Church, the church of the Danish people.

The Role of Christianity and the Folk Church in the Danish Welfare Society

When immigrants with an African or Asian cultural background and with a Muslim, Hindu or Buddhist religious background are being integrated into the Danish society they will encounter a society where there is still a relatively strong link between state and church, people and church, and between culture and Christianity.

Through the Christianization of the Danes in the years or maybe rather centuries after the baptism of King Harald Bluetooth around 965 Christianity became the religious foundation of the kingdom. That this was so is evident from "Jyske lov" (Law of Jutland) from 1241, where even the first sentence states that only children who are baptised can inherit their parents estate. Being a citizen in the Danish kingdom and being a member of the Christian church soon became two aspects of the same matter. This situation was cemented with the reformation in 1536, where the protestant church became a state church.

During the religious wars in the 16th century the principle of *cujus regio ejus religio* was adopted, and in "Danske Lov" (The Danish Law) from 1683 conversion to Catholicism (and attempts at converting Danes to Catholicism) was made a criminal offence. A Dane who chose to convert to the Catholic Church could be exiled, and Catholic missionaries who tried to convert Danes

[17] Mogensen 2005a:35-36.

were threatened with capital punishment. While it was, practically speaking, impossible to convert away from the Lutheran faith and the Lutheran church, conversion the other way was allowed. With the church ritual from 1685 a baptism ritual for adults was authorised, according to which for example Jews and Muslims could be baptised and thereby gain full rights as citizens in the Danish society.[18]

This means that for more than 600 years it was – with very few exceptions – impossible to be a Dane, in the sense of a Danish citizen, will full civil rights without at the same time being or becoming a Lutheran Christian. For non-Christians and non-Lutherans who wanted to become integrated into the Danish society the only way to follow was through conversion to the Lutheran faith and membership of the Lutheran church.

The passing of the Constitution – and as a part of this the introduction of freedom of religion – in 1849 changed this situation formally. The reality, however, was that the Lutheran Church continued to function as a state church, although it was now called the Folk Church. For the following 100 years only about a couple of percent of the population were not members of the Lutheran Church (most of them belonged to other Christian denominations), and in this way the close connection (or almost symbiosis) between the Danish people and the Lutheran Church was maintained. Many of those who decided not to be part of the Folk Church – e.g., those who converted to the Roman Catholic Church – often felt marginalised in relation to the Danish people, and some of them were even considered to be traitors against the Danish people and the Danish culture.[19]

The Constitution from 1849 stated that "The Evangelical Lutheran Church shall be the Folk Church of Denmark, and as such shall be supported by the State" (par. 4), and that "The King shall be a member of the Evangelical Lutheran Church" (par. 6) These paragraphs are carried over into later constitutions and are also part of the present 1953 constitution. The church is still integrated into the Danish State apparatus, and this integrated status has not diminished during the latest decades. In an analysis of the close links between state and church in Denmark, bishop Jan Lindhardt concludes that "when you have a state church, you also have a church state". He goes on to say that "we Danes find it easy to follow the word in the Bible about giving Caesar what belongs to Caesar, and to God what belongs to God because in Denmark God and Caesar have the same address, namely at Christiansborg [where the parliament and the government resides]".[20]

---

[18] Iversen, Hans Raun, red., *Dåb og medlemskab i Folkekirken* (København: Anis, 2000): 72-85.

[19] Mogensen, Mogens S., *Når danskere skifter tro. Omvendelse mellem religionerne i Danmark* (Frederiksberg: Unitas, Denmark, 2005b): 17-28.

[20] Lindhardt, Jan, *Folkekirke. Kirken i det danske samfund* (Beder: Hovedland, 2005): 48. My translation.

In spite of the effects of the secularisation over the last 50 years Christianity and the Folk Church are still key elements of the foundation of the Danish society. The Danish welfare model is based on a particular interpretation of Christianity and Christian ethics.[21] It is not based on the principle of "something for something" ("noget for noget"), but on "something for nothing" ("noget for ingenting") and on the principle of collectively taking responsibility for each other and in particular for those who cannot take care of themselves. It may be argued that the Danish welfare system is borne out of a particular Christian understanding of what it means to live together in society, and that the Christian commandment of love for your neighbour has been reduced to an idea that has been translated into a social and legal system where the citizens are forced practice a solidarity, which is a secularised version Christian love, even if they do not feel love for their fellow citizens. Along the same line the welfare state has taken over many of the diaconal task of the church and to a large extent finance (and thereby also exerts influence on) the remaining diaconal institutions of the church.[22]

When Muslims, Hindus and Buddhist become integrated into the Danish society they cannot avoid indirectly getting in contact with Christianity, and to the extent that they acquire Danish culture they in a sense and to a certain degree will acquire elements of a Danish culture Christianity ("kulturkristendom").

Even when the membership percentage of the folk church has fallen to 83 % and some Danes use their freedom of religion to convert to non-Christian religions, there are indications that many Danes still have a hard time imagining that it is possible to be truly Danish and to be fully integrated into the Danish society if you are not in some sense a Christian – or at least if you do belong to

---

21 Østergaard, Uffe, "Lutheranismen, danskheden og velfærdsstaten", in *Den nordiske protestantisme og velfærdsstaten*, Tim Knudsen red. (Odense: Syddansk Universitetsforlag, Denmark, 2003), argues that "No matter what Social Democratic party programs and generations of party members have said the Danish welfare stat is a result of a secularised Lutheranism in a national attire rather than a democratised socialism". Østergaard 2003:33.

22 Jørn Henrik Petersen claims that the Danish theologian K. E. Løgstrup in many respects is the philosopher of the Danish welfare model. Jørn Henrik Petersen, "Kan den danske velfærdsmodel videreføres?", in Jens Holger Schjørring & Jens Torkild Bak, red., *Velfærdsstat og kirke*. (København: Anis, Denmark, 2005). Løgstrup transfers the ethical demand ("den etiske fordring") from its basic location in the life world of direct face to face relationships to the collective context in society (24). Petersen, however, also points out that this welfare model is under pressure these years due to secularisation since an absolute demand of solidarity with other people only may be based on an ultimate authority and therefore is dependent on a religious foundation for society (32).

a non-Christian religion. In a feature article in the Christian Daily (Kristeligt Dagblad) entitled "De fædrelandsløse" (those without a mother country) the former dean at the Cathedral in Odense Poul E. Andersen voices the opinion that Danish converts (from Christianity) to Islam will face serious problems in their relationship with the Danish society. "Those people who convert to Islam will have to give up essential elements of their cultural and historical identity so that they to a large extent will be people without culture and motherland in their own land".[23]

Leo Kamstrup, who is a dean on Amager (in Copenhagen), said in 2002 in an interview about the establishment of a mission project on Amager focusing on Muslims, that Christian mission is to make Muslims into good Danes by making them into good Christians. In order to be a Dane you have to be a Christian. "I am of the opinion that we have an obligation to endeavour to make the many people here in this area who have a foreign background into Danes," he said in a news broadcast in 2002. When confronted with the claim that his position represented cultural imperialism, he maintained that "the best way to handle part of the integration of Muslims in Denmark is by making them into Christians. Many Muslims simply cannot become a part of the Danish society, because there are all the time held back by their religion".[24]

There are many indications that the Folk Church/Christianity in the integration process of immigrants from a non-Christian religious background works as a sort of a "pull & push" factor. Some immigrants feel attracted by the dominant Christian religion and the Folk Church and therefore are very inclined to adapt to the Danish Christian culture and society, while others may feel that the dominant position of Christianity and the Folk church puts them under pressure to adapt in order to be accepted.

The religiously dominant position of the Folk Church in the Danish society is, among other things, reflected in the close cooperation between the church and the state concerning the keeping of a register of all citizens in Denmark, the coordination of the timetables of the public schools and the church's

---

[23] Andersen, Poul E., "De fædrelandsløse", in *Kristeligt Dagblad*, February 1 2000.

[24] Sørensen, Leif Kiil, "Omstridt provst under pres", in *Kristeligt Dagblad*, January 4, 2003. Many politicians and representatives of the Folk Church, however, have strongly dissociated themselves from the point of view of Leo Kamstrup. The spokesman for the governing Liberal Party (Venstre) concerning church issues Birthe Rønn Hornbech appreciated that the church conducted mission among Muslims but strongly objected to making mission a tool for integration. "As Danes we are part of a people whether we are Christians, Jews or pagans. Christianity has played a key role in the history of the Danish people, but this does not mean that you have to be a Christian in order to be considered to be Danish". Hornbech, Birthe Rønn, "Mission og integration", in *Kristeligt Dagblad*, January 10, 2003.

confirmand classes, the official role of the church concerning weddings and burials and the church's provision of "civil religion" services in connection with catastrophes and crises. Since the vast majority of the population are still members, it is for all practical purposes still this church which establishes a liturgical framework around the most important events in the life of people in Denmark such as birth, transition from child to adult, marriage and burial. This being so, Muslims, Buddhist, Hindus and others will quite often be in contact with the church and Christianity. A few examples from my study will be presented here.

Several pastors report that they have had positive contacts with Muslims in connection with births and the issue of birth certificates. This often leads to conversations about Christianity, and such conversations have occasionally resulted in the baptism of children as well as parents.

Mini-confirmation and confirmation classes have also attracted children with another religious background than Christianity and children from religiously mixed families. When their class mates go for these confirmand classes, which are most often coordinated with the timetable of the classes in the public school, a number of these children want to join these classes too. A pastor who had good relations with a Muslim family reported the following experience:

> Their adult children and grand children seem to be well integrated, and one of their youngest grand children attends confirmand classes with me together with his class mates. The family and I have a mutual respect for each other; I would certainly never make them objects of mission, and the question of baptism has never come up.

This attitude to mission is shared by many pastors in the Folk Church, but nonetheless this study has shown that what contributed to the process of conversion and to baptism for many children of immigrants has been the fact that their families had been so well integrated that it was natural for their children to attend confirmand classes together with their class mates.

Some immigrants with another religious background than Christianity come into contact with the Folk Church in connection with their attendance at funerals of Christian neighbours and friends. It seems as if a church funeral is perceived to be a meaningful ritual framework of death. Some seem to have converted to Christianity in order to make sure that they would receive a Christian funeral.

The Integration-Conversion Pattern in Migrant Congregations

It is possible to find indicators of an integration-conversion pattern in relation to the folk church, but the question is whether similar dynamics are at work when immigrants and their children convert to Christianity in the context of migrant congregations. I did not collect reports on the circumstances around conversions and baptisms from pastors and other church leaders in the migrant churches, but some of the pastors in these congregations have shared their perspectives and experiences in the book "Andre stemmer. Migrantkirker i Danmark" (Other Voices. Migrant Churches in Denmark).[25]

In the migrant congregations 113 former Muslims and 111 former Hindus were baptised in the period 2000-20004. Most of the converts from Islam are Farsi-speaking migrants from Iran and Afghanistan, and most of the converts from Hinduism are Tamil migrants from Sri Lanka.

John Bala, who came to Denmark as a refugee from the civil war in Sri Lanka in 1986, was a Tamil and a Hindu. His wife, who came to Denmark a couple of years later, had been raised in a Christian (Baptist) family and wanted to go to church, and John Bala decided to follow her. In 1991 he was baptised in a Baptist Church in Svendborg, where they conducted Sunday services in Tamil. He is very open about the fact that for him and the congregation there, whose pastor he is today, there is a connection between integration and conversion.

> I would like to show the Tamils that it is easer to live in Denmark when you are a Christian than when you belong to another religion. After I became a Christian I made many more Danish friends. As a Christian you are part of a big community. Our congregation works together with the Danish Baptist Church in Svendborg, and sometimes we are invited to big meetings in other places in Denmark where we meet many people – both Danes and other foreigner.[26]

According to John Bala conversion to Christianity will lead to a faster and better integration into the Danish society, and this situation can be a motivating factor for those who consider becoming Christians.

Massoud Fouroozandeh, who was raised in a Muslim family in Iran, arrived in Denmark as a 15 year old refugee in 1985. His mother, who came to Denmark a few years later, came into contact with a Pentecostal Church and decided to convert to Christianity. Through her and the Christian fellowship to which she belonged he encountered Christianity and in 1996 he was also baptised in the Pentecostal Church in Odense. Today he is the pastor in charge of "Mohabat – Church of Love", which is a Farsi-speaking church with congregations in different parts of Denmark, and whose members are almost all coverts from Islam. Fouroozandeh emphasises that:

> It is important that new congregations do not isolate themselves from others. Personally I make a great effort to establish contacts between Iranian congregations, for which I am responsible, and the Folk Church, the free churches

---

[25] Munck-Fairwood, Birthe, red., *Andre stemmer – Migrantkirker i Danmark set indefra* (København: Religionspædagogisk Forlag, Denmark, 2004).

[26] Munck-Fairwood 2004:36. My translation.

> and Christian organisations. The church has a great task concerning integration of people who convert to Christianity. When people decide to leave their own [pre-migration] religion, they are more flexible and ready to learn more about the Danish culture. Christianity represents a part of the Danish values. Therefore people who convert to Christianity from another religion have already gone a long way in the process of integration.[27]

For Fouroozandeh Christianity represents some of the Danish values, and consequently for him there is a close connection between becoming a Christian and becoming Danish. In his autobiography he elaborates on this perspective.

> The most important thing is to teach immigrants about the new culture to which they have come and the Danish constitution which is based on Christian values. If you can understand the Christian cultural heritage it is ten time easier to be integrated into the Danish society, but if the foreigners just sit quietly in the pews without understanding anything, they have made no progress.[28]

That these conversions take in an ethnic congregation, is here seen as an advantage for the integration since the convert in this way will have a better opportunity to understand and acquire the Danish values in a language with which they are completely familiar. Therefore Fouroozandeh can conclude that "the best way you can integrate immigrants in Denmark is by telling them about Jesus even if it in the beginning takes places in their own language".[29]

Ravi Chandran, who is from Singapore and has lived in Denmark since 1993, was raised as a Hindu but converted to Christianity before he came to Denmark and is now the pastor of a multi-ethnic congregation in Copenhagen, "International Christian Community" which he established in 2002. Ravi Chandran elaborates on the integration strategy which Fouroozandeh indicated.

> Migrant congregations are good at confirming the ethnic identity and self-esteem of new Danes [i.e., immigrants]. Here people get an experience of still being who they once were. It gives them continuity and coherence and promotes psychological stability. Migrant congregations bring new Danes together in a social fellowship which does not exclusively take place on the terms of the Danes.

When immigrants convert to Christianity in migrant congregations their ethnic identity is confirmed so that they do not lose their relationship with their history, culture and people, and at the same time through the Christian faith they establish bonds in terms of values with the Danish society and significant

---

27 Munck-Fairwood 2004:54.My translation.

28 Fouroozandeh, Massoud & Daniel Øhrstrøm, *Den forbudte frelse. Fra koransanger i Iran til kirkefader i Danmark* (København: Lindhardt & Ringhof, 2005): 247. My translation.

29 Fouroozandeh & Øhrstrøm, 2005.

relations with the indigenous Danes.

Social Dimensions in Conversion

What integration and conversion have in common is that they are both processes with significant social dimensions. Both processes lead to incorporation of the persons who are converting or are being integrated into a community or a group or another social entity.

In his study of conversion to Judaism in Copenhagen the anthropologist Andrew Buckser observes that conversion studies often do not focus on "conversion as a social event". "Conversion to a religion is an irreducibly social act: one does not merely join a faith, but one enters into a set of new relationships with members of a religious community" (Buckser 2003:69). The social dimension in a conversion may be so dominant that it may in some cases be a "purely social conversion."

> Membership in a religious community derives from more than a set of beliefs; it also involves a set of relationships with other members, a set of practices and habits, and a set of aesthetic orientations and discursive styles… Converts are able to assimilate such elements without the corresponding beliefs, and indeed these elements may provide a better index of a person's conversion.[30]

There are indications that for some immigrants who have converted to Christianity the social dimension has been so dominant that what we see is an almost "purely social conversion" without much reference to other aspects of the Christian faith. In other cases, however, the social dimension seems to have been one factor alongside a number of other factors.

In all religions, fellowships or communities play a central role in the life of the adherents. All religious traditions require specific fellowships in order that new and old adherents of the religions over time may experience that the religions are plausible and credible. Therefore, the old Catholic maxim still holds true, that *extra ecclesiam nulla salus*, i.e, outside the church – here understood broadly as the religious fellowship or community – there is no salvation – here understood as the experience that the religion and what the religion promises are still probable and credible. Without relations and interactions with people with the same faith or religion it will in the long run be very difficult for a religious person to hold his or her religion for true and real and thereby maintain his or her new identity. Religious fellowships or communities are, as the sociologist of religion Peter Berger has drawn attention

[30] Andrew Buckser, "Social Conversion and Group Definition in Jewish Copenhagen", in *The Anthropology of Religious Conversion*, Andrew Buckser & Stephen D. Glazier (red.) (Lanham, UK: Rowman & Littlefield Publishers, 2003): 81.

to a kind of a "plausibility structure" for the adherents of the religions.[31] With reference to Saul from Tarsus, Peter Berger and his colleague Thomas Luckmann conclude that the phase of incorporation is the most difficult in all the conversion process.

> Saul may have become Paul in the aloneness of religious ecstasy, but he could remain Paul only in the context of the Christian community that recognized him as such and confirmed the 'new being' in which he located this identity.[32]

The religious fellowship is thus the indispensable "plausibility structure" which helps the convert to take his conversion experience seriously and maintain a sense of the plausibility and credibility of his or her new faith.

When Muslims, Hindus and Buddhists leave their homeland, their town or village, and their local religious community and settle in Denmark, they are uprooted from the plausibility structure which nurtured their faith in their home country. If they do not find an equivalent community, which may nurture their faith, there is a greater possibility that they may go through a de-conversion from their pre-migration religion and perhaps also a conversion to another religion.

The immigrants enter a Danish society, which on a national and on a local level may be seen as a "plausibility structure" that tends to make a number of "Danish" assumptions and ideas, values and attitudes plausible for the citizens in this society. Even though secularization for many decades has impacted the Danish society and its citizens so that the church and Christian faith no longer have the same strong position as previously, then still Christianity – often in the form of a more subdued culture Christianity (kulturkristendom) and a view of man and society, which is related to the Christian tradition – is an essential part of common understanding of what is implied in being Danish. Therefore the integration of immigrants into the Danish society – apart from their attitudes and desires – may push or draw them in the direction of Christianity.

Lewis Rambo refers to the following phases or dimensions in the conversion process: context, crisis, encounter, interaction, engagement and consequences. Of special interest in this context is the phase or dimension of interaction. Rambo describes this as an establishment of a sphere of influence where four different forms of interactions are at work:

Relations – With whom does the convert interact?
Rituals – Which unique religious activities does the convert carry out?

---

[31] Berger, Peter L., *Religion, samfund og virkelighed. til en sociologisk religionsteori* (Viborg: Lindhard og Ringhof, 1974): 55.

[32] Berger, Peter L., & Thomas Luckmann, *The Social Construction of Reality. A Treatise in the Sociology of Knowledge* (Garden City, NY: Doubleday, 1966): 145.

Rhetoric – How does the convert begin to think and talk differently?
Roles – Which behavior does the convert do in consonance with the expectations which are directed to converts? The change of role is an internalization and integration of the changes in relations, rhetoric and rituals and will provide the convert with a new life style, new faith concepts and new networks of relationships.[33]

When migrants with a Muslim, Hindu or Buddhist background engage in such an interaction with church/Christianity and thereby become members of the church of the majority or another church that also is related to the religion of the majority and thus adopts the religion of the majority – through relations, rituals, rhetoric and roles – the process of religious conversion comes close to the process of social integration whereby the convert's membership of the Danish society and his or her Danish identity are strengthened.

It may also be argued that the social integration into the Danish society, due to the Christian or culture Christian character of the society, may occasionally lead to a "religious integration" into the church of this society, i.e., a religious conversion. Finally, it may be argued that a religious conversion to the dominant religion of the society may further a social integration into the society. The relationship between conversion and integration can thus take a variety of forms:

- Integration as a motive for conversion.
- Conversion as a means for or a condition for integration.
- Conversion as an effect of integration.
- Conversion as the religious expression of integration.

Conversion of migrants to Christianity in the Folk Church or in the migrant churches may for some of the converts best be explained with reference to the integration-conversion patterns outlined above. It does not make a very big difference whether it was the social integration which brought the converts in contact with church and Christianity and thereby led to the conversion and baptism of these migrants. Or whether the migrants consciously have desired to convert and be baptized in order to be most effectively integrated into the Danish society and to be recognized to be truly Danish. In both cases the religious conversion process is dynamically connected with the social integration process. All this does not go to say that these patterns apply to all immigrants. There are, as mentioned above, also other significant conversions patterns at work in the conversion of immigrants in the Danish society.[34]

---

33 Rambo, Lewis R., *Understanding Religious Conversion* (New Haven: Yale University Press, USA, 1993): 123.

34 Mogensen, Mogens S., "Conversion between Islam and Christianity in a Danish Context." I *Theology and the Religions. A Dialogue*, Viggo Mortensen red. (Grand Rapids MI: Eerdmans, 2003): 287-317.

INCULTURATION AND IDENTITY: A REFLECTION ON CHINESE CHRISTIANITY AND MISSION

Nicholas Tai Ho-fai

Rt Rev Prof Nicholas Tai Ho-fai, Bishop, Evangelical Lutheran Church of Hong Kong, Lutheran Theological Seminary, Hong Kong

Introduction

To reflect on one's identity is always a help for one's own existence. This paper is a reflection on inculturation and identity. First of all, to confirm one's own identity we need to review the living context, and then through Biblical and theological reflections on our identity as Chinese Christian in a metropolitan city like Hong Kong, we will trace how culture affects our identity.

Hong Kong as a context for identity of the Chinese Christianity

Hong Kong is a metropolitan city with great wealth. She is one of the biggest U.S. dollar reserves because of her monetary stability. Hong Kong is an affluent society but with a great disparity between rich and poor. As a developed city, Hong Kong has the highest rate of the Gini coefficient on disparity between rich and poor. Because of the open door policy of China in the 1980s, capitalists in Hong Kong started to move their factories and firms northward, and left large numbers of unskilled workers without jobs. Hong Kong experienced globalization effects already twenty years ago. Besides tourism, Hong Kong is practically almost without job opportunities. It is a monetary centre with the so-called "tertiary sector of industry". But the population strategy of the government and the economic do not match. It leaves a great number of unemployment among the unskillful middle aged people. Although Hong Kong has unemployment subsidizes, this welfare system is not well developed. It leads to misuse of the system or limitations in helping the disadvantaged.

Hong Kong is religiously pluralistic. People have freedom to choose their own religion and political parties. Therefore, cults and political parties are flourishing. Christians face a lot of challenges. Most people confess their own religion as being Buddhist. Buddhism has been flourishing since it took up different forms of mission. It now uses mass rallies like Christian evangelistic meetings and also offers different courses of religious education and meeting places for meditation etc.

In this affluent society, people tend to think that anything can be purchased for money, even religion. The Protestant churches in Hong Kong are traditionally conservative evangelical. Their teachings are very strict and from a Lutheran point of view, focus on righteousness by deeds. But the old strict teachings do not satisfy the needs of contemporary members of society. So some Christians become church shoppers. Within these twenty years the percentage of Christians in Hong Kong has not increased at all. The population has grown from around four millions twenty years ago up to almost seven millions. But the ratio of Christians to the population has at the same time dropped from 10% to 8% despite the fact that the actual number of Christians has increased. During this period, quite a few of successful mega churches emerged. The Lutheran churches have stagnated.

The people in Hong Kong have no problem in access to the world of communication. All sorts of information with its influence come to our youth without any problem. The phenomenon of the so-called post-modern generation X can be seen also in Hong Kong. A group of youngsters want to learn witchcraft but they do not have any access to witchcraft in Hong Kong. Therefore, they search on the internet and learn witchcraft from the net and practice witchcraft accordingly.

Biblical and Theological Reflections on Identity as Chinese Christian

Protestant Chinese Churches in Hong Kong were molded by evangelicals with a strict fundamentalist faith. To help the church coming out from this form of Christianity, one must start with the Bible. The Bible is for them the paper pope. Salvation for this kind of Christians is personal and private. Once people become Christians, they will mostly care for the afterlife. But in society, people tease the Christians by using the phrase "don't talk [about] Jesus". It means, don't talk about nonsense or don't just talk without any action. The name "Jesus", therefore, has through the negative witness of some Christians become a mocking word. The pragmatic way of Chinese thinking confirms that every religion which benefits the society is a good religion. Thus Christianity is for them a religion that does not 'work'. In ecountering this situation it is necessary to help fellow Christians to understand both the mission context of Hong Kong and the Bible. God's message does not come in a religious vacuum, in which it had to create the religious world of symbols from scratch.

In this portion of reflections I will make use of some models in the Old and New Testament in order to show how faith, situation and culture go hand in hand, since the so-called inculturation took place in ancient Israel as well as in the mission work of the early Church.

Inculturation in Old and New Testament

It is important to notice that in the ancient Israel inculturation happened all the time. I take as an example the Israelites' faith in a Canaanite culture. First of all, we must acknowledge the rivalry between the faith of Israel in Yahweh and the Baalim. But it was not all Canaanite gods that were rejected by the Israelites. The God of the fathers was identified as El, the highest god of the Canaanite pantheon.[1] The discovery of Canaanite texts in the ancient city of Ugarit has shed light on the identity of the gods of Canaan. El was praised as the highest god, "father of years", "eternal king" and "creator of earth" etc.[2] According to the the scholars, the psalms that praise Yahweh were former Canaanite songs.[3] The form and practice of offerings of the Canaanites and the Israelites were also very similar. We do not know much about the process of assimilation of Israelite religion to the Canaanite. But we do know that when Israel became a state in Canaan, there were still many Canaanites living together with Israelites. For instance, when David and his men took Jerusalem,[4] the Jebusites probably were accepted as part of the population of Israel.[5] According to some historians, the mysterious story of Melchizedek in Gen 14 was based on this historical fact. According to the report of Judges 1:18-36, there was a considerable number of Canaanite cities within Israel. It is reasonable to believe that during the time of David and Solomon, the Canaanite lived under Israelites' rule. Therefore, one may conclude that, demographically speaking, Israelites and Canaanites could not be segregated in the time of the monarchy – as later the deuteronomist and the deuteronomistic history presented it.The epithets of El which were taken by Yahweh show a certain degree of adaptation of Canaanite religion to the Yahweh religion. The Israelite faith in Yahweh stood on a solid basis of Canaanite religion. By this inculturation method, Israelite religion was enriched. However, the danger of syncretism was not easily avoided. The prophetic ministry of the eight century prophets – especially Hosea in the north – criticized the worship of Baal, or more precisely, the worship of "Baalized" Yahweh. Therefore, inculturation could either be an enrichment or a danger to the true faith.

In the New Testament, we can also name two incidents to reflect the inculturation of the early Church. In Acts 15:1-21, the early Church decided on the basis of a theological conviction (Acts 15:11) that the converted gentiles

---

[1] El Bethel in Gen 31:13, 35:7. El Roi in Gen 16:7. El Olam in Gen 21:33. El Elyon in Gen 14:18. El Shaddai in Gen 17:1 etc.

[2] Frank Moore Cross, *Canaanite Myth and Hebrew Epic*, 16, 43. Patrick Miller, *Israelite Religion and Biblical Theology* (Sheffield: Sheffield Academic Press Ltd., 2000), 24.

[3] For example Ps 29 is a Canaanite song, see J. Day, *Psalms, Old Testament Guide* (Sheffield: Sheffield Academic Press, 1990), 42.

[4] 2 Sam 5:6-10 .

[5] In Zech 9:7, the reception of Jebusites into Israelite community was echoed.

didn't need circumcision. It is in some degree a kind of inculturation. For the Jewish Christians, circumcision was non-negotiable. But the new situation had dawned. And, following the new decisions of the apostles and elders, the mission to the whole world came into full force without a Jewish cultural sign – circumcision. A second example of New Testament inculturation is found in Acts 17:22-31. When Paul in Athens found an altar with the inscription, "To an unknown god", he used it as a tool for his proclamation and related it to Jesus. We may criticize his way of using a polytheistic situation to proclaim the Lord of the universe. But his zeal to let the Gospel to meet a culture is to be affirmed.

Christianity and the Hong Kong Chinese Context: Cultural Tradition

Since the protestant mission work in China started in the early 19th Century, the missionaries tried their very best to proclaim the Gospel. Beside the revelation of God in Jesus Christ, missionaries believed that God revealed himself through this world, although it was corrupted by sin. Hence God could use culture and religion to revel himself. Therefore, one should find ways for the Gospel to grow in Chinese soil. The Bible translation, with for example the translation of "logos" into *Dao* – which is a concept of Daoism (the only native religion of China) –, and the translation of God the father of Jesus Christ into *Shangdi* – the highest god of Daoist pantheon –, demonstrates this effort in the past of inculturation. In the early 20th Century, Chinese scholars attempted to reorganize the Bible by taking away the five books of Moses and introducing the four books and five scriptures of ancient Confucianism. We do appreciate their effort to make Christianity grounded in Chinese soil. Whether we welcome this move or not is another matter.

The New Context

What is the context as Hong Kong Christian in the 21st Century Hong Kong? Do the traditional Chinese cultures really matter? How can Christianity really be a part of Hong Kong culture? These questions shape our quest for identity and inculturation. I would like first of all to draw our attention to the latest development of Buddhism in Hong Kong and Taiwan. Their development is well planned and their growth fast. The "renewal" of Buddhism in Hong Kong is by no means a traditional one. Buddhists have taken up what Hong Kong Christians have always done. They are not confined to temple activities, but set up Buddhist centers, "Sunday schools", Radio broadcasting, websites etc. They have even translated Christian songs, e.g. "Amazing Grace" into Buddhist songs. In this post modern world, the so-called "fusion" of different religious elements can be an advantage for these religions. The Buddhists also involve themselves in social service, public education, and the use of mass media. The Buddhist religion presents itself as progressive, with care for the society. It is a religion in the public that "works".

From this fact we have to think of the context of our inculturation. If Buddhism has tried to modernize and "westernize" itself and we try hard to identify ourselves with a historic Chinese heritage that is rather weakly represented nowadays, we may miss the 'Zeitgeist' of our time. In fact, Chinese theologians in Hong Kong are putting their effort in recovering the local history, tradition, and ancient teachings of Chinese philosophers in order to connect it with Christian thinking.[6] It may be a waste of time and energy. For after the May-fourth Movement (starting 1919) and later, the establishment of the People's Republic of China (PRC) in 1949, China and Chinese culture have changed tremendously. The picture in Hong Kong is also quite the same. Under the British rule, Hong Kong was a westernized colony. After the return to the Motherland, Hong Kong identifies herself as metropolitan in China. If we ask what is our cultural context, the historical heritage is after all not a dominant factor at all. Therefore, it is time to reflect on the cultural context of Hong Kong and even China. We cannot, of course, alienate ourselves from the rest of the universal Church. Different theologies that shape our Church and society are part of our culture. It is not enough merely to trace back into history and traditions that once shaped us. In this globalized world and information era, our existence and being are molded by a complex sum of cultures and ideologies.

Identity and Mission of the Lutheran Church in Hong Kong

Identifying with the Poor

The Evangelical Lutheran Church of Hong Kong (ELCHK) was a refugee church *par excellence*. It was founded by graduates of the Lutheran Theological Seminary, who fled with the move of the Seminary from the Mainland during the civil war in the late 1940s. They started to do evangelistic work among refugees from China. During the time of 1960s and 70s, the Church worked mainly among the poor who lived in resettlement estates. This history shaped the mission direction of this church. A lot of our congregations were started in a social service center or a public school, which were run by the church. Through service to the world, the church witnessed to the risen Lord. When we face the new context of the 21st Century, globalization brings blessing as well as curse to Hong Kong. The economy is still booming, but the disparity between rich and poor is worsening. The experience of our Church and the teaching of our Lord (Lk 4:16-20) already define our mission and the preference for the poor.[7] Our congregations and social service centers are helping people to struggle for a better future. The long term goal is to help people to extricate themselves from poverty. Without the power of God's love in Christ, this work is only an other humanitarian service to the society. As long as we identify ourselves with

---

[6] Risto A. Ahonen, *Mission in the New Millennium: Theological Grounds for World Mission* (Helsinki: The Finnish Evangelical Lutheran Mission, 2000), 165.

[7] Ahonen 2000:235f.

the poor, we will imitate Christ, who for our own sake, became poor.

. *Identity and Mission in a Post-Modern World with Its Internet Culture*

I already mentioned that we live in a post-modern world. It is a world of individualism and alienation. Through computers and the internet world, we sometimes live in a virtual reality. Computer and Internet is nowadays a must for modern people. It is a good tool for our daily life. But it can also lead us into problems. In fact, a lot of people spend hours to "talk" to his/her virtual friend on the other side of the computer. One could write all his/her feelings in a "Blog" everyday, but never express himself/herself to others orally. By the addiction to the virtual world, people thus alienate themselves from reality. Only God can satisfy this hunger created by our technology. Only Christ, through his resurrected power, can mend our alienation. Therefore, it is our privilege and duty to help people who are in isolation and alienate themselves from others. Christians should realize the existence and mission of the Church in their context. The relevancy of the Church depends on whether it speaks to their situation.

Lutheran Identity of Justification by Faith and the Place of Good Works

As Lutherans we are well aware of our theology and identity. Since the suggestion of Justification by love by Bishop K. H. Ting, many may think that Bishop Ting has suggested to do away with the Christian understanding of Justification that is especially cherished by Lutherans. This is the point where Chinese and Western theologians depart. For Chinese, a theology that does not have ethical implications, is not good theology. The relevancy of a theology lies is in her application in daily life. The "metanoia" (conversion) inside one's life should be manifested outwardly by one's deeds. Bishop Ting stresses that the awareness of sin in the world is important. [8] He stresses also that if we say that human beings are nothing but sin, this is another extreme. One could easily see good works among non-believers and communists. On the contrary, when Christians express salvation through faith without work, this can only lead to irrelevancy. Bishop Ting has expressed the problem more acutely than St. Paul did in Galatians 5:6: "The only thing that counts is faith working through love." I do not think that Bishop Ting's intention was to eliminate the doctrine of Justification by faith, but to provoke effects of faith, like the Epistle of James (2:17): "So faith by itself, if it has no works, is dead."[9] The whole issue of "Justification by love" is a quest for the relevancy of the Christians in society. The provocation helps us to rethink the fundamentalistic view of Christian life and to stress a holistic witness to the world. Lutherans should follow what the Roman Catholic and Lutheran *Joint Declaration of the Doctrine of Justification*

---

[8] K. H. Ting, *Collection of Bishop K. H. Ting's Essays* (Hong Kong: Chinese Christian Literature Council Ltd ., 1999), 87.

[9] See also The *Joint Declaration on the Doctrine of Justification* (1997), § 25.

(1997, §25) already stated, namely that Christians cannot and should not live without "good works". In a Chinese context, this is a practical quest for relevancy of our faith.

Conclusion

Inculturation is found throughout the Bible and in the history of the Church. It is important for Christians in Hong Kong to read our context as Chinese in a globalized metropolitan city, so that our identity and mission will not be out of focus.

"GOING GLOBAL": A REFLECTION ON BEING A WESTERN CHRISTIAN IN A GLOBAL CHURCH

Kjetil Aano

Kjetil Aano, General Secretary, Norwegian Missionary Society, Stavanger, Norway

The times they are a-changing

In the time span of a couple of generations, the Christian faith has changed from being a basically Western religion to becoming a global faith. Much emphasis has been put on the southward shift. Philip Jenkins, among others, have argued that on a north-south axis the point of gravity of Christianity today is somewhere in Africa.[1] An equally important point of view, however, is presented in the following statement: "The north-south axis is hugely significant, and we shall remain in Jenkins' debt for this timely reminder, however, within Europe it is important not to ignore the significance of the East-West axis".[2]

The reality of the changes that face us is more than radical enough. We are just now starting to explore how we in the North and West are – and even more will be – challenged by the emerging fact of world Christianity. Here, I am not primarily preoccupied by trivialities relating to how we as Westerners will have to cope with becoming a minority in the world. The question is more how we as western Christians can cope with becoming one among many. The churches beyond the West are finding their own structures and their own ways of thinking and doing.[3] And even in our own world, the West, our Churches are taken over by the believers of the majority world, and they are not asking our

---

[1] Philip Jenkins, *The New Christendom. The Coming of Global Christianity,* (Oxford, New York: Oxford University Press, 2002).

[2] Darrell Jackson, "Pax Europa: Crux Europa" in *Researching European Mission*, Report, 2007.

[3] Fernando F. Segovia, *Decolonizing Biblical Studies : A View from the Margins*, (New York: Orbis 2000); Hwa Yung, *Mangoes or Bananas? The Quest for Authentic Asian Christian Theology*, (Oxford: Regnum, 1997).

permission to do things in their own way.[4] What is going to happen when we in the West do not have the power to make the rules any more?[5]

These changes are the point of departure for my reflections. How will this impact the churches and the Christians in the West?

It is my conviction that if we are to act and believe coherently, we need to see ourselves not primarily as westerners, but as members of the one and global church. We need to go global.

I write these lines in honour of Knud Jørgensen. He has throughout his career, constantly challenged his churches in Denmark and Norway regarding these matters. He has taken his manifold experiences from the northern hemisphere, where he has served in a number of Christian organisations in a wide variety of capacities, and his long life in service for the churches in the south, particularly Ethiopia and China, and not least, his keen interest in serving international bodies (The Lutheran World Federation, The Lausanne Movement and Africa Evangelistic Enterprise), and united them in his approach. He has done it in a challenging and sharing way. Therefore these thoughts presented here, are both in honour of Knud and inspired by his collegiality.

The shift of the centre of gravity

In a recently published article, Philip Jenkins writes:

> Be careful what you wish (or pray) for: you may get it. For some centuries, European and American Christians prayed fervently for the conversion of the wider world, especially in Africa and Asia, and many devoted their lives to achieving this end. And to an astounding degree, they succeeded. (…)
>
> Already we do not represent the norm within Christianity, whether in racial, social or economic terms. By 2050, white non-Hispanics would represent just 15 or 20 percent of the world's Christians.[6]

This shift has taken place within the time-span of a couple of generations, historically speaking a very brief period. The change has been so rapid it is difficult for those of us who are at the losing side, to grasps the realities of it. And if we have a hard time taking in what is happening, it's even harder working out how to react to the changes taking place.

---

[4] Sten Sørensen (ed), *Kirkens utfordring. Kirke av folket eller kirke for folket* (Kvinesdal, Dawn-Norge, 2005), 95-100. Grace Davie, *Europe: The Exceptional Case. Parameters of Faith in the Modern World.* (London: Darton.Longman+Todd 2002), 107-111.

[5] Michael Amaladoss, S.J., "My Pilgrimage in Mission," *International Bulletin of Missionary Research*, Vol. 31, No 1, Jan 2007: 21-24.

[6] Philip Jenkins, *Companions of Life. A supple faith.* http://www.christianitytoday.com/bc/2007/002/9.18.html

Facing the grim reality of diminishing membership, many churches have retracted to a strategy of denial. It is not until the reality of empty churches and financial restraints have hit hard that one realises that new strategies are not an option, but a matter of survival as churches. In Scandinavia, where formal membership is still surprisingly high, at least compared to regular church attendance, and where furthermore the majority and minority churches are generously funded by government money, the underlying long-term changes are hard to detect, and even harder to admit.

The point here is not to paint a totally bleak image of a dying Western Church. Rather it is to argue that unless our churches understand that a new situation requires new strategies, this may well become a reality.[7] The history of the mighty combination of political and spiritual power exercised by a union of state and church (whether through a state-church union as in Scandinavia or other models, as in southern and Eastern Europe) is over.

We have reached a time of reorientation. The question is where we are heading. History tells us of a number of cases where the forces of change were not detected in time, and the needed will to act and to reform was not sufficiently strong. In consequence, churches have dwindled, and died.[8] The same can be said about societies that chose to lose.[9] But there is no inevitability about this.

On the other hand, it has become both politically and theologically correct in the West to talk about the global South as a source of inspiration and renewal. But we often do it as if spirituality and discipleship were merely a matter of emotion and experience. The Western Church has not yet fully grasped the real theological challenges from the global South that is growing in faith and confidence. Philip Jenkins' protest is timely, when he comments on and challenges the view of among others Father Andrew Greeley, who has suggested that: "We [the West] will depend on them for vitality, but they will continue to depend on us for the ideas".

In my own Scandinavian setting similar ideas are sometimes clothed in expression such as "South as source of inspiration and renewal". Jenkins answer is pretty much to the point: "I somehow doubt that the global South's contribution to theological inquiry will be confined to rhythmic dancing or hand-clapping".[10]

On the other hand, in spite of all the changes, an unequal distribution of

---

[7] Steven Croft, *The Future of the Parish System. Shaping of the Church of England for the 21 st Century.* (London: Church House, 2006).

[8] Jenkins 2007:1;3. Kenneth Scott Latourette, *A History of the Expansion of Christianity. Volume 2: The Thousand Years of Uncertainty 500 A.D. to 1500 A.D.* (Grand Rapids: Zondervan): 286-307.

[9] Jared Diamond, *Collapse. How Societies Fail or Succeed.* (New York: Viking Books, 2005).

[10] Jenkins 2007.

academic and financial power is still a lasting legacy of Western dominance. Although western churches have been losing power in their own societies, the West is still a powerful player in the world arena. And that reflects the position that we as westerners play, globally, and as Western Christians play within much of the Global Church. Even if we are not powerful in our own societies, western churches and church organisations still have enough economic and cultural power to dominate north – south relations, and we still make the rules that the churches have to play by on the international scene.

This is a criticism that has been put to Western missions on a number of occasions, and like much criticism, it is not ungrounded. However, at this point in history the criticism may as much be pointed at the role of the global academic world, where Western traditions are unquestioned; or to the global aid-agencies whose ideologically tainted development-strategies dominate south-north relations. All of this points to the mere fact that Western political and financial forces still dominate relations on all levels, as well as international, ecumenical relations Everything is contextual, but to a large extent the Western world still makes the rules that the players have to play by. But for how long?

Where are we heading? A shift in the profile of Christianity

What do we mean by Global Christianity?

In 1977 Walther Bühlmann's book, *The Third Church,*[11] appeared, where he presented his visions of a global Church. Like many Western theologians he was influenced by the then dominant theology of liberation. His visions for the coming global church were heavily inspired by political coloured language of liberation. Thus, Bühlmann is one of many Western thinkers who have prophesised a future church in the image of their own wishful thinking. In spite of that, Bühlmann's book is an important contribution to our understanding of the reality of a global Christian faith.

Also, on another side of the theological spectrum we find similar tendencies. In David Aikman's *Jesus in Beijing,*[12] a fascinating picture of an emerging Chinese church is drawn. The author makes a genuine contribution to a better understanding of the complex relationship between what Western conservatives have preferred to see as opposites: A pro-communist three-self-church and the house-church-movement. However, his gains fall short when he tries to argue that the development of these church movements in turn will open up not only a Western inspired idea of democracy, but an American understanding of the

---

[11] Walter Bühlmann, *The Coming of the Third Church: An Analysis of the Future of the Church*, (Maryknoll, Maryknoll: Orbis Books, 1977).

[12] David Aikman, *Jesus in Beijing: How Christianity Is Transforming China and Changing the Global Balance of Power* (Washington, DC: Regnery Publishing, 2003).

relationship between the freedom of movement of capital and freedom of ideas.

In working with the development of the global Church, there is a temptation to draw it or see it in one's own preferred image. In order to truthfully interpret the world we live in, we, as Western Christians, are constantly challenged by a number of issues. I will mention the following:

First, we need to accept that what is in the making, what is rapidly growing in the two-thirds world, is not asking for permission from the modern paradigm to grow and develop as it wishes.[13] The discussion relating to post-modernism, is part of this. According to Robert Schreiter, post-modernism is a sum reaction to modernism, on the basis that modernism has failed. He shows how these reactions are made in three directions: either as a reappropriation of the pre-modern; as a strategy to overcome the shortcomings of modernity (it hasn't quite succeeded); or thirdly, as a response to fulfil the post-modern condition of deconstructing reality, particularly the value of the great narratives.[14]

Secondly, we need to learn to exceed our categorizations. The categories by which we have learned to order the Church are gradually being broken up and combined in totally new ways. Schreiter calls this "the new catholicity as fullness of faith".[15]

Thirdly, we need to accept that much of what has been Western cultural tradition and academic insights that have become almost part of our own Christian identity hardly makes any sense beyond the West, and if it does make sense, it looks like secularism in disguise.

Fourthly, we should learn that what we are accustomed to look at as the norm, in many cases are specific Western contextualizations of faith. Such a point of view carries a potential for liberation and creativity.

Global and translatable

It is remarkable that the Christian religion appears to be able to express itself in any given language. The mere fact that the Word of God in the Bible comes to us not in a given and unchangeable linguistic form, but as something that is translatable is a powerful expression of universality and diversity.

Lamin Sanneh has forcefully argued that what goes for language also goes for culture. Christianity is expressed not only through a multiplicity of

---

[13] Amaladoss 2007.

[14] Robert Schreiter, *The New 'Catholicity: Theology between the Global and the Local* (Maryknoll, N.Y: Orbis Books, 1997, and Robert Schreiter, "Globalization, Postmodernity and the New Catholicity" in Else Marie Wiberg Pedersen, Holger Lam, Peter Lodberg (ed), *For All People. Global Theologies in Context.* (Grand Rapids: Eerdmans, 2002).

[15] Schreiter 2002: 28-29

languages, but also through a diversity of cultures, shapes and forms.[16] But in a global world like ours, many of the culturally specific expressions of Christian faith become trans-cultural. As Western Christians we relate to many of these expressions, and even encounter them in new ways.

Allow me to suggest some emerging patterns of Christian faith.

We need a new interpretation of Pentecostalism. The Pentecostalization of Christianity has been pointed to by a number of scholars.[17] Pentecostal and Neo-Pentecostal Churches and movements are flourishing practically all over the world. In mere numbers the growth of these churches is breathtaking. By a conservative estimate around 25% of Christians belong to these churches.[18] In general terms they have been placed on the conservative side of the spectrum both theologically and politically. To a large extent, this may still well be true. But things are not that simple, and movements are not so easily positioned any more. Paul Gifford has given an interesting analysis of a number of larger Pentecostal churches in Ghana.[19] Outwardly these churches present themselves as arenas where economic prosperity and individual success are the only things that matter and are the given results of true, Christian faith. But Gifford successfully demonstrates that the role that these churches play is much more diverse. The help they offer is wider and their profile varies more than what first impressions show.

The processes presented in Gifford's study from Ghana, could easily be copied.

The two Norwegian scholars, Berge Furre and Sturla Stålsett, have analysed the Brazilian neo-charismatic, financially successful media mega church, Igreja Universal do Regno de Deus, The Universal Church of the Kingdom of God. The scholars retain a critical attitude to the church, but they have admittedly changed their perspective by what they observe.[20] The two scholars verify the image that Pentecostal leaders present the effects of liberated lives. During the Conference on World Mission and Evangelism that took place in Athens, Greece, in May 2005, Rev. Wonsuk Ma quoted a Pentecostal leader who, when he was asked whether his church had any social programs, responded: We don't

---

[16] Lamin Sanneh, *Translating the Message. The Missionary Impact on Culture.* (Maryknoll, New York: Orbis Books, 1998).

[17] David Martin, *Tongues of Fire: The Explosion of Protestantism in Latin America*, (Oxford: Blackwell, 1990).

[18] David Barrett, Todd M. Johnson, Peter F. Crossing: "Missionmetrics 2007: Creating Your Own Analysis of Global Data", *International Bulletin of Missionary Research* Vol. 31, no. 2. Jan. 2007, 25-32.

[19] Paul Gifford: "A view of Ghanas New Christianity" in Lamin Sanneh & Joel E. Carpenter (ed.): *The Changing Face of Christianity* (Oxford: Oxford University Press, 2005), 811-96.

[20] Berge Furre, "Nypinsevenner – på veg mot Europa" *Kirke og kultur, No 1,* 2003, 3-15.

have any social programs, we are a social program.[21]

The pentecostalization of global Christian faith will most probably continue, and it challenges our categories. For Western Christians "going global" means learning to live with this challenge. The Pentecostal movements on the other hand need to strengthen their efforts to dialogue – primarily locally and nationally – with other Christian traditions.

One of them is a bold and growing Roman Catholic tradition. In Europe, the Catholic Church is facing the challenge of dwindling membership and lack of candidates for the priesthood. But the Roman Catholic Church is a world power. In spite of ecumenical setbacks of late, on many levels the relationship between Roman Catholics and members of other Christian traditions are better and closer perhaps than ever. Any process that overlooks the Roman Catholic Church will at best have a lopsided result. In a global church, where the power of the Spirit is moving, there will definitely be a need for longer historic perspectives, and for order and structures. The Roman Catholics will always be reckoned with. This we have always known.

Of newer date to North-Western European Christians (perhaps with the exception of Finland, if that ever was Western) is the resurgence of the Orthodox traditions. The Orthodox renewal after the fall of communism is astounding.[22] Also, globally, the Orthodox churches are playing a much more prominent role than previously. In promoting environmental consciousness the Patriarch of Constantinople has been able to unite Christians from many traditions to his cause.[23] But also in the field of world mission, the Orthodox churches are making great strides[24]. With the resurgence of interest for religion, an Orthodox theology with a deep trinitarian approach attracts a number of people that the more pragmatic Protestant traditions do not necessarily communicate that well with. One of the real challenges facing the Orthodox tradition as it emerges into the global context is the notion of 'Orthodox lands' where any activity by all other churches is seen as unwarranted proselytism. There is a definite need for entering into real dialogue on the meaning of

---

[21] Wonsuk Ma, ""'When the Poor are Fired up." The Role of Pneumatology in Pentecostal.Charismatic Mission". *Plenary no.10, Report, Conference on World Mission and Evangelism.* (Athens, 2005: CWME/WCC). Philip Jenkins, *The New Face of Christianity. Believing the Bible in The Global South.* (Oxford: Oxford University Press, 2006).

[22] Darrell Jackson, "European Churches in Mission. A research Report form the CEC Mission in Europe Programme 2004 – 2007", CEC, 2007.

[23] Bartholomew I, the present Patriarch of Constantinople, has made it one of his main undertakings to organise ecumenical and ecological sailings in order to pint at the need for ecological consciousness and action.

[24] Athanasios N. Papathanasiou, *Future, the Background of History. Essays on Church Mission in an Age of Globalization.* (Montréal: Alexander Press, 2005).

proselytism.[25]

Before I make a few remarks on main-line Western Churches, I wish to draw attention to the Church in China. The Chinese Church is probably the largest national church anywhere in the world today. A large part of the Church may be described as Neo-Pentecostal. However, the official recognised protestant Church, The Three Self Movement, definitely presents itself as a different entity. This Church has survived decades of persecution, and throughout it all stubbornly insisted on its Chinese identity, and refused to be looked upon as a Western institution or as an instrument of westernisation. That may well be one main reason for its survival. However, with the recent opening up for Western influence in general, the Church in China all of a sudden finds itself in the middle of a stream of interest precisely because it is part of a global and Western reality. Globalization of culture and economy challenges the Church in China to express its identity in new ways.[26]

This is not totally different from what is happening within many main-line Protestant churches in the West. These are churches that have lived with the modern paradigm, and have to a certain extent become proponents of modernity. This tends to give them a varying degree of a liberal taint, and relating to the changes of globalization and post-modernity, they interestingly enough become adversaries to change. These are the churches that have played first violin in relating to the public sphere in their respective countries. This is where the ecumenical movements were born, and it is in these churches that the spirit of ecumenism and reconciliation has been fostered. The conservative/evangelical British theologian, Alister McGrath, has dismissed these churches as largely lifeless and the ecumenical movements as irrelevant.[27]

This is an overstatement, but it may turn out to have some truth to it. One great challenge for these churches is to understand the global world in which they live. Many Western European churches have more or less unwittingly and unwillingly become protectors and proponents of modernity. They have historical ties to European secular culture. In good cultural imperialistic tradition, these churches see themselves as forerunners, and whatever they do and wherever they go, the rest of the world will follow suit.

If this ever were true – of which I am not convinced – it is not so any more. A self-critical approach is warranted, and churches need to learn that their choice of profile and world-view is one of many options. They may all be modern options, as there are many modernities.[28] Additionally, there is bound so be something after modernity.

Modernist Western theology is a genuine expression of a wish to be theologically relevant; it is a Western contextual theology. The problem arises

---

[25] Jackson, CEC 2007.

[26] http://www.time.com/time/printout/0,8816,1229123,00.html#.

[27] Alister E. McGrath, *The Future of Christianity*, (Oxford: Blackwells, 2002).

[28] Davie 2002.

when a contextual theology assumes a self-understanding where it exceeds contextuality. To some extent this has been the fate of Western (male) theological tradition.

Reconciliation and mission

Now all can observe that the context in the west is changing and the return of religion is a reality. The world is rapidly becoming de-secularized, and religion is playing a part in the life of individualsin ways partly unexpected, as well as in the public sphere.[29] Post-modernism is – or at least may well be – a cultural expression of the same underlying stream of change. Modernity is no longer the inevitable answer to the challenge of how to face the future.[30] Many churches have only slowly taken these changes in.

So what are the consequences? What does it mean for western Christians to "go global"?

Let me make three points:

Mission is back

The post-colonial period where mission and western insensitivity was seen as two sides of the same coin is gone. However, mission as the very essence of being church is back. This is clearly demonstrated by the central position in the Church of England of the Report *Mission shaped Church.*[31] There is also a new understanding of the dimension of mission, or the missional dimension of the church. And although the theological and ecclesiological consequences may still be debated, this has been a major change in the approach of the Western churches to their mission. This does not in any way exclude an equally important emphasis on diakonia, on the serving with hands and feet, and in advocacy.

Reconciliation is the essence of mission

The church in the west needs to learn from its global partners to reconcile the two dimensions of the gospel; the one that says that being Christian is living for the other: social change, diaconal witness, and advocacy is the way of the church in our time; and the other that underlines the sharing of the Gospel, spreading the Christian faith and making disciples.[32]

Tension between these two approaches runs through most western churches, and has in many instances also been institutionalised. There are weaknesses on

---

[29] Peter Berger, *The De-secularization of the World*, (Grand Rapids: Eerdmans, 1999).

[30] Schreiter, 2002, 20ff.

[31] *Mission Shaped Church*, (London: Church House, 2003).

[32] Tore Laugerud, Rapport fra CECs Mission Project 2004 -2007, 2, (Kirkerådet/Mellomkirkelig råd, 2007)

both sides. Many evangelical movements are reductionist as they see only the soul of the individual as relevant for the church. On the other hand, a number of the mainline Churches and ecumenical bodies have had a tradition of being equally reductionist in that they do not see the sharing of the gospel with respect and cultural sensitivity as an integral part of their mission. Both of these positions are reductionist, i.a. by not taking seriously the basic theological understanding of humankind being created in the image of God.

Secondly, we need to approach European history of religious and cultural/political conflicts in a reconciliatory perspective, and with a reconciling goal. There is in spite of all progress in mutual contact and understanding, all ecumenical development and theological and cultural exchanges, still need for a protestant –catholic process. This is about theology, but even given the theological insoluble problems, it may be more a process of humility. These conflict lines have torn Europe apart – and not only long ago. Frère Roger of the Taizé movement has at the bottom of his understanding of his mission, a cry for reconciliation. The cry for reconciliation between East and West also relate to the orthodox-roman catholic/protestant axis. Miroslav Volf has in several of his books reflected on the conflict lines between east and west.[33] Himself being a protestant from Serbia, he in his own person unites both the catholic-orthodox and the protestant –catholic line of conflict.

Missional and missionary

Thirdly there is the need for reconciliation north-south. How can we learn to live together?

Can Europeans be humble enough to learn from Africans how hatred may be overcome? Are we able to relate on equal terms with African and Asian churches?

This has many elements, I will point out some aspects of the re-discovery of the missional dimension of being church. This has far-reaching consequences for the future shape of the church in the West:

- The missional perspective of being church is prominent in the English-speaking world, but also beyond, i.a. through the CEC mission project. This changes the profile of European churches.
- The Emerging church or Emergent church. Here the focus is discovering the historical contingency of existing divisions of theological traditions and of denominational or confession differences.
- "Fresh expressions" is a response, particularly in the Anglican

---

[33] Miroslav Volf, *Exclusion and Embrace: A theological Exploration of Identity, Otherness and Reconciliation*, (Grand Rapids: Eerdmans, 2005); *Free of Charge: Giving and Forgiving in a Culture Stripped of Grace.* (Grand Rapirds: Zondervan, 2006). *End of Memory, Remembering Rightly in a Violent World* (Grand Rapids: Eerdmans, 2007).

community to the re-discovery of the cultural diversity of the Western population, and Christian freedom of expression.

The understanding of the missional dimension of the church is of great importance. However, since its focus – and rightfully so – is the problem-ridden churches in the West, it risks becoming an expression of western self-centredness. The western notion of *missional* church, therefore, needs to be reconciled with a *missionary* attitude that has a global perspective. Global mission and missional church belong together. Our challenge is to integrate them – on the receiving side – and on the sending side.

Going global?

It has been an underlying thesis of these reflections that renewal of churches in the West is possible, and that perhaps the way to proceed is "going global". By this I mean that we as western churches need to accept the fact that the church is no longer a western dominated institution. We need to learn to accept that others may have taken the lead in spite of our power, academic resources and wealth. At the same time we need to avoid receding into a newfound and safe isolationism – in fear of repeating earlier mistakes where spiritual sharing (mission) and cultural dominance (colonialism) were mixed and fused into an unholy combination.

Andrew Walls has in one of his many fascinating studies, pointed out how renewal always comes from the periphery, and not from the centre of power.[34]

As Western Christians, we are a living expression of just that – in a double sense. For centuries, we were the instrument of expansion and renewal. And our message was accepted with joy. Now the world has been turned upside down. Renewal, change, and inspiration come to us from the periphery. Our challenge is to receive the gifts that are offered, and be influenced, be renewed. Our challenge is to accept that being Christian is being part of a global 'koinonia'. Being true church means going global.

[34] Andrew Walls, *The Missionary Movement in Christian History: Studies in Transmission of Faith.* (Maryknoll, New York: Orbis Books, 1996).

International Diakonia

Kjell Nordstokke

Dr. Kjell Nordstokke, Director of the Department for Mission and Development, Lutheran World Federation, Geneva, Switzerland

Introduction

Conception of the church as a global reality although always rooted in a local context and in the expression of a local community of believers, belongs to Christian faith. This is affirmed in the liturgy when the local congregation confesses its credo together "with the church throughout the world". Solid ground for the ecumenical vision that we already find expressed in the New Testament is found here, namely that all Christians are One in Christ, and that the church as new creation is given a mandate to participate in God's mission of reconciling and healing the world.

The very term *oikumene*, which is derived from the Greek word for house (*oikos*), understands the world as God's household, announcing that the entirety of creation belongs to God and that the world, in Christ, is given promise of hope and future. The same vision calls Christians to be good *oikoumenoi* (economists, or stewards) of this hope. Therefore, mission is not just an activity organized by some Christians; nor can it be limited to the organizational plans and ambitions of a local church. The church is by her very nature *missional* and through God's Holy Spirit empowered to participate in God's mission for the healing of the world.

Throughout history concrete mission work has encompassed both proclamation (*martyria*), service (*diakonia*), and defense of the poor and excluded (*advocacy*). This holistic understanding of mission is rooted in the ecumenical vision of being sent to the whole world. This is not meant only geographically in the sense of all parts of the world, including the traditional Christian global North. It also implies that the wholeness of human reality is the object of God's mission. This relates to Christian anthropology which states that to be human includes physical, mental, social and spiritual dimensions; therefore, care for people in need, as well as advocacy in favor of human dignity, should respect this four-fold dimension of human life. From this brief introduction it becomes clear that

- diakonia is an intrinsic dimension of being church and, as such, an integral part of the church's mission;
- diakonia in today's world must be international and respond to the challenges of the new global patterns of injustice, exclusion and poverty that victimize millions of people, especially in the global South.

International diakonia, therefore, cannot be seen as an option. It is a necessary element of being diaconal church in today's globalized world. As Christians worldwide confess their belief in the Triune God, international diakonia by its action professes this same faith: In the Creator, to who belongs "the earth and all that is in it, the world, and those who live in it" (Ps 24.1). In the Savior who came that we may have "life, and have it abundantly" (John 10.19). In the Holy Spirit who sets "free from the law of sin and of death" (Rom 8.2).

The importance of terminology

During an evaluation in the final session of a consultation on diakonia in Southern Brazil, a woman stood up and said: "Now I know that what I have been engaged in all my life has a name. The name is diakonia." She explained that she came from a village in a rural area, and that she visited regularly persons who were sick, many of them farmers who had been poisoned by the pesticides they had used in their work. Because of what she had seen, she had become active in the struggle for better protection of the environment and for the rights of landless agricultural workers.

She said that her commitment in the first place was motivated by her Christian faith, but she had not received much help from the church to see the link between her spirituality and her everyday engagement. Of course, she had heard about development projects in which her church was involved, and also about social action, but these terms sounded quite technical, mainly for experts to assume responsibility. Therefore, she had difficulty in relating them to what she was doing. Now, however, she had a new word that linked what she was doing to her identity as a Christian and church member. This word was diakonia.

The advantage of the term diakonia is that it refers to broad biblical material. In the Greek New Testament the term diakonia (in English translated as service or ministry) is found in very important passages when Jesus announces the profound nature of his mission. "For the Son of Man came not to be served but to serve, and to give his life a ransom for many" (Mark 10:45); "For who is greater, the one who is at the table or the one who serves? Is it not the one at the table? But I am among you as one who serves" (Luke 22:27). Both passages illustrate how Jesus understood his Messianic ministry as a saving presence in the midst of human reality in order to heal and reconcile. The reference to the table, and thereby to the Holy Communion, conveys that his ministry includes and empowers for participation. This is stated more explicitly in John 13: "I have set you an example, that you also should do as I have done to you" (verse 15).

In this way, both the christological and the ecclesiological foundations of diakonia are affirmed. Diakonia is imbedded in what the Church is and proclaims, yet it points also towards social intervention in order to change situations of suffering, need and injustice. From the time of the New Testament, there has been a long tradition in the church, to use the concept of diakonia to designate concrete action in favor of the poor and marginalized. In Acts 6 diakonia refers to the daily distribution of food. In his letters, the Apostle Paul uses the term for the campaign of collecting money for the poor in Jerusalem (2 Cor 8 and 9). Ever since, such concrete diaconal action has been a part of the church's life and mission to the world. At times diakonia has taken the form of spontaneous action, at others it has been institutionalized, for instance as hospitals and orphanages. Sometimes it has been silent service, other times bold action in favor of the poorest and most vulnerable.

Summing up, the term diakonia encompasses both gift and task. It refers both to the memory of Jesus and his diakonia for us, and to the new life the communion of believers is called to live in Christ, a life of compassion, justice and peace.

The Dictionary of the Ecumenical Movement defines diakonia in a similar way, as the "responsible service of the gospel by deeds and by words performed by Christians in response to the needs of people, rooted in and modeled on Christ's service and teachings".[1]

Since diakonia refers both to theology and to concrete action in social reality, reflection on diakonia must be *interdisciplinary*. Action can be adequate and responsible only if the tools provided by the social sciences reflect the social reality. This is very important in order to avoid a diaconal practice that is paternalistic and limited by charity attitudes.

On the other hand, it is equally important to root this practice in a clear understanding of its specific Christian identity. Representatives of churches in the South, who have often felt a sort of dichotomy between their identity as churches and their action in the world when involved in development projects, have raised this second point frequently. Because development is a secular word, such projects have tended to be limited to secular worldview, formed by modernist/Western ideology, which itself is secular and has little understanding of the church's role in society. This view is also formed by communication with funding partners in the North, as planning, implementation and reporting have to be done according to their requirements, rather than in dialogue with the local church.

[1] *Dictionary of the Ecumenical Movement* (Geneva: WCC Publications, 2002), 305.

If the language of development has been criticized frequently in the past, it is because it is perceived as being mainly formed by modernist optimism and by the Enlightenment's confidence in human morality and readiness to overcome injustice. As an integral part of the church, diakonia is better informed concerning the power of evil, both in human action and worldly structures, and knows that evil must be resisted and sin overcome. Commitment to justice, therefore, is not based on social and political analysis, but on the confidence in God's justification of the lost and excluded, and in God's saving power and reconciliation in Christ, both in its vertical and horizontal dimension.

In all this, some may claim that the term diakonia is too "churchly" to be used in development work. As a concept, it is unknown and will not be understood by secular partners, for instance, governmental back-donors. On the other hand, these same partners challenge church-related development agencies to present their identity and "added values" in their performance. Evidently, the dialogue here will have to continue as new openness to the role of religion in social and political matters grows, and agents of development cannot ignore the various positive and negative implications of religious worldview and value systems.

The advantage of the concept of diakonia is that it offers a rationale that is different from such concepts as development and social action by the fact that is reflects both "what it is to be a church," and "what it means to be in the world." As already indicated, such rationale must necessarily be interdisciplinary, providing both a theoretical and practical framework for understanding the church's action in today's complex world of poverty, suffering and injustice. Interdisciplinary reflection further presupposes conscious interaction between theory and praxis, as diakonia cannot be limited to observation and analysis, but is, in the first place, intervention and action.

All diaconal action, and especially international diakonia, needs critical reflection for the sake of the dignity of those involved – the needy, the suffering, and the excluded.

The internationalization of diakonia

Already in the time of the New Testament, diaconal action helped the local congregation to see beyond its cultural, social and geographical boundaries. The challenge from the Greek-speaking widows belonging to the congregation in Jerusalem caused a restructuring of the leadership in order to overcome patterns of exclusion. It is noteworthy that the seven men, who were given the responsibility for the diakonia of the table, all bear Greek names (Acts 6.5), indicating that inclusiveness implies empowering the social group that has been ignored.

Equally, the campaign that the Apostle Paul organized in favor of the poor in Jerusalem became an example of Christian solidarity across geographical and cultural boundaries. In arguing for support for this campaign, it should be noted that in his writings Paul does not refer to the tragic suffering of the poor. Instead he lifts up the memory of Jesus and of "his generous act (...) that though he was rich, yet for your sakes he became poor, so that by his poverty you might become rich" (2 Cor 8:9). Paul also refers to a general notion of what is "a fair balance" between the abundance of some and the need of others. Again this is in line with what faith remembers as God's gracious action, as witnessed in the Old Testament story of the manna in the desert. "As it is written, 'The one who had much did not have too much, and the one who had little did not have too little'" (2 Cor 8:14-15).

Reading this in today's situation, it should be noted first of all that the church is a worldwide reality, well rooted in all continents and their variety of cultures and social conditions. Following the basic assumption that diakonia is an integral dimension of being church, it becomes evident that this also counts for the worldwide church, and that diakonia must be international, related to global challenges and tasks. It also follows that all churches, not only the rich churches in the North, are mandated to participate in international diakonia in a spirit of mutuality and sharing of resources. No church is so rich that it has no needs, and no church is so poor that it has no contributions to make.

As diakonia knows no geographical borders, when challenged to act it should pay special attention and be ready to respond actively to situations of extreme poverty, need and injustice anywhere in the world. This is even more necessary in today's globalized world. There is a growing conviction among people engaged in diakonia that more than charitable assistance is required. Diaconal action cannot ignore the fact that the growing gap between the rich and the poor is a North-South phenomenon. Nor can it overlook that neo-liberal market-oriented ideology provides mechanisms that contribute to growing imbalances in the world and leave large populations in the global South without very much hope for the future. International diakonia has to denounce unjust economic and political power structures when millions are being deprived of their God given rights and dignity. The question of justice and of basic human right must be lifted up, and advocacy in favor of the poor and excluded made an integral part of diaconal action.

International diakonia thus means diaconal action across geographical boundaries in response to challenges in today's globalized world. It presupposes a critical assessment of the root causes of so many being excluded from welfare, justice and peace. And it seeks forms of action that contribute to justice, peace and reconciliation.

Ecumenical diakonia

When World War II ended in 1945, Christians joined forces across continents to assist millions of refugees in war-torn Europe. When African countries gained independence in the 1960's, church-related agencies, mainly from

Europe and North America, launched a variety of development projects, often in cooperation with churches in the new nations. In some cases, the agencies assumed the main responsibility for the implementation of projects themselves, but there was soon a clear policy to establish partnerships with actors rooted in the targeted country, be it a local church or a non-governmental organization (NGO). Often ecumenical cooperation was considered important, and many agencies related to organizations like the World Council of Churches (WCC), giving them the task of coordinating the presentation of project applications from partners in the global South to funding partners in the global North.

A survey,[2] undertaken in 2003 by the WCC and ecumenical partners, reveals that this form of international diakonia is active in 130 countries throughout the world. They raise and spend more than 740 million US$ every year, far more than any other non-governmental development organization. Of this amount, development agencies collect 33% themselves, while governments make available 47%. More than 50% of the money is used for long-term development, 14% for disaster and emergency relief, and only 6% for advocacy. The WCC receives only 3%. Action by Churches Together (ACT) receives 4% and 6% goes to the Lutheran World Federation (LWF) whose Department for World Service is engaged in refugee work in different parts of the world. Activities of individual congregations, of mission societies and other expressions of partnership are not included in the survey, although they represent far more money than is shared between churches.

The survey referred to above shows clearly that international diakonia has developed into "a multi-million US$ activity with a set of very professional agencies and partner organizations".[3] From one point of view, this is a success-story, as these agencies enjoy high public respect and can count on substantial funding support from their governments. It also shows, however, that ecumenical cooperation is the exception rather than the rule. For instance, since the 1990s, the WCC has lost its leading role of coordinating international church-related development activity. Whether the newly established ACT Development will give the WCC a new role, including that of influencing policies and practices, remains an open question.

A possible consequence of the dimension, as well as the professional structure, of modern international diakonia could be that it becomes alienated from its roots in the church. Diakonia has a long history of initiatives that through the process of institutionalization and professionalism have had this experience in the sense that diakonia has become distanced from the church and especially congregational life. Some would say this is the reality of most of the

---

2 The following information is provided by Martin Robra, "Diakonia – A Central Task of the Ecumenical Movement", Stefan Heinemann/Julia Kalbhenn (Hg.*), Being in Ecumenical Discourse on Concepts of Diakonia* (Heidelberg: DWI-INFO Sonderausgabe 4, 2004), 32.

3 Ibid.

30,000 diaconal institutions in Germany. Financially, ideologically and professionally, they are quite dependent on governmental structures and decision-making, but much less on churches and church authorities. If a church-based development agency receives most of its funding from the government, will that create similar bonds of dependency? What sort of freedom does it give an agency to openly criticize the political positions of its own government? And equally, how are the links to the church and especially to the local congregations nurtured, not only in the North where these agencies have their constituencies, but even more in the global South where the work is being carried out?

How these agencies understand their power in relation to partners in the global South that, at least financially, depend on them more or less fully, is also being discussed. Project-oriented cooperation creates a sort of "project-mindedness" which considers relations according to performance. Demanding requirements in terms of planning and reporting may disqualify committed churches in the South from being partners in international diakonia. They are simply not able to respond to the expectations of partners in the North. On the other hand, easy access to project money may orient diaconal engagement, making important initiatives dependent on foreign money and expertise. Most agencies are aware of these risks and participate actively in discussion of how to cope with them.

In this discussion, ecumenical organizations can play an important role in securing fairness and participation of all partners. Over the last decades, diakonia has become a key concept in ecumenical theological reflection. There has been a process of collecting experiences and insights from different parts of the world and new directions for diaconal commitment have been elaborated. The following quotation from a study from the WCC is an example that clearly indicates how the concept of diakonia has been renewed and gained a privileged position within the Ecumenical Movement:

> Diakonia, as the Church's ministry of sharing, healing and reconciliation, is of the very nature of the church. Diaconal ministry is the active expression of Christian witness in response to the needs and challenges of our communities.
> Diakonia in all its many authentic forms cannot be separated from the struggle for justice and peace, and it is directly linked to the empowerment, transformation, and liberation of marginalised and excluded people in every community.[4]

A landmark in this development was the international consultation organized by the WCC in Larnaca, Cyprus, in 1986.[5] It took the lead in dissociating the

[4] *Diakonia: Creating Harmony, Seeking Justice and Practicing Compassion. A Study on Ecumenical Efforts in Diakonia and Justice* (Geneva: World Council of Churches, 2005), 1.

language of diakonia from its rather traditional Northern European background, understanding of diakonia as charity and humble service, often expressed in terms of pietistic spirituality.[6] Instead, it linked diakonia to the global challenges of poverty and injustice, to the radical analysis of their root causes, and to bold advocacy in defense of marginalised groups.

The Larnaca consultation pointed at "*prophetic diakonia*" as "*essential for the churches' role in shaping the future*". The overall context of globalization was referred to as the immediate reason for giving focus to this theme:

> In this context ecumenical diakonia cannot be divorced from prophetic diakonia. This in turn is intertwined with ecumenical advocacy, which places the affected people at the centre stage, acting as their own advocates. Ecumenical diakonia must thus embrace a variety of forms, including crisis intervention and direct aid for the victims, but it was also strongly affirmed that Christian commitment to diaconal action must be coupled with transformative prophetic diakonia, which is change-oriented and boldly addresses root causes.[7]

Prophetic diakonia was the theme of a global consultation held by the LWF in Johannesburg, in 2002. In a letter from the meeting, the participants affirmed that diakonia "*is central to what it means to be the church. As a core component of the gospel, diakonia is not an option but an essential part of discipleship*." The message continues that,

> While diakonia begins as unconditional service to the neighbour in need, it leads inevitably to social change that restores, reforms and transforms. […] We must challenge all theological interpretations that do not take seriously the suffering of the world, a world afflicted with poverty, violence and HIV/AIDS. As Lutheran churches, we are to be shaped by a theology of the cross, which compels us to identify with and for the suffering rather than the successful. A theology of the cross calls things what they really are, moving beyond politeness and pretence, breaking the silence and taking the risk of speaking truth to power, even when this threatens the established order and results in hardship and persecution. This is at the heart of the prophetic diaconal calling.[8]

---

5 Klaus Poser (ed.), *Called to be Neighbours: Diakonia 2000. Official Report WCC World Consultation, Inter-Church Aid, Refugee and World Service Larnaca 1986* (Geneva: The World Council of Churches, 1987).

6 An important contribution to breaking with this tradition was made by the Australian scholar John N. Collins, *Diakonia: Reinterpreting the Ancient Sources* (New York/Oxford: Oxford University Press, 1990).

7 Working paper of the Advisory Group on Regional Relations and Ecumenical Sharing to the WCC Programme Committee, dated March 2000.

8 *Prophetic Diakonia: "For the Healing of the World." Report Johannesburg, South Africa November 2002* (Geneva: The Lutheran World Federation, 2003).

Without any doubt, ecumenical diakonia challenges churches in the North and their diaconal action. It addresses the question of whether the cause of justice is sufficiently integrated in diaconal practice. Is advocacy emphasized? Can it be seen as prophetic action proclaiming God's justice in favor of the poor and the excluded? It points anew to the question of *political diakonia* that was raised already in Germany after World War II, asking for a conscious and critical presence in the political arena. The question was raised then because of the silent and submissive role of many diaconal institutions during the Nazi regime, when quite a few diaconal workers even took part in the atrocities in the concentration camps. The hard lesson learned then was that silence implies co-responsibility.

Today, it is broadly understood that inevitably diaconal action has political implication, but there may still be different opinions when it comes to how to assume a more explicit political responsibility. Many would express reservations if this were to lead to open alliances with political parties or movements. Lately the concept of civil society has made it easier to elaborate some principles for political diakonia. Just as many civil groups and organizations have a role to play in the public sphere, each according to its identity and constituency, the church and her diakonia also have an important role to play.

Speaking out publicly will be convincing only if the words are rooted in diaconal action, but, of course, the words will not carry weight if such action does not bear witness to justice and the dignity of the poor and excluded. Political diakonia can be critical only if diakonia is self-critical. A link to prophetic diakonia, which, motivated by its faith in God's righteousness, defends the rights of the poor, can be seen here. As was the case at the time of the Old Testament prophets, so also today prophetic diakonia must first address its own structures before questioning those in power on their exercise of religious authority. From this perspective, questions related to good governance, transparency and mutual accountability are not primarily project-oriented concepts, but deeply rooted in diakonia's value system and its mission to empower people for participation in church and society.

Summing up, ecumenical diakonia has been developed in reaction to the many challenges presented by today's globalized world, focusing on the following items:

- The regaining of a holistic perspective on the mission of the church
- The need of relating social work/action to the identity of church
- The rediscovery of diakonia as empowering service, and
- The prophetic dimension of diakonia.

Diakonia as an integral part of the church's mission

As already mentioned above, the elaboration of ecumenical diakonia has been closely related to a growing understanding of the holistic nature of Christian mission. In a recently published LWF document, mission is said to encompass proclamation, service (or diakonia), and advocacy.[9]

It is important to underline that this is not a modern concept of mission, influenced by liberal worldview. From its very beginning, Christian mission has always had this holistic feature. It is clearly modeled on the example of the mission of Jesus, who preached, cared for the needy, and defended the excluded. It understands Gospel to be all three elements of his mission held together. It remembers the mission commandment of the Gospel of John as a call to follow his example: "As the Father sent me, so also I send you" (John 20.21).

A consultation on mission, organized by the LWF in Nairobi in 1998, gave the following description of the three interrelated dimensions of holistic mission:

> Mission encompasses proclamation, service and advocacy for justice. Mission as proclamation is an attempt by every Christian to tell and interpret the gospel story in his/her context as a way to discover God's saving action and meaningful presence in the world. Mission as service highlights the diaconal dimension of a faith active in love, working for the empowerment and liberation of those in need. Mission as advocacy for justice denotes the church's praxis in the public arena as affirmation and reaffirmation of the dignity of human life, both as individual and as community, as well as a widened sense of justice, encompassing the economic, social and ecological spheres.[10]

The LWF Mission Document affirms the same understanding, and underlines that holistic mission has to be contextual:

> "Mission is holistic and contextual with regard to its aim, practice, and location. Its aim encompasses the whole of creation (ecological concerns), the whole of life (social, political, economic, and cultural), and the whole human being (i.e., all people and the whole person – spiritual, mental, relational, physical and environment needs). Its practice calls for the participation of the whole church, women and men, young and old. Being holistic, mission flows from the being of the church as worshipping, messenger, serving, healing, and oikumene community".[11]

In order to deepen the understanding of holistic mission, the document presents three key concepts: transformation, reconciliation and empowerment. All three are relevant for the understanding of proclamation, diakonia and advocacy as integral dimensions of mission. At the same time, they all have the special

9 *Mission in Context. Transformation, Reconciliation, Empowerment* (The Lutheran World Federation, Geneva 2004).

10 The LWF Consultation on Churches in Mission, Nairobi 1998, Report, 20.

11 *Mission in Context*, 36.

quality of being interdisciplinary, rooted both in social sciences and in theological language, and, therefore, can help to make connections between the context of social reality and Christian identity.

Transformation

Better than "development" and "social change", the word "transformation" takes into consideration the complexity of human reality and the need to relate to economic, social, cultural and religious factors. It also makes clear that in order to have real change, all involved are in need of being transformed. Thus this concept helps to overcome the division between "donors" (those with resources) and "recipients" (those with problems) that so often have been a part of development work.

As a theological concept, transformation recalls God's constant renewal of creation (*creation continua*), as every morning graciously provides the experience of the night's darkness being transformed into the light of a new day breaking forth.

The people of God see transformation as God's gift, for which they owe him praise, above all for the gifts of Word and Sacraments by which sinners are transformed and sanctified as God's children. Therefore, the Apostle Paul exhorts the believers in Rome to no longer be conformed to this world, but be transformed, according to God's will (Rom 12:2).

Empowerment

This concept was developed within the social sciences and became important in the struggle for overcoming apartheid in South Africa. Empowerment is referred to both as the process by which marginalized people assume a leading role as agents and to the goal of that same process of liberation, from oppression into a participatory and just society.

As a theological concept, empowerment refers to the biblical understanding of creation that every human being is created in the image of God, with capacities and abilities, independent of the apparent social situation.

It also refers to the event of Pentecost and the promise that "you shall receive power when the Holy Spirit has come upon you" (Acts 1:8). The theology of baptism affirms this by saying that every baptized member of the church is empowered to be a partner in God's mission. It is here that we discover the real "power structure" of the church, founded in the priesthood of all believers. Although this is a central ecclesiological principle, it easily remains theoretical and difficult to put into praxis. Nevertheless, this should be considered a provocative and liberating alternative to the power structures of exclusive powerful leaders in the church. Jesus reminded his disciples that they should not exercise power according to the model of worldly leaders, but according to his example of diaconal leadership (Mark 10:38-45).

If there is a concentration of power in the church, among the clergy or others with exclusive power, then its mission is hampered. Therefore, it is very important to empower the whole congregation, especially youth and women, to assume roles of active participation and of leadership. In the context of international diakonia this points at inclusiveness as an essential value and task. For this reason, the inclusion of women, youth, differently abled and others, who tend to be marginalized in the church, is crucial.

Reconciliation

In situations of conflict and war, people, especially the victims, long for reconciliation. Fear is a growing reality all over the world, for which there may be many reasons: economic, social, cultural or religious.

For Christians, reconciliation is God's merciful gift grounded in the message that God has reconciled the world in Jesus Christ. This gift is a promise for a broken world. According to 2 Cor 5, the church is given the ministry (Greek: diakonia) of reconciliation as part of her mission to the world. This affirms the holistic nature of mission, namely that proclamation, service and advocacy belong together. Again it should be remembered that service does not mean humble or even self-effacing service, but *prophetic diakonia*. The ministry of reconciliation implies bold witness, courageous action, and committed advocacy. It needs to be carried out in context, addressing difficult issues such as injustice, conflicts, poverty, corrupt leadership, etc.

Summing up, diakonia is an integral part of holistic mission. Transformative diakonia means being an agent of transformation in today's context of suffering, injustice and need.

Empowering diakonia means mobilizing all talents and gifts given to God's people for participation in God's mission, for the healing of the world.

Reconciling diakonia means taking the risk of crossing borders so that truth may prevail, memories are healed, justice restored, and healing take place.

PART ONE

MISSION TO THE WORLD IN WORD AND DEED

(2) Spirituality

Mission and Contemplation: Mission Spirituality in the 21st Century

Tore Laugerud

Rev Tore Laugerud, Project Leader, Cooperative Council for Congregation and Mission, Church of Norway, Oslo, Norway

What is Mission Spirituality?

Spirituality

The word "spirituality" is not an exclusively Christian, or even religious, concept, but has entered the common vocabulary. It is an open concept, inasmuch as there is no single common understanding determining its allusions. Still, some common traits by the use of the concept of spirituality may be indicated:[1]

- Spirituality *focuses on experience*: People long for and experience something/are in touch with something vitalizing
- Spirituality *aims at integrated life*: People often find life fragmented – life should be made whole
- Spirituality *(often) leads to self-transcendence*: In order to integrate, people must transcend the limits of self
- Spirituality *concerns the deepest values of human life*: Simultaneously with the transcendence of limits, a connection is experienced with that which is of fundamental value in life

There are some risks connected with using such an open concept. Different ideas may be mixed up, resulting in a dilution of the content. On the other hand, one may gain possibilities of creating broader dialogues, leading to more depth and renewed insights. As a Christian, I connect the concept of spirituality to theological anthropology, and use it as an expression of the spiritual side of humankind. Humankind is spiritual, thus there is something in its life called

---

[1] See Leif Gunnar Engedal, "Spiritualitet og teologi", *Ung Teologi 2-2003*: 47-56. Here are references to newer English literature on spirituality and Christian spirituality.

spirituality.[2] Human spirituality is deeply personal, and given, and, at the same time, dynamic and in motion. It cannot be reduced to a product of the outward influences on humankind, but communicates with and is formed by them, not the least through our experiences. Spirituality may even be an expression for certain human needs, something one needs to be strengthened and live holistically.

Christian spirituality

As a Christian term, the concept first occurs in 17th Century French Catholic literature.[3] It is employed to express the individual's response to God through attitudes, ascetic practice, forms of prayers etc., what previously had been termed "asceticism" or "devotional life". In the 20th Century it is commonly used within Roman Catholic theology, and one begins to talk of different kinds of Christian spiritualities: Franciscan spirituality, Benedictine etc.[4] Christian spirituality is thus no homogenous entity. It exists in a tension between unity and diversity.

Beginning in the 1960-70-ies, there is an explosive increase in the use of the concept of spirituality. At the same time, the field of meaning is extended, with the result that it might be rather imprecisely used in all personal elements influencing the way people are living out their faith, and theologians such as Raymond Panikkar begin to use the term even for other religious traditions.[5]

After a while, the term came into use also in Protestant circles. The (Anglican) theologian Kenneth Leech[6] describes Christian spirituality as a process where Christ acts, in other words, grace. The aim is to become like Christ. The core of spirituality is to learn to know love. Characteristic for Leech is his strong emphasis that the process even contains confrontation, challenges, and fight. It corresponds with a Lutheran understanding of the work of God in us through Law and Gospel.

A simple definition of Christian spirituality is that it is a matter of *the Christian's awareness of and response to the presence and acts of the Triune God in one's life*. The presence of God may be experienced as *challenging* or *inviting*. There are two basic directions in human response: A person may *let oneself be led out of something* in one's life to devote oneself to Him who

---

[2] For a theological interpretation of human as spiritual being, I refer to Wilfred Stinissen, *Indre vandring* (Tromsø, Sofiaforlaget, 1999), 157-175.

[3] Lawrence Nemer, "Spirituality and the Missionary Vocation", *Missiology 11* (1983): 420. Nemer gives resymees of some importnat Roman Catholic books on mission spirituality, e.g., from Asian contexts.

[4] Ibid.

[5] Ibid: 421.

[6] See, e.g., Kenneth Leech, *Soul friend: a study of spirituality* (San Francisco, CA: Harper, reprint 1992).

touches one, or one may *actively strive towards* a deeper relation with God. Together, those two movements constitute *conversion.* Sadly, this term, as the concept of piety, has been damaged through being used to separate people according to religious or moral qualities. Conversion, when understood as a daily exercise in a lifelong process, is a key concept in Christian spirituality.

Mission Spirituality

In mission circles, there is often claimed to be a close connection between mission and spirituality, but systematic studies and theological reflection on this connection are rare. Carl F. Hallencreutz commented, early in the 1980-ies, that newer research on mission has had other foci:

> At present there is a rewarding ambition in international scholarship to give particular attention to indigenous reactions to different missionary ventures and explore what these responses imply in terms of local factors and initiatives which form an indigenous interpretation of Christianity in different milieus. Another approach is to focus particularly on the ever-controversial interaction of missionary enterprises and colonial expansions during different epochs, particularly during the heyday of the modern missionary movement from the late 18th century onwards.[7]

Hallencreutz wishes to emphasize another aspect that "should be further assessed in continued studies on the interaction of Christianity and other religions – the question of missionary spirituality".[8] Thus, Hallencreutz understands *mission spirituality* (missionary spirituality) as a new research field, and he links it to studies of the interaction of Christian faith and other religions, a subject that has not become less relevant since Hallencreuz wrote this.

The concept *mission spirituality* first occurred in Roman Catholic missiological literature in the second half of the 20th Century, and spread to Protestant missiology in the 1970-ies. It is also worth noting that the prevalence of this term in the Roman Catholic area seems to be related to the rediscovery of the missional nature of the Church by the Second Vatican Council. Walbert Bühlmann points to *Lumen Gentium,* the basic document of the Council, as an important source:

> We have now, in Lumen Gentium, for the first time in church history, the expression that the church is by nature a missionary church. From Lumen Gentium missionary spirituality entered practically all the other documents. The church now has missionary spirituality and mission commitment as an essential

---

7 Carl F. Hallencreutz, "Missionary Spirituality – the case of Ansgar", *Studia Theologica 36* (1982): 105.

8 Ibid.

> dimension. I think the sentence which says that the church is by nature a missionary church is a bomb which has not yet exploded in most countries but which should explode.[9]

In Norway, I have not registered mission spirituality as a concept and theme in the missiological debate until in 1997. Then, the Council for Congregation in Mission (Samarbeidsråd for menighet og misjon, SMM) made use of the term in connection with the work on a new strategy plan. SMM wanted to focus on three aspects: 1. The relationship of Church and mission to spiritual experiences made within the framework of other religions/spiritualities, abroad and at home. 2. Spirituality in churches in the South as source and vitalizer for churches in the North. 3. The relationship between inward life and outward service.[10] From 1999 on, much of the concerns of SMM for mission spirituality was channelled towards preparing the theme *The Church Encountering the Religious Longing of Our Time (Kirken i møte med den åndelige lengsel i vår tid)* for the Church of Norway, General Synod.[11] Later, SMM entered into cooperation with the Church of Norway, National Council, and Areopagos to follow up this theme. Here, also, there was a connection between the concern for mission spirituality and missionary church.

Not surprisingly, the various partners in SMM had somewhat different approaches to the theme of mission spirituality. This is shown, e.g., in a series of articles on mission spirituality published in "Over Alt – Tidsskrift for bønn, meditasjon og Kristusmystikk" (Above All – Journal for Prayer, Meditation and Christ-Mysticism)[12] The series was inspired by Edin Løvaas, the revival preacher who founded the retreat movement in Norway. The mission leaders' words on mission spirituality brought to light again an old concern of Løvaas, to link retreat and mission.

I assume that behind the decision of SMM to highlight mission spirituality by the turn of the millennium, was the realization that although the written word of the Great Commission has been there throughout the history of the Church, that alone is not sufficient to create a missionary Church. The Church becomes missionary when the written word, through the Spirit of God, becomes an inner drive in people, when faith is renewed. The history of the Church contains many renewal movements. They show a wide variety of experiences

---

[9] Walbert Bühlmann, "Missionary spirituality", *New missionary era* (Maryknoll, NY: Orbis books, 1982) 113-118.

[10] Minutes from the meeting of Samarbeidsråd for menighet og misjon, 11. May 1998.

[11] A preparatory paper was presented to the Church of Norway, General Synod: *Kirken i møte med den åndelige lengsel i vår tid* (Kirkerådet 1999).

[12] Edin Løvaas, *Over Alt 3-1999*: 12-17; Tor B. Jørgensen, *Over Alt, 1-2000*: 25-29; Tore Laugerud, *Over Alt 2-2000*: 26-31; Tormod Engelsviken, *Over Alt 4-2000*: 32-35 og Knud Jørgensen, *Over Alt* 1-2001: 21-25.

with God, as well as of spirituality. Through the variety, we find a basic pattern: Individuals have spiritual experiences, and they share them with others. Thus, living devotional movements are formed and strengthen the Church in its mission.

A final delineation: All missionary religions have its mission spirituality/sprritualities. Superficially, there might be some relationship between them, but if we look deeper, we come to the determining question of the understanding of God. The word *mission* spirituality implies a certain view of God, that God is an actively sending God. Mission is *sending*. The Christian understanding of sending receives its characteristics from the faith in the *Triune* God.

What this implies, we will return to later. Here, we will give a temporary definition of (Christian) mission spirituality. Mission spirituality is *the Christian's, and the Christian community's, awareness of and response to the work of the Triune God to become the God of mercy and justice in us, and through us for all humankind.* It concerns, among others, the motivation and driving force of the ministry, how we form our life and our attitudes to the task and to the people we encounter.

Below, I will first draw attention to some fundamental concerns in the Biblical texts. Then, I will review some newer forms of mission spirituality, as well as some older forms that, in our context, have been re-actualized, before I focus on mission and contemplation – mission spirituality in the 21th Century.

Biblical Concerns

The Old Testament

The connection between the experience of God and mission (sending) is expressed already in the story of Abraham. As a response to the encounter with God, Abraham departs from his home and his habitual life, beginning a journey according to God's commands (Gen 12:1-4).

Subsequently, God reveals himself to Moses (Ex 3:2-10), and to the prophets, with a message not only for them as individuals, but for the whole people. The prophetic departure is not only a departure according to the word of God, but a departure to go *with the word of God.* Moses and the prophets become messengers (Greek: apostle = Latin: missionary). God wants to become the God of mercy and justice in them, and through them for the whole people. There are thus good reasons for the Church of Norway to apply the story of the calling of Isaiah (Is 6:1-13) as an Old Testament reading for missionary consecrations.

God's calling of individuals developed with time towards a kind of institutional prophecy, but the prophetic ministry vanishes when the experiences that created it ceased occurring in the Hellenistic time. Judaism describes this as the "extinguishing of the prophetic spirit". The term alludes to the Spirit of God as the source and life of the prophetic ministry.

The New Testament

In The New Testament, we hear of a new experience of God, bringing up again aspects of the Sinai-event, but simultaneously carrying with it something new. God is experienced at Pentecost through an intense presence and powerful acts, affecting and renewing all those present. Public testimonies of God's salvific acts, and appeals to conversion and faith, are immediate responses to this God-experience: "Then Peter stood up with the Eleven, raised his voice and addressed the crowd ..." (Acts 2:14 ff.). Through this event, *a missionary Church* is formed and appears.

Seen in continuity with the Old Testament, we may say that through the death and resurrection of Jesus, the prophetic spirit is reawakened, and the prophetic institution reformed to an "apostolic institution". We may also say that through the death and resurrection of Jesus, the Spirit is poured out on "the whole God's people" and makes it a missionary people of God. We sense a characteristic duality by the missionary/apostolic Church. On the one hand, God continues calling individuals to go with his message, cfr. the call of Paul on the way towards Damascus (Acts 9:1-19). Paul is putting much emphasis on this experience when telling of his motivation and role, but also in his theological reflection and forming of his message.[13] At the same time, he maintains the general New Testament insight that (the whole) Church is missional, as it has received the gift of the Spirit.

Thus, the specific calling and the specific "mission institution" is not in conflict with the general apostolicity of the Church. Through the encounter with God and the reception of the gift of the Holy Spirit in baptism, all the members of the Church participate in the same calling and task. The calling of baptism has a missional dimension. From Pentecost onwards, God works though his Spirit to become the God of justice and mercy, in all baptised and through all baptised. Simultaneously, he calls and endows individuals and creates renewal movements that in a special way become tools for the mission of God.

Mission Spirituality – Some Historic Types

The Church contains in its history many different types of mission spirituality. An important question is how to relate to that theologically. This is not the place to take up that discussion, but we may indicate various perspectives. The diversity in mission spirituality may be seen as a reflection of the diversity in the Spirit, or as a fruit of the diversity, differences, and riches in the gifts of the Spirit. Another perspective is to view the diversity in mission spirituality from

[13] See Seyoon Kim: *The Origin of Paul's Gospel* (Tübingen 1984).

the diversity and complexity of the contexts into which the Spirit incarnates the Word.

19th Century Society mission[14]

By the middle of the 19th Century, almost all Protestant churches and movements had their own mission societies with their respective ethos. Also within the Roman Catholic tradition, several new missionary orders were formed, clerical and lay, women and men. In spite of great diversity, the similarities are more striking than the differences. The purpose was basically the same; to save souls, through preaching or through baptism, and to improve living conditions. One important feature of this spirituality is that it is anthropocentric. It appears as a practical, action-oriented aid and mercy-spirituality. The motivation was mixed. The mission movement was based on the encounter with God in reading of the Bible, preaching of Law and gospel, and intercessory prayer. It made individuals conscious of their responsibility towards other people, spiritually as well as temporally. Some gave "the spiritual aspect" priority, often with reference to "the seriousness of eternity". Others gave more emphasis to timely concerns. Often, spiritual and timely concerns were tightly woven together in the metaphor of the "heathen darkness".

Seen in retrospect, this mission spirituality was tightly woven together with the Western civilizing project. The vast majority employed military metaphors and language, talking of "the great commission", "march order", "the King's errand", "troop reinforcements", "fell on his post" etc. Such language reveals a strong "conquering spirit", and the enterprise could become rather aggressive, especially when directly connected to colonization. The Dominican Pierre Claverie, Bishop in Algeria, murdered in 1996, wrote: "I lived in what I now will call a "colonialist glass bulb", without even seeing the others".[15] In spite of this harsh (self) criticism, mission still often represented the best of Western civilization in its encounter with "the others". Another important feature of the picture is that mission from minority churches and from countries without colonial ambitions (e.g., Norway) often had another motivation and attitude towards the task and towards "the others", than mission proceeding from the churches of the colonial powers. However, virtually all mission of this epoch was characterized by ethno-centrism, giving a special role to Western culture. This led to relations between missionaries and locals were affected by a cast-iron helper-receiver type, having strongly adverse effects on independence and reciprocity.

---

[14] See Lawrence Nemer, *Anglican and Roman Catholic Attitudes on Mission* (St. Augustin: Steyler Verlag, 1981).

[15] Jan Erik Rekdal, "Jesu små søstre og livet i Nasaret" *St. Olav 2-2007*. Theme issue on Charles de Foucauld and The Little Sisters of Jesus.

Charles de Foucauld[16]

Approximately midway through this epoch, however, a diametrically opposite type of mission spirituality evolved. The Roman Catholic Father Charles de Foucauld (1858-1916) began living among the Moslem Tuareg in Southern Algerie, not from a missionary zeal to convert them, but from zeal to live as a priest on places with the greatest need, understood as places where God cannot be present in the sacraments or in the Church.[17] After a while, the life of Jesus in Nazareth, prior to his public ministry, became Foucauld's source of inspiration and his model. As Jesus did, through most of his life, Foucauld wanted to live among the others in quiet life, work for the daily bread, without any specific attention. Behind this was a radical interpretation of the mystery of incarnation; with emphasis on descending, bowing down and encountering the world from below.

The spirituality of Foucauld was marked by testimony through acts and quiet patience. The Tuareg respected a holy man, so he practiced prayer and fasting. They appreciated hospitality, so he practiced it towards everybody passing by. He regarded that the time to preach to the Tuareg had not yet come. Instead, he learned the language, wrote dictionaries and grammars, translated Scripture parts and catechisms, and hoped the day would come when someone could preach. Little sister Magdeleine, the founder of *The Little Sisters of Jesus*, developed this further to a mission spirituality for a movement. She regards the *relations* of the Sisters, rooted in the Word, as a "word preaching the love of God", calling their service *the apostolate of friendship*: "The apostolate of friendship is really our way of mission, our way to communicate God".[18]

Celtic Mission Spirituality[19]

In the recent generation, we have seen in Norway as elsewhere a renewed interest for an old kind of mission spirituality: Celtic spirituality. Medieval Celtic monks contributed strongly to the spread of the Gospel throughout the British Isles, to Greenland, Canada, and to the European continent. The main motivating force for the travels of the monks was neither to bring the faith to non-believers nor to renew the faith of unenlightened baptised. Rather, it was the paramount ascetic act of their devotional life: to leave home, walking or sailing, 12 monks together for the sake of Christ; "peregrinatio pro Christo". Wherever they landed, they founded monasteries according to the Celtic tradition without accommodation. Many visited their monasteries and came to

---

16 S.C. Lorit, *Charles de Foucauld: The Silent Witness* (New York: City Press, 1966).

17 Lillesøster Gaby, "Møtet med Islam" ("The Encounter With Islam"), referred to in *St. Olav* 2-2007.

18 Ibid.

19 See W. Marnell, *Light from the West: The Irish Mission and the Emergence of Modern Europe* (New York: Seabury Press, 1978).

faith through the encounter with the worship and devotional life and through their teaching. Remarkably swift, local names would appear in the monastery records, even as abbots.

We know that Celtic mission spirituality played an important role when the Christian message reached Norway and took root here. For the last generation, Norwegian churchgoers have once more felt the appeal of this spirituality through the hymn, *"Be Thou My Vision", Deg å få skode*, building on a 8th Century text by St. Colomba. In recent decades, the old monastery fellowship of Iona in Scotland has become a central re-creator and transmitter of Celtic spirituality. The Celtic mission spirituality puts much emphasis on the pilgrim motif, the worship services, God in nature, and God in contemporary events. An interesting trait is that Utstein Pilegrimsgård, a pilgrim centre in a former monastery, in the Westward (mission) Diocese of Stavanger strives to re-establish the old Celtic traditions, among others by contact with Lindisfarne monastery.

The Jesuits[20]

Ignatius Loyola, the founder of the Jesuit Order, (the 16th Century) described in his book *Exercitia Spiritualis* (Spiritual Exercises) a new prayer practice, emphasising the presence of God in everything, consciousness of the longings as a basic force in human life, and trust in the power for change of the love of God. The Jesus Meditation is central in this prayer tradition. The Jesuits are not a monastic movement, but a movement living and working within society. The early Jesuits were pioneers for the Catholic mission enterprise from the time of the Reformation. Through the practice of the *spiritual exercises*, they became ready and willing to go wherever they were sent. The driving force was the saving of souls to the honour of God. The Jesuits were convinced that the life style had to be adjusted to the work, and were thus, unlike the Celts, willing to adapt to the local way of life. They emphasised the relationship between culture and religion, and worked to understand the traditional culture and religion, and to harmonize it with Christianity. When this proved impossible, they tried to reorganize the social life of the people. Through the film *The Mission*, their work became known for a broader public.

Currently, many places in Europe witness a strong flourishing and spreading of Jesuit spirituality. This momentum takes place outside of as well as within the Roman Catholic Church, and is a remarkable sign of how contemporary Christians are drawn towards each other. Magnus Malm is a well known example of a Scandinavian Evangelical who, without denying his background, follows the roots deeper down and back in history. The central point of orientation for Malm and for "Compass", the network he leads, is the Ignatian spirituality. Ignatius and his *Spiritual Exercises* were also an important source

20 See Michael Collins Reilly, *Spirituality for Mission* (Maryknoll, New York: Orbis Press, 1978).

for Edin Løvaas, not the least for the Jesus meditation.[21] The Retreat Centres belonging to his tradition, the Sandom tradition, has as its purpose " to lead people into a close fellowship with Jesus Christ, according to the mission commandment of Jesus".[22] As of today, the whole Norwegian retreat movement draws inspiration from the Ignatian spirituality.

A central source for the spreading of Ignatian spirituality in Norway is the St. Joseph Retreat Centre, where for decades the Jesuit Sisters of St. Joseph have offered spiritual counselling according to Ignatian principles. The Sisters of St. Joseph were founded in France in the 17th Century, during a period of great need. They wanted to enter into the need and protect the vulnerable life, after the pattern of St. Joseph protecting Mary and her child. In Norway they became pioneers for health (cf. "Vår Frues hospital", "The hospital of Our Lady") and school work. When the state in 1988 took over all health work, they found a new field of service in Norway: Retreats and spiritual guidance. This development is connected to the missional renewal of the Church taking place after the Second Vatican Council. The Council encouraged every branch on the catholic tree to seek deeper in its roots. The Sisters of St. Joseph found their spiritual roots in the *Spiritual Exercises.* Their work within retreat and spiritual counselling has clearly a missional purpose: to help and guide every searching human in their walk with God.[23] Their mission perspectives are the pilgrim motif and the accompaniment.

New Patterns of Mission Spirituality from the 20th Century

In the 20th Century two important new types of mission spirituality have emerged, *Charismatic mission spirituality* and *liberation theological mission spirituality.* Charismatic mission spirituality has its starting point in a strong experience of the Holy Spirit as a moving force in our life here and now. It emphasizes the Holy Spirit's equipment for mission through spiritual gifts, development of caring fellowships, and powerful communication of the victory and power of Jesus in word and praise. Mission may be followed by signs and miracles. The charismatic mission spirituality is of major importance, not least as it characterizes much of the new mission wave from the South. In an international perspective, a major shift of gravity has taken place, from the mission spirituality of the modern society missions to the charismatic mission spirituality, a move that is related to the general shift of the centre of gravity of the Church from North to South.

Some Southern Churches are also influenced by a *liberation theological*

[21] See Knut Grønvik (red), *I stillhet og tillitt* (Oslo: Verbum, 2005).

[22] By-laws for Sandomstiftelsen.

[23] The purpose of the Sisters of St. Joseph is: "That we ourselves and our neighbour may become totally one with God, that all people may become one with us, and with each other, but all in Jesus and in God, his Father", see www.stjoseph.no

mission spirituality. The starting point for this tradition is the experiences of poor and marginalized people of having a special place in the heart of God. They recognize in their lives God's "solidarity from below", as expressed already in the Incarnation. The experience of God's accepting, solidaric, and liberating presence transforms the congregation socially and humanly, empowering it to a diaconal mission relating to the whole context of human life: socially, politically, culturally, and spiritually. This mission spirituality is especially widespread in Latin America, South Africa, and parts of Asia, but has also gained importance in many traditional Northern Churches. After the dismantling of the Iron Curtain in 1989, liberation theology has moved towards *theology of reconciliation*[24] in a gradually more globalized world, marked by conflicts between people groups and wounds from broken relations. As a reflection of this, "reconciliation and healing" have been persistent themes for the major ecumenical conferences of the last decade.

In this context, even another kind of God-experience ought to be mentioned. Many African revival movements were initiated by an experience of *divine revelation*, for instance the Malagasy revival of the 1890-ies. The movement was from the outset strongly missional, and contributes even today, over 100 years later, to make the Malagasy Lutheran Church a dynamic, missionary Church. Currently, stories of divine revelations increase. Not the least in the Muslim world, stories are told of people coming to faith through experiencing God in visions or dreams. Similar experiences are told from China and from other places. The stories have many similarities with the Biblical revelation stories.

These revelation experiences show the image of an actively seeking God. The presence of God is experienced in a very concrete manner, mediating strong concepts of holiness, peace, reconciliation, purpose, and love. People are invited into this reality, to a fellowship with God, and the invitation overwhelms and scares, fascinates and attracts.

These various patterns of mission spirituality carries with them a common experience that the Triune God is close, active, and transforming, here and now. The experience of God taking part in human life sets the Church in motion. The invisible God and his reality, the Kingdom of God, take shape in the world. It happens through good words and good deeds, through the water of baptism and the bread and wine of the Eucharist. It happens when people are turned towards God, are raised up and transformed.

---

[24] See Gunvor Lande, "Frigjeringsteologien går mot forsoningsteologi" ("From Liberation Theology Towards a Theology of Reconciliation"), *Norsk tidsskrift for misjon*, No.3-2001: 185-192.

Mission Spirituality in the 21th Century

Critical Perspective

The examples above show through their diversity that we must avoid making patterns when emphasising the connection between experience of God and mission. The diversity bears witness of God as the sovereign subject of mission. The actions of humankind are characterized by making and following patterns. God is able to create something new, to create from nothing. Therefore, he acts in constantly new ways, and is again and again experienced as the God of surprises.

After the Second World War, the mission spirituality has lost much of its basis in revival. The 19th and 20th Century European revival movements have ceased, and critical questions are raised concerning many aspects of the spirituality of the revivals. This contributes to a marginalizing of mission in its traditional sense. At the same time, the historical ties between mission and the devotional life of this tradition, motivation, and action, are so strong that new images of mission have difficulties in emerging. In Norway, this is reinforced by a, until recently, very homogenous Church situation. The reasons for this marginalization of mission are not only of an outward, organizational kind. The deeper reasons for the marginalization are of an inner, spiritual character. We lack sustainable mission spirituality for our time.

By closer scrutiny, we will see that a major shift in the spirituality of the mission movement already has taken place. The founder of the church growth thinking, Donald Mc Gavran, criticized the traditional Evangelical pattern, where music and preaching should bring people to a dramatic point, in which to decide on God. He formed a program, consisting of helping people embark on the lifelong journey called Christian discipleship, and to create fellowships of believing pilgrims. With several variations, this has been the dominant Evangelical mission strategy of the last generation. This has, however, been partly obscured, by reserving the concept of mission for more traditional thinking, and terming the new as "Church growth" or "evangelization".

Mc Gavran opened up for a new and important mission perspective: the Christian journey and accompaniment. At the same time, the quantitative focus of the church growth thinking has been one of several entrances for secular market thinking in the church. The adaptation of the church to the market has been a result of *the influence of secularization on our spirituality*. Where secularization is admitted into the faith and thinking of the church, mission is reduced to a question of communication and relevance, in the worst cases mere advertisement. Another result of secularization of spirituality is that, even by the Church, prayer and spiritual counselling is relegated to the private sphere.

Actually, secularization was present already in the 19th Century mission spirituality. Is it not evidence of secularization to talk of "propagating" the Christian faith, and assume that people will receive the Christian message by realize its "superiority"? The message from the 1910 Edinburgh World Mission

Conference: "The Evangelization of the World in our Generation", is to a large extent an expression of this mentality. There existed a deep conviction that Christian mission would progress together with the victory procession of the Christian civilization (science, democracy, and religion) throughout the world. Today, even this thinking has lost its sustainability.

Tear and impoverishment is another important factor for understanding the marginalization of the traditional mission spirituality. The popularity and breadth in the Norwegian revival created practical mission spirituality with clear focus on action, organization, and activities. When the revival ceased, preaching even tended to cease nourishing new life. Gradually, attention turned towards perpetuating the established patterns for service and activities. When this spirituality, with its strong emphasis on action, activities, and organization, encounters our packed and hectic life style, a considerable wear and tear takes place. The price for the Christian activism is hardly seen in any statistics, but may be read in the eyes of the co-workers and the active volunteers. Do their eyes mirror an inner peace?

Spirituality and Theology are Closely Connected

Christian spirituality is not individualistic, but fellowship-oriented. That is, it lives and takes form in encounter with its context, with the biblical word of God, and with the faith of the worldwide church. In our time, we see that Christians are drawn towards each other in a new way. It is simply not possible to isolate spirituality within the framework of one particular confession or theological tradition. Perhaps we are on the threshold of realizing new depths in the Prayer of Jesus in John 17; when the church in its mission mirrors the Trinitarian relation, the world will believe that the sending is from God (v.21-23). The way towards such a unity can only go through the churches turning towards each other in a joint search for its roots. To seek deeper in the sources does not imply turning away from those conditions and incidents in society that occupy and form human life today. Spirituality must let itself be formed by whatever forms human life, in constant reflection over "where is God in this", prayer, and action.

21st Century Mission spirituality will have to retain the crucial realization of the 20th Century, that mission first and foremost is the mission of the Triune God. As Creator, God is near and active by his Spirit in the whole of his creation. By sending his Son, he shows his nature as being *love seeking relationship*. That means that the mission of the Church does not "bring God to people". The Triune God is already present in every nook and cranny of the universe. Out of his own nature, that is love and fellowship, he constantly seeks fellowship with us humans, through interior and exterior means.

The Church is drawn into the sending of the Triune God, as the body of Jesus on earth (1 Cor 12:27) by receiving the Holy Spirit: "As the Father has sent me, I am sending you. And with that he breathed on them and said, "Receive the Holy Spirit" (John 20:21-22). The word "as" relates to the act as well as the content of sending. The Church shall in the execution of its mission be like Christ in his mission; it shall, by the Holy Spirit, do his works with his purpose: that the World shall be saved (cf. John 3:15-17). This similarity with Jesus is not on the level of the individual, but of the *fellowship*. It is the Church as fellowship that is the body of Christ, continuing his mission, through the diversity of gifts given by the Spirit (1 Cor 12:4 ff.). That Jesus lives in his disciples by his Spirit implies that the Spirit is the real actor in the mission of the Church.

Through its mission, the Church makes the invisible God visible, in Word and sacraments. Paul speaks of his service as revealing "the mystery that has been kept hidden for ages and generations" (Col 1:26), God's salvific plan. Salvation in Biblical sense is fellowship (*koinonia*) with God and with other creatures, in Christ. In salvation's dimension of fellowship, the unique character of the Gospel is expressed. Fellowship is a key, to Christian openness towards the presence of God in and under other forms of faith, as well as to Christian testimony towards people of other faiths.[25]

The purpose of mission is *conversion*, basically understood as the human turning its face towards him who has beheld it with the look of love its whole life. In the movement of conversion towards The One, true, lies also a movement away from "the false gods", i.e., away from all those substitutes filling the place of God in human life. We see that the most profound driving force in mission is not to "help", but to *search for fellowship with*. When this is realized, the motivation for mission is moved from the "end point of eternity", the judgement and perdition, to "the starting point of eternity": The fellowship-seeking love of the Triune God. However, the possibility of those loved becoming lost to God is present as a necessary contrast. It is inherent in the nature of love that its reply comes from within, in freedom.

By the beginning of the 21st Century, we stand on the threshold to a reorientation from a Christo-monistic to a Trinitarian understanding of Missio Dei.[26] This reorientation implies that the work of the Spirit is not only understood in view of the Christ-event, but also that the Christ-event is understood in view of the work of the Spirit. Scripture shows that the whole act of Christ is done by the Spirit (Luke 1:35: the conception; Matt 3:16: the baptism; Luke 4:18 ff: the introduction to the public work of Jesus; Rom 1:4: the resurrection). The original work of the Spirit is a *creative and life-giving* action in the whole of Creation (Gen 1:2; Psalm 104:30). It is not until the unity of Creation is broken by sin that the Spirit in addition takes up his *reconciling and healing* work. This, however, should not be taken to imply that the creative

---

[25] S. Mark Heim, "Sharing our differences: Koinonia and the Theology of Religious Plurality" (Faith and Order paper 2004).

[26] I refer to the preparatory papers for the World Council of Churches (WCC) Mission Conference, Athens 2005, cited in *International Review of Mission*, Vol 94, no. 372 (Jan 2005).

and life-giving ministry of the Spirit is *substituted* by its reconciliatory and healing ministry, but that the creative and life-giving work forms the basis for the reconciliatory and healing work. Thus, the dimension of creation becomes the very foundation for and an integral part of the salvific work of the Spirit.

This further challenges us to move from an *anthropocentric* to a *creation-oriented/ecological* understanding of mission. The starting point for the mission of God is God's love towards *the whole of Creation.* God's love towards the individual and towards humankind must be understood within the framework of God's love towards the whole of his Creation. God seeks fellowship with humankind in Creation and as a part of Creation. This means that mission cannot be reduced to "recruiting" people to a "Jesus-club".[27] *Missio Dei* has a far larger scope, to lead us back to all our God-given relations, or put differently, to make the world whole. The Trinitarian reorientation has as its starting point that Missio Dei concerns all processes involving true reconciliation and healing in the world. What is determining is that this reconciliation and healing has its basis in the suffering, death, and resurrection of Christ. Thus, when the Church is called to take part in the mission of God, this takes place by boldly witnessing of Jesus Christ as the source of reconciliation, and by active participation in the reconciling and healing ministry of the Spirit in the World, within all dimensions affected by this God-given reconciliation: reconciliation and healing in relation to God, in relation to ourselves, in our interpersonal relations at all levels, and in relation to the whole of Creation.

To take this challenge seriously implies a reworking of our previous definition of mission spirituality, in order to include the ecological perspective. An attempt reads as follows: Mission spirituality is the sensitivity of the Christian's, and the Christian community's, awareness of and response to the work of the Triune God to become the God of mercy, justice, *reconciliation and healing* in us and through us, for all humankind *and for the whole of Creation.* Briefly and simply, we may express it thus: *Mission spirituality is to search for our place in God's work for the redemption of the earth and humankind.*[28]

---

[27] Tore Johnsen, Norwegian delegate to the WCC Athens 2005 Mission Conference, in report to the Church of Norway, Council on Ecumenical and International Relations.

[28] Freely adapted from *Helingsgudstjeneste*, (I Mesterens Lys, 2007).

Mission and Contemplation[29]

The Way Inwards and the Way Outwards

The realization that Christian spirituality is not individualistic, but oriented towards the community, implies that there even must be structural consequences. The spirituality and theology of the Church must correspond to its structures, so that the three reflect each other. However, it is important to realize, as Magnus Malm points out in his last book,[30] that all system building begins within ourselves. Thus, the real basis for a renewal of Church and mission consists of neither structural nor theological changes, but prayer, and a spiritual guidance, helping us to confront our own fear, our own need for control, and teaches us to read the signals that can lead us out to new freedom. Malm maintains that Church history contains no examples of any other ways for the Church to find its identity. Prayer and spiritual guidance is the innermost and most reliable compass in the mission of the Church in the world.

Mission is often associated with the way outwards. Contemplative mission spirituality aims at focusing on the way inwards. Pentecost implies that the Spirit has been given. But why is the Spirit given? And what does it mean to be spiritual? In a Christian context, someone spiritual is "a person in whom God's Spirit lives". Our self-designation, "Christian" literally means the same: "to be anointed", that is, to be inhabited by the Spirit. That is what humans are created for. The Holy Spirit is the life-giver and the architect of the new Creation, who intends to inhabit all people and all of Creation, and to draw them towards himself in unity. The realization of the destiny of human life and Creation is a process *beginning in the Triune God.* It is here the particular traits of Christian mission spirituality really become visible.

Contemplation and mission are central and indivisible concepts within the intra-Trinitarian relation. Contemplation is to *behold,* to *see.* The Son beholds the Father, and the Father sends the Son and the Spirit. *Within this intra-Trinitarian union of contemplation and mission lies the foundation to all creation.* This union of contemplation and mission is what Jesus alludes to when saying: "The Son can do nothing by himself; he can do only what he *sees* (beholds) his Father doing" (John 5:19). The creative element in the relation between contemplation and mission is a mystery unattainable through thinking. For that reason, mission spirituality must rediscover the beat of the pulse of the mystical theology. It must realize that faith is not an answer to a question, but a trust of the heart which in itself is the answer to all riddles.

The purpose of Pentecost, the outpouring of the Spirit, is that people are drawn in to the fellowship of the Trinity, that we shall see God. Contemplation is the utmost goal of the outpouring of the Spirit. Jesus expresses this goal in

---

29 The paragraph relies on Peter Haldorf, in a seminar on "Mission and Contemplation", Bergen Diakonissehjem (24.02.2007).

30 Magnus Malm, *Hviskninger fra katekombene* (Oslo: Luther forlag, 2007).

one of the Beatitudes of the Sermon of the Mount: "Blessed are the pure in heart, for they will see (behold) God." (Matt 5:8). We notice that Jesus describes "the pure heart" as a condition for contemplation. The Desert Fathers were ardently occupied with the question of when a human has a pure heart. One of their great, Isaac the Syrian (350-440), answered the question thus: When one can regard every human as unsullied. Isaac helps us to see that the "pure heart" is not a moral, but a relational category. It implies that the opposite of pure is not "impure", but "mixed". When the Spirit makes the human heart pure, in the meaning of "unmixed", it is enabled to recognize the image of God in the other. Then, the human can reach its purpose: to see God.

Contemplation does not come easy. It demands practice, and practice demands *silence*. "Let silence be the criterion measuring everything, and keep to silence", one of the greatest of the Desert Fathers, Evagrios of Pontos (345-399) said. In silence, the human is opened for the life-giving and re-creative work of the Spirit. " But when he, the Spirit of truth, comes, he will guide you into all truth" (Joh. 16:13). The Desert Fathers again and again emphasise that there is only one counsellor: The Holy Spirit. At the same time, they realize that the Spirit counsels through people.

Dominicus (1170-1221), the founder of the Dominican Order, and one of the great medieval missionaries, always brought with him the book "Principles" by Johannes Cassianus (360-435) as his counsellor. Johannes Cassianus is wholly reliant on the Desert Father Evagrios. Likewise, Benedict of Nursia (480-550), the creator of a Monastic Rule that formed Christian Europe, relied on Johannes Cassianus. The Monastic Rule is concerned with finding "the proper measure". It is about balancing silence, prayer, rest, and action, in the life of the fellowship. The great medieval missionaries had the same concern. To find the right balance between silence, prayer, rest, and action, is a fundamental challenge for a missional Church.

Salvation – The Great Question in the Desert

In Scripture, the purpose of the gift of the Spirit (God's mission) can also be described as " so that through them you may participate in the divine nature" (2 Pet 1:4). Here, the rationale is that salvation, mediated by the Spirit, fulfils human nature by letting us partake in divine nature. Even this must be relationally understood. To be a person is to be "able to relate", able to turn the face towards another. Since God is "personal", he cannot be solitaire. God is relation: "tri-une". The implication of humankind being created in the image of God is that it is created to be drawn into the fellowship of the Trinity. This final destiny of humankind is described in Scripture by various terms: to "see God", to "participate in the divine nature".

The Cross of Christ, his death and resurrection, is the determining salvific act, since humankind because of sin became unable to be what it is: the image of God. The Desert Fathers regarded contempt as the most fundamental sin; to regard one's neighbour as defiled. Sin is to exclude the love of God from humans. In baptism, we die from sin and are opened to the love of God. A mission spirituality emerging from this perspective will understand its commission as winning one's neighbour for the love of God.

The Desert Fathers took the fight against sin seriously. The New Testament baptism exhortation unites the active sense "put to death … your earthly nature" with the medium form *"let the Holy Spirit fill you"* (Eph 5:18). Here, the Desert Fathers found a deep connection. We can only "put to death the earthly" by "*letting the Holy Spirit fill us*". This corresponds with an understanding of sin that realizes that sin reflects something originally good. Sin is not "negative through and through". Such an attitude opens up for contempt for one's neighbour, and for self-contempt. Rather, sin makes use of human's good potential and twists it towards the ego. In accordance with this, the mission of God is not "to break the vices asunder", but to "liberate the human potentialities" from the ego. That happens when we let us be filled by the Spirit. A mission spirituality aiming at break vices asunder risks ending up in contempt for Creation, in "impurity of heart".

What can humans do to let themselves be filled by the Spirit? We have already mentioned *repentance* as a fundamental movement in the Christian spirituality. Through conversion, we turn towards the face of God. Two other important movements in the Christian spirituality are renunciation and discipline. *Renunciation* is to *freely let go of* something that in itself may be good, in order to achieve a higher goal; an inner urge to enter on a journey bringing us in harmony with our true nature. Renunciation is individual; it is a matter of drawing a borderline according to personal need.

Discipline is *the repeated practice* of turning away from something in order to turn towards God. In our time, it is not only a challenge to take time for the practice. It is a major challenge to trust that the simple and "boring" repetition bears fruit. The whole culture resists this. But without renunciation and discipline, the awareness of the presence of God is not developed to create presence in the life of oneself and others. It is important to emphasise that renunciation and discipline in itself can never give a pure heart. The Spirit is the only one able to cleanse a human heart (cf. Ezek. 36:25-27), in grace. But renunciation and discipline are about seeking openness and receptivity for the Spirit. As human disposition is ambivalent, we have to fight. But the fight is not to shut evil out, but rather to open up for good.

The spirituality of revival emphasised the need for action now, immediately. Sometimes it may be right to catch the moment and make a decision, but the danger of manipulation is just around the corner. The contemplative spirituality gives more emphasis to slow growth and ripening. The spirituality of revival was ardently concerned with seeing God and learning to know him. The contemplative spirituality emphasises the importance of *letting oneself be seen by God and let oneself be known to him*. The desert way goes from asceticism (practice) to seeing (theory), not the opposite direction. Truth is not something to gain and own. Truth is something attained throughout life by turning to God, who is the truth, and let oneself be seen through by him.

Contemplative mission spirituality is realistic on behalf of humans. It knows that, in phases, it is hard to endure the journey. Scripture tells us why: The Spirit is willing, but the flesh is weak. If one does not take account of bodily frailness, failure will be the result. That is why "rules" for the spiritual life is needed, to keep the right balance. A practiced and experienced person may be able to make one's own "training manual for the soul". Most of us need the support given by the monastery, the retreat, and the spiritual guidance. Secularization is a mighty centrifugal force that constantly slings us towards the periphery, towards the superficial. We need help from the retreat centres and from work of silence in our own congregation to resist this and be drawn towards the centre, towards what gives foothold and where roots may fasten. To re-establish retreat as an integral part of missionary preparations, and to work towards establishing spiritual guidance for missionaries and mission leaders, are two important challenges. By entering into the desert, the Desert Fathers created a mission movement that has borne rich fruits in the history of the church.

To experience God in a relation of love

The church of the West has lived through a time when it has been occupied with building defences. One such defence is abstraction of faith. Abstraction creates endless debate, and is a major obstacle to the renewal of the church as a missional church. Seen from the other side, from the outside, the defences of faith appear as impenetrable fortifications. Contemplative spirituality shows a way out of abstraction, by highlighting again Christian mysticism. The Christian mysticism is concerned with experiencing God in a relation of love. It has its roots in the great poem of love, the Song of Songs.

In strong images, the Song of Songs describes how the bridegroom entices, draws, and leads the bride out of her house, her hidden confined ego, towards encounter with him. Faith cannot be confined. Faith is a vulnerable encounter with the other. Faith is to go out of oneself and encounter the other. The enticement of the bridegroom succeeds because it meets the yearnings of the bride. Here is the starting point of the Song of Songs: "Let him kiss me with the kisses of his mouth" (1:2). Yearning is not resigned impotence, but an immense driving force, if only people dare to give it room and to follow its compass.

Another obstacle for renewal of the Church as a missional Church is the individualization of faith. We see the individualization whenever faith becomes a matter of my needs, my taste, or my experiences. Parts of the Church growth movement have tried to answer to this by offering what is demanded. Contemplative spirituality is not about individualization of faith. It springs from a realization that humans cannot love (the world) until they become free (from the world). By seeking the "desert", the quiet place of encounter with God, humans experience freedom – freedom from using the world to confirm humanity in order to know its worth. Simone Veil has pointed out that no human – and no "thing" – must be an overpowering necessity for another person. God is the only overpowering necessity in every human's life. The "desert" is the place to make that experience.

The experience of God in a relation of love is a matter of entering the way of relation, i.e., the way of prayer. The innermost nature of prayer is contemplation. In the repeated refrain of the Song of Songs, it is expressed: "I am my lover's and my lover is mine" (2:16; 6.3; cf. 7:10). In such a God-relation, what draws us towards God is neither fear of punishment, nor any wish for reward, only yearning, thirst, and desire. Such a relation has room for taking the long road: "Do not arouse or awaken love until it so desires" (2:7). Living in a relation of love for God is a matter of delineation (renunciation), slowness (ripening), and repetition (discipline), just as in any other relation of love. Renewal is not to find something new, but to penetrate deeper into what one already has.

The passage in the Song of Songs concerning "the coming of the bridegroom", begins with a curious question: " Who is this coming up from the desert like a column of smoke (i.e., cleansed for his beloved)" (3:6 ff.) The mission of Jesus is to lead the bride home. This flows from his contemplation of the Father. In the same manner, the mission of the Church can only become a true Christian mission when it flows from contemplation. Thus, the movement drawing inwards, towards the centre, the centripetal force, is as important in the mission of the Church as the outward moving force, the centrifugal force.

Mission Spirituality – A Holistic Concern in the Centre of the Life of the Church

These paragraphs on mission spirituality in the 21st Century are in no way exhaustive. They endeavour to lead towards the core of the question of how the church of the West may be renewed as a missional church. I see signs many places of the work of the Spirit and the renewal of faith. Then we also have to raise the question of whether we shall regard the various kinds of spirituality alive in our church as alternative or as complementary. And how are we to understand their complementarities? How may different types of spirituality legitimately live side by side in our church, encounter in respect and cooperation, in order for the whole body to be nourished?

From a Trinitarian perspective, it is possible to unite different spiritual experiences. Tri-unity gives a platform to confirm the truth and reality in diverse manifestations of God. Many experience the power of God in nature. It may be in a violent storm, in the quiet germination of spring, or in the birth of a child. People crying for the mercy of God, in danger or under oppression, may experience divine liberation and new possibilities of life. Some experience a mystical union, and a self-transcendence, overflowing their natural identity.

Trinity as an understanding of God opens up for regarding all those experiences as being of the same reality, not of different realities. Simultaneously, each experience has integrity of its own, and should not be reduced. They need not be separated and measured against each other. The doctrine of Trinity gives the same validity to the experiences of God as the utmost source of being, as a close friend to talk confidentially to, and as the force of one's most profound identity. The doctrine of Trinity can join and unite those disparate elements. Each of them is needed to give full sense to human existence. This insight, often used in daily life, we also need to use to see God in diverse kinds of spirituality.[31]

Therefore, I dare repeating my appeal from the conclusion of the paper *the Church Encountering the Spiritual Yearning of Our Time*: "We are called to look, behind the polarised reality of the Church, for a more holistic spirituality, a spirituality where Bible reading and prayer, mission and evangelization, worship life and the display of the gifts of the Spirit, go hand in hand with concern for justice, human rights, and the protection of Creation. We are called to search together, together as church, and together with the world wide church".[32] However, the relation to God must regain its central place. The silence before the face of God is the necessary beginning, and prevailing condition, to see what it is all about. That mission is *God's* mission – and ours.

> The fruit of silence is prayer.
> The fruit of prayer is faith.
> The fruit of faith is love.
> The fruit of love is service.
>
> Mother Teresa, founder of the Missionaries of Charity

---

[31] Heim (2004). In his paper, Heim applies the doctrine of Trinity on the question of theology of religions.

[32] Kirkerådet 1999, 53.

Spirituality in the Chinese Context

Ekman Pui Chuen Tam

Dr Ekman Pui Chuen Tam, Director of Spirituality Programs, Tao Fong Shan Christian Centre, Hong Kong

"Spirituality" as a concept remains elusive. At this time, instead of enlightening the reader, examination of the literature only increases confusion. There seems to be no consensus regarding the definitions of the term "spirituality." It may be useful to remember that the word derives from Latin, *spiritus*, meaning "breath." "*Spiritus*" was a translation of the Greek, *pneuma*, meaning "lungs, breath, breathing." In the biblical tradition both were connected to the Hebrew, *ruah*, meaning also "breath." It is said in Genesis 3: With God's given "breath," human beings become alive.

The ancient meanings of the word "spirit" indicate a strong bodily locus – the lungs. It is only in the modern usage that the bodily locus has been changed and the word "spirit" begins to carry meanings about the invisible world of ghosts and spirits. Linguistically, one could say that the word "spirit" in these latter days has departed the bodies of men and women and gone to dwell in the ether.

Spirituality as Spiritual Ability

With a long history of association with breathing, the word "spirit" can still be defined as that something that gives life and vitality, as in giving the breath of life. Human beings are "spirited"; without "spirit," we die. The "spirit" is the life force of human beings. In this sense, human beings are intrinsically spiritual. A spiritual person is visibly full of life and filled with exuberance. A "spirited" life does not refer to the richness of dreams and beliefs of a joyful future after death or magical association with the ethereal. A "spirited" life is actualized in the here and now in everyday activities and experiences.

In four dimensions of human life we could identify or recognize the manifestation of the spirituality – spiritual ability – of human beings. The first is concerned with life-giving acts and deeds: sharing the only piece of bread with another starving person, risking one's life to save a baby from a fire scene, or loving someone by whom one's life has been gravely damaged. Such life-giving acts and deeds are seen as "spiritual," for they transcend human aggressive instinct. The Chinese consider a brutal killer “human face with animal heart,” (人面獸心) but admire life-giving people as “human above humans” (人上人). Genuine sacrificial behaviors are not normal acts and deeds of ordinary people. Ordinary people often look up to the life of those rare individuals who share life unto the point of death. The life stories of the “spiritual” persons are often narrated in religious literature.

The second spiritual quality of human existence is our compassionate affectivity toward other living beings. It is “compassion,” the “passion with” the suffering others, that moves one to commit deeds of sharing, helping, and loving. As human beings, when we see our neighbors who have lost their loved ones in accidents, natural disasters, or murders, we cannot help but are moved by their sorrow. We may be more compassionate toward those we know than toward strangers. But in some ways our thoughts and feelings are disturbed in seeing unknown civilians die in tsunamis, suicidal bombings, air crashes, tornados, volcanic eruptions, etc. Compassion is the kind of affectivity that feels not for one’s own well-being, but for the others. It draws us out from our little comfortable world and nudges us into solidarity with those who are suffering. The Chinese value compassion as an intrinsic quality of a human person: “Compassionate and merciful heart is everyone’s making.” (惻忍之心人皆有之) A spiritual person is one filled with compassion toward the living beings on the earth. The many religious figures, especially the “founders” of a religion, are all depicted as individuals with a tremendous capacity of compassion, with Buddha being the typical example. Expectedly, compassion is strongly emphasized in religious teachings.

If the first spiritual quality of human beings concerns the deeds and the second compassionate affectivity, the third has to do with our mind, which I call “reflectivity” – ability to reflect. Human beings are not satisfied with just filling up the stomach or quenching the thirst. We ask troubling questions: Who am I? What am I? Where do I come from? Where am I going? Why am I here, but not there? Why do I do this, but not that? These questions arise because we look at ourselves as the “other,” like looking into the mirror. In order to know the self reflected in the mind’s mirror, we ask many questions. Sadly, the reflected self could never be fully known, for the reflected self appears exactly the same as the bodily self. We know that the reflected self does not exist without the bodily self, but we doubt if the bodily self is the totality of one’s sense of Self. To be spiritual, we imagine, is to discover the true Self. A Chinese sage teaches: “I reflect on myself three times a day.” (吾日三省吾身) A wise, insightful, responsible, compassionate person always reflects on oneself. Spiritual figures of various religious traditions are enlightened in their search for the truth of their identities and existence. Knowing self and knowing the divine are two, sometimes one, common themes in religious literature.

The last spiritual quality of human beings is seen in the person’s aspiration for and connection with the unseen reality, which we may call the Divine, the

Transcendent, the Mystery, the Ultimate. Graves, in many forms, were always found in places where early human history was identified. Human beings, with an intrinsic ability to reflect, contemplate an unseen world – the world where the dead go, the world before all life exists, the world of invisible beings of power. Accounts of mystical experience or supernatural encounters are an attractive motif in literature, movies, dramas, paintings, and dances. Victor Frankl recalled a numinous experience of a woman who was dying in the concentration camp and was holding onto "something" invisible that gave her consolation and hope and meaning about life and death:

> This young woman knew she would die in the next few days. But when I talked to her she was cheerful in spite of this knowledge.
> "I am grateful that fate has hit me so hard," she told me. "In my former life I was spoiled and did not take spiritual accomplishment seriously." Pointing through the window of the hut, she said, "This tree here is the only friend I have in my loneliness."
> Through that window she could see just one branch of a chestnut tree, and on the branch were two blossoms.
> "I often talk to this tree," she said to me.
> I was startled and didn't quite know how to take her words. Was she delirious? Did she have occasional hallucination? Anxiously I asked her if the tree replied.
> "Yes."
> What did it say to her?
> She answered. "It said to me, 'I am here – I am here – I am life, eternal life.'"[1]

For the Chinese, human beings exist in close connection with Tien (天) (the Heavens) or Dao (道) (the Way) . Tien or Dao is the invisible reality that embraces, permeates, and yet transcends human existence. Human life is blessed when harmony is maintained with Tien and Dao. The breath of life seems to bond the visible and invisible in a harmonious whole. Although diverse religions (even among theistic religions) hold different views of the invisible, human beings seek to relate to, connect with, embrace, or enter into the unknown. Human beings are characterized with numinous sensibilities.

The four intrinsic elements that reveal the spirituality – spiritual ability – of human beings are interconnected. They form a coherent whole. Human activity, affectivity, reflectivity, and numinousity are like facets of a diamond. Spirituality involves life-giving behaviors, compassionate affection, meaning seeking, and numinous experience. Either one of these dimensions may stand out at one time, but the rest should not be absent. We would suspect the authenticity and healthiness of a person's spirituality, if, for example, the report of a numinous experience is clearly incompatible with the behavioral, affective, and cognitive sides of the person's life.

---

[1] Victor Frankl, *Man's Search For Meaning* (New York, NY: Washington Square Press, 1963), 109-110.

Sustained and nurtured by the breath of life, human beings, in theoretical terms, are intrinsically spiritual – having the ability to transcend one's own need and to help and care for the others, to seek meaning for one's own existence, and to develop a numinous sense of the invisible. However, the reality of human existence is far from one-sidedly spiritual. Wars, killings, violence, cruelty, discrimination, rejection persist in the human world. The spiritual ability of a person needs to be embodied in everyday life. Spirituality is about lived experience. The more conscious we are in living out our intrinsic qualities as spiritual beings, the more authentic and visible we are in embodying our spirituality. Spirituality is conscious striving to embody the intrinsic spiritual qualities of being human in everyday life.

Spirituality is "conscious" striving, because it requires a deepening of self-awareness and committed self-initiation. A spiritual person is one who has a heightened awareness of self in relation to the world, visible and invisible. It is also a "striving" – a process – that demands much effort in keeping one's mind and heart focused and clear. Meditation, concentration, prayer, chanting are practices helpful in understanding and knowing one's complicated thoughts and feelings, and thereby attuning one's awareness of the inner self, the spiritual connection with others, and the presence of the Invisible. However, "conscious striving" is not simply an internal process but also engages action and behaviors. It should bear fruits in the embodiment of the inherent spiritual qualities in one's life. And the embodiment is a kind of everyday life-style, consistent in the workplace, family, leisure.

What is said above thus far does not explicitly relate spirituality to religion, let alone Christianity. To eclipse the role of religion in spirituality unavoidably elicits questions. One that relates to the interest of this paper is: Can a person be spiritual without following a religion? When the Chinese say a person is rich in "spiritual qualities" (靈性), it does not necessarily refer to the person's religion. On the other hand, the different approaches to the development of spirituality for the Chinese are evolved from either the Daoist, Confucian, and Chan traditions, or the various combinations of the three. The answer to the question about the relation between spirituality and religion should not be a simple yes or no. We may need to take into consideration the different types of spirituality, as we attempt to address the question.

Types of Spirituality

Humanistic Spirituality is put in the outer circle, Religious Spirituality in the middle, and Christian Spirituality in the inmost circle.[2] Although Christianity is put in the inner circle, it should not be seen as triumphal over other spiritualities. The intentional use of dotted wave lines to demarcate the three

[2] Victor Frankl, *Man's Search For Meaning* (New York, NY: Washington Square Press, 1963), 109-110.

types of spirituality suggests that the three are not mutually exclusive or neatly distinguished from each other. It invites a dialogue between the different types of spirituality, for both Religious and Christian spirituality share elements of Humanistic Spirituality, and Christian Spirituality is a specific kind of Religious Spirituality. In fact, all believers, Christians or otherwise, are first and foremost human beings. Religions and Christianity are ritualistic expressions and ways by which human beings attempt to embody the innate spiritual qualities.

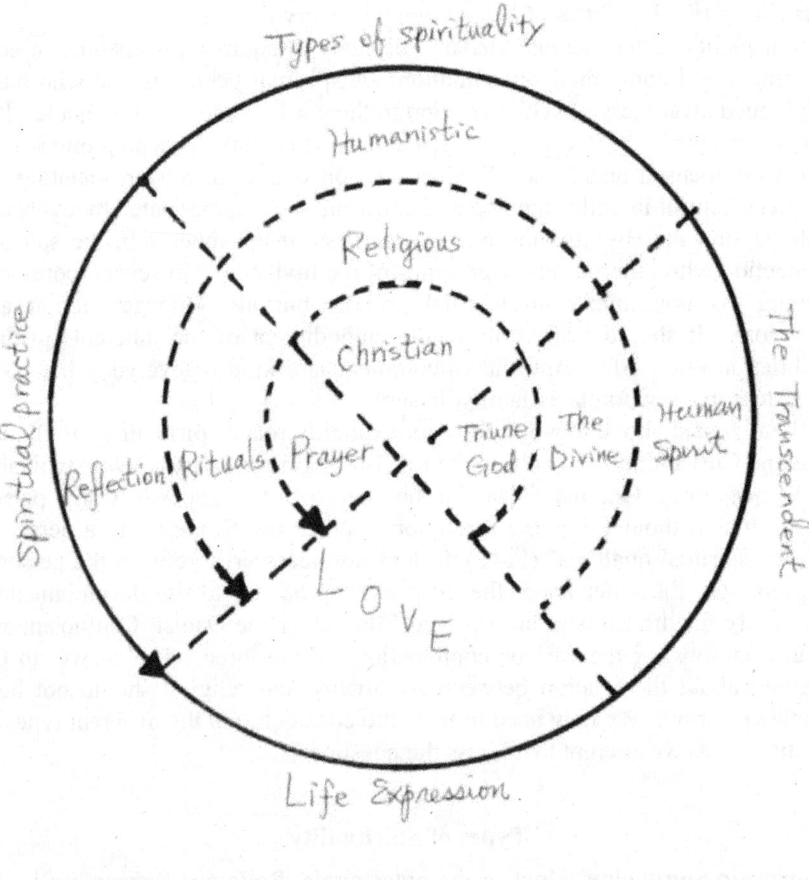

The embodiment or fruit of all three types of spirituality is the same. Love, or compassion, if you will, is the hallmark of authentic spirituality, whether it is humanistic, religious, or Christian. In other words, it is not by the types of spirituality that we define the authenticity of spirituality, but by the fruits of the types of spirituality. An authentic spirituality, be it Christian, religious, or humanistic, bears fruits of love and compassion. At the same, as the arrows also point to the sense of the numinous or the Transcendent, love informs our understanding of the Human Spirit, the Divine, and the Triune God. Whatever it may be, the symbol, image, or name of the Transcendent is not to provoke power of evil or darkness, but, instead, to heal and embrace the evil. Love as the Source or Ultimate of the human spirit or the Divine Spirit nurtures the growth of human life and heals the wounds of the human soul. Love is, therefore, both the inspiration as well as the fruit of all three types of spirituality.

The spiritual practice of the three types of spirituality varies according to the sense each one has of the Transcendent. Humanistic spirituality, focusing on the human spirit, often practices reflection on life and human realities. Religious spirituality adopts rituals in addressing or responding to the Divine. Christian spirituality generally sees prayer to the Triune God as a major spiritual discipline, although there are many approaches or ways of prayer taught in diverse traditions within Christianity.

The three types of spirituality are seen in the Chinese context. Classical Daoist and neo-Confucian approach to life resembles the Humanistic Spirituality. The different sects of the mythical Daoism and Chinese Buddhism, and the various combinations of the two, could be grouped under Religious Spirituality, although we may question if some of these expressions are authentic and healthy. Religious Spirituality, with its diverse and sometimes extreme expressions, is quite dominant in Taiwan and a few of the Asian countries. Christian Spirituality also exists among the Chinese. While the number of Christians remains small in proportion to the general population in Mainland China, Hong Kong, and Taiwan, Christians are convinced of their conversion to Christianity and would therefore maintain a distinct Christian Spirituality. Generally speaking, Christians in Hong Kong, Mainland China, and Taiwan, show little interest in understanding the Humanistic and Religious Spirituality their neighbors follow. They would, however, invest energy and resources in programs and activities that could convert their humanistic or religious neighbors. Humanistic spirituality, for them, lacks a devotion to God the Creator and Jesus the Redeemer. And they would reject any attempt to relate the breath of life or the human spirit to the Biblical concept of Holy Spirit, and particularly not to confuse it with Paul's theology of the Holy Spirit. The majority of the Chinese Christians would interpret the diverse forms of the religious spirituality of their neighbors ungodly, wicked, pagan, or demonic. They feel the burden to convert people from "ungodly religions" to Christianity. Dialogue with people of different types of spirituality is not yet a general concern or interest of the churches in the Chinese context.

Chinese and Christian Spirituality

Many Chinese Christians are converted from either humanistic or some forms of religious spirituality. Conversion is a powerful experience. To choose a new religion and let go of the old implies a detachment from one's family of origin, circles of friends, and even cultural heritage. Teaching that affirms one's new religion and denigrates the old reinforces the difficult and at times risk-taking choice. It would be too confusing and embarrassing to later discover by oneself or be taught by others that there is in fact values in the spirituality one gave up and that there is a link between one's new religion and the old. To bring friends to one's new religion is much more exciting, although not easier, than to dialogue with them. It may take a long journey for Chinese Christians to go from holding a defensive or triumphal attitude to seeing the possibility of building a bridge between Christian and other types of spirituality.

However, there are Chinese Christians (although the number would not be significant) who come to see the fact that human beings are innately spiritual and Christians are spiritual in a uniquely Christian way. With this insight, they change their views of their friends of other spiritualities and also alter their self-understanding as Christian. Christians, for them, are human persons following the way of Jesus Christ who is God incarnated. Indeed, Jesus, being God's incarnation, values life and gives life, to the extent that exemplifies the highest form of humanistic spirituality.

Kenneth Dale, a Lutheran theologian has aptly portrayed the link between humanistic and religious spirituality. According to Dale, the three types of spirituality hold a common concern for life.

> Are not all the tenets of religions for the very purpose of enhancing life? True religion and the salvation, which it offers, are in no way against human life. They point to the fulfillment of life as it can and ought to be lived. Sin is the misuse of life, our own and others. Can there be any question that the divine Spirit is alive in the whole universe that the love of God is present at all times in all places?[3]

Schillebeecks, a Catholic theologian, writes beautifully about the blending of the humanist's concerns for life with the Christian's understanding of God: "God wants life for human family: God is for us. God stands on the side of life and all that belongs to life – liberation, healing, expansion, well-being, growth, joy…The human cause is God's cause."[4] A contemporary monk, Thomas Merton, also writes eloquently on Christian spirituality in humanistic terms: "Spirituality is the highest expression of man's intellectual and spiritual life. It is life itself, fully awake, fully alive, fully awake that it is alive. It is spontaneous awe at the sacredness of life. It is gratitude for life, for awareness

3 Victor Frankl, *Man's Search For Meaning* (New York, NY: Washington Square Press, 1963), 109-110.

4 Quoted in Dale, "Three Perspectives on Spirituality," 3.

and for being."[5] Indeed, to honor and give life is, for Christians, a call from God who came to humanity in Jesus: "I came that they might have life, and might have it abundantly." (John 10: 10) Humanistic Spirituality is not antagonistic to Christian spirituality. Christian Spirituality only affirms Humanistic Spirituality's reverence for life through the symbols and stories of Jesus Christ who is the Incarnation of the Eternal God, the Creator of all life.

Christians are part of the human race. Christians are not special species. Christians are "spiritual," because they are human. If some Christians are more "spiritual" than the people of other religions or no religions, it is not necessarily because of the type of religion (Christianity in this case) they follow. It is because they authentically live their life by following the footstep of Jesus Christ – the God incarnated. Christian spirituality, then, is consciously striving to embody the intrinsic spiritual qualities of being human in everyday life, by following the way of Jesus.

[5] Thomas Merton, *New Seeds of Contemplation* (New York: New Directions Books, 1961), 1.

The Never Ending Song: The Contextualization of Chinese Christian Hymnody

Thor Strandenæs

Assoc Prof Dr Thor Strandenæs, School of Mission and Theology, Stavanger, Norway

Introduction

The Chinese church is a singing church. This is true both concerning Catholic and Protestant churches, within and outside the People's Republic of China (PRC). In the Protestant church there are numerous hymnals, since most of the denominations have issued and still issue their own hymnals.[1] The so-called post-denominational Protestant church in the PRC is, however, an exception, since it has issued one hymnal for common use in all its member congregations – the *Zànměisī Xīnbiàn* (1983). When listening to and partaking in the singing of the various hymns, one becomes aware of many characteristics of Chinese hymnody. In this presentation I will argue, however, that there are two main characteristics which are striking: the Chinese hymnody is truly Chinese, and is at the same time truly transcultural.[2] This means that Chinese hymnody on the one hand includes indigenous – that is, culture specific – expressions of Chinese Christian faith, values and experience. On the other hand it does not

---

[1] Thus already in 1912 a count of 62 different hymnals was made by Donald MacGillivray "A List of Chinese Christian Hymn Books published between 1807-1912," *China Mission Year Book* (Shanghai: Christian Literature Society for China 1912): 253-259. This list was later updated in 1964 by David Sheng, "A Study of the Indigenous Elements in Chinese Christian Hymnody" (D.M.A. Thesis, University of Southern California 1964). But numerous hymnals have been issued since then, both new ones and revised editions of hymnals.

[2] In this article I make use of four categories to identify different aspects of inculturation (/indigenization/ contextualization). These are found in the "Nairobi Statement on Worship and Culture: Contemporary Challenges and Opportunities," in: S. Anita Stauffer (ed.), *Christian Worship: Unity in Cultural Diversity* (LWF Studies 1/1996, Geneva: Lutheran World Federation 1996): 23-28, namely worship (and therefore also hymnody) as transcultural, contextual, countercultural and crosscultural.

neglect expressions of Christian faith, values and experience which it shares ecumenically with Christian churches elsewhere in the world – that is, universal or transcultural elements of Christian hymnody. In the present contribution it is not possible to give a comprehensive treatment of all the inculturation and transculturation related aspects of Chinese Christian hymnody. Instead some important characteristics in the development of Chinese hymnody will be highlighted, as well as some main characteristics of Chinese hymnody itself.[3] The main characteristics of the development will be addressed first, and then some main characteristics of Chinese hymnody.

Historical Development

Development in Phases

The development of a Chinese Christian hymnody may be divided into five phases or stages. These phases may well occur at different times in different churches or denominations – mainly but not entirely due to the number of years these have existed in China or in Chinese communities. Also, some of the phases may overlap or be simultaneous, since the hymnal revision projects involve both the revision and discarding of old hymns, the inclusion of new indigenous hymns and hymn melodies, as well as (undertaking or adopting) translations of hymns not formerly known or used among the Chinese. The five characteristic phases may be listed as follows:

- The phase of translation of hymns, mainly done by expatriate missionaries together with national Christians.
- The phase of indigenous hymn writing and the use of indigenous melodies.
- The phase of hymn revision. This includes the refinement of hymn texts and the discarding of hymns rarely used or regarded as too foreign in their melodies or texts, or even conflicting with Chinese values.
- The phase of translating and adopting new hymns from already cooperating churches or other churches abroad.
- The phase of translating Chinese hymns into other languages for the use of Chinese and non-Chinese Christians in other churches.

In the following I will give some examples to illustrate each of the five stages or phases, starting with the first:

The Phase of Translating Hymns

The initial phase is mainly characterized by the translation of non-Chinese

[3] Some of these characteristics have been identified also in the article by Chen Zemin, "Inculturation of the Gospel and Hymn Singing in China," *Chinese Theological Review* 11(1997)2: 49-57.

hymns into Chinese by expatriate missionaries and national Christians. The first Chinese hymnals contained almost only translated hymns and only very few original Chinese hymns or hymns with Chinese melodies. Although this is true also for the 19th Century hymnals, the point can be illustrated from the development of the following three 20th Century Chinese Hymnals. Hymns – almost entirely in Western languages – were translated into Chinese – an expression of the *crosscultural* aspect of inculturation. The hymns were considered to be relevant expressions also in Chinese for Christian faith, values and experience. And, although these were indeed translated hymns, they nevertheless appeared in Chinese language – more or less refined – and could immediately be learnt and used by the believers. Some times when visitors to Chinese churches make the comment that they hear many Western hymns, they tend to forget that through translation these hymns have become truly Chinese in spite of their foreign origins. Here there is a parallell between the hymnody of Chinese churches and churches elsewhere, such as the Church of Norway and the Evangelical Lutheran Church of Madagascar. Both these churches started out as fruits of European missionary work, but as national churches they have incorporated into their hymnody hymns of both local and foreign origins. Thus the Chinese – like the Norwegian and the Malagasy – Christians were introduced to indigenous hymns used in churches from which the expatriate missionaries had come.[4] But since the hymnody of each of these churches also contained hymns from other nations or linguistic groups – both ancient and modern – the translated hymns at the same time brought the Chinese Christians into contact with the universal heritage of church hymnody – or the *transcultural* aspect of contextualization.[5] The following three examples illustrate this point aptly:

Firstly, the Chinese Lutheran Hymnal – *Hymns of Praise* (/ *Sòng Zhǔ Shèng Shī*) – was published in four editions in the 20th Century (1920; 1924; 1955; and 1994).[6] Looking at the Chinese Lutheran hymnody one finds that it contains a high percentage of hymns translated from other languages, from Lutheran as well as non-Lutheran church traditions. There has only been a slow and gradual increase of the percentage of indigenous Chinese hymns and hymn melodies over the years in the four editions:

- In the 1920 hymnal (1st edition) less than 4 % of the hymns – or 21

[4] E.g., the Norwegian hymns "Hvor to og tre forsamlet er", "Oss er i dag en Frelser födt", "Skriv deg, Jesus, paa mitt hjerte" (In the *Hymns of Praise* # 4, # 56, # 136 respectively).

[5] E.g., the Advent and Christmas carols "O Come, o come Immanuel", "Silent Night, Holy Night", and "O Come, All Ye Faithful" are found both in *Sòng Zhǔ Shèng Shī* (1955), # 118, # 134, and # 153, and in the *Zànměisī Xīnbiàn* (Shanghai: China Christian Council 1983), # 66, # 71, and # 76 respectively.

[6] *Sòng Zhǔ Shèng Shī* – in Chinese actually renders 'Sacred (/Holy) Songs (/Hymns) of Praise to the Lord'.

of 542 – were original Chinese.

- In the 1924 hymnal (2nd edition) less than 6 % of the hymns – or 26 of 450 – were original Chinese.
- In the 1955 hymnal (3rd edition) less than 10 % of the hymns – or 55 of 600 – were original Chinese.
- In the current 1994 hymnal (new revised edition) about 10.7 % of the hymns – or 64 of 597 – are original Chinese.[7]

In the current 1994 edition also the number of Chinese melodies (both for hymns and liturgical texts) has increased, showing signs of indigenous creativity and influence.[8]

Secondly, the hymnal published by the hymnal committee of the China Christian Council (CCC) in the PRC in 1983 – the *Zànměisī Xīnbiàn*[9] – has the highest proportion of indigenous Chinese hymns and hymn melodies found in the Chinese Protestant community. Out of its total 400 hymns some 102 "either have lyrics or melodies composed by Chinese Christians or are adaptations of Chinese tunes".[10] This reveals that, whereas the church on the Mainland still has about three fourths of its hymns as translations from other languages, the Chinese indigenous hymns total some 25% of the hymnal. Thus the politically enforced isolation of China from the West in the second part of the 20ieth Century became a stimulation for Chinese hymn authors and melody composers for creating hymns that reflect Chinese Christian faith and experience with the Gospel in daily life in the PRC. About fifty of these 102 Chinese hymns with Chinese tunes were written before 1949, the rest during the second half of the 20ieth Century.[11]

Thirdly, in the Roman Catholic Church of Hong Kong the effects of the 2nd Vatican Council (1962-1965) have indeed been great also on church hymnody. From a church formerly celebrating mass and singing canticles and hymns in Latin it has developed into a community where the indigenous Chinese

---

[7] 205 of the hymns are retained from the *HoP* 3rd edition (1955), and 292 are new selections.

[8] Most of these may be found from # 543 to # 595 and are melodies to liturgical texts.

[9] An English edition of the foreword to this hymnal – "Foreword to the Chinese Hymnal 1983 Edition" – by the Chinese Christian Hymnal Committee, may be found in *Chinese Theological Review* 1985: 143-147; also found in the preface of the bilingual edition of the *The New Hymnal / Zànměisī Xīnbiàn* (English-Chinese Bilingual edition, Shanghai: China Christian Council 1999): 1-6.

[10] Ibid., "Preface to the Chinese Edition," 2.

[11] Chen 1997:53. The hymnal committee received a total of 2256 hymns between March 1981 and September 1982, from which they made a careful selection (*The New Hymnal / Zànměisī Xīnbiàn* (1999), "Preface to the Chinese Edition," 3).

influence on texts and melodies in liturgy and hymn singing is overwhelming. The Hong Kong Catholic Hymnal – the *Sòng Ēn – Xìnyǒu Gējí*[12] – shows this clearly. Notwithstanding that many of the liturgical and biblical texts are translations, still about 4/5 – or 239 of the 299 – of the hymns and liturgically used prayers are written by Chinese or have Chinese melodies – traditional as well as new. 1/5 (or 60) of the entries, plus a number of biblical and liturgical texts in translation, confirms the local church's links with the church universal, that is, both the transcultultural and crosscultural aspects of hymnody. The vast number of indigenous Chinese hymns and melodies confirm a true belonging to a Chinese society.

The Phase of Indigenous Hymn Writing and the Use of Indigenous Melodies

In spite of a few existing Chinese hymns inherited from the Nestorian and post-Reformation period,[13] most of the hymns written or composed by Chinese Christians are from the 20ieth Century, not including, of course, the traditional Chinese melodies, of which many are found in different hymnals.[14] The list of such hymn writers and composers is long, as may be seen from the indices of authors and composers that can be found in the various hymnals. Some of the hymn writers – such as T.C. Chao – have written numerous hymns, others only one or a few. In spite of the high percentage of indigenous Chinese hymns included in the CCC hymnal – *Zànměisī Xīnbiàn* (1983) – this hymnal only has included some of the most spread and used hymns.[15] Also other hymnals include such indigenous hymns.[16]

The Phase of Hymn Revision, Refinement of Hymn Texts and Discarding of Hymns.

Hymns that have been in usage are normally scrutinized during hymnal revision

---

[12] ["Praise Grace – Collection of Songs for Friends of the Faith"], Hong Kong 1976; rev. Ed., Hong Kong 1985.

[13] E.g., # 385 and # 386 in *The New Hymnal / Zànměisī Xīnbiàn* 1999.

[14] A number of these are found in the *Zànměisī Xīnbiàn* (1983) and *The New Hymnal / Zànměisī Xīnbiàn* (1999) and include such as the (i) ancient *chin* tunes (Nos 13, 178, 198, 380, 381), (ii) ancient tunes (Nos 298, 353), Confucian chant (Nos 184), (iv) folk songs (Nos 30, 31, 43, 51, 83, 101, 138, 175, 202, 204, 379, 382, 383, 384), (v) poetry chanting tune (No 386), and (vi) verse tune (No 59).

[15] *The New Hymnal / Zànměisī Xīnbiàn* (1999), "Preface to the Chinese Edition," p.5 tells that between March 1981 and September 1982 the hymnal revision committee received a total of 2256 suggested hymns. Many of these were indigenous Chinese, but only 102 were included.

[16] E.g., in *Hymns of Praise / Sòng Zhǔ Shèng Shī* (1955) one finds hymns by Wu Ming-chieh (Nos 368, 396), by Wu Pin (No 328), by Louis Yen (Nos 264, 400) and by Luther You (No 595).

projects with a view to improve and refine translations. Also hymns that are considered outdated – not any longer expressing adequately the cultural values of Chinese Christianity –, and those rarely used are left out of the new editions and new ones included. Thus in the Chinese-English bilingual edition of the Lutheran hymnal – *Hymns of Praise* / *Sòng Zhǔ Shèng Shī* (4th ed., 1994) –, only 305 of the 600 hymns were retained from the third edition (1955), and the Chinese texts were "reviewed and changed several times to make the hymns more melodious and a pleasure to sing."[17] 292 new hymns or liturgical texts were introduced.[18]

A similar situation is reflected in the preface of the CCC hymnal – *The New Hymnal / Zànměisī Xīnbiàn* (1999):

> In terms of language and musical style, we have not emphasized uniformity, but sought to preserve variety. Previously published hymnals were all different in terms of language style and words. The Editorial Committee took a cautious attitude toward this in order to preserve as far as possible the composer's original meaning. Those lyrics which were the creation of Chinese Christians were changed as little as possible... In order to show our respect for the tremendous efforts by our predecessors at blending church music more closely with Chinese culture, instances in which their translations employed a more classical vocabulary to express the Christian faith have not been greatly changed. There are also hymns in which the original translation was insufficiently refined, in which the lyrics may not even rhyme; however, in order to show consideration for the preferences of some Christians, we have simply revised or polished here and there and very little new translation has been done.[19]

These two examples suffice to demonstrate that the hymnal committees reflect the churches' development, their contemporary situation and challenges. Also the omission of outdated hymns and the editing of lyrics in use – sometimes only modestly – and the polishing of melodies (and harmonization) express a wish to serve the needs of contemporary Chinese Christians. At the same time the retaining of somewhat archaic lyrical expressions show a respect for hymn tradition as a living tradition.

The Phase of Adopting New Hymns from Old and New Church Connections Abroad.

Long standing relations with European and American churches and increased

[17] *Hymns of Praise / Sòng Zhǔ Shèng Shī* (1994), Preface, p 8. For hymns in the first edition of 1920 which were not retained in the 1924 or 1955 editions of the hymnal, see Thor Strandenaes, "Hymn Concordance for the Lutheran Hymn Book – *Hymns of Praise,*" *Theology and Life* 5(1982): 102-119.

[18] *Hymns of Praise / Sòng Zhǔ Shèng Shī* 1994, Preface, 8.

[19] *The New Hymnal / Zànměisī Xīnbiàn* 1999, "Preface to the Chinese Edition", 4.

contact with churches on other continents have lead the Chinese churches to include in translation new hymns from both sources. To give two examples:

- In the Lutheran hymnal – *Hymns of Praise / Sòng Zhǔ Shèng Shī* (1994) – one finds newly translated hymns not only from America, South America and Europe – including a number of hymns from the Taizé community – but also from Asian countries, such as Japan (Nos 54, 71, 154, 294, 344, 345, 508) and Malaysia (293). This expresses an ecumenical aspect of Chinese hymnody – and therefore also its transcultural nature.
- In the CCC hymnal – both the *Zànměisī Xīnbiàn* (1983) and *The New Hymnal / Zànměisī Xīnbiàn* (bilingual1999) – a few hymns from other Asian countries have been included in translation, such as from Japan (# 218), India (# 32, # 399), and Burma (melody # 390). The total number of such hymns is not high. The hymnal committee has paid most attention to including more indigenous Chinese hymns than to including newly translated ones. As the mutual contacts between the church in and outside the PRC gradually increases, possibly more such newly translated hymns will be introduced.

The Phase of Hymn Export or Sharing Hymns with the non-Chinese

"Export" may not be the most adequate term, as it comes from a market oriented language. Nevertheless the fifth phase is that of hymn export, or the sharing of Chinese hymns with other Christians as a crosscultural and transcultural movement. Many Chinese hymns have been translated into other languages and find their way into ecumenical hymnals[20] or the hymnals of non-Chinese churches.[21] A number of Chinese hymnals have been published in Chinese-English bilingual editions. The main purpose of this, of course, has been to share the treasures of Chinese hymnody with such Chinese communities which consist of both Chinese speaking and non-Chinese speaking members. The following hymnals may serve as examples:

- The Lutheran bilingual hymnal *Hymns of Praise / Sòng Zhǔ*

---

[20] *E.g.*, in the hymnal *Sound The Bamboo. CCA Hymnal 1990* (Trial Edition, Manila: Asian Institute for Liturgy and Music, and the Christian Conference of Asia 1990), which includes hymns from more than 20 countries and 40 languages, and all with English translation, some 24 hymns in Mandarin Chinese (*pǔtōnghuà*) have been included. Six of these are by the famous Chinese theologian and hymn writer T. C. Chao (*Chao Tzu-chen*; 1888-1979), namely # 13, # 155, # 165, # 174, # 200, and # 223.

[21] *E.g.*, the hymnals of the Church of Norway (Lutheran), *Norsk Salmebok* (Oslo: Verbum 1985) has included Psalm 136 (# 87), and *Salmer 1997* (Oslo: Verbum 1997) has included a translation of the hymn by T. C. Chao (cf. previous note), "Golden Breaks the Dawn" (*Qīng zǎo qǐlái kān*), # 126.

Shèngshī (1994)

- The Protestant, ecumenical bilingual *Hymns of Universal Praise / Pǔtiān Sòngzàn* (1994/2006)[22]
- The CCC bilingual hymnal – *The New Hymnal / Zànměisī Xīnbiàn* (1999)
- The Baptist hymnal – *Century Praise / Shìjì Sòngzàn* (2001)[23]

But although the expected main users of the English translations of the hymns have been Chinese who are without the ability to read (or understand) Chinese script (and/or language), the provision of translations of the hymns has equally introduced the non-Chinese Christians of the world to a treasure of Chinese hymns which they were now able to understand and make use of. Thus the Chinese churches through their bilingual hymnals do not only share the Chinese hymnody with their fellow Chinese Christians but also invite the church worldwide to share in the Chinese faith expressions, values and experience. Having formerly experienced the cross-cultural aspect of Christian hymnody mainly as receptors – and therefore in a one-way sense –, the crosscultural experience has become a two-way movement. In spite of a number of Chinese hymns having already been translated into English and other non-Chinese languages prior to the time of the PRC (1949), the big effort of making Chinese hymns available to the non-Chinese took place in the last part of the 20ieth Century. And it is still ongoing, particularly as a result of the bilingual hymnal editions.[24]

Some Main Characteristics of Chinese Hymnody

It is impossible to include all characteristics of Chinese hymnody in this rather short contribution, since a thorough investigation would need much more space. I will therefore concentrate on six of its main characteristics only.

Bible Inspired

A great number of Chinese hymns consist of biblical texts or paraphrases of biblical texts. These hymns are easily learnt by heart, and popular. Thus their function is both to convey key texts and verses in the Bible and to celebrate

---

22 *Hymns of Universal Praise / Pǔtiān Sòngzàn*, New Revised Edition, Hong Kong: Chinese Christian Literature Council Ltd. 2006 (which is based on the 1977 and 1994 revised editions, issued by the same publisher). The first *Hymns of UniversalPraise / Pǔtiān Sòngzàn*, edited by the United Hymnal Committee, was published by the Christian Literature Society, Shanghai 1936, and represented the following denominations: Anglican, Baptist, Methodist, and Presbyterian. It was widely used on the Mainland until 1966, the initial year of the so-called Cultural Revolution (1966-1976).

23 Hong Kong: Chinese Baptist Press 1991.

24 See, e.g., note 16 above.

common faith in the message which they relate. In the Protestant tradition most of the bible inspired texts follow word by word the Chinese texts of the *Chinese Union Version* (Mandarin) bible translation from 1919. Examples found in the Lutheran hymnal are Psalm 23, the *Magnificat* (Luke 1,46-55), the *Nunc Dimittis* (Luke 2,29-32), the *Benedictus* (Luke 1,68-79), and John 14,1-3+27.[25] Others are slight paraphrases of biblical texts in this version.[26]

Further, in many of the Chinese hymnals there is the tradition of giving reference(s) to biblical text(s) under the hymn titles, referring the user to biblical texts which are referred to in or have inspired the individual hymn.[27] In the companion to the CCC hymnal – a historical guide, edited by Huang Shen-le, the *Zànměishī (xīn biān) Shīhuà* (1992)[28] – a biblical reference is given at the entry of each of all the 400 hymns which are introduced. The biblical reference is either to the text which the hymn quotes or refers to more or less directly, or to the text which may have inspired the author, or which is otherwise easily associated by the hymn text. No biblical references or quotes, however, are given for any of the 400 hymns of the CCC hymnal – the *Zànměishī Xīnbiān* (1983) – under the hymn titles or otherwise –, with the exception of the appended 42 *duǎngē* ("short songs"), whereof bible references are given for 16. Interestingly, the biblical books which are most quoted or referred to in the *Zànměishī Xīnbiān* (1983) are the Psalms, the Gospel according to Matthew, the Gospel according to Mark, and the Book of Revelation. This shows that in the life of the Chinese Protestant churches, the Bible has a central position. Further, such scripture passages are mostly used which give references to the teachings, ministry, death and resurrection of Jesus, to Psalms of praise, and to texts which speak about hope, and an afterlife. In other words: to biblical texts which reflect basic biblical truth, inspire faith and contribute to coping with everyday life.

Moreover, a number of the biblical *Psalms* have been included in different Chinese hymnals. In particular the Catholic hymnals have included many of these,[29] but also various Protestant Hymnals, such as the CCC hymnal – the

---

[25] *Sòng Zhǔ Shèng Shī / Hymns of Praise* (1955) – Nos 586, 587, 588, 589, and 591, respectively

[26] E.g., the Lord's Prayer (Matthew 6,19-13) in the Lutheran hymnal – the *Sòng Zhǔ Shèng Shī / Hymns of Praise* (1955), # 590.

[27] In both the 1955 and 1994 editions of the Lutheran hymnal – *Sòngzhǔ Shēngshī* – all hymns are given a reference to a biblical text / biblical texts under their titles. This tradition has also been adopted in the Hong Kong Baptist hymnal – *Century Praise / Shìjì Sòngzàn* (2001).

[28] Shanghai: China Christian Council.

[29] E.g., in the *Hong Kong Catholic Hymnal* (*Sòng Ēn – Xìnyǒu Gējí*) ["Praise Grace Collection of Songs for Friends of the Faith"]; Hong Kong 1976 (rev. Ed. Hong Kong 1985) the following Psalms have been included: Ps 16 (# 134); Ps 19 (# 120); Ps 23 (#115); Ps 25 (# 113); Ps 33 (# 119); Ps 47 (# 130 and #

Zànměisī Xīnbiàn (1983) –, namely Psalms 23, 100, 103, 121, 133, and 150.[30] Chinese Christians have thus taken up a common heritage of the church, dating back to its original Jewish context, of singing the biblical Psalms. Most of the Psalms found in Chinese hymnals are Psalms of hymnic praise, adoration, trust and confidence. Only few laments are in use. Thus, for instance, instead of singing laments in the difficult years of the Cultural Revolution, Psalm 23 became a highly cherished gem among the Christians. Through this psalm the Chinese expressed both confidence in God as lord of history – a god to be trusted also in times of oppression – and protest against persecution and atrocities (cf. Ps 23,4-5) – thus expressing also a countercultural aspect of Christian faith.

Short Songs and Gospel Songs

Also some of the so-called Short Songs (*duǎngē*) and Gospel Songs (*fúyīngē*) belong to the Bible Songs (*shèngjīnggē*), but include many other expressions of Christian faith as well. The short songs and gospel songs are many and very popular among Chinese Proestant Christians. They are, indeed, short, spiritual songs or choruses, often inspired by or conveying a verse from the Bible (Bible Songs or Gospel Songs)[31] or an aspect of Christian faith. Normally they are sung with traditional or popular Chinese melodies, often related to Chinese folk song tradition. Their short form, concentrated and focused message, make them easy to sing and remember. Thus in the CCC hymnal – the *Zànměisī Xīnbiàn* (1983) – 42 such short songs have been appended.[32] Many of these relate one or two bible verses,[33] and two of them consist of scripture names – namely the books of the Old (# 41) and the New Testament (# 42), respectively, listing the books according to the order in which they occur in the Bible – plus a verse which sums up the importance of reading and following the Scripture as the light from God (verses 7 and 4, respectively).

A Chinese woman from a countryside peasant family, Lü Xiaomin has

---

137); Ps 57 (# 133); Ps 66 (# 114); Ps 95 (# 112); Ps 100 (# 79 and # 136); Ps 113 (# 124); Ps 117 (# 129); Ps 123 (# 118); Ps 130 (# 203); Ps 131 (# 131); Ps 136 (# 126); Ps 145 (# 135).

[30] Nos 379, 380, 381, 382, 383, and 384, respectively.

[31] See, for instance, Amy Wang Sit (ed. and comp.), *China Sings: Bible Verses in Chinese Tunes* (Hong Kong: Asian Outreach Ltd. 1981), which is a Chinese-English bilingual collection of 108 such Bible Songs – both from the Old and New Testament.

[32] Unfortunately these have not been included in the bilingual Chinese-English edition – *The New Hymnal / Zànměisī Xīnbiàn* (1999).

[33] Ps 30,5 (# 24), 121,1-4 (# 5), 39,23-24 (# 16); Prov 10,4; 13,11 (# 38) ; Is 54,10 (# 21), Matt 12,20 (# 25); John 3,16 (# 1); Acts 20,35 (# 36); Rom 12,17 (# 30) and 15,2 (# 35); Eph 4,1 (# 28) and 5,17 (# 34); Phil 1,9-10 (# 33) and 3,13-14 (# 32); 1 Pet 5,7 (# 22); 2 Pet 1,5-7 (# 37).

written more than 1000 such short songs – usually referred to as the Songs of Canaan.[34] Also the CCC has issued a collection of 640 short songs – including both Scripture songs and short songs. Both the Songs of Canaan and other short songs and gospel songs are widely known by the Chinese Protestants and used both in non-registered and registered churches in the PRC, as well as in Chinese communities in Taiwan and elsewhere. They normally come with traditional Chinese pentatonic melodies or folk melodies. People easily learn them by heart and sing them in church and home gatherings, and when alone. They are particularly favoured by illiterate people or people with little education, since they find them less difficult to learn than the hymns which are found in the CCC hymnal – the *Zànměisī Xīnbiàn* (1983).

Community Oriented

Traditional Chinese culture has been collectively oriented, likewise main stream Communism in the PRC. Also many of the Chinese hymns focus on the church as a new, extended family and emphasize the duties of Christians to the community – Christians and non-Christians alike. Although there are indeed many of the Chinese hymns which focus on individual faith and ethos, a main characteristic of the Chinese hymnody is its community orientation. This reflects the traditional community oriented aspect found in Chinese culture in general, and in the Christian church in particular – both Protestant and Catholic. Thus a number of hymns affirm this belonging to the church as a family.[35] The following verses of the hymn "I love Christ's Church" (v. 1-2) may serve as an example:[36]

I love Christ's Church, God's own house,
Holy place that He has made.
Heart and soul I worship there,
And I live with sin forgiv'n.

I love Christ's Church, God's own folk,
Heav'nly Father gives them strength.
Brothers, sisters share your love,
Work together, serve the Lord.

---

34 For more information on Lü Xiaomin, cf. http://www.asianoutreach.org/sample/file/AR_04_MarApr.pdf and http://www.globallight.org.uk/Sisters%20Songs.htm . The Songs of Canaan have been published both within the PRC and in Taiwan, see e.g., *Jiānán Shīxuǎn 1-2* ([*Selected Songs from Canaan 1-2*] Taipei: Hosanna Gospel Propaganda Association 2001).

35 See, e.g., hymns Nos 122 – 132 in *Zànměisī Xīnbiàn* 1983, and Nos 289 – 299 in *Sòng Zhǔ Shèng Shī /Hymns of Praise* 1994.

36 *The New Hymnal / Zànměisī Xīnbiàn* (1999), # 125, verse 1-2 (text: Cai Wen-hao 1982; translation by Wendell P. Karsen 1995; alterations by Ivy Balchin and Heyward Wong Wing-hei 1995; melody by Yang Lü-fu 1982).

But also in the Songs of Canaan – for instance in the songs *"Chinese Heart"* and *"Another Home"*[37] – and in other short songs do we find this emphasis.

Emphasizing Models of Faith and Christian Ethos

The long term effect of Chinese Confucianism is a strong emphasis on a common ethos in Chinese society and on right living. Classical Confucianism taught one to behave adequately within each of the specially defined fundamental relations. Thus, within Chinese cultural context also religion is measured according to its effects or results in peoples' lives, especially its ethical consequences. Hence, a religion which produces a good ethos is normally considered a good religion. Nowadays even in the PRC the Christian religion is seen as a moral force in the battle against vices and immorality and as an ally in the promotion of a spiritually based, alternative ethos to counteract pure materialistic values. Thus it is not uncommon that Christians in the PRC are officially declared to be 'model citizens' in a local community – mainly because they have done more to serve the community and their fellow citizens than could justly be expected from them. But also among Chinese outside the Mainland the churches promote filial piety, kindness and respect for the elders, faithfulness and righteous living, and urge believers to love and serve their fellow human beings – be they Christians or not. The Chinese hymnody – Protestant and Catholic alike – reveals this amalgamation of Christian and Confucian ethics. A few examples may suffice to illustrate this point:

Firstly, in the CCC hymnal – *The New Hymnal / Zànměisī Xīnbiàn* (1999) – # 148, *Golden Breaks the Dawn*, verse 2:[38]

Holy Father God, Keep me safe today.
Help me as I plod; Make me kind, I pray.
Let me guide our youth, Honour weak and old.
Let me serve with truth, And God's love unfold.

Other examples are the patriotic hymns. Although there might be various opinions about what it means to be a *àiguó* ("love one's country") person – or a patriotic person, depending who has the right to define "patriotism" –, one finds several hymns or Christian songs, for example in the CCC hymnal – *The New Hymnal / Zànměisī Xīnbiàn* (1999) – and the Songs of Canaan, which praise such patriotic persons and identify further some of the things that make a person appear as loving his or her country. Examples of this kind of hymns are many.[39]

---

[37] # 82 and # 85 in *Jiānán Shīxuǎn 1-2* (2001).

[38] Text by Chao Tzu-chen (1933); translation by Frank W. Price (1953).

[39] CCC hymnal # 351-369 – especially # 350 *Honour God, Serve People*, and # 368 *Help us to do Good* – and the following Canaan Songs by Ms Lǔ Xiǎo Mǐn: Zhōngguóxīn ("Chinese Heart", © 1993), Zhōngguórén yāo qílái ("The

One example in the CCC hymnal – is # 178, *Creator's Artistic Brush*, verse 3:[40]

We strive to build a new world Of justice, love and peace;
To raise the cross in witness, Christ's truth widely to spread.
Everyone with our people Self-reliance we seek;
Until the day when work's done, New heav'n and earth we see.

Finally, two special hymns which are found in the CCC hymnal, are worth mentioning. Both relate biblical stories of persons as models of faith and right life. These are # 330 (*Sage and Virtuous Women of Old*) which presents Ruth, Esther, Mary of Bethany, and Dorca, and # 331 (*Learning from the Saints*) which presents Abraham, Moses, David, Peter and Paul – all biblical persons – female and male, respectively –, as models of faith.

Reflecting the Chinese Experience

For the Protestant churches in the PRC it has been of great importance to follow the "three self principles", that is, self governance, self reliance, self propagation – an expression of which is the hymn *The Church Realizing Three-self's* in the CCC hymnal – *The New Hymnal / Zànměisī Xīnbiàn* 1999 – where the three-self principles are spelled out and further interpreted:[41]

Church of China self govern'd now, Pure and glorius without blemish;
Must in all things follow God's will; Temple of our Lord like a strong rock.

Church of China self reliant now, Following glorious saints' examples,
Dedicating all for His use, His abundant grace transcends all thought.

Chuch of China strives for selfhood, For a gospel pure and whole,
For a spirit witnessing His Words, For a great love cov'ring the earth.

The Church is set guided by Him, Peacefully living under His laws;
All join'd as one body in Christ, Praise to the Father, Son, Holy Spirit.

In fact, the 'three-self-principles', originally introduced by Rufus Anderson and Henry Venn, and later adopted by the CCC, have been supplemented by a fourth – that of being indigenous. Not only in the CCC hymnal but also among the Songs of Canaan do we find these principles expressed in such songs as

---

Chinese Shall Arise", © 1994), and Zhōngguórén ("Chinese", © 1997). *Jiānán Shīxuǎn 1-2* (2001), Nos 82, 76 and 41, respectively.

40 Text by Chen Ze-min (1982); translation by Ng Wenh-in (1994); see further Nos 175-177.

41 *The New Hymnal / Zànměisī Xīnbiàn* 1999, # 124. (Text: Hu Xue-han 1992; translation by Ivy Balchin 1996; melody by Zeng Qing-liu 1982).

Zhōngguórén ("*The Chinese*"), *Zhōngguórén yào qǐlái* ("*The Chinese Shall Arise*") *Zhōngguóxīn* ("*Chinese Heart*").[42]

Striking Balance between the Fellowship of Christians and the Individual Christian

As mentioned above, many hymns and short songs use the 'I'-form, thus stressing the importance of the individual. However, when Chinese Christians sing these hymns and songs they do not only sing them when alone, but even more so when gathered as a community. Examples may be found in all the hymnals, for instance in the hymns *"I Love Christ's Church"* and *"Churches of Christ, Unite"* – both in *The New Hymnal / Zànměisī Xīnbiàn* (1999), # 125 and # 126. Hence the faith community in this 'I' recognizes the collective faith experience of all the believers who join in.[43] The individual 'I' is thereby transcended.

Conclusion

The evidence about Chinese hymnody shows that it contains truly contextual features as well as transcultural ones. Both its history and present day characteristics reveal this. Whereas that part of hymnody which was translated into Chinese in the 19th and early 20th centuries mainly reveals its crosscultural and transcultural features, the hymns written and composed by Chinese in the 20th Century witness its truly contextual or indigenous character. 19th and early 20th Chinese hymnody was mainly the result of translation, but the 20th Century was characterized by indigenous Chinese hymn writing and composing. This study has also shown that, beginning with the latter part of the 20th Century, the hymnody of Chinese Christian churches is increasingly being shared with other churches through translation into English and other non-Chinese languages. Thus the Chinese hymns have not only become an ecumenical contribution to the universal church, in that churches elsewhere through these hymns get to know the faith, values and experience of Chinese Christians. Many of them also have transcultural features, in that churches elsewhere in them recognize and acknowledge essential elements of a universally shared Christian faith.

---

[42] *Jiānán Shīxuǎn 1-2* (2001), Nos 41, 75, and 82, respectively; cf. also Nos 16 and 45.

[43] "*Though I Cannot See*", and "*Who is my Shepherd*", Ibid., # 55 and # 69.

PART TWO

COMMUNICATING THE GOSPEL IN THE 21ST CENTURY

(1) Communication and Contextualisation

Intercultural Communication in Mission: A Tool or a Goal? Missionary Methodology in View of Developments in Intercultural Communication

Øyvind Økland

Asst Prof Øyvind Økland, Gimlekollen School of Journalism and Communication, Kristiansand, Norway

Missiology, the communication sciences and the social sciences have had a close relationship. Mission strategy, as part of missiology,[1] has been pre-occupied with communication of the Christian message, throughout history and across cultures, using variations of strategies. The social sciences have been used in missionary strategizing, in order to be able to communicate effectively.

Most commonly, I will argue, the use of communication science and the social sciences are seen as a tool for an improved communication of a message from a sender, the missionary, to the receiver, the non-Christian, in the most effective way. If the receivers understands the message, and makes it a part of their own belief, the communication has been successful.

Moreover, missiologists have viewed cultures as closed, or homogeneous entities, and where a communication is intercultural when one communicates from one culture to another. In an age of globalization, anthropology has realized that borders between cultures are not fixed. Recent globalization literature has pointed out that cultures constantly are influenced by each others and must be understood as being interdependent,[2] and this should also be a part of a missiological understanding of cultures.

It has been a common way in the communication science to distinguish between two main directions or schools, namely the *process school* and the *semiotic school*. The process school regards the communication as a linear process, where the communication is successful if the message is received according to the sender's intention.[3] The semiotic school focuses on the

---

[1] Jan Martin Berentsen, Tormod Engelsviken and Knud Jørgensen (eds), *Missiologi i dag* (Oslo: Universitetsforlaget, 1994), 16-17.

[2] See e.g. Ulf Hannerz, *Cultural Complexity: Studies in the social organization of meaning* (New York: Columbia University Press, 1992).

[3] See e.g. Harold D. Lasswell, 'The structure and function of communication in society', Lyman Bryson (ed), *The communication of ideas* (New York: Harper and Brother, 1948).

negotiation of meaning between the sender and the receiver, and how the context may play an important part in the interpretation of the message.[4]

In the following, I will discuss some issues in relation to this and argue that there might be ways missiology could be challenged according to developments in the intercultural communication theory, and incorporate recent perspectives from the semiotic school within intercultural communication. This chapter will give some examples from central theorists, both within intercultural communication and missiology. A central concept will be that of *intercultural effectiveness*, as well as discussion of the understanding of *culture*. At the end, I will bring forward some suggestions for possible implications for missiology.

Recent Developments in Intercultural Communication

The field of intercultural communication may, according to the Danish researcher Iben Jensen,[5] be divided into four different traditions: the literature that deals with the *how to do it*, *intercultural competency learning and training*, *functionalistic communication research* and *critical hermeneutical research.* The *how to do it* literature is very practically oriented, and deals with practical advice of what is polite or impolite in another culture, who you should give gifts to, what is proper non-verbal communication and so on. It is about etiquette and is usually directed toward business men. A book like *Do's and taboos around the world*[6] is a typical example. The *intercultural competence learning and training* tradition is very similar to the *how to do it* literature. It is however, more theoretical in the way that is trying to find some criteria for effective communication between one culture and another.

The *functionalistic communication research* is by far the most common and used part of the literature, and consists of the, mostly American, functionalistic research in intercultural communication. Functionalistic in this respect implies the emphasis of the application to the real life situations.[7] Hall and Hofstede are both pioneers in the field of intercultural communication and representatives of this school. Hall is by many regarded as *the* father of intercultural communication. He discovered a need for creating a more practical training that could give the officials some instructions of how to behave in

---

[4] See e.g. Ingunn Hagen, *Medias publikum: Frå mottakar til brukar?* (Oslo: Gyldendal, 2000), 157.

[5] Iben Jensen, *Interkulturell kommunikation i komplekse samfund* (Roskilde: Roskildes Universitetsforlag, 1998), 32.

[6] Roger Axtell, *Do's and taboos around the world* (New York: Elmsford, 1985).

[7] Judith N. Martin and Thomas K. Nakayama, 'Thinking dialectically about culture and communication', *Communication theory* Feb 1999, 3.

foreign cultures.[8] Halls book, *Silent Language*,[9] focused on nonverbal communication in particular, and has become a classic. Typical for him, and several others, are the definition of culture as a limited system, and in reality consisting of national cultures.[10] The same is seen in another well-know theorist within intercultural communication, namely Geert Hofstede. He did a huge research of the many national branches of the multinational company IBM, and labeled a number of differences between the different cultures. The different nations then scored high or low on these criteria. According to his understanding, culture was a mental program that very much corresponded to national cultures.[11]

Common to these, and others, was the belief that culture, whether it was learned or mentally programmed into people's minds, were different from each others, and in order to communicate across these borders on had to overcome such hinders, and avoid the uncertainty that existed when confronted with strangers. It was however, possible to learn about other cultures, about their language, non-verbal communication, beliefs and so on, and by that be able to minimize the difficulties in communication, and even predict some of the outcomes of the communication.

The three different directions mentioned so far all belong within the process school orientation. Within intercultural communication they still are dominant, especially in the American tradition.

A shift in the direction of the critical hermeneutic tradition, or the semiotic school, was seen by the introduction of Fred Jandt's reader.[12] Here he defined culture in a way that focused on how the participants' themselves defined which culture they belonged to, regardless of their citizenship or skin colour. In this tradition Clifford Geertz' definition of culture is used as an analytical concept, where culture is seen as a web that we spin around ourselves,[13] and thus it is the relations between human beings that are important. Communication is seen in a dialogical perspective where both parts in the communication process relate to the other and interpret each other's messages. An example of such a model is Yoshikawa's communication model. It is called the "double swing model" because it goes back and forth constantly and both

---

[8] Dreama G. Moon, 'Concepts of "culture": Implications for intercultural communication research', *Communication quarterly* 44: 1996, 71.

[9] Edward Hall, *The silent language* (New York: Doubleday, 1959).

[10] Edward Hall, *Beyond culture* (New York: Anchor, 1976), 86.

[11] Geert Hofstede, *Culture's consequences: International differences in work-related value* (London: Sage, 1980).

[12] Fred Jandt, *Intercultural communication: An introduction* (London: Sage, 1995).

[13] Clifford Geertz, *The interpretation of cultures: Selected essays* (New York: Basic books, 1973).

parties are changed by the meeting.[14]

Within the Scandinavian tradition, the semiotic perspective has recently become more focused than before. One of the first popular text books in Norwegian, by Dahl and Habert,[15] was clearly within the functionalist orientation. The next book by Dahl[16] has a slightly changed definition of intercultural communication that clearly was more in a semiotic tradition.

Another more recent book, edited by Øyvind Dahl, Iben Jensen and Peter Nynäs, had several articles devoted to hermeneutical models of intercultural communication. Dahl, in his chapter, lists seven different approaches to intercultural communication; the process approach, the functionalist approach, the semiotic approach, the constructivist and social constructionist approach, the poststructuralist approach, the practice theory and the hermeneutic approach.[17] The first two are examples of a traditional understanding of the process school tradition, while the next five represent the semiotic model.

Nynäs showed how important the interpretation process is in intercultural communication. It is crucial how we explain and talk about episodes when for example there is a breakdown in communication. In his article, Nynäs defined intercultural communication as a process where one seeks to achieve a mutual understanding across cultural boundaries.[18]

Iben Jensen has presented a very constructive suggestion of how to explain intercultural meetings according to this new understanding, by using four analytical tools.[19] The first one she called "positions of experience". With this one she meant that all individuals that enter a communication situation will also bring into it their own individual and cultural background, and we have to learn and respect that the other actors also bring their own "positions of experience"

---

[14] Muneo Yoshikawa, 'The double-swing model of intercultural communication between East and the West', Lawrence Kincaid (ed), *Communication theory: Eastern and Western perspectives* (London: Academic Press, 1987).

[15] Øyvind Dahl and Kjell Habert, *Møte mellom kulturer: Tverrkulturell kommunikasjon* (Oslo: Universitetsforlaget, 1986).

[16] Øyvind Dahl, *Møter mellom mennesker: Interkulturell kommunikasjon* (Oslo: Gyldendal, 2001), 65.

[17] Øyvind Dahl, 'Bridges of understanding', Øyvind Dahl (ed), *Bridges of understanding: Perspectives on intercultural communication* (Oslo: Unipub Oslo Academic Press), 8-17.

[18] Peter Nynäs, 'Interpretative models of estrangement and identification', Øyvind Dahl, Iben Jensen and Peter Nynäs (eds), *Bridges of Understanding: Perspectives on intercultural communication* (Oslo: Unipub Oslo Academic Press, 2006).

[19] Iben Jensen, The practice of intercultural: Reflections for professionals in cultural meetings, *The electronic journal of intercultural communication* (Published by Nordic Network of Intercultural communication, NIC) www.immi.se/intercultural/ nr 6.

with them. The second analytical tool is the "cultural presuppositions". Our communication will be colored by the way we view the other actor. The way we will interpret what is going and act will be determined by these presuppositions. The third tool is the "cultural self-perception" which means the way one identifies oneself with certain communities or not. The fourth tool, "cultural fix points", is the focal point for the intercultural meeting, the discussion topic or reason to meet.

These four tools may be used to interpret intercultural communication situations in a way that gives credit to all good knowledge and techniques we might have about the other actor, and still it is not possible to predict the outcome of the meeting, but the outcome is dependent on each particular situation and the participants in it.

As a result of the change in the understanding of culture, due to people's extensive travelling, migration and globalization, we may rather speak about communication in intercultural societies, than intercultural communication, as suggested by Jensen.[20] Haus has a similar viewpoint when he states that in fact we should not talk about intercultural communication in a traditional way any longer. In this understanding, *intercultural co-operation* or *intercultural interaction* is more appropriate terms than *intercultural communication.*[21]

After having looked at some basic developments and positions within intercultural communication, the next step will be to look at developments in missiology. The following will therefore, give some basic developments in the last part the twentieth century.

Recent Developments of Missiology

There are many similar trends between intercultural communication and missiology. One of these is the emphasis on the practical view of communication, as can be seen from the development of what was called missionary anthropology after the Second World War. Similar to intercultural communication, it tried to apply knowledge from the social sciences, such as anthropology. Both fields were pre-occupied with a way of finding a practical and effective way of communicating messages from one culture to another. In missionary anthropology it is more narrowly defined as the Christian message, the gospel.

Missionary anthropology did not primarily, as Conn notes, rise out of cultural anthropology, but out of applied anthropology which developed in

---

20 Jensen, *Interkulturell kommunikation*, 230.

21 Sigurd Haus, 'Knekk koden, forstå og bli forstått! Om fagfeltet interkulturell kommunikasjon og forholdet til kommunikasjonsteoretiske perspektiver', Sigurd Haus, Geir Skeie and Øystein Lund Johannesen, *Kulturformidling fra internasjonale arenaer: Et bidrag til meningsutveksling om kultur* (Kristiansand: Høyskoleforlaget,2003), 67.

North America from the 1930s.[22] The magazine which carried its viewpoints was named *Practical Anthropology*, until in 1973 it became a part of *Missiology*.

Applied linguistics and missionary anthropology have had strong relations, and people like Kenneth L. Pike and Eugene Nida have had a central position. Kenneth L. Pike developed his linguistic principles into a comprehensive theory of language and behaviour, and tried to build a bridge between linguistics and other disciplines, called *tagmemics.*[23] In this theory, he tried to transfer the principles of how languages functioned, to a theory that should explain all human behaviour.

Nida's book on anthropology for missionaries, *Customs and Cultures*,[24] became a foundation for later missiological literature on cultures. Later he published *Message and Mission*,[25] where the communication model in missionary communication is explained and used. Studies in symbolics, psychology, social structuring of experience and theology formed a background for the construction of this model. His thinking has been very influential in missiology the last decades. He introduced the *dynamic equivalence* principle in Bible translation, meaning that the goal of the translation is to transfer the original meaning of the biblical text to the new text. Charles H. Kraft built on Nida's dynamic equivalence model, and claimed that it is the meaning, and not the form that should be translated, and it is possible to distinguish these two from each other. The local church should have its own forms, but they should be able to express the same meaning as these forms had for the first church.[26]

This model gives much freedom in accepting local customs and filling them with Christian meaning.[27] It is clear from Kraft's writings that he viewed culture as a closed entity, and very similar to Hall and Hofstede's view that culture consists of national cultures which again have subcultures. In his book *Anthropology for Christians witness* he devoted several pages to a critique of

---

[22] Harvie Conn, *Eternal word and changing worlds: Theology, anthropology, and mission in trialogue* (Grand Rapids, Michigan: Zondervan, 1984).

[23] Kenneth L. Pike, *Language in relation to a unified theory of the structure of human behaviour*, 2nd ed. (The Hague: Mouton, 1967).

[24] Eugene A. Nida, *Customs and cultures: Anthropology for missions* (New York: Harper and Row, 1954).

[25] Eugene A. Nida, *Message and mission* (New York: Harper & Brothers Publishers, 1960).

[26] Charles H. Kraft, 'Dynamic equivalence churches: an ethnotheological approach to indigeneity', Charles H. Kraft and Tom N. Wisley (eds), *Readings in dynamic indigeneity* (Pasadena: William Carey Library, 1979), 87-111.

[27] Charles R.Taber, *The world is too much with us: "Culture" in modern Protestant missions* (Macon: Mercer, 1991), 145.

the American culture.[28] His indebtedness to a traditional communication model is very clear:

> The principles of effective cross-cultural communication make a third facet of our basic approach. What has come to be called the S-M-R model will help us here. If communication is to be effective, it is important that the communicator (or source, S) present the message (M) to receptors (R) in such a way that the latter will understand and do something about what they receive.[29]

The same accounts for David J. Hesselgrave. He was one of the pioneers in the application of communication theories to missiology.[30] He used Nida's three culture model as a starting point for his theories; the biblical culture, the missionary culture and the respondent culture. The missionary is in the middle, and looks in both directions. He is a messenger for the Scriptures, and never a primary source.[31]

When it comes to emphasizing the need for social sciences in mission, Donald McGavran was a pioneer. His church growth philosophy stressed the need for thorough knowledge of the social stratification of the social network. Without his knowledge, the effectiveness in communication will be minimal.[32] The social sciences are very important to improve this effectiveness. The goal of this communication is church growth, which includes more members in the Church, more members in existing churches and the planting of new ones.[33] McGavran reacted against traditional mission strategies and advocated the *homogeneous unit principle*, which states that people want to become Christians without crossing linguistic or cultural barriers. The homogenous unit principle creates the foundation for an extensive use of the social sciences, sociology and social anthropology, in order to make use of "the bridges of God" in communication.[34]

McGavran and others, like Byang Kato,[35] held the view that there is a gospel

---

[28] Charles H. Kraft, *Anthropology for Christian witness* (Maryknoll: Orbis books, 1996), 81-85.

[29] Kraft, *Anthropology for Christian witness,* 443.

[30] David J. Hesselgrave, *Communication Christ cross-culturally* (Grand Rapids: Zondervan Publishing House, 1978).

[31] David J. Hesselgrave, 'The role of culture in communication', Ralph D. Winter and Stephen Hawthorne, *Perspectives on the world Christian movement: A Reader* (Pasadena: William Carey Library, 1992), C34-C45.

[32] Peter C. Wagner, *Church growth and the whole gospel: A biblical mandate* (San Francisco: Harper and Row, 1981), 12.

[33] David McGavran, *Understanding church growth* (Pasadena: William Carey Library; 1980), 41.

[34] McGavran, *Understanding church growth,* 127.

[35] Byang Kato, 'Evangelism opportunities and obstacles in Africa', J. D. Douglas (ed), *Let the earth hear his voice: International congress on world*

core, and identifiable kernel, that one is to communicate in mission, and that this core therefore is possible to communicate from one culture to another.[36]

Paul G. Hiebert, likewise, has been a central figure within the field of using anthropology in building theories for mission and as tools for effective missionary work.[37] But he distanced himself from church growth school, and also criticized those belonging to this school because "success is measured largely in quantitative terms – in terms of numbers of professed converts. How does this fit with the biblical emphases on faithfulness, hardship, suffering and persecution"? He also criticized their view of people, which "fits tribal peoples best", while "individuals participate in many different groups and cultural frames[38] and do not fully identify with any of them".[39]

Several of these missiologists reveal an antagonistic attitude towards culture, regarding it as a rather closed entity that has good elements in it, but also many elements that need to be fought and overcome. Titles like *Christianity Confronts Culture*[40] and *The Clash between Christianity and Cultures*[41] illustrate this. Kraft however, seemed to take a more positive view of culture, seeing Christianity as an integrated part of the whole, as the title *Christianity in Culture* indicates.[42]

An important question in mission at all times has been how to relate to local cultures, and mission history has given different answers to this at different times. Recently, missiology has debated this with the label *contextualization.*

---

evangelisation. Lausanne, Switzerland. Official Reference Volume: Papers and responses (Minneapolis: World Wide, 1975), 155-158.

[36] T. Yamamori and C. Taber, *Christopaganism or indigenous Christianity* (Pasadena: William Carey Library, 1975); Tippet, Alan R., 'Christopaganism or indigenous Christianity', Charles H. Kraft and Tom N. Wisley (eds), *Readings in dynamic indigeneity* (Pasadena: William Carey Library, 1979); David J. Hesselgrave and Edward Rommen, *Contextualization: Meaning, methods, and models* (Leicester: Apollos, 1989), 172.

[37] Paul G. Hiebert, *Anthropological insights for missionaries* (Grand Rapids, MI: Baker Book House, 1985), 21.

[38] Geertz, *The interpretation of cultures*; Mayers, Marvin K., *Christianity confronts culture: A strategy for cross-cultural evangelism* (Grand Rapids, Michigan: Academic Books, 1987).

[39] Hiebert, *Anthropological insights*, 193-194.

[40] Marvin K. Mayers, *Christianity confronts culture: A strategy for cross-cultural evangelism* (Grand Rapids, Michigan: Academic Books, 1987).

[41] Donald A. McGavran, *The clash between Christianity and cultures* (Washington: Canon Press, 1974).

[42] Charles H. Kraft, *Christianity in culture: A study in dynamic theologizing in cross-cultural perspective* (Maryknoll, New York: Orbis books, 1979).

There are several models of contextualization theologies,[43] and they have different approaches. According to Bevans; Kraft, McGavran and Kato are placed in a translation model, while liberation theologians such as Segundo and Gutierrez are linked to what Bevans called a praxis-model. A semiotic model was developed by the catholic Robert Schreiter, expressing the need for the culture itself to discover God's revelation. Christ is in values, symbols and behaviour patters within the culture itself.

As an evangelical response, Bruce Fleming advocated a need for a contextual indigenization, building on the traditional understanding of indigenization, but seeking deeper, using insights from anthropology, but in a way that these insights are always judged according to the Scriptures.[44]

A natural consequence of the strong belief in the possibility of communicating effectively from a sender to a receiver is the extensive use of media in mission, and much missiological literature has dealt with different models of the use of media. Very often, as tele-evangelism might be an example of, the belief in technology has prevented many from seeing the importance of local and face-to-face communication, and the importance of the local churches has been ignored in many cases.[45]

As the above has attempted to show, mainstream thinking within missiology is very much parallel to and part of the *functionalist* tradition described within intercultural communication. The theories and the research are made for a specific purpose, to reach a goal and to predict possible outcomes. A distinction has to be made here, though. So far theories and theoreticians that we have dealt with here, for the most part belong to what we may label as the evangelical movement within Christianity. The ecumenical movement's missiology have taken different forms, mainly due to a fundamental theological difference. Very simplified, it might be said that ecumenicals have a more dialogical understanding of mission, more similar to Yoshikawa's model, where change of the participants' viewpoints is a goal in itself in the process.[46] As ecumenicals do not see mission so much as a communication of a fixed message from a sender to a receiver, intercultural communication has not been

---

43 Stephen Bevans, 'Models of contextual theology', *Missiology* 13: 1985, 185-202.

44 Bruce C. Fleming, *Contextualization of theology: An evangelical assessment* (Pasadena: William Carey Library, 1980), 53.

45 cf. Knud Jørgensen, *The role and funtion of the media in the mission of the Church* (with particular reference to Africa). A doctoral dissertation (Pasadena: Fuller Theological Seminary, 1986).

46 World Council of Churches, 'Living in dialogue: A Church for others', *Study Encounter* (Geneva: World Council of Churches, 1967), 46; Wesley Ariarajah, *The Bible and other faiths* (Geneva: World Council of Churches, 1985), 68.

an issue to the same extent.[47] Mission takes place on all continents,[48] it is God's mission to the world, and the world takes part in shaping the message, as it is dialogical.[49]

As mission in the evangelical tradition is understood deductively, using Scriptures as a starting point and from there defining the content of the message, the ecumenical movement's understanding of mission is inductively understood, as the Bible and the context, the human experience, play together in shaping the understanding of the content of mission.[50]

Based on this brief presentation of some developments within intercultural communication and missiology, we will in the following discuss some of the implications for this on the view of intercultural communication in mission.

Questioning the Traditional Communication Model

A central focus within intercultural communication, as well as modern missiology, has been how to communicate effectively, based on the traditional communication model, and effectiveness here very often seems to be understood numerically, as how many new Christians have been added to the

[47] Øyvind Økland, *Proklamasjon, dialog eller kommunikasjon: En sammenligning av misjonsteologi og synet på misjonsmetoder i Kirkenes Verdensråd og blant de konservativ-evangeliske i perioden 1961-1980, med særlig vekt på holdninger til ikke-vestlige kulturer og religioner.* M.A. thesis in religious education (Bergen: Universitetet i Bergen, 1986), 96.

[48] R. K. Orchard (ed), *Witness in six continents: Records of the meeting of the Commission on World Mission and Evangelism of the World Council of Churches held in Mexico City 8-19 December 1963* (London: Edinburgh house, 1964).

[49] World Council of Churches, 'On Intercultural Hermeneutics', James A. Scherer and Stephen B. Bevans (eds), *New directions in missions and evangelization 3* (New York: Orbis books, 1999).

[50] World Council of Churches, *The Church for others and the Church for the world: A quest for missionary structures for missionary congregations. Final report of the western European working group and the north American working group of the department on studies in evangelism* (Geneva: World Council of Churches, 1968), 24; Samartha, Stanley J. (ed), *Faith in the midst of faith:. Reflections on dialogue in community* (Geneva: World Council of Churches, 1977), 146; Ellen Flesseman-van Leer (ed), *The Bible: Its authority in ecumenical movement. Faith and Order paper, no. 99* (Geneva: World Council of Churches, 1980), 464; J. D. Gort, 'Human distress, salvation, and mediation of salvation', F. J. Verstraelen (ed) *Missiology: An ecumenical introduction. Texts and contexts of global Christianity* (Grand Rapids: Eerdmans, 1995), 196; James A. Scherer, *A Lutheran perspective on mission and evangelism.* LWF report 10/11 (Geneva: LWF, 1982).

Church.

Kealey, in his study of the Canadian International Development Agency (CIDA) workers, uses the term effectiveness as an indicator of success. Effectiveness is here defined as "the ability to live and work effectively in the cross-cultural setting of an overseas assignment. The definition acknowledges a relationship between an individual's personal adjustment and satisfaction overseas with the person's performance in a cross-cultural setting".[51]

Intercultural communication in Kealey's study is seen as a tool to achieve the goals of culture A, here the Canadian culture. Culture B is the receptor culture, the culture in which culture A transfers its technical skills. According to Dodd's definition of intercultural communication,[52] culture C is where there is a common understanding of the technical skills. Culture C in missionary communication must therefore be understood as the place where the missionary and the receiver/new believer agrees about its content.[53] Recent literature in the field of intercultural communication affirms the fact that there is no exact agreement to what intercultural effectiveness is, let alone how to conceptualize the term and use it consistently in research.[54]

Transferred to missionary communication, the viewpoint of what is an effective missionary seems to be very similar. The use of anthropology as a science has been used as "a power tool to move and change others, to bring about specific desired results",[55] and regarded as "an aid to effective communication".[56] McGavran realized that effectiveness is not only a matter of mechanical effectiveness, as Satan is also at work,[57] but basically he is measuring effectiveness according to the fact that people are in actual fact accepting the message.[58]

In Hiebert's terms culture C is named the bicultural community, and contact between culture A and B, is called the bicultural bridge. "The success of mission work to a large extent depends upon the quality of this bicultural

---

[51] Daniel J. Kealey, *Cross-cultural effectiveness: A study of Canadian technical advisors overseas* (Hull, Quebec, Canada: Canadian International Development Agency, 1990), 5.

[52] Dodd, *Dynamics of intercultural communication*, 4.

[53] Hiebert, *Anthropological insights,* 163.

[54] Geng Gui and Sjef Van der Berg, 'Testing the construct validity of intercultural effectiveness', in *International journal of intercultural relations* 15: 1991, 227-241.

[55] Taber, *The world is too much with us,* 134.

[56] Lyman E. Reed, *Preparing missionaries for intercultural communication: A bi-cultural approach* (Pasadena: William Carey Library, 1985).

[57] Donald McGavran and Arthur F. Glasser, *Contemporary theologies of mission* (Grand Rapids: Baker Book House, 1983), p, 131.

[58] McGavran and Arthur F. Glasser, *Contemporary theologies*, 149.

bridge".[59]

Success and effectiveness are, however, often very difficult to measure. As missionary communication deal with spiritual matters, and is dependant on the Holy Spirit, a scientific measurement of the effectiveness is questionable, as several authors are well aware of.[60] The very essence of the traditional communication model however, tempts us to become too pre-occupied with the measuring of effectiveness in a Western understanding of the word.

If there needs to be a shift in focus from a traditional communication model and its understanding of effectiveness, what would then be the alternative? Some writers within intercultural communication might give helpful insights on the way to a revised understanding of what a healthy and biblically based communication might entail. One example might be the model presented by Iben Jensen. In this model it is possible to label the most important components in an intercultural meeting, and be able to prepare, through learning about the other, and by understanding more of what is going on. It is, however, never possible to predict the outcome of the communication process, based on what one has put into it. One should rather enter with an open mind, willing to also learn from the other, and being conscious of the interpretation that continually goes on from both parties. Instead of thinking in the form of a linear communication model, therefore, a hermeneutic model gives more sense and better explains the processes that are involved.

A Renewed Understanding of Culture

The way culture is defined by Dodd[61] and many missiologists[62] reveal an understanding of culture within functionalistic intercultural communication and missiology that is very similar. Both fields see culture as holistic systems. In missionary communication the cultural element in inter-personal relationships therefore seems to have too much weight, as it explains communication failures, misunderstandings, differences etc. in cultural terms where it otherwise might have been explained in psychological terms, sociological terms and so on. As Collier and Thomas suggest, a critique of a more fixed understanding of culture and intercultural communication might well be

---

[59] Hiebert, *Anthropological insights,* 228-229.

[60] Hiebert, *Anthropological insights,* 18; Steve Grunlan and Marvyn K. Mayers. *Cultural anthropology: A Christian Perspective* (Grand Rapids: Zondervan, 1979), 21.

[61] Carley H. Dodd, *Dynamics of intercultural communication,* 5th ed. (New York: McGraw Hill, 1998).

[62] See e.g. Hiebert, *Anthropological insights*, 30.

justified.[63]

By seeing culture as more open-ended, and with fuzzy borders, it would be impossible to predict outcomes of a communication event, by putting cultural variables into it. Communication events might rather be seen as waves in the ocean, where they melt, and take another form as they move on.[64] This analogy allows at least two perspectives on the analysis of cultural meetings. There is one meeting on the individual level, and these individual communication events are at the same time parts of a greater and global picture; cultures constantly meet and shape each others.

A traditional view of cultures as closed entities should therefore be revised. Several globalization theorists have contributed to alternative conceptual frameworks. Hannerz[65] and Mathews[66] have, among others, provided useful conceptual frameworks for understanding cultures between local and global forces. Boundaries and identities are in fluid and in constant change, "cultural identity becomes, instead, a hybrid, relational affair, something that lives between as much as within cultures".[67] Finally, there is a need to sum up and look at some of the implications for missiology.

Some Final Reflections

As missionary communication theories have drawn upon other sciences, they should continue to do so in the future. Having described two main traditions within intercultural communication, the functionalist and the critical hermeneutic tradition, which one should be preferred? There should be no doubt that in the past missionary communication theory to a large extent has been in the functionalist tradition. The very fact that missionary anthropology came out of applied anthropology and applied linguistics, proves the application orientation, the use of anthropology and other sciences as a tool to meet other ends. And the paradigm in which missionaries have been working, has been how to use these sciences to communicate the gospel most effectively, a purely application oriented definition, and a very closed and static view of culture.

This is not to say, however, that this paradigm is useless and should be

---

63 Mary Jane Collier and Milt Tomas, 'Cultural Identity. An Interpretive Perspective', in Young Yun Kim and William Gudykunst: *Theories in intercultural communication* (New Dehli: Sage Publications, 1996).

64 Jensen, *Interkulturell kommunikation*, 18.

65 Ulf Hannerz, *Cultural Complexity: Studies in the social organization of meaning* (New York: Columbia University Press, 1992)

66 Gordon Mathews, *Global culture/individual identity: Searching for home in the cultural supermarket* (London: Routledge, 2000)

67 Kathryn Tanner, *Theories of culture: A new agenda for theology* (Minneapolis, Minn.: Fortress Press, 1997), 57-58.

rejected altogether. This chapter's main objective has been to focus on the differences of the two and need of a more nuanced view of the communication process, where the usefulness of a functionalistic understanding of intercultural communication is included in a semiotic perspective.

In concluding, two suggestions for a shift of focus in missionary communication will be made. Firstly, the communication event and the individuals involved in it must become more important than an excessive focus on the effectiveness of the transfer of the message from the sender to the receiver, and thus participants in this message as objects, rather than neighbors.

This involves a broadened perspective of all that is involved in an intercultural or even interpersonal communication event, studying not only the effects of non-verbal language, lifestyle and other non-linguistic matters. Very often the focus implied in the traditional communication model, have been mostly on words and verbal communication, or even proclamation.

Hiebert points out the need of focusing on our common humanity rather than our "otherness", stating that "at the deepest level of our identity as humans, there are no others, there is only us".[68] Jesus pointed out as the greatest of all commandments, we should love God, but we should also love our neighbors as ourselves. That is the essence of our calling, and not merely regarding our fellow human beings as objects to be included in the church, since "in mission, our central task is not to communicate a message but to introduce people to that person, Jesus Christ".[69]

Secondly, this shift of focus would also mean a shift away from a culture-oriented definition of intercultural communication towards a view where the communication event is analyzed similar to Jensen's suggestion, on the basis of positions of experience, cultural presuppositions and the actors' self-perception.

In this way, cultural identity becomes extremely important, and in a global world it is not fixed to a particular place any more, but locality and globality both play a part in the identity-making. My own research on youth culture in Vennesla, Norway, showed that the importance of global impulses was very important, but basically where it was made relevant to their daily lives and needs. Therefore, no matter how important internet or the media in general are, they can never become more important than interpersonal communication.[70]

The whole idea about Christian mission is that there is a message, a gospel, to be communicated. It is however, important to be humble in the communication process, being fully aware that whatever one thinks about non-

---

[68] Hiebert, 'The social sciences and missions', 208.

[69] Paul G. Hiebert, *Missiological implications of epistemological shifts: Affirming truth in a modern/postmodern world* (Harrisburg, PA: Trinity press international, 1999), 116.

[70] Øyvind Økland, *Globalization, media, and youth culture: Young high school students in Vennesla, Norway, between the local and the global.* A doctoral dissertation (Deerfield, Ill.: Trinity International University, 2004).

negotiables of this message, it will still remain a human interpretation. Hiebert advocates a hermeneutic model for a new theology. In this model, the theologies from different cultures meet, and as they relate to the biblical revelation, they should develop a global theology.[71]

Whatever model one chooses, there is a need to focus on the meaning production in meetings between Christians and non-Christians, where the meeting has a value in itself, a place to share life and faith experiences and build a mutual understanding. God has called us to go into the world to preach the gospel, and he has also called us to love our neighbors as ourselves. As we bear this in mind, intercultural communication in mission should be a goal in itself, rather than a mechanic tool for a western focus on effectiveness.

---

[71] Hiebert, *Missiological implications,* 113.

Are We to Take a Religion or a Faith?

Charles H. Kraft

Prof Dr Charles H Kraft, School of Intercultural Studies, Fuller Theological Seminary, Pasadena, California

I am honored to be able to contribute this chapter to a book honoring my good friend and former student, Knud Jørgensen. Throughout his career he has been concerned both with how to communicate the Gospel and what it is that we are to communicate. I trust that this presentation will be helpful to others who are asking the above question.

One of the major areas of concern in the communication and contextualization of the Gospel of Jesus Christ is the matter of how Christianity should be compared with the religions of the world. When we talk of Christianity, are we talking about one religion among the many religions of the world? Or are we talking about something that by its very nature is of a different sort? That is, is biblical Christianity a religion or is it something else, something deeper? Or, better, was Christianity intended by God to be a religion in competition with the religions of the world? Or was it intended to be something else and, if so, what?

Given, whatever Christianity was intended to be, people have made a religion out of it. So, at one level, Christianity is a religion. This is necessary, since all human behavior will be expressed in cultural forms and religion is an organization of cultural forms. My question, however, is: Does God intend Christianity to be *simply* a set of cultural forms that we can call a religion or did He intend something more?

If ours is simply a religion, we can speak of *adaptation* when we take it to other peoples. We can see so-called "Christian" forms (i.e. the cultural forms used in the practice of Christianity in the home country) introduced into the cultures of the world with slight modifications to accommodate to the receiving culture. But we cannot speak of *contextualization.* For contextualization is the expression of Christian *meanings and commitment or allegiance* in truly traditional cultural forms that may remain the same or may be adapted but in which the major change will be in the meanings conveyed and the commitment/allegiance chosen rather than in the forms themselves.

We may picture a religion as a box that can be taken

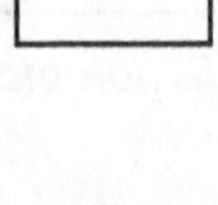

intact from one place to another and, though the corners may be rounded

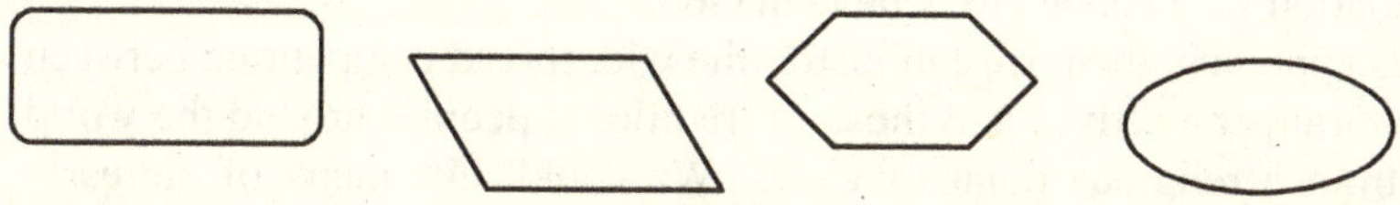

and perhaps other changes can be made to adapt it to the new setting, it is still easily recognizable as a structure that has come from another culture. A

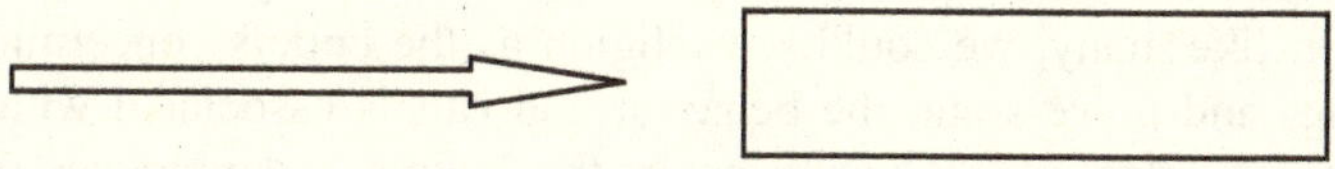

faith, on the other hand, is more like an arrow that is aimed at a particular society, is allowed to enter the culture and then pricks people at various points to elicit a response to God, not simply a response (i.e. acceptance or rejection) to a cultural structure (the religion box) that has its origin in another place, time or culture.

Jesus said He came to bring life (Jn 10:10). Does this mean He came to add one more religion to the list of the religions of the world? Or does it mean He was bringing something that differs from the religions and that, therefore, can be conveyed even through traditional cultural forms, including those cultural forms that are identified with the religion of the people who use them?

Religion Defined

If we are going to answer this question properly, we need to define what we mean by religion. For, not all mean the same thing when they use that term. Some would define religion as the collection of basic assumptions in terms of which a people live their lives (i.e. what I would call worldview) plus the rituals they use to express those assumptions. If that definition is accepted, the religion of most of the members of western societies (including a large number of those who call themselves Christians) would be something called "secular humanism" or, perhaps, "scientism." This is a non- or even anti-supernaturalistic perspective that exalts humans and human thinking above anything claimed to be a revelation from a supernatural being. Such a perspective, then, would function within western societies in a way very similar to the way supernaturalistic beliefs and practices serve within most non-western societies.

If we choose to go in this direction, we can speak of scientists as the priests of western religion and the various rituals of scientific and/or educational activity as the rituals of that religion. A university education, then, would be seen as a religious rite of passage for our youth. And the activities that most people would label religious activities would be seen as the concern of a subset of our population who happen to believe in God.

With this approach, then, we can justify the widespread competition between western cultural perspectives and those of traditional peoples around the world as proper from a religious point of view. We could, like many of the early western missionaries, choose as our motto, "Civilize (i.e. Westernize) in order to evangelize." We who have given our lives to the crosscultural communication of biblical Christianity could then dispense with the whole concept of contextualization and continue in the name of religion the conversion of the peoples of the world to western ways.

Or, like many, we could see religion as the beliefs concerning supernatural beings and powers and the behavior and rituals associated with those beliefs. This definition would nicely cover the beliefs and practices of most of the peoples of the world plus the minority of Westerners who take their relationship with God seriously. It would see religion as embodied in a culture, whether as the core of that culture or as something more peripheral, and as requiring the learning of some important aspects of the originating culture if one converts to it.

As Christians, then, we would see our beliefs and practices as basically *in competition with* the beliefs and practices of nonChristians and seek to convert them to the cultural forms of our religion on the assumption that these forms, our religion, are the best of the competing religious options available. This is, in fact, what has ordinarily been aimed at by Christian witnesses down through history. Christianity has been identifiable by the cultural forms in which it has been encapsulated and it is those forms that are carried from society to society as the religion spreads. Taking the Christian religion to the peoples of other societies, then, involves the taking of our religious forms and adapting them to the culture of the receiving peoples.

A third approach is, however, the one that is basic to any consideration of contextualization. This approach is the one recommended by the Apostle Paul in Acts 15 as not requiring that Gentiles be converted to Jewish customs in order to follow Jesus. Paul had learned this approach by watching God give the Holy Spirit to Gentile converts on the basis of their faith alone, in spite of the fact that they had made no attempt to convert to Jewish culture. Though the early Christians set out to win people on the basis of approach number two above, the Holy Spirit broke their rule and endorsed Gentile cultures as adequate vehicles for Gentile interaction with God. The culture in which Jesus met His followers was not to be the cultural norm for the expression of Christianity.

The focus, then, was to be on the relationship between the converts and God rather than on the cultural forms in terms of which that relationship is expressed. *It became clear to those who agreed with Paul that what God wants is not a certain set of cultural forms but a faith response that can be expressed in a multiplicity of cultural forms.* The battle for the Christians of the early centuries of our faith, then, was to be over whether one worshipped Caesar, calling him Lord (a faith matter), or whether one worshipped Jesus as Lord – not over whether one practiced the religious forms followed by the Jewish Christians.

But down through the centuries, those who have come to Christ have tended to "domesticate" their Christianity. Just as the early Jewish Christians who disagreed with Paul required Gentiles to accept Christ in a Jewish cultural package, so Romans and Germans and Americans have pressured those who convert to Christ to also convert to the culture of those who bring the message. Thus, our faith has come to be known as primarily a cultural thing, a religion wrapped in the cultural forms of the group in power. And from about the fourth century on it has been seen largely as a European cultural thing – captured by our European ancestors and domesticated in cultures very different from that in which the faith was originally planted. Converts to Christianity, then, are seen as those who have abandoned their own cultural religion and chosen to adopt the religious forms and, usually, many of the other forms of European culture. Often such converts are regarded as traitors to their own people and their ways.

If ours is simply a "form religion," as approach number two above assumes, it can be *adapted but not contextualized*, it can be *in competition with other forms of religion* but not flow through those forms because by definition it seeks to replace those forms. But biblical Christianity is not simply a set of cultural forms. Cultural Christianity, however, is. And we get tangled up in our discussions because it is often not clear whether we are speaking of essential, biblical Christianity or of the traditional religion of western societies that is also called Christianity. In one of my books (*Christianity in Culture* 1979, revised ed. 2005) I have attempted to make this distinction by spelling biblical Christianity with a capital C and cultural christianity with a small c.

I would define religion, then, as a cultural thing, a surface-level expression of deep-level (worldview) understandings of the beings or structures or ideas we deem worthy of worship and the rituals and beliefs developed to worship them. At the deep, worldview level, most of the peoples of the world assume the existence and activity of a large number of invisible spiritual beings and powers. Their responses to these beings and powers, then, are what their religion is all about. And much of their cultural life is spent in dealing with this area. So we would say that they are a very religious people. In other societies (e.g. the West), many claim to not believe in supernatural beings or in other things considered religious. In their cultural lives, then, there is very little if any activity ordinarily labeled "religious," though their activities in other areas (e.g. science, sports, career) might rival in function if not in form the dedication of the most ardent religionists.

I would, then, call religion a form thing, the expression through cultural forms of deep-level (worldview) assumptions and meanings. Religious forms are culture-specific and, if the religion has been borrowed from another cultural context, it requires certain of the forms of that other culture to be borrowed. Islam, for example, requires certain forms of prayer, a specific pilgrimage, an untranslatable Arabic book, even clothing styles. Likewise Judaism, Hinduism, Buddhism and culture christianity. These are religions.

Essential biblical Christianity, however, requires none of the original cultural forms. That's how it could be "captured" by the West and be considered Western even though its origin is not Western. *Essential Christianity is an allegiance, a relationship, from which flow a series of meanings that are intended to be expressed through the cultural forms of any culture.* These forms are intended, then, to be chosen for their appropriateness to convey proper biblical meanings in the receptors' contexts.

I believe Christianity is intended to be "a faith," not a set of cultural forms and therefore different in essence from the religions. Religions, because they are cultural things, can be *adapted* to new cultures. Adaptation is an external thing resulting in smaller or larger changes in the forms of the religion. Unlike religion, however, Christianity can be *contextualized*, a process in which appropriate meanings may be carried by quite different forms in various cultures.

Unfortunately, due to the interference of culture christianity, we have not seen all the variety that is possible. Like a religion, the usual form of initiation into Christianity is a first century cultural form involving water and the consolidation ceremony called Communion usually involves the original drink, wine (though many churches have contextualized this to grape juice) and bread (often contextualized to our kind of bread rather than unleavened, Jewish bread). There is, of course, no problem for a people to borrow a few cultural forms from another culture. But true contextualization of these forms could employ a form of initiation similar to that of their tradition and staple items of their diet for the Communion service. It could also employ their methods of communication rather than culture christianity's preaching forms and their forms of worship and music rather than western forms to express these important meanings.

Religion or a Faith?

A way that I have found very helpful to deal with this subject is to ask two questions, What characterizes a religion? And then, What is the essence of biblical Christianity?

I believe the answer to be the distinction between religion or, rather, *a religion* and a faith or commitment. What I mean by "a faith" is a commitment to someone or something, supported by a set of deep worldview-level assumptions. For most of the world, such a faith involves commitment to a God, gods or spirits. In the West, the majority of people both outside and inside of the church seem to have opted for a commitment to human achievement, especially scientific, economic or political achievement supported by human scientific, economic or political structures that serve as the real religion of Westerners, called "scientific humanism."

A religion, then, is a set of cultural forms in terms of which a faith is expressed. These cultural forms are at surface-level in any given cultural structuring, as opposed to the worldview-level forms of a faith, though they are designed to express the worldview-level understandings of the faith. The practicing of the religious forms, further, may or may not involve a deep-level commitment to a God, gods or spirits. The forms may be seen as valuable in and of themselves and, indeed, may be the object of a people's commitment. That is, a people may, in their religious life, in reality be pledging allegiance to the religious forms themselves rather than to any being or thing that exists beyond the forms.

Inherent in this analysis is the distinction between people and structures set forth in my book, *Anthropology for Christian Witness* (1996). That analysis emphasized the fact that cultural structuring and human beings are quite different things. And, even though human beings live by cultural patterns, we are not determined by them. One important implication of the consistent recognition of this distinction is to note that the thing that keeps us following cultural patterns is not the patterns themselves but the fact that we have, along with our learning of the patterns, developed *habits* of following them. The customs themselves have no power to keep us following them. What keeps us following the patterns or customs is something inside of us, not something inside of the customs themselves – human habit. So, in analyzing religious behavior, we need to look at both the cultural patterns and the human activity in relation to those patterns.

Another important implication of this analysis is to note that a major part of human activity in relation to culture is *commitment*. And commitment, like the learning of our customs and the habits of following them is something we learn as we grow up. In childhood, we not only learn our customs and develop the habits that keep us following those customs but we, mostly unconsciously, make a commitment to them. And we practice that commitment habitually as well.

Our commitment, then, is certainly to the culture itself, to the customs that distinguish us from others. But it also involves commitments to *beings*, both beings within our society such as family members and beings outside of the society such as spirits and gods. Our commitment to the people we love, then, is quite a different thing from our commitment to our customs. Likewise, if we commit ourselves to God, gods or spirits, beings that are not culture-bound, these commitments are of a different order than our commitment to the culture or our commitment to some of the people who share our culture with us.

People can, of course, commit themselves to ideas as well as to beings. In such a case, the commitment is to something inside the culture. It is not to beings such as family who are not in the culture but are a part of the society that uses the culture. Nor is it a commitment to someone outside the culture such as

God, a god or a spirit.

The point is, we have in the world both religions and faiths or commitments. *Religions are structure. Faiths are personal or/group commitments.* These are two very different things. Though we may commit ourselves to a religion, an idea or some other structure, the commitment is not the same as the structure. A faith commitment is the first step whereas the expression of that faith in cultural structures, called religion, is a second step. The most obvious part of this two-step process is, however, the cultural expression called religion. This fact confuses some people, especially if the term "religious faith" is used to distinguish the religious type of faith from, say, faith in a government, in an economic system, in a family, in oneself or the like. To make the point that there is a difference between these two things, let's look at ten of the contrasts between them. The various points are discussed below.

RELIGION (STRUCTURAL)	A FAITH (PERSONAL)
1. Structural, Cultural/Worldview	Personal/Group/Social
2. Rituals, Rules	Relationship
3. Beliefs	Commitment/Allegiance
4. Perform	Obey
5. Adapt	Contextualize
6. Borrow/Accept/Imitate (e.g. worship forms of the source culture)	Create/Grow (e.g. cultural forms of the receiving culture)
7. "One size fits all"	Cultural varieties of expression
8. Like a tree, must be transplanted	Like a seed that gets planted
9. Like a loaf of bread that gets passed on	Like yeast that gets put into raw dough
10. An Institution	A Fellowship

Ten Contrasts

These ten contrasts are crucial in distinguishing religion from a faith. The differences are as follows:

1. Religion, being a cultural thing, is structural. It involves religious beliefs and behavior grounded in a cultural worldview. A faith, however, is a personal thing, experienced by people, usually in groups, often as a whole society who make commitments to a being (e.g. God, a god, a spirit, an ancestor, a living human) or thing (e.g. an idol, an idea such as Communism, a structure). This difference is the basic one, opening the way for each of the others.

Though, as discussed below, a faith, like every human commitment, is expressed culturally, it is not the same as the cultural expression. And it is the cultural expression of a faith that I will use the label "religion" to designate, not the faith itself, though popularly this distinction is often not made.

2. A religion is centered around a certain kind and number of rituals accompanied by rules and regulations for ritual behavior and for everyday behavior as well. A faith, on the other hand, is centered around a relationship, usually with one or more supernatural beings, based on a person's commitment to that being or, alternatively, a commitment to an idea, an idol, a structure or a living being. Though the relationship is primary, a faith is usually ritualized, even if it is just a commitment to an idea (e.g. Communism, evolution).

Rituals conducted in worship of God, gods or other beings with which people have established a relationship are well-known. There are, however, also academic, economic and political rituals performed by those with a religion-like commitment to certain ideas and theories.

3. A religion involves a set of intellectual beliefs. These are worldview-level assumptions on the basis of which the religion is practiced and lived. A faith, however, is a commitment, an allegiance to someone or something. There are beliefs underlying the allegiance, to be sure, and these assumptions are also worldview-level. But the allegiance itself is not simply an intellectual thing, it is a matter of a person's will to commit oneself to that something or someone outside of oneself. Commitment, therefore, is a person thing, not a structure thing. It is the act of a person, not of cultural structure in spite of the fact that it results in cultural behavior, as do all commitments.

At this point we need to reiterate that the thing committed to may be any part of the culture, including the religion itself if not to supernatural beings or even in addition to a commitment to supernatural beings. This fact may confuse some people if they fail to understand the difference I am making between structural things such as religion and the personal thing called allegiance or commitment. Since people are entirely immersed in culture, however, they will automatically express whatever allegiances they have in cultural ways.

I have said "allegiances," in the plural. To this point I have been speaking of an allegiance or commitment as if people have only one. In reality, though, each person has many allegiances. And the allegiances that are directed toward supernatural beings or religious structures may not even be at the top of the list. For many of the peoples of the world (including the Jews of Jesus' day), for example, allegiance to family is their primary allegiance. All other commitments or loyalties are secondary to that one. What Jesus intends, however, is that our allegiance to Him be primary with all other allegiances, including family, secondary to that.

The fact that Christianity is basically an allegiance supported by habits, makes witness a difficult thing even though the allegiance is expressed in cultural forms. For we are attempting to bring change at a personal level of commitment that is much deeper than the cultural forms themselves. Cultural forms to which people are only weakly committed can be changed readily. Personal allegiance to supernatural beings or cultural structures (e.g. religion), however, often manifests a tenacity that is genuinely troublesome to those who would like to change such allegiances. For that tenacity is a matter of personal and group allegiance, not a matter of simple tradition or surface-level choice among alternatives.

4. The essence of a religion lies in the performance of the beliefs and behaviors in terms of which that religion is expected to be expressed. The essence of a faith, especially if it is to a personal being, is obedience. If we worship God or gods or spirits, the object is to obey Him/them according to the worldview guidelines that accompany that faith. If we worship a human, we are to obey that person. If our faith is to an academic discipline or some other system of ideas, we are to obey those things specified by the underlying worldview assumptions of that system.

With worldview assumptions underlying both religion and a faith, then, we cannot avoid the structural, cultural requirements for expressing either. But, again, a religion and a faith need to be separated analytically if we are ever to fully understand contextualization.

5. A religion, being a cultural thing, when taken from the originating people to the people of another society can be changed to better fit that culture. The rituals, beliefs and other customs of that religion can be moved from one culture to another. But, since a religion is already a cultural system, when it is moved to another people it will have to be adjusted to those people and their culture. But such adjustment is not contextualization, it is adaptation.

A faith, on the other hand, since it is rooted in personal devotion to beings or ideas, can be expressed in any cultural forms. It does not require as a precondition that the cultural forms in which it was first expressed be carried to another people. The personal relationship between God and Abraham, for example, could have been expressed in other cultural forms if Abraham had been immersed in some other culture. As it was, though, he responded to God in terms of rituals and behaviors that characterized his life before he and God made their covenant. That same faith relationship between a human being and God, then, became the experience of many people within western societies who express that faith quite differently than Abraham expressed it.

This possibility was not in the minds of the majority of Jewish Christians in the early years of Christianity. For they saw our faith as a religion, encased in and wedded to Jewish cultural forms, perhaps allowing for some adaptation by Gentile converts but certainly not to be contextualized in Gentile culture. But God had other ideas. In the events recorded in Acts 10, God attempted to blast Peter out of his ethnocentric view of what Christianity was to be. In Acts 15, then, Paul and Barnabas reported on how God had broken the rules of the Jewish church and given the Holy Spirit to uncircumcised Gentiles on the basis of faith alone, without cultural conversion. Thus God showed that He was in favor of contextualization, not simply adaptation.

6. With a religion, to follow it properly, one accepts, imitates and learns certain cultural forms brought in from the source culture. To become a Muslim, one has to learn to pray in a certain way and in a certain direction. To

become a Buddhist, one has to learn to use incense and clap your hands to awaken the spirits when one goes to a temple. Though certain Christians may prefer certain postures for prayer, there is no cultural requirement. Jewish Christians may prefer to stand, many prefer to kneel or sit. The crucial thing is not the posture (a cultural thing) but the attitude (a personal thing).

Thus, a faith can be expressed creatively in a variety of cultural forms, and people can grow in that faith whether or not they follow the cultural forms meaningful to someone else. Though one Christian may prefer a given posture for prayer and a given musical and communication style, another can be just as committed to God and prefer other postures and styles. One person, in fact, may prefer different styles in different settings because the important things for a faith are allegiance and meanings, not cultural forms.

7. A religion typically is a single entity. Thus, one size, one set of forms is to be carried wherever the religion is taken. A faith, however, is to be flexible and to take on the cultural form of the receiving people. Thus, if a faith is properly contextualized there will be endless variety in the ways in which it is expressed. There should, I believe, be as much difference between the forms in which true Christianity is expressed as there are in the forms of the various cultures of the world. The creativity discussed under point 6 is to be a major feature of properly contextualized Christianity.

8. A religion is like a tree that springs up in one place and then is taken, half grown, to another. It has been nurtured where it was planted with water and nutrients available there and needs a certain amount of such water and nutrients to continue to live in the new context. A seed, on the other hand, is planted where it is to grow and lives for the rest of its life on the water and nutrients of that place.

Unfortunately, though Christianity once came to our Gentile ancestors as a seed, it has often been transplanted as a European religion rather than planted like a seed. Thus, much of the world has gotten the wrong impression of our faith, thinking that they must accept a western package, a western transplant if they are to be acceptable to God. But, as Jesus said, our faith is intended to be a seed, even a very small seed, that sprouts in the soil of the receiving people, being nourished on their water and nutrients. It then is to grow tall and vital becoming a refuge for the birds of the air (Lk 13:19).

9. Or, to refer to another picture that Jesus drew, our faith is to be like yeast, not like the loaf of bread that the yeast has permeated (Lk 13:21). A religion, though, is like the loaf. It has already grown to its full size and then may be taken from one place to another fully formed.

But yeast, like a faith, is small, and may even go unnoticed. Someone inserts it into the dough of a culture and it grows there, spreading throughout the culture and influencing every part. This is what contextualization is all about.

10. A religion is soon institutionalized, leading to all kinds of problems for those who seek true Christianity. For the fellowship that the Christ Way is

intended to be can easily be submerged in the concerns of an institution. Note, for example, what happens in the second, third and following generations of a church or school as it becomes more and more an institution with its primary concern becoming self-preservation. If looked at in terms of its actual function rather than in terms of someone's ideal, many churches and especially training institutions have come to exist mainly to perpetuate themselves.

It is a very sad thing when the actual function of a training institution becomes to train a few people who will fill the teaching positions in that school or others like it with or without much concern for serving the needs of the churches they are supposedly training people for. But this is what most of our seminaries and Bible colleges have become. People learn what they do. And what students in these institutions do is to learn how to conduct classes, buying and selling information, often at the expense of the development of their faith.

Christian churches and training institutions are, however, intended by God to be centered in relationships with God and with others. Note Jesus' statement of the two greatest commandments (Mt. 22:36-40). Fellowship rather than institutionalization should, therefore, be the primary concern of these entities if we are to be true to our calling. The tendency for a faith to become institutionalized is probably the reason why it seems necessary for each church or training institution to experience a faith-renewal movement every generation if the proper relationship with God is to be maintained.

Recombination Theory

Years ago, an anthropologist named Homer Barnett wrote an excellent book on culture change entitled *Innovation, the Basis for Culture Change* (1953). One of the concepts he suggested is called "recombination theory." This concept is intended to assist us in understanding one of the things that may happen when people adopt another society's custom or when we seek to introduce a custom into another culture.

The theory says that when we seek to introduce a custom into another culture, we may divide that custom into its form and its function. We then do the same thing with the custom we would like to displace in another culture. With this done, we can assist the receiving people to combine Form 1 in their culture with Function 2 in the donor culture or vice versa.

The way this would work with a religion can be charted as follows:

Religion 1 of Culture 1	Religion 2 of Culture 2
Forms 1	Forms 2
Faith Commitment 1	Faith Commitment 2

Note that each of the cultures has its "religion," consisting of forms plus faith commitment. If, for example, we look at Islam and Christianity, we would see Muslim forms and Muslim faith in one column, with so-called Christian forms and Christian faith in the other column. If we sought to contextualize one of these "religions" in the opposite culture, we would seek to combine "Forms 1" with "Faith Commitment 2," or "Forms 2" with "Faith Commitment 1." If "religion 1" is Islam and "religion 2" is Christianity, our diagram would look like this:

Islam	Christianity
1. Muslim Cultural Forms	2. "Christian" Cultural Forms
1. Muslim Faith Commitment	2. Christian Faith Commitment

If we wish to contextualize Christianity in Muslim cultural forms, then, the recombination would look like this:

Christianity Contextualized in Muslim Cultural Forms
1. Muslim Cultural Forms
2. Christian Faith Commitment

Note that the opposite combination – Christian cultural forms and Muslim faith – cannot be done if one is to be an orthodox Muslim, since Islam requires certain cultural forms to be brought over into the receiving culture. I believe, though, that many western converts to Islam are attempting to contextualize Islamic faith by committing themselves to the God and religion of Islam without adopting the cultural practices required of the orthodox.

Culture Christianity is Merely a Religion

In popular parlance, Christianity is regularly classified as a "religion." It has beliefs, a faith-allegiance to a supernatural Being, rituals, places of worship, a holy book, a priesthood and many other characteristics that parallel the characteristics of the religions of the world. We can find all of these things in Hinduism, Buddhism, Islam, Animism, etc.

People have taken the teachings of the Bible and worked out a belief system that is supported by Christian leaders and taught to the adherents of the faith. That faith, then, is expressed in personal and group rituals in homes and churches. So are the world's other faiths. Each faith is based on worldview assumptions and personal and group commitments.

When looked at from this point of view, Christianity sure looks like a religion. But is this the way it ought to be seen? Contextualizers need to ask and answer this question. For if ours is simply one of the religions of the world, our relationship with the other religions is a competitive relationship and our aim should be to replace those religions with ours.

As mentioned, culturally naïve missionaries often saw Christianity in this light. They saw their task, then, as introducing people to their own Christian beliefs and practices in the hope that they would convert from their false beliefs and practices and embrace Christianity. And along with conversion to Christ (the faith commitment), the usual expectation was that the converts would embrace the western cultural packaging in terms of which the missionaries expressed their Christianity. To assure this, the missionaries set up western schools to teach children how to live "Christian" (i.e. western Christian) lives. There were additional, and better, reasons for the schools. But winning children to Christ and training them to live as Christians were often articulated as goals of the schools.

When, then, the receiving people were impressed (even intimidated) by the culture of the missionaries, many came to the schools and converted both to the faith of the missionaries and to as much of their culture as possible. Thus, large numbers of the peoples of Korea, Africa, the South Pacific, Latin America and other areas converted to Christ and to western culture at the same time. In places like China, India, Japan, Thailand and the Muslim world, however, if anything the missionaries brought was accepted, it was more likely to be the perceived benefits of the schools and the culture they taught rather than the missionaries' faith. For, though the faith came in western packaging, it was easy for people to see that the schooling did not depend on the acceptance of the faith. They could take the one without having to take the other. It was, though, not so easy in many parts of the world for people to accept the faith without the cultural packaging. Literacy, for example, was often a requirement for baptism.

So, for many of the peoples of the world, Christianity is simply a religion, a cultural thing with or without the faith that is intended to be central to biblical Christianity.

A Christian Worldview?

It is common for western Christians, especially conservative Evangelicals, to speak of *a* or *the* Christian worldview. These have learned that the term worldview is to be applied to the basic assumptions of a people and have come to label the basic assumptions of Christianity as worldview assumptions. So far so good.

But what these people are generally referring to when they speak of a "Christian worldview" is a set of doctrinal assumptions that are important to Christianity – things taught in the Bible that Christians need to give assent to if they are to be truly Christian. These assumptions, then, are to contrast with humanistic assumptions or the underlying assumptions of nonChristian religions. And, once again, Christianity is put in competition with the religions of the world.

The problem here is that the concept of worldview, as defined by anthropologists, those whose expertise is in dealing with culture and worldview, is much broader than this popular usage of the term. For anthropologists, a worldview is the deep level of culture (see Kraft 1996) and includes assumptions concerning time, space and classification as well as concerning persons and power. Though Christian assumptions deal a lot with these latter two aspects of worldview, a so-called "Christian" worldview has little to say about changes required by Christian faith in assumptions concerning time, space and classification. What is apparent to Christian anthropologists, the experts on the subject of worldview, is that the relatively few worldview assumptions focused on by those who use the term "Christian worldview" should not be treated as if they are the whole of a person's worldview. For, though these few things are truly significant, they do not come near comprising a total worldview.

Instead, such a focus gives the misimpression that Christianity offers a total worldview that is in competition with the cultural worldviews of the peoples of the world. This view, then, would assume that Christians are to be radically different from the nonChristians in their society in a much larger number of assumptions than is necessary. This would be competition allowing only for adaptation, not contextualization. Given, we are to differ radically in a few crucial areas. But, as mentioned above, the number of areas is comparatively small. Most of a people's worldview assumptions require little if any change when they convert to Christianity. This is what allows for contextualization within a culture rather than replacement of it.

If, then, Christianity is to be seen as a religion in competition with religions, ours is a worldview in competition with other worldviews. And our job is to convert people from their worldviews to ours. There can in such a case be some adaptation but no real contextualization of our faith. I believe, though, that there is a better way.

A Matter of Meanings

It is, I believe, crucial that we see the essence of true Christianity in the area of meaning and allegiance (both person things) rather than in the forms (cultural things) through which meaning and allegiance are expressed. Our faith is a matter of relationship with a living God and a living Christ and the rituals we perform can vary widely in form as long as the meanings are there. We can worship in a wide variety of ways and even on different days as long as our worship is "in spirit and in truth" (Jn 4:23-24). We can pray in any posture as long as our motivation is right. We can even interpret the meanings of various doctrines differently as long as our allegiance is to the one Christ.

As mentioned, in the religions certain cultural forms are required, usually those that originated in the source culture or, as with Christianity, in the western cultures that have become its primary home. Whether these cultural forms be a certain posture for prayer or a specific language or certain rituals or special artifacts, without them the religion cannot function properly. To practice a religion one has to learn what these forms are and how to use them properly. To practice Christianity appropriately, however, one has only to learn what the supracultural meanings of Scripture are and to set them to whatever cultural forms one feels are appropriate to convey those meanings.

For religion is a facet of culture. And, just as the non-religious forms of a culture are available for the expression of Christian faith, so the religious forms of that culture can also be used – on condition that the satanic power in them is broken and the meanings are Christian. Almost any cultural forms can be captured for Christ.

The tragedy of requiring western rather than traditional forms to be used in Christianity is twofold: that the foreign forms will not be assigned the proper meanings and that Christianity will devolve into simply being seen as a religion. This misunderstanding, then, produces a pull back toward the meanings of the traditional religion. And Christianity devolves into merely a competing religion rather than a faith that is intended to capture the cultural forms once used to express that other faith.

Conclusion

It is my conclusion, then, that true biblical Christianity neither is nor was intended to be a religion in the sense of that cultural structuring that is ordinarily in view as people talk about the religions of the world. It is intended to be, rather, a faith, a commitment to God through Jesus Christ, which, though it must be expessed culturally, can be expressed through any cultural system. Unlike religions, then, Christianity can and should be contextualized, not simply adapted as is required of cultural religions when they are taken from one society to another.

Holistic Contextualisation: Ensuring that Every Facet of Christian Faith is Localized

A Scott Moreau

Prof Dr A Scott Moreau, professor in Intercultural Studies, Wheaton College, Illinois

In most missiological circles today the term "contextualization" is intimately connected with theological paradigms and the development of local theologies that are relevant for particular settings and circumstances. For example, while Stephen Bevans provided a very helpful cognitive map of the models of contextualization developed by people of differing theological strains,[1] going beyond models of *theological* framing to discussing more of a *comprehensive* mapping of contextualized practices and faith expressions has not yet happened. It this theological orientation, framing, and construction truly all that contextualization is supposed to be? It is our contention in this chapter that contextualization cannot be framed or constrained exclusively by theological reflection. It must be comprehensive or holistic; it must include all facets of the Christian faith.

Nigerian evangelical Byang Kato pointed out as early as 1975 that, "Contextualization can take place in the areas of liturgy, dress, language, church service, and any other form of expression of the Gospel truth."[2] While this statement is now over 30 years old, to date the vast bulk of the energy and focus in contextualization has been on theology and theological processes.

Certainly theology must be contextualized. However, there are so many facets of our faith rarely touched by formal theology that we do contextualization a disservice by keeping it confined to theological issues and agendas. Contextualization is more comprehensive – and more holistic than this. It is a more holistic approach to contextualization that we will explore, and we will do that in two stages. First, we offer seven characteristics that should

---

[1] See Stephen B. Bevans, *Models of Contextual Theology* (Maryknoll: Orbis Press, 1992).

[2] Byang Kato, "The Gospel, Cultural Context and Religious Syncretism," *Let the Earth Hear His Voice*, edited by J. D. Douglas (Minneapolis: World Wide Publications, 1975), 1217.

mark out any attempts to holistically contextualize the Christian faith in new settings. Second, we will provide an orientation to seven dimensions that encompass Christian life and provide a framework for holistic contextualization.

Characteristics of Good Holistic Contextualization

We can identify at least seven characteristics of healthy, vibrant, holistic contextualization. Each of them is important in that they set the stage for evaluating contextualizing attempts found in settings all over the world. They can also help establish boundaries for the processes of contextualization that will help ensure an integrity to Scripture that also respects cultures as vehicles through which human beings express our worship of God as creator of both the physical and the social spheres we inhabit.

First, any comprehensive or holistic approach to contextualization must be *concerned with the whole of the Christian faith and not limited to a particular facet of it.* It is absolutely true that we must be deeply concerned with contextualizing theology, but to neglect other components of the entire Christian faith in the contextualization process is to neglect all that the church is and does. This will inevitably short-circuit the process of "translating"[3] the faith into another context.

At one time in evangelical circles, missiologists advocated that there is a supra-cultural core gospel, a "Bible within the Bible," and that our preliminary task is to discern this supra-cultural core. Separating "kernel" from "husk" in this sense, however, was never easily done, as the criteria and procedures of the proposed separation of this core will always be tied to the culture of the one making the proposals.[4] Because of the contextual nature of the theologian, the resulting "core" will always be culturally bound and therefore relative. The reality of the embeddedness of knowledge is certainly one of the significant lessons in post-modern discussion and is a strong reminder that we cannot somehow extract a supra-cultural core of our Christian faith and bring only that core into a new setting.[5]

Failure to recognize that it is the whole of our faith that must be

---

[3] Andrew F. Walls, *The Missionary Movement in Christian History: Studies in the Transmission of Faith* (Maryknoll: Orbis Books, 1996), 26-42.

[4] Donald A. Carson, "Church and Mission: Reflections on Contextualization and the Third Horizon," *The Church in the Bible and the World: An International Study*, ed. D. A. Carson (Exeter: The Paternoster Press, 1987), 248-50; see also Kevin Vanhoozer, "'One Rule to Rule Them All?' Theological Method in an Era of World Christianity," *Globalizing Theology: Belief and Practice in an Era of World Christianity*, ed. Craig Ott and Harold A. Netland (Grand Rapids: Baker, 2006), 100-101.

[5] See Vanhoozer 2006:93-95.

contextualized can lead to "kernel and husk" approaches in which we seek to find only those things (e.g., theology, sacraments, polity) that we (outsiders) consider transcultural and discard the rest. As noted, this has been rejected in theologizing in new contexts, and must be rejected in holistic contextualization as well. It also will inevitably result in the delay of emic faith practices through the imposition of an etic core or, just as bad, the construction of emic theologies in churches that live out their faith through etic practices.

The second characteristic of holistic contextualization is that *it will be a blend of the propositional and the existential.* Over the past century, many American evangelical missiologists, following the lead of evangelical theologians, have rejected existential approaches to theology more as a reaction to their sources (typically mainline and more liberal theologians) than anything else. Certainly one of the lessons learned from the global church of today is that God continues to speak to His people in a multitude of ways, almost universally embedded in the stories and lives of God's children rather than in abstract propositional truths.[6] Holistic contextualization must also engage us on both levels. We cannot ignore the reality of the truth of Scripture, but neither can we ignore the reality of God's ongoing revelation of himself in and through the lives of those who love him and follow his ways. Certainly, however, the normative grounding for understanding God's ongoing revelation is the Bible,[7] which provides the constraints and the filter through which our propositional discussion and existential circumstances must be weighed.

Third, as should be obvious from the second characteristic, *the only sufficient ground for holistic contextualization is the entirety of the Scriptures.* Over the course of the history of God's people, the foundation for understanding our faith has been the canonical scriptures. One of the potential dangers for those engaged in holistic contextualization is to lose sight of the fact that while contextualizing the church into any human setting is something of a dialogical process, it is still a process in which there is one normative pole. Ultimately all of our efforts in contextualization will be based on congruence with Biblical teachings, and thus it is appropriate to apply this as a criterion for holistic contextualization. When we replace the Scriptures as our norm with relative frames of reference – whether cultural values or the latest analytic tools from the social sciences – the result will inevitably be a relativism that will erode the Church and its purpose for existence.

The fourth criterion for good holistic contextualization is that *it will be interdisciplinary in all aspects.* The Bible is our anchor, but the tools with which we seek to better understand both biblical teachings and the contexts of our world will come from a variety of disciplines that have been developed over the past several centuries, including history, theology, anthropology,

---

[6] Philip Jenkins, *The New Faces of Christianity: Believing the Bible in the Global South* (Oxford: Oxford University Press, 2006), 18-41.

[7] Vanhoozer calls this the canonical principle; 2006:112-113.

sociology, psychology, communication, linguistics, economics, international relations, political science, and literature. The tools they offer provide invaluable insights into the human condition, the lived reality of the oppressed in every context of the world, the ways in which we alternately enrich and victimize each other as people, and the processes at work in the systems in every culture on the planet. It is true that no individual human being is competent in all of these disciplines; thus, holistic contextualization can only be accomplished in community.

Fifth, good holistic contextualization *will never be seen as being finished.* Just as human societies are constantly changing, and each new generation within those societies is not identical to the previous generation, the church in those cultures cannot remain static but must be dynamic. This dynamism is not simply the product of a church shifting with trends and fads in its local context, but Spirit-inspired adaptation to and scriptural evaluation of those trends. As long as the anchor of biblical revelation is maintained, the ability to flex with new questions and challenges – while not letting go of the timeless reality of God's sovereignty and love of people, our own human sinfulness, the reality of an enemy who pursues our destruction, and the redemptive work of Christ – will enable the church to be fresh and vibrant in the midst of culture change.

The sixth characteristic of holistic contextualization is that *the reality of our own human sinfulness and brokenness is always recognized as a factor in the contextualizing process*. This sinfulness expresses itself on an individual and societal level, and personal evil as well as systemic evil can be recognized for what it is and fought against with the gifts given by the Holy Spirit. The fallen desire for power and control, our deep longings for security and significance, our reticence to let go of personal dreams and aspirations, and our all-too-common yearning for revenge all interfere with our attempts to communicate and live out the claims of Christ relevantly.

The seventh, and final, characteristic of holistic contextualization is that *it is a two-way* (or perhaps three- or even four-way) *process in which every follower of Christ has something to offer to the rest of the body of Christ.* Contextualization is to be done alongside those in the new culture rather than done to or for them.[8] One of the great recent lessons being brought to Western cultures is how to contextualize for ourselves the things that we have taken for granted within our own cultures.[9] This two-way work ". . . is a form of mission in reverse, where we will learn from other cultures how to be more Christian in our own context."[10] Every society of the world has gifts of contextualized

[8] W. Frederic Sprunger, "Six Lessons about Contextualization," *Mission Focus* 12 (1984):6.

[9] See, for example, Lesslie Newbigin, *The Gospel in a Pluralist Society* (Grand Rapids: Eerdmans, 1989).

[10] Darrell L. Whiteman, "Contextualization: The Theory, the Gap, the Challenge," *International Bulletin of Missionary Research* 21 (1997): 4.

thinking and praxis to offer the universal Church, and the Church not only benefits from each contribution, it also loses when members are denied the opportunity to take part in the process.

The Dimensions of Holistic Contextualization

As noted at the outset, holistic contextualization is deeply concerned with theology but focuses on the entire life of the church rather than simply theological expression or agendas. The ultimate goal of holistic contextualization is to make every facet of the Christian faith embodied in a way that is understandable (and, in-so-far as it is possible, commendable[11]) to the society in which that faith is lived out. This is not to say that all facets simply mirror the cultural values, but that the gospel is incarnated in such a way that those who see the facets can understand them as fitting with local sensibilities rather than foreign ones.

For the rest of this chapter we will explore a seven-dimensional model of those facets and implications for holistic contextualization in each. The model used is derived from religious scholar Ninian Smart's approach to comparing and contrasting religious worldviews in which he explores seven dimensions that can be found across the religions.[12] These seven dimensions are the doctrinal, mythic, ethical, social, ritual, experiential, and artistic (or material).

Dimension 1: The Doctrinal or Theological Dimension

The doctrinal or theological dimension refers most simply to religious beliefs.[13] This dimension is our struggle to answer important questions about the underlying nature of who we are, what powers rule the world (whether natural or supernatural), and what our relationship is with them and with each other. It is the cognitive foundation for the rest of the dimensions. We may express religious truths through doctrinal, theological, or philosophical discourse. As Christians, the truths we hold are found in the Bible, and are typically embedded in narrative rather than outlined in didactic exposition. They include our beliefs about such things as the supernatural (e.g., do angels and demons or other spirits exist?), the created visible world and the universe (e.g., was the world created, and, if so, who created it and how as it created?) and the relationship of people with God or other spiritual or supernatural beings (e.g., do we have direct access to them; if so, how is such access gained?). Religious beliefs may be explicitly stated (e.g., God is sovereign) or embedded in

---

[11] David Hesselgrave. "Contextualization and Revelational Epistemology," *Hermeneutics, Inerrancy, and the Bible*, ed. Earl D. Radmacher and Robert D. Preus (Grand Rapids: Zondervan), 694.

[12] Ninian Smart, *Dimensions of the Sacred: An Anatomy of the World's Beliefs* (Berkeley, Calif.: University of California Press, 1996).

[13] Smart 1996:10.

philosophical literature or symbolically explored through narratives found in a culture (myths, stories, songs and hymns, and so on).

Throughout the history of the Christian Church, we have extracted, organized, and argued these truths about God, humanity, the created order and their interrelationships through systematic, historical, philosophical, political, local, and narrative theologies. Our contemporary world recognizes that there is no single supra-cultural core – or even a single interpretive method[14] – that is expressed the same way in all cultures of the world. Even such simple statements as "God is love" (1 John 4:8) are understood by readers through their understanding of the terms "God" (is he a friendly grandfather, a stern-disciplinarian, an absentee figure?) and "love" (is this brotherly love, love of parent for child, romantic love?). It is through enfleshing such abstract statements in particular languages[15] that we explore theologies in local settings and they take on life.[16] One of the lessons of post-modernism is that, as human beings, we are too much a part of our local contexts and too deeply embedded in our own personal histories to have an objective viewpoint of doctrinal truths.[17]

As noted at the outset, among Christian contextualizers it is this dimension – especially the contextualization of theology – that is most typically discussed and debated.

Examples of contextualized theologies abound. They can be listed by geographic region, from African theologies to Oceanic theologies to Third-World theologies. They can be listed by theological goals or orientations, such as liberation theologies, feminist theologies, and political theologies. They can be listed by ethnic or socio-economic orientation such as black theologies, minjung theologies and dalit theologies. They can be listed by organizational principle or focus, such as waterbuffalo theology and pain of God theology. In addition to these, we can also list Western theologies by their founder or their major focus. Calvinistic, Arminian, Wesleyan, reformed, covenantal, dispensationalist, and Pentecostal theologies are examples of doctrinal systems founded in Western settings. Though not always recognized as contextualized theologies by their adherents, that is precisely what they are. These systems, once thought to be universal, are now recognized as local theologies that are just as much a part of their settings as Latin American liberation theologies are of Latin America.

---

[14] Kevin J. Vanhoozer, "The World Well Staged? Theology, Culture, and Hermeneutics", *God and Culture: Essays in Honor of Carl F. H. Henry*. ed. D. A. Carson and John Woodbridge (Grand Rapids: Eerdmans, 1993), 1-30.

[15] See, for example, X Y. Zhang, "Doing Theology in Chinese," *Chinese Theological Review* 11:2 (1995): 125-39.

[16] Bernard Adeney, *Strange Virtues: Ethics in a Multicultural World* (Downers Grove: InterVarsity Press, 1995), 27.

[17] Vanhoozer 2006:88-99.

Dimension 2:: The Mythic or Narrative Dimension

The second dimension of holistic contextualization is the mythic. While scholars still debate the definition and function of myth,[18] we use it here to refer to the stories and proverbs told in a society that embody that society's values and how it thinks about the world. These range from proverbs used in every day life to fairy tales told to children to the great religious classics. Myth can also include historical figures who personify things valued in the culture (such as stories of heroism, wisdom, sacrifice, valor, generosity) as well as things that are not valued (usually seen in the villains of myth, who cheat, are cowards, and cannot be trusted). These myths serve as mirrors to reflect how a society thinks about the world and what they value in their members. Myth serves societies in several ways: it offers ways of ordering experience, informs people about themselves and validates their beliefs, expresses a saving power in human life, and provides patterns for human actions and social control.[19]

They way the term is being used here should be not confused with the popular idea that myths are untrue fairy tales. In fact, the question of whether a myth is true or not is suspended in the study of myth because the question is not veracity but the way such stories have power to influence people and provide them with a perspective that helps them face life. In this technical sense, all religious scriptures – including the Bible – can be seen as "myth." As followers of Christ, we recognize that the Bible portrays the story of God's interaction with the world, and that it should be considered the one True Myth with all other myths as shadows that derive their value and significance from the way they connect to it.

At the very least, to contextualize in this dimension we must develop and expand our skills in using biblical stories in evangelism and discipleship at all levels.[20] However, there are several additional ways that we can contextualize in the mythic dimension. One is to appropriate powerful mythic ways to explain the biblical story, exemplified by methods such as Chronological Bible Storytelling[21] or movies such as the *Jesus Film* or Mel Gibson's *The Passion of the Christ.* Another way is to develop literature that fits the cultural ethos, embodies (metaphorically or literally) Scriptural truths and captures the cultural imagination, such as Flannery O'Connor's *A Good Man Is Hard to Find, and*

---

[18] Lauri Honko, "The Problem of Defining Myth," *Sacred Narrative: Readings in the Theory of Myth,* ed. Alan Dundes (Berkeley: University of California Press, 1984), 46-48.

[19] Ian G. Barbour, *Myths, Models and Paradigms* (San Francisco: Harper & Row, 1974), 20-23.

[20] See, for example, Jeff Morton, "Narratives and Questions: Exploring Scripture with Muslims," *Evangelical Missions Quarterly* 40 (2004): 172-76.

[21] See http://www.chronologicalbiblestorying.com/Default.htm for helpful explanations and resources.

Other Stories[22] or Susan Howatch's Starbridge novels.[23] A third way to utilize myth is to critically analyze the stories of a local society and use the understanding this analysis provides to help more clearly communicate Christian truths in that society, as Don Richardson did in *Peace Child*.[24] Whichever we use we will be taking advantage of a source of rich emotive language and metaphor that taps into the human heart and connects on the deepest level.

Dimension 3: The Ethical Dimension

As noted above, the doctrinal dimension focuses on what is true. Doctrine speaks to what *is*, while ethics speaks to *how we then should live*. In other words, the ethical dimension focuses on implications of theological truths for how individuals should conduct themselves and how societies should value their members. This includes such things as proper ways to interact with people, our responsibilities towards God's creation, and the extent to which people's behavior should be regulated (usually through law) in conformity to religious values.

To contextualize the ethical dimension, Christians will need to wrestle with what it means to live lives that display God's goodness in ways that people of local sensibilities will see as wise. We are to love God and neighbor under Scriptural standards, applying those standards appropriately in our contexts.[25]

Evangelicals who come from a pietistic heritage typically have no trouble understanding the personal application of this; they have learned from their fellow believers the importance of living lives of integrity, honesty, charity, and so on. However, they do less well at applying Christian ethics in a systemic fashion. By this we do not mean a process of legislating personal morals. Instead, this requires appropriate attention on finding wise ways to confront the multitude of varieties of systemic evil found in every culture in the world, from racism to materialism and rampant greed, from corruption to oppression of the poor and dehumanization of oppressed sub-groups. Certainly this is an area of strength for liberation theologies, which tend to be concerned more with acts of theological significance in relation to justice (i.e., ethical living through championing the cause of the oppressed) than with constructing theoretical theological systems.

As with the doctrinal dimension, we must recognize the limitations of trying to construct a list of supra-cultural moral principles (such as justice or

---

22 Flannery O'Connor, *A Good Man Is Hard to Find, and Other Stories* (New York: Harcourt and Brace, 1955).

23 Originally a six book series by Susan Howatch, starting with *Glittering Images* (New York: Ballantine Books, 1987) and ending with *Absolute Truths: a Novel* (New York: Knopf, 1994).

24 Don Richardson, *Peace Child* (Glendale, Calif.: G/L Regal Books, 1974).

25 Adeney 1995: 79-105.

liberation). Such a quest will always lead to inadequate results because it will focus on abstracting ethical codes of conduct rather than embedding ethical living in concrete settings. For example, while there can be no doubt that the command to "love your neighbor as you love yourself" (Matt. 19:19) applies to all people, just how that will be expressed and appreciated will vary from society to society.

Developing a contextualized personal or systemic ethic requires a deep understanding of Scripture and the local setting, and constant awareness of the dangers of either a calcified legalism or a free-flowing antinomianism. As products of fallen humans created in God's image, all societies are in need of both commendation and condemnation of cultural values and practices. All too often, however, it is easy for the outsider to identify those things that violate her or his conscience and condemn them rather than discerning those things that he or she does that violate local sensibilities.[26] Things that need to be considered in contextualizing this dimension for church settings include formal and informal codes of conduct, standards for leadership, disciplinary measures for those who violate expected behavior, and so on.

Dimension 4: The Social or Organizational Dimension

The social dimension is observed in the social institutions found in every religion, and specifically in how those institutions organize and regulate themselves. For contextualization purposes, this more specifically refers to the way those social institutions are organized and regulated in the Church in light of Scripture and local cultural values. It includes the sense of social identity that comes from participating in ceremonies together (festivals, church services, annual celebrations) as well as the social institutions themselves.

It is within this dimension that we find such things as church associations and how they are joined; kinship practices such as marriage, kin obligations and inheritance; economic systems including exchanges of money, goods and services as well as social capital; educational processes from the informal to the formal; and the means for maintaining law and order within the church, including such things as leadership selection and enforcement of sanctions on those who violate standards set by the church for proper conduct.[27]

Dimension 5: The Ritual Dimension

While the ritual dimension does include those things we normally think of as ritual, such as weddings, baptisms, communion, funerals, and so on, it is defined as any repeated symbolic actions done as part of the Christian faith.

---

[26] Robert J. Priest, "Missionary Elenctics: Conscience and Culture," *Missiology* 22 (1994): 291-315.

[27] See expanded discussion in Paul G. Hiebert and Eloise Hiebert Meneses, *Incarnational Ministry: Planting Churches in Band, Tribal, Peasant, and Urban Societies* (Grand Rapids: Baker, 1995).

Human beings are creatures of ritual. [28] In fact, several glimpses we get of Heaven in Revelation (e.g., Rev. 4:9-11; 5:6-14; 19:1-8) clearly show that our worship of God there will include ritual.

In addition to those things we normally think of as ritual, ritualistic practices seen in churches include such things as sermons, committee meetings, devotional times, small group discipleship practices, revival meetings, prayer meetings, fellowship meetings, church dinners, fund raisers, Sunday School classes, short-term missions trips and so on. In cultures that have practices such as rites of passage, these can also be incorporated into the life of the church.[29]

Three types of rituals found in all cultures have been identified: 1) rituals of transition, when participants change from one status to another through the ritual (such as marriage or baptism); 2) rituals of intensification, when participants renew and energize themselves as believers (such as weekly church worship services and personal or communal devotional times, and short-term missions trips), and 3) rituals of crisis, in which participants deal with unexpected shocks or blows (such as special prayer vigils for the sick, anointing with oil, or deliverance from the demonic).

In many cultures of the world, rituals remain significant in the educational and developmental processes of social maturation, and are available for the Church to adapt in discipleship[30] and even missional[31] practices. Understanding how the rituals in a society work and how – or whether – they can be modified for use by local Christians is an important component of holistic contextualization that is currently underutilized by evangelical missionaries and missiologists.

Dimension 6: The (Supernatural) Experience Dimension

The dimension of supernatural experience is the reality that in all cultures of the world encounters with the supernatural happen through dreams, visions, miraculous experiences, signs and wonders, and so on. Not discounting the power of emotions, the focus of this dimension for holistic contextualization is not on emotional experiences, but on those experiences that are encounters with the supernatural. On the positive side they can range from a gentle sense of peace from God to ecstatic overpowering by the Holy Spirit, and on the negative side from a sense or feeling of the presence of evil to demonic control of individuals or groups.

---

[28] Madge Karecki, "Discovering the Roots of Ritual," *Missionalia* 25 (1997): 169-77.

[29] See, for example, the ROPES approach to rites of passage developed by Tanari Trust (http://www.tanari.org/).

[30] A. H. Mathias Zahniser, *Symbol and Ceremony* (Monrovia, California: MARC, 1977).

[31] See Madge Karecki, "Religious Ritual as a Key to Wholeness in Mission," *Missionalia* 25:4 (December 1997): 598-606.

One of the great losses of Western cultures is the recognition of these encounters as genuinely supernatural together with the tendency to explain them in far more natural terms (usually biological, psychological, or social). The world view behind this tendency was explored by Hiebert and coined as the "Flaw of the Excluded Middle." [32] Many have since picked up this terminology and noted that it is a flaw all-too-commonly found among Western missionaries.

By way of contrast, the church in much of the rest of the world has a vital belief in and expectation to experience supernatural phenomena – including such things as healing miracles, dreams and visions, prophecy, tongues, interpretation, and discernment of spirits.[33]

Unlike the other dimensions, supernatural experiences are not amenable to human control, though attempts to manipulate people through false miracles or other displays of power have been seen through the history of the Church.[34] The Holy Spirit responds to our desires, but he is not controlled by them nor can he be "forced" in ritual or magical ways to produce miracles at our command.

Adapting from Hiebert's model of critical contextualization,[35] holistic contextualization of supernatural experience involves at least three components. First, local Christians together with cross-cultural workers must study the Scriptures and together develop biblically-based perspectives on the experiences people have in the culture. Second, they can then consider developing appropriate rituals that enable encounters with God through Christ (e.g., prayer services) as well as rituals that will help people who struggle with negative experiences (e.g., demonic expulsion). Finally, those who follow Christ need to be given the freedom – and the language – to talk about their experiences and find Bible-centered and culturally-sensitive ways to handle them.

Dimension 7: The Artistic or Material Dimension

The final dimension in holistic contextualization is the artistic or material; we could also label it the technological dimension. Building on an understanding of technology as anything that extends humanity and McLuhan's recognition that we create technology and it then re-creates us,[36] this dimension is included

---

[32] Paul Hiebert, "The Flaw of the Excluded Middle," *Missiology* 10:1 (1982): 35-47.

[33] Jenkins 2006:9-116.

[34] James Randi, *The Faith Healers* (Buffalo, New York: Prometheus Books, 1987) presents a skeptic's investigative reports on contemporary faith healers.

[35] Paul Hiebert, "Critical Contextualization," *Missiology* 12 (1984), 287-96 and "Critical Contextualization," *International Bulletin of Missionary Research* 11:3 (1987): 4-11.

[36] David Lochhead, "Technology and Interpretation: A Footnote to McLuhan" *Journal of Theology* 98 (1994): 60-73.

because of the recognition that Christians everywhere use technology to create things that express their hopes, dreams, values and ideals symbolically. This dimension includes such things as church architecture (including the exterior shape and form as well as the interior use of space to convey religious ideas and ideologies), artistic expressions (from material objects such as paintings, banners, sculptures, symbolic crosses and windows to performances such as song, dance and drama), clothing (what is appropriate to wear – or not wear – to a church service and priestly vestments), and so on. Holistic contextualization will recognize this as a core component that is vital for the growth and development of a local body of followers of Christ and enable them to explore appropriate ways to creatively capture their thoughts, feelings, and values through artistic expression.[37]

Conclusion

Holistic contextualization includes solid theological framing but integrates the entire lives of Christians, including their actions and feelings as well as their thoughts. We must broaden our agenda for contextualization to include not only theology, but every dimension of our walk with Christ in ways that allows Christians in every setting of the world to respect those elements of their culture that honor God and challenge those that do not.

[37] See, for example, the wonderful galleries of art from Asian Christians at http://www.asianchristianart.org/index.html and from African Christians at http://www.jesusmafa.com/index.htm.

Whose Book is it, by the Way? An Aspect of Popular and Scholarly Strategies for Interpreting the Bible in Africa

Knut Holter

Prof Dr Knut Holter, Rector, School of Mission and Theology, Stavanger, Norway

The nineteenth and twentieth centuries made the Bible an African book.[1] First, in the sense that the Bible or parts of the Bible were translated into a large number of languages and cultures throughout Africa. According to Wycliffe Bible Translators, 302 African languages have in 2006 a completed translation project, either in the form of a whole Bible, a New Testament, or a smaller part. And further, 483 translation project are currently in progress. Secondly, the nineteenth and twentieth centuries made the Bible an African book also in the sense that it was used throughout Africa.[2] The Bible was carried in church processions and placed on altars and pulpits. But it was also carried by ordinary Christians on their way to work, and it was placed on their kitchen tables. The Bible was read in the formal settings of churches and assembly halls. But it was also read in the informal settings of homes and shops. Selected verses from the Bible were shared with the masses in evangelisation pamphlets and in stickers found on car and shop windows.[3]

---

[1] It is an honour to dedicate this essay on the role of the Bible in Africa to Dr Knud Jørgensen, a scholar and church leader whose merits include both research and practical work related to the mission of the church in Africa.

[2] Cf. Sigmund Evensen, "Nedtellingen fortsetter", *Wycliffe-Nytt* 28/2 (2006): 4-5.

[3] For general surveys of the role of the Bible in Africa, cf. the following essay collections: Hannah W. Kinoti & John M. Waliggo (eds.), *The Bible in African Christianity: Essays in Biblical Theology* (Nairobi: Acton, 1997), Gerald O. West & Musa W. Dube (eds.), *The Bible in Africa: Transactions, Trajectories and Trends* (Leiden: Brill, 2000), Mary N. Getui, Knut Holter & Victor Zinkuratire (eds.), *Interpreting the Old Testament in Africa* (Nairobi: Acton, 2001), Mary N. Getui, Tinyiko Maluleke & Justin S. Ukpong (eds.), *Interpreting the New Testament in Africa* (Nairobi: Acton, 2001), David T. Adamo (ed.), *Biblical Interpretation in African Perspective* (Lanham: University Press of America, 2006), Knut Holter (ed.), *Let My People Stay!*

Generally speaking, there are no major differences between African and western approaches to the Bible. Nigerian and Norwegian readers do more or less the same thing with the book, and readers from Zimbabwe and the Sweden find more or less the same things in the texts. We all approach the book with our particular questions and concerns, and through the various texts we experience a God speaking words of comfort and hope. Nevertheless, there are some differences. Bible readers in Nigeria and Zimbabwe have some experiences that are missing in the experiences of those from Norway and the Sweden, experiences that have to do with the ownership of the book. The heading of this essay – whose book is it, by the way? – is more than a rhetorical question. It verbalises a problem that has followed (at least modern) African church life and theology from its very beginning, namely its relationship to western colonialism. And it acknowledges that the role of the Bible in Africa is part of this problem, as biblical texts and interpretations were introduced (at least in modern time) parallel to the western colonisation of Africa.

Still, this does not mean that Africa has only been a passive receiver of the Bible. A colonised context does not necessarily imply a colonised mind. On the contrary, encountering assumed western texts and obvious western interpretations, Africa has throughout the nineteenth and twentieth centuries developed her own interpretative strategies, with the conscious or unconscious aim to relate the Bible to Africa, or as it will be expressed her, to Africanise the Bible. Two such sets of Africanising strategies will be focused in this essay; the popular strategies of ordinary readers in homes, schools and churches, and the academic strategies of professional interpreters in universities and seminaries. However, before I go into these two sets of strategies, I would like to draw some lines in traditional western concepts of the relationship between Africa and the Bible, as a general backcloth to the Africanising strategies.[4]

The western ambivalence vis-à-vis the relationship between Africa and the Bible

The geographical and cultural facets of the Bible are many. Jerusalem is located as a junction where Asia, Africa and Europe meet, and the geographical orientation of the Bible stretches from India in the east (Esther 1:1) to Spain in the west (Romans 15:24), and from Sudan in the south (Isaiah 18) to Rome or Philippi (St Paul) in the north.

Nevertheless, throughout most of its history of interpretation the Bible has

---

Researching the Old Testament in Africa (Nairobi: Acton, 2006), and Peter Tomson (ed.), *Lire la Bible en Afrique / Reading the Bible in Africa* (Brussels: Yearbook of the Faculty for Protestant Theology in Brussels, 11, 2006).

[4] On the relationship between popular and academic interpretation cf. Knut Holter, *Yahweh in Africa: Essays on Africa and the Old Testament* (New York: Peter Lang, 2000), 51-60.

been experienced as a western book, partly in the sense that biblical texts and interpretations have influenced western culture, but partly also in the sense that the interpretations themselves have been influenced by their western context and thereby have functioned as carriers of western culture and interests. Not least can this be seen when it comes to Africa. When western biblical interpreters have related the Bible to Africa, their own western contexts have been part of the interpretative framework; negatively when western imperialists used the Bible to legitimise their economic, political and cultural colonisation of Africa during the last couple of hundred years. But also positively, when western missionaries initiated and participated in the translation of the Bible into a large number of African languages, and thereby contributed to a development of a local Christian identity.

Let me start with the negative tradition, the tradition where the Bible has been used to legitimise the western colonisation of Africa. This is a strong tradition. First, the Bible was used to legitimise the military and political colonisation of Africa, thereby depriving African nations of the kinds of political rights western nations were supposed to have. An illustrative example here is the Boers –South African agricultural settlers, of Dutch or French origin, and with a theology of Reformed brand – who in the 1830s and 40s migrated north- and eastwards from the Cape to escape the British colonisation. Although not necessarily emphasised by the pioneers themselves, the next generations developed an ideology and theology where the annexation and colonisation of land was interpreted in the light of the Old Testament conquest traditions, not least as it is expressed in the Book of Joshua. The Boers eventually saw themselves as God's chosen people on their way to the Promised Land, and the African peoples they met on their way were interpreted in the light of Joshua's experiences with various Canaanite peoples.[5]

Secondly, the Bible was also used to legitimise the cultural colonisation of Africa, depriving Africa of cultural identity and value. An illustrative example here is the interpretation western colonisers gave of the ruins of Great Zimbabwe in the latter two or three decades of the nineteenth century.[6] It was a German adventurer who in 1872 (re-) 'discovered' the ruins of a great acropolis-like building complex at the plateau between the Zambezi and Limpopo rivers in southern Africa. It was clear to him and to the first

---

[5] Cf. André du Toit, "No chosen people: The myth of the Calvinist origin of Afrikaner nationalism and racial ideology", *American Historical Review* 88 (1983): 920-952, and Michael Prior, *The Bible and Colonialism: A Moral Critique* (Sheffield: Sheffield Academic Press, 1997), 71-105.

[6] For a survey, cf. Knut Holter, "Interpreting Solomon in colonial and post-colonial Africa", *Old Testament Essays* 19 (2006): 851-862. For further analysis of the early interpretation of Great Zimbabwe, cf. Peter S. Garlake, *Great Zimbabwe* (London: Thames & Hudson, 1973), and Joost Fontain, *The Silence of Great Zimbabwe* (New York: UCL Press, 2006).

generation of observers that such a building complex could not be the product of native Africans; somehow it had to be the result of a non-African colonial project, it was argued. Lines were soon to be drawn between the ruins of Great Zimbabwe and King Solomon's temple in Jerusalem. And the ruins were said to be the remains of the headquarter of the Queen of Sheba, built by Phoenician workers brought to Africa by the queen herself after her visit to King Solomon in Jerusalem. Thereby the late nineteenth century western colonialists in southern Africa had established a biblical predecessor, a three thousand years old non-African colonial project deep into Africa.

What these two examples have in common is that both of them read their own sets of colonial interests into the Bible. As far as the Boers are concerned, they interpret their experiences with the British in the Cape and with various African peoples north and east of the Cape in the light of Joshua's narrative about Israel's conquering of Canaan. Such an interpretative strategy is hardly surprising, however. As Christians we have for two thousand years read our experiences into the Old Testament narratives about Israel or the New Testament portrayal of the early church. Still, in the case of the Boers such a – quite ordinary, principally speaking – interpretative strategy turned out to have severe consequences for the peoples who became their victims, as the Boers lacked an ethical reflection in relation to a use of the Bible that legitimised a colonisation of African land and peoples. A similar lack of ethical reflection in relation to the consequences of their interpretation of the Bible is also the main problem of the Zimbabwe colonisers. At first sight, a paralleling of the supposed colonisation of southern Africa three thousand years ago by King Solomon with the late nineteenth century western colonisation of the same area may seem quite innocent. Still, just under the surface of this paralleling one finds a major ideological concept of the western colonisers, the fact that they take for granted that Africans themselves are not capable of building state or culture, and are therefore in need of assistance from non-African political and commercial enterprises, such as King Solomon three thousand years ago, or western colonisers today.

However, the western interpretative tradition vis-à-vis the relationship between Africa and the Bible had not only an oppressing side. There was also a liberating side, as the western missionary movement initiated and participated in the translation of the Bible into a large number of African languages and cultures, and thereby contributed to religious democracy and to the development of a local Christian identity. There are several explanations to the missionary focus on Bible translation. One thing is that it to some extent grew out of church contexts that emphasised the Bible as a door to the Christian faith, and it was natural for the missionaries to bring their own Bible piety also to Africa. Another thing was the experiences of the first generations of missionaries in Africa, both with regard to high mortality rates resulting from malaria and other tropical diseases, and with regard to the political difficulties of reaching beyond the coastal areas. In both cases a translation of the Bible was seen as the solution. The vernacular Bible would survive the missionaries, and it could be brought into areas where the missionary himself had no access.

Therefore, a number of Bible translations – a single biblical book, the New Testament or the whole Bible – were published throughout the nineteenth century, as the following examples will demonstrate.[7] In West Africa, Sierra Leone got the first biblical book translated into Themne in 1865, and then the New Testament in 1868; Ghana got its first book in Ga in 1843 and the New Testament in 1859; Nigeria got its first book in Yoruba in 1850, the New Testament in 1862 and the whole Bible in 1884; and Cameroon got its first book in Duala in 1843, the New Testament in 1861 and the whole Bible in 1872. In Southern Africa, Zimbabwe got its first book in Ndebele in 1884; Malawi got the first book in Chinyanja in 1884 and the New Testament in 1886; and South Africa got its first book in Setswana in 1831, the New Testament in 1840 and the whole Bible in 1857; South Africa also got the first book in Xhosa in 1833 and the New Testament in 1846, and also the first book in Zulu in 1848, the New Testament in 1865 and the whole Bible in 1883. In Eastern Africa, Tanzania got the first book in Swahili in 1868, the New Testament in 1879 and the whole Bible in 1891; Kenya got the first books in Duruma in 1848 and Kamba in 1850; Uganda got its first book in Luganda in 1887, the New Testament in 1893 and the whole Bible in 1896; Madagascar got its first book in Merina in 1828, the New Testament in 1830 and the whole Bible in 1835; and Etiopia and Eritrea got their first book in Amharic in 1824, the New Testament in 1829 and the whole Bible in 1840; and Ethiopia also saw several translations into Oromo from the 1870s on.

This focus of the western mission movement on Bible translation had many consequences. First, the missionaries were right in assuming that the vernacular translations would serve as doors to the Christian faith. They were of course also right in assuming that the translations would survive the missionaries. And in some cases it would also prove to be correct that the Bible would reach geographical areas and cultural settings where the missionary had no access.

Secondly, however, the vernacular translations would also have other and not necessarily intended consequences. A central point here is the religious democracy that followed in the footsteps of the translations. The word of God was made accessible not only to the western or western-trained religious leadership but to ordinary readers and church members. One consequence of the vernacular translation is that it in many cases became an impetus to political liberation, as oppressed people reading the Bible gradually saw their own dignity and human rights, and therefore eventually demanded corresponding political rights. In this way it can be argued that the modern, western mission movement's focus on Bible translation represents a counterpart to the contemporary colonial use of the Bible to legitimise western colonial interests.

---

[7] Cf. Ype Schaaf, *On Their Way Rejoicing: The History and Role of the Bible in Africa* (Carlisle: Paternoster Press, 1994).

Another consequence of the vernacular translation is that the church leadership lost its interpretative control of the biblical texts. Historically speaking, not least the Old Testament turned out to create problems. It is not difficult to understand that those who had fought African cultural and religious traditions of sacrifice, circumcision and polygamy were somewhat reluctant with regard to translating Old Testament texts demonstrating that similar traditions were practiced by the heroes of faith in the old covenant. Many of the schisms that have occurred in African church life reflect tensions with regard to how such texts are to be interpreted, and it was sometimes argued that a translation of the Old Testament would have to wait until the target group was more spiritually mature.

Popular strategies to Africanise the Bible

A major challenge facing the church in Africa is to find expressions of life and faith – and not least biblical interpretation – that at one and the same time are locally rooted and universally recognisable. At the level of popular biblical interpretation, some of the interpretative subjects are professional interpreters such as evangelists and pastors, but the large majority is made up of ordinary readers of the Bible, lay Christians who interpret the Bible in homes, schools and churches. A couple of remarks as far as their Africanising strategies are concerned should be made.

First, the Africanising strategies of popular biblical interpretation are expressed through a broad spectrum of verbal and non-verbal genres. Verbal interpretation is more than what is expressed by words in a sermons or Bible studies; verbal genres also include hymns, prayers, and personal testimonies. Basically, the verbal genres make use of well-known words and expressions to interpret the biblical texts. So is the case when the preacher makes use of local metaphors to communicate the biblical message. So is also the case when the singer makes use of local poetic conventions to form the biblical text into a lament or praise. And so is especially the case when the Bible translator struggles to find words and expressions in the target language that are fit to convey the message of the source language. It can be central theological terms such as 'creation' and 'salvation', or 'sin' and 'grace'. But it can also be culturally and geographically related terms, such as 'synagogue' and 'snow'. Of particular importance is the need to find a word for 'God'. Most Bible translations in Africa chose to use the name of the local creator god, then complementing the local concepts with biblical material. However, in some cases this approach may increase the interpretative complexity, as a possible tension between the biblical and local creator gods thereby is institutionalised. A quite recent example is the Iraqw (Tanzania) translation of the Old Testament, where the first version (1995) of Genesis tried out the female creator god 'Looa' as a rendering of 'God' in Genesis, whereas the final version (2005) – due to negative reactions from church circles – decided to use the (male) 'Mungu' from neighboring Swahili.[8] Another example is found in the early nineteenth century Malagasy translation, where the British missionaries decided to use the local creator god 'Andriamanitra' to render 'God'. This annexation has in recent years enabled certain religious traditionalists to turn the argument around, claiming that the biblical concepts of 'Andrimanitra' should be corrected according to traditional knowledge of the (assumed) same god.[9] Nevertheless, the traditional annexation of the name of the local creator god has generally speaking functioned quite well – at least as seen from the perspectives of the Bible translators and the church – as it has enabled the vernacular translations to promote an understanding of 'God' that makes sense to a new reading community.

In a similar way non-verbal or symbolic genres, too, make use of local expressions in their biblical interpretation. It can be the visible arts, where local colours and forms may serve to illustrate the biblical message. It can also be dramatisations, where Bible narratives are relocated from Jerusalem or Galilee to an African metropolis or village, with their respective cultures and landscapes. And not least can it be various kinds of rituals that attempt to build bridges between biblical texts and African contexts, either by revitalising a biblical ritual that is assumed to have a parallel in the African tradition, or by transferring a traditional African ritual to church contexts, legitimising it by a reference to a supposed biblical counterpart.[10]

Secondly, the Africanising strategies of popular biblical interpretation are expressed in a broad institutional spectrum; primarily within church contexts – 'western initiated' as well as 'African initiated' churches – but to some extent also outside typical church contexts. As far as church contexts are concerned, the 'African instituted' churches are the ones most open to using the Bible to legitimise traditional African concepts and rituals. There can be dogmatic questions, such as when a local prophet is identified with the Holy Spirit. And there can be ethical questions, such as polygamy. There can also be various kinds of rituals that are transferred from a traditional African context to a church context, generally with an attempt at legitimising it by a biblical reference. A frequently attested example in 'African instituted' churches is the ritual of taking off the shoes before entering the church, a ritual that may refer to Moses and the burning bush (Exodus 3), but it may also reflect more traditional concepts of holiness.

---

[8] Cf. Aloo Mojola, "A 'female' god in East Africa: The problem of translating God's name among the Iraqw of Mbulu, Tanzania", *The Bible Translator* 46 (1995): 229-236.

[9] Cf. Georges Razafindrakoto, "The Old Testament outside the realm of the church: A case from Madagascar" (Holter, ed., 2006), 97-110.

[10] Cf. Zablon Nthamburi & Douglas Waruta, "Biblical hermeneutics in African Instituted Churches", Kinoti & Waliggo 1997:40-57, and Nahashon Ndungu, "The Bible in an African Independent Church", Kinoti & Waliggo 1997: 58-67.

Another example, this from a 'western initiated' church, the Roman Catholic Church in Madagascar, is the development of a Christian version of a traditional fertility and funeral ritual.[11] The Merina people in the inland of Madagascar have a traditional ritual that at certain stages after the burial includes the removal of the body from the grave, to redress it and honour it in various processions. The Protestant churches in Madagascar generally reject this traditional ritual as 'pagan', whereas the Catholic church has developed a Christian version, and legitimised it with a set of biblical references, such as to Exodus 20:12 ('Honour your father and your mother') or Exodus 13:19 (Moses promises to bring Joseph's bones back to Canaan).

This example from Madagascar illustrates how the church in her interpretation of the Bible may be influenced by traditional religious concepts and practices. But the influence goes in both directions. Traditional religion is also influenced by the church and her use of the Bible, and Africanising strategies vis-à-vis interpreting the Bible may therefore also occur outside church contexts. In Nigeria, one finds that certain religious communities influenced by popular Islam write texts from the Book of Psalms on blackboards, then wash it away and drink the chalk water as protection against various illnesses.[12] And one also finds religious communities, more influenced by traditional religion, who make mixtures of herbs and liquids and then read biblical texts over the mixtures, thereby creating a means of protection and healing. Similar practices can be found elsewhere, too, such as in Madagascar, where traditionalists may use the Bible, partly as a 'closed book', that is as a magical instrument in the context of sacrificial practices, and partly as an 'open book', that is as book in which not only Christians but also traditionalists may find texts of value.[13]

Academic strategies to Africanise the Bible

In the last three or four decades, Africa has seen the development of an academic interpretation of the Bible.[14] Whereas popular biblical interpretation is oral and aimed at the masses, academic biblical interpretation is written and aimed at the elites in universities and seminaries. And whereas the question of ownership vis-à-vis the Bible is found just under the surface of popular biblical interpretation, it is found above the surface – visible and explicitly expressed – in academic interpretation.

---

[11] Cf. Georges Razafindrakoto, "The Malagasy *famadihana* ritual and the Old Testament" (Holter, ed., 2006), 111-130.

[12] Cf. David T. Adamo, *Reading and Interpreting the Bible in African Indigenous Churches* (Eugene: Wipf and Stock Publishers, 2001), 47-110.

[13] Cf. Razafindrakoto 2006: 97-110.

[14] Cf. Knut Holter, "Old Testament scholarship in sub-Saharan Africa north of the Limpopo river", West & Dube 2000:54-71.

First, from an institutional perspective, it should be recognised that the quest for an Africanised biblical interpretation has been a major aspect of the development of theological institutions. The strong church growth Africa experienced throughout the twentieth century created a need for competence in academic theology, and then not least in how to interpret the Bible in a meaningful way in contemporary Africa. As far as academic institutions are concerned, a number of Africa's 150-200 universities, but also some of the 1200-1500 seminaries and Bible schools in Africa, have established structures allowing for biblical studies at an academic level. And as far as biblical scholars are concerned, two or three hundred have been educated with a doctoral degree since the 1960s.[15]

Secondly, from a hermeneutic perspective, it should also be recognised that the quest for an Africanised biblical interpretation is becoming more and more focused in African biblical studies. First, African biblical scholars acknowledge their responsibilities vis-à-vis society; academic ivory towers without contact with the practical challenges of church and society are hardly seen here. On the other hand, it is often argued that the questions that traditionally have been posed by western biblical scholarship reflect typically western experiences and concerns of the nineteenth and twentieth centuries, and not necessarily have much to contribute into a contemporary African context. The task of biblical scholarship is not to respond to questions raised by colleagues in another continent and another century, it is argued, but to interpret the texts in a way that creates meaning here and now.[16] Two thematic tendencies in African biblical scholarship can serve to illustrate this point. First, there is a tendency to make use of African cultural and religious experiences as interpretative keys into the biblical texts. What underlies this approach is the assumption that a large number of cultural and religious parallels exist between the biblical world and traditional Africa. Since we have no direct access to the biblical world, the supposed parallels in traditional Africa – which we have still access to – can be used as a key to the biblical texts. Secondly, the same assumption may also be turned the other way round. Rather than using the African parallels to interpret the Bible, there is a tendency to use the Bible as a key to interpret various cultural and religious traditions and practices in Africa.

---

[15] The number is an estimate, as no data is available as far as New Testament dissertations are concerned. For a survey of around ninety Old Testament dissertations written by African scholars from 1967 to 2000, cf. Knut Holter, *Old Testament Research for Africa: A Critical Analysis and Annotated Bibliography of African Old Testament Dissertations, 1967-2000* (New York: Peter Lang, 2002).

[16] Cf. Justin S. Ukpong, "Developments in biblical interpretation in modern Africa", *Missionalia* 27 (1999): 313-329.

Conclusion

The introduction of the Bible to Africa coincided with – and was of course a part of – the western colonisation of Africa. The Bible was the book of the colonisers, a book in which they found support to their imperialism. But the Bible was also the book of the missionaries, a book they – and as time went by also the churches they initiated – wanted to share with all ethnic and linguistic groups. The translation of the Bible to vernacular languages created contexts for liberation from western colonisation. The Bible proved again to be a double-edged sword. The book that was used to oppress Africa, politically as well as culturally, proved to have a potential for liberating its readers. Rather than being a passive receiver, Africa developed active strategies – on popular as well as academic levels – to conquer the book of the colonisers and make it an African book. And that is where we are today. Whose book is it, by the way? Well, throughout the nineteenth and twentieth centuries the Bible changed from being experienced as a typically western book to becoming a typically African book, a book that is able to express central experiences and concerns of African Christianity.

The Southern Phase of Christianity: The Contribution of the Global South to the Church in the Global North

Roar G. Fotland

Assoc Prof Dr Roar G Fotland, MF Norwegian School of Theology, Oslo, Norway

> Christianity in Africa is set to play a crucial role in the future shape of the [Christian] faith and its impact in the world at large.[1]

This statement by the African theologian Kwame Bediako from 1995 is becoming more and more true. While the old European notion was that the church in Europe is the sending church, and the church of Africa is the receiving church, we are now increasingly faced with the other reality, and ask: What can the European church learn from the church in Africa? On these matters, terms like the global South and the global North are used, and I am well aware of the fact that Africa is more than Sub Saharan Africa, but in this article I have chosen the term Africa as the representative for the global South, and Europe as the representative for the global North.

The idea that the European church has something to learn, and that the African church might be the teacher has become a widespread idea among both African theologians and Western missiologists. Knud Jørgensen touches this theme when he tells about his experience coming home to Europe from mission service in Ethiopia in the 1980s. "I started to realise that my experience from Ethiopia and from the East-African revival – and later from the growing church of China – was experiences about how the church was meant to be."[2] Further Tormod Engelsviken claims that "there are many indications that the renewal of

---

[1] K. Bediako, "The Significance of Modern African Christianity: A Manifesto", *Studies in World Christianity* 1.1 (The Edinburgh Review of Theology and Religion 1995), 51-67.

[2] Knud Jørgensen, "Trenger kirken omvendelse? På vei mot en misjonal ekklesiologi", Tormod Engelsviken and Kjell Olav Sannes (eds), *Hva vil det si å være kirke? Kirkens vesen og oppdrag* (Trondheim: Tapir akademiske forlag, 2004), 51-68.

theology and church life will come from the global South"[3]

In my doctoral dissertation, "Ancestor Christology in Context"[4], I have singled out five areas Bediako thinks the African church contributes to the church universal in general and to the European in particular. The first is to give a wider perspective on Christianity than being a Western religion, the second is to recover the significance of the primal religiosity in Christianity, and the third is to regain the missionary sense of theology. Fourthly Bediako suggests that the African sense of wholeness and finally the experience of religious pluralism, might contribute to a renewal of European Christianity.

In 1996, the Organisation of African Instituted Churches (OAIC) wrote a Manifesto where they stated "their own perception of their contribution to the world church."[5] Here they claim to "awaken themes that have become dormant or latent in the universal church due to destructive influence of technology and science on relational life".[6] They identify seven areas such as: a) the wholeness of creation, b) fecundity, c) humans-in-community, d) communion of saints, e) the church as a life-giving organ in society, f) the renewal of the Holy Spirit, and g) spiritual healing.[7]

These two examples, from Bediako and OAIC, show us that the self image of the church in Africa has changed from being the receiver to being a contributor to spirituality and theology of the church, and even to share insights with the European church in order to help her in her weakness. In this chapter I will focus on four of the issues where Bediako finds that the church in Africa has a contribution to make.

Contextuality

> Gospel and culture cannot be separated. It is not possible in Ghana for us to talk about the Gospel and ignore the impact it has on culture and vice versa. It is

[3] Tormod Engelsviken, "Den misjonale kirke og utfordringen fra kirken i sør", Tormod Engelsviken and Kjell Olav Sannes (eds), *Hva vil det si å være kirke? Kirkens vesen og oppdrag* (Trondheim: Tapir akademiske forlag, 2004), 69-92.

[4] Roar G. Fotland, *Ancestor Christology in Context: Theological Perspectives by Kwame Bediako* (Bergen: Universitetet i Bergen, 2004).

[5] J. S. Pobee and G. Ositelu II, *African Initiatives in Christianity: The Growth, Gifts and Diversities of indigenous African Churches, a challenge to the ecumenical movement* (Geneva: WCC Publications, 1998).

[6] Pobee and Ositelu II, *African Initiatives*, 70.

[7] Pobee and Ositelu II, *African Initiatives*, 70-71.

> culture that shapes our response to the Gospel and shapes the kind of church we are.[8]

This is another way for Bediako to say that Christianity does not belong to a specific culture, not even the Western, despite its image of being a Christian culture.

One of the great gifts the church of Africa has given to the universal church is the focus on the importance of contextuality. According to Stephen B. Bevans and Volker Küster, contextualisation was a term introduced in 1972 by the Theological Education Fund of WCC[9] as a response to "the Catholic debate on inculturation."[10] Küster also indicates that the consultation process where the Ecumenical Association of Third World Theologians (EATWOT) participated was crucial to the development, and is crucial to the future of the concept.[11] There are many definitions of contextualisation, Hwa Yung defines it as

> the total process wherein reflection and action are combined as the indigenous church, having properly grasped the meaning of the gospel of Christ from within its own culture, and socio-political and economic realities, seeks, on the one hand, to live out its new faith in accord with the cultural patterns of the local society and, on the other hand, to transform that society and individuals therein, in response to their felt needs under the guidance of the Christian Scriptures and the Holy Spirit[12]

Contextuality has been an element of Christianity since its very beginning, when Peter on the day of Pentecost preached to the Jewish crowd claiming Jesus as the Messiah.[13] Further, we recall Paul's first careful translation of Christianity to the Greek-Roman worldview, Martin Luther's concern to make Christianity culturally relevant for the Germans and John Wesley's desire to contextualise the gospel to the poor masses of England. I also claim that Western theologians in the twentieth century were doing contextual theology, because they, with their philosophically oriented theology, "responded to the

---

[8] Kwame Bediako, "Gospel and Culture, some Insights for our Time from the Experience of the Earliest Church", *Journal of African Christian Thought* 2.2 (1999), 8-17.

[9] Stephen B. Bevans, *Models of Contextual Theology* (Maryknoll: Orbis Books 1992), 21.

[10] Volker Küster, *The Many Faces of Jesus Christ* (London: SCM Press, 2001), 24.

[11] Küster, *The Many Faces*, 25.

[12] Hwa Yung, *Mangos or Bananas? The Quest for an Authentic Asian Christian Theology* (Oxford, Regnum, 1997), 13-14.

[13] Acts 2:36. *The Holy Bible: New International Version* (London: Hodder & Stoughton, 1990).

challenges brought to them by their contemporary culture."[14] This way of thinking is in accordance with John Macquarrie who points to Paul Tillich as a theologian concerned with connecting theology and culture. "Tillich's method of 'correlation' looks to contemporary culture for the questions that are agitating the spirit of the time, and seeks to find answers to them in the Christian faith."[15]

What I claim, is not that the church of Africa invented contextuality, but that, among others, African theologians helped European theology out of its universal captivity, and that we still have something to learn on the issue of contextualisation. At the time when African theology wrestled to be integrated in the global theological scene during the 1960s, most theologians in the Europe thought of African theology as contextual and therefore provincial and provisional, while European theology was universal and therefore global and lasting. In that sense European theologians were in line with the general European understanding, that the European culture was the global culture, and that the concerns of Europe therefore were the concerns of people everywhere. A closer look at Western theology reveals that it is as provisional and contextual as theology always has been. As Kwame Bediako writes; "Western theology was for so long presented in all its particulars as *the* theology of the Church, when in fact, it was geographically localised and culturally limited, European, Western, an not universal."[16]

The main danger of a global theology is that it does not concern anybody. It might become nothing else than an exchange of ideas for the exchange itself, and nobody cares except a few theologians. Pretending to be global, European theology was busy with general philosophical questions derived out of the European context, but with no link to the daily life of the church and the regular church goers. They even thought that African theologians who developed a theology with close links either to culture (cultural theology) or to the political circumstances (South African Black theology), were irrelevant.

Despite lack of enthusiasm from European theologians, African scholars insisted on the need for contextuality, and defended strongly the development of a theology more fitting the African reality than European theology ever could be. In the words of the Ghanaian theologian John S. Pobee their task was "to translate Christianity into genuine African categories."[17] They asked for the African reality, the language, the symbols, the religion, the structure, the daily

---

[14] Fotland, *Ancestor Christology*, 436.

[15] John Macquarrie, "Systematic Theology", in Donald W. Musser and Joseph L. Price (eds), *A New Handbook of Christian Theology* (Nashville: Abingdon Press, 1992), 469-474.

[16] Kwame Bediako, *Jesus and the Gospel in Africa: History and Experience* (Maryknoll, N.Y.: Orbis Books, 2004), 115.

[17] John S. Pobee, *Towards an African Theology* (Nashville: Abingdon Press, 1979), 18.

life, the poems, the joys and the fears of the African people and asked what happened when all this culture and religion were encountered with the Bible and the person of Jesus Christ. By taking into account the African reality and let it meet the Christian reality, not as it was found in the European shape, but as it was found in the Bible and in the person of Jesus Christ, African theologians desired to make Christianity a true African religion relevant for Africans.

At the end of the day, European theologians had to adjust to the new reality, by reconsidering their understanding and accepting their own theology as contextual.

> Part of the impact of the emergence of sizeable Christian communities in areas of the world other than Western Europe and North America has been the recognition that the theological traditions of Western Christianity are culturally determined and therefore not universally normative.[18]

African theology, together with other theologies of the global South, taught us a lesson, and in my opinion we still need to learn contextuality. We still need to learn to ask for the language, the symbols, the spiritualities the joys and the concerns of the people in our culture, encounter our culture with the Biblical story and communicate a relevant, a contextual gospel, to people of today.

Restoring Christianity as religion

> Africa's Christian theologians have contributed in no small measure to reaffirm the place of *religion* itself in the Christian theological enterprise.[19]

With such a statement, Bediako draws the line between African traditional religion, Christianity, and a primal religious outlook. In addition he asserts that European Christianity has lost its sense of religion, and that through the insight of African theology European Christianity has been given the means for a return to Christianity as a religion.

When I was teaching Science of Religion this semester, some students disliked my comments about Christianity as a religion. In their opinion we have religions – at best human beings searching for God, at worst the invention of the devil – and we have Christianity – God's revelation. This way of thinking was not new to me; in my Christian upbringing in the church, I learned that the

---

[18] Kwame Bediako, "African Christian Theology; Theology of African Independent Churches; Black Theology; Culture" in Sinclair Ferguson and David F. Wright (eds), *New Dictionary of Theology* (Leicester: InterVarsity Press, 1988), 8-12; 103-105; 183.

[19] Kwame Bediako, *Christianity in Africa: The Renewal of a Non-Western Religion* (Edinburgh: Edinburgh University Press, 1995), 261.

main difference between Christianity and other kinds of spirituality is that Christianity is not a religion. As a Methodist Seminary student, I learned that John Wesley claimed that Christianity was a social religion, and the religion of the heart, but often I could not resist the temptation to go along with the folk theology, even as a pastor. The statement that Christianity was not a religion became a symbol of a right attitude towards other religions.

It was African theology in general and Kwame Bediako in particular that made me change my mind and my language about Christianity, and it is now important for me to claim Christianity among the religions, with all the implications that follow.

The rejection of Christianity as a religion is based on two main assumptions. First, the idea of the superiority of Christianity, and second the influence of the Enlightenment upon our culture, where religion as such is defined out of the modern context. These two aspects are elements of a European thought pattern, where on the one hand there was a need to find a symbol for Christianity saying it was something else and more than primitive religions found elsewhere in the world, a symbol that at the same time fitted the modern mind. By stating that Christianity was not a religion, these two elements could be paired in one symbol. The Evangelicals were happy and thought they had gained something important over against other religions, and the liberals were satisfied by being able to maintain the philosophical, ethical and cultural aspects of Christianity, putting aside the superstitious elements.

After listening to African theology, I ask if this symbol in fact has reduced Christianity to something *less* than a religion. For me religion has to do with transcendence, with *the something more*, something else and something above the created order. In my Christian language religion has to do with God, the Father, the incarnate and risen Jesus Christ and the Holy Spirit. I might talk about God as a symbol in religious terms. On the other hand God is more than a symbol of transcendence, because Jesus Christ is God revealed in history and the Holy Spirit is God still creating history by actually transforming people and communities after the image of God. If so, by maintaining the symbol of Christianity as not being a religion, all those who want Christianity to be the bearer of transcendence are the losers. The answer for European Christians might be to return to a primal worldview.

A primal worldview

For a Western scholar it is a challenge to encounter African theology and its quest for a return to this pre-Enlightenment – primal – world view. Bediako even claims that

> a serious Christian theological interest in the European primal tradition and the early Christianity amid those traditions, could provide a fresh approach to understanding Christian identity in Europe too.[20]

Bediako has an understanding of European Christianity and theology to be in crisis, and to be marked by philosophy more than by religion. According to Bediako "Christian theology in the West seems, on the whole, to understand the Christian Gospel as a system of ideas."[21] As a result, he argues, theology and Christianity in Europe

> appears to have lost touch with, and to be incapable of answering to, the crucial issues which lie at the heart of human existence, issues which are essentially religious: questions of human identity, community, ecological equilibrium and justice.[22]

It is the rediscovery of Christianity as a primal religion that might be an African contribution to the restoration of the religious element in European Christianity. Bediako draws on Harold Turner's idea and argues that there are "special 'affinities between the Christian and the primal traditions' in religion."[23] A primal worldview is, according to Turner, a belief in[24]

- a sense of kinship with nature
- the deep sense that man is finite and in need of a power that is not his own
- the conviction that man is not alone in the universe, for there is a spiritual world of powers or being more powerful and ultimate than himself.
- human beings can enter into relationship with the spirit world, share its power and blessing and find protection against evil forces.
- the ancestors, "the living dead", remain united in mutual obligations with the "living living".
- human beings live in a sacramental universe where there is no sharp dichotomy between the physical and the spiritual.

One of Bediako's arguments for the massive growth of Christianity in Africa is the earlier mentioned affinity between Christianity and the primal. He further thinks that because Christianity in a primal version grows in Africa,

---

[20] Kwame Bediako, "Five Theses on the Significance of Modern African Christianity: A Manifesto", *Transformation,* 13.1 (1996), 20-29.

[21] Bediako, *Christianity in Africa*, 106.

[22] Bediako, *Christianity in Africa*, 105.

[23] Kwame Bediako, "Christ in Africa: Some Reflections on the Contribution of Christianity to the African becoming" in C. Fyfe (ed), *African Future* (Edinburgh, Centre of African Studies, University of Edinburgh, 1988), 447-458.

[24] Taken from Bediako, *Christianity in Africa*, 93-95.

Christianity in Europe has to turn to the primal in order to grow.[25] By doing that Christianity in Europe is also recovering the religious aspect of Christianity, since true religion for Bediako implies a primal worldview, and since Christianity in its essence is primal.

For us in Europe the big question is if Bediako is right. Worldwide we know he is right. It is not only in Africa Christianity with a primal image is growing, we find the same also in Asia and Latin America. Peter Berger seems to interpret the global context along these lines, when he looks upon the secularisation of Europe as the global exception when it comes to religion.[26] If we add that Eliade claims that human beings are religious in their fundamental nature, we are drawn towards a conclusion which tells us that we might have something to learn from African Christianity.

The objection to this conclusion might for some be the European context. If Christianity is to be a contextual religion, the primal aspect might be questioned on the sole reason that the Enlightenment, the rational outlook, is the context of Europe. This might well contain some truth, but it is not the whole truth, for there are two strands in the European context. One is the rational context and the other is the post-modern open context. Berger suggests that the rational context will remain strong in Europe, because the "principal 'carrier' of progressive, Enlightened beliefs and values [...] are very influential, as they control the institutions they provide the 'official' definitions of reality."[27] If that is the truth the decline of Christianity will continue. I observe a parallel development within the church. A number of the well educated leaders in the church seem to share interests with the educational and political leaders in maintaining Christianity as an element of the establishment observing the need for religious rituals and symbols but without a religious worldview. In this way the rationalistic outlook maintain the power in the church, and Christianity is well under control. The faith in the transcendent God is observed, but Christianity is often reduced to rituals, to ethics and to philosophy. The spirits, the powers, the revelation and the passion for mission are neglected.

The other strand of the European context, the open post-modern, is more flexible and allows the primal to surface. We see it in the new religious movements and the new folk spirituality where the transcendent is obvious and the primal is the norm. The supernatural, the spirits, the powers, the irrational, and the angels flourish. Healing and transformation and revelation are integrated in the perception of reality. This is in line with Bediako's

---

[25] Bediako, "Five theses", 26-28.

[26] P. L. Berger, "The Desecularisation of the World: A Global Overview" in Peter L. Berger *The Desecularization of the World: resurgent religion and world politics (*Washington, D.C.: Ethics and Public Policy Center, 1999), 1-18

[27] Berger, "The Desecularization", 10.

understanding of the primal worldview, the acceptance of the "supernatural"[28] and of a "spiritual outlook".[29] He also contrasts the primal world view with a rational outlook.[30] I observe a parallel development within the church. The emergence of charismatic Christianity, the emphasis on the healing power of the Spirit, the making of a liturgy for cleansing a house for evil or disturbing spirits, the desire for experience and the stress on revelation, are all elements of primal Christianity in the European context.

African theologians did not invent the primal aspect of Christianity, but they have reclaimed it for Christian theology. Even though there are some primal elements in European Christianity, theologising around it is not developed, and here we can learn from African scholars.

Theology as missiological

> African theologians have recaptured the character of theology as Christian intellectual activity on the frontier with the non-Christian world, and hence as essentially communicative, evangelistic and missionary.[31]

Through this sentence, Bediako is first characterising African theology as a theology concerned with mission, concerned with the essence of being a church, the sharing of the gospel. By its very nature, he says, African theology is missiological. Second, he is also characterising European theology through this small word, recaptured. I hear Bediako thinking that European Christianity has lost an important aspect of Christian theology, due to endless philosophical discussions.[32] But, by the help of African theology he thinks it could regain its "missionary sense.[33] Thirdly, Bediako is characterising theology itself, arguing that the very nature of theology is mission. In my understanding he thereby says that theology is for a purpose, the communication of the gospel.

What is a missiological theology? In my understanding it is a theology that is concerned with how to understand mission, how to do mission, and what the content of the message should be in various contexts. Theology as missiological is occupied with shaping the gospel in a language and with symbols people can understand.

My question to Bediako is if he is overstating the crisis in European

---

28 Kwame Bediako, "The Willowbank Consultation, January 1978: A personal Reflection", *Themelios: An International Journal for Theological Students*, 5.2 (1980), 25-32.

29 Bediako, "The Willowbank", 28.

30 Fotland, *Ancestor Christology*, 366.

31 Kwame Bediako, "Understanding African theology in the twentieth century", *Themelios*, 20.1 (1994), 14-19.

32 Bediako, *Christianity in Africa*, 106.

33 Bediako, "Understanding African Theology", 18.

theology. Has European theology completely lost the missionary element? Looking back, it is obvious that mission has been important in European theology. Hundred years ago missionaries were sent all over the world, and due to the way Christianity has spread throughout the African continent, Africa is now becoming the new centre of Christianity. Seeing that, Bediako praises the modern missionary movement to Africa as "a success story."[34] The success is partly ascribed to the missionaries from Europe, because "the historical roots of African Christianity lie in the modern missionary enterprise from the West."[35]

Taking another perspective, the second half of the twentieth century saw a decline of interest in mission in Europe, due to outward, inward and structural aspects. As the quest for de-colonialisation grew in Europe, the idea of mission was increasingly interpreted as imperialistic. As Europe changed and became more multi-ethnic and multi-religious a new understanding of religious tolerance became an element also within theology, and as the church grew in Africa and local leaders emerged while at the same time the trend in Europe was rapid change and no longer life long commitments, the mission work had to be restructured.

Looking at Africa, it seems clear that Bediako is right. African theologians are aware of the need for a theology on the frontier of the non-Christian world, a missionary theology. The history of Christianity in Africa might confirm that it has always been like that. Today we know that the success story of the mission to Africa also is the success story of African evangelists creating a communicative theology they wanted people to grasp the truth in.

Contemporary mission history tells us that the Western missionaries are given too much credit for the Christianisation of Africa. Bediako claims that "the European connection of the Christian presence in Africa in the more recent phase of its development must not be overstated."[36] Bediako points to great African evangelists like the prophet William Wade Harris from Liberia, Joseph Kimbangu from Congo/Zaire and Isaiah Shembe from South Africa when he shows the significant contribution of African prophets to the growth of the church in Africa.[37] Referring to the twentieth century, Bediako claims that Harris is "the one person who in this century has been perhaps the single most important instrument in bringing masses of people within the shortest possible time into the church."[38] But theology as mission is also a concern for

---

[34] Kwame Bediako, "The missionary inheritance", in R. Keeley (ed), *Christianity: A World Faith* (Tring, Lion, 1985), 303-311.

[35] Bediako, 'African Christian Theology', 8.

[36] Kwame Bediako, *Theology and Identity: The Impact of Culture upon Christian Thoughts in the Second Century and Modern Africa* (Oxford, Regnum, 1992), 304.

[37] Fotland, *Ancestor Christology*, 247.

[38] Kwame Bediako, "Scripture as the Hermeneutics of Culture and Tradition", *Journal of African Christian Thought*, 4.1 (2001), 2-11.

contemporary scholars in Africa. In my short conclusion of the personal vocation of Bediako, I write:

> What then is the personal vocation of Kwame Bediako? It is to participate in collaboration with other African theologians, in the future development of Christianity into an African reality, in the spirit of Paul, Origen and Augustine, with the ultimate vocation, in words and deeds, to proclaim Christ.[39]

Looking at the mission history of Africa in general, and the post-colonial period in particular, Bediako finds that "Christian expansion in Africa in the post-colonial era far outstripped its growth in the colonial period. All along, in fact, local African initiative and agency were much more significant than foreign missionary intervention."[40] Mission as an element of European theology seems to have been seriously weakened, while mission as an element of African theology seems to be consistent, if possible even strengthened.

It might be that Bediako is overstating a little bit, but on the other hand, looking at the reality of church and theology in Europe, we must admit that the missionary aspect of both needs to be recaptured. And who should be better equipped to help us with that project than African theologians?

The plurality of religions

> Our affirmation of the unique Christ in the midst of the plurality of religions, which is the task of a Christian theology of religious pluralism, consists in commending the meanings of Christ [...], to men and women in their own worlds of faith, respecting their personality as being created, as ourselves, in the image of the one and the same Creator, and yet seeking to 'move them Christward in the freedom of their personal wills'[41]

The issue of a plurality of religions is not new. Missionaries have lived with that reality all the time, but it is rather new when it comes to how the church in Europe is functioning at home. But as it has become an issue on the home ground, the changes in the global structure has forced the European church to rethink its theology of religions also when other religions are at a distance.

Over the last 50 years Europe has undergone a tremendous change from being primarily culturally homogeneous to becoming a continent with a plurality of cultures and religions. The people that European missionaries visited as strangers and outsiders and whom they tried to convince to leave their

---

[39] Fotland, *Ancestor Christology*, 413.
[40] Kwame Bediako, "Into All the World", in Richard Bauckham et al. (eds), *Jesus 2000* (Oxford: Lion, 1989), 222-225.
[41] Kwame Bediako, "Christ is Lord: How is Jesus Unique in the Midst of Other Faiths?", *Trinity Journal of Church and Theology* 14.2 (1994), 50-61.

culture and religion in order to embrace Christianity and European culture, now have become our neighbours and people whom we need to integrate in our own culture. The religions we earlier wanted people to abandon, are today the religions we make space for and have to accept that our sons and daughters choose. The world experience is now becoming the European experience.

At the same time, as shown above, the idea of a church in mission has been under attack from both outside and inside the church. Within the church a theology of tolerance and equal revelation surfaced, with the result that the whole idea of a church in mission was perceived as old fashioned, intolerant and suiting a time when Christianity was alone on the religious scene.

This change in culture seems to confuse the church in Europe. The church in Europe has for centuries been used to set the scene, but is now frequently challenged to take another role. In a way it became a stranger in its own land without really knowing how to deal with the plurality of cultures and religions. According to Bediako, the "African experience of pluralism"[42] might be a contribution from the church in Africa that can help the church in Europe to cope with the new post-Christian era of pluralism, because religious and cultural plurality is the "normal" experience in Africa.[43]

Bediako's way forward, for the African as well as for the European church is twofold. The first road leads us to accept that all religions are traditions of response[44] to God's revelation[45], or as he puts it, "to the reality and disclosure of the Transcendent".[46] This does not imply that all religions are the same, or are bearers of equal revelation, but he is confirming other religious traditions by ascribing to them that divine revelation is a part of their tradition. On this basis Bediako follows John Mbiti who writes that he "considers traditional religions, Islam and other religious systems to be preparatory"[47] to the Gospel – *praeparatio evangelica*. The second road leads us to hold on to the confession of the uniqueness of Christ. For Bediako, Jesus Christ is the "fulfiller of all human cultures",[48] and Christianity is the only religion able to point to "the Ultimate Identity".[49] John Mbiti, who inspires Bediako, has fronted the axiom

---

[42] Bediako, "The Significance", 62.

[43] Bediako, "The Significance", 62.

[44] A phrase Bediako has borrowed from John V. Taylor.

[45] Kwame Bediako, "How is Jesus Christ Lord? Aspects of an Evangelical Christian Apologetics in the Context of African Religious Pluralism", *Exchange* 25.1 (1996), 27-42.

[46] Bediako, "How is Jesus Christ Lord?", 36.

[47] John S. Mbiti, *African religions and philosophy* (London: Heinemann, Second Edition 1989), 277.

[48] Kwame Bediako, "John Mbiti's Contribution to African Theology" in Jacob K. Olupona and Sulayman S. Nyang (eds), *Religious Plurality in Africa: Essays in Honour of John S. Mbiti* (Berlin: Mouton de Gruyter, 1993), 367-390.

[49] Bediako, "John Mbiti's Contribution", 377.

that the ultimate revelation of God, Jesus Christ, is also looked upon as the yardstick with which we can measure the quality of divine revelation, and Bediako concludes that whatever good is operating in other religions, it is Christ – at least in intention – who operates.[50]

This is just a short summary of Bediako's thinking around these issues. In addition to being a starting point for a continuous conversation, I find it interesting because Bediako gives us insight into an African way of thinking theologically. My experience of European thinking is that it is an either – or culture, while the African thinking is more both – and. In a pluralistic situation the African way of thinking might be more helpful than the old European. And as shown above, it is not a necessary consequence to lose once own identity as Christian with a more open attitude.

By this contribution of the African church, the church in Europe might be guided on a way that can combine the openness towards our neighbour at the same time as we reclaim our right to be a church in mission.

Conclusion

Kwame Bediako sees "African Christianity [as] being the *representative* Christianity at the start of the new millennium."[51] The church in Africa believes that it has something to offer the church in Europe, something that can make it more relevant for people, more enthusiastic about spreading the Gospel and more vital in its worship. The American missiologist Robert J. Schreiter also finds the contribution of Africa promising, writing about the "tremendous human resources" of Africa, and about the Christian churches in Africa that "mirror the vigour and energies of the continent."[52] He further claims that when it comes to Christology, "one finds striking images that contribute not only to the building up of genuinely African theologies, […] but also making distinct contributions to the understanding of Christ for the whole church."[53]

Is it possible to think that the church in Africa can make a difference for the church in Europe? Are we not too different? The human reality in Africa seems to follow the pattern of Eliade when he describes *homo religiosus*, while the European reality by Eliade is portrayed as the first society where the non-religious human being is totally unfolded.[54] Is the church in Europe so

---

[50] Bediako, "How is Jesus Christ Lord?", 38.

[51] Kwame Bediako, "A Half Century of African Christian Thought: Pointers to Theology and Theological Education in the Next Half Century", *Journal of African Christian Thought* 3.1 (2000), 5-11.

[52] R. J. Schreiter, "Introduction: Jesus Christ in Africa Today" in Robert J. Schreiter (ed), *Faces of Jesus in Africa* (London, SCM Press, 1991), vii-xiii.

[53] Schreiter, "Introduction", ix.

[54] Mircea Eliade, *Det hellige og det profane*, (Oslo: Gyldendal, second edition 1994).

interwoven with the desacralized Enlightenment culture, that the impulses from Africa cannot be understood?

On the other hand, we have to remember that the church in Europe is not solely influenced by a philosophical and rational theology. Within the European church we also find theology that is influenced by the primal. Also in Europe Christians say their morning prayer before they go to their working places, believing that God's presence in their lives makes a difference. Also in Europe Christians say a prayer before they eat, thanking God for their daily bread. Also in Europe Christians believe in healing and ask their pastor to anoint them with oil when they are sick. And, also in Europe Christians relate to the world as God's creation, to holy space, holy time, holy myths and the sanctification of life. I have to add that some people also see a return to the primal through the emergence of the new religious movement and through a general ideological shift towards a more open understanding of reality where rationality does not have the answer for everything.

It is not a secret that the church in Europe is deteriorating, while the church in Africa is flourishing. By the end of the twentieth century, we saw a "shift in the centre of gravity in the Christian world,"[55] and as Bediako sees it, we are now moving towards "a specifically 'Southern' phase of Christianity."[56] Looking at the present age, Andrew Walls wrote:

> The recession of Christianity among the European peoples appears to be continuing. And yet we seem to stand at the threshold of a new age of Christianity, one in which its main base will be the Southern continents, and where its dominant expression will be filtered through the culture of those continents.[57]

I believe that the embracement of the Enlightenment ideology has weakened the church in Europe. The divine power to make a change and influence the lives of people and society is diminishing. The divine courage to be a church in mission is fading away. The divine life, expressed though vital worship is to a great extent lost. The divine understanding, that life in its totality is the concern of God, is forgotten. Still, we do experience divine power, divine courage, divine life and divine understanding, but we know it is not enough. Deep in our hearts we recognize that the church in Europe needs revitalisation, and the vital church in Africa offers its help. We cannot just copy their methods and their language, but may God help us to be brave enough to listen and to learn from their spirituality and theology, even to the extent that we accept a modified and contextualised primal view of reality.

---

55 Bediako, "The Missionary Inheritance", 311.

56 Bediako, "The Missionary Inheritance", 311.

57 Andrew Walls, *The Missionary Movement in Christian History* (Maryknoll: Orbis Books, 1997), 22.

The church in Europe can, but it should not, overlook the possibility of God's divine providence that "Once again, Christianity has been saved from the world by its diffusion across cultural lines.[58] We might therefore look for guidance from the church in Africa, because "Christianity in Africa is set to play a crucial role in the future shape of the [Christian] faith and its impact in the world at large."[59]

[58] Walls, *The Missionary Movement*, 22.
[59] Bediako, "The Significance", 44.

Christianity and Society in Today's China – From a Perspective of Experimental Study

Gao Shining

Prof Dr Gao Shining, Chinese Academy of Social Sciences, Beijing, China

The relationship between religion and society can be seen not only in the origin of religion, in its development and its adapting itself to the social need, but also in its influence on the society. As an exotic religion, Christianity has some features in its relationship to Chinese society. This article will discuss these features in today's China from three aspects found in my own experimental study.

Chinese Churches have Different Status

How many Christians are there in China? This is a question attracting many scholars abroad. One of the reasons is that the difference is surprisingly great between the different numbers based on different statistics. According to Tian Feng, an official publication of the Chinese Protestant church, there are 20 million Christians in China; in contrast to that quite low number, the highest number is 70 millions, according to some estimation that has come from abroad.

Why are these numbers so greatly different? It is, I think, because the number in Tian Feng just covers those believers belonging to the Three-self churches – that is, the churches registered with the Chinese government. But the number of believers who do not belong to the Three-shelf church is also great. They belong to various kinds of meeting points in today's China, but are not registered with the government.

From 2002 to 2003, I conducted a one year investigation of Christian Churches in Beijing. As I observed it, the diversity and plurality of Christian churches in Beijing are the basic phenomena worth noticing and analyzing.

From the perspective of sociology of religion, some of the meeting points have certain characteristics of a sect, because they are not open enough and are very exclusivist in their attitudes. Many sociologists have attempted to find out the reasons for the rise of sects. An American scholar, Charles Y. Glock concluded that there were five kinds of deprivation relating to the sect's rising: 1. the economic deprivation, that means the lack of money and materials needed; 2. the social deprivation, that means the lower status and less chances to join some social organization and institution; 3. the bodily deprivation, that means being physically and mentally unhealthy; 4. the ethical deprivation, which means the decline of traditional ethics; 5. the mind deprivation, which means that some members of society are not satisfied with the reality and think they are not accepted by the society.

In China, some reasons for the emergence of the meeting points are related to political factors and the existence of denominations. Even in the very beginning of the "Three Self Movement" in the 1950's, various different voices appeared. The Three Self movement adopted the principles of self-reliance, self-governance and self-propagation. (Later a fourth principle was adopted, that of being indigenous). The dissent opinions did not disappear as a result of one political campaign after the other and could not be suppressed by the administrational orders. On the contrary, they have not only remained but also become stronger with the development of Chinese Christianity.

But in our observation, however, as for the rise of meeting points in recent years, we can see more and more reasons which are not related to politics and denominations. Here I will take Beijing as an example to show that the rise of meeting points relates to the general development of Chinese society and has some specific Chinese features.

In the early 1980's, there were just about 10 meeting points in Beijing. However, according to the statistics by the government in 2004, the number is up to 823. Among them, there are just 57 having been registered. In fact, the number of the meeting points is much more than 823, according to many observers.

Such rapid development of meeting points cannot be explained by one or two reasons. As a matter of fact, there are many elements functioning together in the total development.

The first one is the geographical element. In the recent 20 years, Beijing city has grown very fast. As for the extension of the urban area, some report says that we have got a new Beijing City every 5 years! But the number of registered churches in the city is as the same as 20 years ago – five! Of course, they are far from meeting the demand of Christian services though they have been rebuilt and become larger than before. For most Christians it takes one or two hours and several transfers to go to those Three-Self churches. So, many of them naturally hope that they can attend worship services more easily. Among the 507 Christians who were part of our investigation, 209 transferred at least once to some other churches, and 30% of them did that just for the geographical reason, or transportation reasons.

The second element is the changes in the believers' needs. For the urban believers who do not have basic problems with meeting their material needs, the recent social changes they encounter bring about some quite complicated and varied problems such as psychological and emotional problems. This puts more demands on the quality of care on the pastoral workers. This is especially true for the believers who are more highly educated. Some of them choose meeting points other than Three-Self churches just because they are not satisfied with sermons given by the latter. And often, the latter pastoral work is lagging behind the needs of them.

The third one is the need for fellowship. Many Christians prefer a smaller fellowship which can give them more meaningful social and spiritual life. Of course, some of them also feel happy for being able to communicate with their relatives, friends and acquaintances in the meeting points.

The fourth is that of life style. Many Christians with certain kinds of jobs (such as salesmen) have to work on Sundays, and some meeting points give their service on some workdays to meet their special needs, while the registered churches do not.

The fifth is that of theological differences. Some Christians who have formerly studied abroad and received theological ideas different from those of Three-Self churches, have organized meeting points which reflect their theological understandings.

The sixth is the different dispositions in grouping. Many Christians hope to be together with those believers who have the similar jobs, ages or characters as theirs, so there appeared meeting points mainly made up by nurses, business men, retired persons, even blind persons, and so on.

The seventh, and the last one, is the natural course of split. While meeting points are getting bigger and bigger, they always have a disposition to split into smaller ones, partly because they have to adapt themselves to the limited resources.

All the reasons mentioned above are directly related to the development of Chinese society today.

Of course, the legal status of meeting points is different from that of the established, registered churches. In China, I think we can define the established church as some kind of non-profitable and non-governmental but official Christian organization sanctioned by the government. As we call it a non-governmental organization, we mean that, considering its religious character, the church, as E. Durkheim says, is an ethical community solidifying all the believers in it. As we call it an official organization, we mean that in China, all the Three Self churches, like all other formal organizations, have to be led by Chinese Communist Party and the governments. That is to say, their legal status must be decided by the government, their important decisions must be guided and approved by the Administration of Religious Affairs. Of course, when we talk about their official nature, we are not saying that Chinese established churches have no rights in religious affairs. What we say is just that for the established church freedom and autonomy is very limited. It is not a secret in today's China.

As for the meeting points, because of their legal status, I would like to define them as a kind of non-profitable and non-governmental but legally uncertain Christian organization. In fact, the term 'meeting point' is just a very general title. In Beijing, all the different "meeting points" have their own backgrounds and features. Many people used to call them 'family churches' or 'house churches', and thought that they were against the Three-Self Movement. As I mentioned above, however, the emergence of meeting points was caused by many reasons, which have nothing to do with the attitudes towards the Three-Self Movement. The meeting points have no relationship with the government, except their need of legal status or of being sanctioned by the government. And in fact, since many of them do not hold their worship activities in families or families' houses, the title 'family churches' or 'house churches' is indeed not suitable. What is even more unsuitable is to think they are against Three-Self. On the contrary, most of them are truly characterized by the Three-Self principles, even a Four-Self – they are appearing and disappearing just by themselves!

Although the established church and the meeting point have different legal status, I should say, they have similar social situation in China. That is to say, both of them are not in the mainstream but on the margin of society, which is not only because of their religious nature, but also because of the special political, social and cultural background of China.

The Identities of Chinese Christians

Protestant Christianity did not enter China until the 19th Century and it came to China on a large scale with the West invaders. Therefore, Christianity has been seen as a 'foreign religion', and for many years, branded 'cultural invader' for many Chinese people. In those years, Chinese Christians were thought of as traitors to their country and even to their families. As they looked down upon the ancestors worship, they were even forbidden to take part in the family's sacrifice rituals. That special situation formed some threat to the cultural identities of Chinese Christians.

In the old years, Christians thought their cultural identity in the following order: Chinese, Christians, and then Chinese Christians. This order of identities is reasonable. For choosing to be a Christian, you would have to answer a question from your neighbors: "Why do you as a Chinese want to be a Christian?" And you had to stress that you were still a Chinese and had not betrayed your fatherland; eventually, you should try your best to show that being a Christian and a Chinese in one person was not contradictory. At that time, Christian faith cost the Chinese Christians a lot, even their life.

Today, with the reform and opening in China, and with the efforts of Chinese academics of religious study, the label of 'foreign religion', on the one hand, has begun to be taken off; on the other, the non-Christians' understanding of Christianity has become more and more objective. Generally speaking, Christians do not feel as much press as before and the identities have become not so complex for the Chinese Christians. They think they are both Chinese and Christians; the two identities are not opposite but are integrated, with no questions about which one is primary and which is secondary.

From 2002 to 2003, as part of my investigation, I also did some interviews with nearly 60 Christians. One of the interview topics was about how they think about their double identity: Chinese and Christian. According to my records, all the interviewees think that they are both Chinese and Christians; the two identities are not opposite but are integrated, with no questions about which is primary and which is secondary. That is to say, they understand the two identities as being on different levels: as Chinese, they think they must abide Chinese law and fulfill their responsibility to the country; as Christians, they must preach God's gospel. Some Christians also think that their religious identity can help their civil identity, for the Bible teaches Christians that they should obey the ruler. Indeed, the social situation of today's Chinese Christians has been improved very much. Even so, however, it is still a question for many Chinese Christians whether to confess their Christian identity.

In China with atheism as main ideology, although the number of religious believers now is up to one hundred millions and more, they are still just a minority. China experienced many cruel political campaigns after 1949. All the religions were severely criticized as "opium of the masses" which served the counter-revolutionary ideology. By the time of the "Cultural Revolution", this type of criticism reached its peak. Nearly all religious priests and believers were treated and insulted as "monsters", many were even tortured to death. Even up to today, the influence is so strong that many older believers still tremble when recalling the past days.

In 1998, a questionnaire in an investigation of religious affairs asked the following question: Are you willing to tell others that you are a believer when you travel? In all the answers, the "yes" with "strongly" were 42%, the 'yes' indicating "not strongly" were 24%, only 2% of the answers was "no". It is a great progress, in comparison with the situation before 1980 when nobody dared to recognize or express his or her religious identity. In my questionnaire, I asked the same question. Among the 544 valid answers, those who answered "yes" represented 83.1% of the informants, those who answered "no" only 3.3%. Compared with the questionnaire in 1998, mine has three different features: 1, the participants of my investigation were ten times higher; 2, all were Christians (Christians were just a part of the 1998 case study); 3, the "yes" answers were 17% higher. By the way, even in some academic conferences on religion held in Beijing in recent years, a few scholars have confessed their Christian identity.

How, then, about the non Christians' attitudes towards Christians? This was also a question I wanted to know the answer of. So we distributed 200 questionnaires to some students, to some higher educated clerks in the bank as well as to juridical professionals in order to investigate their recognition of religions. The result was that 70.8% recipients said that they could accept that their most intimate relations were being believers, 95.5% said they did not stand off or keep away from believers. So we can say there is almost no discrimination and bias to the believers in these groups of people. And as a result of the analyses of the questionnaires, a phenomenon attracted my attention: it seems that all the participants are more interested in Christian churches than in Buddhist temples. It is worth studying further whether this shows that the degree of recognition of religion varies according to different religions. As for the young people, there is some kind of tendency that Western culture is becoming more and more popular, for example, many young people and students like Christmas much more than Chinese New Year Festival. All these facts show that the identity of Chinese Christians is now in a quite normal situation and that the social circumstances are better for them now than before.

As Christians, how do they think of traditional Chinese culture? This is another key point which I paid attention to. Judging from my investigation, most of the informants were never conscious of any contradictions between Chinese culture and Western culture when they adopted Christian faith. That is to say, they never thought of the problems of faith from the perspective of it being a cultural conflict. But when asked whether they worship their ancestors, *kowtow* and burn Hades Notes in front of their family graves, they showed different opinions.

Basically there were three different opinions. The first one is that Christians should refuse all this kind of Chinese conventions because it is against Christian faith and is idolatry. The second is that Christians should have a tolerant attitude to the people who do this kind of things as long as one does not do it oneself. The third is that if a Christian in his or her heart has no beliefs in those things, all of them are just a meaningless form for him/her, and it does not matter for him/her whether they join it or not. Most of the Christians I interviewed held the first opinion.

In my questionnaire, I asked the same question in order to know the attitude of more Christians to this matter. We got back 555 valid questionnaires and among them, there were 83.4% of Christians who said that "you cannot take part in such Chinese traditional activities"; 13.5% said it depends on the situations; only 3.1% said that Christian could join these activities. This result is the same as that from my in-debth interviews. It shows that most Chinese Christians have felt the contradictions between their faith and Chinese culture when facing the real problem, but that most of them are able to maintain their faith and dare to abandon that which is not consistent with their faith.

The Influence of Christianity on Chinese Society

Since Christianity has developed so quickly in China, people would ask: what influence does it have on the Chinese society today? How do the Chinese Christians think of this?

Nearly all the interviewed Christians have the same view, namely that Christianity has a positive influence on the development of Chinese modern society, but they cannot say more about that. When I asked a few Christians with master or doctor titles, they said they never discussed this kind of things in their gatherings but that they have been thinking about it.

I put this question in my questionnaire. Among 544 Christians, there were 515 (94.2%) answering that Christianity has a positive influence on the development of modern Chinese society; only 22 persons (4%) had the opposite opinion. Then the following question was, on what aspects of Chinese society the Christian impact can be found? Most of the answers were "on the ethics and morality": 92.8% of Christians thought that Christianity can help in the reconstruction of Chinese morality.

Why do the answers focus on ethics and morality? As every body knows, in today's China, with the huge changes taking place, we observe both the economic development and the breakdown of social norms, we see some kind of rich materialistic life coexisting with a sort of spiritual poverty. There is a kind of serious moral disorder.

In the society of present China, there are three main characteristics of the value system. Firstly, the traditional value systems are gradually disintegrating. Secondly, the contemporary value systems are diversifying, becoming more pluralistic. Thirdly, the 'lower' values are becoming more widespread. In this kind of moral changes, we can find that the decline of the transcendent nature of traditional values is the presupposition of its decline and as for the new diverse values, they have appeared in the absence of such kind of transcendence. So in this situation, what influence can Christianity give to the Chinese society?

The direct influence of Christianity comes from two sides: from the church as organization and from the believer as an individual. Let us take one church in Beijing as example: this church is one of the five churches in Beijing city. It holds four worship services on Sunday with nearly one thousand attendants every time. Nearly every sermon focuses on preaching God's grace, love, man's sin and so on.

Besides the services on Sundays, there are many activities such as bible study, prayers and many special meetings for young people, women on other days; in every month there is Eucharist worship, and there are baptism three times a year. Moreover, the church has some arrangements once or twice a year with social services such as haircutting, bicycle-repairing and simple medical examinations on the streets by some church members with special skills, and some activities as helping the old, the ill and the dependents of army men. The church also gives financial support to a few children whose parents cannot afford their schooling (one in 2004), and helps some theological seminary graduates who are working in some poor regions. And when some disasters happen, the church would make some donations.

The influence of the Christian individuals is an important aspect of my investigation. Nearly all the Christians report they have some changes and gains after they converted to Christian faith. The following is a list of the changes from the records of my interviews and questionnaires.

1. having got sense of happiness and peace in hearts; 2. having begun search for the truth in life; 3. having got confidence in the future; 4. having got some positive views of the life and the world; 5.having overcome some personal difficulties and crisis; 6. having enlarged some knowledge and experiences; 7. having got satisfied with the present life; 8. having learnt to take care and help others; 9. having improved family relationship; 10. having got rid of some bad habits; 11. having overcome selfish mind; 12. having improved the relationship with others outside family; 13. having got more healthy; 14. having been able to take things as they come and receive what happened; 15. having improved economic conditions.

My investigations show that at the level of organization, the church itself cannot exert more important and impressive influences on the society, just due to the limitation of its activities within itself, and even its social work is limited in a small scope. But at the level of individual Christians the influence is much greater. In fact many Christians have influenced the people around them. We have found in our "sociological participations" and "observations" that an invisible power has been forming quietly and is becoming stronger and stronger.

The effect of Christianity in today's China can be seen clearly in these three areas: Firstly, in sustaining, to some extent, the traditional values, including the best of the traditional Chinese values; Secondly, in providing more choices in values for the people in the context of pluralistic value systems; Thirdly, in spreading some higher set of values, at the same time stemming the trend of deteriorating social values.

Even so, our investigation also shows that there is very little interaction between Christianity and the present Chinese society, though the situation for Chinese Christians has been improved; that is to say, the effect of Christianity to Chinese society is still limited.

This limitation is due to, above all, the limitation of resources of the Chinese church. This limitation, above all, is the limitation of manpower resources. No matter whether there are 20 million or 70 million Christians in China, 80% of them are in the countryside, most of them have little influence on Chinese society due to their limited conditions. The urban Christians are much less numerous, even though every one plays his role, their influence is still limited. Taking Beijing' situation as example, according to the census in the year of 2000, the whole population is up to nearly 14 millions, including 3 millions immigrants from provinces. As for Christians in Beijing, there are just 40 thousands not including those in meeting points, according to the official statistics.

Of course, this number is much less than the real number, but in any way Christians in Beijing are still a minority. The fact has some immediate effects on the social resources and social influence of Christianity in today's China.

In China, the reasons that Christianity cannot play a greater role are due to the general political situation and especially traditional culture. Besides, the situation of Christianity itself does not allow it to have some powerful social resources. Taking Beijing as an example again, it is one of the largest cities in the world, but the official churches are just nine – five in the city downtown –, and the registered meeting points are less than 100. The unregistered meeting points are around the city, but there are rarely relationships between them, that is to say, they cannot influence on society as a whole.

Furthermore, a church is not allowed to conduct its worship in other places than the registered "religious places", thus the people outside can hear nothing of what goes on inside. The financial power of the church, generally speaking, is limited too.

The donations from believers of some bigger church are much more than in the meeting points, and the income of some meeting points is just enough to keep the basic living of the pastors and basic church activities.

Even so, we should pay attention to a kind of phenomena. Since the Chinese 'reforms and opening-up', we have had huge changes in many areas – economy, ideology, education, academy and culture. These changes have led to some changes in individual lives. The individuals have begun to have some improved conditions and rooms for their spiritual lives. Therefore all the religions have rooms to play their roles to meet the need for spirituality in today's China. And this kind of changes may provide Christianity or other religions with some chances to enter the public spheres of Chinese society.

CLASH OF CIVILISATIONS OR CONTRACT OF CULTURES?

He Guanghu

Prof Dr He Guanghu, Chinese Academy of Social Sciences, Beijing, China

Introduction

A few years ago, in 1999 when they heard tell something about Samuel Huntington's 'theory of clash of civilizations',[1] most Chinese intellectuals assumed a critical even antagonist attitude towards 'the theory', and many of them even took criticism of it or attack upon it as a fashion. In my observation, most of them neglected the fact that Huntington awakened people to the danger of clash of civilizations just in the hope of advancing 'dialog among civilizations' throughout the world, instead of meaning to advocate the clash,[2] as they said in misunderstanding. Furthermore, they were strengthening the terrible conclusion that the clash of civilizations is necessarily unavoidable when they stressed that Chinese or oriental civilisation has absolutely no commensurability with Western or occidental civilization, as they rebuked Huntington in more or less distortion of his idea.

Two years later, in September 2001 when the United Nations' Group for Civilization Dialogue met in Beijing –as a focus of the 'Year of Civilization Dialogue' proposed by the Iranian President – and following the meetings in Vienna and Qatar, then came the news about the terrorist attack on September 11! As a response to it, many Chinese commentators spoke about the event as a signal or a new start of the clash between Christian and Islamic civilizations, jumping to the side of 'Huntington's viewpoint' that they misunderstood and criticized.

Should we come to, from that and the following events, the conclusion that all the efforts for dialogue and cooperation for peace are doomed to failure, and the clash of civilizations will necessarily or unavoidably break out?

If we arrive at such a conclusion, we are not supporting Huntington, but are

---

[1] The Chinese translation of his *The Clash of Civilizations and the Remaking of the World Order* was published by Xinhua Publishing House in January, 1999.

[2] Cf. the Author's Preface to the Chinese edition of his book, and the last paragraph of the book.

nearly backing the terrorists or the murderers, because that would give their doings some great and profound reasons, some reasons beyond direct political intention, some historical, philosophical and cultural reasons, some unfathomable and irresistible reasons. In one word, that would give them an unexpected gift!

Nevertheless, however, we should never be blind to the existence of so many ethnical and international clashes and hostilities in such a globalization and multi-cultural age.

As for globalization, on the one hand, it has brought the economical principles of efficiency and liberalism to the whole world, and hence a series of important political, ethical and cultural results. On the other hand, it means globalization of many 'risks' such as financial crisis and infectious diseases, hence making so-called 'risk society' into a risk earth where all the nations are interdependent.[3]

And as for the multi-cultural situation, on the one hand, such a situation has made human life much more colourful and richer. On the other hand, it is at least one of the causes of many tragic ethnical and international conflicts. And with the accelerating of 'glocalization' and the lessening of the globe, the danger of conflicts caused by cultural oppositions is becoming much greater and more disastrous.

So, facing the issues vitally fatal to the humankind such as 'glocalization', 'clash of civilizations' and 'opposition of cultures', Chinese intellectuals as the successors to a great culture should not stop at some negative or opposite ideas. On the contrary, we should apply the valuable elements of our inheritance to meet the need of today's humankind and, through positive thinking, put forward some constructive proposals.

Therefore, I will hereby, through the following alternative questions, express my thinking and put forward my proposals

Separation-Unification Circle, or Harmonious Co-existence?

Romance of Three Kingdoms, the most popular Chinese historical novel in hundreds of years, begins with such a sentence: 'The great trend of the world is that a long separation does necessarily lead to unification, and a long unification does unavoidably lead to separation.'

The whole history of China has given the strongest support to this judgment, as it has been indeed a separation-unification circle. And all the roads to all the separations and to all the unifications are unexceptionally through battle-fields, through mountains of bones of the dead and rivers of blood of the victims of wars.

That sentence is true as well to the whole past history of civilizations – the

---

3 Cf. Anthony Giddens and Christopher Piersen, *Making Sense of Modernity* (Chinese edition, Beijing: Xinhua Publishing House, 2001).

histories of the Upper and the Lower Egypt, of the Old and the New Babylonia, of Macedonian Empire and of Roman Empire, of Charlemagne Empire and Byzantine Empire, of Empires of Khalifates and of Mongols, of late Ottoman Empire and late Chinese Empire, even of British Empire and of Soviet Empire.

All the history of separation-unification has given testimony to the well-known lines of Chinese poems: 'One general achieves renown over the dead bodies of 10,000 soldiers', 'a few lines of rulers' names in the history covered the unnumbered tombs in the field'![4]

For some people, today's globalization seems a new kind of unification – at the level of the globe rather than at the level of a country. But we should ask: whether it is a road to the end – the final unity,[5] or just the beginning of a greater separation-unification circle – the circle which will signify the history of the globe? Is it a blessing, or a curse to humanity?

Some people say it is a blessing, because the globalization of market is bringing about the globalization of more reasonable disposition of resources, better circulation of goods, and of higher efficiency of production. And some say it is a curse, because it is deteriorating the consumption of natural resources and the unequal distribution of wealth. Both the sides see things in the same perspective – the economic perspective. However, in '*The Book of Great Unity*' by Chinese thinker and reformer Kang You-wei (1858-1927), as well as in '*De Monarchia*' by Italian thinker and poet Alighieri Dante (1265-1321), we can see some other perspectives which are far more important to the fatal issue – cultural, moral and political perspectives. Dante, for example, points out that a united world government is needed for the world peace, and that is in turn for the realization of human intelligence and innovation of human culture which is the same goal of all the civilizations.[6]

In fact, in many different fields ranging from religious studies to political sciences, we can also see many contemporary academics, such as R. Robertson,[7] U. Beck and J. Habermas,[8] who are dealing with the issue far beyond the exclusively economic perspective and arguing for the necessity for going beyond the nation-state at such a stage of development of humankind.

In order to break through the separation-unification circle and to escape from its bloody tragedy possibly at the global level, we must orient the course of globalization with a widened perspective. For the vitally important matter and thinking about that constructively, Chinese intellectuals could turn their mind to the significant idea in their intellectual heritage – the concept of 'He-He'.

---

[4] The poem in the beginning of *Romance of Three Kingdoms*.

[5] The last sentence of *Romance of Three Kingdoms* reverses the order of the first sentence, suggestion the final unity.

[6] *De Monarchia*, Book I. (Chinese edition, Beijing: Commercial Press 1985).

[7] See his 'Globalization and Traditional Religions', in *Tegent Journal* 3 (2001).

[8] See *Politik der Globalisierung* (Frankfurt am Main: Suhrkamp Verlag, 1998).

The Chinese word 'He-He' (和合) consists of two different Chinese characters, meaning respectively 'harmony' and 'co-existence'.[9] Therefore, the idea 'He-He' means harmonious co-existence or complemental union of different things, an ideal supported by nearly all the intellectual or philosophical schools and religions in China, including Confucianism, Taoism (Daoism), Mohism (Moism), Fa-chia (Legalist School), the Yin Yang School and Buddhism.[10] When we define 'He He' as a 'harmonious co-existence' based on the 'universal love'[11] which is the ultimate resource and core spirit of great cultures and civilizations, I think, we can take this idea as our choice between the two alternatives appearing in the title of this section, and should orient the globalization not to monolithism, but to harmonious co-existence of diverse cultures, which is a sublime ideal of the humankind, including the Chinese people.

Hostility, or Co-operation?

Indeed, the history of separation-unification circle is also a history of hostility. 'The mountains of bones of the dead and the rivers of blood of the victims of wars' are all made by the hostilities in the history. Such a tragic causation can be seen not only between nations and between civilizations, but also within a civilization and even within a nation.

From some Socio-Darwinist viewpoint, one can see all the conflicts between classes, nations and civilizations as necessary and reasonable, looking ruthlessly down upon human beings as tools of 'historical reason'. Addressing this kind of viewpoint, and analysing the cause of ruin of the six kingdoms by the Chin Dynasty (221-206 BC) and giving an account of the short-lived unification of China by Chin, the Chinese poet Du Mu wrote:

> The six kingdoms were destroyed by themselves, not by Chin. And Chin was ruined by itself, not by the uprising [peoples] under heaven. Alas, if the rulers of kingdoms loved or were kind to their peoples, they would have been able to resist Chin. If the rulers of Chin loved or were kind to the peoples of the six kingdoms, they would have been able to be rulers not only for three generations[12] but for ten thousands of generations, and who could destroy them? They had no time for lamenting themselves, but the people in later ages could lament for them. If the

[9] The second character generally means 'union' or 'to unite', but only its other meanings such as 'to co-operate', 'to join together' or 'to get along well with', 'suitable' can apply to this context.

[10] Cf. Zhang Liwen, *An Introduction to He-He Culture in China*, The Party School of CCCPC Press, 2001, 18.

[11] Ibid., 11.

[12] In fact, Chin Dynasty was ruined by the uprisings during the reign of the first emperor's grandnephew.

> later people could not learn their lesson while lamenting, the even more later people could do nothing but lamenting for them![13]

On the other hand, however, the history of China tells us that we can get another kind of result and get rid of the ruthless necessity of 'historical reason', if only we could abandon any hostilities to other peoples and embrace some friendly or co-operative attitude to them. We can see this in the fact that the one and same area – the area connecting the northwest part of today's China and Central Asia – was called the 'Silk Road', associated with birds' singing and flowers' fragrance as well as with terrible battlefields 'with no spring breezes'.[14] The two different kinds of scenes associated with the same place are just the results of different choices or decisions – hostility or co-operation. Neither of the results is necessary or unavoidable. Either is just a choice.

In the age of 'glocalization', such a choice is bound to influence upon not only one area, but also the total earth and the whole humanity. In such a situation, hostilities or conflicts are damaging the interests of not only one side or party, but also of both sides of parties and even of plural sides or parties. Therefore, one's own interests could no longer be the reason for hostility, because it is just our interests that demand our co-operation with others, and because it is just the peace that has become the most important interests of us and of others.

In the field of cultures, the idea of 'zero-sum game', which is held up in many other fields, is utterly false, terribly misleading and fatally harmful. For every culture can be enriched and improved in learning from other cultures, and everybody raised in a culture could get more from other cultures. So, when we think of the spreading of the idea of complementarity and mutual benefit even in the business world, when we think of the original meaning of the word 'compete' (from the Latin word 'competere') as 'to strive together' or 'to drive forward together', and when we think of the original image of the Chinese character '竞竞' (meaning 'to compete') depicting a couple of people running together, will we still refuse to embrace the co-operation as the only choice in today's situation of plural cultures?

Clash of Civilizations, or Contract of Cultures?

Between the two alternatives, of course, we will not choose the former. For the possible clash of civilizations will be the greatest threat to the peace of the world, as S. Huntington said.[15] But, however, what factor or power on earth can we find to prevent or reduce the risk of the clash?

---

[13] An Elegy to the Palace Efanggong (in *Comptele Works of Du Mu*).

[14] From one of the most popular poems that every Chinese schoolchild knows very well.

[15] *Clash of Civilizations and the Remaking of the World Order*, 372.

The globalization of economy seems to be the first great power for this, as it is going to make peoples and nations of different civilizations dependent upon each other in economic life, and to awake them to the fact that the benefits won by maintaining peace are much more than the benefits won by waging wars. However, on the one hand, many conflicts are indeed caused by clashes in the economic area, and on the other hand, more and more conflicts are caused by oppositions in cultural or ideological areas, such as opposition between the nationalisms of two peoples who are hostile to each other.[16] Furthermore, with the decrease of wars caused by economic factors, the conflicts with cultural reasonings would be more and more striking and go to the foreground.

The second great power may be found in the convergent trend of socio-political institutions of various nations, as people have seen less wars between nations with the same socio-political institutions, in comparison with those between nations with opposite institutions. But, however, on the one hand, the history tells us that it is still a possibility for the nations with same or similar institutions to be involved in conflict with each other, and on the other hand, the socio-political institution is forged by many factors among which cultural factors are especially important.

So, in search of a great power to prevent or reduce the risk of the clash of civilisations, we have to move to the cultural area. But, however, we have clearly known that culture could function in this field as a double-edged sword. On the one hand, the essential compatibility of cultures could make the best channels for exchange between nations, and on the other hand, the formal difference of cultures could widen the gap between nations. Cultural factors could make a Silk Road as well as a battlefield of one and the same place.

The reason for that is very simple: the factors which are nearest to the spiritual realm are least controlled by natural laws but most influenced by human free choice. So, the decisive point is the choice of human beings – whether we are inflexibly clinging to the forms or symbols of culture, or liberally loyal to her essence or spirit, which is vital to our future.

On this issue, the movement towards 'Global Ethic' in recent years initiated by some academical and religious people[17] and the developments relating to it have made clearer the following three points:

1. The role of exchange and co-operation of cultures (including

---

[16] The conflicts between China and the former Soviet Union in the 1960s', between China and Vietnam in the 1970s, and what happened in former Yugoslavia are some examples.

[17] Exemplified by the Parliament of World Religions (in Chicago, 1993) initiated by Professors L. Swidler, H. Küng and others, and the Declaration Toward a Global Ethic passed in the Paliament. (Cf. Hans Küng and Karl-Josef Kusche eds., *A Global Ethic: The Declaration of the Parliament of World Religion*s. Guanghu He trans. (Chengdu: Sichuan People's Publishing House 1997).

religions) in preventing and reducing the risk of civilizations has been realized by more and more people, especially many political people.[18]

2. The essential or spiritual compatibility of cultures (including religions) could be discovered and recognized through persistent study and work.[19]
3. It is possible for the representatives of different cultures and common people from diverse traditions to sit together for equal discussion and to agree on some basic principles concerning common interests.[20]

In view of the three points mentioned above, and in the full conviction that the peaceful co-existence of civilizations and harmonious relationship of cultures are in need of some rules or a 'contract', just as such things are needed for a healthy market and equal competition, I put forward hereunder four points as the basic principles of any contract proposed for guiding or regulating the relationship of cultures and of people in any particular culture:

1. Peaceful getting-along and co-existence;
2. Free decision and development;
3. Equal dialogue and exchange;
4. Sincere toleration and complementarity.

The first principle covers the prerequisite for living on the small globe: individuals belonging to or loyal to different cultures ought to get peacefully along with each other, while various cultures ought to co-exist at peace. For on the contrary, hostilities or conflicts will lead either to hurts to both sides, or to suppression of the weak by the strong, hence the vanishing of the former and the stiffening to death through the latter, that of monolithism.

The second principle covers the rights of choice and development: any individual in any particular culture (or cultural tradition or cultural circumstance) ought to have the right to make freely his/her decision concering

---

[18] For example, the efforts to get some 'Universal Declaration of Human Responsibilities' passed by UN, as some proceeding action of the Declaration toward Global Ethic, have been made by the 'Inter-Action Council' whose members include political people such as the former German Chancellor, the former Canadian Prime Minister and the like.

[19] For example, the authors of the Declaration toward Global Ethic have found four fundamental principles in all the great religions and civilizations and succeeded in getting them included in the Declaration.

[20] The Declaration towards Global Ethic was discussed and passed by 6000 and more representatives and common believers of many different religions, denominations and sects throughout the world in 1993 in Chicago. Then, many similar dialogue meetings or seminars were held and arrived at agreement in principle to some degree and in some forms, successively in Vienna, Rome, Naples, Dublin, Qatar and Beijing.

his/her cultural interests or cultural belongings, while any culture itself ought to have the right to develop freely. For on the contrary, coercion or constraint will lead either to succumber or to distortion, both of which will restrain the growth of culture and make it stagnant.

The third covers the prerequisites for mutual understanding and mutual benefiting: individuals and groups under influence of different cultures ought to have coequal status in dialogue with each other, while any particular culture itself ought to have coequal status in any exchange with one another. For on the contrary, unequal status will lead either to coercion or to unidirectional imposition, and will then discontinue the dialogue and exchange, and maintain the barrier between cultures, and even strengthen cultural opposition.

The fourth covers both the basis and the aim of the contract of cultures: only if individuals and groups in any particular culture sincerely tolerate the existence and development of other cultures, could they eventually and really attain the end of complementing each other. For on the contrary, insincerity or dishonesty will make the toleration exist in name only, and keep far away the other cultures, and then disable oneself from influencing upon others and benefiting from others.

In addition, we can say that only those cultures adopting or embracing the above four principles deserve to stand on our small planet, and to have a bright future.

Epilogue

Having considered the positive and negative effects of economic globalization, some western thinkers have proposed some ethical or political contract to advance a global justice.[21] All the proposals have tried to define and direct the globalization in ethical, jural and political perspectives, beyond the one-sided economic perspective.

Having considered the possibility of the clash of civilizations, we have to propose such a contract of cultures as stated above. Of course, it is in cultural perspective that I see the matter. However, in the last analysis, such a contract needs some kind of spirit as a common ground. That spirit is just the often neglected common essence of great cultural traditions. It is expressed in Confucianism as a typically Chinese cultural tradition in such words as: 'When the Great Way was dominant, the world was shared by all alike… and people practised good faith and lived in trust. Therefore, they did not regard as parents

[21] Besides the declaration on 'Global Ethic' proposed by H. Küng and others, we can see the proposals put forward by J. Habermas, A. Giddens and others. For example, Habermas proposed a political nexus of cross-national administration, aiming at harmony other than coercion as guiding principle (see his speech at Fudan University, Shanghai, 26 April, 2001).

only their own parents, or as children only their own children.'[22] That is the spirit of universal love. It is expressed in Christianity in these words: 'How good and pleasant it is when brothers live together in unity!'[23] This is the spirit of universal peace on the basis of brotherly love. It is the resource of the spirit of 'He-He' we mentioned above. Such a spirit is able to offer the correcting guidance we need in the course of globalization.

Facing the irresistible 'express train' of globalization, it is useless and ridiculous for us to spit at the train when it is not in the direction we think to be right. What we should do is to transform ourselves from pessimistic passengers to active members of train-crew, so as to take part in the correcting work. For on board the train, there is no train-master who is alone in charge of it; and ahead of the train, there is no railway which is unchangeable!

---

22 The *Book of Rites*, Chapter of Grand Unity.

23 Psalm, 133:1.

PART TWO

COMMUNICATING THE GOSPEL IN THE 21ST CENTURY

(2) Inter-Religious Encounter and Dialogue

Commonalities Emanating from Religious Scripture

Kjell Magne Bondevik

Rev Kjell Magne Bondevik, Director, The Oslo Centre for Peace and Human Rights, Oslo, Norway; former Prime Minister of Norway

All too often religion is distorted and abused to stir up mistrust and hate, which in turn provide a breeding-ground for conflict and war. A strong religious dimension is often an integral part of unrest and violent power struggles.

Culture and religion could become a resource for peace, rather than a source of conflict. One way of approaching this is to acknowledge the common values shared by the great religions, such as the intrinsic value and dignity of the human being, the commitment to peace and justice, and respect for the sacred. Inter-religious dialogue focuses on these common values.

Human dignity is about respect for life, from conception to natural death. It is about respect for others, respect for the small, the weak and those who are considered outsiders in the world. For me, human dignity means a commitment to fight for the poor and the persecuted. I believe in a God who sees the world from the perspective of the weak, the children, and the oppressed. We cannot shut our eyes to poverty and oppression. We are all part of a global fellowship and we must join together with all those who are struggling for justice.

Christian values

When I engaged in politics many years ago, my motivation came from my Christian values. I learned early that my own religious belief and politics, governance and church are two different things, and must not be mixed. Christianity is first and foremost a question of my relationship with God, about the belief in Jesus Christ as our Lord and Saviour. Politics are on the other hand a way of organising the society to the best for the individual and the community. But still there must be a connection between the two. As a Christian I can not leave my Christian faith and conviction at home when I leave for my job. I bring with me some ethical values and principles which also have meaning in political life.

There are three values that are especially important to me. First: the principle of stewardship. God gave us responsibility for taking care of his creation. Second: the double commandment of love; to love God above all, and to love my fellow human being as myself. Third: the idea that man is created by God, in Gods image, and has an inviolable value. This opinion about the human being, must lead us to protect the human life, from conception to a natural death.

My main inspiration to combat an unjust and troubled world, are God's love for his creation and the example of the life of Jesus, with many deep-felt challenges. I still believe that love for my neighbour is the strongest power that any political decision-maker can yield, anywhere in the world.

Common values

Many people around the world carry with them the burden of fear for people different from themselves, especially people with another belief. Religious and political authorities have often used their position to point to differences more than to similarities. Fear and division are unfortunately widely used tools of power to keep the disciples obedient and loyal. We have seen this in Northern Ireland, in the Middle East, in the Balkans, in the Sudan and elsewhere in Africa. Few, if any, religions actually have this aggressive characteristic in their scriptures. This is a man-made phenomenon as religion is always interpreted by someone. One can work against such negative interpretations by enhancing our efforts to promote understanding between people. There are several common values in all main religions, such as respect for the holy, human dignity and the ideas of peace and justice. The knowledge of this helps break down the religious and cultural barriers that have been erected between peoples, societies and individuals. At the Oslo Center for Peace and Human Rights this is a part of our platform; to work towards peace and reconciliation, with strong emphasis on interfaith dialogue.

All major world religions teach the virtue of peace. Not just peace in the sense of absence of war, but peace between people. The Hebrew word for peace, shalom, and the Arabic word, salaam, have the same root. Both have a broader meaning, referring to a state of mind, to relations with other people and relations with God. This is the same as in the Christian blessing: "peace be with you."

The writings of all the world religions call on us to make peace. In the Christian faith we have Jesus' words in the Sermon on the Mount, "Blessed are the peacemakers, for they shall be called the children of God." The holy book of Islam, the Koran, says, "If they incline to peace, make peace with them". Mahatma Ghandi, a Hindu, put it like this: "Every human being can be made to change his or her violent behaviour into a peaceful one, by virtue of human nature itself which possesses an inherent partiality for peace." Other religions have similar messages. We all seek God with the same purpose, to live in peace with God and our neighbours. The Gospel in the Bible, and I think particularly of St. Paul, shows us how the reconciliation between God and Man, due to His mercy, help Men to reconciliation between themselves.

Today we see a strong worldwide tendency to idealize individualism and egoism, and emphasize materialism over spiritual and relational topics. Religion can here represent a counterweight – Islam with emphasis on human dignity, social justice and duties, Christianity with focus on love and compassion, Buddhists with their way of seeing through egoism that destroys our lives; and Hindus with their focus on the balance between good and evil in people. Religious people from different religions are familiar with the language of ethics and values, of spirituality and the soul, aspects so important in the lives of us all.

Religious people believe that human dignity is created by God, and on that ground we confirm the fundamental human rights of individuals and groups, and the mutual responsibilities that evolve from these rights. Everybody is entitled to full and equal citizen rights, to freedom of speech and freedom of religion, wherever they live. That means that anyone also should have the freedom to belong to the religion he or she wishes, and also to convert to another religion. And it is the responsibility of the state to protect the right of religious societies to organise and participate in the public space.

Responsibility of religious leaders

Political and religious leaders have a responsibility to oppose any attempt to exploit social, economic and other injustices in order to stir up religious hatred and suspicion. The world situation demands us to work hard to reduce tension between religious groups. It can start from the top-down, from the grassroots-up, or both ways, at the same time. The dialogue must be based on reciprocity, confidence and cooperation.

Still, one must be careful not to give religion a too heavy responsibility for conflicts in the world. Former President Bill Clinton stated at the Clinton Global Summit in 2006 the following conclusion:

> Most conflicts are over power, politics and resources. Religion is used and becomes a cover for political differences. Therefore we must continue interfaith dialogue.

Religious leaders have a strong influence on their followers all over the world. This influence can be used to build bridges and show in action that cooperation and friendship are possible with people of all faiths.

Knowledge makes dialogue easier

When we feel confident about our own religious belief, it is easier to meet and talk to people from another faith. Knowledge of your own belief is important for the climate of dialogue.

People of different faiths are sometimes afraid of losing their religious identity, or even their own faith, in interfaith dialogue, but my experience and that of others have been the opposite. The archbishop of Canterbury Dr. Rowan Williams said in The World Council of Churches 9th Assembly that two approaches to inter-religious dialogue were unhelpful. One was to claim an exclusive possession of the truth, while the other was to lose confidence in one's faith and "slip into a world-view that assumes every religion is as good as another". He urged his audience to recognize similarities in their own experience of faith and that of others, saying, "Sometimes when we look at our neighbours of other traditions, it can be as if we see in their eyes a reflection of what we see; they do not have the words we have, but something is deeply recognizable". He continued, "When we face radically different notices, strange and complex accounts of a perspective not our own, our perspective must be not, 'How do we convince them of error? How do we win the competition of ideas?' But 'What do they actually see? And can what they see be a part of the world that I see?"

In my view promoting sound values is especially important in schools. Our schools must foster tolerance and understanding. They must be a means of combating hatred and fear of those who are different. In all schools, also in religious schools, pupils must learn compassion and consideration for others. The role of education is also very important in enhancing confidence and reconciliation.

By understanding more about others I also learn more about myself and my own belief. One might be transformed through dialogue, but that is also the intention of the dialogue, to be on the way to greater understanding. Rev Dr. Ingo Wulfhorst explained this beautifully: "Trying to understand the others' spirituality, religious experiences and practices, learning from them, and sharing our own faith and understanding in order to also be enriched and transformed, is part of an interfaith dialogue". And on the way we can even become friends with people from other religions, feel the companionship and fellowship, and bring down barriers in order to make conflicts easier to solve. To talk about our different faiths, is not a competition any of us can win. More understanding is the goal, and through greater understanding it is easier to live together.

The challenge is to teach about all religions in a fair and correct way, filled with respect. We must also get correct information about our different worlds, and get away from stereotypes about each other. You find moderate and extreme Christians and Muslims, Hindus and Sikhs – and in some respects we can even find that we have more in common with people from another religion than from our own.

Dialogue and diapraxis on the local level

The effect of our dialogue should manifest itself first and foremost in local communities, where conflicts often arise. There is a lot of mistrust in many communities. Many people do not feel safe in their local environment because of discrimination. To be a minority in a society can be hard, if the society does not find ways to live with and respect differences.

A Danish theologian and the director of the Islamic-Christian study centre in Copenhagen, Lissi Rasmussen, introduced the term diapraxis 15 years ago. The main idea is to work together on an equal basis. She defines it like this, "Diapraxis is not the application of dialogue, but dialogue in action. It is a process that calls for a contextual approach to dialogue, enabling people to meet in order to try to reveal and transform the reality they share." Religious leaders have a responsibility to give their followers and members of their community room and encouragement to engage in diapraxis.

Religious dialogue must happen from on the grassroots, solving practical questions concerning the everyday life of the people. Common projects like solving the problems of water supply, lack of security in the neighbourhood, conflicts between youths or the need for extra homework assistance for young people or immigrants. Having concrete common problems to solve can help people to develop friendship and fellowship.

We see today also a tendency that different religious communities find common ground in a world that gets more secular. They realize that there is a common understanding between them of the importance of religion in the different aspects of life.

Challenges in interfaith dialogue

Still, we must remember that many religious groups are not interested in dialogue, both among Christians, Muslims, Hindus, Sikhs and others. It is safe to stay within our own community, and there may be an inclination among religious and political leaders to keep their positions of power. Religion may also be used for political and economic purposes.

Different interpretations of a religion can also hamper a necessary development in different areas, and conserve attitudes that need to be changed in order to promote a free and just world with equal rights for all. Old traditions can stand in the way of necessary development. Inequality between the sexes can be a challenge, and is often maintained by laws emanating from a doubtful interpretation of the scriptures of a religion. Certain religious groups are only motivated by the hope of gaining converts, and serve only their own followers. Cultural and religious history is often closely connected, both in negative and positive ways. An example is the tradition of circumcising women. A barbaric tradition that has no place in today's world and must be abandoned.

Challenges in Christian/Muslim relations

We have over the last few years seen a polarization especially between Christians and Muslims. Principal of Indonesia's Christian Batak Church, Rev

Dr Jamilin Sirait, when explaining the Indonesian situation, had a disturbing tale of being a Christian minority: "One of our problems is that we (the Christians) are seen as Westerners. Christianity is linked to Western thinking. Many of our Muslim brothers and sisters see us as enemies, and opponents of Muslim thought, while many Christians see Muslims as extremists". He said in a meeting in Denmark that one of the major challenges of the Christian-Muslim dialogue is to eliminate these wrong views of each other whereby Christians are perceived as representing the West, and Muslims are seen as extremists.

The Muslim writer Tariq Chaudhry says: "Muslims share a common view of a constant onslaught against them and their religion. Their inability to militarily or politically to resist external threats and aggression adds to their feeling of humiliation, which Muslims have been feeling since the time of crusades and colonial occupation, when large parts of the Muslim world were under foreign domination." He also underlines that after independence one Muslim nation after another has experienced defeat at the hands of non-Muslims, whether it be in the Middle East, South Asia or in the Balkans.

This perspective has also been made a point in the final report of the Alliance of Civilization- High Level Group presented in 2006: Muslim communities share a sense of "discrimination, humiliation, or marginalization against them based on ethnic, religious, or other identity markers".

The philosopher Elie Wiesel points to important root causes to conflict, war and terror in the world. They are based on experiences of humiliation, he says. He shows that occupation creates the feeling of humiliation, and the same happens when a culture becomes undervalued. You also find it among people and in countries that are economically oppressed, and where the redistribution of wealth is very unjust. It is important to fight conditions that make people, individuals and ethnic groups feeling humiliated. It must be a priority to develop strong attitudes and communication systems between and within countries, which in words and actions show respect for different groups and treat people equally, both majorities and minorities. This is also a theme of the important UN-project, Alliance of Civilization., which I support.

There have been many conflicts between Muslims and Christians throughout history, but it is important to remember that there is also a history of cooperation between religions. As far back as the Middle Ages, goods and merchandise, but not least, ideas and knowledge crossed the divide between the Christian West and the Islamic Orient. Up till today, there are examples such as South Africa and the overthrow of Apartheid, and Muslim and Christian religious leaders working together to build peace in war-ravaged Sierra Leone. We also see in the history of Egypt, that Christians and Muslims worked closely together and built a strong alliance to fight the British colonialists. History also shows that the communities in our part of the world that were most willing to learn from others have developed most rapidly.

It would be useful to get more insight in the attitudes and organisation of the cultures and countries that have very low internal tension between different cultures, religions or ethnic groups, and try to draw some experience from it that can be used in other countries and contexts. It is furthermore necessary to look at other reasons for violence and conflicts than religious and cultural differences, and seek ways to prevent those combinations of root causes grow explosive.

The religious communities as a strong force

The religious communities have the means and resources to reach the believers. No other groups have the same capacity to reach out, down to the most remote groups. The best example of how efficient the communication among religious communities can be you find in the fight against HIV/Aids. Religious communities have a very strong influence on peoples' beliefs and actions, and have means to reach an enormous amount of people in a short time, both with messages and initiatives for actions to reach special goals.

To reach a common understanding of important aspects of life and society creates greater room for acceptance of differences. Emphasis on the education of children, and observing how different countries try, also with small resources, to teach some basic skills to improve their future, can be a meeting-place for a greater understanding. Religious communities must at the same time be challenged to describe how they practice their religion and teach their followers about human rights and human dignity.

It is important to develop a line of thought between civilizations, that allows cultures to live side by side, albeit with very different characteristics, where dialogues between the ethnic groups are based on respect, and where there is an environment for dialogue about differences and about how to practice different human rights perspectives. A special challenge is to find a way to deal with the gender problem. Discrimination of women can not be tolerated, and it is important to have open discussions about what gender equality means in a human rights context.

Learn from good praxis

Living with differences in religion, ethnicity and identity must be learned, and structures for it must be built. Through greater knowledge about each other and a broad dialogue in all parts of society, we can make wonders. More knowledge reduces fear, and friendship breaks down barriers.

The Council for Religious and Life Stance Communities in Norway was established 30 May 1996. Member communities today include: the Holistic Community, the Bahá'í Community, the Buddhist Community, the Jewish Communities, the Humanist Association, the Islamic Council, the Church of Norway, the Council of Free Churches, the Catholic Church, the Sikh Community (Gurduara Sri Guru Nanak Dev Ji), the Hindu Community (Sanatan Mandir Sabha), and The Mormons (The Church of Jesus Christ of

Latter-Day Saints).

The goals of the Council for Religious and Life Stance Communities are defined in the statutes:

- To promote mutual understanding and respect between different religious and life stance communities through dialogue,
- To work towards equality between various religious and life stance communities in Norway based on the United Nations covenants on Human Rights and on the European Convention on Human Rights,
- To work, internally and externally, with social and ethical issues from the perspective of religions and life stances.

This council has played a very important role in Norway as a bridge builder between religious- and life stance communities. And it has evidenced dilemmas related to religion and faith. The Oslo Coalition on Freedom of Religion or Belief, that aims at promoting freedom of religion or belief as a positive right. The Coalition cooperates with international experts and organizations, such as OSCE and UNESCO. The Oslo Coalition bases its activities on The Oslo Declaration on Freedom of Religion or Belief from august 1998.

Close dialogue between different religious and faith communities during many years, often connected to current political topics and conflicts, contributed strongly to the non-violent reaction to the conflict surrounding the Muhammed-caricatures in Norway. Knowledge of what is considered holy for the different religions, as well as of the common understanding of what freedom of speech means in practice, created a good base for dialogue in this critical situation.

Common values within the great religions can be used as starting point for dialogue. Knowledge both of your own and about the others beliefs make dialogue easier and are a prerequisite for the recognition of common values. The religious communities are a strong force; by turning to them it is possible to use dialogue and diapraxis as tools in conflict mediation.

I truly believe that religious faith is part of the solution, not part of the problem. It is our common endeavour that can make this come true throughout the world.

Christian Spirituality Challenged by Eastern Wisdom: Why Do Western Christians Go East When the East Goes Global?

Notto Reidar Thelle

Prof Dr Notto Reidar Thelle, Senior Professor, Faculty of Theology, University of Oslo, Norway

This essay in honor of Knud Jørgensen is based on almost four decades of involvement in dialogue with Eastern spirituality, but is prompted by a recent course (spring semester, 2007) for Norwegian Lutheran ministers, dealing with challenges to Christian spirituality in the encounter with Eastern wisdom. A brief sketch of the course and some significant experiences must suffice as a background and context for my reflections on the paradoxical situation suggested in the subtitle: why do Western Christians go East when the East goes global?

Western Christians studying the East

The theme of the course was "Eastern religion and philosophy as a challenge to Christian spirituality," and was arranged as a co-operation between the Areopagos Foundation, the Norwegian Association of Clergy, and the Faculty of Theology at the University of Oslo. The main course was twelve days of intensive seminars, workshops and lectures at Tao Fong Shan Christian Centre in Hong Kong, dealing primarily with Zen ad Daoist wisdom, and in addition a brief visit to churches and religious institutions in Guangzhou (Canton). The required reading covered translations of Daoist and Buddhist texts, and articles dealing with the relationship between Eastern and Western spiritualities. In preparation for the course the participants had to write a minor essay, and concluded their work toward the end of the semester with another essay about the theological implications of their experiences. The staff at Tao Fong Shan, the Areopagos center in Hong Kong, was heavily involved with workshops, lectures, and excursions; Knud Jørgensen participated the first morning with a lecture on Christian leadership and spirituality; and I myself was responsible for the entire program and several of the lectures and workshops.

The course also included various types of exposure experiences. A visit to a Zen center in downtown Hong Kong and a monastery in Guangzhou gave vivid impressions of Buddhist spirituality. Instructions in *taijiquan* by a Chinese master gave at least a touch of awareness of the spirituality of the body in the Daoist tradition. Visits to some popular temples showed what most people in Hong Kong are searching for in religion: the relationship to the ancestors, safety for the family, prosperity, guidance for everyday life through divination, and a number of other rather down-to-earth issues. Other lectures and visits gave additional input about the Confucian background of the Chinese culture and the many aspects of Christianity in China. The fact that the course was held at Tao Fong Shan, the institution established by Karl Ludvig Reichelt, the Norwegian pioneer of a missionary dialogue with Buddhism, also added some historical coloring to the course, and established connections to the Norwegian context.

"Eastern" spirituality is not a central concern in the East

A few experiences from the course suggest some of the paradoxical aspects of such a venture.

First of all, Christians in Hong Kong and China are only minimally interested in the spiritual traditions we had come to study. If the churches are interested in traditional Eastern spirituality at all, Confucianism would be the closest dialogue partner. In actual fact, the churches are probably more Confucian in social structures and ethical thinking than they realize – those who do, are partly affirming it positively or regretting it, especially when it comes to gender roles. Buddhism and Daoism are so much associated with folk religious practices, or seem to be so commercialized that they are hardly regarded as a challenge or inspiration for Christians. The aspects of Buddhism and Daoism that are presently felt as challenges to Christians in the West – such as philosophy, meditation and other spiritual practices – are only to a limited extent visible on the religious scene, and are not regarded by the churches as relevant for study and dialogue.

One interesting and rather surprising aspect of this trend among Christians in Hong Kong is the fact that the master who introduced the group to *taijiquan* and some of the philosophy behind this tradition, belonged to an evangelical ministry using martial arts as an outreach for Christian evangelism. Unfortunately, due to language limitations we were not able to discuss the philosophy behind such an outreach, but it suggests that at least some elements among conservative Christians are open for an interchange between Christianity and Eastern spiritual traditions.

A visit to the seminary in Guangzhou allowed the group to engage in quite intensive sharing session with the students and some of the teachers. We tried to explain our reasons for engaging in the study of classical Eastern wisdom and our concerns about the coming dialogue. The students admitted that the study of Buddhism and Daoist philosophy might be rewarding – some had even studied these traditions with interest – but they were much more concerned about such pressing concerns as the churches' relationship to ancestor worship, funeral rites, and folk religious traditions that tended to isolate Christians from their communities. The study of meditation and philosophy seemed to be a somewhat extravagant phenomenon.

Second, the weak interest in Eastern traditions seems to go along with a strong influence of various Western forms of theology, piety, and spirituality. Many of us were aware that a great part of Chinese Christians are characterized by conservative, evangelical traditions. Theological education, liturgical life, art and music, Bible reading and piety have to a great extent conserved traditions that were once transmitted through Western missionaries.

A new and surprising aspect of such influence from the West impressed us in one of the major churches in Guangzhou. Attending Sunday morning service we discovered to what extent global charismatic Christianity had influenced the community. It was a youth worship which could have taken place almost anywhere in the world. The songs were Christian pop-rock in Chinese; the keyboard player was a husky young man with long hair and sagging clothes, who could have played in any Western rock band or movie from the 1990s; the message, presented with fervor and conviction, was an appeal to believe in the promises of God for successful life. Like it or not, at least this community was part of a global trend, and had little concern in dialoguing with Eastern spirituality.

Visiting the Roman Catholic cathedral in Guangzhou, we had another strong reminder of China's global direction. When I visited the cathedral in 1985, it had recently been reopened after the Cultural Revolution, and the faithful had just begun to return. All the windows were broken, the furniture had been burnt, and the pillars were still black from fire and smoke. Now the church was beautifully restored; mass was celebrated several times every Sunday; when we visited the church Sunday afternoon it was packed – this time by hundreds of Nigerians. Nigeria is one of China's important partners in oil industry, and the Nigerian visitors were obviously involved in that venture. China's global turn inevitably makes the Chinese churches more global.

A third aspect of this global or Western turn in China is the fact that many Chinese intellectuals are intensely concerned about finding alternatives to both Communism, still the official ideology for China, and the unchecked capitalist economy which is threatening. All the major universities have new institutes for the study of religion, Western literature, philosophy, ethics, and theology. A number of so-called "cultural Christians" have committed themselves to Christianity, often without being baptized or connected to any churches, but search for new answers and inspiration in the study of Western Christian traditions. The Institute for Sino-Christian Studies (located at Tao Fong Shan, Hong Kong) is involved in an ambitious effort to translate Western theological literature, from the Church Fathers to modern theology, in order to give Chinese intellectuals access to Western Christian classical literature. There are of course Chinese intellectuals who search for alternatives in classical Chinese philosophy and religion, but the interest in Western learning is striking.

"Eastern" spirituality challenging the West

So why does a group of Norwegian clergy go to Hong Kong to study the types of spirituality that most Chinese find irrelevant or even dated?

One of the answers is obvious, but must be given in at least two ways.

First, Eastern spirituality is becoming increasingly popular in the West. Already in the 1930s Carl Gustav Jung observed that "the spirit of the East is penetrating into our pores and reaches the most vulnerable places in Europe." He expected that this might be beneficial, but also warned against an easy appropriation of what the East had earned as its property through centuries. "We must earn it in order to possess it," he argued.[1] In the 1940's the French theologian and Buddhologist Henri de Lubac observed that Europe seemed to be characterized by a sort of exhaustion, with a nostalgia for the Orient that made it ripe for a "spiritual colonization" from the East. Another theologian and philosopher, Nels Ferré, spoke in similar terms about a "penetration pacifique," probably alluding to an influence that was both peaceful (pacifique) and coming from the Eastern cultures in the Pacific rim (Pacifique).[2] The historian Arnold Toynbee argued in 1947 that future historians who looked back upon the twentieth century will not focus on the political and ideological conflicts between east and west, but the encounter between the religious East and West.[3]

It may be discussed to what extent these predictions have come true, but what has happened in the years after the 1950s is perhaps even more overwhelming than these writers imagined; beginning with the so-called counterculture in the United States and Europe in the 1950s and 1960s, and developing in waves of Eastern influence in alternative religious spirituality and New Age. Hundreds of thousands Westerners journeyed to the East; and Eastern gurus, swamis, Zen masters and lamas have established monasteries, and centers for meditation, learning and healing in most Western countries. When I was a student in the 1960s there was one Buddhist in Norway. Now there are perhaps 15 000, most of them Vietnamese and other Asians with their "ethnic" types of Buddhism that hardly appeals to ethnic Norwegians. But an increasing number of ethnic Norwegians are committed Buddhists, and even more people are fascinated by Buddhism, and regard Buddhism as a more attractive way than established Christianity. Quite a few Christians are also in

---

[1] Carl Gustav Jung's essay in the English translation of Richard Wilhelm, *The Secret of the Golden Flower: A Chinese Book of Life* (London: Routledge and Kegan Paul, 1962).

[2] See Hendrik Kraemer, *World Cultures and World Religions: The Coming Dialogue* (London: Lutterworth Press, 1960), 321-339.

[3] Arnold Toynbee, *Encounters Between Civilizations* (Tokyo: Kinseido, 1957).

dialogue with Buddhism, and try to integrate Buddhist meditation practices and insights into their Christian spirituality.

Second, the Western attraction to Buddhism is directed towards a spirituality that is radically different from the Buddhist religion that is practiced in so-called Buddhist cultures. Western Buddhists are only to a limited degree interested in what one might call "ethnic" Buddhism, that is the types of Buddhism that are generally practiced in Asian countries or Asian immigrant communities in the West. It is, for instance, inconceivable for most Norwegians to pay attention to the religiosity that characterizes Vietnamese communities – perhaps apart from intellectual curiosity or academic research – since it is so integrated in alien culture, with practices, notions, and symbols that they would regard as even more superstitious and otherworldly that the established Christianity from which they opt out.

Expressed in more positive terms, Eastern spirituality is challenging to many Westerners because they offer alternatives to inherited religion, primarily Christianity and Judaism. The appeal is so strong because they to a great extent have shed the Eastern religious traditions in which they have developed, and by which they have been nurtured. Some exotic practices of Westerners involved in Oriental spiritual traditions may seem to contradict this observation, such as reciting sutras in Japanese or chanting mantras and dedications in Asian languages, mastering new terminology, using bells and gongs and bowing to images, and adopt Eastern clothes for meditation and martial arts. But basically these are merely symbols for their search for alternatives, and may not be important per se. Westerners seem to opt for a globalized, transformed East, and the "oriental" elements are primarily markers for a new orientation.

A few examples may suffice to clarify what I mean. The classical Western presentation of Buddhism, as it traditionally has been described in textbooks, is a Western construction created by Theosophists and scholars who more than hundred years ago wanted to purify Buddhism from all sorts of religious practices and cultural trappings. The result was a religion that appealed to intellectuals who were alienated from established Christianity. Buddhism was presented as atheistic (or agnostic), rational, a philosophy that rejected all sorts of superstition, emphasizing the individual's search for mental peace through meditation and moral purity. The fact that Eastern Buddhists were offended by such attempts a "purification" and "return" to the true original Buddhism, is quite revealing. "Textbook Buddhism" still tends to be an abstraction that one may not easily find anywhere in the East.

Abe Masao, the Japanese philosopher who for many years was an important interpreter of Zen Buddhism to Western audiences, made a sharp distinction between Zen Buddhism and Zen. Zen Buddhism was the established tradition of Zen which had been swallowed by Japanese culture, while Zen in his imagination was the pure essence of Zen meditation and spirituality, stripped of the social trappings of Japanese religion. Abe's concern was to transmit the spirit of Zen, not Zen Buddhism. One of my first experiences in Japan almost forty years ago was to meet a group of newly-converted French Zen Buddhists who followed their master, Deshimaru Taizen, to experience Zen in its own "homeland." Their encounter with Japanese Zen was a mental shock, for they did not find what they had been taught about Zen. For them Zen was meditation and mental training, but in Japan Zen monks were primarily involved with ancestral rites, funerals, administration and all sorts of popular religious practices. Most of the monks did not even meditate!

Dalai Lama and many other Tibetan lamas have in a remarkable way managed to communicate their message in a way that has fascinated people in the West. In a simple language, with humor and gentleness, they have presented Buddhism as a universal massage for our time, a religion of love and compassion, tolerance and generosity. This is somewhat paradoxical, since Tibetan Buddhism is one of the most inaccessible traditions in Buddhism, an esoteric religion into which one has to be introduced by a master, through initiation rites, intellectual training and esoteric meditation. I am not criticizing Dalai Lama and other Tibetan masters – their ability to adapt their teaching to various levels of understanding and maturity is based on sound Mahayana principles. My only point is to argue that Eastern traditions in the West tend to be radically different from the way they are mostly known in the East.

The gist of my argument here is not primarily to say that Eastern spirituality in the West is different from the East – it certainly is at least in outward forms – but that it is challenging because in various ways one has tried to extract the spiritual essence of Eastern ways and presented them without the cultural and social captivity of established religions. It is so to say the "entrecôte" of Eastern spirituality, the marrow, the heart, the center, or whatever one chooses to call it.[4] A parallel to that may be the attempt by Christian preachers and missionaries to convey the "pure gospel" of Christianity: as the Gospel of love and forgiveness, as charity and social concern for the downtrodden, as the story of Jesus, as a source for moral renewal, or whatever one chooses to call it.

Christians challenged and inspired by the East

When Western Christians – in this case a group of Norwegian clergy – go to Hong Kong in order to study of Eastern spirituality, the point is not to study Eastern religions in general. It is a preparation for the coming dialogue in Norway by getting in direct touch with the essential core of these spiritual traditions, the life which is still there, in spite of all the much more visible cultural trappings. From what I have already written above, one might assume that it would be even better to study Eastern spirituality in their Western settings. Perhaps so, and that also happens, of course, but the exposure to the

[4] I am, of course, not saying that there are not "worst" examples of Eastern traditions also in the West, in terms of power struggle, discrimination, authoritarianism, oppression.

East adds an element of motivation and inspiration, a feeling of being in direct touch with the sources that is not always possible in the West. An additional aspect is that the direct presence in the East gives a more realistic impression of the Eastern traditions that are generally so idealized in the West.

When I in the following sketch some aspects of the challenges and inspiration from Eastern spirituality, I will focus on the two traditions that were the central concerns in our studies and dialogues, Zen Buddhism and Daoist philosophy. I will first suggest some of the problems and critical issues that face Christians in their encounter with these traditions, then sketch some of the positive challenges to Christian spirituality.

The question of God

From one point of view, Buddhism and Daoism seem to be so different from Christianity in their basic understanding of the cosmos that a meaningful dialogue seems problematic. Daoism has a basic understanding of the origin of the universe that may open for an awareness of some divine mystery behind all things. Buddhism has an awareness of a transcendental wisdom, and modern Buddhist sometimes speak about God in ways that may appeal to Christians. But neither can accept the traditional Biblical belief in a "personal" God who created the cosmos "in the beginning", who guides and protects creation, who rules through his law, sends prophets and messengers, intervening through a savior, and who in the end of times will judge the living and the dead. In Buddhism there is no beginning and no end, no creator God, no savior who has the power to forgive sins, no judge who will vindicate the victims of injustice. All things are rather ruled by an impersonal karmic law, all living beings are bound by karmic consequences that cannot be forgiven but only changed by one's own actions and mental training. Buddha is a savior in the sense that he had the saving wisdom that anyone can practice, and he and other masters are merciful helpers that may guide people toward awakening. But any idea of a merciful God who forgives sins for the sake of the saving act of a "Son of God" is utterly unacceptable.

From a Buddhist or Daoist point of view, the Christian faith in God is seen as a childish superstition, an immature clinging to imaginary supernatural powers. One may accept the value of such beliefs for people at certain stages of civilization, but they are bound to lose meaning in the encounter with the modern science and philosophy, or in the dialogue with Buddhist and Daoist thinking.

Such a rejection of traditional Biblical faith in God is well known from Western philosophies, but coming from religious traditions it may provoke a new and somewhat different reconsideration of traditional theological language, the understanding of the reality of God, the meaning of believing in God as a person, and the classical questions of theodicy, etc. Such a reflection may also be important as part of another dialogue, the encounter with modern Western attempts to speak of God in impersonal categories as energy, a cosmic order or principle, etc.[5]

Jesus Christ as savior

Another serious challenge is the relationship to history. Buddhism and Daoism have numerous stories, legends, and mythological elaborations that are understood as historical facts by many devotees. For the philosophically trained, however, the historical reality behind the stories is of little interest. In principle, not even the historical Buddha or Laozi are important. To use a Buddhist expression, they are just *upaya*, efficient means of elucidating the people and giving them aspirations for wisdom and liberation. The Biblical tradition, on the other hand, is intimately related to God's interaction with the world. The stories are told in order to affirm the conviction that God intervenes in history. Historians, whether or not they affirm in the resurrection of Christ, would generally agree that unless the first Christians believed that they had encountered the risen Christ, Christianity would never have become more than just another Jewish sect. Buddhist scholars have seldom felt threatened by demythologization or similar relativizations of historical happenings, while Bultmann's views shattered the Christian community.

Buddhists and Daoists find it almost incomprehensible that salvation in this way may be based on a historical happening, as Christians confess. For Christians it is important to say that salvation is based on an objective fact, once and for all. For people steeped in Eastern spirituality it is difficult to understand why and how something that happened once in a concrete historical situation can have eternal significance.

Different language worlds, different goals?

One of the questions that arise in the encounter with Buddhism and Daoism is whether we are actually are speaking the same language or even seeking the same goal. I have discussed this in detail elsewhere and shall not repeat it here,[6] but it seems quite adequate to describe Buddhism as religion of the eye, with awakening and insight as its primary concern, while Christianity – along with Judaism and Islam – is primarily a religion of the ear, with relationship as its central concern. Salvation in Buddhism is spiritual enlightenment, awakening, clarity, and liberating wisdom. Salvation is a radical change in mental awareness. Salvation in Christianity is a reconciled relationship with God and human beings, with forgiveness, atonement, justification, love, friendship as

---

[5] See my reflections on different religious languages in "Relation, Awareness, and Energy – Three Languages, Three Worlds? An Approach to Mutual Understanding", *Japanese Religions* 30:1(2005): 113-127; also presented as a chapter in my book, *Kjære Siddhartha! Brev og samtaler i grenseland mellom Øst og Vest* (Dear Siddhartha! Letters and Dialogues in the Borderland between East and West) (Oriens Forlag, 2005).

[6] See note 5.

central concerns, all expressed in relational categories.

The encounter with the East inevitably means that one will have to master different types of languages in order to understand and dialogue with the other; but that process will usually enrich one's own reflection. The process may challenge one's faith, even shatter one's inherited convictions. But my basic experience is that they challenge us because ultimately the questions are not only coming from outside, from two different traditions, but because they are already present within the critical Christian reflection about faith. From that point of view such challenges are a vital part of a continual reorientation that characterizes a sound search for theological meaning.

Mutual attraction

It is a paradoxical fact that religious traditions that are so different in their orientation as Christianity and the two Eastern traditions, still attract one-another. Especially between Buddhism and Christianity there seems to be an almost magical mutual attraction. Numerous Christians both in the East and the West are drawn to Buddhism, and engage in a process of testing out some of spiritual practices or probing its philosophical insights. In a similar way, numerous Buddhists make spiritual journeys into Christianity; they are challenged and inspired, and somehow become disciples of Christ. It happens that people convert, and abandon or even actively reject their previous faith. In most cases, however, they return to their original path, but with new insights and experiences that change their relationship to their old faith. In a similar way there are numerous Christians who have found Daoist philosophy, represented primarily by Laozi (Daode-jing) but also Zhuangzi, so challenging that they feel compelled to give room for its wisdom in their own spiritual life.

I will conclude my reflections by suggesting a few aspects of Buddhism and Daoism that may inspire Christians, and add new insights and perspectives to the way they practice their Christian faith.

The conversion of the missionaries

Since the course for Norwegian clergy was arranged at Tao Fong Shan, the institution founded by Karl Ludvig Reichelt, I will add an observation that is relevant for the understanding of the process of change that often happens when Christianity encounters Eastern traditions. An American observer published in 1919 an interesting article about the new generation of missionaries who came to China around 1900, entitled "Converting the missionary":

> He had gone out to change the East and was returning, himself a changed man … The conversion of the missionary by the Far East results in his being not only a

> missionary but an internationalist, an intermediary between the two great civilizations that inherit the earth."[7]

The new generation of missionaries came with an ardent vocation to proclaim the Christian message, but in the process they discovered that the East had proclaimed its own message to them. In China they wanted to change the society they had come to serve. At home they helped people to see better the greatness of the East.

Karl Ludvig Reichelt was one of these. He arrived in China in 1903 with all the negative notions about non-Christian religions, but he soon developed interest in Chinese religion and philosophy, particularly in Buddhism. He spent many years in study and contact. He made many friends in Buddhist monastic communities all over China. He founded places for dialogue in Nanjing and Hong Kong where Buddhists and religious seekers could meet Christians in an atmosphere of friendship. They were "friends in Dao" (*daoyou*). He wrote about his experiences and translated Buddhist and Daoist writings. In this way, he became the most important disseminator of knowledge about Chinese religion and philosophy in Norway in the first half of the twentieth century. Reichelt was the first to translate *Daode-jing* into Norwegian. We used it for our course, even though it is somewhat dated, but it still conveys some of the inspiration from Chinese wisdom.

The "conversion" of the missionaries did not mean that they abandoned their Christian faith to become Buddhists and Daoists. But they were converted to a *larger* faith – a Christian vision which discovered that God is present and active in all cultures. The encounter with the East made them not only preachers abroad, but also cultural missionaries at home, where they shared their new insights as a grateful gift in return for all that they have received.

Nowadays one does not have to be a missionary or a traveler to encounter Eastern traditions. Christians all over the world are in different ways in touch with the East, and one of the consequences might be described as "the conversion of the Christians," that is, an increasing numbers of Christians who are faithful to their Christian way but are converted to a broader vision that opens for the insights and experiences of Easter ways.

Meditation

One of the gifts Reichelt brought to Norway was a new interest in meditation. He had seen the importance of meditation in Buddhist training, and returning to Norway also saw the need for a deeper personal experience of faith. In 1926 he

---

[7] Earl H. Cressy, "Converting the Missionary," *Asia: Journal of the American Asiatic Association* 19:6 (June 1919): 553-556. The theme is analyzed in great detail in Lian Xi, *The Conversion of the Missionary: Liberalism in American Protestant Missions in China, 1907-1932* (Pennsylvania: Pennsylvania State University, 1997).

gave a lecture which later was published as a booklet, *Christian Meditation*.[8]

He saw the need for "quiet absorption and reflection, pious rumination about the deeper questions of life, notably the religious questions." He was aware of the fascination of the East in Europe, and wanted to investigate how we in the West could be inspired by the "sacred mysticism of meditation," from the "springs" where the deeper spirits of Asia had received so much inspiration.

Of course prayer and meditation was part of his Christian heritage, but he mentions some important elements from Eastern meditative traditions: the sitting position, the breathing, the silence and quiet reflection. The way to the inner sanctuary of meditation is, first of all, "to be … emptied of all one's own," to let go of ones concerns, one's troubles and burdens, letting the quietude open the mind for God's presence.

Reichelt was a pioneer in the Norwegian context, but both in China and Japan a number of Christians had already experimented with ways to include Buddhist meditative practices into Christian spirituality. As early as in the 1890s Japanese Christians began to practice Zen meditation as part of their spiritual life, and a series of prominent Christians followed up in different ways. Later, missionaries of various categories, both Protestant and Catholics, have experimented with Buddhist meditation. After the Second Vatican Council (1962–1965), a number of Roman Catholic priests and monastics, such as Enomiya Lassalle, William Johnston, and Thomas Merton have inspired Christians also in the West to integrate Buddhist meditative practices in Christian spirituality. This is not the place to evaluate such ventures, but it seems that the inspiration from Zen and other meditative traditions have added new energy to many Christian communities.[9]

Transformation of the self

Another challenge to Christians encountering Buddhism and Daoism is the emphasis on spiritual search as a search for the true self. The center of Buddhist search is to search for one's true nature, one's original self, or, to use a classical Zen expression, "one's original face" (*benlai mianmu, honrai no menmoku*). Daoism is also a search for the original mystery of all things, the Dao (Way), which is at the same time a return to the original self, the pure, unsophisticated, spontaneous person who lives in harmony with the Way of heaven and earth.

Both Buddhism and Daoism are often regarded as self-occupied and self-centered. That easily happens with religions that turn inwards. But the deepest concern in both traditions is to let go of the egoistic self and become a true

[8] *Kristelig meditation* (Oslo: Buddhistmisjonens Forlag, 1926).

[9] For a review of such process in Japan, see Notto R. Thelle, *Buddhism and Christianity in Japan: From Conflict to Dialogue* (Honolulu: University of Hawaii Press, 1987), 174-181, 247-260; see also Thelle's chapter, "The Christian Encounter with Japanese Buddhism", *Handbook of Christianity in Japan*, ed. Mark R. Mullins (Leiden: Brill, 2003), 227-247.

human person.

When Reichelt in his liturgies praised Christ as the "original face of all sentient beings," he used a Buddhist term to express a deep Christian conviction that Christ is not only revealing the true image or face of God to us, but that he also shows the true original face of what it is to be human.[10] Buddhism and Daoism challenged him to take seriously that Christianity is not only a teaching (*jiao*), but a way (*dao*) to walk, a practice in which we are expected to be transformed to his image, which is the true image of being human. One of the gifts of Buddhism and Daoism is to remind us that to become a true human person we have to forget ourselves, just as Christ, the true face of God, emptied himself and became one of us.

With the radical emphasis on justification by faith alone in Lutheran traditions, one has often been less concerned about spiritual transformation or the restoration of the original image of God. The encounter with Buddhism and Daoism may actually turn out to be an impulse to recover such an aspect of classical Christianity that has often been dormant.

The spirit of the valley, the power of the water

One aspect of returning to the true self in Buddhism and Daoism is the emphasis on forgetting oneself, or to let selfish desires yield to humble service. It is described in Daoism by a series of symbolic virtues or qualities, such the quality of weakness, softness, the female power, the spirit of the valley, or the spirit of water which always seeks the lower places in order to serve. Both China and Norway are fond of mountains, the lofty peaks that tower up in their beautiful majesty. The mountains are often symbols of God, of power, majesty, glory, religious aspiration. Reichelt followed Chinese traditions establishing his centers at mountains or hills, such as Ching Fong Shan and Tao Fong Shan. But he also learned that the true Way, the real *Dao*, does not remain in the lofty peaks, but seeks downwards.

Reichelt was inspired by *Daode-jing* to see this as the central quality of the Gospel. The water always seeks its ways downwards, down to the valleys, to the lower places in order to give life to fields and trees, to nurture animals and human beings, always serving. In the same way God, or Christ as the Dao, is always seeking the lower places. In the story about the temptation of Jesus, we are told that the Devil took him to a high mountain where he showed him all the kingdoms of the world and their glory. All these would be his if he would only worship him (Matt 4:1-12). But Jesus was not seeking power and glory. His way was different. He left the mountain and descended to the valleys where people were struggling with their lives, even accepting suffering and death. In

[10] For a thorough analysis of these liturgies, see Notto R. Thelle, "A Christian Monastery for Buddhist Monks. Part II: Buddhist Rhetoric in Karl Ludvig Reichelt's Christian Liturgies," *Ching Feng* (New Series) 6:2 (2005): 131-177 (published in 2007).

this way he made God present where nobody expected that God could be or should be: the lowliest place we might conceive. We often say: Glory be to God in the highest. *Daode-jing* and the Gospel remind us that we might also say: Glory be to God in the lowest.

To follow Christ is to follow him down towards the valleys and low places, like the water, in order to serve and share.

Going across the creek to fetch water?

The Norwegian proverb speaks about "going across the creek to fetch water" if someone is searching for something far away when it is actually available in one's own backyard. A similar question often surfaces when Christians try to share their experiences from the encounter with Eastern traditions with friends and colleagues: Why on earth do we search for these types of experiences in Eastern religions when they are available in our own Christian traditions?

The question is valid, for it often happens that people who have been inspired and challenged by their new discoveries in Eastern traditions, after a while realize that their discoveries are not necessarily so alien to Christianity. The Christian church is a treasure house of religious insight, experience, wisdom and beauty. One does not have to go East to learn to meditate, or to learn about the dimension of quietude, the unspeakable mystery, the intimate relationship between faith and practice, or the discipline of mental transformation; even the strenuous path of critical reflection and questioning of inherited truths are deeply rooted in Christian spirituality.

The problem for many Christians is that these treasures have not been available in the communities where they grew up. They had to get out in order to search for a deeper understanding and greater visions. When they return – or if they return – to their own Christian home, things somehow change, sometimes radically. They have mastered new knowledge, experienced new types of spirituality, met people who shared their insights, the world has expanded. But perhaps more important, their eyes have been opened to a new appreciation of unknown dimensions of their own faith; they are inspired to reflect critically on their own tradition; and they search for ways to integrate new experiences in their own spiritual life.

So what happens when a group of Norwegian clergy go to Hong Kong in order to study Buddhist and Daoist spirituality? Twelve days of seminars, workshops, and exposure in the East, plus a few weeks of reading classical text and writing a couple of papers, of course, only represent a superficial touch with a different world and do not necessarily make a lasting impact.

For some such a course does not necessarily lead to any change at all. It is only a welcome break in the busy rhythm of pastoral duties, a refreshing confirmation of their conviction that Christianity has the answer anyway, and that the East is only for people with exotic interests. For some it will certainly be an invitation to move on intellectually and spiritually. They may be disturbed by critical questions, inspired by new insights and experiences, and begin a process of integrating what they have learned. But it also happens that even a superficial touch with the East is the beginning of a spiritual journey with unexpected consequences for one's entire outlook.

Whatever happens, I am sure that such experiences enable the participants to see more clearly to what extent the East is penetrating even into the Norwegian culture, and prepare them for the encountering the Eastern fascination with more confidence and openness than before. For the East is not only in the East; it is not only somewhere in the alternative communities outside the boundaries of the church. The East is present within the congregations, represented by faithful who experiment with faith, search for new spiritual experiences, and long for deeper dimensions. It is important that the church has leaders who have confidence and competence in this dialogue, with a hospitality of the mind that is able to integrate whatever is "noble, good, and pure" (Phil 4:8).

TAO FONG SHAN – WHAT HAVE WE DONE? REFLECTIONS ON THE POST-WAR SEARCH FOR A NEW IDENTITY

Rolv Olsen

Dr Rolv Olsen, Director, Egede Instituttet, Oslo, Norway

The story of Karl Ludvig Reichelt and of Tao Fong Shan, the beautiful institute he founded on one the hillsides surrounding the then tranquil village of Sha Tin, New Territories, Hong Kong, is familiar to all acquainted with the Scandinavian Christian Mission to the Buddhists (CMB), now Areopagos.[1] The effort to reach to the Chinese Buddhist monastery community with the Christian Gospel has been frequently retold, and continues to inspire and to provoke.

Still, it only consists of a minor part of the story of Tao Fong Shan. The mission enterprise to the Buddhist monks basically came to an end with the Second World War and the Japanese occupation of Hong Kong. CMB was left

---

[1] Karl Ludvig Reichelt (1877-1952) is probably the most well known Norwegian missionary internationally, and undoubtedly the most controversial. He endeavoured to reach the Chinese monastic Buddhist community with the Christian Gospel. In 1922, he founded an institute in Nanjing. In 1926, CMB became an independent mission organization. In 1930, the Tao Fong Shan Christian Institute was founded. For a more comprehensive rendering of the story and Reichelt and Tao Fong Shan, see Sharpe, Eric, *Karl Ludvig Reichelt: Missionary, Scholar and Pilgrim* (Hong Kong: Tao Fong Shan Ecumenical Centre, 1984); Riisager, Filip, *Forventning og oppfyldelse* (Expectation and Fulfilment) (Hjørring: Forlaget Aros, 1973); Riisager, Filip, *Lotusblomsten og korset* (The Lotus and the Cross) (Copenhagen: Gads forlag, 1998); Eilert, Håkan, *Boundlessness: Studies in Karl Ludvig Reichelt's Missionary Thinking with Special Regard to the Buddhist-Christian Encounter* (Aarhus: Forlaget Aros, 1974); Holth, Sverre, *Karl Ludvig Reichelt* (Oslo: Egede Instituttet, 1952); Prenter, Regin, "Theologen Karl Ludvig Reichelt" (*Karl Ludvig Reichelt, the Theologian*), *Norsk tidsskrift for misjon* (Norwegian Journal of Missiology), Vol. 32, 1978, No.1:1-20; Thelle, Notto Reidar, "A Christian Monastery for Buddhist Monks: Part I: Karl Ludvig Reichelt's Sacred Mountains", *Ching Feng*, New Series, Volume 6, No. 1, 2005; Olsen, Rolv, *Prevailing Winds. An Aanalysis of the Liturgical Inculturation Efforts of Karl Ludvig Reichelt* (Lund: Studia Missionalia Svecana CIV, 2007).

with a purpose no longer possible to fulfil and with a property designed for an encounter no more taking place, and with vastly more obligations than resources. A search for a new identity began, and the search more or less continued for the rest of the century. What were the main challenges, and how did the people in charge of Tao Fong Shan respond to the new demands? What identity, what purpose, was found for Tao Fong Shan after the Buddhist monks ceased to come? To what degree could those responses be regarded as adequate to the challenges? Those are the questions this study attempts to give some answers to.

Below, I will try to critically review this search, highlight some of its salient points, and suggest some lessons to be learnt. I have the advantage and disadvantage of having spent several years of my life serving as Superintendent, later called President, at Tao Fong Shan. Whereas this gives me "inside information", it naturally also gives a certain bias to my views. Which bias, though, is harder to determine. Would I be more likely to try to hide or excuse my shortcomings, or would I rather run the danger of being overly self-critical? Most likely, I will make both mistakes; possibly, if possible, simultaneously doing so.

The period covered by this article has a span of approx. fifty years, from the end of the Second World War until towards the end of the Millennium. Firstly, I will briefly describe the post-war situation at Tao Fong Shan, the various enterprises of that time, and the theological reorientation taking place after the death of Reichelt. From there, attention will be turned to the second reorientation, instigated by Sverre Holth. Finally, the period of the last two Scandinavian superintendents will be considered; a period of promises, finally fulfilled, of a vastly improved economy.

Shelter and Community

The Second World War more or less put an end to the original work of Tao Fong Shan. Swiftly after the attack on Pearl Harbour, Hong Kong was conquered by the Japanese forces, and remained occupied until the end of World War II.[2] During the Japanese occupation, the missionaries were interned at Tao Fong Shan. Donations from abroad practically ceased. The brotherhood came to an end, as most of the brothers and students fled to the unoccupied parts of China or left for other reasons, lack of food at Tao Fong Shan not the least among them. [3] The "golden age" of Tao Fong Shan and its brotherhood

---

[2] *Karl Ludvig Reichelt, Dagbøker* (Karl Ludvig Reichelt, Diaries), Kopier fra Riksarkivets privatarkiv nr. 592, K.L. Reichelt (Copies from the Norwegian National Archives, Private Literature Archive no. 592, K.L. Reichelt), VA:08-15/12/41; VIA:16/08/45. In the following referred to as "Diaries".

[3] Upon leaving Tao Fong Shan, the students were furnished with a letter or recommendation. See Diaries VB:31/03/42. For wartime working restrictions

congregation were gone, never to return.[4]

Admittedly, many of them came back after the war, and with the stream of refugees from the revolution coming to Hong Kong, more monks came to Hong Kong, and some even to Tao Fong Shan. Nevertheless, basically, an era was ended, and a new purpose for Tao Fong Shan needed, as Reichelt and others were well aware of.[5] The 1949 Revolution, with its influx of refugees and subsequent closing of borders, resulted in a totally new situation even at Tao Fong Shan. Previously, monks had come from all over China. Now, only those who lived in or had been able to flee to Hong Kong could visit. It is hardly surprising that the number of visiting pilgrims dwindled, even more so since the initial success of the work and the ensuing controversies resulted in the monks receiving warnings against having anything to do with the "sheep stealers" at Tao Fong Shan.[6] The last baptism of a monk took place in 1962.[7] To meet the new demands, the leaders of Tao Fong Shan responded with what may be described as a *threefold reorientation*; of work, of partners, and of theological approach.

The influx of *refugees* resulted in a desperate housing situation in Hong Kong. It was of course impossible to provide housing to more than a million people suddenly arriving, and many had to live in whatever shelter they were able to find.[8] It was inevitable that some found their way to the hill of Tao Fong Shan. As most other churches, missions and charitable organizations, CMB and Tao Fong Shan did respond to the need of the refugees in various ways. Rooftop schools were organized. Several refugees were provided housing, while others acted on their own initiative. Some were baptized, and eventually became co-workers.

The perhaps best-known feature of Tao Fong Shan in the post war period is within *indigenous Christian art*.[9] Through pottery with Christian motifs, painted in traditional Chinese style, a visible expression to its conviction that Christianity is not a Western religion, but as much for Chinese as for

---

and overall conditions, see, e.g., Diaries VB, 17, 20 and 22/04/42, and the *Statement in Connection with the Christian Mission on Tao Fong Shan, Shatin, N.T.*, enclosure to the latter entry.

[4] See, e.g., Diaries VA:08/01/42; VB:10-12/03/42 and 25/08/43.

[5] For the policy deliberations at Tao Fong Shan, see Diaries VIB:09/05/51; VIII:10/01/57.

[6] See Diaries VIB:11/11/48, VIII:09/10/56.

[7] See "*Registration of Baptisms of the Members the Tao Fong Shan Christian Congregation*", 1930-, Tao Fong Shan Congregation Archives, no. 160, 21/01/62.

[8] Even in 1998, some people lived in cage like dwellings, and average flat size was less than 40 square meter.

[9] Diaries VIB:05-16/03/48 and 15/04/48; *Østen og vi* (The East and Us), Den Nordiske Kristne Buddhistmisjon, Oslo, No. 4/81:7.

Westerners, was to be given. At the same time, the danger of creating "serfs" would be avoided by ensuring self-reliance of its students through creating a "self-supporting community" at Tao Fong Shan.[10] A school for trade, agriculture and art was set up, and students recruited among, e.g., former monks, refugees, and art students, several of them having physical disabilities. Not all Chinese Christians equally appreciated this attempt at contextualization, and it may well be argued that the paintings of Jesus and the disciples in traditional Chinese dress might prove a kind of *fossilization* or *cultural romanticism*. Still, the paintings have become a source of inspiration for several Chinese Christian artists in their attempts at expressing their faith in a way that gives justice to their own context.

Another characteristic aspect of the life of Tao Fong Shan in the post war period has been the *Ai Dao Yuan*, Ai Tao Yuen, "Love Tao/the Way Garden", a Christian community for women, patterned after the Buddhist *Cai Tang*, "Vegetarian Halls", where women without a family to support them, for a minor investment in money or work, may live after retirement. The women at Ai Tao Yuan were provided with a rather large piece of land where they were able to do small farming for a living. Leaders were Elisabeth Pettersen and Lau Ng Man Lo.[11]

The tradition of *study and dialogue* was continued through the establishment of the Christian Study Centre on Chinese Religion and Culture (CSCCRC) in 1957.[12] Establishing such study centres might be called a general trend in the first decades of post war Christian mission. As has often been the case with

---

[10] See Diaries VIA:19/05/47.

[11] See Ellingsen, Svein, Måsø, Ragnhild, Nøttveit, Aud, Rimington, Greta (Eds.), *Fra Nanking til Tao Fong Shan* (From Nanjing to Tao Fong Shan) (Oslo: Den Nordiske Kristne Buddhistmisjon, 1987), 36-39. For the initial deliberations, see Diaries VII:20/02/53 and a letter from Pettersen, dated 19/05/53, enclosure to Diaries VII:25/05/53. Pettersen worked at Tao Fong Shan between 1948 and 1972. She was ordained pastor after returning to Norway. See Østen og Vi No. 3/77:8f, 14. Mrs. Lau worked at Tao Fong Shan from 1950 until retirement, and is still *de facto* in charge of Ai Tao Yuen. See Østen og Vi No. 2/1972:17f. The area was later sold to provide an economic foundation for CMB, and Ai Tao Yuan was resettled in 1992. Given the present socio-economic situation in Hong Kong, a continuation of this community, beyond the life of the current members, is unlikely.

[12] See Diaries VII:04/03/55 and 23/11/55; VIII:16/11/56, for the deliberations prior to establishment. The speaker at its first arrangement was Hendrik Kraemer. Diaries VIII:21/09/57. In view of his previous critique of Reichelt, this is somewhat ironic. See Lee, Peter K.H., "Forty Years in the Wilderness: A Former Director's Account of the Christian Study Centre on Chinese Religion and Culture's Past Forty Years", in *Ching Feng*, Vol. 40, No. 1, March, 1997:57-77, for a survey of the history of CSCCRC.

similar institutions in other Asian countries, focus of attention has to a large degree been on the social situation of the country of location.[13] Gerhard Reichelt was its first director. From 1973 until his retirement, Peter K.H. Lee, an internationally renowned authority on interreligious dialogue, was director.[14]

The post war *congregation* was of a markedly different character than the old brotherhood. The flow of monks was reduced to a tiny trickle. The former monks married and started to raise families. Tao Fong Shan had its share of the influx of refugees, and several of them joined the congregation. The Lutheran Theological Seminary moved to Tao Fong Shan, and teachers and students joined the worship services. Some adjustments were probably inevitable as the context changed so drastically. The cushions were removed and pews installed. The Sunday worship liturgy was revised and some of the typical Tao Fong Shan elements removed. The congregation became more like an ordinary congregation. At the same time they signify a new climate at Tao Fong Shan, as will be seen below.

One new *partner*, arriving from China, had a notable effect on Tao Fong Shan. In 1948, the Lutheran Theological Seminary (LTS) wanted to move to Hong Kong, and was invited to establish itself at Tao Fong Shan.[15] This coincided approximately in time with the acceptances of CMB as members both of the Chinese Lutheran Association and the Norwegian Missionary Council and may be understood as evidence of far more cordial attitudes towards CMB from other church bodies.[16] Further, the request from LTS for locations at Tao Fong Shan might have been very welcome during this CMB search for a new identity, and it was approved without much hesitation.[17] This arrangement continued until the new LTS campus was finished in 1955.[18] The effects of suddenly receiving this large, strictly confessional Lutheran, body of

---

[13] See Cobb, John B. jr., "The Buddhist-Christian Dialogue Since 1945", Fu, Charles Wei-hsun and Spiegler, Gerhard E. (eds.), *Religious Issues and Interreligious Dialogues: An Analysis and Sourcebook of Developments Since 1945*, 571-589 (New York: Greenwood Press, 1989), 573.

[14] *Østen og Vi* No. 3/1985:4; 2/1979:4f, 11.

[15] See Diaries VIB:13/11, 23/,11, 26/11 and 29/11-06/12/48; Carlberg, Gustav, *The Changing China Scene: The Story of the Lutheran Theological Seminary in Its Church and Political Setting over a Period of Forty-Five Years: 1913-1958*, (Hong Kong: Lutheran Literature Society, 1958), 104, 106-109.

[16] Diaries VIB:04-04/11/49; Hsiao, Andrew, *A Brief History of the Chinese Lutheran Church* (Hong Kong: Taosheng Publishing House, 1999), 24p, 43.

[17] In addition, as shortage of personnel and funds caused the cessation of the "Religion Study Courses", Tao Fong Shan would welcome the opportunity for continued training of co-workers. Hsiao 1999:42.

[18] Carlberg 1958:112p; Hsiao 1999:24. Thus LTS, as the only theological seminary in China, was able to relocate to Hong Kong and continue its existence there after the revolution.

theological teachers and students at Tao Fong Shan should not be underestimated. Neither the co-workers nor the converts were likely to be unaffected.

Thus, it was almost inevitable that Tao Fong Shan underwent a *theological reorientation* as took place shortly after the death of Reichelt, entering its "iconoclastic period". As early as August to October 1952, a reassessment of the work was conducted, one of the items of the agenda "How to change the conditions which we think are wrong". A new set of guidelines were approved, indicating a clear redirection of the work, the most important change for our purposes saying: "The mixing of Christianity with Buddhism. All plaques with non-Christian quotations and proverbs should be removed".[19] The original liturgies were modified. Several wooden tablets were removed, some said to be destroyed.[20] The swastika on the altar was removed, and lotus crosses less frequently displayed. The redirection became official policy after the Tao Fong Shan 1955 Annual Conference.[21]

Should the redirection be understood as signifying an adequate response to a new context with work among refugees rather than among Buddhist monks, as a differing, more cautious approach to the Chinese environment, as evidence of a more conservative understanding of the Christian faith and the relation between Christianity and Buddhism, inspired by dialectical theology, or even as a lack of understanding of the special character of Tao Fong Shan? It is difficult to determine with certainty the rationale behind the shift.[22] It is likely, however, that it, to a large extent, was motivated by the major change in the congregation from Buddhist monks to refugees, and thus could be seen as a necessary adjustment. Nevertheless, it is entirely possible the reorientation of the fifties might not have taken place, if not for the different theological climate of the

[19] Diaries VIB:11/08/52; 08-09/10/52.. Apart from this, the guidelines mainly warned against creating "rice Christians", stressed the importance of the students being self-supporting, not having to rely on Tao Fong Shan for their living, and the need for unity among the co-workers. While self-reliance at best was only partially obtained, the other changes were more easily carried through.

[20] Choi told me once that he hid some of them in his house to avoid destruction.

[21] See Diaries VII:25/03/55.

[22] One reason for this is that it difficult to reconcile the recollections of those involved, where the missionaries commonly are seen as the main movers, where the Diary records, where the Chinese co-workers play a much more active role. Several contradictory conclusions might be drawn from this, all entirely possible; e.g., subsequent modifications of views, incomplete records, conscious downplaying of the role of some of those involved, the real decisions being taken elsewhere, etc.

missionaries.[23]

C.C. Wang, one of the converts from the Nanjing period and later one of Reichelt's most prominent co-workers, became in 1962, as Gerhard Reichelt left Hong Kong for good, the first Chinese Superintendent of Tao Fong Shan, a position he held until 1966.[24] Wang was a skilled artist. The Lotus Crypt tablets, and the "Narrow Gate" and "Thanksgiving Pavilion" built by the large cross overlooking the Shatin Valley, are among his main contributions to Tao Fong Shan. His theology, at least in his later stages, is characterized by a somewhat more antagonistic understanding of the relationship between Buddhism and Christianity than that of Reichelt, as evidenced by his book *Ye Fo hecan* "A Comparison of Jesus and Buddha", where, according to Whalen Lai, Buddhism is dismissed as pessimistic, escapist, fatalist and depreciative of God's good creation.[25] Of other co-workers, Kung T'ien-ming was among the most prominent. After graduating from LTS in 1952, he travelled to Japan to study Buddhism, and later worked as a missionary among the Buddhists in Taiwan.

Study and Dialogue

In 1967, the respected sinologist Sverre Holth, a Norwegian Anglican and an old friend of Reichelt, became superintendent. With him, a new impetus was given to the work.[26] Holth strongly advocated the return to the original purpose

---

[23] There is definitely a rather long distance between Reichelt's understandings of the relationship between worship and culture, and between Christianity and other religions, and those of his successors. Seen at a distance of fifty years, it may well be that it is the theology of Reichelt, at that time rejected as syncretistic or outdated, which now seems most in conformity with mainstream Christian views.

[24] Wang (1908-96) first came to the CMB Centre in Nanjing in 1925, and remained with CMB for most of his working life. December 6, 1936, he was ordained pastor at Tao Fong Shan. In 1970, he moved to California, for several years continuing the mission work there. *Østen og Vi* No.5/70:53.

[25] Lai, Whalen, "The Buddhist-Christian Dialogue in China", Fu and Spiegler 1989:620. According to the same source, Wang recalled at the same time having written a book defending Buddhism against Christianity", but that "the new missionary did not agree with that", and that it was never published.

[26] Holth (1902-1995) worked as a missionary in China from 1925 to 1951. He was a respected Sinologist who published several translations of and commentaries on Taoist classics. 1941, he was ordained Anglican priest, and was Chief Editor of the Southern Chinese version of the Book of Common Prayer. He has been described as a "second founder" of Tao Fong Shan. His main contributions to Tao Fong Shan were the founding of the "Reichelt Memorial Library" and the two "Houses of Friendship" in Kowloon and

of Tao Fong Shan. Holth advocated concentration on the interreligious dialogue and established to that purpose, as Buddhists refrained from coming to Tao Fong Shan, a meeting place on "neutral ground" in Kowloon. The chapels and preaching points established at various places in Hong Kong were transferred to the Evangelical Lutheran Church of Hong Kong (ELCHK), so that Tao Fong Shan should be able to concentrate on its "special calling". The meeting places were called *Zongzhao Youyi She*, "Religion Friendship Society", in English called "House of Friendship". Confucian, Buddhist, Taoist and Christian scholars were invited to give lectures, and an interreligious committee was set up to direct the work.[27]

Even though it may be said that House of Friendship never really managed to fulfil the intended role, a not insignificant number still attended the meetings regularly. A similar meeting place was established in 1969 in Taiwan, but after a promising start, even developing local chapters, various difficulties resulted in CMB gradually losing contact with the work.[28]

After the retirement of Holth in 1970, poor finances and rapid changes of leadership made consequent direction and further development of Tao Fong Shan virtually impossible. Within twelve years, there were six different superintendents at Tao Fong Shan, the Swedes Daniel Nelsson, Holger Bennettsson, Johan Ohlson, and Gunnar Sjöholm, the Dane Erik Kvan, and the Chinese Bishop James Y.K. Pan, the latter using "rector" as his title.[29] The main attention of CMB seemed to have shifted to Japan.[30] At Tao Fong Shan, it might have been difficult enough just to keep the existing work going. In 1976, an agreement was made between CMB and Church of Sweden Mission (CSM) whereby CSM took over the financial and administrative responsibility for Tao Fong Shan. This arrangement continued until the withdrawal of CSM from CMB and Tao Fong Shan in 1986.[31] CSCCRC published two periodicals, "Tao Fong" *Dao Feng,* published since the time of Reichelt, and the bilingual "Bridge", the latter concentrating on the life and conditions of the church in China. In 1980, Tao Fong Shan and the Study Centre amalgamated to the *Tao Fong Shan Ecumenical Institute*, with emphasis on studies and dialogue, mission and education, and art and worship life, under the direction of Hong

---

Taiwan. See Diaries VIB:19/12/51; VIII, 19/10/56; *Østen og Vi* No. 6/1967:67p; 7/1968:76-78; 11/1970:114-116; 1/1983:4p, 14.

[27] *Østen og Vi* 10/1968:107; 11/68:121p.

[28] *Østen og Vi* 5/1983:14.

[29] *Østen og Vi* 3/1979:4p, 15; 5/1979:4p, 15; 9/79:4-6; 2/1980:4-6, 14; 4/1980:6, 14p; Hsiao 1999:112.
The surname of Bishop Pan is sometimes spelled "Pong".

[30] See Ellingsen, Måsø, Nøttveit and Rimington 1987:42f, for the work in Japan; Diaries VII:08/08/53, for the reaction at Tao Fong Shan to the appointment of their co-worker Ragnvald Hemstad (1923-) to Japan.

[31] *Østen og Vi* 3/1986:5p.

Kong Christian Council (HKCC).[32] In 1986, however, CSCCRC moved to its present location in Kowloon.[33]

Worship life centred round the congregation, with Choi To Tang, himself a former Buddhist monk, as pastor from 1954.[34] In 1984, the congregation became a member of ELCHK.[35] For Tao Fong Shan, this both signified acceptance and created a potential obstacle to further experiments in contextualization of worship, as the ELCHK liturgy became the norm. The "Pilgrim's Hall", the Guest House, continued to function, although receiving guests from Hong Kong and abroad, most of them Christians, instead of Buddhist monks.[36]

From Rags to Riches

Within the last two decades, as a result of the changes in the political situation, it has again become possible to maintain relations with the church in China and even to enter into cooperation with Chinese institutions. The Chinese church has undergone a period of enormous growth, and an unprecedented curiosity for and interest in Christianity has arisen.

Simultaneously, a new reorientation of CMB and Tao Fong Shan has taken place, and conscious attempts made to become more relevant to the people of Hong Kong and China.

---

[32] *Østen og Vi* 4/1980:7-10.

[33] Harbakk, Ernst, "The Tao Fong Shan Christian Centre: A Statement of Purpose", *Areopagus*, Fall 1987 (Vol. 1, No. 1), 52.

[34] Diaries VII:23/05/54. Choi (1919/20-) was raised in a Buddhist Monastery from childhood and ordained as a monk in 1931, Diaries VIB:19/03/52. In 1937, he visited Tao Fong Shan and was overwhelmed by the warm welcome from Reichelt. He was baptised on Easter Day, 1940, and gave his first public testimony approx. one month later, Diaries IV:07/05/40. During World War II, he was enrolled as student at the Lutheran Theological Seminary, then in Chungking. He graduated in 1951, was ordained May 23, 1954, and served as pastor of the Tao Fong Shan congregation until his retirement in 1991, and even later, albeit in an assisting and advisory capacity. Although Choi is a Mandarin speaker, I choose to use the official Hong Kong rendering, based on Cantonese pronunciation, of his name.

[35] *Minutes from the Meetings of the Board of Deacons of the Tao Fong Shan Christian Congregation*:08/01/84.

[36] Diaries VII:07/12/53, relates that C.C. Wang was the first to suggest the idea of a guesthouse. In 1970, 3,000 visitors were reported. At the new peak in 1997, approx. 10,000 guest nights were recorded. Several major renovation works have been undertaken, the latest in 2000/ 2001.

In 1983, Ernst Harbakk became superintendent and remained so until 1992.[37] For the first time since Holth, leadership remained unchanged long enough to give consistency to the work. At the same time, the anticipation of a vastly improved economy in the near future helped making it possible not only to continue with the existing work, but also to venture into new areas. These nine years were marked by major accomplishments as well as probably the most serious conflicts in the history of CMB and Tao Fong Shan since the split with NMS in 1926, resulting in the withdrawal of CSM from CMB, of CSCCRC moving from Tao Fong Shan and of Hong Kong Christian Council (HKCC) withdrawing from its involvement with Tao Fong Shan.[38] The conflict has often been described as predominantly a personal conflict, a clash of personalities, but this may have been of secondary significance.

The origins of the conflict seem to have been manifold, of theological, missiological, political, organizational, and personal character. Theologically, the CSM representatives tended towards a so-called inclusivist outlook on the relation between Christianity and other religions, while the Danish and Norwegian branches preferred a more cautious view. Missiologically, CSM emphasised ecumenical ties and local leadership, while Danes and Norwegians rather wanted to strengthen their ties with the Hong Kong Lutherans. Politically, some Tao Fong Shan co-workers were critical to the apparent pro-China bias of CSCCRC. Organizationally, the parties disagreed on who had the deciding power in matters concerning Tao Fong Shan. On the personal level, the relations between the key figures were undoubtedly difficult at times, but their effect on the outcome ought not to be exaggerated. The decisive factor in the struggle seems to have been the question of power. For a foreign charitable organization to be registered in Hong Kong, property or at least an office address in the home country is necessary. CMB consisted of three branches, one for each of the three Scandinavian countries. As the Norwegian branch was the only one owning property, a precondition for a foreign company to being

---

[37] Harbakk (1940-) had formerly been a NMS missionary in Taiwan and Hong Kong with his wife Kari, who was born in China of missionary parents. During his years at Tao Fong Shan, its English speaking community grew and regular Sunday and Friday services were inaugurated. Much inspiration was received from their neighbour Murray Rogers, an Anglican missionary formerly living in India, who for several years headed the small Christian community "One Bamboo Hermitage" a little further up the hillside, and from Brant Pelphrey, an Evangelical Lutheran Church of America (ELCA) missionary pastor and the first editor of Areopagus, who some years later returned to Hong Kong as an Orthodox priest. Harbakk welcomed LTS to Tao Fong Shan and envisioned worshipping and working fellowship of the two institutions, a vision that to a large extent yet remains to be realized.

[38] See *Østen og Vi* No. 5/1984:7; 6/1985:15; 1/1986:3, 12, 15; 2/1986:3-5; /1986:26.

registered in Hong Kong, the Norwegian branch was registered as owner of Tao Fong Shan, and thus had the final say as to its future. April 1986, CSM withdraw from CMB and CSCCRC moved to its present location in Kowloon. The international reputation of Tao Fong Shan was at low ebb, but at the same time, new optimism could be discerned internally.[39]

This optimism was to a large extent based on the agreement with Sun Hung Kai Properties, one of the foremost constructing companies in Hong Kong, on development of the old Ai Tao Yuen, laying a solid economic basis for CMB and Tao Fong Shan. Actually, regardless of which side of the conflict might have been "right" or "wrong", the abandonment of the first agreements on the property turned out to be an unequivocal blessing for CMB and Tao Fong Shan, as the revenue eventually acquired was more than tenfold the original amount.

During this period, several new initiatives were taken, the most important accomplishments summarized as follows:

- The move of LTS to its new campus at Tao Fong Shan. In this, history may be said to have repeated itself. Reorganization of land made it necessary for LTS to find a new campus site, and a large piece of land was donated to them by CMB at Tao Fong Shan. This campus was inaugurated in 1992 and has been in use since 1993.[40]
- The decision to register Tao Fong Shan as an independent company, a surprisingly complicated process that took approx. ten years to finalize.
- The starting up of new fields of work, such as the periodical "Areopagus – A living Encounter With Today's Religious World" and the "Ascension House", a Christian guest home for back packers, and regular worship services in the English language, strengthening the international ties of Tao Fong Shan, as well as providing CMB with a group of young "goodwill ambassadors", fascinated by its history and purpose.
- The formation of four main objectives for the further work of Tao Fong Shan. In short, these are: Spiritual and religious renewal; interreligious dialogue; contextual Christian art; and studies and research, especially on matters concerning China and the church.
- The building up of relations and cooperation with the China Christian Council and the Amity Foundation, a preliminary to the contemporary social work of CMB/Areopagos.[41]

---

[39] See *Østen og Vi* No. 2/1986:5; 3/1986:8-13; 4/1986:7, 13.

[40] Hsiao 1999:111.

[41] See, e.g., Harbakk 1987.52; Harbakk, Ernst and Riisager, Filip (ed.), *Veien videre* (The Way Ahead), written for the 75th Anniversary of the CMB (Oslo: Den Nordiske Kristne Buddhistmisjon, 1997), 46-48.

Through this, CMB and Tao Fong Shan were given new life and new direction. Naturally, this was not the accomplishment of one man only, but Harbakk's pivotal role cannot be denied.

However, in 1990, shortly after Tao Fong Shan celebrated its 60th anniversary, the community was deeply shaken by the discovery that the cemetery manager, who was also treasurer for the congregation, had embezzled funds on a large scale. In the wake of the investigation, it was realized that mission and co-workers did not necessarily agree on who had the right to the funds to be accrued from the property development, whether they rightly belonged to the mission or to the co-workers and congregation. Not long before, the building of the agreed retirement home for old co-workers had to be postponed due to lack of funds. Many of the old co-workers were deeply troubled and afraid that CMB would not live up to its promises. The tension continued to trouble Tao Fong Shan until the retirement home finally was purchased and inaugurated in 1996.

One way to ensure increased staff participation in the decision making process was the creation of Tao Fong Shan Staff Executive Meetings.[42] Still, it was difficult to keep sufficiently up with times, the reorganization of structures complicated the decision making process, and the impatience these years, especially among younger staff, with the slow pace of increase of influence on events was palpable. Parallel with these attempts at more democratic structures, the search for Chinese leadership started. Harbakk had hoped that he would be the last Scandinavian superintendent, but, apparently, at that time it was still too early; for the mission, the Chinese board members, and the Tao Fong Shan staff, for such a move. Six years later, however, the ground was ripe. Possibly, one might even say overripe.[43]

In 1992, Harbakk was succeeded by Rolv Olsen, who happens to be the author of this article. I endeavoured to develop Tao Fong Shan according to the direction already given, rather than devising another purpose.[44] During my six years tenure, Hong Kong ceased to be a British colony, and in 1997 became a Special Administrative Region of China. At Tao Fong Shan, these years witnessed the completion of the sale and subsequent development of the old Ai Tao Yuen, laying a solid financial foundation for the future work. In 1996, after years of deliberations between three Lutheran churches in Hong Kong, ELCHK, the Tsung Tsin Mission, Hong Kong Synod (TTMHK), and the Chinese Rhenish Church, Hong Kong Synod (CRCHK) and CMB, Tao Fong

---

[42] Sadly, all minutes and other relevant documents from these meetings were destroyed in the 1999 Tao Fong Shan office fire.

[43] I hope it was not solely due to mistakes and/or poor leadership by the superintendent of those years …

[44] Olsen (1956-), and his wife Olaug Karin, had formerly been a NMS missionary in Taiwan. He succeeded Harbakk as Superintendent in 1992 (from 1997: President) and resigned in 1998 to localize leadership.

Shan Christian Centre (TFSCC) was registered as an independent body.

During these years, a new generation of Chinese co-workers appeared, three of whom are still serving at Tao Fong Shan, namely the Program Directors Yeung He Nam, Daniel, later Executive Director of the Institute of Sino-Christian Studies (ISCS), the Spiritual Director Ekman P.C. Tam, and the administrator Jacob S.K. Wong. For approx. two decades, Chow Chuk Nam, South (1937-), took care of the administrative duties, contributing immensely toward smooth running of the daily business in spite of the repeated leadership shifts.[45]

In my own opinion, the main achievement of those years was the establishment of the ISCS, the brainchild of its Academic Director Liu Xiaofeng, which started operating in 1993 as a part of Tao Fong Shan, and has been a separate body since 1995.[46] ISCS is cooperating with several academic institutions in China and with many of the so-called "Cultural Christians" in today's China. ISCS publishes the periodical *Tao Feng* "Logos and Pneuma", and a series of theological literature, "Chinese Academic Library of Classical Christian Thought". The honour for coming up with the two inspired ideas, to employ Dr. Liu, and to establish such an Institute, independent of the Tao Fong Shan structure, belongs to Dr. Liu and Mr. Yeung. My own contribution was merely administrative; to realize that both ideas were brilliant; to convince the

---

[45] Yeung (1958-) was appointed Assistant Superintendent and Program Director in 1992. In 1993, he took the initiative to invite Dr. Liu to Tao Fong Shan. Together, they built up ISCS, first as part of TFSCC, and from 1995 as an independent entity, though not formally established until 1997. Yeung resigned by the end of 1995 to work full time at ISCS. Tam (1957-) was appointed new Spiritual Director, but as he was in the process of finishing his doctoral studies in Ottawa, he could not resume his duties until autumn 1998. In the interim, Chan functioned as Spiritual Director on top of his other duties, and at the same time pursuing his own doctoral studies. Wong (1959-) was appointed General Manager in 1998, and is now General Manager of the Service Unit. Chow (1937-), began his career at Tao Fong Shan as a painter, but later was appointed Administrative Assistant. Finally, in 1996, he was appointed Director of Administration, a role he in reality had filled for a long time. After his retirement in 1998, he emigrated to Canada. Other prominent co-workers of those years were, Program Director Chan Kwong Pui, Frank, Spiritual Director To Nim Kam, Herman and the administrator Leung Kam Fong, Janet.

[46] Liu (1956-), born in Sichuan, is probably the best known of the Chinese "Culture Christians", sometimes nicknamed "the Chinese Apollos". See, e.g., Lee, Peter K.H., "The 'Cultural Christians' Phenomenon in China", in *Ching Feng*, Vol. 39, No. 4, December 1996, 308f. Liu is a prolific writer and editor. After completing his D.Th. in Basel, Switzerland, he was invited to Tao Fong Shan in 1993, first on part time, later on full time basis. Liu is now a professor of Zhongshan University, Guangzhou.

CMB administration of the same (not a difficult task); to ensure that the necessary facilities, and economic means, were to be found; to serve as Chairman of the Board during the initial period; and to lend my name to serve as publisher until ISCS could be recognized as an independent juridical body.

Another feature of the nineties was the increased focus on Hong Kong. In the preceding years, emphasis had been on the relations internationally and to the Chinese mainland. Now, more attention was given to the local context, as evidenced by the appointment of a Program Director, later accompanied by a Spiritual Director. Through this, a foundation for the present work of Tao Fong Shan was laid. At the same time, the anachronistic nature of Scandinavian leadership became evident. Thus, I saw the smooth transfer of leadership into Chinese hands as one of my main responsibilities.

Chia Phin Yin, Philip *Xie Binren* took over as TFSCC President in 1998.[47] He emphasised strengthening the academic profile of Tao Fong Shan. By the end of 1999, he resigned from his position. For some time, leadership was divided between a quartet, the Academic and Executive Directors of ISCS, the Spiritual Director of Tao Fong Shan and the General Manager of what is now called the Tao Fong Shan Service Unit. Subsequently, The Service Unit and the Spirituality Department were established as independent units.

The name and symbol of Tao Fong Shan has recently become a cause for acute concern. In English, the name has been several times altered through the years. Originally, it was called Tao Fong Shan Christian *Institute*. In Chinese, the name long remained unaltered, *Dao Feng Shan Jidujiao Conglin*. Originally, *Conglin* signifies "dense forest", and is used to designate an institute for teaching, usually implying teaching of Buddhism. By the end of 1998, it was resolved to change the word *Conglin* to *Zhongxin*, Centre".[48]

In 1997, TFS was invited to become a member of HKCC. At that time, full membership was impossible for formal reasons, as it required three years existence as a registered body. Also, some of the staff preferred not to enter into new obligations at a time with so much instability. In the meantime, thus,

---

[47] Chia (1957-), is from Sabah, Malaysia. He moved to Hong Kong in 1991. Before coming to Tao Fong Shan, he was Professor in the Old Testament at the Alliance Seminary in Hong Kong. Formerly he was Chairman of the Malaysian Christian Writers' Association and active in Christian-Buddhist-Moslem dialogue in Malaysia.

[48] There were two major reasons for this move. To many Buddhists, the usage of *Conglin* was felt offensive. Although probably not a solely Buddhist word at the outset, *Conglin* did obtain the status of a *terminus technicus* for a Buddhist Institute providing teaching in Buddhism. In addition, in modern colloquial Mainland Chinese, the expression *Conglin* is said to have connotations, similar to "a robber's den". For this reason, *Zhongxin* to some extent was adopted on letterheads for correspondence in China, even some years before the formal decision to change the name.

an associate membership was opted for. In 2001, the HKCC Executive Committee recommended the application to its September Annual General Meeting for final acceptance. Thus, one more "ghost of the past" may be said to have been put to rest.

The main obstacles to the development of Tao Fong Shan during the 90-ies were related to economy and personnel. From the limitations set by the lack of funds, CMB suddenly found itself far richer than envisioned. However, the new wealth brought not only manifold possibilities, but also new problems, as it predictably was followed by bitter conflicts.[49] Nevertheless, conflicts are not dangerous. The many new members and supporters, as well as the conflicts concerning the profile of CMB, the future direction of the work, and the power, all contributed to the setting of the present course. Still, the conflicts had strongly adverse effects on CMB, and the strain on the people involved was considerable.

Conclusion

To a remarkable extent, life at Tao Fong Shan for a long period continued in its own fashion, largely undisturbed by outside events. Until recently, Tao Fong Shan may have been described as an island of tranquillity in the midst of a raging ocean. Within two decades, Tao Fong Shan has been transformed, from a close-knit community of former Buddhist monks and refugees, to a multi-faceted working community for modern, urban Hong Kong Chinese. It is still too early to predict in which direction the life of Tao Fong Shan will develop, but the adjustment to the new contexts has begun.

Judging from the original vision of creating a community of Christian believers with monastic Buddhist background, bringing their testimony to the Chinese Buddhist community, one might say that Tao Fong Shan is a failure, and that the various redirections merely aggravated the failure. Even the subsequent visions never were more than partly achieved, and the relevance for the life of the people remained limited. The main reason for this, however, simply is that to expect such mass conversion of Buddhist monks to Christianity, as Reichelt seems to have envisioned, was unrealistic.

The reality may not have lived up to the visions. Nevertheless, with the limited resources in mind, the achievements were by no means negligible, and the effects on people, whether as inspiration, encouragement, rest, or other, considerable. If there is a gap between vision and reality, that is to be expected. As the Norwegian author Arne Garborg said, paraphrasing a statement from the Sermon of the Mount, "He who seeks finds, but what he finds is not always

---

49 As Mrs. Kari Rognstad, then administrative leader of CMB, dryly commented; it was touching to see how many people who suddenly realized how relevant the purpose of CMB was, and how important and constructive its contributions had been.

what he seeks for".[50] Also, there is no shame involved in failing to do the impossible. Rather, to aim for the impossible, to act on one's visions, may be seen as the key to great achievements, as Piet Hein concludes in his *Gruk* on Julie, the supreme tightrope walker, who decided to try walking without any rope:

> "The secret of achieving the difficult
> Is hidden in attempting at the impossible."[51]

[50] "Den som leitar, han finn, men ikkje alltid det han leitar etter." My English translation.

[51] "For kunsten at klare det svære, er at forsøke på det umulige." My English translation.

Including Gender Perspective in Muslim-Christian Dialogue in Europe and Scandinavia – A Disturbance to Bridge-Building or a Contextual Necessity?

Anne Hege Grung

Rev Anne Hege Grung, Research Scholar, Faculty of Theology, University of Oslo, Norway

In Norway and in Europe in general, interreligious and interfaith dialogue is an expanding field in different arenas, with a growing number of religious communities and participants involved and with a multiplicity of aims. In the theological rhetoric of the churches and of different Islamic organisations and faith communities the call for dialogue is generally high on the agenda. This does inspire several people and organisations to strive for bringing people together across religious borders. The current development has several reasons, which are clearly aimed at counteracting a growing atmosphere of islamophobia[1] in Europe amongst the majority non-Muslim population. It also aims at addressing an attitude of fear both amongst Muslims and non-Muslims linked to occasionally increased tension, ongoing armed conflicts which in some ways include a more or less conscious constructed image of "the West" and "Islam" as enemies, and acts of terror. This situation can easily result in distorted images of those who are considered to be the 'other'. Edward Said launched the notion of 'orientalism' to describe the attitude of the so-called West towards the so called 'Orient', consisting of a view of the 'Orientals' and Islam in essensialistic, stereotypical images as 'irrational, fanatic and traditional', opposite the supposedly 'rational, democratic and dynamic 'West''.[2] This view leads to the use of 'the Orient' and Muslims as a negative mirror by the 'West', a wish to create an identity in opposition to the negative 'Other'. Orientalism is still used as a key notion to describe many of the attitudes of fear and demands of assimilation amongst the majority population

---

[1] The word 'Islamophobia' is from the 1990's in use as a new word as a "useful shorthand way of referring to dread or hatred of Islam – and therefore, to fear or dislike of all or most muslims" – p.1 in the Report "Islamophobia – A Challenge For Us All", by the Runnymede Trust, Commission on British Muslims and Islamophobia, London 1997.

[2] Said, Edward: *Orientalism* (London: Routledge & Kegan Paul, 1978).

towards Muslims. This means that not only people living in the 'Orient' but Muslims living in the 'West' still are defined as 'Other'. This results in difficulties amongst Muslims to enjoy equal social status and equal possibilities to get jobs, and suspiciousness toward them when practising the Muslim religion and acting out cultures of African, Middle Eastern, or Asian origin.

The need for Muslim-Christian dialogue is clearly coming from 'within' – as a the need for believers and communities of Christianity and Islam to relate to each other in the religious and social landscape in which they exist. But the need comes maybe even stronger from the 'outside', from a political and social context where the need is articulated to build bridges and decrease tension between people of Christian and Muslim faith – and between Muslims and 'general society'. Looking at the present European and Scandinavian context it is necessary for Christian theologians and churches in Europe to relate to the Muslim minorities and to their situation in the countries, cities and neighbourhoods in which we live in order to relate adequately to our own context.

The context demands Muslim-Christian dialogue. But what are the aims and the content of these dialogues? The notion of dialogue used in different contexts is at the moment fragmented and ambiguous, due to the fact that the word has increasingly become popular and used about all kinds of activities which include some extent of articulation and exchange of opinions. Additionally the word 'dialogue' has been regarded by many minorities as becoming part of a repressive language used in order to confirm and perhaps strengthen the existing status quo in the power balance between majority and minority population groups. To qualify the notion of dialogue in interfaith and interreligious context is necessary, in addition to critically analyzing and evaluating the current praxis of such dialogue work continuously.

Let me sketch up the notion of dialogue in the way I will use it here: when talking about dialogue in an interreligious or interfaith setting the aim is to meet across religious tradition barriers to talk, to increase the knowledge of the other part and get new views upon one's own tradition, sometimes agree upon common action, to build personal and maybe institutional relationships in order to decrease tension and increase understanding, and peace-building efforts between people of different faith. One is not entering a dialogue with the aim of transforming the other(s), but to take part in the possible mutual transformation which might be the result of the encounter. The necessary respect required to start and to continue a dialogue is based on the principle that the partners in the dialogue are equals – equally controlling the themes, the presentation of themselves, the physical circumstances, and the aim of the effort. A dialogue of this type has spiritual, social, political, cultural and personal dimensions.[3]

---

[3] In my article "Begrepet *dialog* i Emmaus – noen refleksjoner om bruken av begrepet på grunnlag av erfaringer i et flerreligiøst landskap" ("The notion of *dialogue* in Emmaus – reflections upon the use of the notion of dialogue based

As for the contents and aims of the different Muslim-Christian dialogues in Europe and Scandinavia, there are generally speaking two main areas dealt with in these: Long term process dialogues aimed at peace-building and community building in different forms, or more ad-hoc addressing to emergency situations where there is a need to address fear, to correct constructed enemy images of each other and to act together to increase knowledge and understanding in general society. There are also dialogues where common religious praxis such as praying and relation to Holy Scriptures are the main focus, but these are largely overwhelmed by the more political and socio-ethical. The majority Christian churches in countries like UK (The Church of England) Sweden (Svenska Kyrkan/Church of Sweden) and Norway (Den norske Kirke/Church of Norway) have played important roles in defending religious rights of the Muslim minority communities within general society, both by acting on their own behalf as majority religious communities with at least a partly acknowledged particular responsibility for developing tools for politicians and the general society to handle issues concerning the growing multi-religious context, but also, and perhaps more important, by acting out based on dialogues established together with Muslim organisations and faith communities. The issues dealt with in this last way are both principal issues concerning different practical aspects of the freedom of religion, and socio-ethical issues such as Muslims and Christians together rejecting violent actions like the war in Iraq or terrorist acts in Europe or the US. Since 1992 a contact group between the Church of Norway and The Islamic Council in Norway has been meeting regularly, including leaders from both sides.[4] This group has dealt both with matters of practical importance for Norwegian Muslims, such as possibilities to establish graveyards for Muslims, and possibilities for Muslim prisoners to be served by imams, but the group has also addressed the situation after 9.11.2001, urging Norwegian Christians and Muslims to pray for each other and to struggle against fear and islamophobia together, and discussed the situation for the Christian minority in Pakistan, the country from which most Muslims in Norway originate.

In the Scandinavian context, particularly in Norway and Sweden, gender issues can be identified as the area where conflicts between particularly the Muslim minority and general society have been most strongly articulated. This is due to the fact that gender equality stands out as one of the most important

---

upon experience in a multi-religious landscape") in *Kirke og Kultur 1/2005, Oslo.* I am exploring how my experience in practical dialogue work in the Center for Dialogue and Spirituality Emmaus in Oslo influences the use of the notion *dialogue:* Its possibilities, its limits, and how working with this notion is a dynamic process between praxis, religious and political context(s) on the one hand and philosophical and theological theory on the other.

[4] Leirvik, Oddbjørn: *Islam og kristendom – konflikt eller dialog? (Islam and Christianity – conflict or Dialogue?)* (Oslo: Pax, 2006), 29.

community values and political aims in these countries, to the lack of knowledge in general about Muslim communities which easily can lead to stereotypical images also in this field, and to the cultural differences between immigrants from Africa, the Middle East and South East Asia, and the majority of Norwegians. The release of the so-called 'Barometer for integration 2005' in January 2006 – the first larger survey in Norway so far mapping attitudes in the Norwegian population towards immigration and cultural plurality – shows this with great clarity. The field covered in chapter 6 of the survey, called 'Attitudes towards current social issues', the respondents were asked questions in four areas. These were: Arranged marriages, circumcision (of girls), attitudes towards wearing the hijab, and family reunion. There were no questions about other cultural or political potential conflict areas – the concentration was entirely at gender (particularly women related) issues and 'family questions'. Being meant to be a 'Barometer' for measuring attitudes in the general Norwegian population, the survey is surely also a 'Barometer' concerning which questions the Norwegian ruling authorities consider the most central. This shows that the question on gender issues in general and women's issues in particular have become much of a test-question where your answer is defining your cultural identity, and questions of great symbolic value in addition to the importance they carry in their own weight. These questions in Chapter 6 of the survey also highlight questions relating to Muslim praxis, as the hijab and partly the circumcision of girls are questions relevant for the Muslims. Dealing with gender put as *the* conflict issue between 'Muslims' and 'General society' needs careful exploration to sort out the cultural, religious, political and social levels and to some extent to differentiate between them so that gender issues raised concerning women's situation and women's rights, including wearing hijab for Muslim women, circumcision of Muslim women, forced marriages and domestic violence, is not stuck on all Muslims in general and thus becoming part of a stereotypical image of Muslims as in Orientalism. Unfortunately, this exploration is often not done, and the following process leads to more islamophobia, which is damaging both for 'general society '*and* for the Muslims (both women and men) because it can easily freeze or polarize positions without pointing at any solutions or strategies of cooperation.

A report done by a group of researches in Europe, financed by the EU, investigated how Muslim women in different European countries (Germany, Denmark, UK, Italy and Spain) experienced multiple types of discrimination.[5] The report itself concluded that the discrimination the women experienced did take place in the religious communities and that this was the most important hindrance for them in order to live a fulfilled life socially and politically, but the women themselves stated that the most urgent problem for them was the discrimination perpetrated against them by social institutions, by state laws and

---

[5] Blaschke, Jochen (ed.): *Multi-level discrimination of Muslim Women in Europe,* Berlin 2000.

regulations and mechanisms in the labour market. The discrepancy between the report's own conclusion and what most of the informants actually presented as their interpretation is interesting – and disturbing. It shows how the patterns of orientalism can be traced also in serious, up-to-date European research. Even if this report did not include Norway it is very likely that the same pattern is present to a certain extent here. The view of Muslim women as 'subjugated' in society represents a devaluation of Muslim women's individuality and resources, and a hindrance for their possibilities to obtain a life with the qualities one can expect to have in Norway. In addition to the current discourse of islamophobia in the 'West' this deprivation of possibilities for Muslim women is a hindrance in itself for having the strength to work on their situation and challenges related to gender models within Islam, and also for having the necessary surplus to enter into a interreligious dialogue. But the most important hindrance coming out of this is how the image of Muslim women is settled as collectively 'subjugated', also amongst possible Christian dialogue partners. This may create a very uneven power balance putting all dialogue initiatives qualified as dialogue between equal partners at risk.

To summarize: The outside context – or more precisely the socio-political context in Norway and the rest of Europe is presenting challenging issues related to Islam and gender. Christianity as being the dominant religion and an important part of the cultural heritage is to a certain extent used together with Islam in a dichotomy to construct an image where women and women lives are dragged into the construction of mutual enemy images of Muslims and so-called "Western culture". In Scandinavia, particularly in Norway and Sweden, the main conflict areas presented in the media between "the Muslims and the majority citizens" are not about terrorism – it's about women's rights. Muslim women are considered collectively "subjugated" because they are Muslims (which implies that Muslim men are collectively "subjugators"). On the other side many Muslims consider "Western women" to be lonely, likely to be unfaithful to their family and husband, and oppressed by the commercial industry. Both these views are regarding women more or less "property" or at least victims of cruel men – the men being part of the "feared other". In these ways women can become a battlefield for religious and cultural identity.

Interreligious dialogue and Gender Issues

How can Christian-Muslim dialogue relate to gender issues? Firstly, I will draw attention on a more general level to Professor Ursula King and her reflections on interreligious and interfaith dialogue in general relating to gender issues and women. She states in her article "Feminism: The Missing Dimension in the

Dialogue of Religions"[6]

> Narrowness is evident with regard to the marginalisation, invisibility and exclusion of women, for wherever interreligious dialogue has developed, women seem to have little part in it at least at the official level. Proof for this is found en every single book on interfaith dialogue ... can these 'religious leaders' today still legitimately 'voice' the concerns of women and speak on their behalf, as if women could not speak for themselves?[7]

Ursula King uses the notion feminism – which needs a careful consideration when used in a Christian-Muslim context. But her point about men in dialogue speaking on women's behalf, and women's perspectives as missing from the agenda, is clear enough. It must be a crucial step to include women participants in dialogue, as well as including women's issues – in order to make a dialogue relevant. This gives a possibility of breaking up the stereotypical images as well as offering an arena of process and discussion.

The need for addressing gender issues in Muslim-Christian dialogue

I will argue that the needs for this come not only from the social and political context in Europe and in Scandinavia, but also from within the Christian and Muslim religious communities and organisations. Both the Christian and the Muslim religion are (together with Judaism) traditions heavily rooted in a patriarchal structure, and both the sacred texts and the religious practices shows this in different ways and to a different degree when in comes to present religious praxis. John Esposito states in his introduction "Women, Religion and Empowerment" to the book *Daughters of Abraham: Feminist Thought in Judaism, Christianity, and Islam:*

> However different, the daughters of Abraham, Sara, and Hagar have inherited a religious legacy that is not only the product of divine revelation but also of human interpretation ... overwhelmingly male and patriarchal ...As a result, the image of women has been shaped by patriarchy as much as by revelation.[8]

So what happens when two of these religions enter into an encounter – will they confirm or challenge this particular part of their respective traditions? For every Christian or Muslim who wants to transform her own religious

---

[6] King, Ursula: "Feminism: The Missing Dimension in the Dialogue of Religions" in May, John (Ed.): *Pluralism and the Religions: The Theological and Political Dimensions,* London 1998.

[7] Ibid.

[8] Haddad, Yvonne Yazbeck, and Esposito, John (Eds.) : *Daughters of Abraham. Feminist Thought in Judaism, Christianity, and Islam*, Florida 2001, Esposito, John: "Introduction. Women, Religion, and Empowerment", 1.

community into a space of more gender equality, this has to be explored. Within many Christian and Muslim communities there is a struggle going on at different levels concerning gender issues. This includes struggling with scriptures, tradition, and gender roles within the religious tradition. A Muslim-Christian dialogue capable of including these efforts might be able to provide new tools for transformation from within. This can be through tools of raised awareness, more knowledge of oneself and the other, having "blind spots" in one's own tradition revealed, and finding new insights. In this way the challenge to distinguish between culture and religious norms can become more visible. For women engaged in dialogue the very experience from it can be empowering to enter into addressing new questions and in being more aware of oneself as an acting subject.[9]

The book *Scriptures in Dialogue – Christians and Muslims studying the Bible and Qur'an together*[10] is the result of a seminar in 2003 where different Christian and Muslim scholars reflected upon Christian and Muslim texts and the aim and scope of dialogue. Gender issues were not addressed in particular, but in the summary it is stated that

> There is clearly ample scope for further engagement of Christians and Muslims together in a dialogue grounded in reading the scriptures together.( ) This is especially obvious in relation to gender issues ... dialogue cannot be only with one another ... it must also engage with the secular understandings and forces in our religious and secular world.[11]

How should one interpret this: Is it an indicative of openness towards including 'secular' European gender perspectives including 'Western feminism', or does it rather express a resignation on behalf of Christianity and Islam as religious traditions, suggesting that both religions are lacking the necessary discourses or theoretical tools to deal with gender issues? The important first step is nevertheless clear: Christians and Muslims need to address this, together in a dialogue, but not isolated from the particular challenges and resources which arise from different contexts.

There should be plenty of reasons why dialogue arenas should be acknowledged as gendered space and "gender issues" discussed and articulated openly: The participants always are present in the dialogue either as a man or a woman, the religious space and praxis of both Christianity and Islam is marked

---

[9] Grung, Anne Hege: "Kvindeperspektiv på kristen-muslimsk dialog" ("Women's perspective in Christian-Muslim dialogue") in Larsen, Lena and Rasmussen, Lissi (Eds.): *Islam, Kristendom og det Moderne (Islam, Christianity and Modernity)*, Copenhagen 2004.

[10] Ipgrave, Michael (Ed.): *Scriptures in Dialogue – Christians and Muslims studying the Bible and the Qur'an together,* London 2004.

[11] Ibid., 146.

by a patriarchal heritage, and one gender (men) is dominating the level of leadership both in civil society and in the religious communities of Christianity and Islam.

Gender issues and Gender perspective in Norwegian Christian-Muslim dialogue

So what about gender issues in the Christian-Muslim dialogue arena in Norway? Is the dialogue arena able to contribute constructively to dealing with gender issues?

The experience from the Norwegian dialogue context is ambiguous: On the one hand, we do have examples from the Norwegian context of Christian-Muslim dialogues dealing with gender issues and women issues in particular. The formerly mentioned Contact group between Islamic Council in Norway and the Church of Norway initiated and supported a project where Lena Larsen from Islamic Council of Norway and myself representing the Church of Norway, as members of the contact group were asked to produce relevant material of interest about experiences of Christian-Muslim dialogue. Our choice was to establish a group of Christian and Muslim women and go through a dialogue process, meeting regularly, and then write and publish a book about it later on. The contact group was supportive of this, and the book *Dialog med og uten slør (Dialogue with and without veil)* was published in 2000.[12] This project was simply giving different women in a group an opportunity to explore Christian-Muslim dialogue, and then telling the story about the process and the reflections which arose, in addition to sharing more general information about both Islam and Christianity in Norway. It did not particularly take into use a feminist analysis of the two religions or the dialogue – but the voices heard in the project were women's voices, and there were reflections upon the meaning of women being subjects in sharing and articulating traditions and experiences. In the larger dialogue projects and processes which have taken place in Norway involving more broad participation, there has been an effort to have a gender balance amongst the participants – and this has to a large extent succeeded.

One the other hand, it seems that rather than acknowledging a gender perspective as integrated in Muslim-Christian dialogue processes, this field and particularly so-called 'women issues' are also sometimes put aside in order not to create 'unnecessary tensions'. And even if there has been a gender balance amongst participants in different dialogues, as most religious leaders from all religious communities are men, a balance in gender participation does not necessarily imply an equal power balance. Often 'gender issues' or 'women issues' are either fragmented into single-case discussions without including an overall gender perspective, or put as secondary issues under headlines like

[12] Grung, Anne Hege and Larsen, Lena: *Dialog med og uten slør (Dialogue with and without veil)* Oslo 2000.

'family issues', 'discrimination against Muslim women because of the use of hijab' and so on. Most dialogue participants in the different ongoing dialogues would agree that 'gender issues' and 'women issues' are very important to deal with in the dialogue, some will say 'time is not right yet' – one needs to wait for the right moment to appear sometime in the future. Being polemic towards this quite familiar argumentation is relatively easy, but what are the issues needed to be addressed, and how is it possible to create a discourse in the Muslim-Christian dialogue for discussing gender related issues? Is it too ambitious to throw this into a dialogue arena as some of the religious communities are still struggling amongst themselves to have open discussions about this? Or perhaps the dialogue arena can be an open space for discussing 'gender issues' and 'women issues' to a greater extent than within the respective traditions, because the aim in this dialogue is not to achieve agreements so much as to explore the differences? These questions are to be asked in the current Norwegian Christian-Muslim dialogue contexts.

A gender perspective is necessary for a qualified and relevant Christian-Muslim dialogue

To qualify a Muslim-Christian dialogue requires a consciousness of the context in which it takes place. Gender issues and issues concerning women's rights and women's lives are an important part of our context, and Christian and Muslim wrestling with their own tradition, in different ways. An overall gender perspective is necessary, as well as securing participation of both women and men, but also to address issues both from within the traditions of Christianity and Islam (scriptures, tradition, praxis and culture) and from the socio-political reality. It is, in the European and Scandinavian context of growing islamophobia, of utmost importance that both traditions refuse to enter into a construction of stereotypes on both sides, but rather address current problems and challenges openly and thoroughly in dialogue processes.

PART THREE

LEADERSHIP AND TRAINING IN MISSION

(1) Leadership in Church and Mission

Women as Mission Leaders – A Historical Perspective[1]

Kristin Norseth

Assist Prof Dr Kristin Norseth, MF Norwegian School of Theology, Oslo, Norway

A striking feature characterising the expansion of Christianity in the nineteenth century, is the participation of women in mission work.[2] Never before in the history of Christianity had women played such an outgoing role, neither in foreign mission work nor in domestic religious life. It applies to Protestantism as well as Catholicism indicating it as a phenomenon connected with the modernisation of the Western world.[3] This article is, however, concerned with the Protestant context. Since there is a close connection between what happened at home and abroad, it is necessary to deal with women as leaders in the broader context of both domestic and foreign mission. Foreign mission meant to evangelize the "unsaved souls" of the non-Christian peoples, home mission aimed at saving the souls of unbelieving or indifferent, baptized fellow citizens. Reflecting general tendencies, examples will be drawn from

---

[1] The article's primary source is Kristin Norseth, *"La os bryte over tvert med vor stumhet!" Kvinners vei til myndighet i de kristelige organisasjonene 1842-1912* ("Let's break with silence!" Women acquiring authority in [Norwegian] religious organizations 1842-1912) (Dr. theol thesis in church history, MF Norwegian School of Theology, Oslo, 2007). When no references are made, the material is drawn from this.

[2] Kenneth Scott Latourette, *The Great Century in Europe and The United States of America A. D. 18000- A. D. 1914* (A History of the Expansion of Christianity, 4: New York: Harper and Row, 1970 [1941]), 98.

[3] Latourette, *A History of the Expansion of Christianity*, 1970, 23-34, 108. Never before had the Catholic world seen such a prospering of female orders engaged outside the convent, primarily in teaching and nursing. In the Nordic countries nuns played a vital part in the re-establishing of the Catholic Church in the 19th century. Else-Britt Nilsen, *Nonner i storm og stille. Katolske ordenssøstre i Norge i det 19. og det 20. århundre* (Nuns in turbulence and peace. Catholic sisters in Norway in the 19th and 20th Century.) (Oslo: Solum, 2001); Yvonne Maria Werner (ed), *Nuns and Sisters in the Nordic Countries after the Reformation. A Female Counter-Culture in Modern Society* (Uppsala: Swedish Institute of Missionary Research, 2005).

Norwegian Lutheran church life, which by the end of the nineteenth century came under direct influence of Anglo-American revivals and evangelical movements. The article's main focus is the period 1842 to 1914, when lay people took command and religious life was significantly altered. It also includes an outlook to the latter part of the twentieth century.

Outnumbering men

By the turn of the twentieth century women outnumbered men in mission work at home and abroad. The latter part of the nineteenth century had seen an increasing multitude of independent female missionary societies pursuing women's specific objectives and goals. They had been set up partly because women were denied access to missionary societies run by men, partly because of the difficulties men encountered when trying to evangelize women in societies where strict gender boundaries were the rule. On the mission field female mission workers accounted for approximately half the missionary force.[4] They ran a variety of schools and hospitals; they worked as teachers, nurses and doctors educating and evangelizing the "heathens" with the physical and spiritual welfare of children and women as their specific task. Back home women's auxiliaries[5] were counted in the thousands making up the financial backbone of most missionary societies in which men and women joined forces as well as in solely female enterprises. For instance, America alone had 41 female missionary societies which employed 1200 single female mission workers and was supported by at least 3 million women. They outnumbered lay men's organizations as well as student movements usually credited for the explosive growth in protestant mission work.[6]

Norway, a community dominated by the Lutheran Church counting 2 million people in 1900, can serve as another slightly different example. Contrary to Britain and America Norway only had two minor female missionary societies, both founded in 1902. Neither of them developed into

---

[4] Latourette, *A History of the Expansion of Christianity,* 1970, 49, 98. Female missionary workers were single women employed by a missionary society. Adding missionaries wives who were usually not accounted for, women made up two third of the total amount of persons being sent by all missionary societies.

[5] In Norwegian: Misjonskvinneforening. The term auxiliaries underline the non-formal aspects of women's work.

[6] Latourette, *A History of the Expansion of Christianity,* 1970, 95-98; Patricia Hill, *The World their Household. The American woman's foreign mission movement and cultural transformation 1870-1920* (Univerity of Michigan Press, 1985), 2-5; R Pierce Beaver, *American Protestant Women in World Mission: a History of the First Feminist Movement in North America* (Grand Rapids, Michigan: William B Eerdmans, 1980).

full-fledged missionary societies due to the fact that women in 1904 acquired formal organizational rights (eligibility and the right to vote) within the dominating general society, the Norwegian Missionary Society (NMS).[7] Generally, women joined in enterprises with men. In 1904 more than 3500 women's auxiliaries, estimated to organize 90 000 women, supported the NMS, facilitating two thirds of its annual budgets.[8] Without formal attachments to NMS prior to 1904, they outnumbered the 900 ordinary mission associations which were governed by men and constituted the NMS body. Although women took part in ordinary association's meetings, women's auxiliaries were the most popular. Spread as they were all across the scarcely populated country, no rural area or school district was left untouched by missionary fervour. Not only did they support a variety of religious and philanthropic enterprises financially and in prayer. Through monthly meetings for their own edification and production of handicrafts for sale, annual bazaars, lotteries and the running of children's auxiliaries *women* were locally the most effective diffusers of information on missionary work, recruiting new supporters and missionaries as well as socializing younger generations to missionary efforts at home and abroad.

An international revival

Internationally missionary fervour reached a peak during the third great awakening (approximately 1885 to 1914). The revival had an international scope and an ecumenical impact, giving Americans a lead in protestant mission work. It gave birth to transnational Protestant organizations such as the Student Volunteer Movement (SVM) and the World's Young Women's Christian Association (YWCA, founded 1894), who fervently insisted on female leadership. It also coincided with the rise of the World Woman's Christian Temperance Union (founded 1883) and the women's movement sweeping across the Western world. This is significant in relation to women's involvement in Christian mission work. Generally speaking, at the end of the nineteenth century women went public involving themselves in matters of political, social and religious concerns. They not only claimed the right to vote

---

[7] KMA: Kvinnelige Misjons Arbeidere (Female mission Workers); LMF: Lærerinnenes Misjonsforbund (Female Teacher's Mission Association). Kristin Norseth, "To alen av hvilket stykke? Tvillingsøstrene LMF og KMA i norsk, nordisk og internasjonalt perspektiv" ("Two of a kind? The Female Teacher's Mission Association (LMF) and Female Mission Workers (KMA) in a Norwegian, Nordic and international perspective"), *Norsk Tidsskrift for Misjon*, 56.2 (2002), 91-106.

[8] Kristin F Tjelde, *Kvinder hjælper Kvinder. Misjonskvinneforeningsbevegelsen i Norge 1860-1910* (Women helping Women. The Women's Mission Auxiliaries movement in Norway 1860-1910.) (Master Thesis, University of Oslo, 1990), 105-106, 108.

in general elections. They also insisted on their right to perform leadership, to preach in public and participate in evangelistic work as men's equals. Not only men but women as well had a personal calling to leave everything behind to serve the Lord.

General conditions

Women's active participation in religious life was due to a complex interaction of structural, demographical, cultural, political and ideological alterations that changed societies and old ways of living and affected the relationship between public and private, men and women. Industrialization had a profound effect on individuals as well as civic society and institutional life. Production was taken out of the households/families, leaving unmarried women to earn their own income outside the household. Married women were made the emotional, moral and spiritual cornerstone of the modernized home, having been reduced from an economic productive household to a small, emotionally tightly knit unit of a wife, a husband and their children. Romanticism furthered the modern concept of family and home by underscoring the difference between the sexes as complementary as well as emphasizing sensibility and piety as female characteristics and the individual as a personality whether man, woman or child. The insistence on the difference and complementary lifted woman up by man's side as a companion or an assistant neither he nor home nor society could manage without. As different from men, women were assigned a role primarily in the private sphere, while men's main responsibility was public affairs and matters in civic and institutional life. Women touched the cradle. The task entrusted to women by nature itself, was to bring up morally good, devoted and useful citizens for the common good. As such they held the nation's future in their hands. Mothers possessed the key to people's hearts. Women then became of vital importance in transferring religious and moral values to future generations and disbelieving husbands. By the end of the nineteenth century father was so to say dethroned as the family's religious leader for the benefit of the ever present, caring, religious, sensitive and morally exalted mother. Reaching and educating women and children then became vital in mission work and a task appropriate for single female missionary workers, female missionary societies – and missionaries' wives, off the record.

Motherhood was not granted all women. The generally large surplus of women in Europe left a high percentage unmarried and childless. Still, by nature any woman was the bearer of motherly qualities that *civic* society needed and could benefit from. On the basis of difference and complementarity, women claimed access to public life and a role for women not only in the private household of the family, but in church and society as well. This applied especially to single women, making them more prominent in public and civic life than wives. The model of the modernized family was transferred to the public sphere. Nations, public institutions and organisations were thought of as major households where men and women were needed alongside each other just as in the private lives of families. The world became women's household.[9] Insisting on the common need for female gifts, values, virtues and purity, women entered the public sphere and its institutions with special obligations towards the poor and the sick as well as children and women.

This had bearing on the concept of leadership. Leadership understood as any position facing the public was originally a task for men. Men therefore filled the boards and headed private and public institutions of all kinds. But, the insistence on difference opened up for women to hold leadership and exercise authority on their own terms locally, nationally and internationally. In the latter part of the nineteenth century gender patterns were fundamentally changed in society as well as in religious life. On certain conditions women were granted leadership and authority alongside men in religious life. It could be achieved basically in two different ways. Either women could run their own organizations according to the principle women's work for women, or, they could obtain formal organizational rights (the right to vote and eligibility to general assemblies and boards) in general organizations, implying the above understanding of gender relations. According to the understanding of men playing a leading role in private and public life, the number of men in joint boards always exceeded that of women, and men always played the leading role as chairman or general secretary. Patriarchy and subordination was transferred to the public sphere. But taking place under new conditions, it served to give women access to the same arenas as men. In the long run, the development later served to provide access for women on the same conditions as men.

A significant vehicle of reform was the establishment of religious organizations furthering democratization and lay influence in church life and society. So also was a new conception concerning the calling. It was no longer merely understood as an institutional matter tied to natural relations given in everyday life. Rather it was conceived as something personal and extraordinary taking place between God and the individual, having as its consequence a breaking up from conventions as well as natural contexts to serve the Lord in other places.

Mission work – a voluntary enterprise

In the nineteenth century Christian missions were no longer a governmental responsibility but a voluntary enterprise carried out by devoted, believing church members. Throughout the century religious revivals swept the Western world, mobilizing laity, men *and* women, in the spreading of the faith in foreign countries and at home. To pursue their calling, objectives and goals men and women more often than not joined in setting up a variety of private,

[9] Cf title, Hill, *The World their Household,* 1985.

specialized organizations, being independent of authorities whether ecclesiastical or governmental. By the end of the century there existed a broad spectrum of religious organizations for different purposes aiming at a variety of target groups.

In Norway most voluntary religious organizations were clear-cut Lutheran, working freely within the framework the constitutional Lutheran State church, Church of Norway.[10] They were mainly based on modern democratic principles. An elected board of men answered to a general assembly consisting of representatives from local mission associations headed by men. This was the principles on which the Norwegian Missionary Society was founded jointly by Moravians, Haugians[11] and State church clergy in 1842. In the middle of the eighteen hundreds men having the lead was in accordance with custom, legislation and the understanding of Scripture. As family heads they represented their household publicly. Women had the legal status of minors. Unmarried women were dependent on either fathers or brothers, wives on their husbands. This was reflected in the NMS statutes. Women did not have a direct say or a vote in organizational matters nor were they eligible for public positions as board members on local, regional or national levels. Though, as believers women were not at all excluded from attending the meetings of an ordinary mission association. They could also sign up as individual members, if unmarried or widowed. Neither were women excluded from exercising influence indirectly through male relatives or acquaintances.

Women's auxiliaries – a means of empowerment

Women's auxiliaries were promoted and encouraged by NMS from the very beginning. Their establishment can be seen as a female counterpart to the ordinary mission associations in accordance with the pattern private – public. Not formally attached to any organizational body, women's auxiliaries were defined as private entities. They belonged to everybody and nobody, deciding for themselves where to channel their interests and money. More often than not they divided the money they obtained between different organizations and enterprises, seldom forgetting NMS, the mother of women's auxiliaries and a highly prominent and influential organization throughout the century.

Women's auxiliaries proved a useful tool for female influence outside

---

[10] Churches of other denominations were allowed settling in the kingdom following legislation in 1845. At the end of the century just a minor percentage was members of other churches than Church of Norway.

[11] Haugians were affiliated to the Norwegian revivalist pietistic movement named after its founder, the peasant, preacher and author Hans Nielsen Hauge (1776-1824). It gained numerous followers from 1796 to 1804, especially among prominent farming families, and left a lasting effect on religious as well as societal life.

women's own families and households. They became a channel for women to influence civic society, as the following examples illustrate. Around 1860 women's auxiliaries initiated two major national projects: The building of a vessel taking NMS missionaries to and from the mission field, and the establishment of an educational institution for deaconesses (nurses). Both projects were realized in cooperation with men. But they aroused especially women's interests and thus the formation of women's auxiliaries. The latter initiative was taken by a small group of upper class revivalist women. Among them were the sisters Ulrikke Eleonore (Rikke) Nissen (1834-1892) and Bolette Gjør, born Nissen (1835-1909). They wanted to improve hospital treatments as well as give women an opportunity to serve church and society as deaconesses, a calling esteemed highly suitable for single religious women. Their idea was a professional nursing school and hospital. They influenced the opinion by writing articles in magazines – anonymously. They contacted influential men, trying to convince them to take responsibility for realizing their idea. Through their auxiliary they raised money which was donated to the Christiania (Oslo) home mission association on the condition that it was set aside for the establishment of a deaconess institution. They succeeded. *Diakonisseanstalten* (The institution of deaconesses) opened in 1868. Two years later the first deaconesses had concluded their training to work in public hospitals and in charity and health programs for the poor run by local home mission associations in the cities as well as serving on the mission field.[12] The gifted Rikke Nissen, educated as deaconess in Neuendettelsau in Germany, became head of the educational department. In that capacity she wrote Norway's first textbook in nursing. She wanted an institution run by women, in accordance with the principle of *women leading women*. In this matter she did not succeed. In 1886 the board structured what was by then almost a little village of institutions, as a family. A pastor became director and head (father), leaving the education and the deaconesses' home to the matron (mother) as a subordinated department.

Being trained in nursing as well as spiritual guidance, deaconesses played a leading role in local religious life. They gained authority being professionals having a religious calling. They were set apart for a special service, ideally assisting the clergy as "assembly mothers". In addition to their work among the poor and sick, they attended meetings in local home or/and foreign mission associations, they organized and ran women's auxiliaries, and taught in Sunday schools. Later in the century they engaged in religious youth work. Wearing uniforms, they were easy to spot. That made them a symbol of womanly virtues and visualised the possibility for middle class and peasant women of climbing the social ladder.

---

[12] Kari Martinsen, *Freidige og uforsagte diakonisser. Et omsorgsyrke vokser frem 1860-1905* (Free and easy (candid) deaconesses. The origin of a profession of 1860-1905) (Oslo: Aschehoug, 1984).

Fostering female leadership

Education fostered female leadership on a local and a national level. So did women's auxiliaries. Even though keeping chairman, secretary and treasurer was thought of as unwomanly, women's auxiliaries needed administering and organizing. The ideal was for women to lead women, according to Moravian, romanticism's and modern pedagogical ideas.[13] Men often gave a helping hand, sometimes to the annoyance of women. Numerous women took responsibility leading auxiliaries locally. The upper class Bolette Gjør was one of them. The activities in which she engaged, reflects what fields the religious organizations opened to women. As young unmarried converts of the 1850-revival that especially mobilized the upper classes, she and her sister ran an auxiliary in the rural area where they lived, primarily supporting NMS – the organization Bolette Gjør happily served the rest of her life. She also engaged in caring for the poor, counselled men and women seeking her spiritual advice, taught Sunday school and ran educational programs for peasant girls. When asked, she also gave Bible instruction to a group of young women having been spiritually awakened and left in spiritual confusion by a non-Lutheran emissary. This developed into meetings, gathering so many, women and men alike, that she considered it coming close to public preaching. As there was no one else willing to take over, she carried on holding to the "principle of emergency": Whenever there was no man suitable or wiling to preach, women could. Evangelizing had priority over church order and traditional Scripture reading, holding women to silence in public assemblies. Whenever she had the opportunity, Bolette Gjør attended NMS regional and general assemblies as did ordinary women. Listening in on the debates, they learnt the rules of democracy.

At the age of 37 Bolette Gjør married Rev Julius Gjør (1839-1916). Being a pastor's wife was in itself an influential role, and with only one foster daughter and servants she was free to pursue her own interests and goals. Throughout her life she acted according to the norm: Women leading women. It is reflected in her authorship: From 1884 onwards she published 15 widely read fiction books for children and adults, aimed at women, as well as being an editor of a women's and a children's magazine. It is reflected in her deeds: Wherever she came, Bolette Gjør initiated and conducted women's auxiliaries as well as public women's meetings. In 1887 she was one of the founders of the Kristiania (Oslo) Young Women's Christian Association, being a board member well into the twentieth century. Year after year during the 1890s she gave weekly Bible lessons. In these capacities, through authorship and deeds, she became a role model to younger and older women, publicly contributing to the reform of

---

13 Hartvig Nissen, *Om kvindelig Dannelse og kvindelige Underviisningsanstalter* (On Women's Refinement and Women's Education) (Christiania: Malling, 1849).

woman ideals within church and society.

Bolette Gjør – a woman of national importance

In 1884 NMS started publishing a mission magazine for women, *Missionslæsning for Kvindeforeninger* (Mission-reading for women's auxiliaries). Bolette Gjør became editor, seeing it as a calling from the Lord. As such she was authorised to speak on behalf of the most influent religious organization in the country, making her equally influential. The magazine was initiated by her long-time friend, the teacher and missionary wife to Madagascar, Johanne Borchgrevinch (1836-1924). On furlough she had been upset to learn how little women in mission auxiliaries knew about mission work. A magazine for and by women would resolve the problem as men did not know what interested women. Bolette Gjør shared her view. The magazine hit home from the start, getting 3600 subscribers the first year. By the turn of the century it had 10 000, equalling some of the major newspapers. The magazine raised an enormous interest in mission work among women. From 1882 to 1892 women's mission auxiliaries increased from 1600 to 3000, reaching 3500 in 1904 and 4500 in 1940.[14] Women had gotten a voice.

The importance of the magazine can hardly be overestimated. It made ordinary women, single mission workers and missionary wives visible to each other *and* to the public. It also made Bolette Gjør a national leader of what emerged as a nationwide movement of women auxiliaries bound together by a magazine, its editor and her ideology of international sisterhood. Yet the bond between NMS and the individual women's auxiliaries was informal, resting on women's loyalty toward the organization and its work. In times when new organizations and causes contested old loyalties, Bolette Gjør found it necessary to discuss the issue of formal connections between women's auxiliaries and NMS with the general secretary Lars Dahle (1843-1925). Even though he was a true friend of democracy, he hesitated, waiting for the ripe moment to act. Due to their interaction, as well as that of regional boards, women supporting NMS in 1904 acquired individual members' rights to vote. They were made eligible as deputies to all formal assemblies as well as to boards in local mission associations, the pattern being consistent to that of the family with men as heads as well as having the plurality. Women did not gain access to regional boards or the main board.[15] Everybody knew it was just a

[14] Tjelle, *Kvinder hjælper Kvinder,* 1990:122, 108. Tjelle estimates 25 members per auxiliary. In 1900 NMS auxiliaries not only was the oldest but also the largest women's movement in Norway – as e.g. in America.

[15] For a more detailed account on this, see Karina Hestad Skeie and Kristin Norseth, "Creating a voice – acquiring rights. Women in the Norwegian Mission Society and the process towards formal organizational rights in 1904", *Nora. Nordic Journal of Women's Studies* 11.1 (2007), 5-13.

question of time, though, as they all realized that a new principle had been introduced.[16]

The decision was a major breakthrough, furthering the political process according to a leading suffragette.[17] It was also of principal importance, opening leadership and the right for women to speak in public. What Scripture prohibited then, was, according to the new interpretation introduced in 1904, that women were being authorized to preach the word of God in public, whether from the pulpit in a church or a prayer house. The general assembly argued that women deserved influence in the constitutional body of NMS because of their great efforts. Those who provided the most money should also have a say in the use of it.

Bolette Gjør favoured the decision, arguing that women should be granted rights not because they deserved it but because NMS needed women's specific gifts and abilities. She looked upon the organization as a household, where men and women sought each other's advice and supplemented each other. On this background, she favoured a woman in the main board, which made decisions concerning women and children at home and on the field. The reason for this was recent experiences. In 1900 Bolette Gjør and friends had founded a school for female mission workers, with the permission of NMS. As head and leader of the committee running it, she often had to deal with the secretary and the main board, coming to realise their inadequacies concerning female mission workers and women's interests and requirements. This led her to acknowledge the need for women on the main board.

International aspects – missionary feminism

When Bolette Gjør commenced as editor in 1884, she introduced *women helping women* as the magazine's slogan. Echoing international trends, she made it the basic principle of women's mission work, perceiving it a special branch of the general mission. Her point of departure was sisterly solidarity between the "mission sisters" in Norway, the "serving sisters" in the field, i.e. female mission workers and missionary wives, and the "sisters out there", i.e. Zulu and Malagasy women whether Christian or not.[18] By the end of the century this had developed into an ideology advocated by world movements. It was based on the presupposition that Christianity above any other religion had lifted women to dignity. Evangelizing then became a tool of liberating women

---

[16] Women became eligible to regional boards in 1916, to the main board in 1939. From then on there were constantly two women at the main board. Since the nineteen-eighties, 50 % of the main board members have been women.

[17] Norway was the first sovereign state to endorse their women's citizenship, based on income, in 1907. Full citizenship on the same conditions as men was given in 1913.

[18] Tjelle, *Kvinder hjælper Kvinder,* 1990, 137-146.

in non-Christian lands from restricting traditions, prejudices and oppression as well as combating Scripture interpretations, preventing women from participating in mission work and public preaching.

Researchers have characterized this position as *missionary feminism*, seeing it as a religious expression of conscious efforts to change women's lives and living conditions for the better of the individuals and society as a whole.[19] This kind of feminism was part of a broad and universal phenomenon, the women's movement, having as its overall aim "to secure for the social influence of women, richer inward development and freer social activity". It was protean in its manifestations and transcended "religions and prejudices of class, race, or colour". By the turn of the century modern women had enshrined "their ideals in world organizations", Ruth Rouse (1872-1956)[20] wrote, mentioning eight at work on a large scale. Among them were the World's Young Women's Christian Association, with 657 485 members in twenty-one countries, and the World's Women's Christian Temperance Union, with auxiliaries in at least fifty countries counting millions of members. She identified two spiritual forces behind the women's movement in the West, determining them as "distinctly Christian in their origin"; firstly the striving for liberation understood as a desire for the development and expression of personality, secondly the striving for opportunity to serve the community. Criticising foreign missionary leaders who were "impatient" with the women's movement, she emphasized the necessity of liberation as a first stage, "to the end of service". Having individual and relational aspects, the dominating note in the women's movement was not the interests of one sex, but that of the community.[21]

Ruth Rouse – "Miss International"

The gifted and manifold Ruth Rouse was not *any* English woman; she was Protestantism's Miss International herself, "a pioneer woman among pioneer

---

[19] Line Nyhagen Predelli, *Issues of Gender, Race and Class in the Norwegian Missionary Society in nineteenth -century Norway and Madagascar* (Studies in the history of missions, 24: Lewiston, N.Y.: Edwin Mellen Press, 2003); Lisbeth Mikaelsson, *Kallets ekko. Studier i misjon og selvbiografi* (Echoes of the calling. Studies in mission and autobiography) (Kristiansand: Høyskoleforlaget, 2003).

[20] Born in London, educated from Cambridge, member of Church of England, missionary to India 1899-1901.

[21] Ruth Rouse, "The Ideal of Womanhood as a Factor in Missionary Work", *The International Review of Missions* II.5 (1913), 148-164. The others mentioned: The International Council of Women, the International Women's Suffrage Alliance, the Traveller's Aid Society, Les Amies de la Jeune Fille, L'Association Catholic Internationale des Oeuvres de Protection de la Jeune Fille, Le Secrétariat Internationale de l'Action Sociale des Femmes.

women". She represented the new type of women about to conquer the world: the unmarried, educated women preoccupied with women's issues. Since 1897, she served as travelling secretary under the umbrella of the Student Volunteer Movement; from 1905 to 1924 she worked with the World's Student Christian Federation (WSCF). In that capacity she toured the world as missionary, evangelist, secretary and pioneer in reaching students in universities and colleges, visiting more than sixty-five different countries, many of them several times.

Ruth Rouse is referred to as a "female John R. Mott". Since the 1890s, she was his close fellow worker in student work, also being his assistant general secretary in the WSCF, thus reflecting the family pattern. Independent and capable in her own right, she was "a perfect balance in the WSCF for Mott". Like him she had the same zeal for evangelization and the same ability to inspire people. To numberless women she became the embodiment of WSCF. She correlated her WSCF-work with that of the World's YWCA, where she served as member of the World Executive Committee (1906-1946) and president (1938-1946). During her lifetime she attended innumerable international conferences, among them the Edinburgh World Missionary Conference in 1910 and the World Council of Churches first conference in 1948.[22] Being involved mainly in non-denominational organizations and work, Ruth Rouse has a major part in the development of modern world ecumenism.

On visiting Kristiania (Oslo) in 1897, Ruth Rouse conveyed missionary fervour and missionary feminism. Her stay left a lasting imprint on Norwegian religious life, shaping female religious leaders of national importance, such as e.g. Henny Dons (1874-1966).[23] A small association of Christian women students was founded while she was still in the city. More striking is the change that took place within the Kristiania YWCA and its sister-associations. Young women spoke up and claimed their right to participate in direct evangelizing work. Echoing arguments comparable to international rhetoric labelled as missionary feminism, they influenced religious and political life through decades.

Conclusion and outlook

Religious organizations and women's auxiliaries are so to say twins, having their origin in an early phase of the modernization of Western societies. This indicates women's auxiliaries as means modernizing the role of women in religious and societal life. The 1880s was the decade when women went public

[22] Ruth Franzén, "Ruth Rouse 1872-1956. Missionary, Student Evangelist, Ecumenical Pioneer", in Gerald H Anderson, Coote, R.T., Horner, N. A., Phillips, J. M. (eds), *Mission Legacies. Biograpichal Studies of Leaders of the Modern Missionary Movement* (Maryknoll, N.Y.: Orbis, 1994), 93-191.

[23] Norseth, "To alen av hvilket stykke?", 2002.

and started to organize themselves in national and international organizations of their own. This, as well as a transfer of the family model to public societal life, made women visible and influential on certain fields, according to what was determined as womanly. During the period 1890 to 1914 Norwegian women acquired the right to vote and became eligible in most national religious organisations. The admission was based on the concept of difference and complementarity. But when acquired, it furthered a development of equality.

In a worldwide context, women organizing themselves in separate religious organisations decreased from the 1930s, almost ebbing away during the 1970s, when a new feminist wave had occurred. The new wave created as much discussion and disagreement between the political feminists and the church as the nineteenth-century one had. Still, in the wake of it, women came to positions and influence in religious organisations and Church of Norway, unheard of at the beginning of the century. Today they hold leadership positions on all levels. In the NMS they serve as pastors, making up half of the main board members as well as having been elected chair. The organic family pattern and the system where women's religiosity was the one that mattered, is left behind to the advantage of the abstract ideology of equality. The church has so to say become nothing in gendered terms. According to Callum C. Brown this has a bearing on secularisation and death of Christian Britain as well as Norway.[24]

---

24 Callum C Brown, *The Death of Christian Britain. Understanding secularisation 1800-2000* (London and N.Y: Routledge, 2001), 193-198.

Leadership and Ministry – An Evangelical Lutheran View

Kjell Olav Sannes

Prof Dr Kjell Olav Sannes, MF Norwegian School of Theology, Oslo

The question of leadership in the Christian church has been addressed in many different ways during the history of the church. The much more open and fluid situation of the present time, poses new challenges for the reflection on church leadership. This is a subject area to which Knud Jørgensen has dedicated quite a bit of attention, e.g. in his *Visjon og hverdag. Lederskap i misjon og menighet* (Vision and everyday. Leadership in mission and congregation), 1991. Although this book is primarily dealing with leadership in mission, he includes leaders in the church and in Christian organisations as well.[1]

This issue is indeed not new. Traditionally it has often been put forward in the way of emphasizing the unique character and importance of bishops, pastors or priests of the church, often with special reference to the relationship between different offices. Thus the question of church leadership has often been transformed into the issue of church hierarchy. The threefold ordained ministry of the Roman Catholic Church, also in use in the Anglican tradition, is a significant and important example, both historically and currently. According to this view, the *ordo* consists of bishops, priests and deacons, with the bishops at the peak, delegating power to the priests and being assisted by the deacons. The traditional Reformed-Presbyterian Calvinistic tradition, on the other hand, stresses the supposedly Biblical pattern of e.g. apostles, prophets, teachers and deacons. This thinking is the basis for much modern or postmodern teaching on the subject.

The question is not, however, just what leaders or officers there should be in church and mission, how they should be selected or what kind of authority or even power they are supposed to have. Basically one should also address the fundamental theological question what we mean when we talk about 'leadership', 'ministry' or 'office' in the church. One thing is the use of those and other terms, often used very differently and thus confusing rather than clarifying the matter at hand. In this article, I use 'ministry' in a somewhat

---

[1] *Visjon og hverdag. Lederskap i misjon og menighet* (Oslo: Verbum, 1991), 14.

broader sense, as the mission or service as such; different opinions and usages will be mentioned later. In my terminology, 'office' on the other hand denotes a more formal, defined kind of ministry, i.e. a position or "job".

Another and even more important part of it is the theology of the ministry or office ("embetsteologi") as part of a theological ecclesiology and within the framework of a comprehensive theology. In this article, *the theological or doctrinal understanding of the ministry* is the topic. It is not, however, just a theoretical question, an issue for discussion by far-from-reality scholars. I think Knud Jørgensen is right when he argues that a good theory is the most practical thing there is, being a good map of the terrain that enables us to organize and explain the practical reality.[2] Himself being a man of both theoretical reflection and forceful practical achievement, Dr. Jørgensen is an example of the necessity of combining the two. Following this, I will first address the theological issue and then venture to draw some conclusions for our contemporary situation.

It is my intention, as the title says, to present an Evangelical-Lutheran view. The Ministry of the church is, however, a topic where Lutheran theology has not developed a common doctrine. Although Lutheran theologians during the Reformation period were joined in a common theological thinking contradicting many aspects of Roman Catholic understanding of the priest's office, the subject as such was not a matter of great dispute at the time. Traditionally, however, the minister/pastor has played a very dominant role in the Lutheran congregations, and often the theology on the subject may have reflected this fact. This poses the background on which to discuss a Lutheran theology of the ministry today.

Contemporary challenges and different types of theology of ministry

This dominant role of the minister in the Lutheran church and the corresponding teaching about the office of the ministry has been challenged in many ways and should be discussed in several contexts:

1. Minister-church relationship: In the wake of democratization and lay movements there has been a discussion about who has the "right" to preach in the congregation, and more generally about the relation between the pastor and the congregation and its members. The relation between the ordained and the non-ordained leadership in the church is also on the agenda. The relevant theological question would be about the relationship between the offices in the church and the congregation as a whole, included that of the ordained to the non-ordained, so called "lay" members of the church. But it is also a question of different structures of leadership, represented by the pastors and the parish council or even the

---

[2] Jørgensen, *Visjon og hverdag,* 21.

bishops and the Church council.

2. Internal church order: In the churches other offices have emerged beside the pastor, as those of the catechist and the deacon, or even the organist and the missionary. There has been, and indeed are, discussions of whether they are part of what is called the one ministry of the church or somehow outside of it. Which offices should there be in a Lutheran church, how should they be understood and defined in relationship to each other, and what is the theological significance of such offices?
3. Ecumenical situation: The contacts and talks, and in some cases even agreements, with churches of other traditions (Roman Catholic, Presbyterian, Anglican etc.) pose a challenge to the Lutheran churches. The same is the case with newer Charismatic and Faith Movement views of the anointed leader basing his ministry upon a special God-given vision. Some Lutherans are influenced by such views, and the question is to what degree one could do that within the framework of a Lutheran ecclesiology. The issue of mutual recognition – or rather: non-recognition – of offices is also relevant here: When a Lutheran minister is not recognized as such by the Roman Catholic Church, not only one's pastoral self understanding but also one's theology of ministry is challenged.
4. Sociological context: The traditional offices and ministries are shaped by patterns of Hebrew, Greek, Roman and Western origin. When the Christian faith and the Gospel are communicated into new contexts, those traditional offices may be challenged by other forms of leadership. In an African context, witch doctors, elders, tribal chiefs and even kings might represent patterns for church leaders to relate to. In general, does the church have to adhere to certain fixed traditions, or is it free to interact with the existing culture in a both constructive and critical way?

Some of those challenges are ancient, existing for hundreds of years. Others are relatively new, increasingly characterizing the situation of the Western and even the Two-Thirds world in the last decades. Different churches and schools of theology are responding to them, in line with the traditions of their churches respectively. In this way, many different views of church leadership and ministry are developed.

One can categorize such views in different ways. One approach to the matter is to look at it from a confessional or denominational perspective. This might not be the best way, for two reasons: The theological thinking and even order of ministry is not necessarily tied to one specific confessional family; there are significant similarities between e.g. Roman Catholic and Anglican understanding. Similar challenges by the sociological context may also lead to similar models and practises, across the confessional dividing lines. On the other hand, a plurality of opinions can be found inside the same denomination.

As mentioned above, Lutheran theology is an example of this.

I consider it more promising to distinguish between different types of theological understanding of what the church ministry or office is, types that to a certain degree exist across the denominational spectrum. Four types can be mentioned as main ecclesiological categories:

1. A *personal* or clerical understanding of the ministry, focusing on the persons who are able or empowered to hold the office of leadership, teaching and administering the sacraments of the church. The rite of ordination is seen as the transmission of this authority and is therefore imperative.
2. A *functional* understanding, according to which the main thing is the actual preaching of the Word of God and the giving out of the holy sacraments. This view focuses on the means of grace as such. Although the church's calling and ordination of its leaders may be highly appreciated, this is seen as a matter of good order and not as a theological and ecclesiological necessity.
3. A *biblicist* understanding, that seeks to establish which the main offices of the congregations of the New Testament were and to copy those in the present situation. A New Testament congregational order is supposed to be important, although the holders of this view may disagree among themselves what this order actually is.
4. A *charismatic* understanding, concentrating on leaders claiming to have a direct calling from God himself, through a vision or revelation of some kind or another. Such a leader, supposedly having received a divine anointing or divine authority, assembles a congregation around himself and his vision, preferably a large one to prove the validity of his calling.

It should be noted that there are similarities and even combination forms of opinions. One might argue that the charismatic view in some ways resembles both the personal and the biblicist view. In practical life, this is actually often the case.[3]

A Lutheran understanding of the ministry of the church

As already mentioned, there is no general agreement among Lutherans as to which of these views should be considered genuinely Lutheran, or indeed the one and only Lutheran understanding. One usually agrees that the charismatic view is highly problematic for Lutheran theology, but the other opinions might

---

[3] This categorization is a revised version of the one given in Kjell Olav Sannes, "Kvinners tjeneste i kirken i lys av embetssyn – skriftsyn og synet på forholdet mellom mann og kvinne", in Gunnar Eikli (ed.): *Kvinner i Bibelen, i kirken, i misjonen* (Oslo: Nye Luther Forlag, 1991), 144-148.

all find their spokesmen.

This fact is probably to a large degree due to the fact that the theology of ministry is not a core issue in the main Lutheran confessional writings as e.g. the Augsburg Confession (AC). Not even the Lutheran teaching about the priesthood of all believers is explicitly taught there, although it is clearly presupposed when AC 28 talks about the right of the congregation – indeed the divine command – not to obey the bishops in case of wrong teaching: "when they [i.e. the Roman Catholic bishops] teach or establish anything contrary to the gospel, churches have a command from God that prohibits obedience."[4] This is only possible on the basis of a teaching of the fundamental equality of all believers. But the teaching itself is not spelled out in any of the doctrinal articles of the AC.

This does not mean that the Lutheran confessional writings are without references to the ministry. Although the AC has not elaborated on it, this confession – being the main Lutheran doctrinal confession – has actually been a major focusing point in the discussion about the ministry in Lutheran theology. The article most referred to is AC 5, which is traditionally understood as stating that God has instituted the one ordained office of ministry, commonly identified with that of the pastor, including the bishop. This clerical interpretation has been challenged by a functional one: What is divinely instituted is not the clerical office but the function, the means of grace in use according to the institution of Christ. This became an important issue in the debate between theologians such as A.F.C. Vilmar and J.W.F. Höfling in the 19th century, a debate that has been continued in the 20th century by Scandinavian theologians such as Regin Prenter and Per Erik Persson.[5]

Much of the same goes for AC 14. In the 19th century Norwegian theologians discussed – on the background of the lay preachers following the lay Norwegian church reformer Hans Nielsen Hauge – what it means that nobody should preach *publice* (publicly) in the church unless he is *rite vocatus* (properly called). Does *publice* mean that the preaching is done on behalf of the church, or that it is done openly, for everyone to hear? In the first case, the lay

---

[4] AC 28, §23 (LT), Robert Kolb and Timothy J. Wengert (ed): *The Book of Concord* (Minneapolis: Fortress, 2000), 95. The German text is very similar to the Latin one, ibid.: 94. Cf. Bernhard Lohse, *Martin Luther's theology. Its Historical and Systematic Development* (Minneapolis: Fortress Press, 1999), 289-291.

[5] Cf. Holsten Fagerberg, *A new look at the Lutheran Confessions (1529-1537)* (St. Louis: Concordia, 1972; original 1952); Per Erik Persson, *Kyrkans ämbete som Kristus-representation. En kritisk analys av nyare ämbetsteologi, Studia Theologica Lundensia 20 (*Lund: Gleerup, 1961); articles by Walter Sundberg and Todd Nichol in Todd Nichol and Mark Kolden (eds.), *Called and Ordained. Lutheran Perspectives on the Office of the Ministry* (Minneapolis: Fortress Press, 1990).

preachers could not speak 'publicly' in the meaning of 'on behalf of the church' with the same authority as the ordained ministers. They could, however, be messengers of the good news of the Gospel as a kind of non-official supplement to the ordained pastors of the church, a kind of 'principle of emergency' ("nødsprinsipp"). With the second interpretation, the preaching of laymen – and indeed: laywomen! – would be restricted to the more private sphere of the family or perhaps the closest neighbors. This then would invoke the question of the authority of this regulation, whether it was a matter of doctrine or of church law and order.

The Augsburg Confession on the ministry

As the confession, together with and subordinated to the Scriptures, is an important part of the basis of Lutheran theology, the teaching of the Augsburg Confession on the subject must be dealt with. I will not go into every detail, just point out some important reasons for my interpretation of three relevant articles.[6]

My first thesis can be formulated in the following way:

Thesis 1

> AC 5 should not be interpreted as teaching an institution by God of a certain office of the church, e.g. the office of the pastor with the administration of the means of grace as the main "job description". Strictly speaking, AC 5 is just about the Word and the sacraments, instituted by God as the means of grace through which the Holy Spirit is given and acts.

The most relevant part of AC 5 on this issue shall be rendered here, both in the Latin version and the German version. I consider both versions as equally authentic and thus of equal importance.[7] The two versions are given first in the original form, then in English and Norwegian translation:

> Latin text (LT): Ut hanc fidem consequamur, institutum est ministerium docendi evangelii et porrigendi sacramenta. Nam per verbum et sacramenta tamquam per instrumenta donatur spiritus sanctus, qui fidem efficit …

---

[6] Cf. Kjell Olav Sannes, "Det kirkelige embede etter de lutherske bekjennelsesskrifter", *Ung Teologi* 1973, hf. 1, 13-26; Kjell Olav Sannes: "Det kirkelige embete og den offentlige embetsutøvelse etter de lutherske bekjennelsesskrifter", *Ung Teologi* 1975, hft. 1, 59-70.

[7] For this and other principles of interpretation and use of the AC, see Kjell Olav Sannes, "Kristen bekjennelse i en annen tid", in Jan-Olav Henriksern, Gunnar Heiene and Svein Olaf Thorbjørnsen (eds.), *Teologi for kirken. Festskrift til professor dr.theol. Torleiv Austad på 65-årsdagen* (Oslo: Verbum, 2002), 130-133.

[English:] So that we may obtain this faith, the ministry of teaching the gospel and administering the sacraments was instituted. For through the Word and the sacraments as through instruments the Holy Spirit is given, who effects faith …

[Norwegian:] For at vi skal komme til denne tro, er det innstiftet en tjeneste med å lære evangeliet og meddele sakramentene. For ved Ordet og sakramentene som midler blir Den Hellige Ånd gitt, han som virker troen …

German text (GT): Solchen Glauben zu erlangen, hat Gott das Predigamt eingesetzt, Evangelium und Sakrament geben, dadurch er als durch mittel den heiligen Geist gibt, welcher den Glauben … virket …

[English:] To obtain such faith God instituted the office of preaching, giving the gospel and the sacraments. Through these, as through means, he gives the Holy Spirit who produces faith …[8]

[Norwegian:] For å oppnå en slik tro har Gud innstiftet preketjenesten, gitt evangeliet og sakramentene, gjennom hvilke han – som ved middel – gir Den Hellige Ånd, han som virker troen …[9]

The personal or clerical interpretation of AC 5 focuses on the terms *ministerium docendi evangelii et porrigendi sacramenta* (LT) and *Predigamt* (TT). Those terms, in English often rendered with office or ministry (above), are supposed to be about a certain, specified position or "job" held by a specific person, namely the pastor or minister. The addition is then understood as a kind of "job description".

Against the latter view, and in favor of a functional interpretation of AC 5, several reasons can be mentioned:

1. It is often argued, or rather taken for granted, that the commonly used title of the Latin text of AC 5, *De Ministerio Ecclesiastico*, indicates a personal/clerical interpretation. This title is found in many recent editions of the *Book of Concord*, and in the critical text edition by Heinrich Bornkamm, *Die Bekenntnisschriften der evangelisch-lutherischen Kirche*. It is therefore also used in many translations: In English translations it is rendered with "The Ministry of the Church" or "Ministry in the Church", in Danish and Norwegian editions with "Det kirkelige embede" or similar. The titles of AC 1-19 and 21

---

[8] Here and later the original AC texts are quoted from the critical edition by Heinrich Bornkamm, *Die Bekenntnisschriften der evangelisch-lutherischen Kirche* (Göttingen: Vandenhoek & Ruprecht, 1930, 5. Aufl. 1963), 58. The English translations are from Kolb/Wengert, *The Book of Concord*, 40f, the Norwegian translation of the LT is from Jens Olav Mæland (ed.), *Konkordieboken. Den evangelisk-lutherske kirkes* bekjennelsesskrifter (Oslo: Lunde Forlag, 1985), 31.

[9] The translation is mine.

are generally seen as not original, but by many considered to be included in one of the very early editions.[10]

In a not yet published study I try to show that these now commonly used titles are not only non-original, but that they are in fact from a much later period. Actually, they can not be found in editions from the 16th century; the very first time they all seem to be present is in an edition of the Book of Concord from 1669. This means that the commonly used Latin title of AC 5, "De Ministerio Ecclesiastico", expresses a later interpretation of the article and therefore is no indication of what the reformers saw as its content.[11]

2. The term *ministerium* in the Latin text can mean both an office, e.g. the office of the pastor, and the ministry as a function, i.e. something which is done. The parallel German text reads that God has instituted *das Predigamt*, which is also a rather open term. The German text does, however, give a key to the interpretation of this first part of the text, as it adds an expression that serves as an explanation and interpretation: *hat Gott das Predigamt eingesetzt, Evangelium und Sakrament geben*. That God instituted *das Predigamt* means, therefore, that he gave the gospel and the sacraments.

3. The German *Predigamt* is defined in the Schwabach article 7, which states that to give us this – i.e. the saving – faith *hat Gott eingesetzt das predigambt oder muntlich wort, nämlich das Euangelion*. In the English translation by William R. Russell this reads: "God has instituted the preaching office or spoken Word (that is the Gospel)". I think Russell's translation is rather misleading. Obviously, *das predigambt* is here equivalent with the oral word, the gospel, or we could say: with the preaching of the gospel ("preketjenesten"). It is interesting that the Marburg article 8 states that the Holy Spirit is not given without previous *predigt oder mundlich Wort oder Euangelion Christi*; here *predigt* (sermon) takes the place of *predigtambt* in Schwabach 7, and is clearly identical with it.[12]

---

[10] Theodore G. Tappert (ed.): *The Book of Concord* (Philadelphia: Fortress, 1959), 31; Kolb/Wengert, *The Book of Concord,* 41; Leif Grane, *Confessio Augustana* (København: Gyldendal, 1959), 15; Peder Nørgaard-Højen, *Den danske folkekirkes bekendelsesskrifter. Tekst og oversættelse* (København: Anis, 2. korr. Udgave, 2004), 49; Mæland, *Konkordieboken*, 31.

[11] Kjell Olav Sannes, *Artikkeloverskriftene i Confessio Augustana* (unprinted manuscript, 2002); cf. Kjell Olav Sannes, *Å tolke Den augsburgske bekjennelse. Forståelse og prinsipper for tolkning av Confessio Augustana i Danmark og Norge 1530-1980* (Oslo: Det teologiske Menighetsfakultet, 1996), 451-453. The commonly used set of titles in the GT is even younger that those of the LT (ibid.).

[12] Those documents from 1529, used by the writing of the AC and thus significant parts of its background, are quoted after Theodor Kolde, *Die Augsburgische Konfession lateinisch und deutsch* (Gotha: Fiedrich Andreas Perthes, 1895, 2. verbesserte Aufl. 1911), 127, 131. See also *Die*

4. The line of argument is clear with, and only with, a functional interpretation. If the meaning were that God instituted the pastoral office, there would be a break in the line of reasoning: The article would then start by mentioning the office and then move away from it to an elaboration of the means of grace. The article, however, solely deals with the administering of the gospel and the sacraments, as is evident from the German text.

5. This interpretation is clear also from the condemnation of the Anabaptists in the last part of AC 5. In general the condemnation in the AC articles corresponds with the teaching of the article, thus the negation gives us an indication of the correct understanding of the doctrinal position. In AC 5, § 4, the Anabaptists are condemned not because they reject the office of the pastor, which they by the way actually did, but because they teach that humans obtain the Holy Spirit without the external word: "They condemn the Anabaptists and others who think that the Holy Spirit comes to human beings without the external Word [*sine verbo externo*] through their own preparations and works."[13] This fact strengthens the interpretation given above, i.e. that it is the means of grace as such, as the means of the Holy Spirit, that is the point in AC 5.

6. This can also be seen from the *Confutatio*, the Roman Catholic response to the AC, written and presented in the name of the emperor at the Augsburg diet August 3rd 1530. The *Confutatio* renders the content of AC 5 by stating that "Article Five, which says that the Holy Spirit is given by Word and sacrament, as through instruments, is approved." It then goes on to mention the gift of the Spirit in relation to the word and to baptism, and furthermore addresses the subject of faith. It does not at all mention the office of ministry. This indicates that the theologians behind the *Confutatio* did not interpret AC 5 as an article about the clerical office.[14]

Bekenntnisschriften, 59. Russell's translation is in Robert Kolb and James A. Nestingen (eds.), *Sources and Contexts of the Book of Concord* (Minneapolis: Fortress Press, 2001), 85.

[13] Kolb/Wengert, *The Book of Concord*, 41. In Norwegian the condemnation reads as follows: "De fordømmer gjendøperne og andre, som mener at Den Hellige Ånd kommer til menneskene uten det ytre ordet, ved deres egne forberedelser og gjerninger." (Mæland, *Konkordieboken*, 31) In this case I have quoted only the LT, as the Latin and the German versions are pretty much alike concerning what view they are against.

[14] Kolb/Nestingen, *Sources and Contexts,* 109. The original text is given in Herbert Immenkötter, *Die Confutatio der Confessio Augustana vom 3. August 1530, Corpus Catholicorum Bd. 33* (Münster Westfalen: Aschendorff, 2. verb. Aufl. 1979), 87. The German text, which according to Immenkötter is the original, renders it thus: "Als in dem funften artickl bekennet wirt, das der Heilig Gaist gegeben werde durch die wort und sacrament als durch instrument, wirdet billich zugelassen" (ibid., 70. 86).

Thesis 2

AC 14 regulates that the administering of the means of grace that is done openly in the church, should be done by persons properly called by the relevant authority. It is not a doctrine about ordination as such.

Latin text: De ordine ecclesiastico docent, quod nemo debeat in ecclesia publice docere aut sacramenta administrare nisi rite vocatus.

[English:] Concerning church order they teach that no one should teach publicly in the church or administer the sacraments unless properly called.

[Norwegian:] Om kirkeordningen lærer de at i kirken bør ingen lære offentlig eller forvalte sakramentene uten at han er rettelig kalt.

German text: Vom Kirchenregiment wird gelehrt, dass niemand in der Kirchen offentlich lehren oder predigen oder Sakrament reichen soll ohn ordentlichen Beruf.

[English:] Concerning church government it is taught that no one should publicly teach, preach, or administer the sacraments without a proper [public] call.[15]

[Norwegian:] Om kirkestyringen blir det lært at ingen skal i kirken offentlig lære eller preke eller meddele sakramentet uten ordentlig kall.[16]

1. AC 14 states that nobody but the called should (*debeat/soll*) preach, teach and give the sacraments publicly. This indicates that for the Reformers this is not a doctrine, not a dogma, but a kind of regulation, part of the church order. The LT states that this article is about *ordine ecclesiastico*, which may here actually mean church order. It is not suggesting a doctrine of calling as a condition of this activity, just stating who should – and who should not – do this.

2. The subject of the article is that preaching/teaching and administering of the sacraments that is done *in ecclesia publice* (LT)/ *in der Kirchen offentlich* (GT). The two parts of the expression, 'in the church' and 'publicly', belong together. The words *publice* and *offentlich* as used in the AC do actually refer to something that is open, for everyone to see, as different from what is private, secret.[17] AC 14 is about how that ministry with the means of grace, i.e. that preaching and giving of sacraments, ought to be done when it is performed

---

[15] *Die Bekenntnisschriften* 69; Kolb/Wengert, *The Book of Concord*, 46f; Mæland, *Konkordieboken,* 34.

[16] The translation is mine. The structure of the sentence imitates that of the German.

[17] Sannes, "Det kirkelige embete og den offentlige embetsutøvelse etter de lutherske bekjennelsesskrifter", 63-66.

openly in the church.

3. This service should not be performed by someone who is not *rite vocatus* (LT)/ without *ordentlichen Beruf* (GT). The Latin phrase could seem to suggest a ritual, but the German text shows us that this is actually not the case. The point is that it should be done properly, in an orderly manner. This interpretation is confirmed by AC 15, where the German equivalent to the Latin *De ritibus ecclesiasticis* actually is *Von Kirchenordnungen*: In AC *ritus* means the same as *Ordning*.[18] This indicates that the term is not referring to a liturgical act, such as an ordination ceremony.

4. The view that *rite vocatus* should refer to the rite of ordination, is an impossible interpretation also for historical reasons. Actually, the church in Kursachsen did not have a regular order of ordination until 1535, 5 years after the AC was written. Luther ordained Georg Rörer to being a deacon already in 1525, but that was just a one-time event. Also in the following years ordinations occurred only sporadically, although more often after 1530. Ordination as a regular church order was not institutionalized in Wittenberg before 1535.[19]

5. The situation in Germany at the outset of the Reformation was that different persons and institutions had the authority to call a preacher or a pastor. It could be a prince, a city council etc. that held the prerogative to call someone to such an office. In this context, to be properly called would most likely mean to be called in accordance with the commonly accepted order.[20]

Thesis 3

> According to AC 7 it is essential to the existence and the unity of the church that the means of grace are administered according to the Word of God. The ordained ministry as such is not mentioned.

1. When AC 7 describes and almost gives a definition of the church, it not just points out that the church is One (according to the Nicene Creed) but it also says what is necessary for true unity. What constitutes the being of the church is that "the gospel is purely preached [*rein gepredigt*] and the holy sacraments are administered according to the gospel [*lauts des Evangelii gereicht*

---

[18] *Die Bekenntnisschriften*, 69.

[19] Ralph F. Smith, *Luther, Ministry, and Ordination Rites in the Early Reformation Church, Renaissance and Baroque Studies and Texts Vol. 15* (New York, Washington et.al.: Peter Lang), 87, 98-108; Lohse, *Martin Luther's theology*, 295.

[20] In Kolb/Wengert's edition of the AC, note 81, that may be written by the translator of the AC, Eric Gritsch, states that "*Rite vocatus* means called in a regular manner by a proper public authority." (Kolb/Wengert, *The Book of Concord*, 47, cf. viii)

werden].” It is important to note that this is the same that constitutes the unity of the church:

> ...this is enough for the true unity of the Christian church that there the gospel is preached harmoniously according to a pure understanding [*einträchtiglich nach reinem Verstand*] and the sacraments are administered in conformity with the divine Word [*dem gottlichen Wort gemäss gereicht werden*].[21]

The unity is not just constituted by the “horizontal” agreement between Christians, AC also demands that the preaching has to be in conformity with the divine Word (“vertical” agreement). In the GT it is also clearer than in LT that it is not sufficient with theological agreement, but that there has to be a common preaching according to the Bible. In short, it is the use of the means of grace that is necessary for the church, both for its existence and its true unity.

2. This corresponds closely with the interpretation of AC 5 that is given above. When AC 5 says that the ministry of the means of grace is instituted so that we may obtain the justifying faith, it is equivalent with the teaching of AC 7 stating that these means of grace are constituting the church and its unity. A clerical interpretation of AC 5 would have caused problems when confronted with the fact that AC 7 does not mention the office of ministry. The ministry in the clerical sense of the word is not implied in what AC 7 sees as necessary for true unity in the church. This office is clearly not a constitutive element of the church. It seems by implication that it is understood as one of the “ceremonies, instituted by human beings” that the article states as “not necessary for true unity of the Christian church”.

The interpretation of the AC given above gives reason to argue some important points:

- There is no foundation in the AC for the claim that God has instituted a specific office of ministry or a pattern of offices in the clerical sense.
- The main point is the divine institution of the means of grace, the Word and the sacraments, as the way to obtain faith and thus to salvation and to incorporation into the church.
- The means of grace may be administered in different ways, through especially called persons but also through others.
- There should be a good order in the church, to serve the life and the ministry of the means of grace in the church. This order is not, however, as such constitutive for the church.

[21] Here and later I use the translation of the German text of AC 7 that is found in Kolb/Wengert, *The Book of Concord,* 42. LT is from *Die Bekenntnisschriften,* 61.

An outline of a Lutheran theology of the ministry of the church

When we also take into consideration the Lutheran doctrine of the priesthood of all believers, I propose the following way of thinking as the most fruitful for the Lutheran theology and church. I also indicate a few important lines of thinking according to the New Testament.

1. God has given his commission to the whole church and all its members. This can be seen from Matt. 28:16-20, Christ giving his disciples his Great Commission of making disciples. The church and all its members – of different ethnicity, gender, age and social status – are thus taking part in the mission of the Triune God himself and have a common supreme responsibility for its accomplishment.[22]
2. The mission of the church is an integral part of the life of the church, basically the same whether it is done inside or outside one's own congregation, i.e. regardless of whether it is foreign mission or inner mission. Thus the church is of necessity a 'missional church'.[23]
3. The understanding of the ministry of the church should be centered on the means of grace. The Great Commission corresponds closely with the institution of the actual means of grace. In Matt. 28:19-20 baptism and teaching are especially mentioned when the becoming disciples of Jesus is the issue.
4. The Great Commission should be carried out in different ways, both by certain persons given special, defined responsibilities and duties in the congregation(s) and also by all members of the congregation. This is already the case in the NT congregations; se e.g. Acts 8. A theological understanding that limits the right of carrying out God's commission to just one group of believers, is not in accordance with the Word of God.
5. The order and the offices of the church are not as such a matter of doctrine but are related to what best serves the accomplishment of the Great Commission – communication skills, good insight in the message of God and the Christian doctrine, personal qualifications, good order etc. – in the given context. It may therefore differ

---

[22] Kjell Olav Sannes, "Kirken i bevegelse med et oppdrag", in Tormod Engelsviken og Kjell Olav Sannes (eds.), *Hva vil det si å være kirke? Kirkens vesen og oppdrag. Bind 3 i Ekklesiologi-prosjektet ved Det teologiske Menighetsfakultet* (Trondheim: Tapir Akademisk Forlag, 2004), 31-49.

[23] Cf. Knud Jørgensen, "Trenger kirken omvendelse? På vei mot en misjonal ekklesiologi", in Engelsviken/Sannes, *Hva vil det si å være kirke?* 51-68; Tormod Engelsviken, "Den misjonale kirke og utfordringen fra kirken i sør", in Engelsviken/Sannes, *Hva vil det si å være kirke?* 69-92.

somewhat from time to time and from place to place, in order to serve the life and ministry of the church.

6. The church must be open to the possibility of different patterns of office or ministry; cf. the different patterns in the NT congregations. It can not dogmatize any office or pattern of offices as essential to the church, nor make it/them part of a theological self-understanding or of an ecumenical agreement.[24]
7. A doctrine of the ministry of the church can not just barely accept the service of "lay" people but should hold it in high esteem as an important and integral part of the ministry of the church. The notion of "laity" is a problematic one because it may be understood to indicate the existence of different classes among the believers, and should in my opinion rather be avoided altogether.[25]
8. Obeying the Great Commission is not just something that the members of the congregation may do on their spare time, but a major aspect of their whole life as believers. This emphasizes the Lutheran teaching of "calling".
9. The ordination of persons for special offices in the church should be understood as a way of orderly conferring the calling of God and the church for a special ministry and responsibility in the church, according to the order of the particular church. It is not, however, a necessary condition for the validity of certain sacraments or for the preaching of the Word.
10. The pastor and other holders of church offices are neither masters of the congregation nor its functionaries carrying out its orders, but ministers serving in it and together with it according to the will and commission of God. The notion of 'leadership' has to be purged for all ideas of leaders being something similar to directors of large business companies. A Christian leader is by definition a servant.

This way of thinking has obvious advantages as a guide line for the life and the ministry in the congregation, both in a local and a world wide context. Let me mention some:

- It might entail a spirit of *cooperation* in the congregation. When God's commission and the basic responsibility for it is entrusted to the whole congregation, both the staff, the elected leaders and all the members have it in common and should work together to fulfill it. If the church work is seen basically as "the pastor's business", then any work by the rest of the church staff and by other members of the congregation will be seen as a kind of practical assistance

[24] Cf. Kjell Olav Sannes, "Karakteristikk og vurdering av 'Porvoo-erklæringen' som økumenisk dokument", *Tidsskrift for Teologi og Kirke* 1997, 83-96.

[25] R. Paul Stevens, *The Abolition of the Laity. Vocation, Work and Ministry in Biblical Perspective* (Carlisle: Paternoster Press, 1999).

and help to the pastor in what is really his/her duty. If the work is seen in the context of competition among different staff members or offices, it obstructs the common mission. The ministry is not just ministry *in* the church but also *by* the church.

- This understanding of the church's ministry is more *on the offensive* and less static. We should not primarily ask who has the "right" to do something (as e.g. whether the un-ordained preacher has the right to preach or the catechist or deacon may administer baptism), but rather how we together can obey the common, overwhelmingly Great Commission of God. The pastor has special opportunities that others do not have in the same way, but so do actually all the members of the congregation in their encounter with people. If the work of the church was identical with that of the pastors, it would not go far and could certainly not reach out "to the ends of the earth".
- In this way, the ministry of the church can be more *flexible* and less bound by traditional patterns. It opens for discussion of new forms, also of the offices in the church, which are responding to new challenges in any given context. This may be important in the traditional churches living in an ever changing context, but obviously even more so in younger churches. The church should not necessarily introduce forms of leadership and ministry that are developed in Western societies through hundreds of years, but consider what forms are functioning well in the cultural context where the given church actually lives and serves.

I have argued for an understanding of the ministry of the church that includes both ordered (ordained) ministries and the ministry of non-ordained members, on the basis of Christ's Great Commission to his church. This is important in order to get a comprehensive, Lutheran understanding of the ministry and the mission of the Church, both in a local and an international context. In a changing world, confronted with ever new challenges, it is an important legacy of Lutheran theology for the future ministry of the church to affirm a conviction of the Lord's commission to make disciples through the means of grace, given to the whole people of God, combined with an appreciation that this mission should be carried out in an offensive, flexible way in the different contexts where the church lives and serves.

Preparing Leaders for an "Emerging" Church

Eddie Gibbs

Prof Dr Eddie Gibbs, professor, School of Intercultural Studies, Fuller Theological Seminary, Pasadena, California

The rapidly changing ecclesiastical landscape throughout the Western world is presenting some radical challenges to the traditional models of educating and training leaders. In North America the megachurch movement has not yet run out of steam, although it is struggling with the problem of aging congregations due to the fact that its strongest appeal was to the baby boomer generation (born between 1946 and 1964). Among the younger generations there is a desire for authenticity, intimacy and involvement, which has caused them to question a consumer-driven version of church. As Western societies witness the crumbling of Christendom and the questioning of many of the assumption that undergirded modernity, so the Church needs to re-imagine itself as a missional movement working from the margins of society divested of its position.[1]

Two movements, both arising from the pioneering work of Lesslie Newbigin, are seeking to address the issues that Western churches need to face with the realization that simply inviting the de-churched and never-churched to come to us on our terms is no longer adequate as an evangelizing strategy. These two movements are described as "missional church" and "emerging church." As a broad generalization, the first of these represents a theology in search of practical expressions, and the second represents pioneering initiatives in search of a theology! In this contribution I am using "emerging church" in the broadest sense of Western churches seeking a new identity as it emerges from the constraints and compromises that have shaped the church from the fourth until the mid twentieth centuries.

What Is an Emerging Church?

Ryan Bolger and I, in our book *Emerging Churches* defined an Emerging Church as one that consists "of followers of Jesus who are seeking together to

---

[1] See Craig Carter, *Rethinking Christ and Culture: A Post-Christendom Perspective* (Grand Rapids: Brazos Press, 2007).

be faithful in their place and time."[2] We then expanded this to encompass nine practices that characterized the churches we included in our survey: (1) identify with the life of Jesus, (2) transform the secular realm, and (3) live highly communal lives. Because of these three activities, they (4) welcome the stranger, (5) serve with generosity, (6) practice as producers, (7) create as created beings, (8) lead as a body, and (9) take part in spiritual activities. We devoted a chapter to each of these nine practices.[3]

In this session I want to expand this concept of "emerging church." I do so in order to avoid dismissing the emerging church as simply a fad or a fringe, rather then perceiving it as a frontier in western mission. I believe that every church that is engaged in mission is an "emerging church." Among all of our traditional denominations (which we used to call "mainline"), as well as many independent churches across the theological spectrum, we have witnessed chronic membership and attendance decline during more than four decades. Congregations are not only shrinking, they are aging, resulting in frustration among many pastors in young adult ministries because the churches in which they serve resemble senior care institutions. If a church is not emerging, it is submerging or trying to keep its head above water!

When shrinking congregations number less than 100 active members the result is fewer entry-level, salaried positions for pastors who have to pay off their student loans accumulated during their undergraduate and graduate programs. This is less of a problem for students who have received financial support through state subsidies, denominational or local church contributions, or who have attended universities and seminaries that offer generous student grants. Here in the United States, where educational costs are high, increasing numbers of graduating students find that in training for ministry they have mortgaged their ministry and end up in secular employment at least for a time, while they pay off their loans!

Confusion Surrounding the Term "Emerging Church"

There is a widespread misconception, especially in North America that "emerging church" refers to trendy churches seeking to be relevant to the youth culture. This arose because of the early sponsorship of conferences by youth ministry organizations. Aging Boomer megachurches caught on to the concept as a way of holding on to their young adults by providing alternative worship services for a generation that did not identify with the prevailing "blended worship" and soft-rock "contemporary music." But they failed to appreciate that many of the younger generation were not merely looking for a different

[2] Eddie Gibbs and Ryan K. Bolger, *Emerging Churches: Creating Christian Community in Postmodern Cultures* (Grand Rapids, and SPCK, London, UK: Baker Academic, 2005, 44).

[3] Op. cit. 45.

style of worship, but of a different way of envisioning church.

As emerging churches gained wider attention they were regarded with increasing concern among some evangelical scholars who considered their most prominent spokespersons to be liberalizing evangelicalism. This reaction was triggered by the post-evangelical debate questioning foundationalism as a modernist lens through which the ancient texts were being interpreted.[4]

But "emerging church" is not so easily categorized as it is not a cohesive movement. It is also more than a conversation, because there are many local expressions that are not part of a broader network. Consequently, I think it is best described as a spontaneous phenomenon emerging from the ground level. In the early days there was no foundational body of literature and the conferences and conversations being held were did not always represent the range of expressions to be found in many cultural contexts.

Furthermore, emerging churches, as their name implies, are still in the process of evolving. Some emerging church leaders are clear and forceful in expressing what they are not rather than what they are. Also, because this is a church birthing movement there are some stillbirths, a high infant mortality rate, and birth defects.

Three Broad Streams of Emerging Churches

As emerging churches have evolved, so three broad streams have become apparent. First, are the *independent faith-communities* that represent individual initiatives that are usually, but not in every case, engaged in a broader conversation. Second, are the *entrepreneurial networks* led by apostolic leadership types. One such leader is Neil Cole, a church starter and pastor who is the founder and director of *Church Multiplication Associates*, an organization that has helped start over seven-hundred churches in thirty-two states and twenty-three nations in the course of six years![5] Third, are *Fresh Expressions* of church within traditional denominations? At the present time this stream is most confined to the United Kingdom, where traditional denominations, such as the Church of England and the Methodist Church, have come to the realization that they need to identify a new kind of leader, train them in a different way, for a different kind of church.[6]

---

[4] See Dave Tomlinson, *The Post-Evangelical* (London: Triangle, 1995), and the writings of Brian McLaren, and the response of D.A. Carson, *Becoming Conversant with the Emerging Church* (Grand Rapids: Zondervan, 2005).

[5] Neil Cole, *Organic Church: Growing Faith Where Life Happens* (San Francisco: Jossey-Bass, 2005).

[6] See http://www.cofe.anglican.org/info/yearreview/dec05/freshexpressions and the Church of England report, *Mission-Shaped Church: Church Planting and Fresh Expressions of Church in a Changing Context* (London: Church House Publishing, 2004).

Here in the United States, though less so in Canada which is closer to the European and Australian post-Christendom experience, denominational and megachurch leaders can still play for time because the money hasn't run out yet! But are they simply postponing the inevitable and leaving the next generation of leaders to deal with the impending crisis?

Emerging Into What?

Emerging churches are making it up as they go along, endeavoring to re-envision the church in a missional, post-Christendom context. They are seeking to reconnect ecclesiology with missiology, which separation characterized so many of the Western churches under the prevailing influence of Christendom.[7]

Churches in the Western world must recognize that they are a pilgrim church on a faith journey. As such they will always be emerging from a specific cultural context and into new context. They understand "church" not as a place, but as a people; not as a weekly gathering but as a community that provides their core identity; not as a refuge from the world but as a training ground for mission in the world. You don't GO to church; you ARE the church. In short, it is a church seeking to reconnect with the mission of Jesus. They identify with the Johannine emphasis that the mission of Jesus' disciples is nothing other than a continuation of his own ministry. *"As you sent me into the world, I have sent them into the world"* (John 17:18). *"As the Father has sent me, I am sending you"* (John 20:21). When Jesus breathed on his disciples in the upper room it represented an act of re-creation as well as commissioning.

Jesus' Model of Mission

In the mission of Jesus we see a sequence that must not be overlooked in our contemporary engagement in mission. That sequence is: first the announcement and demonstration of the good news of the kingdom; second, comes the mission of the followers of Jesus commissioned by him, and who have an irrepressible desire to pass on that message and invite people to join their communities; third, their mission results in the formation of the churches with a high reproduction potential. We see in this progression that the church must recognize that it is the product of mission before it can become an agent of mission.

We might summarize Jesus' ministry under the following points:

- *Authenticity that exposes hypocrisy.* Those closest to Jesus describe him as "full of grace and truth" (John 1:14). He was accessible ("pitched his tent among us") and his life open to scrutiny. Therein lies the difference between a celebrity and a saint.

---

[7] See Loren B. Mead, *The Once And Future Church* (Washington D.C.: The Alban Institute, 1991).

- *Servanthood replacing domination.* Jesus was prepared to do anything, yet resisted pressures to do everything. Therein lies the difference between wearing a towel and becoming a doormat. Jesus' prior commitment was to his heavenly Father.
- *Forgiveness absorbing hostility.* Reconciliation was at the heart of his message; reconciliation with God through the Cross and with one another as evidenced in the life of the church (2 Corinthians 5:18-21).
- *Association challenging separation.* Jesus' attitude towards those who could not keep the Pharisaic regulations surrounding the law was in sharp contrast to other rabbis. He had the reputation of hanging out with the lawbreakers and disreputable members of society. The mission of Jesus is not one of judgmental separation but of grace-filled identification with a view to transformation.
- *Grace superseding law.* Jesus' message was one of good news that liberates, setting people free that they might know reconciliation with God and the privileges of their adoption as sons and daughters in his family.

It is this mission what shapes the character of the church. As Archbishop Rowan Williams reminded the General Assembly of the Church of England, *"It is not the Church of God that has a mission, but the God of mission who has a Church."*

I believe that the emerging church profile has profound implications for seminary education. How can seminaries connect with these leaders? What challenges do they present both in terms of curriculum content and delivery systems?

Context of Emerging Church

The emerging church phenomenon has not evolved in a cultural vacuum. It comes on the heals of the crumbling of Christendom in the West, which is now increasingly recognized as a failed project.[8] Under Christendom the church accommodated its radical message to the secular state, which used it to bolster an ill-defined civil religion and to legitimize nationalistic ambitions. The Church has been tried and found wanting. However, it cannot return to the pre-Constantinian era. It has to re-imagine itself in a radically different post-Constantinian context.

Many, though by no means all, emerging church leaders are seriously questioning the assumptions of modernity and its impact on the church. They are protesting against the separation of spheres, public and private, with the relegation of religious conviction to the private sphere. Such a separation of spheres has contributed to a crisis of values in the public sphere of politics,

[8] See Craig Carter, op. cit.

business and military, etc. In response they are insisting on a holistic spirituality that embraces every area of life. They are rejecting a reductionist gospel with its privatized, otherworldly emphasis, and that is focused on the needs and aspirations of the individual.

Emerging church leaders are also suspicious of institutionalized Christianity, regarding hierarchical and controlling denominational structures as the ecclesial counterparts of big government and big business. They are also highly critical of consumer driven, *seeker-sensitive* churches, which includes those suburban megachurches that grow at the expense of smaller churches and who adopt a come-to-us philosophy of ministry. They are more concerned for churches to become *seeker-sending* agencies, following the pattern of Jesus' ministry, who came to seek and save the lost, than in being seeker-attracting church, inviting people to come on our terms.

Consumer/Missional Congregations

We need to pause to consider, "In what kind of churches are we training seminarians to serve?" The consumer model of church is ill-suited for the present context. Such churches may well grow in newer suburban contexts, which are upwardly mobile, homogeneous and in areas of the country being settled by people who had previous strong church connections or who are looking for a more relevant expression of church.

A *consumer* church consists typically of 1-2 percent paid staff assisted by 18 percent volunteers who assist in the running of programs and leading various areas of ministry. They endeavor to satisfy the demands of the 80 percent of the congregation who are consumers needing to be satisfied in order to ensure their continuing support.

By contrast a *missional* church is one in which the paid and volunteer staff equip the members to engage in their God-given mission in the world where they are already strategically placed. An emerging church pastor does not *dismiss* a congregation at the end of a worship service–the implication being out of sight, out of mind–the emerging church pastor *disperses* the congregation to continue throughout the week as the church in dispersion.

Leadership Profile[9]

The emerging church's commitment to incarnational ministry means that the faith community *engages popular culture* that has such a pervasive influence. However, as the majority of leaders have no formal cross-cultural training they are prone to succumb to naïve contextualization, baptizing the culture, rather than recognize the complex relationship between gospel and culture. If this

[9] For a study of the leadership style of younger leaders see, Eddie Gibbs, *LeadershipNext* (Downers Grove: InterVarsity Press, 2005).

complex issue is not addressed, emerging churches will be subverted by an uncritical acceptance of postmodern culture, just as the church in previous generations was subverted by modernity.

Second, as the leaders are either in their 30s or have older leaders that have made the transition into the Internet age, they are *cyber-space connected.* An older generation that has not made this transition is largely ignorant of the extent of the website and blog networks with which younger church leaders are regularly connected.[10]

Third, they are *highly relational* in their leadership style. They represent a contrast to many older leaders who tend to be hierarchical and controlling. Younger leaders are looking for an alternative model that is more functional in the present context characterized by unanticipated, chaotic change; a style that encourages developing networks, creativity and empowerment. Some have experimented unsuccessfully with leaderless groups. Leadership often rotates according to the specific challenges and opportunities.

Fourth, they are *risk-takers*, believing it is better to try and fail than not to try at all. They recognize that we often learn more from our failures than our successes. So they provide a learning environment in which you can fail with dignity and then learn the lessons from that painful experience.

Fifth, they usually operate with *meager financial resources,* as they do not have the backing of denominational home mission departments or wealthy congregants. Their financial situation also means that many are priced out of the seminary track for ministerial preparation.

Sixth, many of the leaders have *short attention spans* and quickly become disillusioned or bored. This results in instability in a number of promising emerging churches. They were highly creative and attracted younger people who had become disconnected from the church, or who had never associated with the church. But when they moved on they left behind no viable church.

Seventh, the majority of the younger leaders we interviewed were *well read.* The most significant authors, apart from Brian McLaren, were N.T. Wright, especially his studies on Jesus–which are no light reading![11] – and Dallas Willard in the area of spiritually integrated with the radical teaching of Jesus.[12]

Lastly, they had *various levels of theological education.* Some had been through seminary and had advanced degrees in theology, while others were well taught. I would describe many of them as lateral thinkers with a broad range of interests and able to relate their reading across the disciplines of theology and the social sciences.

---

[10] For example see http://www.emergingchurch.info/; http://tallskinnykiwi.typepad.com/; theooze.com

[11] See N.T. Wright, *Jesus and the Victory of God,* vol. 2 of *Christian Origins and the Question of God* (Minneapolis: Fortress Press, 1996).

[12] Dallas Willard, *The Divine Conspiracy* (SanFrancisco: Harper, 1998).

Establishing the Relevance of Theological Education

Theological schools that offer traditional theology programs are widely perceived among emerging church leaders as institutions that prepare people for yesterday; that is for churches shaped by Christendom and modernity. The majority has not received formal education, nor would they seriously consider attending until first they are convinced of its relevance. They perceive the need to be trained IN ministry rather than FOR ministry, and for ministry BY the church in the world rather than confined TO the church's existing members. They look for a curriculum that is responsive to the issues they are facing, namely, one that demonstrates a missional approach to theology and ecclesiology.[13] But they are not anti-intellectual, as we have mentioned many are well-read and are eager for conversation and mentoring. Also, they recognize that the educational approach must be based on adult learning models and that adopts a life-long learning approach.

Those leaders who have attended seminary value their experience and the knowledge gained. It has provided a foundation on which they can build and which they can critically relate to a changing cultural context for ministry and mission.

The Equipping Ministry Matrix

Their model of ministry is not the omni-competent, professional clergy person. They take as a useful framework the ministry matrix found in Ephesians 4:1-16. As we review the five roles mentioned there we begin to ask where the traditional, Christendom-focused school of theology places its emphasis?[14] And then to ask whether they need to broaden the scope of their training? The one-size-fits-all Master of Divinity curriculum, or its equivalent in European contexts, may need to be re-examined, some would say, as a matter of urgency.

I am grateful to one of our on-line Master's students, J.R. Woodward of *Kairos* who leads an emerging church movement based in Hollywood for providing some fresh terms to throw light on old language. He calls the Apostle, "the Dream Awakener," the Prophet, "the Heart Revealer," the Evangelist, "the Story Teller," the Pastor "the Soul Revealer," and the Teacher

---

[13] A few colleges and seminaries in both the UK and the USA are taking steps to radically reshape their program so that it is more missional in emphasis and integrates theory and praxis.

[14] To this five-fold pattern of ministry Alan Roxburgh argues the need for the poet to enable people to move forward. He writes, "Poets listen for the stories, symbols, signs, and language beneath people's words. He believes that many within the church need help in relating their personal stories to the grand narrative of Scripture. Alan J, Roxburgh, *The Sky Is Falling!* (Eagle, Idaho: ACI Publishing, 2005), 163-168.

"the Light Giver."[15]

The calling to which seminaries traditionally respond is that of *providing leaders to serve established churches*, namely pastors-teachers as a hyphenated gift. This role must not be neglected in the future because the pastoral and educational needs of the churches are greater than ever.

- *Teacher* as *Light Giver* – This role is crucial bearing in mind that we have a biblically illiterate generation. This is the assessment of many seminaries as they receive fresh intakes of students who have come for graduate level education despite their having received such little biblical formation in their churches. Their ignorance represents the downside of topical preaching and a therapeutic gospel. It also reflects the religious pluralism and relativism of the society in which they have been nurtured and educated. The broader culture is no longer shaped and undergirded by biblically based moral values.
- *Pastor: Soul Healer* – The increasing stress of living in a culture in rapid transition places a heavy counseling burden on the pastor. Many people experience job insecurity resulting from new technologies, outsourcing and downsizing. Furthermore, they received less emotional and material support and inter-generational wisdom from their extended family due to family fragmentation resulting from mobility and dispersal. We have also witnessed during past decades a dramatic increase in separation, divorce, co-habitation, alternative life-styles, and blended families.

  We also have to recognize that the churches overall are losing ground. In Europe we are acutely aware of this, but the United States is no longer immune from this trend. Church leaders in the US have been lulled into a sense of false security by an over-reliance on the findings of telephone polls, which have given an average weekly church, synagogue, temple attendance at between 39-43 percent for the past four decades. However, when you compare people's claims with actual practice you get a very different picture. According to Dave Olson, director of church planting for the Evangelical Covenant Church, the true figure is around 18-20 percent.[16] This overall statistic hides the considerable regional variance between the South and the Pacific North West,

---

[15] www.kairos.la

[16] Dave Olson's website: www.theamericanchurch.org. See also C. Kirk Hadaway, Penny Long Marler and Mark Chaves, "What The Polls Don't Show: A Closer Look at U.S. Church Attendance," *American Psychological Review* 58 (December 1993, 742). The same 100 percent inflation was also evidenced by research conducted in Australia. See, Peter Kaldor, *Who Goes Where? Who Doesn't Care?* (Homebursh West, NSW: Lancer Books, 1987), 20.

where church attendance may be as low as Canada and Northern Europe. The lower figure may also represent a churchgoing trend that churchgoers are attending less frequently.

The fact that the majority of established congregations are aging and declining means that here in North America we are in urgent need of fresh expressions of church across the traditions. This being so, local congregations, church leaders and theological and ministry training schools need to be address the other three roles in the ministry matrix, namely apostle, prophet and evangelist. As one denominational home-missions leader in Australia expressed it, "We have a chronic shortage of APEs!" The three most neglected roles in traditional settings are the dominant leadership models in emerging churches that are birthing new faith communities.[17]

- *Apostle: Ground Breaker* – For emerging church leaders the term "apostle" does not refer to a megachurch pastor with a super-charged ego. To the contrary, it refers to those intrepid leaders who ventures where the church does not yet exist. They make a clear distinction between the *apostles of Christ* and the *apostles of the church.* Luke uses the term in the former sense, whereas the apostle Paul never used '*apostolos*' to refer to Jesus' twelve disciples as a group. He mentions Barnabas, Silas, Timothy, James the Lord's brother, Apollos, Junia[s], Andronicus, Epaphroditus as well as himself as apostles.

  Martin Garner has written, "These missionary apostles identified in the New Testament always worked with a team and were often called by God to a specific group or place. They work with a team and they had no guaranteed source of support. They were prepared to endure opposition, suffering and face hardship joyfully. What scares most of us is fulfillment for the apostle."[18]
- *Prophet: Truth Teller* – The role of the prophet is to apply God's word to specific situations, whether at the local, regional or global level. Sometimes it is in the form of *forth-telling*–speaking out boldly on issues where there is a conspiracy of silence or where we are too involved to be able to step back and see the broader issues. At other times it is *fore-telling* – the seer is able to see further and more clearly than the rest of us.
- *Evangelist: Story Teller* – The evangelist is the bearer of God's

[17] Please note that in referring to the Apostle and Prophet I have used a different descriptor from that of J.R. Woodward, who refers to the apostle as "dream awakener," and the prophet as "heart revealer." ("The Equippers, " Unpublished paper, 2007).

[18] Martin Garner, *A Call for Apostles Today* (Cambridge, UK: Grove Books, 2007).

> good news. We are called upon to fulfill the role of witness, but the evangelist has a special burden for the spread of the gospel and an ability to proclaim and explain it in simple terms in appropriate ways. In our day, when our culture has become disconnected from the Biblical narrative, we need to tell the Jesus story and the unfolding salvation drama of the entire Scriptures. More specifically we need to share the gospel from the Gospels, because we can no longer assume that people know the Jesus story.

As we review these five leadership roles we must not consider them in isolation from the ministry of the entire congregation. Indeed, the context of the ministry matrix is the unity and resourcing of the whole church.[19] Emerging Churches need pastor-teachers to ensure both maturity and continuity in their churches, providing a base from which they can move on to face fresh challenges. On the other hand, established churches need apostles, prophets and evangelists to ensure they break out of their cultural cocoons to impact wider society and to give birth to new faith communities. In other words, established churches and emerging churches need each. The churches of the New Testament were reproducible, with households of faith begetting other household. They reproduced at the rate of rabbits, whereas so many of our churches are either sterile or reproduce at the rate of giant pandas.

Proposals for Consideration

Here is my radical proposal for theological schools to establish relevance among emerging church leaders: They need to give serious consideration to making available free of charge all that they teach on-line. I say this because this is the age of the democratization of information through powerful search engines. We have access to the latest research, experience and ideas through Google and Wikipedia. The information is instantly available and is free of charge. I believe that MIT to mention one university has taken this bold step. This raises the question as to what students then pay for? Answer: they pay for mentoring and credentials. Younger leaders long for opportunities to engage in interactive learning experiences. I believe that placing our course content on line would be the most effective form of advertising. We used to say that it was publishing that attracts students to faculty. This is still true to an extent, but many more curious individuals start their inquiries and have their interests sparked through on-line contact (e.g. course resources and faculty blogs).

In making the above proposal I am not suggesting that on-line education is the complete answers. Rather that it provides an adult learning model in which

---

[19] See, Mike Breen and Walt Kallestad, *The Passionate Church* (Colorado Springs: Cook Communications, 2005, Chapter 16), and Alan Hirsch, *The Forgotten Ways: Reactivating the missional church* (Grand Rapids: Brazos Press, 2006).

students take responsibility for accessing information through required reading and on-line interaction. Contact time with professors consists of week long, week-end, or evening intensives in which the students identify issues, contextualize their learning in relation to their ministry experience, develop discernment, integrate in a creative way, and generate passion. When class-time is taken up with imparting information, then weariness sets in due to overload!

Lastly, as we continue to face escalating costs, we urgently need to establish think tanks composed of academics, administrators, church and Christian leaders in the public sector to address the following: *How can we make available to the people who need to know, what they need to know, when they need to know it and at a price they can afford.*

LEADERSHIP DEVELOPMENT – SYSTEMS DEVELOPMENT AND INDIVIDUAL FORMATION

Jørn Lemvik

Cand polit Jørn Lemvik, Consultant, Norwegian Church Aid, Oslo, Norway

> We think with our worldview, and because of our worldview – not about our worldview! (James W. Sire)

Introduction

Leadership is a challenge wherever in the world it is being performed. In the research world, the leadership thinking has been moving from leadership traits, through situational leadership to transformational leadership (Yukl 2002). During the first decades, the focus was on the leader. Later the sub-ordinate or follower has been more and more seen as a vital actor (Bass and Stogdill 1990). And now, during the recent years, the cultural issue has been put on the agenda. Hofstede's study of leadership in IBM started a discussion on how leadership is influenced by culture (Hofstede 1991). It was recognised that leadership is not performed in the same way in different cultural settings. There are cultural aspects influencing the way the leader leads, and the way the co-worker[1] follows.

Leadership is experienced in all settings, in all countries all over the world. Experience indicates that leadership makes a difference as to how teams, units, organisations or countries are functioning (Nahum 2003). Bad leaders may kill the potential of a group of people, while good leaders may develop the potential beyond what people thought possible.

The spiritual side of leadership has received more focus during recent years. Leadership researchers are developing the concept of charismatic leadership and transformational leadership (Bass and Avolio). Some researchers are focusing more on the actual religious leadership (Fry 2003), but there is almost no research work done linked to churches in an African setting, although these churches have a special place in the civil society of their countries (Roy 1998).

---

[1] I prefer to use the words co-worker when talking about leadership. The word sub-ordinate easily gives negative connotations as to a person's worth, and is therefore not used.

Leadership in an African setting is a challenging adventure. African nations do not necessarily have a national culture (Nahum 2003). People working in organisations and government have different ethnic backgrounds, with a different understanding and practice of leadership. In some tribal settings, there is a “strong man” system, where the leader is very powerful. In other tribes, like the Oromo tribes in Ethiopia, a more democratic[2] system used to function (Legesse 1973).

When leaders, with such a diversity of understandings and experiences with cultural leadership meet in a national organisation or institution – how is leadership then defined and practiced? This is an important question to which the answer is relevant for the development of the institutions, and also for society at large (Nahum 2003).

Dr Knud Jørgensen has been working on leadership development over the years. He has been involved in the work of Ethiopian Evangelical Church Mekane Yesus (EECMY) for many years. He has served, and is still serving, as a mentor to several of the Mekane Yesus church leaders. He is the person who was instrumental to the development of a Leadership and Communication Department at the Mekane Yesus Theological Seminary in Addis Ababa. Not many European theological seminaries have established leadership departments, Dr. Jørgensen saw the need for focusing on leadership development, give the Church leaders a sound, theoretical leadership competence as well as helping them to develop leadership character and leadership skills.

Jørgensen saw the traditional Ethiopian leadership system as a system with a fear aspect to leadership (Jørgensen unpublished). The leader holds power and should be honoured. This power may strongly affect the co-workers if they do not keep the leader happy. The co-worker is afraid of the leader. In such leadership systems, initiative may be seen as opportunistic behaviour, and feedback usually means praising the leader. Leaders do no admit mistakes. When mistakes are done by a leader, someone else will be blamed. Learning and development is often not taking place at all. It is my experience that fear hinders development, and the fear aspect needs to disappear if good leadership shall take place.

Leadership systems are often part of, or strongly influenced by cultural systems. Is it possible to change leadership systems – if at all wanted? The initial quote indicates that it is difficult to challenge our own basic thinking and attitudes. We have seen and learned leadership throughout our upbringing, and our grown-up lives. We often react on instinct, based upon our cultural understanding and habits. It is my experience that change in leadership systems or other cultural patterns needs a strong and united conscious effort and commitment. It usually goes beyond what the individual leader can do on

---

[2] It should be noted that the democracy is defined to be only among men, the women are not taking part in the decision-making.

his/her own.

This chapter presents a new leadership development model. The challenge of leadership and leadership development is a global one. The aim here is to describe a double model where

- the leaders in an organisation/church in a conscious and reflected manner develop their own leadership system (the way they want leadership to be done)
- the leaders implement the system, and help each other to make actual changes in their way of performing leadership

The chapter is organised as follows: The second part is dealing with leadership. Part three gives some personal experiences on the importance of process and follow up, while the fourth part touches the issue of churches as change agents in society. The new leadership development process is then presented in part five. Part six underlines the importance of involving research institutions and documents actual development and the last part presents some closing comments.

Leadership

In many contexts (tribal cultures, national cultures and also organisational cultures), the issue of leadership is not on the debate agenda (Vaughan and Tronvoll 2003). Leadership is performed, not discussed! Discussing leadership is easily experienced to be discussion of the leader, which is generally difficult, and in some cultural settings not even "allowed".

Relatively spoken, leadership is a new word. It did not become part of the English language until the 19th century, and it was not found in the Oxford English Dictionary until 1933. Even though the leadership word is relatively new, the concept of leadership is old. Leaders have been around always, and it seems that in all cultures leadership in one form or another develops (Smith and Kreuger in Bass and Stogdill 1990). The understanding of leadership, however, and what roles and responsibilities should be connected to the leadership position in different cultures and at different times in history, have varied and may vary (ibid).

If, however, leadership shall be defined, there are challenges arising. It seems that there are as many definitions of leadership as there are writers publishing on the issue (Bass and Stogdill 1990, Yukl 2002).

Yukl is summing up most of the main points in his definition,

> Leadership is the process of influencing others to understand and agree about what needs to be done and how it can be done effectively, and the process of facilitating individual and collective efforts to accomplish the shared vision. (Yukl 2002)

Although this definition will be challenged somehow by the actual practice of the fear leadership system which is touched in this document, it will serve as a starting point on working with the leadership challenge.

Competence, tools and integrity

When leadership is being looked at, it is my experience that there are at least three major aspects to be considered:

- competence
- tools
- character and integrity

Much of the leadership training available today is focusing on the two first ones. Seminars and workshops – or shorter courses – present leadership theories and leadership tools – often more on the tools side. The challenge is that the third one is absolutely vital if good leadership is to be experienced. Leaders without character and integrity are usually a threat to their organisations. It is therefore important to make sure that a leadership development process also focuses on the character and integrity side of the leaders, as well as building competence and develop practical skills in handling leadership tools.

Ownership of the leadership system

Experience shows that it is challenging and difficult for leaders to change their attitudes and leadership behaviour. Cultural patter and systems are very powerful. Leaders are children of their cultures. All societies seem to have leadership systems and leadership understanding as part of the culture, which the leaders have adapted as part of their upbringing and socialisation (Vaughan and Tronvoll 2003).

As mentioned in the introduction, quite a few leadership systems are strongly influenced by the fear element (Nahum 2003, Vaughan and Tronvoll 2003). Some of the visible implications of fear are: no feedback given, lack of initiative, blaming, and no sharing of information. When discussed, my experience is that most leaders agree that fear, and the consequences mentioned, are negative for the development of the work of the organisation. In such discussions they also indicate that they see the need for a leadership system where fear is not a central element.[3]

If a leadership system should be changed, however, forced change from the outside seldom works. The leaders need to believe in and own their leadership system. Therefore it is of vital importance that leaders take part in discussing and defining the way they want leadership to be done – and the practical consequences it holds for the leaders.

[3] I have organised leadership training in Ethiopia and other places, where the fear element makes a strong part of the leadership system,. The experience referred to is taken from these groups.

Leadership and culture

> "Sometimes I behave like a feudal leader exercising power. At other times my sub-ordinates make me a feudal leader even though I do not like it. I feel trapped, and I do not know how to get out!" (Ethiopian Church leader)

In many countries and organisational settings, leadership development is a new word. Based on upbringing and cultural understanding, the leaders and the co-workers know their roles and responsibilities (Vaughan and Tronvoll 2003). They are aware of acceptable and unacceptable leadership behaviour. This is known, not necessarily because there is much reflection on the issue – but because the knowledge and understanding have been part of their upbringing, and is "in their backbone", like reflexes.

Many leaders feel uncomfortable discussing their own leadership style. It takes courage to stand forward and invite comments and feedback as to how the leadership is performed, more so in cultural settings where the leaders is seen as someone who knows it all, and will loose face if criticised. In such cultures inviting feedback or giving negative feedback is seen as weak and unacceptable behaviour (Lemvik unpublished). If challenged or criticised, the leader shall hit back hard in order to make sure that the challenge or criticism disappears, and to make sure that everybody is aware of who the leader is and how the leadership is performed.

As it is indicated in the quote above, leaders sometimes feel trapped in their cultural contexts and systems. The leaders see the challenges and consequences of their leadership, but they do not know how to break out.

Leadership and change

> "If you want to see changes in our system, there is only one way to do it. Telling us what is wrong and giving us the "right" answers will never work. You have to knock on our door. If we open our door, you have to come into our house. You have to live with us, and learn how things are working in our place. You have to show that you understand and respect us. Then you may start asking questions – not giving answers. And we will reflect upon your questions and discuss the consequences of our system – then change may come. But it will take a long time to change! (Abuna Paulos, Patriarch of the Ethiopian Orthodox Church)

Rick James, together with Julius Oladipo, Moses Isooba, Betsy Mboizi and Ida Kusiima has been doing some research on how African leaders change (James et al. 2005). First they indicate that even though carloads of books are written on leadership, very little is written on the challenges that African civil society leaders are facing – and even less on factors that may help these leaders to change their leadership behaviour. They discuss the situation today, present their experiences, and come up with the following list of recommendations:

Content of leadership development

- Assist leaders to work out their own coherent concept of leadership
- Deal with leaders as whole persons leading congested lives
- Explore an empowering style of leadership
- Address issues of leadership succession

Methods of leadership development

- Leadership development – in-house development processes
- Mentoring and coaching
- Peer support networks
- Exchange, exposure visits and sabbaticals

Principles of leadership development practice

- Create space for reflection
- Challenge leaders to discover answers themselves
- Ensure peer/facilitator feedback
- Provide good resource materials
- Use role models where possible.
- Ensure that learning is applied
- Follow through – it is a process, not a happening

Leadership and values

During the recent years, the issue of organisational values has been put high on the agenda. Organisations should have a value fundament, and this fundament should influence the way the organisation is working. Through organisational projects and activities, people should recognise the values. Much time has been spent in seminars and processes, defining and developing value bases of organisations. Not so much time has been spent in looking at the practical consequences of the values, for example for leaders. What influences should the values bring e.g. to the leadership system and the way the leaders behave. If involvement is an organisational value – what implications should this have for the leaders in their daily work?

Personal Experience

I have been working on leadership development in different African and Asian cultural settings during the last 15 years.[4] At present I am doing a research project focusing on "leadership in multi-cultural settings", focusing on an

[4] I have been working in around 10 different African countries in East and West Africa. In addition I have also been working in India and China.

Ethiopian context.

My research work, and my work as facilitator in leadership development processes, have opened my eyes to the truth of the initial quote of this document: We think with our worldview, and because of our worldview – not about our worldview! (James W. Sire)

Leaders are not always aware of why they are leading the way they do. In the Ethiopian setting, I have tried to map the cultural leadership system and mirrored it back to the leaders. This has created interesting discussions. "I have never been thinking of this as a leadership *system*", is a comment often heard.

When the leaders see the characteristics of the system practiced in their group or their organisation, they have a fundament for discussing the general *consequences* of this system, and in particular the consequences linked to leadership. Challenging the leaders on the practical consequences of the leadership system they know, and asking them if the effects of the leadership system are good or wanted, opens up discussions where they themselves may start looking at different ways of performing leadership. If a group of leaders starts discussing and agreeing on wanted leadership behaviour, it brings possibilities of developing a new leadership system, new ways of actually doing leadership.

Church leaders as change agents

In the African context, few actors hold the potential of Christian churches and other religious institutions (Roy 1998). The churches represent organisational structures reaching from a national level down to the smallest village. Although the actual functioning of these church structures are varying, the potential of reaching people through the structures, is never questioned.

Church leaders are familiar with the texts of the Bible. In the Bible, Jesus Christ and some of the Biblical authors brings up issues linked to leadership. Stewardship (Matt 21 – the fact that the leader is accountable to someone), servant leadership (Matt 20 – where the focus is on the leader being a servant and not a master), empowerment and delegation (Matt 28), honesty (Exodus 20), transparency (1 John 1) etc. are major Biblical concerns. All the above mentioned issues are strongly influencing leadership thinking and leadership systems.

Church leaders do know these texts, and are familiar with the theoretical ideas of being servants and stewards. The practice, when these principles meet a cultural leadership understanding which is totally different, creates challenges for the leaders. Mirroring the Biblical texts, looking at the leadership principles found, and discussing together on the practical consequences of these principles for leaders may be valuable input when trying to develop a new leadership system.

Church leaders hold the potential of being change agents in their societies. Often they are not representing a power threat to the political leadership in the country, and thereby they hold a potential for developing and practicing an alternative leadership system: a system, where e.g. the fear aspect and the lack of initiative may be exchanged with systems of respect, cooperation, learning and development. If new leadership systems may be developed, systems where the leaders and the followers may hold more constructive roles, this may bring a situation where quality results may be reached. The bigger picture is that such changes may ultimately bring positive change to the organisation and to the society.

A new leadership development process

In the following few pages, a new leadership development approach will be presented. This approach is based upon findings like the ones presented by Rick James and his co-workers – and upon my own experiences.

Basic principles

This leadership development process is based upon the following basic principles:

a) Organisational arena – Involvement and ownership.

If the development of a leadership system is to hold potential for change, this will be made possible through an organisational focus. The leaders of an organisation should be participating in such a leadership development process together. This will help them in developing new understanding of leadership, and implementing new leadership principles together. The leaders must be involved in the development of their own leadership system, and all of them should take part in the process. Ownership is created through participation, reflection, discussion and common development. As the process is moving forward, the other employees will also be involved through departmental discussions, invitation of feedback etc.

The organisations participating in such a project should be invited and accept the invitation voluntarily. Based upon a project sketch (like the one outlined here), the organisations with their leaders should accept to take part. The detailed planning of the process should be done together with the actual leaders.

b) Team approach – Facilitation

It is difficult for individual leaders to bring substantial changes into their organisations on their own. There is a need for the leaders to discuss and agree on wanted changes, and find ways of putting this into practice *together*. As an integrated part of the leadership system development, the team development takes part.

Experience shows that it is useful to have facilitators who can help keep processes on track. The role of the facilitator is to facilitate and ask questions.

The answers to the challenges of leadership, however, should not come from the facilitator – but from the leaders themselves.

c) Transparency and information – Feedback and learning

There is a need, from the very beginning of a leadership system development process, to be transparent towards the rest of the organisation. Information should be given to the employees on what such a leadership development process is, how it will be done, and how the employees will be involved in the process. Invitation for input and feedback from co-workers should also be welcomed from the very beginning.

Leaders need to discuss the consequences of their present leadership system (there has to be a mapping of the system, and "mirroring" the findings) on a general basis. As the process develops, there is also a need for the leaders to invite feedback to their individual way of performing their leadership. From the very beginning of the project, learning should receive a key focus. This indicates that a learning culture where feedback, reflection, discussions and change should be part of the way the leaders lead, and the project is moving. There is a need for the leaders to be able to discuss and ask advice as they change their leadership role. A system of peer-mentoring, or individual mentoring, should be set up to facilitate for this need.

d) Process – homework – and change

Development and implementation of a leadership system takes time. Therefore such a project should have a time horizon of at least five years. This is not a competence building project, where the idea is only to equip the leaders with new knowledge and teach them tools. The integrity and ethical side of leadership should also be focused. It should be a leadership development process where the development of a new leadership system and thereby the leaders themselves, is just as much focused on attitudes and the ethical side of leadership. One of the major issues in such a development process is how the new leadership system has to be implemented. In between each leadership development workshop (see below for more details), each of the leaders have to practice the agreed systems, principles etc. and report back how the experiences have been. In this way reflection and learning may take place.

e) Establishing networks

Network arenas for experience sharing, discussions and learning should be established. This should be done on several levels. There could be internal networks where employees could come and follow the development of the leadership training, meet and discuss with the leaders, and bring their input to the process. There could also be networks established on a regional or national level. Here leaders from several organisations could meet together, share experiences of leadership system development and implementation, and learn from each other.

Leaders who participate in these networks are responsible to bring back experiences, learning and reflections from these forums to their own organisations.

A practical way of organising the project

The actual leadership development process holds 8 different stages:

Information stage

Transparency is a key word linked to this process. The organisation should be informed on the planned process, so that all employees know what is going on. Information should also be made available to the organisation throughout the process.

Mapping and identification stage

In order to use this concept, it is a precondition to map the actual cultural and organisational leadership systems. A way to do this mapping should be developed, and the actual system(s) should be described. At this stage, the documented organisational values should also be identified. Identification of Biblical principles linked to leadership should also be done at this stage.

Mirroring stage

In this part of the process, everything which was mapped and identified in the previous stage should be presented to the leaders. This goes for

- the actual leadership system(s)
- the documented organisational values
- the Biblical leadership principles

Analysing/connecting – discussions on consequences

When the mirroring has been done, it is time for reflection and discussion. The leaders should talk together, and help each other *see the practical consequences* of the leadership system related to the co-workers, partners and organisational functioning. At the same time they should also discuss logical consequences for leaders related to the organisational values and the Biblical principles.

Development of a new leadership system

After the mirroring and the reflections and discussions related to consequences are done, the leaders have the background to start discussing and developing a leadership system they would like to see functioning in their organisation. Leadership principles should be worked out, and the new leadership system should be developed. The practical consequences of this new system should also be spelled out to secure that the leadership system is "producing" the consequences wanted.

Development of plan for implementation of the leadership system

It is now time to plan how to implement the system. A thorough plan should be worked out. In order to be able to implant the system, a follow-up system has to be developed so that the leaders are finding support for the actual day-to-day implementation of their new leadership system.

Implementing the new system

The system should be put into practice according to the plan developed and agreed upon. Enabling structures have to be developed for each of the stages presented above to support the development of the new system, and the implementation of it.

Monitoring, learning and change

In order to make the new system work, there is a need for close monitoring and reporting. The leaders will be needing support from each other, from the organisation, and probably also from a facilitator/mentor to make the new system function. The actual change lies in the follow-up – and therefore this stage is really challenging and important.The learning circle (planning, implementation, reflection, change) could be used as a practical tool in the implementation and development of the new leadership system.

Practical organization

There should be three meetings a year set aside for this leadership development process, each of the duration of four days. Mapping, mirroring, development of a leadership system, discussion on practical implementation, competence building, experience sharing and learning should be making up the program. A facilitator should be engaged to plan the detailed program together with the leaders, and follow up on the development and implementation of the new leadership system. In order to secure even more learning, it is advisable that several organisations within the same country are moving into such a process. If e.g. three organisations take part in the project and each of the organisations develops their own leadership system, a network of organisations could be established to create space for experience sharing and learning. Bi-annual meetings should be organised where the organisations meet together on a national level to share experiences, to learn from each other, to develop new ideas etc. Such meetings should be planned as two day workshops. A facilitator should be made available also for the planning and facilitation of these meetings. There is a reporting obligation, all that is going on in all meetings and workshops shall be reported back to one's own organization.

Who could use the leadership development system?

The leadership development concept may be used by any organisation[5] in any part of the world where the leaders want to look at the way the culture influences their leadership, and where the goal is to develop an organisational leadership system based upon the organisational value foundation. (In practical terms this means that every organisation should benefit from running such a process). It is important that the leadership group should be motivated for such a leadership development process. It usually puts the heaviest challenge on the top leadership.

Organisational change

Change in leadership practice automatically leads to changes in the way the organisation is functioning. Therefore leadership development processes are usually followed by organisational development processes.

In order to secure lasting changes, there is a need for such a process to run for some time. Church leaders are often elected for periods of three to four years (they usually may be re-elected). Experience shows that leadership changes take place quite often. I would therefore recommend that such leadership processes should run for at least five years (Lemvik 2006).

Research and documentation

This approach describes a way of organising leadership system development and leadership formation, which has not been tested out and documented before. Research institution(s) could be invited in to follow and document the process and the results. This will assure that activities, analysis and learning linked to the leadership system development will be documented, and may be shared with other milieus through articles or other publications.

It should also be investigated with universities if it is possible to link such a leadership development program to a formal leadership education program. In this way the participants may be able to develop a leadership system, implement it – and at the same time study leadership and have this recognised as formal competence.

The project outlined is a leadership system development as well as a leadership formation process. As such it is a learning process to see if it is possible to find effective ways of developing leadership systems and leaders

[5] The process outlined here is focusing on Christian churches and the potential for these churches and church leaders to be influencing the civil society. Instead of using Biblical principles for leadership behaviour, one mirror may be set up with ethical standards linked e.g. to human rights – and the same process may be used for the leadership system development.

where the ownership of the system and the change processes is embedded in the leadership group of an organisation.

At the same time, it is a learning process on how to organise leadership development activities. It is therefore of vital importance that a proper documentation is done from the outset of the process, so that the experiences and learning will be made available to other actors and organisations (Lemvik 2006).

Closing comments

Will such a process as the one outlined here guarantee a change in leadership systems, in leadership behaviour and in organisational functioning? It is not possible to bring such guarantees. It is quite certain, however, that unless we try to find good ways of developing leadership systems – and of helping leaders to develop their leadership potential, the present challenges we are facing will remain.

This is an attempt to find a way in a new landscape where we have not been before. As such it will bring an important contribution to the leadership process development thinking, and hopefully put this important aspect of organisational functioning on the agenda in a positive and constructive way.

TRANSITION OF LEADERSHIP

Dag Håkon Eriksen

Cand philol Dag Håkon Eriksen, Project Advisor, Church of Norway, Oslo

Introduction

Every successful organization will at some point face the challenge of transition of leadership. There comes a time in every organization's life when the founding leader has to hand the leadership over to someone else.

This is more than mere change; this is a leadership transition with major organizational implications. This is a process where the defining elements of the organization must be transferred from the founder to the next leaders. In the beginning the organization's vision and mission are defined and materialized by the founder. As a lasting legacy they must institutionalize the organizational genetic code in a way that balances the need for both continuity and flexibility, thus sustaining the long-term viability of the organization. Transition of leadership is extremely deciding in this process.

An example of this can be found in the reports of the New Testament (NT) on how Jesus secured long-term viability of the emerging movement called "the way" by imparting vision and leadership to his followers through an empowering relationship.

The transition of leadership can be an opportunity for growth, focus and shared vision. It can be seen as organizational development through renewal of its leadership. But without preparation, this process may be accompanied by organizational conflict, unease and a frantic search for new leadership and organizational identity.

In this article we are looking into the different dynamics involved and the factors contributing to this process of leadership transition from the founder to the second generation leaders in young independent organizations. Transition of leadership is seen as the process of *transferring leadership* where the practicing leader increasingly releases leadership tasks, functions and roles to an emerging leader that increasingly accepts responsibility for this in an organization.[1] We will focus on the factors that affect the transition. The

---

[1]Robert Clinton & Kathrine Haubert: *The Joshua Portrait. A Study in leadership development, leadership transition & destiny fulfillment* (Altadena,

transition of leadership can also be seen as a process of *empowerment*. The ultimate task of any leader is to empower followers, to equip them and help them realize their potential. Ephesians 4 points out that God gave leaders to the church to equip its members for service. This is the kind of leadership Jesus exercised: "Come follow me," Jesus said, "and I will make you into fishers of men" (Mk. 1:17) He turned followers into leaders. From this we see that Jesus can serve as a model for such *empowering leadership.*[2]

The purpose with this article is to provide the reflective practitioner with models and theories on how leadership in organizations can be transferred from the founder to the second generation leaders, in a way that can contribute to the dynamic long term viability of the organization. The article is based on theoretical studies and case studies of a church planting movement in the US and a para-church organization in South Africa.[3]

Through these studies different factors contributing to the process of transition of leadership in organizations were identified. The factors fall into different categories. Organizational, Extra-organizational, Leadership and the Hand-over process itself. These categories will provide the structure of this article.

Organizational Factors Affecting the Transition of Leadership in Organizations

Here we are exploring the organizational context for the specifics of transition management, factors like organizational history, structure and culture.

The term "organization" is used as an overall term meaning "psychological groups united to achieve a common goal."[4] This means that both churches and para-church organizations fit this term. Christian organizations have both an eschatological-transcendent and a socio-historical dimension.[5] The eschatological-transcendent dimension implies that it is God who ultimately is building his church. This article will focus on the socio-historical dimension the Christian organization shares with all other organizations.

CA: Barnabas Resources 1990).

[2] Leighton Ford: *Transforming Leadership. Jesus' way of creating vision, shaping values & empowering change* (Downers Grove, Ill.: InterVarsity Press 1991).

[3] The study was conducted in 1998-1999. Knud Jørgensen gave considerable input and feedback to this study. Another article based on this study has been published in "Norwegian Journal of Missiology".

[4] Bjørvik in Henning Bang: *Organisasjonskultur* (Oslo: TANO 1988, (3rd ed)), 17.

[5] Olav Skjevesland: *Kirken i Det nye testamente* (Oslo: Andaktsboksforlaget 1976), 109

Organizational History

Different writers describe the development young organizations go through. They use different concepts and terms, but basically they describe the same phenomenon: As young dynamic organizations grow, they go through different phases, often leading to more formalized structures and bureaucracy.[6] This basic understanding is reinforced by the case studies. One of the founders said:

> "One (stage) is the burst of vision at the beginning and the conveying of vision to others. Then the organizing of those others along with oneself into the fulfilling of that vision and letting it grow and get under way. Then consolidating it and maintaining it, and finally, as in a cycle, of reaching the time for a fresh burst of the entrepreneurial to push the organization off the plateau and into the second generation."

Organizations need different leadership styles at different stages. Many writers say an autocratic and entrepreneurial leadership style must change to a more administrative and delegating style, at the same time as the creative element must be upheld. The charismatic leadership that often is the moving force behind new organizations must be transformed and transferred to others in the organization.[7] How transition of leadership is prepared and managed plays a major role in this process. There is a crucial phase in the organizational development when the leadership should be transferred from the founder to the second generation leaders. The tension and confusion connected with this transitional phase is found in both the cases.

The organizational development leads to a phase where the organization needs more administration and structure to sustain performance. It has outgrown the initial coordination and communication procedures sufficient in the entrepreneurial stage. It is often in need of alignment and integration. This stage that Adizes called *adolescence*, is often characterized by tensions between the administrative and entrepreneurial elements in the organization. Mintzberg said that a well managed and administrated bureaucracy might be needed to

---

[6] Max Weber: *On charisma and institution building. Selected papers edited and with an Introduction by S.N. Eisenstadt* (Chicago, Ill.: The University of Chicago Press 1968); Ichak Adizes: *Corporate Life Cycles* (Englewood Cliffs, N.J.: Prentice Hall 1988); Mintzberg, Henry: 1983 *Structures in Five. Designing Effective Organizations* (Englewood Cliffs, N.J: Prentice Hall, Inc.); Greiner, Larry E: "Evalution and Revolution as Organizations Grow" *Harvard Business Review*, July-August 1972. Reprinted as HBR Classic 1998.

[7] Max Weber: *On charisma and institution building. Selected papers edited and with an Introduction by S.N. Eisenstadt* (Chicago, Ill.: The University of Chicago Press, 1968); H. M. Trice and J. M. Beyer: "Charisma and its routinization in two social movement organizations", *Research in Organizational Behaviour*, vol 8, pp.113-164.

achieve the original mission of the charismatic organization.

Adizes points to the need for more administration, but at the same time the entrepreneurial elements should be emphasized. If administration and innovation are integrated the organization will reach its *prime* stage where Adizes claims it can make change occur as it likes, and it can control what it wants to do.[8]

Preparation in itself is a crucial factor. Steffen emphasizes the need to start the preparations for this early in a missiological endeavor. Rothwell says the major difference is between planned and unplanned transition strategies.[9] In both cases the organizations were forced to change the leadership because the founders either passed away or approached retirement. This is a simple observation; all people, included founders, grow older and will at one stage not be capable of leading the organization, but it seems that the application of this fact is easily postponed in the everyday life of a busy organization.

Organizational Structure

Mintzberg explains how the entrepreneurial structure is fragile and dependent upon the leader.[10] Both cases had established some structures that preserved continuity parallel to the founder, making the organizations somehow independent from the founder.

The board plays a major role in the transition process. It facilitates long term viability of the organization, independent of the founder. Adizes called this process a *depersonalization* of the management process. The individual's knowledge, capacity and network should be transferred to the organization. Trice and Beyer see this as an important component of the routinization of charisma.

However, there is a danger in developing rigid structures, loosing the initial flexibility of the organization. The organizations need to develop structures that secure the balance between control and flexibility. One of the two cases was aware of this possibility and tried to counter work this bureaucratic process by nurturing organizational values like 'form follows function'. This brings us to the next category.

Organizational Culture

There are informal sides of an organization that affect the transition of leadership. The term organizational culture tries to capture the formal or informal rules and values that guide the thinking and behavior of the members

[8] Adizes, 1988

[9] William J. Rothwell: *Effective Succession Planning. Ensuring Leadership Continuity and Building Talents from Within* (New York: Amacom, 1994).

[10] Mintzberg, 1983.

of any organization. From the cases it seems apparent that organizational culture plays a major role in the transition of leadership.

The organizational culture was different in the two cases. One had been very conscious in developing and nurturing what they call their "genetic code". Relevant for us is the strong value placed upon participation, equipping and releasing emerging leaders expressed in the slogans like "We all get to play" and "Equipping the Saints". They sought a church culture where it was accepted to try new things, and to succeed or fail. The other did not place the same value upon equipping and releasing people into ministry. They rather recruited people already with a recognized ministry. This led to alignment problems and nurtured a 'Lone Wolf' mentality not very functional towards transition. It seemed that the organizational culture was formed and influenced by the founders. Their way of operating and functioning had served as an example for the rest of the organization. The cases support Schein's understanding that the founder deeply influences the organizational culture.[11]

The incorporation of the founder's mission and message into the organization's written and oral tradition is an important element in the routinization of their charisma. This tradition will provide direction and integration for the second generation organization surviving beyond the founder. Synnes says this was the major focus in the transition that took place from Paul to Timothy. He should guard what had been entrusted to his care, the Gospel Paul had preached.[12]

It seems that the role of the founder in forming the organizational culture has been reinforced, and that cultural values are important factors affecting the transition of leadership in organizations. Among these crucial values are the willingness, habits and infrastructure needed to share knowledge and experience. This might facilitate organizational learning enabling dynamic organizations to cope and thrive with change.[13]

We have now discussed some central organizational factors in the transition of leadership. All of these factors are within the organization itself. But organizations as open systems are influenced by their surroundings. It is therefore important to consider the influence extra-organizational factors have on transition of leadership.

---

[11] Edgar Schein: *Organizational Culture and Leadership* (San Francisco, CA: Jossey-Bass Publ. 1985).

[12] Martin Synnes: *Vakthold om den skjønne skatt. Innføring i Pastoralbrevene og kommentar til første Timoteusbrev* (Oslo: Luther Forlag, 1996), pp.107f and 275ff. See also: 1 Tim 1:18ff; 6:11-14, 20 and 2 Tim 1:12ff; 2:2.

[13] For more on organizational learning see Chris Argyris: *On organizational Learning* (Cambridge, Mass.: Blackwell, 1994). Peter Senge: *The Fifth Discipline: The art and practice of the learning organization* (New York: Doubleday, 1990). I. Nonaka: "The knowledge creating company", K. Starkey (ed.): *How organizations learn* (London: Int. Thompson Business ,Press 1996).

Extra-Organizational Factors Contributing to the Transition of Leadership

Organizations are *open systems*, interacting with and being influenced by their surroundings. The member's identity is influenced by the surrounding national or regional culture. This has major implications for how leadership should be exercised in general and also for how a transition of leadership should be worked out in that culture. Hofstede has worked on the relationship between organizations and the national cultures they act within. He has recognized four dimensions in the surrounding culture influencing the leadership in organizations.[14] Leaders should adjust their leadership style to both the factors within and the factors surrounding the organization. The ability to discern the situation and adjust one's leadership style accordingly is as an essential part in empowering situational leadership.

Jørgensen presents some theses on leadership and culture.[15] Leadership in culture has to do with communication in culture. The message of communication is not primarily in the signals, but in the receivers who interpret the signals. This implies that leadership in one culture is not the same as leadership in another culture. There is a need for dynamic-equivalent leadership.[16]

Leadership Factors Affecting the Transition of Leadership in Organizations

Leadership is seen in relation to the situation. We are concerned with the dynamic relationship between leadership and organization. What kind of leadership will empower the organization and make the transition of leadership easier?

The theoretical and empirical studies this article is building on have pointed to different leadership factors that are mutual and interconnected; Personal aspects of leadership, Leadership style, and Leadership development.

The Personal Aspects of Leadership

The personal aspects of leadership are important because they influence how

---

[14] 1. Power distance, 2. Uncertainty Avoidance, 3. Individualism-Collectivism, and 4. Masculine-Feminine from: Hofstede, Geert: *Cultures and Organizations. Software of the Mind* (London: McGRAW-HILL, 1991).

[15] Knud Jørgensen: *Equipping for service. Leadership in Church and Mission.* Addis Ababa. Ethiopia:.Mekane Yesus Seminary, 1995), 32

[16] Kraft, Charles H.: *Christianity in Culture. A study in Dynamic Biblical theologizing in Cross-Cultural Perspective* (Maryknoll, New York: Orbis Books, 1979), 103.

leaders exercise their leadership functions, influencing thereby the organization and, in the end,also transition. The values embodied by the founder deeply influence the organizational culture.[17] Both theory and the case studies underline the importance of the personal aspects of leadership. Our task is to identify what personal aspects of leadership seem relevant and functional in regard to transition.

The NT contains elements crucial for an effective transition of leadership in any context. Leaders in the Biblical sense are servants and followers first. This implies that the leaders first and foremost should realize the vision given within the Great Commission and the Golden Rule, and not their own grand ideas. The NT offers an alternative base for self-worth and identity than performance. This enables servant leaders to rejoice when emerging leaders are empowered to take the baton and bring it further. Jørgensen identifies the primary task of the servant leader as equipping others for service, on the background of Ephesians 4:11-16.[18] This must involve humility and a willingness on the servant leader's behalf to see others excel and succeed. The willingness to empower others and rejoice when they are elevated is a major factor in the transition of leadership found both in theory and in the cases.

In Mark 3 we see Jesus in the process of choosing his disciples. From then on he spent most of his time with them. He sought to reproduce himself and his performance in the lives of his followers. After three years of preparation in word, deed and example, he was ready to hand over leadership to them. This was no last minute plan. He prepared for this moment. From the reports in the NT it is clear that Jesus devoted himself steadfastly to the twelve, and spent more time with them than with the crowds. This says something about character.

He was not swayed by popularity, but stayed committed to investing himself into others who would do greater things.[19]

The Biblical concept of the leader as a steward highlights that the leaders are not the owners, but that they only manage someone else's property. If taken seriously this concept might prove to be of major importance for transition of leadership. In the beginning of the organization's life cycle, the founder's commitment is crucial to its very existence. But as time passes the parental embrace might turn into an unhealthy grip choking initiative and freedom to grow for the organization in the adolescence stage.

Jesus handed over leadership and responsibility for his church to 12 rough men who few founders would have trusted as successors. But they grew to the challenge and took the baton further by the help of the Holy Spirit.

---

[17] Edgar Schein: *Organizational Culture and Leadership* (San Francisco, CA: Jossey-Bass Publ., 1985).

[18] Knud Jørgensen: *Visjon og Hverdag. Lederskap i misjon og menighet* (Oslo: Verbum, 1991).

[19] John 14:12

Another aspect concerns criteria for success. If success is achieved individually and the founders only seek to prove their own success, not success through others, this will contribute to what Adizes calls the "founder's trap."[20]

When or at what stage is success measured? At the peak of the founder's career or some time later when their lasting legacy or contributions are to be measured? At what time success is measured relates to what vision the founders have pursued. If their vision surpasses their possible capacities, if the vision was truly great, they have to develop others and release them to pursue the vision further. Since Christian leaders are followers themselves, they should actually never pursue their own vision. Ultimately they pursue the Kingdom of God, which they can never own. Working out a God-given vision transcends individual possibilities and requires multiplication and reproduction. We see this expressed in Paul's instruction to Timothy; to entrust what he had heard from Paul to reliable men, who will be qualified to teach others.[21]

On the other side not every organization should live forever. Some achieve their goal. Then what do they do? One of the case studies reflected upon this. Were their vision and mission completed? They answered 'no' to that fundamental question, and thereby found the *raison d'être* for the second generation organization.

The discussion above concerns different aspects of the role attitude plays in the transition of leadership. From this we see that some of the unique aspects of Christian leadership might prove functional towards transition. This is if these values are internalized and thus become the leader's *theory-in-use* and not only their *explicit-theory.*[22] The personal aspects of leadership are decisive for transition, because those personal aspects influence other factors such as leadership style, leadership development, organization culture etc.

The personal aspects that seem most important are the understanding of oneself as a steward and a servant leader, set to equip others for service, fulfilling the grand vision through others.

Let us now turn to another category of leadership factors that is influenced by the personal aspect of leadership, and which in turn affects the transition of leadership.

Leadership Style

There is a relationship between leadership style and the transition of leadership. Here we will discuss the theoretical and empirical findings identified as important in regard to transition.

---

[20] Adizes 1988.

[21] Martin Synnes: *Vakthold om den skjønne skatt. Innføring i Pastoralbrevene og kommentar til første Timoteusbrev* (Oslo: Luther Forlag, 1996), 107f and 275ff.

[22] Argyris 1994.

The major principle concerning leadership style is that of a situational leadership style combining relational and task-oriented behavior, so as to match the follower's readiness level. As the readiness level of the followers increases, the leader's style should change accordingly.[23] But there is a need for considering other situational factors as well.

In the case studies I found indicators that supported the major idea of situational leadership. When it comes to which situational factors that should be considered, as leadership style is selected to fit the situation, my case studies support the importance of the follower's readiness level. But at the same time it is also apparent that other factors need be considered. The case studies showed the need to consider factors within and around the organization as we have briefly mentioned.

In a Christian organization there is a spiritual dimension that must be considered. The organizations in my case studies recognized the role the ultimate Lord of the church plays. In some ways the practicing leaders must widen their horizon beyond management principles and consider what the ultimate Lord is doing and where He is leading the organization and its people.

Empowering situational leadership style describes a leadership style that seeks to equip people and release them into ministry. The cases reflected that a relational leadership style creates a learning environment where the trust and confidence needed for growth can be established.

The practicing leader needs to facilitate learning, helping the emerging leaders and the organization to learn and develop the relevant capacity. The competent leaders have to restrain themselves, giving others an opportunity, even if they could have done it far better themselves.

We see from this that it becomes decisive for the leader to delegate critical tasks and functions and let others do their part gaining experience and a feeling of ownership. D'Souza says that delegation is a major leadership development tool.[24] To optimize the learning experience the delegated task should be challenging, but possible to achieve. It is also important that the leaders, who have delegated authority, respect that authority themselves. Both cases showed how dysfunctional vacillation in this area can be. Emerging leaders became uncertain whether they really had been given authority or not. This uncertainty may lead to frustrations and conflicts.

Leadership development

Leadership development in itself is of major importance for transition of leadership. Here I would like to discuss the different aspects of leadership development.

---

[23] Paul Hersey & Kenneth H. Blanchard: *Management of Organizational Behaviour* (Englewood Cliffs, N.J.: Prentice Hall, 1988).

[24] D'Souza, Anthony: *Leadership* (St. Paul's Publ., 1989).

From the case studies, it seems important to start leadership development as early as possible. Everybody in an organization should be given the opportunity to grow and develop. In modern organizations, the people themselves are the major assets. The organizations cannot grow or develop beyond their people. Such development programs could build both on their present abilities and be related to the perceived future needs of the organization according to its strategy. This future assessment, together with the personal aspects of leadership that we discussed earlier and the dynamic-equivalent Biblical criteria should guide the selection of successors. This should also guide the content and form of the leadership development programs. Designing the development program according to these guidelines will facilitate a fit with the overall organizational strategy, thus utilizing the full organizational developmental potential of the preparations toward a transition of leadership.

Rothwell stresses this and says assessments of future needs should guide the other components of the development process. He says that transition planning programs should fit into the organization's overall strategies. Gilmore did the same as he addressed how an organization should assess its strategic situation and let this assessment determine the other elements of the transition.[25]

Specific Elements in Transition of Leadership in Organizations

In this section we are narrowing our focus down to the specific elements of leadership transition and how they can be managed.

We are seeking factors and dynamics which are important to consider in different situations. The outworking of these factors should be related to each specific situation.

The specific elements of transition are, of course, intimately connected to the other factors related to the organization, the leadership, and the surrounding environment. Therefore no 'quick fix' solution to the transition problem will work if it has been neglected for years.

If, for example, the leadership style has been very autocratic, and no leadership development has taken place, it will not work to suddenly hand over authority to unprepared followers.

If the organizational or leadership factors have been characterized by qualities dysfunctional toward a transition, it requires time to change those qualities and prepare the organization for a transition of leadership. For these organizations, reactive models might be most useful. It might be a golden opportunity for organizational development, resulting in a more flexible organization on a long term basis.

---

[25] William J. Rothwell: *Effective Succession Planning. Ensuring Leadership Continuity and Building Talents from Within* (New York: Amacom, 1994). Thomas North Gilmore: *Making a leadership change* (San Fransisco, CA: Jossey-Bass Publ., 1988).

For other organizations that are able to start the preparations for a transition of leadership earlier, it is possible to nurture qualities in the organization and in the leadership that will both facilitate the transition of leadership and the long term flexibility of the organization. In a way these organizations can be said to have implemented proactive models. Let us first turn to the reactive models.

The Reactive Models

The Center for Partnership in Development has developed some tools to tackle the complexities of the process of handing over health care projects from foreign initiators to national agencies.[26] Even if this setting differs from my cases, these tools still apply.

The *sustainability assessment tool* defines sustainability as a match between activities and capacity within a given context over a period of time. The *power assessment tool* measures how far the leadership transition has come in terms of decision making. It would help assess how ready the acting leadership felt to make decisions in its own right in the founder's absence.

The power assessment tool can be used in conjunction with Clinton and Haubert's leadership transition model. Their model encompasses more than decision making, describing how the practicing leader can transfer leadership tasks, functions and roles to the emerging leader.[27] Their basic point of graduality has been confirmed in the cases. The founders transferred over time what you can describe as leadership tasks, functions and roles. Clinton and Haubert's model is a simple workable model for thinking about transition of leadership that also facilitates organizational learning. Implied in their model is the idea of rising up leaders from within the organization, or letting emerging leaders from the outside enter into leadership positions at a slow pace.

<table>
<tr><th colspan="5">Replacement of Leadership--------------->Replacement of Leader</th></tr>
<tr><td>Simple Task</td><td>More or complicated Task(s)</td><td>Take on some functions</td><td>Major Responsibility for functions</td><td>The Leader's Role</td></tr>
<tr><td colspan="5">Practicing Leader Increasingly RELEASES responsibility</td></tr>
<tr><td colspan="5">Emerging Leader Increasingly ACCEPT responsibility</td></tr>
</table>

Collin and Poraas stress the need to develop and promote insiders who are

---

[26] Mirjam Bergh: *Caring Sharing Daring. Development work in transition* (Oslo: "Norsk Misjonsråds Bistandsnemnd" and "Diakonhjemmets Internasjonale Senter" 1995).

[27] Robert Clinton & Kathrine Haubert: *The Joshua Portrait. A Study in leadership development, leadership transition & destiny fulfillment* (Altadena, CA: Barnabas Resources, 1990).

highly capable of stimulating healthy change and progress, while preserving the core.[28] According to Gilmore, the sociopolitical and technical changes occur so fast that the organization often needs totally new qualities in its leadership to keep up. Thus he encourages organizations to seek new leadership from the outside.[29]

The cases show that there is a major difference between organizations that have prepared themselves for transition and those suddenly awakening to the urgent need for a successor. Rothwell stresses the need to make a commitment to a systematic transition planning program. His model might help facilitate the continuous organizational development process culminating in the consistent development of new leaders, as the transition planning program is directly linked to organizational and human resource strategic plans.[30]

Reactive models can be implemented and help organizations prepare themselves for a transition of leadership and benefit from the organizational development process which a transition is. Now we will see how the proactive models can facilitate this.

The Proactive Models

Typically the concern for leadership development and transition is introduced in the strategy at a later stage. Hesselgrave goes so far as to say: "If there is one subject in church-planting evangelism that does not receive adequate attention either in the literature or in the actual planning for a new work, it is that of the withdrawal of the pioneer worker(s)."[31] Steffen and Brock suggest strongly that to see an effective succession of leadership and the establishment of an indigenous church, those concerns must determine the whole process from its very start. [32] Traditionally the indigenous church has been characterized by the three-self formula: self-governing, self-supporting and self-propagating. In addition to these characteristics, Smalley claims that an indigenous church has found its own cultural expressions. Hiebert says it also develops its own theology, while Onsrud points to its ability to write its own history.[33] Brock, in

---

[28] James C. Collin & Jerry I. Porras: *Built to Last. Successful Habits of Visionary Companies* (New York: Harper Business, 1994).

[29] Thomas North Gilmore: *Making a leadership change* (San Fransisco, CA: Jossey-Bass Publ., 1988).

[30] Rothwell, 1994.

[31] David J. Hesselgrave: *Planting Churches Cross-Culturally. A Guide for Home and Foreign Mission* (Grand Rapids, Mich.: Baker Book House, 1980).

[32] Tom Steffen:. *Passing the Baton. Church Planting that Empowers* (La Habra, CA: Center for Organizational and Ministry Development, 1993). Charles Brock: *The Principles and Practice of Indigenous Church Planting* (Manilla: Baptist Center, 1980).

[33] Smalley 1967 in Charles H. Kraft and Tom N. Wisley: *Readings in Dynamic*

his strategy for how to plant an indigenous church, emphasizes the need for thinking reproducibility in every aspect of the process, i.e. material things, strategy, leadership etc., from beginning to end.[34] Hesselgrave develops a strategy called the "Pauline cycle," based on a study of Paul's strategy as reported in the NT.[35] Hesselgrave claims that this model is found in the NT, and that this strategy is applicable today. In the "Pauline Circle" there are 11 phases. Starting with the sending of the missionaries and completed when the missionaries returns to their sending body ready for another mission. Hesselgrave describe how the newly established fellowship can identify leaders among them, how these leaders can take on leadership, and then finally how the relationship between the missionaries and the indigenous church can be maintained.

Steffen gives us a model for church planting driven by a concern for an effective transition of leadership and its crucial role in the planting of indigenous churches. Our cases are not churches planted by foreigners, but some of the issues do apply to our cases. Steffen presents a proactive phase-out oriented approach where all aspects of the strategy, starting with the selection of the workers, are determined by transition concerns. Steffen's model can be seen as an effort that can guide the establishment of an indigenous entity. He defines phase-out activities as "activities that empower nationals to develop leadership among them selves with an eye toward ministry that reproduces." Often church planters fail to withdraw in a responsible way, hurting the church they have worked so hard to plant. The first step on the way is to define responsible phase-out: "The planned absences of church planters, protracted over time, so that national believers can immediately strengthen their spiritual roots and wings, as responsibility for the church shifts as quickly as possible to them from the church planters." Steffen claims this is something desperately needed in missions today.

Steffen is strong on the issue of letting the whole strategy be determined by phase-out perspectives. So does Brock, claiming that our strategies must be reproducible in all aspects.[36]

We will now focus on the aspects of Steffens model that deal most directly with the empowerment and succession of leadership. As we see from this

---

Indigeneity (Pasadena, CA: William Carey Library, 1979). Paul Hiebert: *Antropological Insights for Missionaries* (Grand Rapids, Mich.: Baker Book House 1985). Line Marie Onsrud: *History and Contextualization. A study of Church History and Cultural Identity in East African Pentecostal Churches as Narrated by Former and Present Leaders of the Church* (an unpublished masters thesis at MF Norwegian School of Theology. Oslo. 1998).

[34] Brock 1980

[35] Hesselgrave.1980, 396.

[36] Charles Brock: *The Principles and Practice of Indigenous Church Planting* (Manilla: Baptist Center, 1980).

model, the goal is responsible phase-out. To facilitate this, church planters must be prepared for a series of changing roles that will propel national leaders into ministry roles.

The first role, "Learner", begins in pre-entry stage and continues through phase-out. A church planter must always keep a learning posture. In the pre-evangelism stage, the church planters take on the role of "evangelists" by living out their faith in daily life. As they move into the evangelism stage, the church planters must adapt their role in evangelism from doing to modeling to releasing national Christians. The modeling takes place in the post-evangelism stage. As the church planters become more successful in modeling evangelism to nationals they begin to take on teaching roles, initiating the post-evangelism ministry. Also this role should aim at empowering the nationals to do the direct ministry through a process of doing, modeling and releasing. As the nationals gain experience in teaching a life changing, culturally relevant curriculum, presenting an accurate Gospel, the church planter moves into the role of "resident advisor". This is one of the most difficult roles a church planter can go through. The goal of this role is to allow the local Christians to win or lose the game on the basis of their own efforts, without entering the game to save it for them. It is a hard thing emotionally to release the ministry in such a way. Nevertheless, the church planters must never do for the national believers what they can do for themselves. This is the crucial point. Steffen claims this point is where most church planting fails, and responsible phase-out is delayed. Church planters must be willing to die to self-serving ambitions so that national believers can live up to their full potential. This requires a certain type of individuals and preparations. Phase-out strategy must therefore also determine recruitment and training of the church planters.

During the time as resident advisor, the local leaders take the lead. The effective 'resident advisors' will now begin programmed absences, becoming 'itinerant advisors.' They will be there and help them out, but more and more they must learn to trust the Holy Spirit to guide them. The final role is the "absent advisor." The church planters have worked their way out of a job, but not out of a relationship. Through letters, visits etc. relationships will continue and advice may be received. According to the role changes the church planters passes through, the role of responsive nationals will also change, from 'companions', 'participants' to 'leaders' and 'trainers'.

Steffen says wise church planters concentrate their efforts on faithful national believers. He defines faithful believers as those who are "capable" (Ex 18:21), who seek to "obey everything I have commanded you" (Matt 28:20), and who are "qualified to teach others" (2 Tim 2:2). They possess character, commitment, a certain degree of competency to handle complex tasks, and a willingness to coordinate efforts. They advance through four levels to become effective church leaders/planters. Such a developmental model allows an advance from one level to the next within the national's own time frame. It also encourages drawing of strength and confidence from the Holy Spirit instead of the church planter who will soon move on to become an absent advisor. As the church planters move through the various roles they should continually look for corresponding changes on the part of their national counterparts. This model is designed for cross-cultural church planting in tribal settings, but its main principle can be applied in other settings as well.

The cases show that it is decisive for the future transition what sort of culture that is created in the early stages of an organization, during what Holmberg calls the primary institutionalization.[37] These organizational values and norms are hard to change later, and they guide 'how things are done' in the organization.

Steffen's strategic contribution is to emphasize the need for a perspective and attitude that would facilitate transition from the beginning. But would this reduce some of the commitment needed to start a work? It might, if the vision is to elevate oneself and build one's own empire, but if the vision and heart is bigger, it might not reduce commitment. This relates to our discussion on criteria for leadership selection.

Steffen's model requires a setting were there is a body overseeing the process of starting a new organization, from selecting the founders to taking care of the continued relations to the second generation leaders after the transition. Independent founders could find a lot of help in his model as well, as they seek to build an organization that could live on beyond them.

One model that emerges as a possible way of starting a new work is to have an executive body or board that is in charge. This is what DuBrin called *subsidized entrepreneurship.*[38] They would recruit and support entrepreneurial founders committed to a vision of a viable organization. As the founder builds the organization the executive board would develop sustainer type leaders, which manage to balance entrepreneurial and administrative capacities. Alternatively the executive board might develop and appoint several leaders to a leader team, to creating the balance needed to sustain a dynamic and viable organization. The executive board could ideally guide the timing and tempo of the leadership transition, optimizing organization and leadership factors.

Specific Elements in Transition That Should Be Considered In Most Situations

One such element is criteria for selection of successors. Rothwell underlines that criteria for selection of successors should be related to the assessment of the future needs of the organization. Drucker says leaders tend to select a

---

[37] Bengt Holmberg: *Paul and Power. The structure of authority in the Primitive Church as reflected in the Pauline Letters*. Coniectanea Biblica New Testament Series 11. (Lund: CWK Gleerup, 1978), 180.

[38] DuBrin, Andrew J.: *Foundations for Organizational behavior. An applied perspective* (Englewood Cliffs, N.J: Prentice Hall, Inc., 1984), 334.

'carbon copy' of themselves that seldom works, because the organization needs another leader emphasis. Flamholtz says: "This transition (from entrepreneurial to professionally managed firms) requires stepping back from the day to day activities of the enterprise and understanding that the skills and personality needed to establish a successful entrepreneurship are different from the skills needed to take the organization into its next stage of development."[39]

It is therefore important that the board is active in the selection and appointment of the new leader, avoiding the selectivity of the practicing leader. From this we see that the successor should be selected from among emerging leaders that are able to meet the future organizational leadership needs and requirements. At the same time, Christian organizations have a spiritual dimension, implying that ultimately it is God who selects and appoints. This 'call' can be perceived subjectively, but it should also be confirmed by other authorities.

The cases highlight the need for planning ahead and preparing the organization for the transition of leadership. Timing emerges as one of the primary specific elements of leadership transition. From the cases it seems that rearticulating the vision is an important part of the transition process. The organizations were born out of the founder's vision, and now there is a need for a more shared ownership of the vision for the second generation organization. Although the founding vision did create commitment and attracted people, it seems that it needs to be renewed and rearticulated by a new leadership for a new time. This process should include large sections of the organization's staff and members. Their input should be incorporated and considered. Such a bottom-up process facilitates ownership of the vision. Ownership of vision for the second generation constitutes both commitment and participation. The rearticulation of vision might also contribute to increasing the entrepreneurial emphasis in the organization. In short, a new shared vision provides the organization a continued reason to exist.

At the same time we should be aware that *goal replacement* can occur. Etzioni described this phenomenon as when the organization's original goal is made a means to ensure organizational survival.[40] This again points to the question of whether the organization should continue into the second generation at all, or whether it should release its resources, providing new emerging organizations with a flying start.

Restructuring the organization also seems to play a part in the transition

---

[39] Rothwell 1994, 183 Eric G. Flamholtz: *How to make a Transition from the Entrepreneurship to a Professionally Managed Firm* (San Francisco, CA: Jossey-Bass Publ., 1986). Peter Drucker: *Innovation and Entrepreneurship. Practice and Principles* (New York: Harper & Row, 1985), 188. Gilmore: *Making a leadership change* (San Fransisco, CA: Jossey-Publ., 1988), 39.

[40] Amitai Etzioni: *Moderne Organisasjoner* (Oslo: Forlaget Tanum Norli, 1978), 20.

process. A restructuring might contribute to the flexibility of the organization on a long term basis, contributing to broader participation and ownership. This is a central part in the process of depersonalizing the organization, as it shifts from a founder-dominated structure to a more democratic structure. According to Mintzberg, organizations often move from a simple to a more complex structure in the second generation.[41]

From the cases, we see the need for some form of ritual facilitating the transition. Even if the transition of leadership should be a gradual process, there comes a point in time when power has to be transferred in a tangible and definitive way. This can be done in symbolic, ritual ways. From the reports in the NT, Skjevesland says ordination is an element in the process of institutionalization that took place in the early Church.[42] The ordination or coronation ritual is a classical example of how power, or charisma, is extended or transferred to the next generation leaders, leaving no doubt as to who has the authority. In a tangible way the power has been transferred from the founder to the successor. At the same time rituals can also transform the persons holding power.

One function of such a ritual is that it might give the successor a basis for withstanding the founder's vacillation. We saw this as a major dysfunctional element in both cases. The founder should promote the successor, not step in and overrule what the successor has decided, thus undermining the present leadership. A form of ritual might help the founders process their feelings around shedding leadership and constitute their new positions. During such a *rite de passage*[43] the founders should be honored for their achievements, and given some emeritus positions. It is important that the founder sees an attractive alternative to holding on to the leadership, but the *rite de passage* must leave no doubt as to who's in charge.

A balance must be sought between honoring the founders and benefiting from their wisdom, and providing freedom for the successor and the second generation organization to pursue the vision for the new era. We have seen some specific elements of transition that probably would be relevant to address in most situations where a transition of leadership is in process.

Concluding comments

Transition of leadership in organizations can be conducted in a way that could balance the need for structure and flexibility, securing the long term dynamic

---

[41] Mintzberg 1983a,b, 1989

[42] Olav Skjevesland: "Ordinasjonen i Det nye testamente". P.O. Gullaksen et al. (ed.), 201.

[43] Van Gennep and Turner in T.H. Eriksen, *Små steder. Store spørsmål. Innføring i Sosialantropologi V Reform og embete* (Oslo: Universitetsforlaget, 1994).

viability of the organization.

The reflection on whether the organization should live on beyond the founder is preliminary and fundamental. There are many forces at work in organizations that lead to goal replacement and bureaucracy serving itself rather than the vision. Later this might counterwork the original vision. One radical conclusion from this is to simply let the organization die with the founder. In this article we assume that the organization will move on to the second generation.

In this article we have found indications that the factors contributing to a smooth transition of leadership also would contribute to the long term viability of a dynamic organization. Considering all the stilted organizations once started out as dynamic, relevant movements, this might be the most promising finding of this study. To expand and explore this relationship, longitudinal studies following these factors in several organizations over longer periods of time could be conducted.

PART THREE

LEADERSHIP AND TRAINING IN MISSION

(2) Theological Education and Formation

FORMATION FOR MINISTRY AND MISSION: REFLECTIONS ON VOCATIONAL SPIRITUALITY

Ole Christian M. Kvarme

Rt. Rev. Ole Christian M. Kvarme, Bishop, Church of Norway, Oslo, Norway

Recently a student of theology asked me the following question: "Does the church really care about my calling?" The question took me by surprise, and the immediate impulse was to answer: "Of course it does!" But I did not say that. Rather I expressed my surprise, we talked for a while, and the student told about struggling with God's calling, being drawn in different directions and missing a companion who would see what the student did not.

"Does the church really care about my calling?" The question has stayed with me and made me reflect on how we actually do this. The following reflections are dedicated to Knud Jørgensen as a colleague and friend. Knud Jørgensen has inspired many young and old to pursue a life in the ministry and mission of the Church of Jesus Christ. He has done so through a distinct leadership in preaching, writing and various ways of communication, and as a friend and companion. The last is not the least important for people considering God's calling in their lives.

Vocation and Profession

Not long ago a stage director said to a group of pastors in our country: "I can think of no other vocation which is more meaningful and exciting than being a pastor." Coming from a man of the theatre, we would expect him to point to the fact that religious faith and spirituality again have a place in popular interest. But he pointed in a different direction. Pastors always have to be involved with the real lives of people. They have to be at the cutting edge of God's presence and doing in the real lives of men and women, young and old.

The stage director also shared examples of pictures drawn of pastors in Norwegian literature, and he made the following point: Pastors described with sympathy are probably not those whom we would consider successful, but pastors struggling with their lives and calling. A point well taken; and it brought to my mind the wisdom of the great Pietist leader and theologian Johan Albrecht Bengel who said that the calling of a pastor is not to be successful, but faithful.

In dealing with the issue of God's calling to pastoral or missional ministry, I want to begin with the question indicated by the mentioned references: What are the vocational marks of the pastoral profession? A teacher or professor is not only concerned to convey certain amounts of knowledge, but understanding. A physician is not only concerned to cure a specific disease, but about the total health of a person. The task of a pastor is not only to perform religious rituals or convey religious knowledge, but to be concerned with the basic God-relationship – that people may know God in their lives in a personal relationship to Him. As Jesus says: "This is eternal life: that they may know you, the only true God, and Jesus Christ, whom you have sent" (John 17:3).

When the issue is ministry and mission, "vocational integrity" goes deeper than "professional integrity". "Vocation" may be synonymous with "profession", but carries at the same time a deeper connotation – the calling that lies behind the exercise of the profession. It involves the calling of God and the calling of the Church; it involves the God-relationship of the actual person prior to and in the midst of the exercise of the pastoral or missional profession. In my talks with ordinands I therefore often bring up the mentioned quote of Jesus and ask them what this has meant and means to them – to know the only true God and the one He has sent, Jesus Christ.

It is inevitable that the professional dimension – the exercise of the profession – has focus in theological education and training for ministry and mission in addition to the various theological disciplines. I believe now is a time to renew a distinct focus on the vocational dimension and the personal calling to ministry and mission, the involvement of the real life of the persons themselves being trained. It is time for vocational spirituality, to focus upon the personal formation for ministry and mission.

Holy Calling and the Priesthood of all Baptized

In our church the ordination liturgy ends with the statement by the bishop: "I hereby declare that you are a rightly called pastor (or: minister; Norwegian: prest) in our church, with the responsibility and authority which accompany your holy calling." It should be noted, however, that the expression "holy calling" in the NT is used about the general calling of God to all believers.

In addressing Timothy Paul encourages his friend to renew the gift of grace which was given to him when Paul laid his hands upon him. But then Paul goes on and points to the fundamental saving grace: "God saved us and called us with a holy calling, not in virtue of our works but in virtue of his own purpose and the grace which he gave us in Christ Jesus ages ago" (2 Tim 1,:9).

The words "calling" and "vocation" are semantically related. "Vocation" comes from "vox" – voice. God acts with His voice, through his words. With His voice He calls light and life, heaven and earth into being. Jesus Christ is the Word of God from eternity, and through Christ He addresses human beings and calls us "out of darkness into his wonderful light." Salvation implies vocation, and it is proper to speak of baptism as "the ordination of believers" – ordination to the priesthood of all believers: "You are a chosen people, a royal priesthood, a holy nation, a people belonging to God, that you may declare the praises of him who called you out of darkness into his wonderful light" (1 Pet 2:9).

Our ordination liturgy actually also starts with this basic dimension, that baptism is the starting point of a life in service and ministry: "In baptism we became members of the people of God, and we were all consecrated to be God's servants." The calling of God begins with His grace and salvation in Christ; it involves our daily lives and natural gifts and continues with the equipment of the special gifts of the Spirit. Baptism is a gift and at the same time a calling to follow Jesus and belonging to a people of servants, a people in mission – called and sent.

But is the fellowship in our parishes conducive to being attuned to the voice of God and his calling to us as community and as individuals to serve His Kingdom? With the strong emphasis upon baptism in our Lutheran churches, I propose that we need a renewed focus upon the calling of God to all baptized to a life in service – the priesthood of all baptized. Each and every Christian is called to follow Jesus in holy living in all contexts of their daily lives and in these contexts be part of the ministry and mission of the whole people of God.

The Inner Calling – the Voice of the Heart

It is in this context of the general calling to each and every Christian that the specific calling to pastoral and missional ministry also grows. But the ordinands have come a long way to the public affirmation of their calling in the ordination service, struggling with or at least clarifying their own inner calling. Their stories reflect a variety of roads that they have walked before applying for ordination.

Today our theological education and pastoral training provide space for the students to tell the stories of their faith and lives. In my conversation with ordinands some tell of a direct calling, a quiet, but powerful voice speaking to them in their prayer. Some tell that they had a desire to pursue a different profession, but that an inner voice has left them with no option but to seek the pastoral ministry. Others have had a natural interest in pastoral studies and appetite for worship, preaching and ecclesiastical ministry. Many tell about a pastor or an older person who have said to them: "May be you should study theology?" Or: "You will make a good pastor!" This variety of ways towards ordination is as it should be. God has a variety of ways addressing us and calling us – also to pastoral and missional service.

Two writers in the classical, Christian tradition have provided wise counsel in achieving clarity about the calling of God. The first one is St. John of the Cross. In one of his writings he speaks of our past and present experiences as the finger of God writing his presence into our lives. These experiences – and this writing – also provide direction for our lives in following Christ and serving His Kingdom. I have always found it meaningful to talk with ordinands and older pastors about their life's experiences as an eye-opener to discern the direction of their calling – not only in their choice of vocation or profession, but with regard to God's particular calling and road ahead for them.

In recent years the "Spiritual Excercises" of Ignatius of Loyola have become a source of renewal also in Protestant and Evangelical circles. In these exercises Ignatius provides wise counsel on how to deal with major choices in one's own life. One way is to describe for oneself the possibilities that lie ahead and consider what will be to God's greater glory. One should pray to God to move one's spirit and will, and in this process one should also use reason. Then one should make a decision and ask God to confirm this decision through trustful confidence.

Another way to come to clarity in making a major choice, according to Ignatius, is to focus upon the love to God that moves me. Then I should think of another person in the same situation and consider what advice I would give him or her with regard to what would be to God's greater glory. I could also reflect on my own situation on death-bed, as I am to appear before the throne of God, asking myself: What would I then have chosen as I look back? Which choice would I then regard to be to God's greater glory?

There are many ways to achieve clarity about the calling of God and in making the proper choice. The exercises proposed by Ignatius are certainly both practical and helpful. But clarity about God's calling is seldom achieved in "solitary confinement". Normally we need someone to talk to, not only head to head, but heart to heart: a teacher or a student pastor in the seminary, a close friend or companion, an older and more experienced Christian. In my personal conversations with young students and ordinands, I usually ask them if they have a spiritual director or a companion with whom they can regularly talk about their own lives and God's calling to them.

Our lives are not static. The ministry and mission of the Church are not static. The calling of God is not static, but dynamic. God is constantly at work in our lives and surroundings, and so is His Son (John 5:17). Are we attuned to His voice and calling as we pass the crossroads of choices in our lives – smaller and major crossroads determining the direction of our lives and ministries? The choices and the calling of God do not stop with ordination or consecration, but follow us throughout our lives – in our daily ministries and at those major crossroads when we may move on to another place or field of ministry.

The External Voice – the Calling of the Church

It is fundamental to our faith in Christ that we live in communion with Him and with one another in His Church. The one body is a key metaphor to Paul: "In Christ we who are many form one body, and each member belongs to all the others" (Rom 12:5; cf. also 1 Cor 12). This is a major concern when it comes to the identity and the exercise of the pastoral vocation, and the inner calling has to be confirmed by an external calling – the calling of the Church. In our ordination liturgy it is also stated: "God has given His Church the mandate to call people to the ministry of preaching and administering the sacraments." How then does the clarification of this external calling of the Church take place?

In the end it is the bishop who has the exclusive authority in our church to decide upon ordination of a person to the pastoral ministry and consecration of deacons, catechists and cantors. At the same time it is the Diocesan Council which appoints pastors, and regional councils in the Diocese which appoint the other categories, and appointment to an office is usually also the prerequisite for ordination or consecration. In both ordination and appointment process room is given to the personal story, to their calling and their experience as well as their expectations to the ministry. Clarifying the external calling of the Church is also a process, often overlapping with clarification of the inner calling of God.

When focusing upon the formal process to clarify the calling of the Church, one should not overlook the organic presence of the Church in the individuals′ own reflection upon their inner calling from God. When a pastor or an older Christian says to a young person: "You will make a good pastor!" this is also the voice of the Church, albeit preliminary. The same could be said when young and old are confronted with the church's need for pastors and missionaries, or when the calling of God is the topic of preaching and teaching. Theological education and training for the ministry should also be regarded as an ongoing dialogue between the inner calling and the calling of the Church.

But is such a dialogue actually taking place? The question from the student quoted at the beginning of this paper: "Does the church really care about my calling?" is just one example indicating that we still need to develop a culture and instruments in our church and parish life that provide companionship and counsel to young and old struggling with or reflecting on God's calling to them.

As mentioned above, the study of practical theology in our seminaries today provide space for the students to tell the story of their lives and faith. In our church theological students considering the ordained ministry are also invited to regular seminars with their bishops, and the bishops usually have three counselling conversation sessions with the individual students before the final conversation before ordination. This is a good start. Other churches have more comprehensive programs for companionship and counselling sessions, and we are in a learning process.

Ordination is the public confirmation of the calling of God and the Church, and the statement "rightly called pastor" should confer a spirit of freedom as well as responsibility and authority on the person now entering the pastoral vocation. But ordination is at the same time only the starting point of a life in ministry, and the road ahead may not always be strait. This is also a challenge to the Church that both calls and appoints. The calling of the Church does not stop with ordination; it follows the pastor, church workers and missionaries throughout their ministry. I believe we still have work to do to develop a culture and instruments that provide companionship and counsel as the ministries of these servants develop and they pass major crossroads in their lives.

Formation for Mission – Vocational Spirituality

How do we then in our church and in pastoral training develop a culture that takes care of and provides room for the calling of God? I believe we need a new consciousness about and emphasis upon the calling of God to all baptized to be part of the ministry and mission of the church – the priesthood of all baptized. In our folk-church setting this is not self-evident and need careful attention in preaching and teaching as well as in personal counselling with young and old. It is also a quite practical challenge, to give room for the natural talents and the spiritual gifts of the members in the life and ministry of the community. With regard to pastoral and missional ministries I believe we have to go one step further.

In his book *Working the Angles. The Shape of Pastoral Integrity* Eugene H. Peterson speaks of the three visible lines of pastoral work as preaching, teaching and administration. In a Lutheran context we probably would describe the visible lines somewhat differently. But more important are the angles that keep the lines together in a triangle and give the pastoral ministry its shape and integrity: prayer, Scripture and spiritual direction. The integrity of the pastoral vocation is rooted in attention to God in prayer, in listening to God in His Word, in attention to God in conversation with another person. This attention to God involves the totality of the pastoral ministry and the community, and it begins with attention to God in relation to the pastor's own life.

I refer to this pastoral triangle of Peterson, not because it is something new, but rather because it implies the recovery of something original – inherited from the classical tradition of the Church. It comes close to a classic statement of Martin Luther, that prayer, meditation and being tested are what makes a theologian: "Oratio, meditatio et tentatio faciunt theologicum." These are elements that will carry a pastor's ministry and keep it fresh, give it integrity in new surroundings and in the face of new challenges.

I believe these elements are basic in the formation for ministry and mission and in sustaining a healthy vocational spirituality, for persons considering the pastoral vocation as well as pastors in ministry:

- Disciplined prayer, immersing oneself in the Book of Psalms and the wealth of prayers from the Church's long tradition, as well personal prayer in conversation with our Lord and Father.
- Reading Scripture, not only with the eyes of historical-critical exegesis, but listening to His Word in meditation and contemplation.
- Seeking spiritual direction in the company of a friend, another

pastor or an experienced counsellor, for the sake of one's own life and in order to be equipped as spiritual director oneself.

"Does the church care about my calling?" I must admit that we are not good at this, but there are signs of a growing awareness on many levels. We still need to develop a pastoral culture which emphasizes prayer, Scripture and spiritual direction. This is not an easy task, but hard work, and it should not be left to each and every individual. It is a collective responsibility, and we have to detect and find ways to establish proper instruments for counselling and spiritual direction, for communal prayer life and meditative Bible-reading. It is my hope that we shall be able to answer the student's question with an affirmative "Yes!" and do so with confidence and credibility.

ARE YOU CALLED OR JUST PERSONALLY MOTIVATED?

Ingrid Eskilt

Assoc Prof Dr Ingrid Eskilt, Ansgar School of Theology and Mission, Kristiansand, Norway

Introduction

In one of the leading theological seminaries in Norway, a large wooden wall carving, titled: "Follow the call" was some years ago moved from the front wall to a less visible location. Is this relocation just accidental, or is it a symbolic expression of the position of the call in contemporary society as well as in Christian service at home and abroad? Is call still the main issue in recruiting for mission, or are personal preferences and subjective motivation and interests the only factors? When young people today are talking about commitment and call, they talk less about sacrifice and struggle and more about their own interests and gifts. Does this necessarily mean that the younger generations are less occupied with world mission and have a reduced willingness to pay the necessary costs of fulfilling the Great Commission? Do the self-realization and the self-expressive vocabulary necessarily mean a more egocentric attitude?

This is an article about recruitment for mission and historically this has primarily been a question of call. This chapter gives therefore a brief historical overview of the notion of call, and describes thereafter the so-called subjective turn in the Western culture. A main body gives an account of the findings of a research project about the changing perspectives on the understanding of the missionary call in the Mission Covenant Church of Norway (MCCN). Even if this is a fairly limited qualitative study, it indicates general trends or tendencies which confirm the subjective turn also in the area of missionary call and recruitment. On this background the article ends with a few reflections on the future of recruitment in mission.

A brief history of the status of calling

During the first decades of the 20th century, people in Norway were familiar with the concept of "call." It was an important part of the early modern industrial society where identity was found through volunteerism, in societies with members from different social strata who shared a common vision of commitment that created a deep new sense of "we." Christian and missionary organizations constituted a vital part of the volunteer or civil society.[1] The concept of call was used in secular society by artists and by people in caring vocations, such as teachers, nurses and medical doctors.

This was the heyday of the Norwegian missionary societies when the missionary vocation was well known and respected in the Norwegian society even outside the churches. Early in the 20th century the country had more cross cultural missionaries per capita than any other country in the world. The missionary call was the main motivational factor for going into a missionary vocation. "The missionary call has been the stuff of modern missions. There is little agreement on precisely what it is, but without it, overseas missions could never have taken hold."[2]

Today the number of European and Norwegian missionaries is decreasing[3], and the Western hegemony of world mission is largely taken over by people from the Eastern and Southern countries. World mission and the call to the divine vocation is not dead as a theme in Norwegian churches, but it has fallen on hard ground compared to the heyday of mission a century ago. The Lutheran vocational ethic is no longer a natural part of contemporary Norwegian culture and the concept of call is felt outdated in the secular Norwegian society and it seems to be a less popular theme also in Christian preaching and teaching.

A subjective turn

A cultural shift has taken place in Western societies from the 1970s to 1990s. The shift is linked to the pluralistic society and the freedom of choice. The change is given different names, but is well documented.[4] The shift is a "subjective turn" (Heelas and Woodhead 2005) from collective subjectivism to individualism (Lorentzen 2004), from materialism to post-materialism (Inglehart 1997) from modern to late modern conditions (Giddens, 1992) where

---

1 Lorentzen, Håkon, *Fellesskapets fundament: Sivilsamfunnet og individualismen* (Oslo: Pax, 2004)

2 Tucker, Ruth, *Guardians of the Great Commission: The story of women in modern mission* (Grand Rapids: Academic Books, 1988), 13.

3 Kjøde, Rolf and Darryl Krause. "Norsk råd for misjon og evangelisering: Misjonsstatistikk 2001, "*Norsk Tidsskift for misjon 57* (2003): 27-39.

4 Inglehart, Ronald, *Modernization and Postmodernization: Cultural, economic, and political change in 43 societies*(Princeton: Princeton University Press , 1997). Heelas, Paul and Linda Woodhead, with Benjamin Seel, Bronizlaw Szerszynski, Karin Tusting, *The spiritual revolusion: Why religion is giving way to spirituality* (Oxford: Blackwell, 2005)
Giddens, Anthony, *Modernity and self-identity*: *Self and society in late modern age* (Cambridge: Polity Press, 1992)

continuation, security and obedience are given way to the advantages of flexibility, self-realization, self-reflection and individual authenticity and anti-authority attitudes. There is a consensus among missiologists that a paradigm shift in mission is a part of the same shift.[5] Bosch calls the old paradigm: "Mission in the Wake of Enlightenment," and the new: "An emerging ecumenical missionary paradigm." The crises and bewilderment, which always accompany a paradigm shift, have been evident in world mission for some decades now. In most descriptions of the new paradigm in mission, the call is mostly out of the picture or at least not in focus.

As a part of the shift, there seems to be a fundamental change in the recruitment or motivation for entering into Christian vocations. The Finnish researcher Kati Niemela[6] looked into motivation for studying theology in Finland and her studies showed a shift away from spiritual towards a more secular vocation among applicants to studies in theology:[7] "something I feel good about doing, something which is in line with my abilities, a shift from obedience to a divine calling, towards an understanding of calling as self actualization or realization."[8]

British researchers Heelas and Woodhead confirm the extreme turn towards subjectivity as the most striking element of contemporary culture. It can be seen most evidently in what the researchers are calling "the ethic of subjectivity," which is shown through actions of self-expression and self-fulfilment, through expressions like: "what feels right," "following your heart," and "being true to yourself."

Norwegian researcher Håkon Lorentzen has studied the Norwegian civil society and confirms the same subjective turn. He names the shift "a transition from collective subjectivism to individualism": from the realization of the self in a community with others towards the realization of the self with solely personal goals.[9] His study has shown a deep variation between the oldest and youngest part of the population. The oldest are more organized on the basis of ideology; they are more closely linked to the organization and are more focused on membership. For many of the oldest participants, membership in an organization is part of their identity. The youngest, however, are generally less interested in voluntary work; they are more pragmatic and less ideologically

---

[5] Bosch, David, *Transforming Mission: Paradigm shifts in theology of missions* (Maryknoll, New York: Orbis, 1992).

[6] Niemela, Kati,"Calling or vocation? A shift from spiritual toward secular vocation among applicants to studies in theology and theological candidates in Finland", *Tidsskrift for kirke, religion og samfunn 14*(2001): 43-52.

[7] Ibid, 43.

[8] Ibid , 51.

[9] Lorentzen 2004, 62.

engaged.[10] British sociologist of religion, Grace Davie, sees in this trend a profound change in the social life in the Western/European world. As a part of that change, churches and all activities which require gatherings on a regular basis are experiencing decrease.[11] This will also include engagement in mission societies.

The subjective turn and authority

"The subjective turn" is most of all a question of authority, many will say a loss of religious authority, others a transfer of authority from institutions to individuals. Individuals have on most levels been granted a new freedom of choice. The individual acts as the ultimate authority concerning herself and her own life. Individual reflexivity is more a question of transference of authority than lack of authority, says Lisbeth Mikaelsson. In the religious arena individual experiences play an increasing role as a source of religious authority. The structural change of individualism, which deals with choices and authority, explains why the self has become the pivotal point in much of contemporary religion. Old and new traditions are chosen in accordance with the worth and relevance they have for the individual.[12]

Paradigm shift in missionary calling: A qualitative study

In the same way as Bosch talked about an old and a new paradigm in mission, so it is reasonable to talk about an old and a new paradigm of the missionary call. In 2005, Ingrid Eskilt completeted a qualitative study among missionaries in three different generations in the Mission Covenant Church of Norway (MCCN) on their changing perspectives on the missionary call.[13] (Veterans, retired missionaries; baby boomers: people between forty and sixty; generation X: people in their thirties.) In most ways her research confirmed the subjective turn which so far has been described. She found an old and a new paradigm, at the same time as she found continuity and discontinuity between the paradigms.

---

[10] Wollebæk, Dag, Per Selle, and Håkon Lorentzen: *Frivillig innsats. Sosial integrasjon, demokrati og økonomi* (Bergen: Fagbokforlaget, 2000), 249.

[11] Davie, Grace:"Religion in Europe in the 21st century", *Religion in late modernity. Essays in Honor of Pål Repstad*, eds Inger Furseth and Paul Leer-Salvesen (Trondheim: Tapir 2007), 40.

[12] Mikaelsson, Lisbeth , " Religionens individualisering og retradisjonalisering. En kommentar til Jan-Olav Henriksen". *Forankring eller frikopling? Kulturperspektiver på religiøst liv i dag,* eds. Tone Lund-Olsen and Pål Repstad (Kristiansand : Høyskoleforlaget. 2003), 35-41.

[13] Eskilt, Ingrid, *An analysis of changing perspectives on the understanding of the missionary call in the Mission Covenant Church of Norway, Ph.D. dissertation in intercultural studies* (Deerfield, Illinois: Trinity International University), 2005.

Continuity in perspectives across the generations

All generations had representatives who regarded themselves as called by God to different ministries. A so-called "mystical call" was not weaker in the youngest generation than in the oldest. All generations had representatives who had met the call as an encounter with external needs.

Changed perspectives

The time perspective on the call had changed.

There were still younger people with longer perspectives on their calls. The youngest generation seemed, however, more hesitant in using the wording "life long". They didn't know how life would develop, but so far as they could see today they had devoted themselves to a call which was for the rest of their lives. This life perspective which was distinctively pronounced by two of the eight of the youngest informants was living parallel with shorter life perspectives.

The calling could be more easily redefined. If the youngest for different reasons didn't return to the mission field it was not regarded as a deceit. Generation X considered their own country as a mission field. The calling could therefore more easily be realized everywhere in the world.

The attitude towards the mission organization has changed. This could be recognized in different ways:

All in Generation X said they did not regard it as problematic to work for other organizations than MCCN. The oldest, however, were much more linked to MCCN and had their identity and belonging linked to that connection. For the youngest, however, the organization mostly had an instrumental role to play in the realization of their personal calling.

For the oldest the organization was a bearer of the call. The organization therefore had a stronger mandate to define geographical places and forms of service. Missionaries in the oldest generation were often generalists, prepared to do all kinds of work they were asked to do. The younger were more conscious about their spiritual gifts and God-given talents. The youngest wanted more clearly defined job-descriptions before they left for the mission field. At the same time were also the youngest well aware that they went as servants and not primarily for their own self-fulfillment. The organization was among the youngest informants regarded as an employer and not as a stake-holder of identity and belonging. They were looking for mentors, not primarily in organizations but through closer net-works.

The oldest generation regarded the organization's acceptance of their missionary candidacy as their objective and external call. For the youngest generation the organization did not have the same position. Still there was a need for a confirmation of the subjective call, but it seemed to have been replaced, either in favor of a local church or closer networks of friends.

The needs and demands within MCCN were often the releasing factor of the missionary call in the oldest generations. Also today external needs were releasing missionary calls. These external needs were, however, conveyed trough all the modern mass media or own travel experiences. Most of the youngest missionaries had some missionary experience before they came to MCCN as candidates. Before their first encounter with the organization most of them already had a call or a clear awareness of where they wanted to serve or in what kind of service.

The objective call seems to have weakened.

For the oldest, the objective confirmation of their call was very important. Internal struggle before this confirmation was not uncommon. In this struggle Bible verses seemed to be of great importance. The youngest talked little about external confirmation, and their experiences of call were also seldom linked to specific Bible verses.

The understanding of obedience has changed.

For the oldest obedience to God was shown through obedience to external authorities, most likely to organizations and their rules and regulations. For the youngest the authority had moved inward and had become a question of authenticity: to be faithful to oneself, one's own God-given gifts and what the individual experienced as his/her calling. Typical utterances among the youngest were: "God said to my heart," "I followed my heart." Obedience to external authorities without internal subjective affirmation was regarded as a lack of genuineness.

From obedience to relationship

The oldest experienced the calling as an order. An order demanded obedience. The youngest experienced the calling, not as a demand, but as a request from a loving father who asked if the child was willing to go and where there was a freedom of choosing.

For the oldest the Great Commission was probably the most important motif for their missionary service. The youngest experienced their relationship to Christ as the most important motivation for their service. Saving sinners from being lost did not seem to be that important for their motivation as the possibility for all people to get into a close relationship with Christ. Close relationships to God and other people were important in a much stronger way for the youngest generation than the others.

The identity in the missionary role has changed.

The oldest had their identity in their missionary role. " Once a missionary, always a missionary" was their ideal. Even if they had worked only a few years in Africa, they would still, thirty years later, have their identity as African Missionaries. The youngest were strongly against this form of missionary identity. Life was for them very changeable and they had their identity in different roles dependent on where and with what they were working.

The missionary calling does not place people on pedestals any more.

The old missionary paradigm separated the missionaries from other Christians.

The youngest generation was strongly opposed to that attitude. They powerfully proclaimed that all Christians have a call. Serving in another culture did not place any person on a pedestal. A specific missionary call does not single out some Christians as more specific than others. All Christians are called to different ministries.

Changing spiritual contexts

All the Veterans had backgrounds from the spiritual awakenings which influenced Norway before and during The Second World War. They had clear dates for the experience of salvation. The Boomer generation had partly been in contact with the Jesus movement. Most of them were well acquainted with a preaching style which expected specific experiences for salvation as well as call to service.

The youngest came from a less homogeneous spiritual background. Only one had a clear date for his experience of salvation. Many had backgrounds from Youth with a Mission (YWAM). This organization has a clear teaching about all Christians' having a call and can expect daily divine guidance.

Changed discourse

There has been an evident generational change in how Christians talk about their Christian experiences, life and service. An archive study on the introductory letters sent from the MCCN pioneer missionaries (from 1900 to 1940) to their organization found descriptions which were strongly "spiritual." They described the missionary life as a sacrifice where they had to leave the good life behind in order to serve God. Often the call was described as something coming from outside demanding them to enter a service which they initially disliked and felt very incompetent to accomplish. They often had great battles with their call and were in need of strong experiences of confirmation in order to give in and obey. They often felt peace in the moment they surrendered all their self-life and said yes to what they experienced as the will of God.

Much of the same discourse was recognized also among the Veterans. They also said explicitly that they were supposed to write about their victories and not about difficulties in the service.

They did not talk about problems as single missionaries or as missionary couples. The only subject they clearly described as difficult was the separation from their children. The Boomer generation had a much more open attitude towards the difficult parts of the missionary life.

The open discourse was quite obvious for the youngest generation. The youngest were also much more open about their own interests for foreign cultures and exotic places. They didn't talk so much about sacrifices. On the contrary, they wanted to serve God in mission and believed they had something to contribute. This did not mean that the youngest were freed from battles related to the calling. The battles were not as often related to their own lack of qualifications as to fights against the fear of loneliness and of untimely death.

A turn towards self-realization?

The changed discourse can easily lead to such a conclusion, but it is not necessarily the fact. The awareness about own adequacy is greater, but still there is a clear consciousness about sacrifice in the service of God, they know there will always be a price to pay.

The call and the changing cultural categories

Religious experiences, like a missionary call, are interpreted in accordance to one's frames of reference. People are experiencing what they have cultural categories to experience, says Lisbeth Mikaelsson.[14] The contemporary Norwegian worldview is much more secular then the prevailing culture fifty years ago. The plausibility structure for the missionary role and the missionary call has decreased.

The Swedish religious psychologist Hjalmar Sunden says in his theory of social role-taking that a religious experience depends upon a good knowledge of the Holy Scriptures within a religious tradition, the status of the role taker is also important for understanding such an experience.[15] Secularization has reduced church-activities and biblical knowledge, weakened the preaching of call and minimized the status of the missionary. During such circumstances the experience of a call will probably decrease, but not necessarily disappear. The interpretation of the experience will, however, probably change in accordance with the changed reference frames.

A missionary traditionally identified herself as an actor in a cosmic drama, says Mikaelsson,[16] where the plot was clear: a spiritual warfare where people could be lost or saved and where the missionary was the co-worker with the living God. Perhaps the plot is less clear today than a generation ago, not only for secular people but even for church members and missionaries. At least it is more open for individual interpretations. The missionary call fitted well into a clear black/white description, which made reality simple and the roles clear. Today the new paradigm of mission is more complex also among Evangelicals.

The application forms to the MCCN schools and missionary service have

---

14 Mikaelsson, Lisbeth, *Kallets ekko: Studier i misjon og selvbiografi* (Kristiansand: Høyskoleforlaget, 2003), 235

15 Spilka, Bernhard, Ralph W.Hood Jr, Bruce Hunsberger and Richar Gorsuch, *The psychology of religion: an empirical approach* 3.ed. (New York: The Guilford Press, 2003), 255.

16 Ibid, 235

also changed. There is a reduced emphasis on call in the forms. It has partly been abandoned or replaced with "motivation". However, collaborational agencies and young missionary agencies, like YWAM which are profoundly influencing the younger generation, still focus on calling in their application forms.

Conclusions

There seems to be confusion about the notion of call. The old paradigm is broken and the concept has become multifaceted, but it is still in use, but with different focus in different contexts. Therefore, there is a need for a clarification when call is used in recruitment for mission. Motivation seems to be a word which has started to replace the call.

The headline of this article poses a question: Will recruitment for mission in the future be a question of divine call, or a question of the individual's preferences, and personal motivation? These are not necessarily contradictory questions. The sending ministry of the Church and the calling into such a vocation is constant.[17] The main motives for sending people into cross-cultural mission have been "profoundly influenced by the overall context in which Christians lived and worked", says David Bosch.[18] The same is the case with how the sending is carried out and in what way a person perceives and interprets her call to work in the sending ministry of the church. If the use of the notion call is diminished and the word sacrifice no longer is a part of the common recruitment vocabulary, it does not necessarily mean that the responsibility for the spreading of the good news is neglected among the coming generations. The rapid changes and the globalization of the world have a tremendous influence also on the recruitment to mission and the duration and content of the missionary work. The time of the lonesome Western pioneer missionary seems to be gone. The use of multicultural teams seems to increase. The local churches seem to play a much more important part in world mission in the future probably at the expense of the old mission agencies. The coming missionaries need to be flexible and have a great variety of backgrounds, culturally, personally, spiritually, professionally and educationally. They seem to need a closer network and spiritual leaders who can serve as mentors. Every generation needs to ponder the questions of being true disciples and followers of Christ in their generation and what the costs will be in order to be authentic followers in words and deeds.

---

[17] Berentsen, Jan-Martin, "Misjonstjenestens misjonale identitet og karakter", *Norsk Tidsskrift for Misjon 57*(2003): 221-234, 227.

[18] Bosch 1992, 349.

Theological Education and Mission

Vidar Leif Haanes

Prof Dr Vidar Leif Haanes, Rector, MF Norwegian School of Theology, Oslo, Norway

Introduction

When we are discussing theological education and mission, we often discuss on two different levels. On the first level we are concerned with mission studies or missiology as an academic discipline. This level belongs primarily to the period before the last paradigm shift in theology of mission, as explained by David J. Bosch.[1] In a modern, enlightenment setting, it was vital to place missiology among the academic disciplines, to deserve a position in the academic world. But after the transformation of theology and mission, as a result of the "emerging, ecumenical missionary paradigm" (Bosch), we discuss the place and role of missiology on another level. We are more concerned with missiological approaches to theology as such, and for theological education this has implications for the entire curriculum. We are further concerned with the formation of theological students, encouraging spiritual life and congregational engagement. Several theological institutions have taken these criticisms seriously. New courses in practical theology, pastoral psychology, cross-cultural studies, missiology, studies in leadership and spirituality and so on, have been added to an already over-stretched syllabus. The problem is that the timetable cannot take the strain, for hardly anything already in the curriculum is allowed to drop out. We may ask which elements are necessary for theological education to serve properly the Church's obligation to respond in obedience to the *missio Dei*.

Missiology as an academic discipline

In the 1950s Professor Olav G. Myklebust (1905-2001) at MF Norwegian School of Theology wrote his dissertation on "*The Study of Missions in Theological Education*" in two volumes, still an international standard

---

[1] David J. Bosch, *Transforming Mission: Paradigm Shifts in Theology of Mission* (Maryknoll, N.Y.: Orbis Books, 1991), 349-362.

reference work.[2] Myklebust, a graduate from MF, started his work as missionary at Umpumulo in Natal, Kwa-Zulu, and in 1933 he became the principal of the training institution there. Umpumulo is the first permanent Norwegian mission station in South Africa, founded by the famous Norwegian pioneer (and devout academician) Hans Paludan Smith Schreuder (1817-1882). Myklebust was an admirer of Schreuder, who had passed his theological examinations at the University with highest distinction, and later wrote readers, a grammar and a hymnbook in Zulu.[3]

In 1939 Myklebust was called to MF, to a chair in Church History with a special obligation to lecture in Mission Studies. Myklebust stressed the importance of scholarly study of the missionary enterprise, and he became the founder of Missiology as academic discipline in Norway, required in theological education. He was instrumental in founding the Egede Institute of Missionary Research (1946), and later in establishing the Nordic Institute for Missionary and Ecumenical Research (NIME). But Myklebust had a wide vision. In 1951 he published a proposal for "An International Institute of Scientific Missionary Research", but it took 20 years for the first part of that dream to materialize in the International Association of Mission Studies (IAMS). He had important positions in national and international organizations such as the International Missionary Council and the Commission of World Mission and Evangelism in the World Council of Churches. Myklebust encouraged others to do research and to write, to choose dissertation topics of missionary interest.[4]

Myklebust credits Schleiermacher for appending missiology to one of the four main disciplines, namely to practical theology.[5] But Schleiermacher did not really see mission as a task to be encouraged, rather an activity to be permitted: Mission as the propagation of the Christian faith is a task entrusted to the believers as church (gemeinschaftlich) in those countries which have connection with non-Christian countries and areas, especially through colonialism.[6] Missiology, or the Study of Mission, including Ecumenics, was

---

[2] Olav Guttorm Myklebust, *The study of missions in theological education: An historical inquiry into the place of world evangelisation in western protestant ministerial training with particular reference to Alexander Duff's chair of evangelistic theology. Vol 1, until 1910* (Oslo: Land og Kirke, 1955), *Vol 2, 1910-1950* (Oslo: Land og Kirke, 1957).

[3] O.G.Myklebust, "The Legacy of H.P.S.Schreuder", *International Bulletin of Missionary Research,* Vol. 8 Issue 2 (1984):70-75.

[4] Vidar L. Haanes, " The first Professor of Missiology in Norway: Professor O.G. Myklebust (1905-2001)", *Norsk Tidsskrift for Misjon* 59:4 (2005):239-246. Cf. Tormod Engelsviken, "Olav Guttorm Myklebust: 1905-2001", *Mission studies* 19:2 (2002):12-13.

[5] Myklebust 1955:85.

[6] Myklebust 1955:87.

nevertheless for the first time permitted a place in the theological curriculum.

As a theological faculty, established for the education of Lutheran clergy in the Church of Norway, MF is based on the German-Scandinavian model. Theological study came to mean the study of a number of discrete disciplines pertinent to the ministry, a theory of practice about those tasks. "Theology as personal quality continues as practical know-how, necessary to ministerial work. Theology as discipline continues as one specialized scholarly undertaking among others, as systematic theology."[7] The very definition of theology as a set of disciplines or knowledge resulting from there is tightly correlated with education needed by the professional leadership of the religious community. In the 1980s the heritage from Schleiermacher was heavily debated among scholars and educators in theology, especially the problems created by the conventional fourfold model of the theological curriculum. Edward Farley wrote that Schleiermacher's legacy had contributed to these problems: "The fourfold pattern is not now a genuine theologically based pattern, but a school-catalogue phenomenon, a way of organizing courses. Accordingly, it is more accurate to label the fourfold pattern catalogue-fields than disciplines."[8]

The first struggle for missiology was to be counted among the theological disciplines, and in the 1980s it was recognised as such at most theological schools and seminaries, as a subject in the theological curriculum in its own right. But after David J. Bosch wrote in his comprehensive work that a new paradigm for theology of mission was emerging, the discussion started again. Bosch was advocating "a pluriverse of Missiology in a universe of mission".[9] The questions raised by mission studies about the contextual nature of theology mean that missiology is party to the post-modern critique of theology, as Bosch tried to demonstrate. The modern era is not the last epoch of world history to exercise an influence on the thought and practice of mission. Modernity has now become the past, and is followed by the post-modern paradigm.[10] Though whether Bosch's paradigm is post-modern is questionable.[11] But the importance of this is the insight that missiology represents not the past but the future of theology.

---

[7] Edvard Farley, *Theologia. The Fragmentation and Unity of Theological Education* (Philadelphia: Fortress Press, 1983):39.

[8] Farley 1983, 141.

[9] Bosch 1991:8. Cf. G.M.Soares-Prabhu, "Missiology or Missiologies?", *Mission Studies*, no. 6, (1986):85-87.

[10] Bosch 1991:349ff.

[11] Kirsteen Kim, "Postmodern Mission: A Paradigm Shift in David Bosch's Theology of Mission?" *International Review of Mission* LXXXIX/353 (2000):172-179.

Missiology as the future of theology

Which came first, theology or mission? This is like the question on what comes first of the chicken or the egg. With a quotation of Martin Kähler, David J. Bosch stated that "mission is the mother of theology".[12] Martin Kähler (1835-1912) was a devout Lutheran, and Professor of Systematic Theology and New Testament Studies in Halle, Germany. He was much read and admired a hundred years ago by the first teachers at MF Norwegian School of Theology. What Kähler wrote (in German), was more like: "Mission in the old church became the mother of theology".[13] The New Testament is mostly written within a missionary context. Theology, according to Kähler, began as an accompanying manifestation of the Christian mission, and not as "ein Luxus der weltbeherrschenden Kirche" (a luxury of the world dominating church).

Mission is the mother of theology, and not the illegitimate daughter. But we must add that to be the mother of theology doesn't mean that the time for mission is over, but that true theology grows out of mission. Thus, mission is not primarily the precedent, but the future of theology. Mission is the future of theology because we are entering a future with many cultural similarities to the first centuries, which were primarily an epoch of mission.

Stephen Neill used to say that "if everything is mission then nothing is mission".[14] Even if not everything is mission, we may widen the understanding of mission to more than the act of sending missionaries to proclaim the Gospel. At least it is clear that the study of mission interfaces with a wide range of disciplines in theology, history, cultural studies and social sciences. With the words of Kirsteen Kim: "Theology of mission is therefore concerned with the relationship of truth and proclamation, gospel and society, salvation and history, Christian witness and other faiths, scripture and culture, church and kingdom, Word and world, revelation and theologies."[15]

When it comes to theological education, we may ask whether we should take the next step, and let a missiological understanding permeate all theological disciplines and be a premise for all theological thinking. "Missiology contends against all theological provincialism, advocating an intercultural perspective in theology", said the Puerto Rican missiologist and contextual theologian

---

[12] Bosch 1991:16.

[13] „Die älteste Mission wurde zur Mutter der Theologie", Martin Kähler, „Die Mission – ist sie ein unentbehrlicher Zug am Christentum?" In: *Schriften zu Christologie und Mission*, Herausgegeben von Heinzgünter Frohnes, Theologische Bücherei Bd. 42 (München: Chr. Kaiser Verlag 1971), 190.

[14] Stephen Neill, *Creative Tension* (London: Edinburgh House Press, 1959), 81.

[15] Kirsteen Kim, "Mission Studies in Britain and Ireland: Introduction to a World-Wide Web", *British Journal of Theological Education* Vol. 11.1 (2000):76.

Orlando Enrique Costas (1942-1987).[16] And he goes on:

> Missiology questions all theological discourse that does not seriously consider the missionary streams of the Christian faith; all biblical interpretation that ignores the missionary motives that shape biblical faith; all history of Christianity that omits the expansion of Christianity across cultural, social, and religious frontiers; and all pastoral theology that does not take seriously the mandate to communicate the Gospel fully and to the heart of the concrete situations of daily life. By fulfilling such a critical task, missiology also enriches theology because it puts theology in contact with the worldwide Church with all its cultural and theological diversity.

In a keynote address at the Faith and Learning Institute on the Internationalization of Curriculum in Christian Higher Education, Costas critiqued the provincialism of the Christian worldview of the schools and called for the willingness to "cross intercultural, interethnic and interracial boundaries."[17] In the same address, he set forth three goals for theological education. The first was to equip the student for reaching out to persons who have no appreciation or knowledge of the Christian faith. Next was the spiritual formation of women and men in ministry for the praxis of mission in the world. Lastly, in response to the fragmentation of the Christian church along racial, class and denominational lines, seminaries should prepare persons to promote Christian unity and human solidarity. This is to begin by becoming sensitive to the people who live among us from different ethnic and cultural groups. For this crossing of boundaries to take place students, faculties and trustees are to be involved in learning experiences that expose them to perspectives other than their own. According to Costas, theological education is about discipleship, and theological and spiritual formation. In addition Costas helped especially Hispanic Evangelicals to open up for a new understanding and doing theology from the perspective of marginalized people.[18] Education was political for him. It was about the work of evangelization as well as social justice. He mobilized different denominations to respond to the needs of theological education of minority groups. The worldview of much of the emerging younger churches is much closer to that of the New Testament than is true of Western culture. These Christians read the Bible as a book that connects with amazing and revolutionary relevance to their own worldview and experience. These

---

[16] Orlando E. Costas, "Theological Education and Mission" in C. René Padilla (Ed.), *New Alternatives in Theological Education* (Oxford: Regnum Books, 1988), 15.

[17] Orlando E. Costas, "Internationalizing the curriculum in Christian higher education" in Robert A, Hess (Ed.), *Internationalizing the curriculum* (St. Paul, Minnesota: The Christian College Consortium, 1986), 11.

[18] Cf. Samuel Escobar, "The legacy of Orlando Costas". *International Bulletin of Missionary Research*, 25 (2001):50-56.

churches are vigorously missionary; they have not been intimidated by the relativism and critique of missions that permeate much of Western culture today. This was formulated in the Manila Manifesto (Lausanne II) in 1989: "For the great new fact of our era is the internationalization of missions. Not only is a large majority of evangelical Christians now non-western, but the number of Two-Thirds World missionaries will soon exceed those from the West.[19] On this background Kirsteen Kim concludes her article on Mission Studies in Britain and Ireland: "The study of mission is an introduction to a world-wide web. It is a subject which crosses theological and academic boundaries in its reflection on the mission of God to the world expressed in the living Word and the life-giving Spirit."[20] With the words of James A. Scherer, mission theology should assist with the task of creating a fresh vocabulary for missionary function in the new missionary era, taking into account that mission is the task of the church in all six continents.[21]

Missiology and Church

Mission may be the mother of theology, but not the mother of the theologian. Mission puts the theologian in close contact with his/her mother: the church. Missiology is a discipline that studies the expansion of the church, and missiology addresses the crossing of barriers with the gospel of Jesus Christ. Its concern about crossing boundaries is now becoming a central concern in theology as a whole. Theological education is about the facilitation of learning and obedience to this missiological concern. "A theology of theological education must be grounded in *missio Dei* and in a proper understanding of the church (this faith community), her purpose and mission in the world." This is a statement from an "Issue Group" within the Lausanne Movement, working with "Effective Theological Education for World Evangelization" (Pattaya 2004). [22] The statement is probably representative for evangelical seminaries and colleges today. In Norway "missio Dei" and "missional" are rather new concepts in the theological vocabulary. As we often use the words missionary and mission to express the sending of the church, we are in danger of understanding this as an activity only. Mission has been understood as an activity for missionaries and for especially "mission-minded" people in the

[19] J.D.Douglas (Ed.), *Proclaim Christ Until He Comes* (Minneapolis: World Wide Publications, 1989), 34.

[20] Kim 2000:81

[21] James A. Scherer, *Gospel, Church, Kingdom. Comparative Studies in World Mission Theology* (Minneapolis: Augsburg Publishing House, 1987), 245.

[22] Lausanne Occasional Paper No. 57, *Effective Theological Education for World Evangelization*. Produced by the Issue Group on this topic at the 2004 Forum for World Evangelization hosted by the Lausanne Committee for World Evangelization In Pattaya, Thailand, September 29 to October 5, 2004, 17.

congregations, and not as an indispensable part of being church. Again we can turn to Martin Kähler: "If you first recognize the insoluble connection between church and mission", Kähler wrote a hundred years ago, "the relation between mission and theology follows".[23] Kähler was addressing equally theologians sceptical about mission and "Missionsfreunde" sceptical about theology. A theology of mission is an important factor in overcoming the limitations in a local, culture-bounded ecclesiology. As Knud Jørgensen has stated, we have to develop a missional ecclesiology, as the church inherently is a missionary church, as the people of God in the world.[24] What are the issues at stake for theological education to recover a focus on the church? It is to participate fully in the Son's redemptive work as the Spirit creates, leads, and teaches the church to live as the distinctive people of God.[25] Moltmann's connection of *ekklesia* and mission becomes another aspect of locating theological education in mission: "Today one of the strongest impulses towards the renewal of the theological concept of the church comes from the theology of mission".[26] We may ask whether contemporary theological education is properly focused on the real needs of local churches and mission agencies as leaders are being trained for church and mission work. It is no doubt that praxis-based theological education conduces to ministry and mission.

Mission and educational practice

Andrew J. Kirk wrote a paper in 2005, showing an alternative way of looking at theological education, trying to provoke serious critical reflection and hoping to encourage "a rethinking of the content and methods of educational practice, in the light of God's missionary activity and purposes for his people".[27] Kirk tries to re-envisage a process of theological education, which deliberately attempts to respond to the claim that proper theology, and therefore theological education, is through and through missionary in character.[28] According to Kirk, there is an apparently wide gap between his own, missiologically informed

---

[23] Kähler 1971:184, 189.

[24] Knud Jørgensen, "Trenger kirken omvendelse? På vei mot en missional ekklesiologi?" (Is the Church in need of conversion? Towards a missional ecclesiology.) URL: http://intercultural.dk/icms/filer/kj-omvendelse-art.pdf

[25] Craig Van Gelder, *Confident Witness – Changing World. Rediscovering the Gospel in North America* (W.Eerdmans Publ.: Grand Rapids, 1999), 31.

[26] J. Moltmann, *The Experiment Hope* (London: SCM Press 1975), 7.

[27] J. Andrew Kirk, "Re-envisioning the Theological Curriculum as if the Missio Dei Mattered", *Common Ground Journal* v3 n1 (Fall 2005):23. URL: www.commongroundjournal.org.] Cf. J. Andrew Kirk, *The Mission of Theology and Theology as Mission* (Valley Forge: Trinity Press International, 1997).

[28] Kirk 2005:40.

programme and the more traditional, university-based style of education. He then admits that the real distinction is between a genuinely theological programme of education and one which has as its presupposition the study of religion. Whether called theology or not, what happens in most universities is the latter rather than the former. Many theological education programmes fail, precisely because they are trying to combine two quite distinct aims and methodologies, Kirk concludes.

I understand Andrew Kirk to say that the main problem is the aim and methodology of Religious Studies, not being able to focus on the uniqueness of Christ and Christian theology, and not necessarily the academic tradition of theology as such. In their interest in being relevant to the needs of the secular culture around them, some theological colleges are in danger of making the Gospel irrelevant. On the other hand, that may also happen if we are neglecting the culture we are rooted in. One has to run the risk of being put to question, to test one's own inherited set of values and ideas. Even for theological students, may be especially for them, this is a necessary part of their formation. In the paper by the Lausanne Issue Group already mentioned we find the same critique against theological institutions as in the essay of Andrew Kirk.[29] Theological colleges and schools are said to imbibe secular values on the one hand, and on the other hand there is a tendency for them to be isolated from the realities of the world around them. It is true that theological faculties in many European universities have suffered from fear of not being relevant for the academic audience, which has resulted in a liberal theology, usually not relevant for the church. But the opposite is also possible, that theological schools and colleges leaving the university sphere or academic level are in danger of being irrelevant for both society and church. Isabelle Stengers, a 'non-Christian' philosopher belonging to a tradition marked by relations between philosophy and theology, regrets that theology no longer figures as an argumentative or creative force opposing the exclusive authority of the sciences, or assisting them in guarding against the arrogance and stupidity to which their present-day lack of fearless, imaginative interlocutors makes them prone.[30]

An important part of the European cultural heritage is to recognize various kinds of knowledge. Scientific reason alone cannot provide life with values or directions. We need wisdom and insight as well, as Karl Jaspers said: "There is a form of thought which requires our personal commitment in order to achieve the status of truth".[31] Education and research must aim for formation of the whole person, education in the broad sense of the term, not only the

---

[29] Lausanne Occasional Paper no. 57, 10.

[30] I. Stengers, "Science and Religion. Beyond complementarity", In: Nils H. Gregersen and U. Görman, *Design and Disorder. Perspectives from Science and Theology* (London: T & T Clark, 2002), 120.

[31] Karl Jaspers, *The Idea of the University* (Boston: Beacon Press 1959), 12.

transmission of facts and skills. The aim of theological education is not only to transmit Christian beliefs, but also to foster the characteristic values, attitudes and dispositions of the Christian life. As such, it is also concerned with spiritual formation. Growing in the knowledge of God and in his purposes for his world is the ultimate purpose of all theological education. Consequently, a missional approach to theological education is vital.[32]

MF, Mission and Theological Education

In the following I will use my own institution, MF Norwegian School of Theology as a lens for examining the connection between theological education and mission.[33] MF has a special place in the history of theological education in Europe, as a private, evangelical school having defended the position as the leading theological faculty in Norway since the 1930s. A majority of the ministers and all the present bishops in the Church of Norway are graduates from MF, as well as a majority of Norwegian mission leaders, and many missionaries and Free Church pastors. Dr. Knud Jørgensen has been connected with MF for many years, as lecturer, board member, and at present one of the trustees.

MF is not a seminary, and never has been. While the Catholic Church after the Council of Trent renewed the seminary, and placed the education and formation of priests within the control of the Church, the Lutheran Churches in Germany and Scandinavia placed the education of the clergy in the universities. When MF Norwegian School of Theology was established in 1907, one had no choice but to follow the same curriculum as in the Faculty of Theology at the University of Oslo. This continued more or less until the 1950s. Until recently, the difference in curriculum between the two faculties has been marginal. The difference between the two was more a matter of theological and spiritual formation. At MF the students learned theology from teachers, who in a special way focused on vocation, congregational work and mission. MF did not receive any financial support from the state until the 1970s, so students and faculty members were travelling all around Norway to preach, sing and collect financial and spiritual support. The late history of the Student Volunteer Movement and the early history of International Fellowship of Evangelical Students are in many ways connected with MF. The Norwegian IVF-movement (NKSS) was started in 1924, by Professor Ole Hallesby, for theological students at MF as an evangelical alternative to SCM. The Norwegian Student Volunteer Movement (AFMF) joined the new evangelical group in 1926. Robert Wilder and John R. Mott started the Student Volunteer Movement in 1888, with the watchword: "The Evangelization of the World in this Generation". Wilder resigned in 1927 as general secretary of his own

[32] Lausanne Occasional Paper no. 57, 46.

[33] http://www.mf.no

organisation, as the watchword faded. In 1934 he wrote to the British IVF, urging them to adhere to the basic essentials of the evangelical faith, and the missionary obligations of the Christian. IVF then formed their own Missionary Fellowship for intending missionaries. Robert Wilder arranged a meeting between the British students and two Norwegian graduates, his wife's niece and her future husband: Carl Fredrik Wisløff, secretary in the Norwegian IVF since 1932. The result of this meeting was an international conference for evangelical student leaders, held in Oslo 1934. Professor Ole Hallesby was giving an address on "The Hour of God", talking about the evangelical student movements, suddenly and spontaneously springing up in so many countries at the same time. "For many years a rationalistic theology has held most of our churches. On Christian work amongst students this theology has also laid its clammy hand... Today we are here, representatives of many nations... we can each tell of a Christian student work based on the Bible as the Word of God."[34] After the War, in August 1947, The International Fellowship of Evangelical Students (IFES) came into being.[35] The founding members were Australia, Britain, Canada, China, France, Holland, New Zealand, Norway, Switzerland and the USA. Martin Lloyd-Jones was the new chairman, Stacey Woods general secretary and Prof. Ole Hallesby was appointed president of the IFES (1947-1954). The same year Carl Fr. Wisløff became principal of the Practical Theological Seminar at MF, a position he held until 1962, when he was appointed Professor of Church History (until 1975). Wisløff was IFES chairman 1959-1967, and then president 1967-1977. The Professors Ole Hallesby, Olav G. Myklebust and Carl Fr. Wisløff had substantial influence on the theological students at MF. But you wouldn't find traces of this in the curriculum, except for some small courses in Mission Studies. The formation of the students belonged to what we today call "the hidden curriculum".

Today MF has full accreditation as a specialized university, with two PhD-programs, several master's and bachelor's programs. The national, and therefore international (because of the Bologna process) accreditation has been very important, as MF now is treated as an equal member of the *Norwegian Association of Higher Education Institutions* and *Nordic University Association* (NUS). This gives MF freedom to establish degrees, programs and courses, and therefore an opportunity to meet the demands for a renewal of theological education in light of the paradigm shift.

Many evangelicals working with theological education are ambivalent to academic accreditation. Accreditation is seen as a problem for the missiological perspective in theological education, and a hindrance to changes in the areas of contextual and inductive learning. Several examples can be found in Bernhard Ott's monograph on mission studies in evangelical theological education in

---

[34] Pete Lowman, *The Day of His Power* (Leicester: Inter-Varsity Press, 1983), 66-68.

[35] Lowman 1983:79.

Germany and German-speaking Switzerland, especially the schools in membership with the Konferenz Bibeltreuer Ausbildungsstätten (KBA).[36] He gives a detailed examination of the paradigm shifts which have taken place in recent years in both the theology of mission and the understanding of theological education. According to Ott, their requirements for certification or accreditation do not match the educational aspirations and aims of the institution. They are in conflict because the accrediting agency is working with a different set of parameters and a different definition of what makes an educating institution effective. These schools are theologically conservative, and resist the challenge of Bosch's mission paradigm shift in the areas of contextual and inductive learning, mostly because of disagreement in hermeneutics. Ott's thesis is that the evangelical Bible school movement, which historically has embodied many of the features of this new paradigm, nevertheless has jeopardized these by their pursuit of academic accreditation. The result, says Ott, is a continuation of the same downward spiral towards mediocrity and irrelevance.

I have no reason for arguing with Ott's thesis, but I wonder why the accreditation agencies would turn their thumbs down for the reason of adjusting to a contextual and inductive learning process. Recently, OECD's Directorate for Education visited Norway for a review of tertiary education, also commenting on the private theological schools, like MF Norwegian School of Theology and the smaller School of Mission and Theology in Stavanger. The review mentions that students who attend private institutions benefit, under the same conditions, from the same basic financial support as in State institutions to cover costs of living. They also have access to extra loans to help them cover their tuition fees. The OECD-group especially gives positive attention to this, as it clearly facilitates students' *freedom of choice* and enables the development of institutions with *distinct approaches and purposes*.[37]

In Norway, the governmental Quality Reform in Higher Education led to a reform of the theological education. The higher degree of theology (cand.theol.), which is obligatory for ministers in the Church of Norway, was a 7 year degree, the last year containing practical theology and praxis. Practical theology (homiletics, pastoral counselling etc.) has traditionally been placed after biblical and historical studies and systematic theology, as we are disposed to think in linear terms.

Because of the Bologna-process, working towards a European Higher Education Area, Norway adopted the 3+2+3 year degree structure (bachelor,

---

[36] Cf. Bernhard Ott, *Beyond Fragmentation: Integrating Mission and Theological Education. A Critical Assessment of some Recent Developments in Evangelical Theological Education* (Oxford: Regnum Books, 2002).

[37] Organisation for Economic Co-operation and Development (OECD): Directorate for Education; Education and Training Policy Division, *Thematic Review Of Tertiary Education, Norway, Country Note* (September 2006).

master, PhD). But at the same time the reform put much emphasis on "Professional Studies", with the result that the education of ministers, medical doctors and psychologists were allowed a 6 year degree, including one year of integrated praxis. We keep the structure from the Schleiermacher model, with emphasis on the four main disciplines, including Biblical studies built on obligatory courses in Greek and Hebrew. But the applied and practical theology, including periods of praxis, is put as several integrated courses in the curriculum, the first rather early.

In addition the students will take several inter-disciplinary courses, some obligatory and some elective. Among the 20 inter-disciplinary courses offered are "The Meaning of the Death and Resurrection of Christ", "Let Your Kingdom Come", "The Work of The Holy Spirit in Acts and in Today's Mission", Ecclesiology and Spirituality", "Missiology and History of Missions".[38] MF also offers inter-disciplinary bachelor-programs in "Youth, Culture, Faith" and courses in "Youth, Church and Mission" or "Cross-Cultural Communication", including praxis or "field-studies". It is necessary for theological education to be characterized by *praxis* rather than by persisting polarities such as theory and practice. The theological education has to prepare the student for the realities of Christian ministry, and thus be in communication with the local churches. According to Robert Banks for theological education to be missional, means that it is wholly or partly field-based, and that involves some measure of doing what is being studied (life-engaging). It requires observant participation and not merely participant observation. Only by maintaining its close link with mission will it remain relevant to changing circumstances, and hold true to the missionary impulse that gave rise to the church and theology.[39]

The theological students at MF Norwegian School of Theology will have several periods working in a congregation, in a hospital, prison or another institution, to put their skills, attitudes and understandings to work in real-life settings. During this praxis, they will have the opportunity for theological reflection upon these experiences, guided by a teacher. The most effective experiential learning takes place when an appropriate level of oversight and support is offered and the experience is reasonably similar to the context in which the student is expected to eventually put their new learning into practice. A teaching approach that has become important in many professional studies, and also at MF, is Problem-Based Learning (PBL). It is an approach designed to connect theory with real life experiences, to encourage dialogue between reality and theory about it. PBL is a helpful way to overcome the fragmentation of disciplines in curriculum. Often the specialization of teachers to narrow

---

[38] http://www.mf.no/

[39] Robert Banks, *Reenvisioning Theological Education: Exploring a Missional Alternative to Current Models* (Grand Rapids: William B. Eerdmans, 1999), 131-132.

subject areas creates obstacles to learning which could be overcome by a closer connection with the church and society and by finding and verbalizing central problems for PBL exercises. In the course of the development of this fresh way of doing theology, a number of traditional truisms have been challenged. Missiology is still a distinct discipline at MF, but also more than one section of the theological curriculum. During the annual "mission week", the lecturers in all the disciplines are encouraged to focus especially on the mission perspectives. In addition there is a various programme for the students, with seminars and discussion panels. Mission agencies are invited to MF, for exhibition and information, inspiration and focus on their special mission field.

European universities have been a model for unity in diversity and diversity in unity.[40] There is not *one* uniform culture in Europe, but different cultures and different religious traditions, be it Christian, Islamic or Jewish. In Oslo, having once a homogeneous, Lutheran population, there is now a strong Muslim population, but in addition we find as much as 100 immigrant churches of all denominations. Only twenty years ago, mission studies were about foreign mission, especially Western mission in other continents. Today, missiology's concern about crossing boundaries is becoming an ever more central concern in theological education for those going to serve as pastors in Norwegian congregations.

MF started as a confessional, Lutheran school, but is today an ecumenical school with a Lutheran platform. The Church of Norway is still the most important stakeholder. But MF also educates pastors for the Methodist Church, Pentecostal Churches, as well as priests for the Catholic Church. We have a few faculty-members belonging to the same churches. Some of our Lutheran students now follow courses in spiritual leadership designed for Pentecostal ministry, and Pentecostal students may follow courses in Catholic Pneumatology and initiation. Many of these "cross-denominational" courses are fitting the concept of ecumenical Missiology, or "Mission as Theology" described by Bosch.[41] Hopefully the students now preparing for ministry will be able to cooperate and communicate when they one day become leaders of various churches and religious institutions.

Finally, some words about lay people. In this essay, on theological education and mission, focus has been on the education of pastors or ministers. But theological education of lay people is vital for renewal of the church in mission. The "Mission Issues and Strategy Advisory Group II of the Anglican Consultative Council", stated some years ago that "the effectiveness in mission depends upon the whole people of God being adequately equipped and trained

---

[40] Vidar L. Haanes, "Unity in Diversity and Diversity in Unity: The Role and Legitimacy of the European Universities", *Higher Education in Europe* 31:4 (2006):443-448.

[41] Bosch 1991:489-498.

for the task whatever their sphere of involvement."[42] Theological education of lay people is of fundamental importance for the process of equipping the people of God for their mission and ministry, communicating the Gospel in the 21st Century. But this is the topic for another essay.

[42] *Towards Dynamic Mission renewing the Church for mission.* Final Report of Mission Issues and Strategy Advisory Group II (MISAG-II) of the Anglican Consultative Council (London, 1992), part VI.

TEACHING MISSIOLOGY IN A SECULAR UNIVERSITY

Viggo Mortensen

Prof Dr Viggo Mortensen, Theological Faculty, University of Aarhus, Denmark

> The situation for missiology as an academic discipline [is] insecure and struggling, but [I am] convinced that although it might be placed at the margins, it plays a central role within culture and theology; and maybe it is after all the right place to start, from the margins.[1]

This was the conclusion I had to draw in 2001 after a survey of the Nordic attempts to conduct missiological and ecumenical studies. Knud Jørgensen has always had a keen interest in academic studies and missiological training both in East and West. That is why my contribution to his Festschrift is an updated attempt to reflect on how it is possible today to pursue academic studies and teaching in missiology outside the confined walls of the churches and their institutions. In this respect I draw on my experience in teaching missiology within a secular university. Because of the historical development this is still a possibility in the Nordic countries, where we still have theological faculties within state supported secular universities.

But as is well known: the universities are changing dramatically in these years, adapting to a globalised market for academic research and teaching. In this contribution, I am going to analyse how that might influence the discipline of missiology.

Missiology in the Nordic countries

In regular intervals those of us involved in the study of missiology in the Nordic countries as organised in the Nordic Institute for Missiological and Ecumenical Research (NIME) try to take stock and evaluate where the development is leading us. So again in 2006 a survey of the status of missiology and ecumenics in the Nordic countries was carried out.[2] It is

---

[1] From a paper given at the Annual Meeting of NIME, Uppsala 2001. Printed in *Swedish Missiological Themes (2001) 89/4:*439-453 with the title: Nordic Missiology and Ecumenics.

[2] *Swedish Missiological Themes 2006/4.* Special Issue on Nordic Mission Studies.

fascinating to observe how the picture changes and it becomes obvious that people matter; it becomes clear how much the concrete people that inhabit the chairs in missiology mean for the development. That the Swedish chairs of missiology in Lund and Uppsala are secured through outside funding and in 2006 got new incumbents makes it possible to evaluate the future of the discipline in Sweden as rather stabile; other places it might be more precarious.

Tormod Engelsviken points to the fact that "mission studies in the more traditional sense are threatened in the universities in Europe and are often replaced by religious or global studies."

Engelsviken does not want to denigrate those studies, but he states that "there is a need to uphold missiology proper as an academic discipline" and he expresses the hope that "new challenges for research and teaching in the area of religion and religious encounter in the contemporary world may go along with an approach to mission studies that are both relevant for the present global situation and faithful to the church's missionary obligation." (SMT 2006/4:466f.)

Notto R. Thelle, outgoing professor at the University of Oslo, foresaw early that the discipline of missiology hardly would survive because it was so much related to a certain historical phase and its theological culture – the modern missionary movement, tied up with colonial expansion and Western dominance and a certain group of missionary societies. As this historical phase disappears the discipline must also disappear, or change. And that is in fact what Notto Thelle observes; missiology must develop into a "complementary science" (SMT 2006/4: 452) Therefore he does not deplore that his chair disappears and is replaced by a chair in interreligious studies; he sees encouraging signs of missiological themes being integrated in a number of other disciplines and this is the direction one should pursue. In addition one should define a discipline – he calls it intercultural studies – that should take responsibility for some of the traditional concerns of missiology.

David Kerr, Lund, makes it very clear in his contribution how and why mission and ecumenical studies have become multidisciplinary, drawing on the resources of ethnographers, social anthropologists, intercultural studies and even political studies. In particular he adds, "mission and ecumenical studies must span the gulf that exists, ideologically and practically, between theology and religious studies. Too often mission studies colluded in this division, captured as they have been by the tension between mission and dialogue. Mission and ecumenical studies demand an open-ended engagement with both theology and religious studies." (SMT 2006/4: 500)

It is not only the Nordic missiologists that reflect on the fate of the discipline. German colleagues have also been engaged in a thorough reflection of the future of the discipline.[3] The starting point is of course the changes in the

---

[3] Missionswissenschaft als Interkulturelle Theologie und ihr Verhältnis zur Religionswissenschaft. http://web.uni-marburg.de/hosting/wgth/

cultural climate, where the growing religious pluralism in Europe sets a new agenda. The solution for the German colleagues is also to reformulate mission studies as intercultural theology, whereby mission studies come in close contact with religious studies.[4]

Missiology and interdisciplinarity

The conclusion of this brief overview is that missiology is struggling at public universities. The themes addressed by missiology have not become less important, on the contrary, but the way they are dealt with are coloured by the development of the general tendencies within the academy. Thus, missiology research is increasingly becoming an interdisciplinary subject that appears in many different contexts. To the extent that it is preserved as an independent discipline, its main area will be defined as *religion and globalisation*, *world Christianity or intercultural theology*, thereby approaching anthropology and cultural studies and sharing a common area of interest with the study of religion.

At the University of Aarhus we have also experienced this development, but we have taken the consequences of the inter-relationship between theology and the study of religion by organising the two disciplines within one faculty with the aim of a possible fruitful collaboration between the two. This is, for example, the idea behind the introduction of the subject 'religious studies for theologians' (Da: religionsfag) within the curriculum at the BA level in theology.

Although it was already clear from the very inception of the theological faculty at the University of Aarhus that mission should be one of the subject areas taught, it took some time before mission studies was established as a discipline. When this happened, theology of mission was seen as part of

---

religionsgeschichte/textauswahl.htm (seen 1/4 2007) The objective of this 'Positionspapier' is "den Gegenstandsbereich der Interkulturellen Theologie/Missionswissenschaft innerhalb der Evangelischen Theologie deutlich zu profilieren.", 1)

4 "Das Fach in seiner heutigen Ausrichtung widmet sich in einer breiten theologischen Perspektive der Begegnung und Ausienandersetzung des Christentums mit nicht-christlichen Religionen sowie der theologischen Reflexion nicht-westlicher kultureller Dialekte des Christentums in engem Bezug auf allgemeine ökumenische Fragestellungen. Hinzu kommt die ausdrückliche und bewusste Hinwendung zur religionswissenschaft als festem Bezugspunkt missionswissenschaftlicher Forschung. Im ergebnis hat sich die Missionswissenschaft zu einer breit angelegten, empirisch fundierten christlichen Theologie der Kulturen und Religionen entwickelt. Vor diesem Hintergrund is Interkulturelle Theologie/Missionswissenschaft als eine theologische Disziplin zu beschreiben". Positionspapier S. 3.

systematic theology and in close cooperation with confessional and ecumenical studies. The biblical foundations for mission were dealt with in the exegetical disciplines and history of mission was seen as part of church history and general historical studies. The founding father of missiology in Aarhus, Dr. Johannes Aagaard started out as a scholar in history of mission, but later took on a strong interest in new religious movements, especially the more occult among them. When he retired in 1998, the chair in missiology was renamed to cover Global Christianity and Ecumenical Concerns, and when I was called to the chair in 1999, there was a need for a new beginning. In the meantime Religious Studies had grown within the Faculty, and it was decided to establish a Centre for Multireligious Studies in order to promote the cooperation between systematic theology and religious studies (www.teo.au.dk/cms).

Today missiology is challenged by the same factors also affecting the development of society in general:

- the rapidly increasing secularisation of the traditional Christian countries;
- the end of the absolute cultural supremacy of the West;
- the growing self-consciousness and increasing political influence of other religions;
- the return of religion as a normative factor for the individual as well as in society.

This return comes in new forms disguised as either fundamentalism or spiritualism. Therefore, the concept of mission is also changing and as a result the academic discipline that studies the concept must change.

The crucial questions are what constitutes mission studies, and how can such studies be compatible with a theological curriculum. Here, the development of the concept of mission in relation to the triune God (Missio Dei) has led to mission being anchored in the Trinity, and thus an essential part of systematic theology. If mission is to participate in the Trinity's own loving movement through the Son, with the Holy Spirit, into the world, then mission must be part of all theological activities, and the study of mission must be included in all the disciplines of theology. But in order not to forget the subject matter, it is also important to emphasise its special role and treat missiology as an independent discipline, e.g. in the academic study of theology.

When missiology has to work under the conditions of the present age, one thing is certain: It is only possible through the inclusion of many other disciplines. Thus, mission theology or missiology is an interdisciplinary discipline by nature. To accomplish its tasks it must apply the methods and results of other scholarly disciplines. Here I will focus on two neighbouring disciplines. First, the study of history, in which the history of mission has been and still is a productive research area (I). And second, the study of religion, where missiology has a lot to learn from the different disciplines within the field of religious studies, first and foremost when it comes to specific knowledge about other religions, their life, work and history; but also the general knowledge of the history of religion becomes relevant (II). In return, mission theology can contribute to opening the eyes of the study of religion for the mechanisms at play when living organisms such as religions interact, spread and collide.

Missiology and history of mission

Mission history often describes history as a movement consisting of transcending borders: geographical, ethnical, cultural and religious. History research always faces the problem: How does one do justice to the past? The minimum demand is the willingness to attempt to see persons and events in the true historical contexts that motivated their actions. Thus, mission history is a part of history as a whole. It cannot simply restrict itself to account for the actions of the missionising, but must also focus on the dissemination of local Christianity. When mission is to transcend borders, geographical as well as cultural, it comes to deal with co-habitation between people with different cultural backgrounds. Therefore, mission history approaches multicultural studies.

Not all passing on of religion is mission, but a religious socialisation can be found in all religions. It is found in the family or other social units, like e.g. the tribe, and this is of course the most commonly used way of passing on religion. Mission, however, is characteristic for certain religions at certain times and happens only where people are convinced that their specific religion provides them with a life that should be shared by people outside their own narrow society; which is far from obvious. The most common feature is to see "the others" as strangers and enemies with whom you do not wish to share, and against whom you need to protect yourself. Only when a culture opens itself up to the unknown or strangers is the interaction within mission possible. Generally speaking, mission viewed separately seems to be the most influential factor in the development towards seeing different groups of peoples as partners in the common life. The very notion that we share life with everybody – and that we have to share it with everybody – is an idea we may not even have had, had it not been for the missionary impulse of Christianity.

The transition of cultural borders is a consequence of the transition of religious borders. It is characteristic that religious transition is experienced as more problematic than cultural transition. This may be because religious transition is perceived as identical with conflict and repression. However, the actual mission has not worked that way. It has rather contributed to creating a new religious self-consciousness and connection between religions that furthers diversity and plurality. This is a consequence of the fact that the set of ideas the mission invites you to internalise calls you out of the existing family and tribe community, as it builds on the idea of the equality of every human being, of turning yourself to the world and not away from it, and a search for the divine.

If it is not a missionary religion meeting a tribal religion, but rather a meeting between two missionary religions, the religious encounter is different. In this case an uncomplicated symbiosis is not possible, but rather competition. Of course, such a competition for souls can take many forms, which has been documented many times throughout history. However, underneath there is also a fruitful exchange between the different religions. Converts bring their ideas with them and thereby add an inter-religious dialogical element to the new religion.

If one looks back on the last 200 years, it is easy to focus on the relationship between colonialism, imperialism and mission. The motivations behind may vary: one motive could be to collect arguments against the accusation that mission is merely colonialism under a different name. But also here the patterns of reaction among the missionaries are better understood if the development is analysed in a larger perspective. When Middle Age churches were to decide which course to take, they took the consequence of the persecution they had suffered during the Roman Empire and in the missionary fields to abstain from missionary endeavours in areas without Christian political supremacy. Therefore, great efforts were made to convert the political ruler. Just think of our own Nordic mission history: "The Harold who Christianised the Danes". The Christening is initiated by the political ruler, sometimes followed by a military conquest, like Olav Tryggvason's christening of Norway.

Freedom of religion and the history of mission

It is not until far later, when politically motivated persecutions were acknowledged as a possible risk, mission was attempted in areas ruled by non-Christians. Examples are the mendicant order's mission in the Islamic world and China in the 13th and 14th century. Other examples are the Jesuits in India, Japan and China in the 16th century. All these attempts have in common that they were unfruitful and often ended in persecution.

It is therefore striking that the missionary movement mostly turned to these areas when it renewed itself through the missionary societies in the 19th century. Why? Because of religious freedom, an idea which is rooted in Protestantism, but is spread through the enlightenment.

When the idea of religious freedom through the American Declaration of Independence and the French revolution became politically effective, it also penetrated protestant missionary thinking. The present generation had a unique chance to organise a worldwide mission. With the opportunity came the obligation.

This line of thought culminated with John Mott and Edinburgh 1910. The foundation of the newly established Christian missionary movement was not a wish to extend a Christian colonial rule. The motivation was a strong belief that the idea of religious freedom would spread, which is why Christian mission no longer needed to fear persecutions.

The same ideas are already expressed by William Carey and repeated by

John R. Mott. The freedom of religion is interpreted as a chance for one's own religion; as it is now possible to preach the gospel without the risk of persecution. Of course, to these pioneers of mission, freedom of religion would apply to all religions, but they had an amazing confidence in the power and supremacy of the Christian gospel as the definitive redeeming message for salvation.

However, the idea of religious freedom did not become as widespread as imagined by these pioneers. What instead spread was their idea that in areas with religious freedom, religion could sever links with the political power. This idea is also transferred to other religions. Mission history then becomes the history of the development of inter-religious relations.

Why history of mission is important

In the previous reflections we have continuously touched upon the relation between religion and politics. That is the way it is. It is inescapable. It is impossible to study mission history and at the same time ignore the political history. The relation between mission and politics may vary, but an inter-dependence will always exist between them. In the course of history, different models have been applied. On the one hand, there are examples of mission convincing politics that it should take the missionary cause and make it its own. The mission movement played a decisive role in the abolition of slavery.[5] On the other hand, there are examples of conflict between religion and politics. For instance in the case of the Confessing Church in Germany in the 1930's and in the struggle against apartheid in South Africa in the last half of the 20th century. Finally, there are examples of mission utilised as a political instrument. In these cases, mission has been used to justify political or military expansion. This last example in particular has brought mission into disrepute.

Research in mission history – and necessarily taking a long perspective – is a prerequisite for understanding the plurality of society. Taking its starting point in 1705/06 with the dispatch of Ziegenbalg and Plütschau, the Protestant research in mission history often only deals with the last 300 years. A more mission critical approach may choose to begin with the Spanish and Portuguese colonial period from the 16th century. If one wants to base one's research on archival material, the situation usually is such that only material dating 100 years back is preserved. Of course, the source material is exciting, but the excitement should not overshadow the fact that the mission has a much longer history. It is important to remember this history, as it also provides the foundation for a broader perspective on current and topical mission historical events.

It is crucial to be acquainted with the inter-related history of the missionary

---

5 See for instance Lamin Sanneh: *Abolitionists Abroad* (Cambridge: Harvard University Press ,1999).

religions in order to get a clear picture of how people of different ethnicities are able to live together. In these religions, a human identity which was able to join together different cultures was formed. A secular counterpart is not experienced until today under the keyword globalisation. When people of different ethnicity and culture have to live together, religion must not be excluded. Many religions have strived to become market leaders by repressing other religions, but they have seldom succeeded, which can be explained by the dynamic of the missionary process. The local religions, which belonged to the tribal society, were included in the new religious reality. And the co-existence of the missionary religions only became possible following their encounter. Thus, it is the missionary religions that have founded the basis of inter-religious dialogue. A modern pluralistic and secular society can only survive as a liberal and tolerant one if it succeeds in fertilising such experiences of co-existence. This is the explanation why mission history is so important in our society. It analyses models for a fruitful life together and thus approaches multireligious studies.

Missiology and religious studies

The two disciplines, theology and religious studies, have a common history, and this past still affects their mutual relationship. It is well-known that theology is the oldest one of the two disciplines, and the first universities are founded around theology. The study of religion is far younger. The discipline was born at the end of the 1890's, and its relation to theology was problematic from the outset. Some attempted to define the relationship as a close one, thereby minimising the distance between the study of religion and theology. Others were eager to create a distance. It is possible to construct a typology of the attempts to determine the relation between theology and the study of religion as ranging from *cooperation* over *complementarity* to *confrontation* and *emancipation*.[6]

The person most often mentioned as founder of the study of religion is the indologist Friederich Max Müller (1823-1900). As a pioneer within the discipline it was natural for him to focus on liberating the growing impartial comparative study of religion from the embrace of theology. And as a matter of course, he attracted scepticism from theologians, who insisted on the sovereignty of Christianity. However, one of Müller's favourite arguments against the sovereignty of Christianity was taken from theology itself. He introduced the idea of a common revelation as the basis for all religious manifestations. Müller is well-known for his statement: He who knows only one religion knows none. It was formulated as a counterargument against another famous statement dating back to Adolf Harnack and his Rektoratsrede,

---

6 See S. Hjelde: Religionswissenschaft und Theologie. Die Frage ihrer gegenseitigen Abgrenzung in historischer Perspective. *Studia Theologica* 52/1998

in which he, in the style of liberal theology, insisted on the superiority of Christianity with the statement that: he who knows this religion knows all ("Wer disese Religion kennt, kennt alle").[7]

Other pioneers saw in the study of religion a potential renewer of theology and did not believe that Schleiermacher's explanation for the cohesion and unity of theology, that is the need of practical theology and church organisation for theological reflection, was a sufficient argument for placing theology at a university. If theology were to have domicile at a university, it had to be as an integral part of a general study of religion, also a point of view often maintained today. The ideal seems to be to have two equal disciplines that can work side by side and be mutually supportive. Very often the potential conflicting relationship between theology and the study of religion burst into the open, leading to the logical conclusion to subordinate theology under the general study of religion. In most cases, however, this solution was impossible theology being a historically well-established discipline. Today this possibility is closer and often leads to a lack of clarity and talk of complementarity and co-operation. Historically, co-operation usually turned into a division of labour: Theology would deal with Christianity and the study of religion would deal with the "foreign" religions. But this neat division is no longer tenable.

Co-operation and complementarity

The reason for a long-standing period of peaceful co-operation can be found in the prevalent theological conception that theology, in addition to analysing Christian religion, was supposed to study the phenomenon religion as such with the aim of determining "the true religion". A distinguished Nordic representative of this almost melting together of theology and the study of religion is Nathan Söderblom, a Swedish archbishop and prime mover behind the church meeting in Stockholm in 1925, and thus one of the founders of the World Council of Churches. Söderblom claimed that the world of religions in general belonged to the area of theology. More strongly than most, Söderblom emphasised the theological nature of the study of religion. He sees no conflict between an analysis pertaining to the study of religion and a theological occupation with the phenomenon religion.

The vision of a peaceful co-existence was primarily linked to an understanding that from a liberal theological point of view it was possible to establish a synthesis between Christianity and culture. However, it is this same synthesis that is blocked by dialectical theology and its revolt against religion as a universal concept. In the 2nd edition of his commentary on Romans, Karl Barth declares war on the cultural synthesis of liberal Christianity. Religion is

[7] See also the discussion in Armin W Geertz, Søren Jensen , Peter Widmann (eds.): *Medspil og modspil. Teologi og religionsvidenskab* (Aarhus: Faculty of Theology, University of Aarhus, 1996).

viewed as a part of man's general attempt to master his life and establish security. The Gospel, however, which comes direct from above, is the destroyer of all security. Therefore, the study of religion may very well be invited to analyse all the religious behavioural patterns of human beings, including the ones that emanate from Christian religions, but it can never access the Gospel itself. Religion is in fact the most cunning form of idol-worship and sin. As a result, this dialectical-theological viewpoint leads to an increasing alienation between theology and the study of religion.

When dialectical theology pours acid on the synthesis between culture and religion, religious experience becomes sinful human's pathetic attempt to gain advantages over God. Thus dialectical theology lays the foundation for the religious criticism of the 20th century. It turns against the modern subjectivist religion that creates God in its own image, which thereby also leads to a break with the prevailing opinion among scholars of the study of religion that religion is a man-made construction.

In view of Barth's influence on the protestant theology of the 20th century it is legitimate to ask whether it is necessary for a protestant theologian to know anything about other religions. Will it lead to confusion instead? Will it not rather raise doubts in the souls of less firm believers about the truth of Christianity? Or is it only a contribution to syncretism?

Barth's response has been normative for large parts of the protestant theology in the 20th century. To him, religion was human beings futile attempt to get closer to God by his own efforts through religious behaviour. By doing good deeds, humans will force God to be more kindly disposed. But in reality, this only expresses sin and revolt against God. Only God can remedy the wronged relationship between God and human beings. Only God can stretch out the hand of reconciliation. Faith is to assume this and is thus opposed to all religion.

As mentioned, Barth's response has been extremely influential. The belief in progress and optimism of the 19th century received its deathblow in the trenches of World War I and was replaced by a pessimistic vision of humanity and its future. In this situation, Barth's focus on revelation was felt as a relief. But as revelation is not an event accessible to common scientific methods, a logical conclusion could be to abandon the scientific study of Christianity altogether and instead to focus on the "practising of Christianity" and define theology as a science of faith. However, this did not become the dialectical theological position, which on the contrary wished to maintain the scientific study of religion, leading as a natural consequence to treating Christianity on par with other religions.

Thus, there seems to be an inner contradiction in the position of the dialectical theology. In the end, the Barthian resistance against including the study of religion in theology was seen as an immunisation strategy: theology did not wish to be challenged by the other religions. There are several reasons why this would not work today. First of all, nobody understands such a position. Most theologians will side with Müller: He who knows only one religion knows none. There is also a potential for religious criticism in the meeting between the study of religion and theology, which may be worth activating. It could be the responsibility of theology to remind the study of religion of the original religious criticism that is behind its activities, which was there from the beginning, but which sometimes has been thrust into the background under the shelter of a positivist umbrella. And confronted with the vital new agenda of the second half the 20th century, with the growth of religious pluralism, the position becomes meaningless. When religious plurality and diversity become pronounced, Christianity is not able to understand itself without the comparison with other religions. The monopoly is broken and pluralism reigns.

In some instances the debate about the relationship between theology and the study of religion has been characterised by anticlerical viewpoints. The study of religion is a child of the enlightenment and the religious criticism that followed in its footsteps. Naturally new positions sprang up, demanding the study of religion to replace theology. The harmonious division of labour envisioned by some of the pioneers, where theology would deal with Christianity and the study of religion with other religions, did not seem defensible. Sometimes the housing of theology at the university was attacked. Thus, the Norwegian professor of the study of religion, Wilhelm Schencke, quarrelled with his Faculty of Theology by calling it the appendix of the university. Today, not many would express themselves this sharply, but sometimes the intention is the same, and the conclusion is clear: Theology should be removed. It does not belong among the other respectable scholarly disciplines.

Others have thought to see a way out through historical development. When different areas of society become increasingly secularised, it also becomes possible to question why the university houses theology. Today this argument is not heard that often, because the big question confronting the secular university today is how to handle Islam. The traditional orientalist study of Islam has come under heavy criticism on the one hand; and on the other hand the tradition for Islamic scholarship on the basis of revealed scripture and divine guidance is difficult to swallow for a liberal secular university tradition formed in the wake of the enlightenment. However, I have been in several academic conferences where it was quite normal for the academic presenter to begin "In the name of Allah, the most Beneficent, the most Merciful".[8] Should missiologist in the future start presenting their academic papers "in the name of the triune God, the Father, the Son and the Holy Spirit"?

It will be very interesting to watch how Islamic theology and Islamic studies

---

8 Thus Fatih Okumus, Vrije Universiteit, Amsterdam at the European Society for Intercultural Theology and Interreligious Studies (ESITIS) conference, Birmingham 11.-13. April 2007: The resurgence of Religion in Europe.

will be integrated in the modern secular university in the West. It might be possible to pursue Islamic cultural studies descriptively, but when it comes to Islamic theology it will of course express itself normatively, like Christian theology and missiology have always done. It is not possible for systematic theology and mission theology to do their job properly if they cannot express themselves normatively. But how can a secular university handle clashes within normativity?

It is not a new experience for Christianity to exist in a mulitreligious society. This was also the case at the times of the early Church, in which the Christian theologians were preoccupied with reformulating the Christian truths in dialogue with the philosophical and religious flows of the time. When theology today wants to become familiar with the living faith in other religions, it is among others in order to become better to express its own. Multireligiousity challenges Christianity to state its case and to advance it as a public truth (*Leslie Newbigin*). In order to relate to other religions, it is necessary to be able to account for the lived faith in Christianity in a critical and reflective way.

Confrontation and emancipation

With two parallel disciplines, theology and religious studies, it is only logically possible to work with a limited number of relations: An equal collaboration based on the division of labour and complementarity or opposition and contrast with possible relations of superiority or subordination. However, at the root of the study of religion project lies a striving for liberation. Therefore, the history of religious studies has often been described from a liberation perspective, usually the liberation of the sensible study of religion from the metaphysical and biased theology. As a consequence, it is emphasised that the study of religion works historically and systematically with empirical religions without considering any normative statements, whereas it is assumed that theology expresses itself normatively, at least within dogmatics, which is why it has difficulties finding its place within the academy. It is also true that the study of religion is an empirically oriented discipline that works inductively. This feature has often been promoted as the most important feature of the study of religion in contrast to theology, which works normatively and deductively. However, this is not the entire truth; it is not fair to present the study of religion as unconditional and objective and theology as biased and subjective. Within theology as well as within the study of religion, there is an extensive pluralism of methodology and working methods.

The study of religion meets theology in two ways, partly as subject for research and partly as a neighbouring discipline. When theology or Christianity becomes the subject for investigation with methods and theories pertaining to the study of religion, visible plurality is unavoidable. That is why the study of religion often talks about Christianities and avoids speaking of Christianity in the singular.

As neighbouring disciplines they share this complex history, which I have tried to describe by means of the mentioned typologies. The practical division of theology as a study of Christianity and the study of religion as a study of all other religions cannot be maintained. Letting them collaborate from their individual perspective with religion as the common denominator is not possible either. It is true that the study of religion deals with the phenomenon religion, but it becomes apparent in a number of ways why the various disciplines of the study of religion must come into play. On the one hand, it is possible to establish a number of overlaps. On the other hand, there are visible differences. Indeed, theology can be said to deal with religion, but it does so with itself at the centre, and, in our cultural sphere, theology is therefore usually limited to only dealing with Christian religion. But as already mentioned chairs in Islamic theology are now being established, sometimes as a supplement, sometimes as a substitute for chairs in missiology and Christian theology.[9] How this will influence the teaching and research in missiology remains to be seen. Christian theology has a tradition for dealing with other religions, but often one would approach them with the methodologies shared with the other disciplines of the study of religion.

Co-operation, complementarity, confrontation or liberation; these seem to be the possibilities in the process of determining the relationship between the study of religion and theology/missiology. The relation will never settle down, but this is only beneficial for the academy, which to a large degree is based on criticism and contradiction. It would therefore be a loss, if one discipline succeeds in replacing the other. So co-operation is the order of the day and also represents the most fruitful way. But it requires openness from both sides.

The present multireligious situation requires such a co-operation. If we are to reconcile the tension in the wake of the establishment of multireligious and multicultural societies and thus contribute positively to the peaceful development of society, inter-religious dialogue is crucial. For a missiologist it is natural to engage in dialogue with other religions. Religious studies can assist in this endeavour by establishing a respectful approach to people of a different faith. And the theological practices enable a creative approach to one's own tradition and maintain a normative concept of truth. If one engages in religious dialogue, it is not sufficient to try to understand the other person by means of questions that are relevant only within one's own tradition. An attempt must be made to understand the other from within, to learn the languages, to get familiarised with the concepts and thoughts. That is the challenge.

---

9 In January 2007 Jørgen S. Nielsen was appointed professor and chair in islamic theology at the theological faculty; University of Copenhagen (see http://www.ku.dk/satsning/Religion/)

-o-

Here I have argued that missiology has a legitimate place in the secular university because it helps to better understand the dynamic at play in the intercultural and interreligious encounter, so important a factor in the development of today's society. Missiology can nurture interreligious understanding and co-operation that is a vital ingredient for the well-being of society. How to nurture a culture of dialogue and mutual exchange is at the heart of the missiological endeavour. Missiological themes will surface within many disciplines, and they will have to be dealt with according to many methods and on the background of several theories. In addition it should as a distinct discipline be given a place in the theological curriculum. In order for that to happen the traditional discipline will need to be flexible and able to change. It is bound to work interdisciplinarly, and it must be open to interreligious dialogue.

The whole idea of the secular university is for the moment much in dispute. The traditional virtues of the university, that it can offer a neutral academic space where truth can be pursued for its own sake in a spirit of critical openness, are contested. Will the post-modern university become a multiple space which is no longer concerned to impose a secular agenda but is rather a sort of consortium of different methodologies or even confessions? One thing is certain: Teaching and research in the university no longer take place in a pristine environment but are seen in the context of the society that also supports its activities and expects a certain return on its investment. This is not new to a discipline such as missiology. Traditionally it analyses tensions in society created by introducing new beliefs. So the future should look bright for the discipline. But it will be interesting to watch how the departments for religious studies and the theological faculties will adapt and define their new role.

BIBLIOGRAPHY OF KNUD JØRGENSEN
THE LITERARY WORKS OF KNUD JØRGENSEN: 1976-2007

Inger Johanne Gillebo

Librarian Inger Johanne Gillebo, MF Norwegian School of Theology, Oslo, Norway

The bibliography includes book chapters, multi-authored and co-edited contributions, and articles. Newspaper articles, interviews, speeches and book reviews are not included.

1976

Evangelisation og kirkevækst – Hellerup: DMS-Forlag, 1976 – 57 p.
"Kirkevækst: et forsøg på en indføring" in *Evangelisation og kirkevækst* – Hellerup: DMS-Forlag , 1976, 9-33.
"Models of communication in the New Testament" in *Missiology*, vol. 4, 1976, 465-484.

1978

"Mediemission i Afrika" in *Evangeliet til verden,* 1978, 40-45.

1982

"Kirkevækst og missionsforskning" in *Mission,* vol. 93, no. 4, 1982, 150-189.

1983

"Innledning" in *Misjon og kommunikasjon: veiledningshefte* – Kristiansand: IMMI, 1983, 2-3.
"Kommunikasjon er mennesker" in *Misjon og kommunikasjon: veiledningshefte* – Kristiansand: IMMI, 1983, 4-14.
"Evangelisasjon og kirkevekst" in *Misjon og kommunikasjon: veiledningshefte* – Kristiansand: IMMI, 1983, 49-55.
"New and old media in Norway" in *Communicatio socialis,* vol. 16, no. 2, 1983, 155-159.

1984

Arbeidsbok til Radioarbeid: programproduksjon og radiojournalistikk. Oslo: NKS-forl., 1984 – 12 p.
Nærradio, nærmiljø og lokalmenighet: Veiledningshefte for menigheter og

organisasjoner / Jørgensen, K., K. Melhus, G. Mykletun. - Kristiansand: IMMI, 1984 – 107 p.
Radioarbeid: programproduksjon og radiojournalistikk / Colbjørnsen, H., K. Jørgensen, K. Melhus – Oslo: NKS-forl., 1984 – 203 p.
Kirken og de elektroniske mediene i informasjonssamfunnet: nordisk konferanse om kristen mediekommunikasjon, Drammen 1.-4. mars 1984 / redaksjon: Brommeland, H-G., K. Jørgensen – Kristiansand: IMMI, 1984 – 95 p.
Proclaiming Christ to his World / Brommeland, H-G. and K. Jørgensen (editors) – Oslo: Luther, c1984 – 148 p.
"Närmedier, närmiljø och församlingen" in *Kristen i medierna* / redigerad av Holgersson, T – Stockholm: EFS-förlaget, c1984 – 129-133.
"Mangfold og amatører" in *Radio: radiojournalistikk: lydmediets framtid* / Torsvik, A. (red.) – Oslo: Universitetsforlaget, c1984 – 83-94.
"Ansvar i en ny medietid: Mangfoldighet og amatører" in *Kirke og kultur,* vol. 89, no. 2, 1984, 84-91.

1985
Medie- og kommunikasjonsstrategi / redaksjon: Brommeland, H-G., K. Jørgensen – Kristiansand: IMMI, 1985 – 115 p.
"Om kirkernes internationale mediearbejde" in *Gammel og ny informationsorden* / Berntsen, K – Hellerup: DMS-forlaget, 1985 – 84-92.

1986
The role and function of the media in the mission of the Church (with particular reference to Africa) – Ann Arbor, Mich.: University Microfilms International, 1986 – 701 p.
Bruk av små medier i evangelisering og undervisning / redaksjon: Brommeland, H-G., K. Jørgensen – Kristiansand: IMMI, 1986 – 98 p.
Nærradio og oppsøkende arbeid / redaksjon: Brommeland, H-G., K. Jørgensen – Kristiansand: IMMI, 1986 – 73 p.
Planlegging og evaluering i misjon / redaksjon: Brommeland, H-G., K. Jørgensen – Kristiansand: IMMI, 1986 – 60 p.

1987
Åpen kanal: misjon og medier. – Oslo: Luther, 1987 – 94 p.
Radioarbeid: programproduksjon og radiojournalistikk / Colbjørnsen, H., K. Jørgensen, K. Melhus – 2. utg – Oslo: NKS-forlaget, 1987 – 203 p.
Samtale og tiltale: radioandakten som forkynnelse og formidling / redaksjon: Jørgensen, K., T. Sandsdalen Jerstad. – Kristiansand: IMMI, 1987 – 65 p.
Det trykte ord / redaksjon: Jørgensen, K., H-G. Brommeland – Kristiansand: IMMI, 1987 – 82 p.
"Misjon i en forandret verden" in *Norsk tidsskrift for misjon,* vol. 41, no. 1, 1987, 7-14.

1988

Local churches and missions: a report from a working party on local churches and missions / editor: Jørgensen, K – Kristiansand: IMMI, 1988 – 106 p.

Tverrkulturell kommunikasjon / redaksjon: Jørgensen, K., H-G. Brommeland – Kristiansand: IMMI, 1988 – 86 p.

"Fra industrisamfunn til informasjonssamfunn" in *Informasjonssamfunnet* / redaksjon: Gjørv, L-I., T. Sandsdalen Jerstad – Kristiansand: IMMI, 1988, 1-8.

"Hvordan skal kirkens budskap "overleve" i et nytt samfunn?" in *Informasjonssamfunnet* / redaksjon: Gjørv, L-I., T. Sandsdalen Jerstad – Kristiansand: IMMI, 1988, 61-70.

"Kirken og kommunikasjonskrisen" in *Ung teologi,* vol. 21, no. 2, 1988, 1-11.

1989

"Lederskap på tvers av grensen" in *Santalen,* vol. 107, no. 24, 1989, 18-19.

"Misjon er åndskamp" in *Santalen*, vol. 107, no. 12/13, 1989, 14.

"Misjon må plante misjon" in *Santalen,* vol. 107, no. 5/6, 1989, 28-29.

"Misjonærbagasjen" in *Santalen,* vol. 107, no. 8, 1989, 8.

"Rike kristne i en fattig verden" in *Santalen,* vol. 107, no. 10, 1989, 18-19.

1990

"Medier i misjon i 90-årene" in *Medienes rolle i evangelieformidlingen* – Oslo: Kristelig institutt for ledelse og administrasjon, 1990, 29-35.

"Kirke i informasjonssamfunnet" in *Tidsskrift for teologi og kirke,* vol. 61, no. 4, 1990, 273-282.

1991

Visjon og hverdag: lederskap i misjon og menighet – Oslo: Verbum, 1991 – 249 p.

Vitner i arbeid og fritid: teltmakertjeneste til jordens ender / Jørgensen, K. og B. Helgøy Kloster – Oslo: Credo, 1991 – 62 p.

"Åndskamp – mer enn slagord" in *"Reis deg Guds menighet": impulser til kristenliv i Norge i nitti-årene* / utgitt av Kontaktforum for evangelisering – Oslo: Credo: Nye Luther, 1991, 75-85.

"Misjonens og historiens Herre" in *Santalen,* vol.109, no. 2, 1991, 4-7.

"Kristelig lederskap i relasjon til organisasjon og struktur" in *Tidsskrift for kirke, religion, samfunn*, vol. 4, no. 1, 1991, 34-52.

"Misjon er åndskamp" in *Visjon*, no. 2, 1991, 11.

1992

"Fra industrisamfund til informationssamfund" in *Medierne og os: et årsskrift om medier, samfund og kirke* – Vejle, Kristelig Lytter- og Fjernseerforening, Kirke og Medier, 1992, 59-64.

"Misjonærrollen under lupen" in *Santalen,* vol. 110, no. 6/7, 1992, 16-19.

"Missionærrollen under lup" in *Santal posten,* vol. 97, no. 6, 1992, 4-6.

1994

Missiologi i dag / redaktører: Berentsen, J-M., T. Engelsviken, K. Jørgensen – Oslo: Universitetsforl., 1994 – 486 p.

"Modernity, information technology and Christian faith" in *Faith and modernity* / edited by P Sampson, P., V. Samuel and C. Sugden – Oxford: Regnum, 1994, 273-286.

"Avslutning: misjon i kirkens liv og lære" av Berentsen, J-M., T. Engelsviken og K. Jørgensen in *Missiologi i dag* – Oslo: Universitetsforl., 1994, 437-440.

"Grunntrekk i misjonens teologi" av Berentsen, J-M., T. Engelsviken og K. Jørgensen in *Missiologi i dag* – Oslo: Universitetsforl., 1994, 173-185.

"Innledning" av Berentsen, J-M., T. Engelsviken og K. Jørgensen in *Missiologi i dag* – Oslo: Universitetsforl., 1994, 15-19.

"Misjon og kirke" in *Missiologi i dag* – Oslo: Universitetsforl., 1994, 275-305.

1995

Communication means people. Manual on communication in society and culture. Addis Ababa: Mekane Yesus Seminary & Kirkens Nødhjelp, 1995 – 87 p.

Equipping for service. Leadership in church and mission. Addis Ababa: Mekane Yesus Seminary & Kirkens Nødhjelp, 1995 – 137 p.

1996

"De fattige har dere alltid" in *Ansikt til ansikt: folkelig bibellesning verden rundt* / redigert av Hasle, J – Oslo: Genesis: I samarbeid med Kirkens nødhjelp, 1996, 54-59.

1998

"Missiologiske udfordringer på vej mod år 2010" in *Mission*, vol. 109, no. 2, 1998, 5-10.

"Misjonsforståelse på norsk" in *Norsk tidsskrift for misjon*, vol. 52, no. 2, 1998, 97-116.

"De troendes prestedømme" in *Årbok for Den norske kirke*, vol. 47, 1998, 131-132.

2000

"Areopagos" in *Norsk tidsskrift for misjon,* vol. 54, no. 3, 2000, 191-194.

2001

"Kom, sannhets ånd, og vitne giv!" in *Over alt*, vol. 13. no. 1, 2001, 21-25.

2002

"Spiritual conflict in socio-political context" in *Deliver us from evil: an uneasy frontier in Christian mission* / edited by Moreau, A. Scott ... [et al.] – Monrovia, Calif.: Marc, c2002, 213-230.

"Om å drive misjon eller være misjon" in *Luthersk kirketidende*, vol. 137, no. 18, 2002, 473-476.

2003
"Spiritualitet og åndskamp" in *Ung teologi*, vol. 36, no. 2, 2003, 57-65.

2004
Missiologi i dag / redaktører: Berentsen, J-M., T. Engelsviken, K. Jørgensen – 2. utg – Oslo: Universitetsforl., c2004 – 498 p.
"Trenger kirken omvendelse?: på vei mot en misjonal ekklesiologi" in *Hva vil det si å være kirke?: kirkens vesen og oppdrag* / Engelsviken, T. og K. O. Sannes (red.) – Oslo: Det teologiske Menighetsfakultet ; Trondheim: Tapir akademisk forl., 2004, 51-68.
"Avslutning: misjon i kirkens liv og lære" av Berentsen, J-M., T. Engelsviken og K.Jørgensen in *Missiologi i dag* – Oslo: Universitetsforl., 2004, 455-458.
"Grunntrekk i misjonens teologi" av Berentsen, J-M., T. Engelsviken og K. Jørgensen. in *Missiologi i dag* – Oslo: Universitetsforl., 2004, 173-186.
"Innledning" av Berentsen, J-M., T. Engelsviken og K. Jørgensen in *Missiologi i dag* – Oslo: Universitetsforl., 2004, 15-19.
"Misjon og kirke" in *Missiologi i dag* – Oslo: Universitetsforl., 2004, 295-326.
"Mission er et must" in *Ikon,* no. 48, 2004, 19-22.
"Lederskap i bevegelse" in *Luthersk kirketidende*, vol. 139, no. 1, 2004, 8-10.
"Ikke frelse i nogen anden" in *Ny Mission*, no. 7, 2004, 43-56.

2005
"Lesslie Newbigin. Fader til en bevægelse" in *Ny Mission*, no. 6, 2005, 36-47.
"Et levende møde i et multireligiøst samfund" in *Ny Mission,* no. 9, 2005, 75-90.

2006
"Obstacles to leadership in culture, society and church" in *Enabling organisations: supporting articles* / Lemvik, J. (editor) – Oslo: Bistandsnemnda, 2006, 51-56.
"Time management" in *Enabling organisations: supporting articles* / Lemvik, J. (editor) – Oslo: Bistandsnemnda, 2006, 57-68.
"Missiologien udfordrer teologien" in *Ichthys*, no. 33, 2006, 25-36.
"Steps into a pluralist world" in *Norsk tidsskrift for misjon*, vol. 60, no. 3/4, 2006, 255-268.

2007
"Communication – the future. Where to go from here?" in *Festschrift for Charles H. Kraft.* Maryknoll, NY: Orbis, 2007 – (NP)
"Misjon og fortapelse" in *Luthersk kirketidende,* vol. 142, no. 5, 2007, 144-146.

BIBLIOGRAPHY

Adamo, David T. (ed.), *Biblical Interpretation in African Perspective,* Lanham, UK: University Press of America, 2006.

-, *Reading and Interpreting the Bible in African Indigenous Churches*, Eugene: OR: Wipf and Stock Publishers, 2001.

Adeney, Bernard, *Strange Virtues: Ethics in a Multicultural World*, Downers Grove: Ill., InterVarsity Press, 1995.

Adizes, Ichak, *Corporate Life Cycles,* Englewood Cliffs, NJ: Prentice Hall, 1988.

Ahonen, Risto A., *Mission in the New Millennium: Theological Grounds for World Mission*, Helsinki: The Finnish Evangelical Lutheran Mission, 2000.

Aikman, David, *Jesus in Beijing: How Christianity Is Transforming China and Changing the Global Balance of Power,* Washington DC: Regnery Publishing, 2003.

Alighieri, Dante, *De Monarchia*, Book I., Chinese edition, Beijing: Commercial Press 1985.

Amaladoss, Michael, S.J., "My Pilgrimage in Mission," *International Bulletin of Missionary Research*, Vol. 31, No 1, Jan 2007: 21-24.

Andersen, Poul E., "De fædrelandsløse", *Kristeligt Dagblad*, February 1, 2000.

Andersen, Øyvind, *Grunnsannheter til frelse: Romerbrevet 1-8*, Oslo: Gry, 1958.

Ariarajah, Wesley, *The Bible and other faiths,* Geneva: World Council of Churches, 1985.

Argyris, Chris, *On organizational Learning*, Cambridge, MA: Blackwell, 1994.

Axtell, Roger, *Do's and taboos around the world*, New York, NY: Elmsford, 1985.

Bakke, Johnny, *Christian Ministry: Patterns and Functions within the Ethiopian Evangelical Church,* Oslo: Solum Forlag, 1987.

Banks, Robert, *Reenvisioning Theological Education: Exploring a Missional Alternative to Current Models*, Grand Rapids, MI: William B. Eerdmans, 1999.

Barbour, Ian G., *Myths, Models and Paradigms,* San Francisco, CA: Harper & Row, 1974.

Barnett, Homer G., *Innovation, the Basis for Cultural Change*, New York, NY: McGraw-Hill, 1953,

Barrett, David, Todd M. Johnson and Peter F. Crossing: "Missionmetrics 2007: Creating Your Own Analysis of Global Data", *International Bulletin of Missionary Research* Vol. 31, no. 2. Jan. 2007, pp. 25-32.

Bass, B. M., *Bass and Stogdill's Handbook of Leadership,* 3rd edition, New York: The Free Press, 1990.

Bauman, Martin, "Religion und ihre Bedeutung für Migranten". Antrittsvorlesung 20.06.2002 in Luzern, http://backupuni.bison-web.com/gf/3259_9399.htm 06-11-2006.

-, "Religion und ihre Bedeutung für Migranten", *Religion - Migration – Integration*, Beauftragte der Bundesregierung für Migration (red.), Flüchtlinge und Integration., Berlin & Bonn: Beauftragte der Bundesregierung für Migration, Flüchtlinge und Integration, 2004, pp. 19-30

Beaver, R. Pierce, *American Protestant Women in World Mission: a History of the First Feminist Movement in North America,* Grand Rapids, MI: William B Eerdmans, 1980.

Bediako, Kwame, "The Willowbank Consultation, January 1978: A personal Reflection", *Themelios: An International Journal for Theological Students*, 5.2 (1980), pp. 25-32.

-, "The missionary inheritance", R. Keeley (ed), *Christianity: A World Faith,* Tring: Lion, 1985, pp. 303-311.

-, „African Christian Theology; Theology of African Independent Churches; Black Theology; Culture", Sinclair Ferguson and David F. Wright (eds), *New Dictionary of Theology*, Leicester: IVP, 1988, pp. 8-12; 103-105; 183.

-, "Christ in Africa: Some Reflections on the Contribution of Christianity to the African becoming", C. Fyfe (ed), *African Future,* Edinburgh: Centre of African Studies, University of Edinburgh, 1988, pp. 447-458.

-, "Into All the World", in Richard Bauckham et al. (eds), *Jesus 2000,* Oxford: Lion, 1989, pp. 222-225.

-, *Theology and Identity: The Impact of Culture upon Christian Thought in the Second Century and Modern Africa,* Oxford: Regnum, 1992.

-, "John Mbiti's Contribution to African Theology" in Jacob K. Olupona and Sulayman S. Nyang (eds), *Religious Plurality in Africa: Essays in Honour of John S. Mbiti,* Berlin: Mouton de Gruyter, 1993, pp. 367-390.

-, "Understanding African theology in the twentieth century", *Themelios*, 20.1 (1994), pp. 14-19.

-, "Christ is Lord: How is Jesus Unique in the Midst of Other Faiths?", *Trinity Journal of Church and Theology* 14.2 (1994), pp. 50-61.

-, *Christianity in Africa: The Renewal of a Non-Western Religion,* Edinburgh: Edinburgh University Press, 1995.

-, "The Significance of Modern African Christianity: A Manifesto", *Studies in World Christianity* 1.1, The Edinburgh Review of Theology and Religion, 1995, pp 51-67.

-, "How is Jesus Christ Lord? Aspects of an Evangelical Christian Apologetics in the Context of African Religious Pluralism" *Exchange* 25.1 (1996), pp. 27-42.

-, "Five Theses on the Significance of Modern African Christianity: A Manifesto", *Transformation* 13.1 (1996), pp. 20-29.

-, "Gospel and Culture, some Insights for our Time from the Experience of the Earliest Church", *Journal of African Christian Thought* 2.2 (1999), pp. 8-17.

-, "A Half Century of African Christian Thought: Pointers to Theology and Theological Education in the Next Half Century", *Journal of African Christian Thought* 3.1 (2000), pp. 5-11.

-, "Scripture as the Hermeneutics of Culture and Tradition", *Journal of African Christian Thought* 4.1 (2001), pp. 2-11.

-, *Jesus and the Gospel in Africa: History and Experience,* Maryknoll, NY: Orbis Books, 2004.

Berentsen, Jan-Martin, 'Background and emergence of Norwegian missions: Historical sketch and brief outlook', in Japanese translation, *Senkyo to shingaku,* Kobe Lutheran Theological Seminary, No. 28, Fall 2006, pp. 15-25.

-, "Misjonstjenestens misjonale identitet og karakter", *Norsk Tidsskrift for Misjon* 57(2003), pp. 221-234, 227.

Berentsen, Jan Martin, Tormod Engelsviken and Knud Jørgensen (eds), *Missiologi i dag*, Oslo: Universitetsforlaget, 1994

Berger, Peter L., *Religion, samfund og virkelighed: elementer til en sociologisk religionsteori.* Viborg: Lindhard og Ringhof, 1974.

-, *The Desecularization of the World: resurgent religion and world politics,* Washington DC: Ethics and Public Policy Center, 1999.

Berger, Peter L. and Thomas Luckmann, *The Social Construction of Reality. A Treatise in the Sociology of Knowledge.* Garden City, NY: Doubleday, 1966.

Bergh, Mirjam, *Caring Sharing Daring. Development work in transition,* Oslo: Norsk Misjonsråds Bistandsnemnd and Diakonhjemmets Internasjonale Senter, 1995.

Bevans, Stephen B., *Models of Contextual Theology*, Maryknoll, NY: Orbis Books, 1992.

-, "Models of contextual theology", in *Missiology*, 13: 1985, pp.185-202.

Bjerke, B., *Business Leadership and Culture*, Cheltenham UK – Northampton, MA: Edward Elgar, 1999.

Bjørvik in Henning Bang: *Organisasjonskultur,* 3rd Ed., Oslo: TANO 1988.

Blaschke, Jochen (Ed), *Multi-level discrimination of Muslim Women in Europe*, Berlin, 2000.

Bonhoeffer, Dietrich, *Ethik,* herausgegeben von Ilse Tödt *et al.*, Munich: Chr. Kaiser Verlag, 1992.

-, *Nachfolge,* herausgegeben von Martin Kuske und Ilse Tödt, Munich: Chr. Kaiser Verlag, 1989.

-, *Sanctorum Communio. Eine dogmatische Untersuchung zur Soziologie der Kirche,* herausggegeben von Joachim von Soosten, Munich: Chr. Kaiser Verlag, 1986.

Boris, Stephen, *The Land of the Living. The Danish Folk High Schools and Denmark's Non-violent Path to Modernization,* Nevada City: Blue Dolphin, 1991.

Bosch, David, *Transforming Mission: Paradigm shifts in theology of missions,* Maryknoll, NY: Orbis Books, 1991.

Breen, Mike and Walt Kallestad, *The Passionate Church,* Colorado Springs, CO: Cook Communications, 2005.

Brock, Charles, *The Principles and Practice of Indigenous Church Planting.* Manila: Baptist Center 1980.

Brown, Callum C., *The Death of Christian Britain. Understanding secularisation 1800-2000*, London and New York, NY: Routledge, 2001.

Brunner, Emil, *The Word in the World*, London: SCM Press, 1931.

Bühlmann, Walbert, "Missionary spirituality" in P. Flanagan: *A New Missionary Era*, Maryknoll, NY: Orbis books, 1982, pp. 113-118.

-, *The Coming of the Third Church: An Analysis of the Future of the Church*, Maryknoll, New York: Orbis Books, 1977.

Bäckström, Anders, *Svenska Kyrkan som välfärdsaktör i en global kultur,* Stockholm: Verbum, 1999.

Bäckström, Anders et al, *Religious Change in Northern Europe. The Case of Sweden,* Stockholm: Verbum, 2004.

Børgesen, Inger-Marie, *Folk og folkekirken. Kirkens plads i menneskers hverdagsliv og tankeverden*, Copenhagen: Akademisk Forlag, 1991.

Buckser, Andrew, "Social Conversion and Group Definition in Jewish Copenhagen", *The Anthropology of Religious Conversion*, Andrew Buckser & Stephen D. Glazier (eds.), Lanham, UK: Rowman & Littlefield Publishers, 2003, pp. 69-84.

Campbell, John L., John A. Halland and Ove K. Pedersen (eds.), *National Identity and the Varieties of Capitalism,* Copenhagen: DJØF Publishing, 2006.

Carlberg, Gustav, *The Changing China Scene: The Story of the Lutheran Theological Seminary in Its Church and Political Setting over a Period of Forty-Five Years: 1913-1958*, Hong Kong: Lutheran Literature Society, 1958.

Carson, Donald A., *Becoming Conversant with the Emerging Church*, Grand Rapids, MI: Zondervan, 2005.

-, "Church and Mission: Reflections on Contextualization and the Third Horizon," *The Church in the Bible and the World: An International Study*, ed. D. A. Carson, Exeter: The Paternoster Press, 1987, pp. 248-50.

Carter, Craig, *Rethinking Christ and Culture: A Post-Christendom Perspective,* Grand Rapids: Brazos Press, 2007.

Chen, Zemin, "Inculturation of the Gospel and Hymn Singing in China," *Chinese Theological Review* 11(1997)2, pp. 49-57.

Chinese Christian Hymnal Committee, "Foreword to the Chinese Hymnal 1983 Edition", *Chinese Theological Review* 1985, pp. 143-147.

Christoffersen, Lisbet (ed.), *Gudebilleder, ytringsfrihed og religion i en globaliseret verden,* Copenhagen: Tiderne Skifter, 2006.

Clinton, Robert and Kathrine Haubert: *The Joshua Portrait. A Study in leadership development, leadership transition & destiny fulfillment*. Altadena, CA: Barnabas Resources, 1990.

Cobb, John B. jr., "The Buddhist-Christian Dialogue Since 1945", Fu, Charles Wei-hsun and Gerhard E. Spiegler (eds.), *Religious Issues and Interreligious Dialogues: An Analysis and Sourcebook of Developments Since 1945*, New York: Greenwood Press,1989, pp.571-589.

Cole, Neil, *Organic Church: Growing Faith Where Life Happens,* San Francisco, CA: Jossey-Bass, 2005.

Colin, James C., and Jerry I. Porras: *Built to Last. Successful Habits of Visionary Companies*. New York, NY: Harper Business, 1994.

Collier, Mary Jane and Tomas, Milt, 'Cultural Identity: An interpretive perspective', Young Yun Kim and William Gudykunst (eds.), *Theories in intercultural communication*, New Delhi: Sage, 1996.

Collins, John N., *Diakonia: Reinterpreting the Ancient Sources,* New York, NY/Oxford: Oxford University Press, 1990.

Confessio Augustana, Augsburg, 1530, English Edition, Pelikan, Jaroslav and Valerie Hotchkiss (eds.), *Creeds & confessions of faith in the Christian tradition, Vol. 2: Creeds and confessions of the Reformation era*, New Haven, Conn.: Yale University Press 2003, pp. 49-118.

Conn, Harvie, *Eternal word and changing worlds: Theology, anthropology, and mission in trialogue*, Grand Rapids, MI: Zondervan, 1984.

Costas, Orlando E., "Internationalizing the curriculum in Christian higher education", Robert A, Hess (ed.), *Internationalizing the curriculum,* St. Paul, MN: The Christian College Consortium, 1986.

-, "Theological Education and Mission" in C. René Padilla (ed.), *New Alternatives in Theological Education,* Oxford: Regnum Books, 1988.

Cressy, Earl H., "Converting the Missionary," *Asia: Journal of the American Asiatic Association* 19:6 (June 1919): 553-556.

Croft, Steven, *The Future of the Parish System. Shaping of the Church of England for the 21 st Century*, London: Church House, 2006.

Cross, Frank Moore, *Canaanite Myth and Hebrew Epic*, 16, 43. Patrick Miller, *Israelite Religion and Biblical Theology,* Sheffield: Sheffield Academic Press Ltd., 2000.

Cui, Geng and Sjef van der Berg, 'Testing the construct validity of intercultural effectiveness', *International journal of intercultural relations* 15: 1991, pp. 227-241.

Dahl, Øyvind 'Bridges of understanding: Perspectives on intercultural communication', in Øyvind Dahl, Iben Jensen and Peter Nynäs, *Bridges of understanding: Perspectives on intercultural communication*, Oslo: Unipub forlag, Oslo Academic Press, 2006, pp. 7-22.

-, *Møter mellom mennesker, Interkulturell kommunikasjon*, Oslo: Gyldendal Akademisk forlag, 2001.

Dahl, Øyvind and Kjell Habert, *Møte mellom kulturer: Tverrkulturell kommunikasjon*, Oslo: Universitetsforlaget, 1986.

Davie, Grace, *Europe: The Exceptional Case. Parameters of Faith in the Modern World.* London: Darton, Longman, Todd 2002, pp. 107-111.

-, "Religion in Europe in the 21st century", in *Religion in late modernity. Essays in Honor of Pål Repstad*, eds Inger Furseth and Paul Leer-Salvesen, Trondheim: Tapir 2007.

Day, J., *Psalms, Old Testament Guide,* Sheffield: Sheffield Academic Press, 1990.

Diakonia: Creating Harmony, Seeking Justice and Practicing Compassion. A Study on Ecumenical Efforts in Diakonia and Justice, Geneva: World Council of Churches, 2005.

Diamond, Jared, *Collapse. How Societies Fail or Succeed.* New York, NY: Viking Books, 2005.

Die Bekenntnisschriften der evangelisch-lutherischen Kirche, Göttingen: Vandenhoek & Ruprecht, 1930, 5. Aufl. 1963

Dodd, Carley H., *Dynamics of intercultural communication,* 5th ed. New York, NY: McGraw Hill, 1998.

Douglas, J.D., (Ed.), *Proclaim Christ Until He Comes,* Minneapolis, MN: World Wide Publications, 1989.

Drucker, Peter, *Innovation and Entrepreneurship. Practice and Principles*. New York, NY: Harper & Row 1985.

D'Souza, Anthony, *Leadership*, St. Paul's Publ. 1989

DuBrin, Andrew J.: *Foundations for Organizational behavior. An applied perspective*. Englewood Cliffs, NJ: Prentice Hall, Inc.,1984.

du Toit, André, "No chosen people: The myth of the Calvinist origin of Afrikaner nationalism and racial ideology", *American Historical Review* 88 (1983), pp. 920-952

Dyrkøb, Jan Ulrik, *Northrop Fryes litteraturteori,* København: Berlingske Forlag 1979, pp. 61ff.

Eilert, Håkan, *Boundlessness: Studies in Karl Ludvig Reichelt's Missionary Thinking with Special Regard to the Buddhist-Christian Encounter*, Aarhus: Forlaget Aros, 1974.

Eliade, Mirclea, *Det hellige og det profane,* Oslo: Gyldendal, Second Edition, 1997.

Ellingsen, Svein; Måsø, Ragnhild; Nøttveit, Aud and Rimington, Greta (Eds.), *Fra Nanking til Tao Fong Shan*, Oslo: Den Nordiske Kristne Buddhistmisjon, 1987.

Engedal, Leif Gunnar, "Spiritualitet og teologi", *Ung Teologi* 2-2003, pp. 47-56.

Engelsviken, Tormod, *Besettelse og åndsutdrivelse i Bibelen, historien og vår egen tid,* Oslo: Lunde, 1978.

-, 'Den misjonale kirke og utfordringen fra kirken i sør', Tormod Engelsviken and Kjell Olav Sannes (eds), *Hva vil det si å være kirke? Kirkens vesen og oppdrag,* Oslo, MF /Trondheim: Tapir akademiske forlag, 2004, pp 69-92.

-, "Divergene or Convergence? The Relationship between Recent Ecumenical and Evangelical Mission Documents", *Swedish Missiological Themes*, No. 2 (2001), pp. 197-220

-, "Exorcism and Healing in the Evangelical churches in Ethiopia", *Journal of Mission Theology,* Vol.1, Fasc. 1 (1991), pp. 41-48.

-, "Misjonstenkningen fra 1900 til vår tid", Jan-Martin Berentsen, Tormod Engelsviken and Knud Jørgensen (eds.), *Missiologi i dag*, 2nd ed., Oslo: Universitetsforlaget, 2004, pp. 140-158

-, "Olav Guttorm Myklebust : 1905-2001", *Mission studies* 19:2 (2002), pp.12-13.

Engelsviken, Tormod and Kjell Olav Sannes (eds.), *Hva vil det si å være kirke? Kirkens vesen og oppdrag. Bind 3 i Ekklesiologi-prosjektet ved Det teologiske Menighetsfakultet,* Trondheim: Tapir Akademisk Forlag, 2004

Engen, Charles van, *God's Missionary People. Rethinking the Purpose of the Local Church,* Grand Rapids, MI: Baker Book House, 1991.

Eriksen, Thomas Hylland, *Små steder. Store spørsmål. Innføring i Sosialantropologi*. Oslo: Universitetsforlaget, 1994.

Escobar, Samuel, *Changing Tides. Latin America and World Mission Today,* Maryknoll, NY: Orbis, 2002.

-, "The legacy of Orlando Costas", *International Bulletin of Missionary Research*, 25 (2001):50-56.

Eskilt, Ingrid, *An analysis of changing perspectives on the understanding of the missionary call in the Mission Covenant Church of Norway*, Ph.D. dissertation in intercultural studies, Deerfield, IL: Trinity International University, 2005.

Etzioni, Amitai, *Moderne Organisasjoner*. Oslo: Forlaget Tanum, Norli 1978.

Evensen, Sigmund, "Nedtellingen fortsetter", *Wycliffe-Nytt* 28/2 (2006), pp. 4-5.

Fagerberg, Holsten, *A new look at the Lutheran Confessions (1529-1537)*, St. Louis, MO: Concordia, 1972; original 1952.

Farley, Edvard, *Theologia. The Fragmentation and Unity of Theological Education,* Philadelphia, PA: Fortress Press, 1983.

Flamholtz, Eric G., *How to make a Transition from the Entrepreneurship to a Professionally Managed Firm*. San Francisco, CA: Jossey-Bass Publ., 1986.

Fleming, Bruce C., *Contextualization of theology: An evangelical assessment*, Pasadena, CA: William Carey Library, 1980.

Flesseman-van Leer, Ellen (ed), *The Bible: Its authority in ecumenical movement. Faith and Order paper, no. 99*, Geneva: World Council of Churches, 1980.

Ford, Leighton, *Transforming Leadership. Jesus' way of creating vision, shaping values & empowering change*. Downers Grove, IL: InterVarsity Press, 1991.

Fotland, Roar G., *Ancestor Christology in Context: Theological Perspectives by Kwame Bediako*, Bergen: Universitetet i Bergen, 2004.

Fontain, Joost, *The Silence of Great Zimbabwe,* New York, NY: UCL Press, 2006.

Fouroozandeh, Massoud and Øhrstrøm, Daniel, *Den forbudte frelse. Fra koransanger i Iran til kirkefader i Danmark*. København: Lindhardt & Ringhof, 2005.

Frankl, Victor, *Man's Search For Meaning,* New York, NY: Washington Square Press, 1963.

Franzén, Ruth, "Ruth Rouse 1872-1956. Missionary, Student, Evangelist, Ecumenical Pioneer", Anderson, Gerald H., R. T. Coote, N. A. Horner, J. M. Phillips (eds), *Mission Legacies. Biograpichal Studies of Leaders of the Modern Missionary Movement,* Maryknoll, NY: Orbis, 1994, pp. 93-191.

Fry, L. W., "Toward a theory of spiritual leadership", *The Leadership Quarterly*, v.14, I 6, Dec. 2003.

Furre, Berge, "Nypinsevenner – på veg mot Europa", *Kirke og kultur, No 1,* 2003, p. 3-15.

Galvin, J. C, *Streams of research*, Draft article in progress, 2004.

Garlake, Peter S., *Great Zimbabwe,* London: Thames & Hudson, 1973

Garner, Martin, *A Call for Apostles Today,* Cambridge, UK: Grove Books, 2007.

Geertz, Armin W., Søren Jensen and Peter Widmann (eds.): *Medspil og modspil. Teologi og religionsvidenskab*, Aarhus: Faculty of Theology. University of Aarhus, 1996.

Geertz, Clifford, *The interpretation of cultures: Selected essays*, New York, NY: Basic books, 1973.

Getui, Mary N., Knut Holter and Victor Zinkuratire (eds.), *Interpreting the Old Testament in Africa,* Nairobi: Acton, 2001

Getui, Mary N., Tinyiko Maluleke and Justin S. Ukpong (eds.), *Interpreting the New Testament in Africa,* Nairobi: Acton, 2001

Gibbs, Eddie, *LeadershipNext,* Downers Grove: InterVarsity Press, 2005.

Gibbs, Eddie and Ryan K. Bolger, *Emerging Churches: Creating Christian Community in Postmodern Cultures,* Grand Rapids: Baker Academic and London, UK: SPCK, 2005.

Gibbs, Eddie and Ian Coffey, *ChurchNext. Quantum Changes in Christian Ministry,* Downers Grove, IL: InterVarsity Press, 2001

Giddens, Anthony, *Modernity and self-identity: Self and society in late modern age,* Cambridge: Polity Press, 1992

Giddens, Anthony and Christopher Piersen, *Making Sense of Modernity,* Chinese edition, Beijing: Xinhua Publishing House, 2001.

Gifford, Paul, "A view of Ghana's New Christianity" in Lamin Sanneh & Joel E. Carpenter (eds.) *The Changing Face of Christianity,* Oxford: Oxford University Press, 2005, pp. 81-96.

Gilliland, Dean S. (ed), *The Word among us: Contextualization theology for mission today*, Dallas, TX: Word, 1989.

Gilmore, Thomas North, *Making a leadership change*. San Francisco, CA: Jossey-Bass Publ. 1988

Gort, J. D. 1995, 'Human distress, salvation, and mediation of salvation', in F. J. Verstraelen (ed), *Missiology: An ecumenical introduction. Texts and contexts of global Christianity*, Grand Rapids, MI: Eerdmans, 1995, pp.194-210.

Grane, Leif, *Confessio Augustana*, København: Gyldendal, 1959

Greiner, Larry E: *Evalution and Revolution as Organizations Grow*. Cambridge, MA: Harvard Business Review, July-August 1972, Reprinted as HBR Classic, 1998.

Grung, Anne Hege, "Begrepet dialog i Emmaus – noen refleksjoner om bruken av begrepet på grunnlag av erfaringer i et flerreligiøst landskap" in *Kirke og Kultur,* No. 1/2005.

-, "Kvindeperspektiv på kristen-muslimsk dialog" in Larsen, Lena and Lissi Rasmussen (eds.) *Islam, Kristendom og det moderne*, Copenhagen, 2004.

Grung, Anne Hege and Lena Larsen, *Dialog med og uten slør*, Oslo, 2000.

Grunlan, Steve, and Marvyn K. Mayers, *Cultural anthropology: A Christian perspective*, Grand Rapids, MI: Zondervan, 1979.

Grønvik, Knut (red), *I stillhet og tillit,* Oslo: Verbum, 2005.

Guder, Darrell L., *Mission in a Pluralist Society – Why and How? Mission Conference of the Folk Church at Nyborg Strand June 9 2006, Presentation I.*

-, *The continuing Conversion of the Church,* Grand Rapids, MI: William B. Eerdmans, 2000.

Gumperz, John and Dell Hymes (eds), *Directions in sociolinguistics: The ethnography of communication*, New York, NY: Holt, Rinehart and Winston, 1972.

Gundelach, Peter and Ester Nørregaard Nielsen, *Etniske gruppers værdier,* Copenhagen: Ministeriet for Integration, 2007.

Gustafsson, Göran and Thorleif Pettersson (eds.), *Folkkyrkor och religiös pluralism – den nordiska religiösa modellen,* Borås: Verbum Förlag, 2000.

Habermas, Jürgen, *Politik der Globalisierung,* Frankfurt am Main: Suhrkamp Verlag, 1998.

Hadaway, C. Kirk, Penny Long Marler and Mark Chaves, "What The Polls Don't Show: A Closer Look at U.S. Church Attendance," *American Psychological Review* 58, December 1993.

Haddad, Yvonne Yazbeck and Esposito, John L (Eds.), *Daughters of Abraham – Feminist Thought in Judaism, Christianity and Islam*, Florida, 2001.

Hagen, Unni, *Medias publikum: Frå mottakar til brukar?*, Oslo: Gyldendal, 2000.

Hall, Edward, *The silent language*, New York, NY: Doubleday, 1959.

-, *Beyond culture*, New York, NY: Anchor, 1976.

Hallencreutz, Carl F. "Missionary Spirituality – the case of Ansgar", *Studia Theologica 36* (1982).

Hambrick, D. and Mason, P. A., "Upper Echelons: The organisation as a reflection of its top managers", *Academy of Management Review*, Vol. 9, No. 2, 1984.

Hannerz, Ulf, *Cultural Complexity: Studies in the social organization of meaning*, New York, NY: Columbia University Press, 1992.

Harbakk, Ernst, "The Tao Fong Shan Christian Centre: A Statement of Purpose", in *Areopagus*, Fall 1987 (Vol. 1, No. 1), Hong Kong: Dialog Centre International and Tao Fong Shan Christian Centre.

Harbakk, Ernst and Riisager, Filip (eds.), *Veien videre* (The Way Ahead), written for the 75th Anniversary of the CMB, Oslo: Den Nordiske Kristne Buddhistmisjon, 1997.

Haus, Sigurd, "Knekk koden, og bli forstått! Om fagfeltet interkulturell kommunikasjon og forholdet til kommunikasjonsteoretiske perspektiver", Haus, Sigurd; Geir Skeie og Øystein Lund Johannesen (eds.), *Kulturformidling fra internasjonale arenaer: Et bidrag til meningsutveksling om kultur*, Kristiansand: Høyskoleforlaget, Norway, 2003.

Heelas, Paul and Linda Woodhead, with Benjamin Seel, Bronizlaw Szerszynski, Karin Tusting, *The spiritual revolution: Why religion is giving way to spirituality,* Oxford: Blackwell, 2005.

Hegstad, Harald, *Folkekirke og trosfellesskap. Et kirkesosiologisk og ekklesiologisk grunnproblem belyst gjennon en undersøkelse av tre norske lokalmenigheter*, Trondheim: Tapir Forlag, 1995.

Heim, S. Mark, "Sharing our differences: Koinonia and the Theology of Religious Plurality", Faith and Order paper 2004.

Heisler, Barbara Schmitter, "The Sociology of Immigration. From Assimilation to Segmented Integration, from the American Experience to the Global Arena", in *Migration Theory. Talking across Disciplines*, Caroline B. Brettell & James F. Hollifield (eds.), New York, NY & London: Routledge, 2000, pp.77-96.

Helingsgudstjeneste, Copenhagen: I Mesterens Lys, 2007.

Hersey, Paul and Kenneth H. Blanchard: *Management of Organizational Behaviour*. Englewood Cliffs, NJ: Prentice Hall, 1988.

Hesselgrave, David J., *Communicating Christ Cross-Culturally*, Grand Rapids, MI: Zondervan Publishing House, 1978.

-, "Contextualization and Revelational Epistemology," in *Hermeneutics, Inerrancy, and the Bible*, ed. Earl D. Radmacher and Robert D. Preus, Grand Rapids, MI: Zondervan.

-, *Planting Churches Cross-Culturally. A Guide for Home and Foreign Mission.* Grand Rapids, MI: Baker Book House, 1980.

-, 'The role of culture in communication', in Ralph D. Winter and Stephen Hawthorne: *Perspectives on the world Christian movement*, Pasadena, CA: William Carey Library, 1992.

Hesselgrave, David J. and Rommen, Edward, *Contextualization: Meaning, methods, and models*, Leicester: Apollos, 1989.

Hiebert, Paul G., *Anthropological insights for missionaries*, Grand Rapids, MI: Baker Book House, 1985.

-, "Critical Contextualization," *Missiology* 12 (1984), pp. 287-96 and *International Bulletin of Missionary Research* 11:3 (1987).

-, *Missiological implications of epistemological shifts: Affirming truth in a modern/postmodern world*, Harrisburg, PA: Trinity press international, 1999.

-, "The Flaw of the Excluded Middle", *Missiology: An International Review,* No. 10, 1982, pp. 35-47

-, 'The social sciences and missions: applying the message', in Edward Rommen and Gary Corwin (eds), *Missiology and the social sciences: Contributions, cautions and conclusions*, Pasadena, CA: William Carey Library, 1996.

Hiebert, Paul G. and Eloise Hiebert Meneses, *Incarnational Ministry: Planting Churches in Band, Tribal, Peasant, and Urban Societies,* Grand Rapids, MI: Baker, 1995.

Hill, Patricia, *The World their Household. The American woman's foreign mission movement and cultural transformation 1870-1920,* Ann Arbor. MI: University of Michigan Press, 1985.

Hirsch, Alan, *The Forgotten Ways: Reactivating the missional church,* Grand Rapids, MI: Brazos Press, 2006.

Hjarvard, Stig, "Medialisering af religiøse forestillinger", in Højsgaard, Morten Thomsen and Hans Raun Iversen (eds.), *Gudstro i Danmark*, København : Anis, 2005, pp. 175ff.

Hjelde, S., Religionswissenschaft und Theologie. Die Frage ihrer gegenseitigen Abgrenzung in historischer Perspective, *Studia Theologica* 52/1998.

Hofstede, Geert, *Cultures and organisation: Software of the Mind*, London: McGraw-Hill, 1991.

-, *Culture's consequences: International differences in work-related value*, London: Sage, 1980.

Holmberg, Bengt, *Paul and Power. The structure of authority in the Primitive Church as reflected in the Pauline Letters.* Coniectanea Biblica New Testament Series 11. Lund: CWK Gleerup, 1978.

Holter, Knut, "Interpreting Solomon in colonial and post-colonial Africa", *Old Testament Essays* 19 (2006): 851-862.

- (ed.), *Let My People Stay! Researching the Old Testament in Africa,* Nairobi: Acton, 2006.

-, *Old Testament Research for Africa: A Critical Analysis and Annotated Bibliography of African Old Testament Dissertations, 1967-2000,* New York, NY: Peter Lang, 2002.

-, "Old Testament scholarship in sub-Saharan Africa north of the Limpopo river", West, Gerald O. and Musa W. Dube (eds.), *The Bible in Africa: transactions, trajectories, and trends,* Leiden: Brill, 2000, pp. 54-71.

-, *Yahweh in Africa: Essays on Africa and the Old Testament,* New York, NY: Peter Lang, 2000, pp. 51-60.

Holth, Sverre, *Karl Ludvig Reichelt*, Oslo: Egede Instituttet, 1952.

Hong Kong Catholic Hymnal (*Sòng Ēn – Xìnyǒu Gējí*) ["Praise Grace Collection of Songs for Friends of the Faith"]; Hong Kong 1976, Revised Edition, 1985.

Honko, Lauri, "The Problem of Defining Myth," in *Sacred Narrative: Readings in the Theory of Myth,* ed. Alan Dundes, Berkeley, CA: University of California Press, 1984, pp. 46-48.

Hornbech, Birthe Rønn, "Mission og integration", in *Kristeligt Dagblad*, January 10, 2003.

Howatch, Susan, *Absolute Truths: a Novel,* New York, NY: Knopf, 1994.

- *Glittering Images,* New York, NY: Ballantine Books, 1987

Hsiao, Andrew, *A Brief History of the Chinese Lutheran Church*, Hong Kong: Taosheng Publishing House, 1999.

Hunsberger, George and Craig Van Gelder, *The Church between Gospel and Culture*, Grand Rapids, MI: Eerdmans, 1996.

Huntington, Samuel, *The Clash of Civilizations and the Remaking of the World Order,* Chinese translation, Xinhua Publishing House, 1999.

Hwa, Yung, *Mangos or Bananas? The Quest for an Authentic Asian Christian Theology,* Oxford: Regnum, 1997.

Hymns of Praise / Sòng Zhǔ Shèng Shī, 1955, Hong Kong: Taosheng, Revised Edition, 1994.

Hymns of Universal Praise / Pǔtiān Sòngzàn, United Hymnal Committee, Shanghai: Christian Literature Society, 1936, New Revised Edition, Hong Kong: Chinese Christian Literature Council Ltd. 2006.

Højsgaard, Morten Thomsen and Hans Raun Iversen, *Gudstro i Danmark,* Copenhagen: Anis, 2005.

Haanes,Vidar L., " The first Professor of Missiology in Norway: Professor O.G. Myklebust (1905-2001)", *Norsk Tidsskrift for Misjon* 59:4 (2005), pp. 239-246.

-, "Unity in Diversity and Diversity in Unity: The Role and Legitimacy of the European Universities", *Higher Education in Europe* 31:4 (2006), pp. 443-448.

Immenkötter, Herbert, *Die Confutatio der Confessio Augustana vom 3. August 1530, Corpus Catholicorum Bd. 33*, Münster Westfalen: Aschendorff, 2. verb. Aufl. 1979

Inglehart, Ronald, *Modernization and Postmodernization: Cultural, economic, and political change in 43 societies,* Princeton, NJ: Princeton University Press, 1997.

Integreringsbarometeret 2005, Integrerings- og mangfoldsdirektoratet IMDi, (The Barometer of Intergration 2005, The Directorate of Integration and plurality IMDi), Oslo, 2005.

Ipgrave, Michael (Ed), *Scriptures in Dialogue. Christians and Muslims studying the Bible and the Qur'an together*, London, 2004.

Iversen, Hans Raun, red., *Dåb og medlemskab i Folkekirken.* København: Anis, 2000.

-, "Folk Church as Mission to Cultural Christians", *Swedish Missiological Themes*, 85/3-4, (1997), pp. 237-264

-, "Gudstro i den danske religionspark", in Morten Thomsen Højsgaard and Hans Raun Iversen: *Gudstro i Danmark,* Copenhagen: Anis, 2005.

-, "Incarnation, Congregation and Mission", *Identity and Conflict. Essays in Honour of Johannes Aagaard,* New Delhi: Munshiram Manoharlal Publishers Pvt. Ltd., 1998, pp. 203-218.

-, *Karma, Koran og Kirke. Religiøs mangfoldighed som folkekirkelig udfordring,* Aarhus: Univers 2007.

-, "Kulturkristendom, kirkekristendom og karismatisk kristendom. Kristendomsformernes baggrund og samspil i folkekirken", in Jørn Henrik Olsen (ed.): *Kulturkristendom og kirke. Ny Mission 1,* Copenhagen: Unitas Forlag, 1999, pp. 6-43.

-,, "Leaving the distant Church. The Danish Experience" in Mordecai Bar-Lev and William Shaffir (eds.), *Leaving Religion and Religious Life,* London: Jai Press Inc.1997.

-, "Palau og Ansgar", *Nordisk Missionstidsskrift* 100/1 (1989), pp. 8-12.

-, "Secular Religion and Religious Secularism", *Nordic Journal of Religion and Society,* 19/2 (2006), pp. 75-92.

-, *Tanzania tur/retur. Syv tekster om socialisme og mission,* Aarhus: FK-Tryk, 1981.

-, "Tidevarv komma, tidevarv försvinna... Overvejelser omkring en spørgeskemaundersøgelse af salmesang i de nordiske lande", *Hymnologiske Meddelelser* 31/1 (2992), pp. 76-82.

Jackson, Darrell, "European Churches in Mission. A research Report form the CEC Mission in Europe Programme 2004 – 2007", CEC, 2007.

-, "Pax Europa: Crux Europa", *Researching European Mission,* Report, 2007.

James, Rick, "Realities of change. *Understanding how African NGO leaders develop.* Moses Isooba Praxis paper no 6, July 2005

Jandt, Fred, *Intercultural communication: An introduction,* London: Sage, 1995.

Jaspers, Karl, *The Idea of the University,* Boston, MA: Beacon Press 1959.

Jenkins, Philip, *Companions of Life. A supple faith.* http://www.christianitytoday.com/bc/2007/002/9.18.html

-, *The New Christendom. The Coming of Global Christianity,* Oxford, New York: Oxford University Press, 2002.

-, *The New Faces of Christianity: Believing the Bible in the Global South,* Oxford: Oxford University Press, 2006.

Jensen, Iben, *Interkulturell kommunikation i komplekse samfund,* Roskilde: Roskildes Universitetsforlag, Denmark, 1998.

-, 'The practice of intercultural communication: reflections for professionals in cultural meetings, in *The Electronic Journal of Intercultural Communication,* Nordic Network of Intercultural Communication, NIC, 2003 www.immi.se/intercultural/No. 6.

Jiānán Shīxuǎun 1-2 ([*Selected Songs from Canaan 1-2*] Taipei: Hosanna Gospel Propaganda Association, 2001

Joint Declaration on the Doctrine of Justification, Final Proposal, Geneva: Lutheran World Federation, 1997.

Jung, Carl Gustav, *The Secret of the Golden Flower: A Chinese Book of Life*, English translation by Richard Wilhelm, London: Routledge and Kegan Paul, 1962.

Jørgensen, Knud: See separate bibliography.

Jørgensen, Knud and Berit Helgøy Kloster, *Vitner i arbeid og fritid: teltmakertjenesten til jordens ender* (Witnesses during work and leisure time: tentmaker ministry to the ends of the earth), Oslo: Credo, 1991.

Kähler, Martin, "Die Mission – ist sie ein unentbehrlicher Zug am Christentum" in: *Schriften zu Christologie und Mission*, Herausgegeben von Heinzgünter Frohnes, Theologische Bücherei Bd. 42, München: Chr. Kaiser Verlag 1971.

Kaldor, Peter, *Who Goes Where? Who Doesn't Care?*, Homebursh West, NSW: Lancer Books, 1987.

Kallenberg, Brad, "Conversion Converted" in *Evangelical Quarterly*, Vol. 67, No. 4/1995, pp. 335-364.

Karecki, Madge, "Discovering the Roots of Ritual," *Missionalia* 25 (1997), pp. 169-77.

- "Religious Ritual as a Key to Wholeness in Mission," *Missionalia* 25:4 (December 1997), pp. 598-606.

Kato, Byang, 'Evangelism opportunities and obstacles in Africa', in J. D. Douglas (ed), *Let the earth hear his voice: International congress on world evangelisation. Lausanne, Switzerland.* Official Reference Volume: Papers and responses, Minneapolis: World Wide Publications, 1975, pp.155-158.

-, "The Gospel, Cultural Context and Religious Syncretism," in *Let the Earth Hear His Voice*, edited by J. D. Douglas, Minneapolis: World Wide Publications, 1975.

Kealey, Daniel J., *Cross-cultural effectiveness: A study of Canadian technical advisors overseas*, Hull, Quebec, Canada: Canadian International Development Agency, 1990.

Kim, Kirsteen, "Mission Studies in Britain and Ireland: Introduction to a World-Wide Web", *British Journal of Theological Education* Vol. 11.1 (2000).

-, "Postmodern Mission: A Paradigm Shift in David Bosch's Theology of Mission?" *International Review of Mission* LXXXIX/353 (2000), pp. 172-179.

Kim, Young Yun, 'On theorizing intercultural communication', in Young Yun Kim and Willam B. Gudykunst (eds), *Theories in intercultural communication*, London: Sage, 1996.

King, Ursula, "Feminism: The Missing Dimension in the Dialogue of Religions" in May, John (ed.): *Pluralism and the Religions: The Theological and Political Dimensions*, London, 1998.

Kinoti, Hannah W. and John M. Waliggo (eds.), *The Bible in African Christianity: Essays in Biblical Theology,* Nairobi: Acton, 1997.

Kirk, Andrew J., "Re-envisioning the Theological Curriculum as if the Missio Dei Mattered", *Common Ground Journal* v3 n1 (Fall 2005):23. URL: www.commongroundjournal.org.]

-, *The Mission of Theology and Theology as Mission,* Valley Forge: Trinity Press International, 1997.

Kirken i møte med den åndelige lengsel i vår tid, Oslo: Kirkerådet, 1999.

Kjøde, Rolf and Darryl Krause, "Norsk råd for misjon og evangelisering: Misjonsstatistikk 2001", in *Norsk Tidsskift for misjon*, Vol. 57, 2003, pp. 27-39.

Kolb, Robert and Timothy J. Wengert (eds.): *The Book of Concord*, Minneapolis: Fortress Press, 2000.

Kolb, Robert, and James A. Nestingen (eds.), *Sources and Contexts of the Book of Concord*, Minneapolis: Fortress Press, 2001.

Kolde, Theodor, *Die Augsburgische Konfession lateinisch und deutsch*, Gotha: Fiedrich Andreas Perthes, 1895, 2. verbesserte Aufl. 1911.

Kraemer, Hendrik, *World Cultures and World Religions: The Coming Dialogue*, London: Lutterworth Press, 1960.

Kraft, Charles H., *Anthropology for Christian Witness*. Pasadena, CA: William Carey Library, 1996.

-, *Appropriate Christianity*. Pasadena, CA: William Carey Library, 2005.

-, *Christianity in culture: A study in dynamic theologizing in cross-cultural perspective*, Maryknoll, New York: Orbis Books, 1979.

-, 'Dynamic equivalence churches: an ethnotheological approach to indegeneity', in Charles H. Kraft and Tom N. Wisley (eds), *Readings in Dynamic Indigeneity*, Pasadena: William Carey Library, 1979.

Kraft, Charles H. and Tom N. Wisley: *Readings in Dynamic Indigeneity*. Pasadena, CA: William Carey Library, 1979.

Küng, Hans and Karl-Josef Kusche (eds.), *A Global Ethic: The Declaration of the Parliament of World Religions*. Guanghu He trans., Chengdu: Sichuan People's Publishing House, 1997.

Küster, Volker, *The Many Faces of Jesus Christ*, London: SCM Press, 2001.

Kvalbein, Hans, *Jesus og de fattige og hans bruk av ord for "fattig"*, Oslo: Luther, 1981.

Lai, Whalen, "The Buddhist-Christian Dialogue in China", in Fu, Charles Wei-hsun and Spiegler, Gerhard E. (eds.), *Religious Issues and Interreligious Dialogues: An Analysis and Sourcebook of Developments Since 1945*, New York, NY: Greenwood Press, pp.613-631.

Land, Stephen J., *Pentecostal Spirituality: a Passion for the Kingdom*, Sheffield: Sheffield Academic Press, 1993.

Lande, Gunvor, "Frigjeringsteologien går mot forsoningsteologi" ("From Liberation Theology Towards a Theology of Reconciliation"), *Norsk tidsskrift for misjon* 3-2001, pp. 185-192.

Larsen, Christian A., *Danskernes forhold til religionen – en afrapportering af ISSP98*, Ålborg: Aalborg Universitetscenter, 2002, pp. 86-88.

Lasswell, Harold D., "The structure and function of communication in society", Lyman Bryson (ed), *The communication of ideas*, New York, NY: Harper and Brother, 1948.

Latourette, Kenneth Scott, *A History of the Expansion of Christianity. Volume 2: The Thousand Years of Uncertainty 500 A.D. to 1500 A.D.*, Grand Rapids, MI: Zondervan, 1971 [1938].

-, *The Great Century in Europe and The United States of America A. D. 1800- A. D. 1914* (A History of the Expansion of Christianity, 4: New York: Harper and Row, 1970 [1941].

Lausanne Occasional Paper No. 57, *Effective Theological Education for World Evangelization.* Produced by the Issue Group on this topic at the 2004 Forum for World Evangelization hosted by the Lausanne Committee for World Evangelization In Pattaya, Thailand, September 29 to October 5, 2004.

Lee, Peter K.H., "Forty Years in the Wilderness: A Former Director's Account of the Christian Study Centre on Chinese Religion and Culture's Past Forty Years", *Ching Feng*, Vol. 40, No. 1, March, 1997, pp. 57-77.

-, "The 'Cultural Christians' Phenomenon in China", *Ching Feng*, Vol. 39, No. 4, December 1996, pp. 307-321.

Leech, Kenneth, *Soul friend: a study of spirituality*, San Francisco, CA: Harper, reprint, 1992.

Legesse, A, *Gada. Three approaches to the study of African Society*, New York: The Free Press, 1973.

Leirvik, Oddbjørn, *Islam og kristendom – Konflikt eller dialog?* (Islam and Christianity – Conflict or dialogue), Oslo: Pax, 2006.

Lemvik, J., *Enabling organisations. Stories and tools*, Oslo: Bistandsnemnda, 2006.

-, *The feudal leadership system. A first view,* Undated, Unpublished article.

Lian, Xi, *The Conversion of the Missionary: Liberalism in American Protestant Missions in China, 1907-1932,* Pennsylvania, PA: Pennsylvania State University, 1997.

Lillesøster Gaby, "Møtet med Islam" ("The Encounter With Islam"), referred to in *St. Olav* 2-2007.

Lindhardt, Jan, *Folkekirke. Kirken i det danske samfund,* Beder: Hovedland, 2005.

Lochhead, David, "Technology and Interpretation: A Footnote to McLuhan" *Journal of Theology* 98 (1994), pp. 60-73.

Lohse, Bernhard, *Martin Luther's theology. Its Historical and Systematic Development,* Minneapolis, MN: Fortress Press, 1999

Lorentzen, Håkon, *Fellesskapets fundament: Sivilsamfunnet og individualismen*, Oslo: Pax, 2004.

Lorit, S.C., *Charles de Foucauld: The Silent Witness*, New York, NY: New York City Press, 1966.

Lowman, Pete, *The Day of His Power,* Leicester: Inter-Varsity Press, 1983.

Lund, Birthe and Hans Raun Iversen (eds.), *Livshjælp. Undersøgelser af begravelsespraksis og begravelseskultur i Danmark*, Århus: Landsforeningen af Menighedsrådsmedlemmer, 1993.

Løgstrup, K. E., *Etiske begreber og problemer*. København: Gyldendal, 1996.

Ma, Wonsuk, ""When the Poor are Fired up." The Role of Pneumatology in Pentecostal.Charismatic Mission". *Plenary no.10, Report, Conference on World Mission and Evangelism,* Athens: CWME/WCC, 2005.

MacGillivray, Donald, "A List of Chinese Christian Hymn Books published between 1807-1912," *China Mission Year Book,* Shanghai: Christian Literature Society for China, 1912, pp. 253-259.

Macquarrie, John, "Systematic Theology", Donald W. Musser and Joseph L. Price (eds), *A New Handbook of Christian Theology,* Nashville, TN: Abingdon Press, 1992.

Malm, Magnus, *Hviskninger fra katekombene,* Oslo: Luther forlag, 2007.

Marnell, W., *Light from the West: The Irish Mission and the Emergence of Modern Europe*, New York, NY: Seabury Press, 1978.

Martin, David, *Tongues of Fire: The Explosion of Protestantism in Latin America*, Oxford: Blackwell, 1990.

Martin, Judith N. and Thomas K. Nakayama, "Thinking dialectically about culture and communication", in *Communication theory*, Feb 1999, pp.1-25.

Martinsen, Kari , *Freidige og uforsagte diakonisser. Et omsorgsyrke vokser frem 1860-1905*, Oslo: Aschehoug, 1984.

Mathews, Gordon, *Global culture/individual identity: Searching for home in the cultural supermarket*, London: Routledge, 2000.

Mayers, Marvin K., *Christianity confronts culture: A strategy for cross-cultural evangelism*, Grand Rapids, MI: Academic Books, 1987.

Mbiti, John S., *African religions and philosophy*, London: Heinemann, Second Edition 1989.

Mboizi, Betsy, Corat Africa, Intrac and CDRN, *Ida Kusiima*, 2005.

McGavran, Donald A., *The clash between Christianity and cultures*, Washington: Canon Press, 1974.

-, *Understanding church growth*, Pasadena, CA: William Carey Library, 1980.

McGavran, Donald A. and Arthur F. Glasser, *Contemporary theologies of mission*, Grand Rapids, MI: Baker Book House, 1983.

McGrath, Alister E., *The Future of Christianity*, Oxford: Blackwells, 2002.

Mead, Loren B., *The Once And Future Church,* Washington D.C.: The Alban Institute, 1991.

Merton, Thomas, *New Seeds of Contemplation,* New York, NY: New Directions Books, 1961.

Mikaelsson, Lisbeth, *Kallets ekko. Studier i misjon og selvbiografi* (Echoes of the calling. Studies in mission and autobiography), Kristiansand: Høyskoleforlaget, 2003.

-, " Religionens individualisering og retradisjonalisering. En kommentar til Jan-Olav Henriksen". *Forankring eller frikopling? Kulturperspektiver på religiøst liv i dag*, eds. Tone Lund-Olsen and Pål Repstad, Kristiansand : Høyskoleforlaget, 2003, pp.35-41.

Mintzberg, Henry, *Structures in Five. Designing Effective Organizations* Englewood Cliffs, NJ: Prentice Hall, Inc., 1983.

Minutes from the meeting of Samarbeidsråd for menighet og misjon, 11. May 1998, Oslo: Samarbeidsråd for menighet og misjon.

[*Minutes from the Meetings of the Board of Deacons of the Tao Fong Shan Christian Congregation*], Hong Kong: Tao Fong Shan Congregation Archives.

Mission in Context. Transformation, Reconciliation, Empowerment, Geneva: The Lutheran World Federation, 2004.

Mission-Shaped Church: Church Planting and Fresh Expressions of Church in a Changing Context, London: Church House Publishing, 2004.

Missionswissenschaft als Interkulturelle Theologie und ihr Verhältnis zur Religionswissenschaft, http://web.uni-marburg.de/hosting/wgth/religionsgeschichte/textauswahl.htm, seen 1/4 2007.

Mogensen, Mogens S., "Conversion between Islam and Christianity in a Danish Context.", *Theology and the Religions. A Dialogue*, Viggo Mortensen red., Grand Rapids, MI: Eerdmans, 2003, pp. 287-317.
-, *Dåb og religionsskifte*. Frederiksberg: Unitas, 2005a.
-, *Når danskere skifter tro. Omvendelse mellem religionerne i Danmark.* Frederiksberg: Unitas, 2005b.
Moltmann, Jürgen, *The Experiment Hope,* London: SCM Press, 1975.
Moon, Dreama G., 'Concepts of "culture": Implications for intercultural communication research', in *Communication quarterly* 44:1996, pp. 70-84.
Moreau, A. Scott, "Contextualization: From an Adapted Message to an Adapted Life," in *The Changing Face of World Missions* by Michael Pocock, Doug McConnell and Gailyn VanRheenen, Grand Rapids: Baker, 2005, pp. 321-348.
-, "Contextualization that is Comprehensive," *Missiology* 34 (2006), pp. 325-335.
Mortensen, Viggo, *Betydningen af religion og religiøsitet for integrationsprocesserne*. Aarhus, 2002.
-, "Nordic Missiology and Ecumenics", *Swedish Missiological Themes* (2001) 89/4, pp. 439-453.
Morton, Jeff, "Narratives and Questions: Exploring Scripture with Muslims," *Evangelical Missions Quarterly* 40 (2004), pp. 172-76.
Munck-Fairwood, Birthe, red., *Andre stemmer - Migrantkirker i Danmark set indefra*. København: Religionspædagogisk Forlag, 2004.
Myers, Bryant, *Walking with the Poor. Principles and Practices of Transformational Development,* Maryknoll, NY: Orbis, 1999.
Myklebust, Olav Guttorm, "The Legacy of H.P.S.Schreuder", *International Bulletin of Missionary Research,* Vol. 8 Issue 2 (1984), pp. 70-75.
-, *The study of missions in theological education: : an historical inquiry into the place of world evangelisation in western protestant ministerial training with particular reference to Alexander Duff's chair of evangelistic theology, Vol 1, until 1910,* Oslo: Land og Kirke, 1955, *Vol 2, 1910-1950*, Oslo: Land og Kirke, 1957.
Nahum, F., *Visions of transforming Africa: The challenge of leadership*, Ethiopia: Brenna P.E.P, 2003.
Ndungu, Nahashon, "The Bible in an African Independent Church", Kinoti, Hannah W. Kinoti & John M. Waliggo (eds.), *The Bible in African Christianity: Essays in Biblical Theology*, Nairobi: Acton, 1997, pp. 58-67.
Neill, Stephen, *Creative Tension,* London: Edinburgh House Press, 1959.
Nemer, Lawrence, *Anglican and Roman Catholic Attitudes on Mission,* St. Augustin: Steyler Verlag, 1981.
-, "Spirituality and the Missionary Vocation", *Missiology 11* (1983).
Newbigin, Lesslie, *Foolishness to the Greeks. The Gospel and Western Culture,* Grand Rapids, MI: Eerdmans, 1986.
-, *The Gospel in a Pluralist Society,* Grand Rapids, MI: Eerdmans, 1989.
Nichol, Todd, and Mark Kolden (eds.), *Called and Ordained. Lutheran Perspectives on the Office of the Ministry*, Minneapolis, MN: Fortress Press, 1990.

Nida, Eugena, *Customs and culture: Anthropology for Missions*, New York, NY: Harper and Row, 1954.

-, *Message and mission*, New York, NY: Harper & Brothers Publishers, 1960.

Niemela, Kati,"Calling or vocation? A shift from spiritual toward secular vocation among applicants to studies in theology and theological candidates in Finland", *Tidsskrift for kirke, religion og samfunn* 14(2001), pp. 43-52.

Nilsen, Else-Britt , *Nonner i storm og stille. Katolske ordenssøstre i Norge i det 19. og det 20. århundre*, Oslo: Solum, 2001.

Nissen, Hartvig, *Om kvindelig Dannelse og kvindelige Underviisningsanstalter*, Christiania: Malling, 1849.

Nonaka, I., "The knowledge creating company", K. Starkey (red): *How organizations learn*. London: Int. Thompson Business Press, 1996.

Nordlander, Agne, *Väckelse och växtvärk i Etiopien*, Stockholm: Verbum, 1996.

Norseth, Kristin, *"La os bryte over tvert med vor stumhet!" Kvinners vei til myndighet i de kristelige organisasjonene 1842-1912*. Doctoral dissertation, Oslo: MF Norwegian School of Theology, Oslo, 2007.

-, "To alen av hvilket stykke? Tvillingsøstrene LMF og KMA i norsk, nordisk og internasjonalt perspektiv", *Norsk Tidsskrift for Misjon* 56. 2 (2002), pp. 91-106.

Norsk Salmebok (Norwegian Hymn book), Oslo: Verbum, 1985.

Nthamburi, Zablon and Douglas Waruta, "Biblical hermeneutics in African Instituted Churches", Kinoti, Hannah W. and John M. Waliggo (eds.), *The Bible in African Christianity: Essays in Biblical Theology*, Nairobi: Acton, 1997, pp. 40-57.

Nygren, Tomas; Lars Olov Eriksson and Sebastian Rehnman (eds.), *Med smak av nåd : hur skall tron utformas och gestaltas idag? Festskrift til Agne Nordlander*, Örebro: Libris, 2000.

Nynäs, Peter, "Interpretative models of estrangement and identification", in Øyvind Dahl, Iben Jensen and Peter Nynäs (eds), *Bridges of Understanding: Perspectives on intercultural communication*, Oslo: Unipub Oslo Academic Press, 2006.

Nørgaard-Højen, Peder, *Den danske folkekirkes bekendelsesskrifter. Tekst og oversættelse,* København: Anis, 2. korr. Udgave, 2004

O'Connor, Flannery, *A Good Man Is Hard to Find, and Other Stories,* New York, NY: Harcourt and Brace, 1955.

Olsen, Rolv, *Prevailing Winds. An Analysis of the Liturgical Inculturation Efforts of Karl Ludvig Reichelt*, Studia Missionalia Svecana CIV, Lund, 2007.

Onsrud, Line Marie, *History and Contextualization. A study of Church History and Cultural Identity in East African Pentecostal Churches as Narrated by Former and Present Leaders of the Church*. Oslo: MF Norwegian School of Theology, Unpublished Masters Thesis, 1998.

Orchard, R. K. (ed), *Witness in six continents: Records of the meeting of the Commission on World Mission and Evangelism of the World Council of Churches held in Mexico City 8-19 December 1963*, London: Edinburgh House, 1964.

Organisation for Economic Co-operation and Development (OECD): Directorate for Education; Education and Training Policy Division, *Thematic Review of Tertiary Education, Norway, Country Note* (September 2006).

Ott, Bernhard, *Beyond Fragmentation: Integrating Mission and Theological Education. A Critical Assessment of some Recent Developments in Evangelical Theological Education*, Oxford: Regnum Books, 2002.

Over Alt 3-1999, pp. 12-17; 1-2000, pp. 25-29; 2-2000, pp. 26-31; 4-2000. pp. 32-35 and 1-2001. pp. 21-25.

Papathanasiou, Athanasios N., *Future, the Background of History. Essays on Church Mission in an Age of Globalization,* Montréal: Alexander Press, 2005. http://www.time.com/time/printout/0,8816,1229123,00.html#

Park, Chris C., *Sacred Worlds. An Introduction to Geography and Religion.* London & New York, NY: Routledge, 1994.

Persson, Per Erik, *Kyrkans ämbete som Kristus-representation. En kritisk analys av nyare ämbetsteologi*, Studia Theologica Lundensia 20, Lund: Gleerup, 1961

Petersen, Jørn Henrik, "Kan den danske velfærdsmodel videreføres?", Schjørring, Jens Holger and Jens Torkild Bak (eds.), *Velfærdsstat og kirke*. København: Anis, 2005

Pike, Kenneth L., *Language in relation to a unified theory of the structure of human behaviour,* 2nd ed., The Hague: Mouton, 1967.

Pobee, John S., *Towards an African Theology,* Nashville, TN: Abingdon Press, 1979.

Pobee, John S. and Ositelu, G. II, *African Initiatives in Christianity: The Growth, Gifts and Diversities of indigenous African Churches, a challenge to the ecumenical movement,* Geneva: WCC Publications, 1998.

Poser, Klaus (ed.), *Called to be Neighbours: Diakonia 2000. Official Report WCC World Consultation, Inter-Church Aid, Refugee and World Service Larnaca 1986,* Geneva: The World Council of Churches, 1987.

["Praise Grace – Collection of Songs for Friends of the Faith"], Hong Kong 1976; Rev. Ed., 1985.

Predelli, Line Nyhagen, *Issues of Gender, Race and Class in the Norwegian Missionary Society in nineteenth -century Norway and Madagascar,* Studies in the history of missions, 24: Lewiston, NY: Edwin Mellen Press, 2003.

Prenter, Regin, "Theologen Karl Ludvig Reichelt", Vol. 32, 1978, No.1, pp.1-20.

Preparatory papers for the World Council of Churches (WCC) Mission Conference, Athens 2005, *International Review of Mission* Vol 94, no 372 (Jan 2005).

Priest, Robert J., "Missionary Elenctics: Conscience and Culture," *Missiology* 22 (1994), pp. 291-315.

Prior, Michael, *The Bible and Colonialism: A Moral Critique,* Sheffield: Sheffield Academic Press, 1997).

Prophetic Diakonia: "For the Healing of the World." Report Johannesburg, South Africa November 2002, Geneva: The Lutheran World Federation, 2003.

Rambo, Lewis R., *Understanding Religious Conversion*. New Haven, CT: Yale University Press, USA, 1993.

Randi, James, *The Faith Healers,* Buffalo, NY: Prometheus Books, 1987.

Razafindrakoto, Georges, “The Malagasy *famadihana* ritual and the Old Testament”, Holter, Knut (ed.), *Let my people stay! Researching the Old Testament in Africa*, Nairobi: Acton, 2006, pp. 111-130.

-, “The Old Testament outside the realm of the church: A case from Madagascar”, Holter, Knut (ed.), *Let my people stay! Researching the Old Testament in Africa*, Nairobi: Acton, 2006, pp. 97-110.

Reed, Lyman E., *Preparing missionaries for intercultural communication: A bi-cultural approach*, Pasadena, CA: William Carey Library, 1985.

[*Registration of Baptisms of the Members the Tao Fong Shan Christian Congregation, 1930-,*], Tao Fong Shan Congregation Archives.

Reich, Ebbe Kløvedal, *Kun et gæstekammer. Historien om den danske folkekirkes fødsel*, Aarhus: Landsforeningen af Menighedsrådsmedlemmer, 1999.

Reichelt, Karl Ludvig, *Kristelig meditation,* Oslo: Buddhistmisjonens Forlag, 1926.

Reichelt, Karl Ludvig, Dagbøker (Karl Ludvig Reichelt, Diaries), Kopier fra Riksarkivets privatarkiv nr. 592, K.L. Reichelt (Copies from the Norwegian National Archives, Private Literature Archive no. 592, K.L. Reichelt), Oslo: Riksarkivet, Vol. IV, 1938-1940, Vol. V A, 1940-1942, Vol. V B, 1942-1944, Vol. VI A, 1944-1948, Vol. VI B, 1948-1952, Vol. VII, 1952-1955, Vol. VIII, 1955-1961.

Reilly, Michael Collins, *Spirituality for Mission,* New York, NY: Orbis, 1978.

Rekdal, Jan Erik, ”Jesu små søstre og livet i Nasaret”, *St. Olav* 2-2007.

Richardson, Don, *Peace Child,* Glendale, CA: G/L Regal Books, 1974.

Riisager, Filip, *Forventning og oppfyldelse*, Hjørring: Forlaget Aros, 1973.

-, *Lotusblomsten og korset*, Copenhagen: Gads forlag, 1998.

Robra, Martin, “Diakonia – A Central Task of the Ecumenical Movement”, in: Stefan Heinemann/Julia Kalbhenn (Hg.*), Being in Ecumenical Discourse on Concepts of Diakonia*, Heidelberg: DWI-INFO Sonderausgabe 4, 2004.

Rothwell, William J., *Effective Succession Planning. Ensuring Leadership Continuity and Building Talents from Within*. New York, NY: Amacom, 1994.

Roxburgh, Alan, *Constructing the Bridge: Developing Missional Ledarship,* Unpublished manuscript, 2003.

-, *The Sky Is Falling!* Eagle, ID: ACI Publishing, 2005, pp. 163-168.

Rouse, Ruth , “The Ideal of Womanhood as a Factor in Missionary Work”, *The International Review of Missions* II.5 (1913), pp. 148-164.

Roy, A. van, *Civil Society and the Aid Industry*, London: Earthscan publications, 1998.

Ryman, Björn et al (eds.), *Nordic Folk Churches. A Contemporary Church History,* Grand Rapids, MI: William B. Eerdsmans Publishing Company, 2005.

Said, Edward, *Orientalism – Western concepts of the Orient*, London: Routledge & Kegan Paul, 1978.

Salmer 1997 (Hymns 1997), Oslo: Verbum 1997.

Samartha, Stanley J. (ed), *Faith in the midst of faith: Reflections on dialogue in community*, Geneva: World Council of Churches, 1977.

Sanders, Hanne, *Nyfiken på Danmark –klokare på Sverige,* Göteborg: Makadam/Center for Danmarksstudier, 2006.

Sanneh, Lamin, *Translating the Message. The Missionary Impact on Culture,* New York, NY: Orbis Books, 1998.
Sannes, Kjell Olav, "Det kirkelige embede etter de lutherske bekjennelsesskrifter", *Ung Teologi* 1973, hf. 1, pp. 13-26
-, "Det kirkelige embete og den offentlige embetsutøvelse etter de lutherske bekjennelsesskrifter", *Ung Teologi* 1975, hft. 1, pp. 59-70.
-, "Kvinners tjeneste i kirken i lys av embetssyn - skriftsyn og synet på forholdet mellom mann og kvinne", Gunnar Eikli (ed.): *Kvinner i Bibelen, i kirken, i misjonen,* Oslo: Nye Luther Forlag, 1991.
-, *Å tolke Den augsburgske bekjennelse. Forståelse og prinsipper for tolkning av Confessio Augustana i Danmark og Norge 1530-1980*, Oslo: Det teologiske Menighetsfakultet, 1996.
-, "Karakteristikk og vurdering av 'Porvoo-erklæringen' som økumenisk dokument", *Tidsskrift for Teologi og Kirke* 1997, 83-96.
-, *Artikkeloverskriftene i Confessio Augustana,* unpublished manuscript, 2002.
-, "Kristen bekjennelse i en annen tid", Henriksen, Jan-Olav, Gunnar Heiene and Svein Olaf Thorbjørnsen (eds.), *Teologi for kirken. Festskrift til professor dr.theol. Torleiv Austad på 65-årsdagen*, Oslo: Verbum, 2002, pp. 125-134.
-, "Kirken i bevegelse med et oppdrag", Engelsviken, Tormod and Kjell Olav Sannes (eds.), *Hva vil det si å være kirke?* pp. 31-49.
Schaaf, Ype, *On Their Way Rejoicing: The History and Role of the Bible in Africa,* Carlisle: Paternoster Press, 1994.
Schein, Edgar H., *Organisational culture and leadership*, San Francisco, CA: Jossey-Bass Publ., 1985, 3rd edition, 2004.
Sheng, David, *A Study of the Indigenous Elements in Chinese Christian Hymnody*, D.M.A. Thesis, University of Southern California, 1964.
Schenk, Wilbert R., *Changing Frontiers of Mission,* Maryknoll, NY: Orbis, 1999.
Scherer, James A., *A Lutheran perspective on mission and evangelism*. LWF report 10/11, Geneva: LWF, 1982.
-, *Gospel, Church & Kingdom. Comparative Studies in World Mission Theology,* Minneapolis, MN: Augsburg Publishing House, 1987,
Schjørring, Jens Holger and Jens Thorkild Bak (red.): *Velfærdsstat og kirke,* Copenhagen: Anis, 2005.
Schreiter, Robert, "Globalization, Postmodernity and the New Catholicity" in Else Marie Wiberg Pedersen, Holger Lam, Peter Lodberg (eds.), *For All People. Global Theologies in Context,* Grand Rapids, MI: Eerdmans, 2002.
-, 'Introduction: Jesus Christ in Africa Today' in Robert J. Schreiter (ed), *Faces of Jesus in Africa,* London: SCM Press, 1991, pp. vii-xiii.
-, *The New 'Catholicity: Theology between the Global and the Local,* Maryknoll, NY: Orbis Books, 1997.
Segovia, Fernando F., *Decolonizing Biblical Studies : A View from the Margins*, New York, NY: Orbis 2000.
Senge, Peter, *The Fifth Discipline: The art and practice of the learning organization.* New York, NY: Doubleday, 1990.
Sharpe, Eric, *Karl Ludvig Reichelt: Missionary, Scholar and Pilgrim*, Hong Kong: Tao Fong Shan Ecumenical Centre, 1984.

Sit, Amy Wang, (ed. and comp.), *China Sings: Bible Verses in Chinese Tunes,* Hong Kong: Asian Outreach Ltd. 1981.

Skarsaune, Oskar, "Hvor mange typer menigheder huser folkekirken?", *Halvårsskrift for Praktisk teologi*, 1/1997, pp. 20-25.

Skarsaune, Oskar, "Noen overveielser om norsk folkereligiøsitet", *Halvårsskrift for Praktisk teologi*, 2/1993, pp. 13-18.

Skeie, Karina Hestad and Norseth, K, "Creating a voice – acquiring rights. Women in the Norwegian Missionary Society and the process towards formal organizational rights in 1904", *Nora. Nordic Journal of Women's Studies*, 11.1 (2007), pp. 5-13.

Skjevesland, Olav, *Kirken i Det nye testamente,* Oslo: Andaktsboksforlaget, 1976.

-, "Ordinasjonen i Det nye testamente", Gullaksen, P. O. et al. (eds.), *Reform og embete: festskrift til Andreas Aarflot på 65-årsdagen den 1. juli 1993*, Oslo : Universitetsforlaget, 1993, pp. 199-212.

Smalley, William A. (ed.), *Readings in Missionary Anthropology*, Tarrytown, NY: Practical Anthropology, 1967.

Smart, Ninian, *Dimensions of the Sacred: An Anatomy of the World's Beliefs,* Berkeley, CA: University of California Press, 1996.

Smith, Ralph F., *Luther, Ministry, and Ordination Rites in the Early Reformation Church, Renaissance and Baroque Studies and Texts Vol. 15*, New York, NY: Peter Lang, 1996.

Soares-Prabhu, G.M., "Missiology or Missiologies?", *Mission Studies*, no. 6, (1986), pp. 85-87.

Sound The Bamboo. CCA Hymnal 1990, Trial Edition, Manila: Asian Institute for Liturgy and Music, and the Christian Conference of Asia, 1990.

Spilka, Bernhard, Ralph W.Hood Jr, Bruce Hunsberger and Richar Gorsuch, *The psychology of religion: an empirical approach*, 3.ed., New York, NY: The Guilford Press, 2003.

Sprunger, W. Frederic, "Six Lessons about Contextualization," *Mission Focus* 12 (1984).

Stauffer, S. Anita (ed.), *Christian Worship: Unity in Cultural Diversity,* LWF Studies 1/1996, Geneva: Lutheran World Federation, 1996.

Steffen, Tom, *Passing the Baton. Church Planting that Empowers*. La Habra, CA: Center for Organizational and Ministry Development, 1993.

Stendahl, Krister, "De nordiske folkekirkers fremtid", Nilsson, Kjell Ove (ed.), *Folkekirkerne i Norden.* Uppsala: Nordiska Ekumeniska Instituttet, 1986.

Stengers, I., "Science and Religion. Beyond complementarity", Gregersen, Nils H. and U. Görman, *Design and Disorder. Perspectives from Science and Theology,* London: T & T Clark, 2002.

Stevens, R. Paul, *The Abolition of the Laity. Vocation, Work and Ministry in Biblical Perspective*, Milton Keynes and Carlisle: Paternoster Press, 1999.

Stinissen, Wilfred, *Indre vandring,* Tromsø: Sofiaforlaget, 1999.

Strandenaes, Thor, "Hymn Concordance for the Lutheran Hymn Book – *Hymns of Praise,*" *Theology and Life* 5(1982), pp. 102-119.

Synnes, Martin Synnes: *Vakthold om den skjønne skatt. Innføring i Pastoralbrevene og kommentar til første Timoteusbrev*. Oslo: Luther Forlag,

1996.
Sørensen, Leif Kiil, “Omstridt provst under pres”, in *Kristeligt Dagblad*, January 4, 2003.
Sørensen, Sten (ed), *Kirkens utfordring. Kirke av folket eller kirke for folket*, Kvinesdal: Dawn-Norge, 2005.
Sørensen, Øystein and Bo Stråth (eds.), *The Cultural Construction of Norden*, Copenhagen: Scandinavian University Press, 1997.
Taber, Charles R., *The world is too much with us: "Culture" in modern Protestant missions*, Macon: Mercer, 1991.
Tanner, Kathryn, *Theories of culture: A new agenda for theology*, Minneapolis, MN: Fortress Press, 1997.
Tappert, Theodore G. (ed.): *The Book of Concord*, Philadelphia, PA: Fortress Press, 1959.
The Holy Bible: New International version, London: Hodder & Stoughton, 1990.
The Life and Ministry of Rev. Gudina Tumsa, General Secretary of the Ethiopian Evangelical Church Mekane Yesus (EECMY): Report Volume & Lectures of the Missiological Seminar Sponsored by the Gudina Tumsa Foundation at Mekane Yesus Theological Seminary, Makanissa, April 18-21, 2001, Addis Ababa: The Gudina Tumsa Foundation, 2003.
The New Hymnal / Zànměisī Xīnbiàn, English-Chinese Bilingual edition, Shanghai: China Christian Council 1999.
Thelle, Notto Reidar, "A Christian Monastery for Buddhist Monks: Part I: Karl Ludvig Reichelt's Sacred Mountains", in *Ching Feng*, New Series, Volume 6, No. 1, 2005.
-, “A Christian Monastery for Buddhist Monks. Part II: Buddhist Rhetoric in Karl Ludvig Reichelt's Christian Liturgies,” *Ching Feng* (New Series) 6:2, 2005 (published in 2007), pp. 131-177.
-, *Buddhism and Christianity in Japan: From Conflict to Dialogue,* Honolulu, HI: University of Hawaii Press, 1987), pp.174-260.
- *Kjære Siddhartha! Brev og samtaler i grenseland mellom Øst og Vest*, Vikersund: Oriens Forlag, 2005.
- “Relation, Awareness, and Energy – Three Languages, Three Worlds? An Approach to Mutual Understanding”, *Japanese Religions* 30:1(2005), pp. 113-127.
- "The Christian Encounter with Japanese Buddhism", *Handbook of Christianity in Japan*, ed. Mark R. Mullins, Leiden: Brill, 2003, pp. 227-247.
Thiessen, Terrance L., *Who Can Be Saved? Reassessing Salvation in Christ and World Religions*, Downers Grove, IL: InterVarsity Press, 2004.
Ting, K. H., *Collection of Bishop K. H. Ting's Essays,* Hong Kong: Chinese Christian Literature Council Ltd ., 1999.
Tjelde, Kristin F, *Kvinder hjælper Kvinder. Misjonskvinneforeningsbevegelsen i Norge 1860-1910* Oslo: Master Thesis, University of Oslo, 1990.
Tomlinson, Dave, *The Post-Evangelical,* London: Triangle, 1995.
Tomson, Peter (ed.), *Lire la Bible en Afrique / Reading the Bible in Africa,* Brussels: Yearbook of the Faculty for Protestant Theology in Brussels, 11, 2006.

Towards Dynamic Mission renewing the Church for mission. Final Report of Mission Issues andStrategy Advisory Group II (MISAG-II) of the Anglican Consultative Council, London, 1992, part VI.

Toynbee, Arnold, *Encounters Between Civilizations,* Tokyo: Kinseido, 1957.

Trice, H. M. and J. M. Beyer: *Charisma and its routinization in two social movement organizations. Research in Organizational behaviour*, vol 8,0, 1986, pp. 113-164.

Trompenaars, F. and Hampten-Turner, C., *Riding on the waves of culture: Understanding Cultural Diversity in Business*, 2nd edition, London: Nicolas Brealey Publishing, 1997.

Van Gelder, Craig, *The Essence of the Church,* Grand Rapids, MI: Baker Books, 1998.

Tucker, Ruth, *Guardians of the Great Commission: The story of women in modern mission.* Grand Rapids, MI: Academic Books, 1988.

Ukpong, Justin S., "Developments in biblical interpretation in modern Africa", *Missionalia 27* (1999), pp. 313-329.

Van Gelder, Craig, *Confident Witness – Changing World. Rediscovering the Gospel in North America,* Grand Rapids, MI: W.Eerdmans Publ., 1999.

Vanhoozer, Kevin J., "'One Rule to Rule Them All?' Theological Method in an Era of World Christianity", Ott, Craig and Harold A. Netland (eds.), *Globalizing Theology: Belief and Practice in an Era of World Christianity*, Grand Rapids, Mi: Baker, 2006.

-, "The World Well Staged? Theology, Culture, and Hermeneutics,", Carson, D. A. and John Woodbridge (eds.), *God and Culture: Essays in Honor of Carl F. H. Henry*, Grand Rapids, MI: Eerdmans, 1993, pp. 1-30.

Vaughan, Sarah and Tronvoll, Kjetil, *The Culture of Power in Contemporary Ethiopian Political Life*, Oslo: SIDA studies no 10, 2003.

Verstraelen, F. J., A. Camps, L. A. Hoedemaker and M. R. Spindler, *Missiology: An ecumenical introduction: Texts and contexts of global Christianity*, Grand Rapids, Mi: Eerdmans, 1995.

Wagner, C. Peter, *Church growth and the whole gospel. A biblical mandate*, San Francisco, CA: Harper and Row, 1981.

Walls, Andrew F., *The Missionary Movement in Christian History: Studies in the Transmission of Faith,* Maryknoll, NY: Orbis Books, 1996.

Warmind, Morten, "Ateisme i Danmark", Højsgaard, Morten Thomsen and Hans Raun Iversen (eds.), *Gudstro i Danmark,* Copenhagen: Anis, 2005, pp. 279-294.

Weber, Max, *On charisma and institution building. Selected papers edited and with an Introduction by S.N. Eisenstadt*. Chicago, IL.: The University of Chicago Press, 1968.

Werner, Yvonne Maria (ed), *Nuns and Sisters in the Nordic Countries after the Reformation. A Female Counter-Culture in Modern Society,* Uppsala: Swedish Institute of Missionary Research, 2005.

West, Gerald O. and Musa W. Dube (eds.), *The Bible in Africa: Transactions, Trajectories and Trends,* Leiden: Brill, 2000.

Whiteman, Darrell L., "Contextualization: The Theory, the Gap, the Challenge," *International Bulletin of Missionary Research* 21 (1997), p. 4.

Willard, Dallas, *The Divine Conspiracy,* San Francisco, CA: Harper, 1998.

Williams, Raymond Bradley, *Religions of Immigrants from India and Pakistan: New Threads in the American Tapestry*. Cambridge: Cambridge University Press, 1988.

Wimber, John, *Power Evangelism. Signs and Wonders Today,* London: Hodder and Stoughton, 1985.

Witness and Discipleship. Leadership of the Church in Multi-Ethnic Ethiopia in a Time of Revolution. The Essential Writings of Gudina Tumsa, General Secretary of the Ethiopian Evangelical Church Mekane Yesus (1929-1979), Addis Ababa: Gudina Tumsa Foundation, 2003.

Wollebæk, Dag; Per Selle and Håkon Lorentzen, *Frivillig innsats. Sosial integrasjon, demokrati og økonomi,* Bergen: Fagbokforlaget, 2000.

Working paper of the Advisory Group on Regional Relations and Ecumenical Sharing to the World Council of Churches Programme Committee, March 2000.

World Council of Churches, "Living in dialogue: A Church for others", in *Study Encounter*, Geneva: World Council of Churches, 1967.

-, *The Church for others and the Church for the world: A quest for missionary structures for missionary congregations. Final report of the western European working group and the north American working group of the department on studies in evangelism*, Geneva: World Council of Churches, 1968.

-, 'On Intercultural Hermeneutics', in James A. Scherer and Stephen B. Bevans (eds), *New directions in missions and evangelization 3*, New York, NY: Orbis books, 1999.

Wright, N.T., *Jesus and the Victory of God,* vol. 2 of *Christian Origins and the Question of God,* Minneapolis, MN: Fortress Press, 1996.

Yamamori, T. and C. Taber C., *Christopaganism or indigenous Christianity* , Pasadena, CA: William Carey Library, 1975.

Yoshikawa, Muneo, 'The double-swing model of intercultural communication between East and the West', in Lawrence Kincaid (ed), *Communication theory: Eastern and Western perspectives*, London: Academic Press, 1987.

"You are the light of the world". Statements on Mission by the World Council of Churches 1980-2005, Geneva: WCC Publications, 2005

Yukl, G. A., *Leadership in Organisations,* Upper Saddle River, NJ: Prentice-Hall Inc., 1981, 5th edition, 2002.

Zahniser, A. H. Mathias, *Symbol and Ceremony,* Monrovia, CA: MARC, 1977.

Zànměisī Xīnbiàn, Shanghai: China Christian Council 1983,

Zhang, Liwen, *An Introduction to He-He Culture in China*, The Party School of CCCPC Press, 2001, 18.

Zhang, X.Y., "Doing Theology in Chinese," *Chinese Theological Review* 11:2 (1995), pp. 125-39.

Økland, Øyvind, *Proklamasjon, dialog eller kommunikasjon: En sammenligning av misjonsteologi og synet på misjonsmetoder i Kirkenes Verdensråd og blant de konservativ-evangelikale i perioden 1961-1980, med særlig vekt på holdninger til ikke-vestlige kulturer og religioner.* M.A. thesis in religious education, Bergen: Universitetet i Bergen, Norway, 1986.

-, *Globalization, media, and youth culture: Young high school students in Vennesla, Norway, between the local and the global.* Doctoral dissertation, Deerfield, IL.: Trinity International University, 2004

Østen og vi, Oslo, Norway, No. 6/1967; 7/1968; 10/1968; 11/68;5-1970; 11/1970; 2-1972; 3/1977; 2-1979; 3/1979; 5/1979; 9/79; 2/1980; 4/1980; 4/1981; 1/1983; 5/1983; 5/1984; 3/1985; 6/1985; 1/1986; 2/1986; 3/1986; 4/1986.

Østergaard, Uffe, *Europas ansigter. Nationale stater og politiske kulturer i en ny, gammel verden*, Copenhagen: Rosinante, 1992.

-, "Lutheranismen, danskheden og velfærdsstaten", *Den nordiske protestantisme og velfærdsstaten*, Tim Knudsen red,. Odense: Syddansk Universitetsforlag, Denmark, 2003.

Websites

http://intercultural.dk/icms/filer/kj-omvendelse-art.pdf
http://www.asianchristianart.org/index.html
http://www.asianoutreach.org/sample/file/AR_04_MarApr.pdf
http://www.chronologicalbiblestorying.com/Default.htm
http://www.cofe.anglican.org/info/yearreview/dec05/freshexpressions.html
http://www.emergingchurch.info/; http://tallskinnykiwi.typepad.com/
http://www.globallight.org.uk/Sisters%20Songs.htm .
http://www.jesusmafa.com/index.htm.

Subject Index

Author Index

BIOGRAPHICAL NOTES ON THE AUTHORS

Jan-Martin Berentsen, b. 1939. Dr. theol.,University of Oslo 1982. Missionary, Norwegian Missionary Society in Japan 1966-1974. Teacher, later Professor, of Mission Theology, School of Mission and Theology, Stavanger, 1974-2006. Former chair of the Nordic Institute of Missiology and Ecumenical Research (NIME) and editor of *Norsk tidsskrift for misjon.* Published books and articles in the field of theology of mission.

Kjell-Magne Bondevik, b.1947. Cand. theol., MF Norwegian School of Theology, 1975, Practical Theological Seminar, 1979. Member of the Norwegian Storting (Parliament), Christian Democratic Party, 1973-2005. Minister for Church and Education, 1983-86, Minister for Foreign Affairs, 1989-90, Prime Minister, 1997-2000 and 2001-2005. Founder and President, Oslo Center for Peace and Human Rights, 2006-. United Nations Special Humanitarian Envoy for the Horn of Africa.

Tormod Engelsviken, b. 1943, cand. theol. 1969, MF Norwegian School of Theology, Ph.D 1981, Aquinas Institute of Theology, Dubuque, Iowa. Teacher at Mekane Yesus Theological Seminary in Ethiopia 1971-73, studies in the USA 1973-76, teacher Fjellhaug School of Mission, Oslo, 1976-78, research fellow at MF Norwegian School of Theology, 1978-1983, associate professor in missiology 1984-98, professor 1998-. Editor of Norwegian Journal of Missiology 2006-, chair of the Egede Institute for two periods, moderator of the Church of Norway Council for Eumenical and Foreign relations 1999-2003, member of Commission on World Mission and Evangelism, WCC 1999-2005, member of the Lausanne Theology Working Group 1985-2000, visiting professor at Central University for Nationalities in China, Beijing. He has written several books and articles on mission, the Pentecostal/Charismatic movement and spiritual conflict.

Dag-Håkon Eriksen, b. 1973. Cand. philol., MF Norwegian School of Theology, Oslo 1999. Previously Executive officer on leadership in youth ministry, Normisjon. Project advisor, Church of Norway. Publication: "Utrustende lederskap i misjon" (Empowering leadership in mission), *Norsk tidsskrift for misjon* No. 3,2001. Married to Elisabeth, the daughter of Eva and Knud Jørgensen.

Ingrid Eskilt, b. 1949. Cand. Philol, MF Norwegian School of Theology, Oslo 1986. Ph.D., Intercultural Studies, Trinity International University, Deerfield, Illinois, U.S.A. 2005. Teacher for mentally handicapped, Egersund,

Norway 1973- 1978, Teacher for missionary children, Congo Brazzaville 1979-1982, Teacher, Ansgar School of Theology and Mission 1986-, Associate Professor 2005-. Publications: "Kimbanguistkirken – Ngunzabevegelser", *Norsk Tidsskrift for Misjon* No. 4,1986, "Misjon og misjonærtjeneste," in *Missiologi i dag,* J-M. Berentsen, T. Engelsviken, K. Jørgensen (eds.), Oslo: Universitetsforlaget, 2.ed. 2004, *An analysis of changing perspectives on the understanding of the missionary call in the Mission Covenant Church of Norway, Ph.D. dissertation in intercultural studies*, Deerfield, Illinois: Trinity International University, 2005.

Roar G. Fotland, b. 1955, ordained Deacon in 1977 and Elder in 1980 in the United Methodist Church, pastor in a local church 1977 – 86, Certificate of Mission from Selly Oak Colleges 1987. Missionary in Liberia 1987-89, Dr. Min. from Washington Theological Seminary 1990, teacher at United Methodist Theological Seminary in Norway from 1991, principal from 1998-, board member of Norwegian Board of Global Ministry (UMC) from 2000-, director of the Egede Institute and co-editor of Norwegian Journal of Missiology 2001-03, chairing the Norwegian Faith and Order Committee from 2002-, board member of Africa University (Zimbabwe) from 2003- and member of the Executive Committee from 2007-, Ph.D at MF Norwegian School of Theology 2005 from the University of Bergen, associate professor in Study of Religions and Missiology 2006-, board member of the Egede Institute from 2007-. Published articles on Methodist theology, UMC mission history and African theology.

Gao Shining, b. 1950. B.A., Guizhou Teachers' University, 1981. M.Ph., Chinese Academy of Social Sciences, 1988. Professor, Chinese Academy of Social Sciences. Visiting Scholar, Toronto University, 1992-1993. Visiting Scholar, Chinese University of Hong Kong, 2000-2001. Visiting Scholar, Aarhus University, 2002. Visiting Scholar, Birmingham University, 2005. Chief editor, "Religious Culture of the World", 1992-1996. Author of several books and papers on sociology of religion.

Eddie Gibbs, b. 1938. B.Div., London University, 1962. D.Min., Fuller Theological Seminary, 1982. Curate, London, 1963-1966. Missionary, Chile, South American Missionary Society, 1966-1970. Home and Education Director, 1970-1977. Program Manager, British and Foreign Bible Society, 1977-1984. Training Director, "Mission England," 1982-1984. Assistant Professor of Church Growth, School of World Mission, Fuller Theological Seminary, 1984-1988. Associate Professor of Evangelism and church Renewal, School of Theology, 1988-1991. Professor of Evangelism and Church Renewal, 1991-1993. Associate Rector for Discipleship, All Saints' Episcopal Church, Beverly Hills, 1993-1996. Professor of Church Growth, Fuller Theological Seminary, 1996-2007. Senior Professor, 2007-. Director, Institute for the Study of Emerging Churches, Brehm Center for Worship, Theology and the Arts. Founding President, British Church Growth Association, 1980. President,

North American Society for Church Growth, 1989. Author of several books and articles.

Anne Hege Grung, b.1965. Cand. theol., University of Oslo, 1991. Pastor, Emmaus Centre for Dialogue and Spirituality, Oslo, 1997-2006. PhD-student, CULCOM (Cultural complexity in the new Norway), University of Oslo, 2006-. Her main field of work is Christian-Muslim dialogue with a gender perspective, and Christian and Muslim feminist theology.

He Guanghu, b. 1950. M.A., The Chinese Academy of Social Sciences. Ph.D., The Chinese Academy of Social Sciences. Professor, .Depts.of Philosophy and Religious Studies, Renmin University of China. Visiting Scholar, Regent College, Vancouver, 1996. Visiting Research Associate, Harvard University, 1997-1998. Visiting Professor, Baptist University of Hong Kong, 2000-2001. Visiting Professor, University of Aarhus, 2002. Author, translator and editor of several books, articles and periodicals, on religions and philosophy.

Knut Holter, b. 1958. Cand. theol., School of Mission and Theology, Stavanger, Norway 1985, Dr. theol., University of Oslo 1993, Associate Professor of Old Testament, School of Mission and Theology 1993, Professor 2003, Rector 2004. Author or editor of ten books on Old Testament interpretation and African Biblical hermeneutics.

Vidar L. Haanes, b.1961. Cand. theol. MF Norwegian School of Theology 1985, Dr. theol. MF 1998. Professor of Church History and President of MF Norwegian School of Theology. Chair of Norwegian Network for Private Universities and Colleges; Chair of the National Council for Theology and Religious Studies and member of the Committee for Study and Academic Affairs in The Norwegian Association of Higher Education Institutions; Member of the General Synod and the Doctrinal Commission in the Church of Norway; Vice Chair of the Centre for Church Research. Dr. Haanes has published several books and articles on the history of theological education and on Reformation studies.

Hans Raun Iversen, b. 1948, Cand. theol., University of Aarhus, Denmark, 1976. Institute of Missiology and Ecumenics, University of Aarhus 1974-1982, Research Associate at University of Dar es Salaam 1977-78, Associate Professor in Practical Theology, University of Copenhagen, 1982-. Among recent publications: *It began in Copenhagen. Junctions in 300 years of Indian-Danish Relations in Christian Mission*, New Delhi: ISCPK, 2005 (ed. with George Oommen) and *Rites of Ordination and Commitment in The Churches of the Nordic Countries*, Copenhagen: Museum Tusculanum Press, 2006.

Charles H. Kraft, b. 1932. B.A. Anthropology, Wheaton College, 1953; B.D. Theology, Ashland Theological Seminary, 1960; Ph.D. Anthropological

Linguistics, Hartford Seminary Foundation, 1963. Missionary in Nigeria,1957-60; Professor of African languages, Michigan State University,1963-68, UCLA, 1968-73; Professor, School of Intercultural Studies (formerly the School of World Mission), Fuller Theological Seminary, Pasadena, California, 1969-. President, Deep Healing Ministries. Author of 30 books and numerous articles dealing with the relationship of Christianity to culture and spiritual warfare.

Ole Christian M. Kvarme, b. 1948. Degree in Hebrew, the University of Oslo; training in Bible Translation, Halle; studies in Rabbinic Judaism, Göttingen and Jerusalem; Cand. theol., MF Norwegian School of Theology, 1974. Ordained 1975. Lutheran pastor in Haifa and secretary of the Bible Society in Israel and the West Bank, 1975-81. Director of the Caspari Center for Biblical and Jewish Studies in Jerusalem, 1982-86. General Secretary of the Norwegian Bible Society, 1986-96; Dean of Oslo Cathedral, 1996-98; bishop of Borg, 1998-2005 and now Bishop of Oslo. Member of the Theologcial Commission of the United Christian Council in Israel and the Lausanne Consultation on Jewish Evangelism; editor of Mishkan, A Forum on the Gospel and the Jewish People; European Committee and Executive Committee of the United Bible Societies; the ecumenical committee for Jubilee 2000 in Norway; Catholic-Lutheran Forum in Norway; council of the Egede Institute. Publications: Kirkens jødiske røtter, Oslo 1985; Evighet i Tiden, Oslo 1992; Åtte dager i Jerusalem, Oslo 1996; Gjennom det gode landet, Oslo 1997; Barnet og Byen. En bok om Betlehem, Oslo 2003; as well as publications on Bible translation, Jewish-Christian relations, Gospel and Culture, pastoral and missiological issues.

Tore Laugerud, b. 1950. Cand. theol. MF Norwegian School of Theology, Oslo 1975. Missionary pastor, Norwegian Missionary Society (NMS), Madagascar, 1977-88, NMS Oslo 1988-94. Director, Egede Institute 1991-2000, Director of the Council for Congregations in Mission 1995-, Advisor to the National Council, Church of Norway 2000-.

Jørn Lemvik, b. 1955. Cand. polit, University of Bergen, 1993. Missionary, Norwegian Lutheran Mission (NLM), Ethiopian Evangelical Church Mekane Yesus. Consultant, BEST Beslutningsstøtte, Norwegian Church Aid, and Freelance, 1992-. Head of Research Department, Holy Trinity Theological College of the Ethiopian Orthodox Church, 2004-06. Ph.D. student of the Norwegian School of Management, BI. Publications: *Enabling organisations. Stories and tools,* Oslo: Bistandsnemnda 2006.

Mogens S. Mogensen, b. 1950. PhD in Intercultural Studies, Fuller Theological Seminary, 2000. Missionary with the Danish Sudan Mission in the Lutheran Church of Christ in Nigeria 1981-1991. General Secretary, the Danish Sudan Mission 1992-98. General Secretary, the Danish Mission Council, 2000-2001. Consultant on intercultural and inter-religious issues and part time lecturer, Faculty of Theology, University of Copenhagen, 2001-. Publications include *Fulbe Muslims Encounter Christ. Contextual Communication of the Gospel to Pastoral Fulbe in Northern Nigeria* (2002); *Dåb og religionsskifte* (2005), *Når danskere skifter tro* (2005).

A. Scott Moreau, b.1955. B.S. Physics Wheaton College, 1977, M.Div. Missions, Trinity Evangelical Divinity School, 1983, D.Miss. Trinity Evangelical Divinity School, 1986. He served fourteen years on staff with Campus Crusade for Christ, ten in Africa, taught science at Ntonjeni Swazi National High School, 1978-1980, and missions at the Nairobi International School of Theology (NIST), 1984-1991. Professor in Intercultural Studies at Wheaton College, 1991-, Department Chair, 2001-07. Managing Editor of the Network for Strategic Missions Knowledge Base, a Web-based database on missions (www.strategicmissions.org), 2000-, Editor of *Evangelical Missions Quarterly*, 2001-. He has written or edited nine books and numerous journal and dictionary articles focused on contextualization, missiology, Internet and Missions, and spiritual warfare.

Viggo Mortensen, b. 1942. Professor in Systematic Theology. Dr.theol. 1988, University of Aarhus, Denmark. Chair in global Christianity and Ecumenical Concerns. Director for the Centre for Multireligious Studies at the University of Aarhus. Director for the Danish Pluralism Project. Coordinator for the European network for Religious Innovation and Pluralism in 21st century Europe (RIPE). Director for the Department of Theology and Studies at The Lutheran World Federation in Geneva, 1991-1999. Member of the Danish Research council for the Humanities (FKK). President for the Nordic Institute for Missiology and Ecumenism (NIME). Has recently published: *Theology and the Religions: A Dialogue*. Grand Rapids: W.B.Eerdmanns 2003 (Ed.), *The role of Mission in the Future of Lutheran Theology*. Aarhus: CMS 2003 (Ed.), "Religious Change as a Challenge to Ecumenical Methods and Processes", *SMT* 92/1, 2004, "What is happening to Global Christianity?" *Dialogue. A Journal of Theology*. 43/1, 2004, *Kristendommen under forvandling. Pluralismen som udfordring til teologi og kirke*. (Christianity Changing. Pluralism as a Challenge to Theology and the Church) Univers 2005, "Global Christianity is changing: how do these changes influence conflict and peace?" in T. Yates (ed.) *Mission and the next Christendom,* Cliff College Academic Series 2006, "Globalization, Civilisation and Reconciliation. The Challenge to Christianity from Religious Diversity", in Anindita N. Balslev (ed.): *Toward Greater Human Solidarity. Options for a Plural World*, Dasgupta & Co. Kolkata 2005, *Religion & Society. Crossdisciplinary European Perspectives*. Højbjerg. Univers 2006 (Ed.).

Kjell Nordstokke, b. 1946. Cand. theol , MF Norwegian School of Theology, Oslo, 1972, Dr. theol, Oslo University, 1991. Missionary in Brazil 1974-81, and 1994-96 (teaching systematic theology in São Leopoldo). Diakonhjemmet College and Hospital, Oslo, 1990-2005, Director 1997, appointed professor of diakonia at Diakonhjemmet College, 2004. Director of the Department of Mission and Development, the Lutheran World Federation, Geneva, 2005-. Has published various books and articles on diakonia, in English: *Through the Mud. Reflections on diakonia* (Durban : Diakonia Council of Churches, 2000). Also published: *Council and Context in Leonardo Boff's Ecclesiology The Rebirth of the Church Among the Poor*, Lewiston, New York: Edwin Mellen Press, 1996.

Kristin Norseth, b. 1949. Cand mag in education 1973; Cand theol, MF Norwegian School of Theology, 1998. Ph.D., MF Norwegian School of Theology, 2007. Research Fellow, later Assistant Professor, MF. Working experience from Christian organizations in Norway (i.e. in the Norwegian Missionary Society as head of the youth desk and the public relation desk), publishing, marketing and public broadcasting. Doctoral dissertation: *La os bryte over tvert med vor stumhet!" Kvinners vei til myndighet i de kristelige organisasjonene 1842-1912* ("Let's break with silence!" Women acquiring authority in [Norwegian] religious organizations 1842-1912), MF Norwegian School of Theology, 2007.

Rolv Olsen, b. 1956. Cand.theol., School of Mission and Theology, Stavanger, Norway 1984. Theol.lic., Lund University, 2001. Theol.Dr., Lund University, 2007. Missionary pastor, Norwegian Missionary Society (NMS), Taiwan, 1985-90. Student pastor, NMS, Oslo, 1990-92. Missionary pastor, Christian Mission to Buddhists (CMB) (now: Areopagos), superintendent (later: president), Tao Fong Shan Christian Centre, Hong Kong, 1992-98. Research Scholarship, CMB, 1998-2000. Director, Egede Institute, 2000-02, 2004-. Lecturer in KRL (Christianity, Religions and Lifestands) in the following University Colleges: Høgskolen i Hedmark, 2000-03, Høgskolen i Bodø, 2003-04, Høgskolen i Telemark, 2004-. Doctoral dissertation: *Prevailing Winds. An Aanalysis of the Liturgical Inculturation Efforts of Karl Ludvig Reichelt*, Lund University, 2007.

Kjell Olav Sannes, b. 1945. Cand. theol. MF Norwegian School of Theology 1968, Dr. theol. MF 1997. Taught dogmatics at MF Norwegian School of Theology from 1972, associate professor 1986, professor 2003. Ordained in 1974, member of boards in the Norwegian Lutheran Inner Mission Society. Doctoral dissertation *Å tolke Den augsburgske bekjennelse. Forståelse og prinsipper for tolkning av Confessio Augustana i Danmark og Norge 1530-1980* (To interpret the Augsburg Confession. Understanding and principles of interpretation of the Confessio Augustana in Denmark and Norway 1530-1980). He has published books and numerous articles in the subject areas of Christian doctrine (principles of theology, Trinity, baptism, ecclesiology, ministry) and the Augsburg Confession, as well as on ecumenical issues and topics related to Roman Catholic doctrine, the Charismatic Movement and the Faith Movement/Kenneth E. Hagin.

Thor Strandenæs b.1949 in Antananarivo, Madagascar. Cand. theol., School of Mission and Theology (MHS) and MF Norwegian School of Theology, Oslo, 1973. Th.D., New Testament, Uppsala University, 1987. Ordained in 1973 for missionary service for the Norwegian Missionary Society and the Norwegian YMCA-YWCA in Hong Kong. Ministry within the Evangelical Lutheran Church of Hong Kong 1973-91, first as school chaplain (1975-79), then teaching New Testament and liturgics at the Lutheran Theological Seminary (1981-91). Associate professor MHS, New Testament 1991-93, Missiology 1993-. Dissertation: *Principles of Chinese Bible Translation as Expressed in Five Versions of the New Testament and Exemplified by Mt 5:1-12 and Col 1* (Coniectanea Biblica, New Testament Series 19), Uppsala: Almqvist & Wiksell International 1987. Other studies deal with the history of Chinese Bible translation, worship and mission, contextualization of Christian worship and hymnody, children and worship etc.

Nicholas Ho Fai Tai, b. 1955. B.R.E., 1979, M.Div., Lutheran Theological Seminary, 1985; Th.D., University of Munich, Germany, 1993; Evangelist and Pastor, Kwai Yan Lutheran Church, 1979-87; Ordained, 1985; Assistant Professor, 1993-96, Associate Professor, 1996-2004, Professor, 2004-, Vice-President, 1996-2002, Acting President, 1998-99, Lutheran Theological Seminary; Vice- President, the Evangelical Lutheran Church of Hong Kong, 1999-2005; Bishop, the Evangelical Lutheran Church of Hong Kong, 2005-. Publications: *Prophetie als Schriftauslegung in Sacharja 9-14* (Calwer Theologischen Monographien Bd. 17), 1996, *An Inquiry into the Exegetical Methods of Chinese Churches*, 1999, *Women and Jewish Exegetes in Bible Reading*, 2000. "The End of the Book of the Twelve. Reading Zechariah 12-14 with Joel" in F. Hartenstein, J. Krispenz & A. Schart (Eds.) *Schriftprophetie*, Festschrift für Jörg Jeremias, Neukirchen: Neukirchener Verlag, 2004. *Covenant, Sermon Series of the Revised Common Lectionary – OT (Year A)*, Taosheng Publishing House, 2004. The New Being, *Sermon Series of the Revised Common Lectionary – OT (Year B)* Taosheng Publishing House, 2006.

Ekman Pui Chuen Tam, b.1957 in Hong Kong. B.Th., Hong Kong, 1987. Church ministry until 1992. He went abroad to Canada in 1992 for further study in psychology and counselling, B.A., M.A., University of Ottawa, and then Spirituality, M.A. and Ph. D., St. Paul University. Spiritual Direction at Tao Fong Shan Christian Centre, Hong Kong, 1998-. Doctorate in psychology, Graduate Theological Foundation, 2006. He is a Clinical Member of American Association of Marriage and Family Therapy and a Counseling Psychologist of Hong Kong Psychological Association. Dr. Tam has published two books in English, the first one on Thomas Merton and the second on spiritual direction and therapy, and several articles in English on spirituality, psychology, and religious dialogue. He also published two books in Chinese and many articles on Christian spirituality.

Notto R. Thelle, b. 1941. Cand. theol., University of Oslo, 1965, Practical theology 1966, Japanese studies, Sheffield University, 1969-1970, and Kobe Language School, 1970-71. Buddhist studies Otani University, 1972-73, Dr. theol., University of Oslo, 1983. Missionary in Japan, Christian Mission to Buddhists (now: Areopagos) 1969-1985, most of the time Associate Director at the NCC Center for the Study of Japanese Religions in Kyoto; Professor of Ecumenics and Missiology, University of Oslo 1986-2006; Senior Professor 2006-. Research, dialogue and pastoral work to a great extent focused on the encounter with Eastern religions, and theological reflection on implications of the encounter, notably related to Japan and China. A number of books on dialogue and spirituality widely read in Scandinavian countries.

Øyvind Økland, b.1956. Cand. philol., University of Bergen, 1986; Ph D, Trinity International University, USA, 2004. Teacher, Nordborg vgs., Oslo, Norway, 1984-87; Danvik folkehøgskole, Drammen, Norway, 1988-98, the last year as Rector. Director, Wycliffe Bible Translators, Norway, 1987-96. Assistant Professor, Gimlekollen School of Journalism and Communication, Kristiansand, Norway, 1998-. Doctoral dissertation: *Globalization, media, and youth culture: Young high school students in Vennesla, Norway, between the local and the global*, Deerfield, Ill.: Trinity International University, 2004.

Kjetil Aano, b. 1949. Cand. theol., School of Mission and Theology, Stavanger, Norway. Missionary pastor, Norwegian Missionary Society (NMS), Madagaskar, 1978-88, as evangelist, as head of the evangelism department of the Central Synod in the Malagasy Lutheran Church, and as director of Atsimoniavoko Regional Theological Seminary. General Secretary, NMS, 2000-. Previous work: immigrant work, Stavanger, editor of the NMS Mission Magazine *Misjonstidende*, parish pastor, and assistant to the Diocesan Bishop in Stavanger. He has written books and articles on mission and the global church.

Tabula Gratulatoria

Marit and Hans Arne Akerø
Knut Alfsvåg
Børge Kaahr Andersen
Einar Lunde and Ellen Westberg Andersen
Nils-Tore Andersen
Peggy Andersson
Thomas Andersson
Solomon Araya
Niels Henrik Arendt
Tore Askildsen
Rune Backlund
Dwight P. Baker
Inger og Jens Bang
Kjetil Bang-Hansen
Kjell-Einar Barreth
Erik Baun
Mehret-Ab Bereke
Åse H. and Jan-Martin Berentsen
Mirjam Bergh
Reidun Løvoll Bildøy
Irene Bjørnsborg
Rigmor and August Bolstad
Ele and Steen Bonde
Kjell Magne Bondevik
Odd Bondevik
Jonathan J. Bonk
Gunnar Breivik
Jørgen Bøytler
Helga Haugland Byfuglien
Nelson Chen
Xida Chen
Choy Wai Man
Berit Schelde Christensen
Helle Christiansen
Øyvind Dahl
Lars Dahle
Arabinda Dey
Ingulf Diesen
Live Danbolt Drange and Helge Drange
Melkamu Dunfa
Jan-Otto Eek
Peder A. Eidberg
Rolf Ekenes
Bertil Ekström
Bodil and Tormod Engelsviken
Elisabeth Almaz Berger Eriksen, Dag-Håkon Eriksen, Iris Almaz Eriksen and Sebastian Berger Eriksen
Per Reinert Eriksen
Ingrid Eskilt
Oddvar Espegren
Turid and Oddbjørn Evenshaug
Christel Eyermann
Naol Ferede
Bjørn Øyvind Fjeld
Hilde Margrethe Sæbø Fjeldstad and Arne H. Fjeldstad
Terje and Kirsten Fonk
Jóannis Fonsdal
Leighton Ford
Roar G. Fotland
Kristen Skriver Frandsen
Ingrid and Lars Fuglsang
Astrid Fylling
Gao Shining
Yenenesh Geleta
Eddie Gibbs
Inger Johanne Gillebo
Inger Marie and Øyvind Gjessvåg
Iteffa Gobena
Louise and Jan Gossner
Egil Grandhagen
Hans Aage Gravaas
Michael Green
Niels Henrik Gregersen

Anne Hege Grung
Joachim F. Grün
Knut Grønvik
Bernhardur Gudmundsson and Rannveig Sigurbjörnsdottir
Henrik Guii-Larsen
Ole D. Hagesæther
Flemming Hansen
Ernst Harbakk
Jon Andreas Hasle
Kari Storstein Haug
Trond Arne Hauge
He Guanghu
Harald Hegstad
Gunnar Heiene
Rolf G. Heitmann
Magnar Helgheim
Christian Morimoto Hermansen
Thor Hesselberg
Georg Hille
Terje Holmedahl
Morten Holmqvist
Jette Holst
Knut Holter
Inge Morten Paulsen Hopøy
Hugh Hudson
Erik Høidahl
Morten Thomsen Højsgaard
Leif M. Haanes
Vidar Leif Haanes
Bent Hylleberg
Yohannes Irenna
Mitsuo Ishii
Tobias Iveland
Hans Raun Iversen
Svein Jacobsen
Göran Janzon
Tove and Niels Johansen
Kurt Johansen
Georg Jørgensen
Henrik Berger Jørgensen
Jonas Adelin Jørgensen
Kristian B. Jørgensen
Lise and Theodor Jørgensen
Tor B. Jørgensen
Fekadu Kanno
Kirsten and Kai Kjær-Hansen
Mogens Kjær
Rolf Kjøde
Helge Kjøllesdal
Inger Margrethe and Flemming Kofod-Svendsen
Charles Kraft
Flemming Kramp
Anne Karin Kristensen
Hans Kvalbein
Ole Christian Kvarme
Anne Birgitta Langmoen and Leif Gordon Kvelland
Reidun Kyllingstad
Audhild Kaarstad
Wendimu Lakew
Aasulv Lande
Poul Langagergaard
Per Inge Langeland
Knut Edvard Larsen
Tore Laugerud
Anna Ramskov Laursen
Moses Lee
Oddbjørn Leirvik
Jørn Lemvik
Runo Lilleaasen
Peter Lodberg
Kåre Lode
Jon Magne Lund
Erling Lundeby
Stig Lundberg
Trond Løberg
Per Lønning
Hans Thore Løvaas
Fergus Macdonald
Ole Skjerbæk Madsen
Lars Inge Magerøy
Lars Immanuel Mandrup
Melese Mekasha
Per Midteide
Nils Aksel Danbolt Mjøs
Kristian Mogensen
Mogens S. Mogensen
Lars Mollerup-Degn
Matthew Monger
A. Scott Moreau

Viggo Mortensen
Stein Mydske
Jacob Birger Natvig and Harriet Backer Natvig
Temsegen Negassa
Lisbet and Arne Kiel Nielsen
Nicolaj Wibe Nielsen
Aage Nielsen
Karsten Nissen
Ragnhild and Arne Nordahl
Lars-Erik Nordby
Halvor Nordhaug
Agne and Karin Nordlander
Randi and Øyvind Nordlie
Kjell Nordstokke
Kristin Norseth
Torill and Geir Magnus Nyborg
Birger Nygaard
Kjell Bertel Nyland
Kari and Ole-Magnus Olafsrud
Jens Olesen
Jørn Henrik Olsen
Rolv Olsen
Svein Johs Ottesen
Moti Lal Pandit
Ingolf Henoch Pedersen
Jens Møller Pedersen
Jørgen Nørgaard Pedersen
Clifton M. Pederson
Henrik Petersen
Henrik Jul Petersen
Erling J. Pettersen and Turid Barth Pettersen
Trond Pladsen
Anne Grete and Per Rasmussen
Henrik Ertner Rasmussen
Leif Rasmussen
Lissi Rasmussen
Hans Erik Raustøl
Arne Redse
Johannes Redse
Karl Ludvig Reichelt
Bodil Rettedal
Torger Reve
Torbjørg and Gunnar Ringøen
Kari and Hans Rognstad
Arild Romarheim
Sissel and Dag Arne Roum
Johan Hermann Rump
Miikka Ruokanen
Trygve Rö
Ole Rølvaag
Oddrun and Finn Aasebø Rønne
Elise Sandnes
Kjell Olav Sannes
Fredrik Saxegaard
Edward H. Schroeder
Gunnleik Seierstad
Dina and Nils Skarsholm
Sune Skarsholm
Olav Skjevesland
Bodil Skjøtt
Åse Snøtun
Arne Solberg
Terje Solberg
Dagfinn Solheim
Anne-May and Asbjørn Stavenes
Ørnulf Steen
Terje Stordalen
Thor Strandenæs
Aslaug and Åge Strøm
Paulo Suess
Bergljot and Olav D. Svanholm
Arne Tord Sveinall
Hans Svelland
Kristjan Sverrison
Martin Synnes
Jørgen Skov Sørensen
Maria and Oddvar Søvik
Tai Ho-fai, Nicholas
Ekman P. C. Tam
Claes Tande
Edmond Tang
Karl Inge Tangen
Jette and Ole Techow
Mona and Notto R. Thelle
Britt R. and Svein Arne Theodorsen
Karsten Thomsen
Svein Olaf Thorbjørnsen
Kjell Børge Tjemsland
Svein Ragnvald Tjora
Arne Tolo

Egil Torp
Inge and Verner Tranholm-Mikkelsen
Guri and Ola Tulluan
Olav Fykse Tveit
Kamma and Gunner Tøttrup
Charles Van Engen
Leif Vestergaard
Bjørn Vilberg
Stein Villumstad
Knut Vollebæk
Finn Wagle
Bjørn A. Wegge
Inger Johanne Wremer
Bjørn Ove and Sissel Ødegaard
Øyvind Økland
Berit Østby
Knut Østbye
Søren Østergaard
Arna and Lars Østnor
Anna Marie Aagaard
Marianne Skjortnes and Kjetil Aano

Ansgar Teologiske Høgskole
Areopagos
Bistandsnemnda
Danish Mission Council
Dansk Bibel-Institut
Den Evangelisk Lutherske Frikirke
Den Norske Israelsmisjon
Den norske kirkes presteforening
Det Norske Misjonsselskap
Det teologiske Menighetsfakultet
Dialogsenteret Emmaus
Egede Instituttet
Familie & Medier, Kristent Medieforum
Fjellhaug Misjonshøgskole
IKON-Danmark
Institute of Sino-Christian Studies
Institutt for Sjelesorg
Kirkens Nødhjelp by Atle Sommerfeldt
Kirkerådet by Jens- Petter Johnsen
Kristent Interkulturelt Arbeid (KIA)
Lutheran Church in Singapore by John Tan
Luthersk Mission
Mekane Yesu Theological Seminary
Menighedsfakultetet, Danmark
Metodistkirken i Norge by Gunnar Bradley
Metodistkirkens Misjonsselskap by Tove Odland
Misjonsalliansen
Misjonshøgskolen
Misjonstidende by Eivind Hauglid
Møre bispedøme
Nidaros biskop and Nidaros bispedømmeråd
Norea Mediemisjon
Norsk Luthersk Misjonssamband
Norsk Misjon i Øst
Oslosenteret for fred og menneskerettigheter by Kjell Magne Bondevik
Peterstiftelsen
Sparebanken Pluss by Vidar Blakseth
Statsbiblioteket/Institutservice/Teologi, Aarhus
Stiftelsen Diakonissehuset Lovisenberg by Torstein Lalim
Svenska Institutet för Missionsforskning
Sykepleiernes Misjonsring
Tao Fong Shan Service Unit
The Lutheran World Federation
Tunsberg Bispedømmeråd